Psychopathology

Psychopathology

ARNOLD H. BUSS

Rutgers University

John Wiley & Sons, Inc.
New York • London • Sydney

Library of Congress Catalog Card Number: 66-13521
Printed in the United States of America

FIRST CORRECTED PRINTING, JANUARY, 1968

For Edith

Preface

Two assumptions underlie the organization and content of this book. The
first is that the exposition should be rigorous and systematic. This means
that observations should be separated from explanations, data from inferences, and facts from theories. We shall start with the facts—the events
to be explained—and then proceed to an understanding of these events.
The "events" of psychopathology consist of symptoms. Once we know what
the symptoms are, we can proceed to the theories that attempt to explain
them.

The theories are described with an attempt at impartiality. Each of
us is allowed to have his personal preferences, but fair play demands that
we allow for and give an adequate hearing to the major approaches to
the field. The assumption is that polemic belongs in a journal, not in a
textbook.

This does not mean that theories are not evaluated. Many theories
are assessed against a body of evidence and found wanting; a few receive
praise. Some theories are amenable to such evaluation because they are
sufficiently precise and quantified to be tested. We have only to examine
the data to discover whether they are correct. Other theories are too broad
or too qualitative to be checked against data. They are approaches to an
area rather than precise formulations that have testable deductions. Their
worth depends on whether investigators and students find them a useful
source of ideas or explanations.

In discussing theories, we shall attempt to state their basic assumptions
and their consequences. Where there are competing theories, comparisons
will be made. In comparing theories, differences among them will be empha-

sized so that the student may understand each theory in its pure form. Of course, similarities will not be neglected.

The second assumption is that progress may be marked by advances from the clinic to the laboratory. In any field, the early, crude, qualitative observations are supplanted by later, refined, quantitative data. At first the clinician's subjective observations and inferences predominate and are the basis of most knowledge. Later the laboratory researcher's objective, quantitative data predominate and are the basis of most knowledge. This appears to hold in medicine, in which progress can be accurately gauged by the extent to which laboratory procedures have replaced clinical impressions in diagnosis and to the extent that treatment is derived from research rather than clinical tradition.

There are analogues in clinical psychology. An intelligence test marks a real advance over clinical impressions of intelligence. Similarly, we favor facts obtained in the controlled context of the laboratory over observations made in the less controlled context of the clinic. Of course, many facts cannot be obtained in the laboratory, and a complete description of psychopathology must include clinical observations. Psychopathology, like medicine, is far from being a laboratory science, although there has been considerable progress in recent years. Clinical impressions will continue to be of value, but they are to be trusted less than the more reliable data that emerge from the laboratory.

One consequence of both assumptions is an emphasis on issues, facts, and theories, and the omission of case histories. Like autobiographies and novels, accounts of patients' lives are interesting to read. They are also of value in that they illustrate how symptoms develop in individuals, but there is almost always a bias built into the case presentation, which can be selected to "prove" or to illustrate any theory or point of view. The bias is usually in favor of social or interpersonal approaches and against impersonal or biological approaches. Furthermore, case histories, although intrinsically interesting, tend to distract the reader from the rich and complex issues of abnormal psychology. There has been a proliferation of research on psychopathology in recent years, and the lines between opposing viewpoints have been drawn more sharply. There is enough to occupy our attention without the addition of case histories.

The book has four main sections. The first three chapters deal with broad issues: the nature of abnormality, definitions, models, and classification. Chapters 4 through 8 are concerned first with neurotic symptoms and then theories of neurosis. The third section, Chapters 9 through 15, involves symptoms and dimensions of psychosis and then theories of psychosis. The last two chapters are expositions of psychosomatic disorders and conduct disorders.

Many persons assisted in the writing of this book. Bertram D. Cohen read most of the manuscript and made many valuable comments. A similar debt is owed to Barclay Martin. Peter Lang helped to sharpen many ideas and collaborated in the writing of two papers that served as a basis for Chapters 12, 13, and part of 14. Neil Murray's questions helped to clarify several sections. The following colleagues offered constructive feedback in their areas of competence: Fred Kanfer, Harvey Lacey, David Lazovik, Oakley Ray, and David Reynolds. The patient and expert typists were Rae Yanoski, Elsie Squitieri, and Lola Scott. Proofreading and indexing were facilitated by Judith Fishman, Virginia Mencher, and Marjorie Schiffman. Sallyanne Riggione was a most efficient copy editor. Arthur Hepner sharpened and clarified the writing. Smoothing the way from the beginning was my good friend and editor, Gordon Ierardi. The largest debt is owed to my wife, to whom this book is dedicated.

ARNOLD H. BUSS

New Brunswick, New Jersey
December 1, 1965

Contents

CHAPTER 1

Normality and Abnormality

There have been many approaches to normality and abnormality, but three of them appear to be fundamental: normality as a statistical concept, normality as ideal mental health, and abnormality as the presence of certain behaviors. The statistical concept is the simplest, stating merely that normality consists of whatever tendencies are most frequent in the population. Abnormality is defined by exclusion, that is, by the presence of features uncommon in the population. Abnormality may be unidirectional, as in vision. Normality is represented by 20-20 vision: seeing at 20 feet what an *average* person sees at 20 feet. Better vision (say, 10-20) is still normal, but poorer vision (say, 20-40 or 20-100) is abnormal. Thus visual acuity becomes abnormal only when it is worse than average, and normality is represented by both average and better-than-average vision. However, abnormality may be bidirectional, as in body temperature. The normal or healthy temperature range is roughly 97 to 100° Fahrenheit, and *both* lower and higher temperatures are abnormal or unhealthy.

One problem with the statistical concept is that it does not in itself supply a basis for deciding whether abnormality should be unidirectional or bidirectional in any given instance. Thus assembling frequency distributions is not sufficient in defining normality. It is also necessary to specify what is being counted, that is, to define the *content* of normality and abnormality. Although the statistical concept is not a sufficient definition of normality, it cannot be ignored. Normality implies that the majority of any population has the attribute in question. It would not be acceptable to define normality so as to exclude most people because that would destroy the meaning of the term *normal*.

Unfortunately, defining normality in terms of ideal mental health makes precisely this assumption, that normality is an ideal state attained only by a selected few. We shall examine this approach in detail in the next section, after introducing the third approach, which focuses on the content of abnormality.

A rough definition of abnormality or maladjustment is needed to carry us through a discussion of the issues, a definition that will suffice until a more precise one can be attempted. Let us define abnormality, then, in terms of misery or an inability to manage one's own affairs. *Misery* refers to anxiety, depression, and allied dispositions. *Inability to manage* is self-defining. This temporary definition uses two vantage points in viewing maladjustment: that of the individual (discomfort) and that of society (not fulfilling a role in society).

The definition states in general terms what abnormality is, but in recent years the mental health movement has supplied the impetus for an alternate approach, defining abnormality as the absence of mental health. This approach emphasizes the positive aspects of adjustment: normality, positive striving, and productivity, as opposed to abnormality, defensive maneuvers, and inefficiency.

IDEAL MENTAL HEALTH AND NORMALITY

Reflecting a psychoanalytic position, Kubie (1954) suggests that in the normal person there is a predominance of conscious over unconscious urges; in the abnormal person there is a predominance of unconscious, irrational urges. This position has been criticized by Redlich (1957), who states that Kubie implicitly assumes that behavior determined by conscious, rational forces is healthier than behavior determined by unconscious, irrational forces. If this assumption were correct, then the behavior of children, lovers, and artists would be considered abnormal. Redlich's argument is that not all unconscious behavior is irrational.

The criterion of consciousness is poor because it emphasizes awareness and neglects behavior. Pseudoliberated individuals can usually give an accurate account of the nature of their problems, especially after a course of unsuccessful psychotherapy, but keen awareness of the roots of their difficulties apparently has no effect on their continued maladjustment. On the other hand, many adjusted, reasonably productive individuals are unaware of their basic motivations. The ability to verbalize correctly about oneself is evidently not highly related to the ability to adapt well to one's environment.

This position is consistent with the current trend among clinicians of downgrading the importance of insight. In psychotherapy, for example:

Insight is manifested when a client makes a statement about himself that agrees with the therapist's notions of what is the matter with him. This is not a particularly useful formulation. (Hobbs, 1962, p. 742)

Consciousness or insight is only one of several criteria proposed by advocates of the positive-mental-health approach to normality. Shoben (1957) listed five other criteria: self-control, personal responsibility, social responsibility, democratic social interest, and ideals. Jahoda (1958), who has written the most comprehensive work on concepts of mental health, lists six criteria. The first is self-insight, which is essentially the same as Kubie's criterion of consciousness. One of the others has been separated into two attributes, making a total of six criteria of positive mental health to be discussed:

> balance of psychic forces
> self-actualization
> resistance to stress
> autonomy
> competence
> perception of reality

Balance of psychic forces implies a set of opposing tendencies which must somehow be reconciled. This notion, which is part of such depth theories as psychoanalysis, is difficult to pin down in behavioral terms. As such, the criterion cannot be dealt with outside of the context of a particular theoretical framework. Since the present discussion assumes a neutral stance regarding theory, balance of psychic forces cannot help in the quest for criteria of normality.

Self-actualization, or the full realization of one's potential as reflected in productivity in science, the arts, or other fields, is an ideal state which few persons attain. If it is a requirement of mental health, then very few persons are mentally healthy. Most segments of society lead a routine life, hemmed in by the petty details and drudgery of everyday existence. Realizing one's potential requires not only the presence of latent creativity but also the motivation and means to break out of the mold of the habits and trivial demands of day-to-day living. Few people possess these attributes, yet the majority who do not possess them are not ordinarily considered maladjusted, that is, they are not miserable and can manage their own affairs.

Conversely, there is the possible coexistence of creativity and abnormality. Vincent Van Gogh had psychotic episodes during his career, and there are many other examples of creative genius' occurring in men who were unquestionably abnormal. Thus self-actualization, in the sense of realizing one's potential, has serious faults as a criterion of mental health.

The next three criteria, *resistance to stress, autonomy,* and *competence,* all appear to be aspects of maturity. The concept of maturity is fairly straightforward in its application to the develoment sequence. During childhood, children are expected to progress through a series of age-graded roles which require increasing self-control and self-help. A child of eight who performs in familial and social contexts at a level expected of eight-year olds is mature; if he were to perform at a six-year level, he would be called immature. Similarly, adults who manifest behavior patterns typical of adolescence or childhood are labeled immature.

The three salient capacities underlying the age-graded roles are autonomy, competence, and resistance to stress. The child is expected to increase in all three as he becomes older, the peak being attained in adulthood. The infant is completely dependent upon its parents; the mature adult is expected to be self-sufficient and in no need of parental assistance. The infant has a very small behavioral repertoire; the mature adult is expected to be competent in work, play, and personal relations. The infant can respond to stress only with diffuse excitement and panic; the mature adult should be able to tolerate threat and failure sufficiently well to persevere in attempting to solve problems and reach goals.

Thus maturity can be grossly defined in terms of autonomy, competence, and resistance to stress, but the basic issue confronting us is its relationship to normality. Presumably most mature adults are normal in that they are not miserable and can manage their own affairs, but a minority might well be abnormal. Consider an individual whose life is plagued with an inordinate amount of stress (disappointments, failures, threats, rejections, deaths of friends or relatives). At first he may respond with resilience, bouncing back to solve problems after each setback, but eventually he would probably become despondent and perhaps even hopeless in the face of continued misfortune. In brief, the definition of normal must take into account the fortunes of life; maturity may not be sufficient to guarantee normality.

Autonomy presents special problems. Independence does not necessarily lead to normality. In the course of moving away from dependence on parental figures, there may be an over-reaction to all control. Thus the adult might be excessively autonomous: he might be insulated from the care and affection of others, negativistic and defiant of authority. Excessive rebellion involves the individual in conflict with authority in its various forms. Consequently he either is not allowed to manage his own affairs or is judged incapable of doing so, that is, he is judged abnormal.

Even if an individual is not excessively autonomous in the sense of being negativistic and defiant of authority, he may become maladjusted. One connotation of the term *adjustment* is accommodation to the pressures of society. Conformists find life easier in the sense of "belonging" and of accruing the material rewards of a prosperous society. The life of the dissenter is more difficult because although we prize rugged individualism as part of our democratic values, we tend to deal with it harshly in everyday life. By nonconformity we are referring to the individual's right to go his own way in his private affairs, not rebellion against authority. An example of such nonconformity is a white man marrying a Negro woman. Although society recognizes this right in the abstract (except for some Southern states in which it is unlawful), such nonconformity usually results in censure, rejection, and a blocking of many means to achieve social and vocational goals. In brief, the nonconformist must face a stressful and frustrating environment, which in turn may lead to misery and difficulty in managing his affairs, that is, abnormality.

Thus maturity is not always identical to normality or adjustment; nor does immaturity necessarily lead to abnormality. It is possible to maintain a childlike dependence on others without being maladjusted, so long as persons are available to play the opposite, parental role. There are moderately successful marriages in which one partner plays a dominant, parental role and the other plays a submissive, dependent role. Similarly, on some jobs an individual can find a niche in which he is protected from facing adult responsibilities. People who do not move all the way to adult independence can still find satisfaction in life and (with help) manage their own affairs. They are immature but not necessarily maladjusted.

Having pointed out the defects of maturity as a criterion of normality, we must be fair and mention that the two are positively related. With the exceptions noted, mature people tend to be adjusted and immature people, maladjusted. The relationship is especially strong when there is extreme immaturity, which leads inescapably to abnormality. Let us note for later discussion that abnormality is more closely linked to immaturity than normality is to maturity, and immaturity is easier to specify than maturity.

Perception of reality is certainly an important aspect of maladjustment, but the proper emphasis must be on its absence. The person who distorts reality is obviously abnormal, and those around him will respond immediately to his bizarreness. However, a relatively accurate perception of everyday stimuli does not guarantee normality. The cognitive apparatus needed to read reality correctly may function very well, but the behaviors necessary for adjustment may be missing. Thus an individual might correctly ascertain that he is in immediate danger and then freeze into immobility, being unable to cope with the threat. Note that here again it is easier to define abnormality than normality.

This examination of the various criteria of normality reveals that although some of them are clear and relevant, others are unclear. In any event, it is obvious that very few individuals will meet all the criteria that describe an ideal person. If this ideal is normal, are the rest of us abnormal? The answer is no, because the concepts of normality and adjustment implicitly refer to most persons.

Are the criteria highly correlated? There are no data to guide us because the criteria have not been used in research. However, it is reasonable to assume that some of them are more closely related than others. Thus attitudes toward the self probably are more closely related to clear perception of reality than to autonomy.

If some of the criteria are not related, how many of them must be met for an individual to qualify as mentally healthy? A person might fail in self-attitudes, self-actualization, and perception of reality but pass in autonomy and competence. Is he mentally healthy? There can be no clear answer to this question because there is no way of deciding which criteria are of greater importance. There are many ways to be adjusted and to lead a reasonably happy and productive life. One mode of adjustment might meet some of Jahoda's criteria, and another mode, other criteria.

The positive striving approach attempts to spell out the psychological values and goals of "the good life" in our society. We can applaud these goals and the attempt to reach them, but this way of dealing with mental health has the following defects:

(1) its ideal nature excludes too many persons;
(2) some of its criteria necessarily lack precision because some goals are excessively vague and abstract;
(3) there are many ways to adjust to the world and achieve some happiness or sense of well-being, too many to allow a reasonably short list of criteria.

This third defect is crucial. Abnormality is a smaller domain and is best defined in its own terms rather than as the absence of normality, which is a larger domain of behavior.

RESEARCH CRITERIA OF ABNORMALITY

An alternative to defining normal or ideal adjustment is specification of the criteria of *abnormality*. Scott (1958) reviews five criteria of abnormality which have been used for research purposes:

psychiatric diagnosis
presence in a mental hospital
social maladjustment
subjective unhappiness
objective psychological inventories

Psychiatric diagnosis is an obvious criterion of abnormality. Individuals diagnosed as psychotic or neurotic are clearly abnormal, being either miserable or unable to manage their affairs. Those with psychosomatic complaints or conduct disorders constitute borderline instances because it is difficult to make these diagnoses. Furthermore, mild neurosis is difficult to distinguish from normality. Aside from the problem of diagnosing borderline conditions, psychiatric diagnosis is a circular kind of criterion because it defines abnormality as what the psychiatrist says it is. The only way out of the circularity is to use the *bases* of diagnoses as criteria of abnormality, but these turn out to be certain kinds of symptoms, which will be described later in the book. Symptoms or complaints, as we shall see, are good measures of abnormality.

Presence in a mental hospital appears at first glance to be a reasonable criterion of abnormality, but closer inspection reveals several faults. As Szasz (1961) has forcefully commented, admission and discharge procedures depend largely on community pressures, the mental hospital being an instrument used to protect the community as well as to help psychiatric patients. Admittance and discharge also depend in part on the financial and personal support offered by the patient's family. Furthermore, whether a disturbed person is admitted to a hospital depends on whether he comes to the attention of professional personnel. Surveys such as the Midtown Study (Srole et al., 1962) have turned up substantial numbers of disturbed persons who have never been inside a mental hospital and have never had professional attention. Lastly, hospital admissions are limited principally to psychotics, the majority of nonpsychotics being seen on an outpatient basis, in clinics, or in private practice. Thus admission to a mental hospital is a limited and incomplete criterion of abnormality.

The third criterion, *social maladjustment*, requires that we specify cultural norms and appropriate reference groups. One norm might be legal, with maladjustment defined as being in trouble with the law. Another possibility is conformity to community values; on this basis a white Mississippian who favors desegregation is maladjusted, whereas if he moved to the North, he would be adjusted. The problem is thus one of spelling out "adjustment to what." Maladjustment, so defined, is too flexible. Furthermore, dissidence in itself does not equal maladjustment, just as conformity does not equal adjustment.

The fourth criterion, *subjective unhappiness*, presents difficulties because the individual's mood may be determined by his immediate environment. In the face of a business failure or military service in Antarctica, unhappiness might be an appropriate reaction. In addition, some individuals who might be abnormal on the basis of other criteria (diagnosed as psychotic and admitted to a psychiatric hospital) might still report feeling happy; a manic probably would. However, these difficulties do not appear to be as serious as those confronting the other criteria. Environmental stress is one of the determinants of abnormality, and therefore its effect on subjective happiness is entirely appropriate. There are no data suggesting that psychiatric patients are as happy as others; on the contrary, Scott (1958) reports studies showing just the reverse. In brief, although subjective unhappiness may be a tricky criterion for the researcher, it is potentially a good measure of abnormality in the broader context of the present discussion. As it stands, unhappiness is not a good criterion of abnormality because it is too subjective and diffuse, but it can be modified to yield a good measure.

The last criterion, *objective psychological inventories,* is criticized by Scott because of scoring problems and because of a close relationship to conformity. A more crucial issue in the present discussion is the content of these inventories. The content obviously must be determined by the test constructor's views about abnormality, that is, his criteria of abnormality.

This analysis of the five research criteria of abnormality reveals that most of them are unsatisfactory, although two of them are potentially useful. Eventually, better ones will be developed, but the problem of the fuzziness of the concept may prove to be a severe limitation.

PRACTICAL CRITERIA OF ABNORMALITY

At first glance it would seem that medical concepts of abnormality and illness are clearer and simpler than psychological concepts. However, as we shall see in Chapter 2, medical concepts of disease are also complex and confusing. These issues do not bother the medical practitioner, the one who actually treats abnormality, because his definition is simple: abnormality is a disturbance in biological functioning serious enough to cause discomfort. This pragmatic definition resembles admission to a mental hospital as a criterion of abnormality, and it suffers from the same defect, namely, that not all medical abnormality is brought to the office, clinic, or hospital.

Whereas the practitioner's definition is incomplete, the approach underlying it may be of help. This approach is pragmatic; it inquires about the kinds of complaints that are serious enough to be brought to professional attention. The value of this line of thinking is that it implicitly recognizes the everyday, rule-of-thumb nature of concepts like illness and abnormality. Like many terms used in biology and psychology, they have definite referents and can be used meaningfully, but they are fuzzy and imprecise. They have meanings that go beyond careful arm-chair or research definitions. They resemble the concept of *intelligence,* which has great practical significance but little scientific stature.

Perhaps the solution to the problem is to regard abnormality as a rough, everyday notion—useful but without theoretical pretensions. This approach still requires a search for criteria of abnormality, but the search is focused on the criteria used in clinical practice. The question becomes: what are the reasons for labeling persons as psychologically abnormal?

There are three practical criteria of abnormality: discomfort, bizarreness, and inefficiency. They are difficult to quantify and depend in part on social context, but they constitute the clinical bases for labeling an individual as psychologically abnormal.

Discomfort

Discomfort may take many forms. There is the kind of *indisposition* that drives people to taking medicine or seeing a physician: aches, pains, nausea, fatigue, etc. These symptoms of bodily distress are often caused by medical illness, and as such they do not concern us here. However, physical (somatic) symptoms may occur in the absence of a medical disease and in fact may be caused by psychological factors. These do concern us, for they constitute one of three kinds of psychological discomfort.

In practice, the client usually seeks a physician's help in relieving bodily distress. If the physician can account for the complaints on the basis of a disease process, the malady will be labeled medical. Otherwise, the patient will be regarded as psychologically abnormal and referred to a clinical psychologist or psychiatrist. The borderline between medical and psychological symptoms involving bodily complaints is diffuse and hazy. Some neurotic symptoms mimic those seen in organic disease (see Chapter 4), and certain kinds of symptom patterns, called psychosomatic disorders (see Chapter 16), are caused at least in part by psychological determinants. Note that the labeling of bodily discomfort as *psychological abnormality* is based upon etiological (causal) variables and not upon the mere presence of symptoms.

The second kind of discomfort is *worry*. The apprehensiveness may be about the present or the future; it may be variable or constant; it may be about any aspect of life, from a fear of heights to a fear of "going crazy." Whatever the nature of the anxieties, they constitute a state of discomfort, and relief from anxiety is much sought after in everyday life.

Allied to worry is *depression*, the third kind of discomfort. Changes in mood are part of normal adjustment, and temporary gloom may be an entirely appropriate reaction to failure, disappointment, or physiological indisposition (say, a hangover). However, the melancholy may endure long after the temporary event that elicited it, or its occurrence may be unrelated to any sorrow-producing event; in such instances the depression is abnormal.

The presence of enduring anxiety or depression is sufficient for labeling the behavior as psychologically abnormal; it is not necessary to establish the psychological determinants underlying these symptoms. Of course, upon closer scrutiny it may turn out that the anxiety or the depression is caused by organic sources, but whether or not this proves to be the case, the symptoms are ordinarily regarded as evidence of psychological abnormality. The opposite situation prevails for bodily symptoms: they are ordinarily regarded as evidence of medical abnormality until proven otherwise.

The discomfort criterion of abnormality resembles *subjective unhappi-*

ness, which was discussed earlier. Unhappiness is a poor criterion of abnormality not only because it denotes a transient mood state, but also because it has manifold and diffuse connotations. Furthermore, it is closely linked with only one of the three kinds of discomfort, depression. Discomfort is preferred as a criterion because it is more comprehensive, including not only depression, but also anxiety and bodily symptoms. In addition, discomfort connotes a less subjective criterion than does unhappiness, which refers to a purely subjective state of affairs. We can learn about an individual's discomfort from his self-report, but we can also *observe* his anxiety (fidgeting, restlessness, sweaty hands), his depression (sad mien, slow movements, no initiative), and bodily distress (pallor, flushing).

Bizarreness

Bizarreness may be defined as *abnormal* deviations from accepted standards of behavior or deviations from (consensually defined) reality. This criterion includes such major deviations as delusions, hallucinations, and severe memory loss, as well as such minor oddities as motor tics, phobias, and compulsive rituals. Not all deviations from accepted standards are abnormal, some kinds of nonconformity being tolerated as more or less normal. For example, women's topless bathing suits represent a deviation from the accepted standard of modesty and wearing one in public is unlawful in most communities, but the wearer would not be considered psychologically abnormal. However, while a woman's exposing her breasts is not considered abnormal, exposure of the genitals in public by either men or women is considered psychologically abnormal.

These examples make it clear that bizarreness is defined *socially,* for it is the community that decides whether a specific act is only a minor deviation from what is allowable or a major deviation from the standard and therefore abnormal. Thus cultural relativism is important in the evaluation of bizarreness. What is bizarre and abnormal in one culture may be accepted and normal in another. Note that this follows from the definition of bizarreness as deviations from accepted standards of behavior. This kind of bizarreness includes most of the behaviors labeled abnormal: individual peculiarities and asocial acts. Normality shades into abnormality imperceptibly; a mild compulsion to note the numbers on automobile license plates seems normal enough, but it is not far removed from the abnormal compulsion of counting and recounting or checking and rechecking one's money, accounts, or possessions. Most neurotic symptoms fall into this class of bizarre behavior. In addition to compulsions, there are obsessive thoughts, phobias (unrealistic fears), diffuse, nameless fears, and an inability to make a decision or choice. On a dimension that ranges from normality to extreme abnormality these symptoms represent moderate abnormality.

Asocial acts, representing more severe abnormality, consist of the chronic breaking of the unwritten and, in some instances, the written rules of society. This includes delinquency, chronic drunkeness, addiction to drugs, and sexual perversions. Sexual perversions are the most difficult deviations to identify because the standard for normality varies not only among societies but also within different segments of a single society. For example, lower-class morality judges masturbation a perversion, but middle-class (especially upper-middle-class) morality does not. Furthermore, some behaviors are considered less abnormal in women than in men. For example, male homosexuality is commonly considered more perverse than female homosexuality.

Thus cultural relativism prevails in assessing sexual perversion, as it does in evaluating the abnormality of any of the behaviors included in this class of bizarreness. In fact, this class is defined by the *social* evaluation of the behaviors. Society is inconsistent in the degree of deviation it will tolerate; in general, it tolerates little nonconformity in sexual behavior and much nonconformity in nonsexual behavior. Individuals who have failed to learn the rules of society or who, knowing them, flout them, are on the face of it abnormal.

Bizarreness also includes a second class of behaviors, deviations from reality. We perceive reality with our sense organs but make corrections for faulty sense impressions when necessary. We learn that distant objects appear smaller than near objects, and we learn to correct for distortions when viewing objects submersed in water. Thus we believe our senses so long as our perceptions do not clash with those of everyone else, and we disbelieve our senses when they counter common knowledge (e.g., we know, despite our senses, that the world is not flat). The major *misperceptions* of reality are called hallucinations: seeing, hearing, feeling what is not there and experiencing peculiar, unrealistic bodily sensations. Delusions are *misinterpretations* of events and others' behavior; being incorrect evaluations, they are less abnormal than hallucinations, which are faulty perceptions. *Disorientation,* or not knowing the date, the month, the year, or the place, is also a clear deviation from reality.

This second class of bizarreness, consisting of hallucinations, delusions, and disorientation, represents a failure of "biological" adaptation. The term *biological* is used here to indicate adaptation to the *physical* environment, as opposed to the social environment. All biological organisms require means of sensing the physical environment to take appropriate action in avoiding danger, obtaining nutrition, etc. In a normal organism the sense organs and the brain process stimulus inputs properly, giving a more or less accurate picture of the environment. When the cognitive apparatus (sense organs and brain) present a distorted picture of the physical world, there is a gross failure in biological adaptation. It is analogous to the failures seen in biological diseases, especially diseases of the nervous system. This does not mean that the cause of deviations from reality is neural damage, only that the symptoms are analogous. In both instances the malfunctioning occurs in relation to the physical or biological aspects of the environment.

In general, this second class of bizarreness is relatively easy to recognize. It constitutes extreme abnormality and is seen only in the most disturbed patients, psychotics. In fact, the most important difference between psychosis and other kinds of psychopathology lies in the cognitive dysfunction seen in psychosis: inability to perceive correctly the nature of the physical world. This kind of bizarreness does not depend on a social evaluation because the stimuli are physical, not social. Since the physical environment, in terms of stimulus inputs, is essentially the same everywhere, this second class of bizarreness is universal. The cognitive symptoms of psychosis are universal in the same sense that medical disease is universal: biological adaptation does not respect geographical or social boundaries.

It has been argued that hallucinations, delusions, and disorientation cannot be accepted universally as signs of abnormality because of differences from one culture to another. Delusions might be acceptable in some "primitive" societies, and hallucinations, especially those involving religion, have been accepted as true and real in relatively advanced Western culture. Although in the past there have been differences among societies in their tolerance of bizarre perceptual behavior, it does not follow that we must accept the cultural relativism. Gross misperception or reality is abnormal wherever it occurs, and if a society is too backward technologically to recognize this fact, it does not alter the matter. The issue concerns the "biological" functioning of sense organs and the brain; the distinction between reality and fantasy is one that must be made in all societies. In every society some members break with reality. Therefore the perceptual symptoms of psychoses are universal, although it may require a professional to judge them. The symptoms are real whether or not they are observed by a professional person, just as the microbes seen by the biology instructor are present whether or not his student sees them.

The point is that whereas cultural relativism is entirely appropriate in evaluating the abnormality of certain deviations from accepted standards (specifically, those included in the first class, described above), it does not apply in evaluating the abnormality of cognitive deviations. In some societies abnormalities of perception are excused or even valued, but they are never considered normal. Misperceptions of reality are not considered the norm nor are they common in *any* society, and the fact that they are dealt with differently in some societies does not make them normal. Reality, in the sense of recognizing the physical world around us, is a universal issue, and failure to be in contact with reality must be considered universally abnormal.

This discussion of bizarreness would not be complete without mentioning danger. Initially, danger would seem to be a separate criterion of abnormality, distinct from bizarreness. Thus when an individual harms or threatens to harm himself, he is considered abnormal. However, it is not the danger that renders such behavior abnormal but the bizarreness. Harming *others* is not in itself considered abnormal, only illegal. The criminal who steals, murders, or embezzles in order to obtain money, is engaged in earning a living. Whereas his methods are illegal, he is not necessarily abnormal. If he suffers no discomfort, is reasonably efficient at his livelihood, and his illegal acts are designed solely to obtain money, he is *psychologically* normal. Most criminal behavior is illegal but psychologically normal in that the individual is plying what is often a lucrative trade. Note that the issue is not one of morality: criminal behavior should not be condoned, but illegal and immoral behaviors are not necessarily abnormal.

On the other hand, abnormality is not restricted to self-inflicted harm. Some acts that are dangerous to others may be so bizarre as to be labeled abnormal. Some "crimes of passion," committed without anticipation of material gain, are considered bizarre enough to be called abnormal. The law recognizes this important distinction, demanding that a defendant must be legally competent in the sense of being "normal" before he stands trial. Defendants judged not responsible are incarcerated in psychiatric institutions and are not tried until they are declared legally sane. The important point to remember is that it is not danger that is the criterion of abnormality when a crime has been committed, but bizarreness.

Inefficiency

Each member of society is assigned social roles on the basis of age, sex, class status, vocation, etc. These roles have both privileges and responsibilities, and it is the responsibilities that concern us here. In fulfilling the responsibilities of a role, each person is expected to maintain some minimal level of efficiency in rendering service, producing goods, keeping house, or attaining passing grades in school. There is a dimension of efficiency in fulfilling social roles, which ranges from expertness to incompetence. Society will tolerate some inefficiency because expertness cannot be required of everyone, but beyond a vaguely defined borderline, inefficiency is considered abnormal.

Efficiency may be assessed in two different ways. The first is to compare the individual's performance with his potential. For example, an individual with an IQ of 140 would be expected to perform very well in intellectual tasks and to be able to hold a responsible position vocationally and in the community. If this person rose no higher in vocational status than the job of janitor, this would represent a clear breakdown in efficiency. Such a pronounced differential between actual and potential performance is indicative of abnormality.

The second way to evaluate efficiency is to compare performance with the requirements of the role. Some positions demand little social, intellectual, or organizational skill. In the example just mentioned, even a person deficient in these skills might be able to meet the requirements of the position; in fact, this is precisely the reason that those with great potential but inefficient performance gravitate toward such positions. The requirements of the role may be so slight that an individual who is inefficient in the utilization of his potential would be able to fulfill the role efficiently. Many occupations and roles do not demand full efficiency from the individual. Minor disorganization is tolerated, and many people manage with only a minimal level of performance. Some positions, especially those involving responsibility for the welfare of others, require considerable organizational skill and top performance; hence inefficiency is discovered more easily than in less responsible positions. Thus the criterion of disorganization is related to the level of efficiency demanded by the role. The greater the status, complexity, and responsibility of the role, the more quickly is inefficiency (and therefore, abnormality) detected.

Inefficiency was one of the two aspects of the rough definition of abnormality presented earlier. It was stated in terms of inability to manage one's own affairs, which represents an extreme degree of inefficiency. Such gross inefficiency usually leads to commitment to a mental hospital: the housewife who neglects the dishes, the meals, and the laundry, and just sits on the floor, staring; or the businessman who suddenly initiates wild and unrealistic schemes that would soon bankrupt his firm. When the inefficiency is this extreme, it is easy to notice. Milder degrees of inefficiency are more difficult to detect, which means that the abnormality involved is more difficult to assess. As noted above, an individual with great potential may be inefficient in the sense of not using his potential but efficient in fulfilling the requirements of an undemanding role. Thus both kinds of inefficiency must be taken into account in evaluating abnormality.

The role of inefficiency in psychopathology has been emphasized by Wishner who pointed out its advantages:

. . . the term efficiency is preferred here to such terms as appropriateness or adequacy because the latter usually involve a priori value judgment, which would make an objective definition of psychological health impossible. Moreover, efficiency immediately implies something quantifiable, whereas appropriateness and adequacy are usually considered in qualitative terms. (1955, p. 70)

Wishner stated a limitation of the concept of efficiency: it is meaningful only when the requirements of the task are all clearly specified. In everyday situations it is often difficult to specify the task requirements precisely and the behaviors called for. In fact, many everyday tasks require behaviors that must satisfy multiple criteria, for example, criticizing a student's paper without rejecting the student as a person.

These limitations emphasize the basic problem of the concept of abnormality, which should be regarded as a rough, practical notion rather
than as a precise, scientific construct. It has been established that severely
disturbed patients are less efficient than normals when efficiency can be
defined precisely and quantitatively (see the laboratory research in Chapters
12 and 13). Efficiency can be assessed precisely in the controlled environment of the laboratory but not in the uncontrolled environment of every-day
life. However, regarded as a practical, qualitative concept that represents
one aspect of abnormality, efficiency is of considerable use in evaluating
psychopathology.

Practical Criteria and Symptoms

It is customary in medical practice to distinguish between so-called
objective symptoms (observed by the physician) and subjective symptoms
(reported by the patient). *Objective* and *subjective* are awkward terms in
this context. They should be replaced by the terms *sign* (indicant) and
complaint. A sign is any aspect of the individual's functioning that indicates
abnormality. In medicine it would be biological dysfunction, which might
indicate an underlying disease process. In psychopathology it would be psychological dysfunction, which might indicate an underlying "disease"
process. A complaint is a verbalization by the patient that something is
wrong. In medicine it is usually *pain;* in psychopathology it is usually
anxiety.

The two kinds of symptoms, signs and complaints, are related to our
practical criteria of abnormality. Inefficiency and bizarreness, which are observed by the clinician, are *signs* of psychological dysfunction. Discomfort,
which is ordinarily reported by the patient, falls under the heading of *complaints.* The analogy between medicine and psychopathology may be carried
a step further. Medical research has concentrated on signs, which can be
observed objectively and quantified, rather than on complaints, which tend
to be unreliable and qualitative. Similarly, psychopathological research has
concentrated on inefficiency (see Chapters 12 and 13) rather than discomfort for precisely the same reasons.

NORMALITY AND MODERATION

It is widely recognized that there are optimal states of the organism,
optimal amounts of food ingested, optimal amounts of discipline, etc. Ex-
cesses in either direction—too much or too little—represent maladaptation,
dysfunction, or perhaps even disease. There are many medical examples
of the association between moderation (an optimal amount or degree) and
normality (health), but one will suffice here. This is diastolic blood pressure, which optimally is between 75 and 85 millimeters of mercury. Extremes of blood pressure, both high and low, are signs of ill health.

X

The association between moderation and normality may also hold for psychological adjustment. Clinicians acknowledge that certain personality dimensions are important in psychopathology. As we shall see in Chapter 4, dimensions relating to dependency, aggression, and sexuality are believed to be especially important in neurosis. In evaluating the relationship between moderation and normality, it is necessary to establish bipolar dimensions, with extremes at each end and moderation in the middle. This is precisely what was done by Buss and Gerjuoy (1957) with 18 dimensions of personality. Adjectives were scaled along each dimension first for intensity and then for abnormality. The judges were clinical psychologists.

The results of the scaling for the Impulsiveness dimension are shown in Table 1.1.

The words connoting the greatest impulsivity have the lowest intensity scale values, and as the intensity scale values increase, the words connote less impulsivity and greater deliberateness. The dimension proceeds from too much impulsiveness (*incontinent, reckless, rash*) to too little (*overcautious, retarded, sluggish*); these are the extremes. The middle of the dimension (*spontaneous, self-possessed*) represents moderation.

TABLE 1.1   INTENSITY AND ABNORMALITY SCALING FOR IMPULSIVENESS

	Intensity	Abnormality
incontinent	2.1	7.8
reckless	2.2	7.0
rash	2.7	6.3
impetuous	2.8	5.8
excitable	3.6	5.1
hasty	3.9	5.0
abrupt	4.1	4.5
restless	4.4	4.8
mobile	4.7	3.8
spontaneous	4.8	1.8
self-possessed	5.5	2.1
cool-headed	5.7	2.0
deliberate	5.9	3.0
controlled	6.0	2.8
restrained	6.6	4.2
staid	6.6	4.3
overcautious	7.3	5.5
retarded	7.8	6.8
sluggish	7.8	5.8

The abnormality scale values vary directly with abnormality, the highest numbers representing the greatest abnormality. Note that abnormality is greatest at the extremes and least in the middle of the dimension. Thus the extremes of too much and too little impulsiveness are associated with abnormality; the moderate range of impulsivness is associated with normality. The relationship is asymmetrical: too much impulsivity represents greater abnormality than too little impulsivity. The asymmetry is present in most of the 18 dimensions scaled by Buss and Gerjuoy. Thus too little self-esteem is more abnormal than too much; too little autonomy is more abnormal than too much, too much anxiety is more abnormal than too little, etc. The asymmetry is probably present in virtually all personality dimensions, one extreme being more abnormal than the other; assymmetry is probably present biologically also. However, the asymmetry is a minor issue. The major point to remember is the relationship between extremes and abnormality, between moderation and normality.

Finally, the analogy between biological and psychological moderation should not be pushed too far. Biological moderation comes about largely through feedback mechanisms similar to a thermostat on a furnace (homeostatic mechanisms). As we shall see in the next chapter, there are no similar mechanisms in the areas of personality and adjustment.

REFERENCES

Buss, A. H., & Gerjuoy, H. The scaling of adjectives descriptive of personality. *Journal of Consulting Psychology*, 1957, **21**, 366–371.

Hobbs, N. Sources of gain in psychotherapy. *American Psychologist*, 1962, **17**, 741–747.

Jahoda, Marie. *Current concepts of positive mental health.* New York: Basic Books, 1958.

Kubie, S. The fundamental nature of the distinction between normality and neurosis. *Psychoanalytical Quarterly*, 1954, **23**, 167–204.

Redlich, F. D. The concept of health in psychiatry. In A. H. Leighton, J. A. Clausen, & R. N. Wilson (Eds.). *Explorations in social psychiatry.* New York: Basic Books, 1957, pp. 138–164.

Scott, W. A. Research definitions of mental health and mental illness. *Psychological Bulletin*, 1958, **55**, 29–45.

Shoben, E. Toward a concept of normal personality. *American Psychologist*, 1957, **12**, 183–189.

Srole, L., Langner, T. S., Michael, S. T., Opler, M. K., & Rennie, T. A. C. *Mental health in the metropolis: the midtown Manhattan study.* New York: McGraw-Hill, 1962.

Szasz, T. S. The uses of naming and the origin of the myth of mental illness. *American Psychologist*, 1961, **16**, 59–65.

Wishner, J. The concept of efficiency in psychological health and in psychopathology. *Psychological Review*, 1955, **62**, 69–80.

CHAPTER 2

Concepts and Models
of Psychopathology

Abnormality is related to disease. The normal-abnormal dichotomy is paralleled by the health-disease dichotomy; normality connotes health, and abnormality connotes disease. We saw in Chapter 1 how the practical medical notion of abnormality helped to define abnormality in psychopathology. Now we shall examine how medical concepts of disease have been applied to psychopathology.

MEDICAL CONCEPTS OF DISEASE

Medical concepts of disease, like concepts of normality, have been essentially pragmatic. Systematic definition came only after many decades of using everyday "rules of thumb." It has been suggested that there are three criteria of disease: a specific cluster of symptoms, a specific etiology, and a specific treatment (von Bertalanffy, 1960). This is a narrower view of disease than is commonly held, and what makes the definition so restrictive is the third criterion, a specific treatment. This criterion appears to be superfluous because its presence may be related to chance variables. When a pattern of symptoms (syndrome) has been described and its cause discovered, there may still be no specific treatment. For example, the complex cluster of symptoms called Addison's disease was known to be the result of a defect in the cortex of the adrenal glands, but many decades passed before the major products of the adrenal cortex were discovered. Subsequently, a specific treatment became available for Addison's disease, but before the discovery of cortisone, the syndrome was a disease. When the etiology of a syndrome is known, curative treatment is *possible*. Whether successful treatment procedures are developed depends on the difficulty of the task and the ingenuity of researchers.[1]

With these considerations as background, let us clarify terminology. *Disease* is defined as a state of ill health marked by symptoms; it is synonomous with *syndrome*. A *disease entity* is a syndrome whose etiology is known. Thus *disease* is the more generic term. Many diseases cannot be cured, principally because their etiology is unknown; some disease entities cannot be cured because knowledge of their cause has not yet led to practical treatment measures.

Types of Disease

Man is subject to many ills, the number of different kinds depending upon how disease is defined. Since our ultimate interest is in psychopathology rather than medicine, we need not construct a list that includes every medical disorder. The center of attention here is the types of disease that have analogues in psychopathology. This eliminates from consideration anomalies such as limbs deformed at birth, cleft palate, etc. There remain three different kinds of diseases: infection, systemic disease, and noninfectious trauma.

Infectious Disease. Infections involve an invasion of the body by a parasite, which attacks a specific organ or an organ system such as the digestive tract. The manifest symptoms are the result of destruction of tissue, products of the parasite's metabolism, or defensive operations of the body. The usual treatment is to attempt to destroy the parasite without harming body tissues, and to this end a large number of antibiotics have been discovered and used successfully. Of more enduring worth is preventive treatment, which enables the organism to build up immunity to the invading parasite. Immunity is established by exposing the host organism to extremely mild attack by the parasite, in either live or dead form. The defensive operations set in motion by inoculation are usually sufficient to resist later attacks of the parasite in full force, for example, the Salk vaccine.

Because of the success of the inoculation method, there has been increasing interest in the host-parasite interaction. This marks a departure from the earlier emphasis solely on germs. The epidemiological approach, which is of great importance in modern medicine, places as much emphasis on the variables determining resistance of the host organism as on the potency of the parasite. Approaching disease in terms of the parasite-host relationship has been so useful in medicine that some have come to identify infectious disease with the idea of disease itself. Infections are regarded as

---

[1] Treatment may also be discovered by trial-and-error and used successfully without knowledge of the reason for success, but this fact is peripheral to the issue under discussion.

diseases, and all other illnesses are viewed as "functional disorders." The rationale for this approach becomes clear if we bear in mind the distinction between disease entities and diseases. The etiology of virtually all infectious diseases is known, but the etiology of most noninfectious diseases is generally unknown. Thus the difference between infectious diseases and functional disorders may be construed as the difference between disease entities and diseases.

Systemic Disease. Systemic diseases are the functional disorders just mentioned: noninfectious ailments involving the malfunction of organs or, more frequently, organ systems. Etiology is sometimes known, or approximately known. For example, in diabetes the defect in sugar utilization has been traced to malfunction of the insulin-producing apparatus, the Isles of Langerhans. Unfortunately, it is not clear what triggers this malfunction, so that only part of the cause is known. For treatment purposes, this knowledge is usually sufficient, and the condition is more or less remedied by administering insulin.

More generally, etiology is unknown, as in essential hypertension, which is a sustained elevation of resting blood pressure level in the absence of kidney malfunction. Treatment of high blood pressure is directed toward alleviating discomfort and attempting to diminish the pressure (as, for example, by hypotensive drugs). This is analogous to treating the fever caused by an infection: symptoms may be alleviated, but there is no attempt to remove the cause of the disease.

These two examples, diabetes and hypertension, demonstrate the difference between infectious disease and systemic disease. In infectious disease the cause is known because it is an invading parasite (for present purposes we omit weakness of the host as a major cause), whereas in the latter, there is usually no unequivocal cause. The consequences of this difference for treatment are obvious, and it is abundantly clear why medicine has had more success with infectious than with systemic disease.

Noninfectious Trauma. This awkward phrase includes bodily malfunction that is due to two kinds of environmental stress. The first is poison, which may not kill the individual but may cause severe illness. For example, men who were gassed during the First World War subsequently developed a variety of respiratory and digestive illnesses.

The second kind of stress is physical force that causes injury. Some injuries have enduring effects, as can be seen from two examples. A blow on the head may lead to brain damage and long-term neurological symptoms. A fractured bone or dislocated joint may lead to improper use of the body part and perhaps eventually to arthritis. The foregoing examples are all sudden stresses, but the trauma may be insidious and long-lasting. The relation between lung cancer and a variety of air pollutants (including tobacco smoke) has been well established. The stress or poison may have so slight an immediate effect that it requires many years to produce symptoms.

The Unified Theory of Disease

During the last century and part of this century the success of germ theory in explaining illness and leading to treatment led to its being accepted as the basic model of disease. Within the last several decades, however, there have been increasing attacks against it as the best way of understanding disease. Now that most infectious diseases have been mastered, physicians are more concerned with systemic diseases like arthritis and hypertension. Systemic diseases cannot be explained by germ theory, nor can the illnesses caused by poisons. In rejecting germ theory some physicians have broadened the entire concept of disease, and the result has been the unified theory of disease.

Engel (1960) rejects the older, mechanistic concepts of disease, according to which the body is a machine and disease is due to a defective part. From him, "Disease corresponds to failures or disturbance in the growth, development, functions, and adjustments of the organism as a whole or any of its systems" (p. 459). Wolf (1961) goes further, stating that *both* health and illness are aspects of man's way of life. Thus disease is not a special state or a temporary derangement, but *part of man's state of being*. This approach regards symptoms as a temporary flare-up or intensification of continuing processes. An individual is not healthy *or* sick; he is more or less healthy (less or more sick).

In this context an invasion of parasites is merely one of many noxious aspects of the environment. The organism must cope not only with germs but also with trauma, poisons, and stresses that tax its adaptive resources. For example, there are adaptive biological mechanisms for handling short-term emergencies, but no organism can cope with an emergency that endures over time. Short-term adaptive mechanisms break down when required to maintain themselves over time, and the breakdown results in symptoms. Thus the unified approach attempts to encompass all three kinds of disease under the general heading of *maladaptation.* The organism must continually adapt to a changing and potentially noxious environment, and disease represents failure or inefficiency in adapting. Failure refers to inability to prevent damage by noxious agents such as germs, poisons, or trauma. Inefficiency refers to victory over the noxious agents but only at the cost of worn or damaged organs or organ systems.

Medical Models of Psychopathology

Infection. The success of germ theory during the last century led psychiatrists to believe that most psychopathology was also caused by an invasion of parasites. This hypothesis was greatly strengthened when the cause of paresis was discovered. The symptoms of paresis closely resemble "functional psychosis" (no known organic etiology), and there were many dynamic speculations about its etiology. Then it was found that the symptoms resulted from neural deterioration, which in turn was caused by the syphillis spirochete. When these facts became known, the infectious disease model of psychopathology assumed greater importance. However, there have been no subsequent discoveries similar to the germ etiology of paresis, and this theory of psychopathology is now mainly of historical interest.

Systemic Disease. In systemic disease there may be an abnormal outpouring of chemical products (too much or too little), as in diabetes, or malfunctioning of a mechanical system, as in hypertension. When this disease model is applied to psychopathology, the emphasis is biochemical. This is especially true of attempts to explain schizophrenia, which is regarded by many clinicians as a biological disease. Some investigators believe that the defect is in the autonomic nervous system and others suggest that endocrine malfunction (especially the adrenal cortex because of faulty reactions to stress) is the basic problem. During the last 15 years there has been mounting interest in brain chemistry and the substances that affect neural transmission. These matters will be discussed more fully in Chapter 14. For the present we may note that the systemic disease model has adherents and may be a fruitful approach, at least in studying psychosis.

It might be argued that the systemic disease model is particularly useful because chemical therapy (insulin coma) has been at least partially successful in treating schizophrenia. This partial success would seem to suggest that schizophrenia may be analogous to a disease like pneumonia. The analogy does not hold. There is a specific pneumococcus in pneumonia, whereas the etiology of schizophrenia is obscure. Chemical therapy in pneumonia kills the etiological agent. Chemical therapy in schizophrenia attempts only to remove the symptoms; the severe physiological stress of sugar deprivation is aimed not at an etiological agent, but at a reduction in bizarre thoughts and behavior. Thus the use of particular therapies in treating certain psychoses is not evidence for the psychoses' being disease entities, and it is not an argument for the systemic disease model.

Noninfectious Trauma. As noted earlier, noninfectious trauma leads either to poisoning or to injury. Poisoning can produce a variety of psychological symptoms, especially cognitive symptoms. A number of drugs, including alcohol, lead to sensory disturbances and sometimes to hallucinations and delusions. Injury of the brain can cause a psychosis with symptoms similar to those seen in schizophrenia. Neither of these conditions is encountered frequently in psychosis. Although they are certainly observed in clinical practice, psychoses resulting from drugs or brain damage are infrequent in comparison to "functional psychoses."

The lack of demonstrated brain damage in most cases of schizophrenia and manic-depressive psychosis is apparently not an obstacle to some theorists, who insist on a traumatic model of psychosis. Some believe that schizophrenics and brain-damaged patients show the same underlying problems, the main difference being in the grossness of the brain damage.

We have been using the word *trauma* to mean a *physical* stress that causes injury, but the term may be defined to include psychological stress as well. Verbal attacks, threats, and rejection, being noxious stimuli, may be regarded as traumatic events. Such noxious stimuli may initiate defensive or emotional reactions, which in turn may lead to abnormality. When clinicians speak of psychological causes of psychopathology, they are implicitly using the noninfectious trauma model. Thus there are two trauma models. The first assumes that abnormal behavior is caused by physically noxious stimuli, which damage the central nervous system. The second model assumes that abnormal behavior is caused by psychologically noxious stimuli, which initiate anxiety, depression, or maladaptive defensive reactions.

The Unitary Concept

This is an analogue of the unitary disease concept. A number of writers, dissatisfied with standard psychiatric classification and the underlying assumption of separate disease entities, have suggested that the disease entities concept be replaced by a unitary concept of psychopathology. Karl Menninger (1960, 1963) has been a forceful advocate of this point of view:

Suppose that instead of putting so much emphasis on different kinds of illness we tried to think of all mental illness as being essentially the same in quality and differing, rather, quantitatively. This is what we mean when we say that we all have mental illness of different degrees at different times, and that sometimes some of us are much worse or much better. (1960, p. 63)

He sets up a continuum of psychological health, with happiness and achievement at one end, and misery, failure, and crime at the other end. This approach denies the importance of qualitative differences among different syndromes, which presumably differ only in severity of disturbance. The attempt to order the various symptom clusters in terms of degree of psychopathology should certainly be applauded, but it is debatable whether they can be aligned along a single dimension. Psychotics are, by professional consensus, more disturbed than neurotics; yet some psychotics have a better prognosis and are more mature than some neurotics. Thus the notion of a single dimension of severity for all the varieties of psychopathology, while intriguing in its parsimony, appears to be an oversimplification.

Underlying the unified concept of psychopathology, according to Menninger and other adherents, is the principle of *homeostasis:* organisms attempt to maintain a steady state and react to any stress (parasites, hormonal imbalance, hunger, threat, etc.) with mechanisms that restore the organism to the central, balanced state. All symptoms are regarded as restitutive reactions by the organism in the face of threat or unbalance.

Ausubel (1961) has shown how this position applies to both medicine and psychopathology. He divides symptoms into three classes: both adjustive and adaptive, adjustive but not adaptive, and neither adjustive nor adaptive:

The plausibility of subsuming abnormal behavioral reactions to stress under the general rubric of disease is further enhanced by the fact that these reactions include the same three principal categories of symptoms found in physical illness. Depression and catastrophic impairment of self-esteem, for example, are manifestations of personality disorder which are symptomologically comparable to edema in cardiac failure or to heart murmurs in valvular disease. They are indicative of underlying pathology but are neither adaptive nor adjustive. Symptoms such as hypomanic overactivity and compulsive striving toward unrealistically high achievement goals, on the other hand, are both adaptive and adjustive, and constitute a type of compensatory response to basic feelings of inadequacy, which is not unlike cardiac hypertrophy in hypertensive heart disease or elevated white blood cell count in acute infections. And, finally, distortive psychological defenses that have some adjustive value, but are generally maladaptive (for example, phobias, delusions, autistic fantasies) are analogous to the pathological situation found in conditions like pneumonia, in which the excessive outpouring of serum and phagocytes in defensive response to pathogenic bacteria literally causes the patient to drown in his own fluids. (1961, p. 72)

Actually, there are only two kinds of symptoms in Ausubel's system: those that are part of an attempt to react to stress and restore balance, and those that are part of a failure of worn-out mechanisms to respond.

Thus the unitary concept regards symptoms in terms of partial or complete failure of the organism to adapt, adaptation consisting of a restoration to the steady, resting state. The concept of homeostasis requires that two conditions be demonstrated: (1) that there is a resting or steady state, which is in essence a zero point with respect to change, and (2) that there are negative feedback mechanisms to reverse the effect of any external event that forces a deviation from a steady state. These two conditions can be demonstrated for a number of physiological systems, and, not surprisingly, the concept of homeostasis originated in physiology.

Body temperature, which is regulated homeostatically, has a central steady state. Heat leads to sweating, which cools the body; cold leads to shivering, which cuts down exposure to the air and warms the body. Using temperature regulation and other physiological systems as models, the concept of homeostasis has been extended to psychology and psychopathology. If the steady state is equated with optimal adaptation, then external stress can be equated with threats to adaptation. Since failure to adapt ultimately means death, some homeostatic mechanisms are required for survival. Survival can refer not only to integrity of the body but also to integrity of the personality. A major exponent of this line of reasoning has been Stagner:

The important features of adult behavior include protecting one's family against economic and other threats, protecting one's feeling of self-respect against attack, protecting the status of one's profession or social group, and so on. It is easy to see that such actions are homeostatic in the sense that the individual has achieved a favorable steady state and acts to defend it, just as he did at the tissue level as regards temperature, water, and food. (1961, p. 20)

Note the similarity in approach to Ausubel's. Homeostasis is assumed to be a generalized description of all human systems, behavioral and physiological, with these differing only in "level."

This formulation has not escaped criticism, the most penetrating being that of Davis (1958). He noted that one physiological steady state may be maintained at the expense of another. Thus temperature regulation is maintained in part by sweating, but sweating causes variability in the water-salt balance; this means that the price of temperature constancy is water-salt variability. This example also demonstrates that homeostasis cannot be equated with adaptation, and therefore, survival. Sweating, which maintains a proper temperature in desert heat, also dehydrates the body; in the desert loss of salt and water could mean death.

Davis doubted that the criteria of homeostasis could be met by most psychological systems. Can we point to a steady state in psychology? The only one to do so was Freud; he did it in his hypothesis about the conservation of instinctual energy. Freud believed that the steady state is tensionless and that defensive efforts are directed toward removing all tension. Note that there is no central *balance* point but a steady state of zero or quiescence. In passing, we need only comment that the assumption that *all* tension is aversive does not stand up in light of what is known empirically.

When the steady state cannot be specified, the concept of homeostasis adds nothing.

Of course, so long as a process has any effect at all, it is always possible to find something or invent something which it regulates, and in each case one would have quite a wide choice. This is a particular danger when homeostasis is taken as a general model. We may be offered variables or entities which exist only to be opposed by homeostasis, and conversely homeostatic processes which are said to exist only because they are opposite to some known effect, according to some Hegelian logic.

An extreme example of such speculation, once offered in all seriousness, runs as follows: People have a homeostatic mechanism for maintaining social esteem, or the awareness of it. So, when they become aware that they have fallen in the opinion of their fellow men, they take action to raise their standing until their awareness of esteem reaches the point of equilibrium. The factual basis of this, so far as visible, is that people do things that others approve of, and it is doubtful that we know any more about this after learning the theory. (Davis, 1958, p. 11)

Davis' argument appears to hold for all of psychopathology. Nowhere is the equilibrium point specified; instead there are speculations similar to the one he noted concerning social esteem. In brief, until *both* the steady state and the precise mechanisms are clearly denoted, the concept of homeostasis will be of dubious value in psychopathology.

INNER ETIOLOGY AND ALTERNATIVES

A basic assumption underlies all medical concepts of disease: outer symptoms are caused by inner dysfunction. The sick person reports complaints, and the physician speculates about internal processes. Symptoms are on the surface, but the cause is deep inside. Treatment is directed toward correcting the inner ailment, and cure of the inner malady results in the disappearance of outer, manifest symptoms. An inner etiology may also be postulated for the overt symptoms of psychopathology, or this notion may be rejected as inappropriate outside of medicine. Two models of psychopathology assume an inner etiology, and three models reject it.

Inner Etiology

The Biological Model. The biological model regards psychological symptoms as a subclass of medical symptoms. Presumably, such symptoms occur because of some inner malady, and the disease model most commonly employed is that for systemic disease. Since this model was described above, we need discuss it no further.

The Psychoanalytic Model. Psychoanalytic concepts of disease and normality have changed somewhat since Freud's early formulations (Hollender & Szasz, 1957). The original model was conversion hysteria, a "disease" with clear-cut symptoms. Gradually, this disease concept was abandoned, replaced by a characterological approach in which the core issue is relationships with others, rather than symptoms. This approach gave way to the present one, which regards abnormality or disease as an unbalance of id, ego, and superego. It is this present-day model that will be discussed.

Psychoanalytic theory adopts the notion of an "inner man," or at least an inner "psychic anatomy." Symptoms are regarded as superficial manifestations of conflicts *inside* the inner person, in other words, intrapsychic conflict. This is "depth psychology." Depth is associated with covertness, unconsciousness, irrationality, and instincts or drives. Surface is associated with overtness, consciousness, rationality, and (in part) defenses against instincts or drives.

The anatomy of this inner man is tripartite: id, ego, and superego. The id is the source of all cravings, of all impulses, and of all "mental energy." It is the source of drives not only for food and warmth but also for sexual release and aggressive dominance. Since the expression of id impulses must at times run counter to the wishes of the outside world, it is necessary to have a kind of executive inside the organism. This executive or ego determines whether an id impulse will be expressed and how it will appear manifestly (in behavior). Fenichel describes the relationship between id and ego as follows:

Underneath the organized periphery of the ego lies the core of dynamic, driving chaos of forces, which strive for discharge and nothing else, but which constantly receive new stimulations from external as well as internal perceptions, influenced by somatic factors that determine how the perceptions are experienced. The organization proceeds from the surface to the depth. The ego is to the id as the ectoderm is to the endoderm. The ego becomes the mediator between the organism and the outer world. As such it has to provide protection against hostile influences from the environment as well as enforcement of gratification even against a restricting outside world. (1945, p. 16)

Note the analogy to anatomy: ego-ectoderm and id-endoderm. The psychoanalytic model is directly analogous to the medical model, and it follows that outer psychological symptoms must be caused by an inner psychic dysfunction. More precisely, the dysfunction must occur in the relationship between the ego and the id, that is, dysfunction of *inner* structures:

Since the normal functioning of the mind is governed by a control apparatus that organizes, leads, and inhibits deeper archaic and more instinctual forces—in the same way that the cortex organizes, leads, and inhibits impulses of the deeper and more archaic levels of the brain—it can be stated that the common denominator of all neurotic phenomena is an insufficiency of the normal control apparatus. (Fenichel, 1945, pp. 18–19)

The third structure comprising psychic anatomy is the superego, which consists of introjected parental attitudes and evaluations. The superego usually acts in opposition to the id, helping the ego to repress and channelize "immoral" id impulses. Of course if the ego allows the expression of "bad" instinctual demands, the superego turns against the ego.

Thus there are two kinds of conflict underlying all symptoms. First, the id may be opposed by the ego and superego. Because of guilt concerning instinctual urges, the superego lines up with the ego against the expression of forbidden desires. Second, when the ego allows some expression of guilt-laden impulses, it must fight both the id, which demands still more expression of its impulses, and the superego, which attacks the ego for allowing transgression of the moral code. Observable symptoms represent the end point or compromise of intrapsychic conflict. The entire etiology is concealed and unconscious, and the appearance of symptoms seems mysterious only because the events leading to psychopathology all occur within the inner man.

It is clear that psychoanalytic theory uses a disease model, with etiology being located inside the organism. The psychic events leading to manifest symptoms can be discovered but only by painstaking investigation of the history of inner conflicts via psychoanalytic therapy. Psychoanalysis leans toward the disease entities model rather than the unitary concept. There is a psychoanalytic etiology for each pattern of symptoms based on fixation or regression in the psychosexual sequence. Thus obsessiveness has its etiology in fixation at the anal stage of development, and depression, at the oral stage. If psychoanalytic theory is accepted, it is entirely appropriate to regard the various neuroses and psychoses as disease entities; not only is there a pattern of symptoms but also a specific psychoanalytic etiology. Those who accept psychoanalytic thinking are therefore entirely consistent in regarding mental illness as analogous to organic disease. This comprehensiveness is one reason for the wide acceptance of psychoanalytic thinking, for it offers a complete account of the various symptom clusters in terms of a developmental sequence of psychological stages. The point to note is that the entire developmental sequence, which may lead to psychopathology, occurs in the inner man: the behaviors of everday life and the inappropriate behaviors (symptoms) are merely superficial aspects of an underlying, dynamic interaction within the inner man. Thus psychoanalytic theory is analogous to the biological model in its assumption of an inner etiology.

Alternatives to Inner Etiology

Before discussing alternatives to inner etiology, we shall illustrate the issues involved by examining two physical phenomena. The first consists of volcanic eruptions, which are explained in terms of processes occurring within the earth. The only accepted explanations of volcanoes are those that point to an inner cause for outer "symptoms." The volcanic eruption is an event on the earth's surface that is explained by hypothetical events inside the earth.

The second phenomenon is the tidal action of oceans, another event occurring on the surface of the earth. Unlike volcanoes, tides are not ascribed to processes inside the earth. They are ascribed to a relationship between the earth and the moon, the crucial concept being a gravitational field between the two. Thus one alternative to an inner cause is a field theory, and two models of psychopathology are of this type.

The Learning Model. The learning model specifically rejects the notion of inner etiology. Although there are variations in particular learning theories, some leaning heavily on psychoanalytic theory (see Chapter 6), the fundamental assumption of the learning model is that the symptom *is* the disease. Psychopathology consists of insufficient learning, excessive learning, learning of incorrect responses, etc., and the explanation must be sought in the same principles underlying any behavior, for example, nature and timing of rewards and stimuli, schedules of reinforcement, and traumatic avoidance conditioning.

The learning model, like that of psychoanalysis, gives an important role to conflict, but the conflict is between habits or response tendencies, not between structures of the inner man. Thus two habits that have been learned in separate stimulus contexts may be called forth by a situation having elements of the stimuli that ordinarily elicit both responses; if the responses are incompatible, there is conflict. When the individual cannot resolve this conflict because of the equivalence of the two habits, he is labeled neurotic.

Other kinds of psychopathology may be listed. Self-defeating patterns may develop because the individual learns responses that are not appropriate (do not lead to reward' often enough or are not efficient in achieving a reward), or he learns not to learn or remember (repression). Habits that were once adjustive in that they led to rewards may no longer be appropriate, but the individual fails to extinguish them. There may be overuse of avoidance and underuse of approach responses. There may be failure to inhibit responses that lead only to punishment. Finally, there may be a simple failure to acquire the responses that are appropriate to the individual's role in everyday life, for example, failing to learn how to carry on a conversation with a member of the opposite sex.

What makes the learning model a "field theory" is its locus of explanation: stimulus-response relationships. Presumably, the crucial variable is the interaction between the individual and his environment. Attention centers on the stimuli that impinge on the individual and the responses that are elicited or emitted. All explanations of symptoms must be sought in the individual's learning history, which consists of stimuli, responses, rewards, punishments, etc. These are overt and manipulable phenomena, and they carry the burden of explanation. Thus the learning model rejects inner etiology for a field theory approach.

The Interpersonal Model. This model is really a restricted form of the learning model, differing in that it considers only one class of stimuli. This class is other people, and the "field" consists of the interaction between the individual and other people around him. Instead of emphasizing the entire learning history, the interest centers on significant personal relations, especially those occurring within the family. Parent-child interactions are of paramount importance, but interactions with siblings and peers are not neglected. Except for these restrictions, the interpersonal model is similar to the learning model in its emphasis on learned patterns, the importance of the organism-environment interaction, and the rejection of inner etiology.

The Regression Model. The regression model is neither an inner theory nor a field theory. It is a maturational theory which assumes a fixed developmental sequence. The individual moves through successive stages from infancy to adulthood. Adulthood represents maturity and normality—the end point of the developmental sequence. The symptoms of psychopathology are caused by a retracing of the steps in the sequence. The dispositions and behaviors appropriate to childhood are inappropriate to adulthood. When an adult can no longer cope with his problems with adult modes of behavior, he retreats to less demanding and less anxiety-laden modes. The inappropriate, childish tendencies result in the symptoms of psychopathology.

Thus it can be seen that the locus of explanation for this model is neither inside the organism, nor in an interaction, but in a kind of "psychobiological clock." Once the timetable is known, psychopathology can be understood: the deeper the regression, the more severe and ominous are the symptoms. The details are described in Chapters 5 and 11. It is interesting to note that psychoanalytic theory employs a regression model, the timetable being called *the psychosexual sequence.* The theory also assumes an inner etiology, and this combination is one of the reasons for the comprehensiveness of the psychoanalytic approach. Since the regression model does not specifically reject an inner etiology, the two can be combined harmoniously.

REFERENCES

Ausubel, D. P. Personality disorder *is* disease. *American Psychologist,* 1961, 16, 69–74.

von Bertalanffy, L. Some biological considerations of the problem of mental illness. In L. Appleby, J. Scher, & J. Cumming (Eds.). *Chronic schizophrenia.* Glencoe, Illinois: The Free Press, 1960, pp. 36–53.

Davis, R. C. The domain of homeostasis. *Psychological Review,* 1958, 65, 8–13.

Engel, G. L. A unified concept of health and disease. *Perspectives in Biological Medicine,* 1960, 3, 459–485.

Fenichel, O. *The psychoanalytic theory of neuroses.* New York: Norton, 1945.

Hollender, M. H., & Szasz, T. S. Normality, neurosis and psychosis. *Journal of Nervous and Mental Disease,* 1957, 125, 599–607.

Menninger, K. Concerning our advocacy of a unitary concept of mental illness. In L. Appleby, J. Scher, & J. Cumming (Eds.). *Chronic schizophrenia.* Glencoe, Illinois: The Free Press, 1960, pp. 54–67.

Menninger, K. *The vital balance.* New York: Viking Press, 1963.

Stagner, R. *Psychology of personality.* New York: McGraw-Hill, 1961.

Wolf, S. Disease as a way of life. Neural integration in systemic pathology. *Perspectives in Biological Medicine,* 1961, 4, 288–305.

CHAPTER 3

The Domain of Psychopathology

The vast domain of psychopathology is traditionally grouped under seven headings: neuroses, psychoses, psychosomatic disorders, conduct disorders, children's disorders, subnormal intelligence, and brain damage. This range of syndromes is so extensive that only the first four kinds of disorders are usually included in textbooks. Children's disorders, subnormal intelligence, and brain damage are ordinarily excluded, perhaps because they require special knowledge (for example, neuroanatomy for brain damage) or because they have little in common with one another and the other forms of deviance. Following traditional usage, we shall include only neuroses, psychoses, psychosomatic disorders, and conduct disorders.

Neuroses are commonly divided into syndromes, which will be discussed in detail in the next chapter. A preliminary description of neurotic symptoms includes the following:

(1) worry, tension, and distractibility—indicants of excessive fear
(2) excessive forgetting, obsessive thoughts, and compulsive rituals—self-defeating attempts to cope with fear situations
(3) depression and fatigue—psychological residuals of prolonged tension

Neurotics tend to be overinhibited, anxious, or guilt-ridden, and these tendencies hinder direct action in solving the problems of everyday life. Accordingly, neurotics tend to meet the need for choice with vacillation, the need for directness with deviousness, and the need for bold action with timidity.

Psychoses comprise more deviant and serious symptoms:

(1) hallucinations—disturbances in perceiving reality
(2) delusions—disturbances in interpreting reality

(3) loose associations, fragmented and incoherent speech—disturbances
of thought
(4) prolonged melancholy or elation—disturbances of mood
(5) isolation and withdrawal from others—disturbances in personal
interaction

Psychosomatic disorders consist of bodily malfunctions produced by enduring states of tension: high blood pressure, ulcers, asthma, etc. In contrast
to medical illnesses, psychosomatic disorders cannot be explained solely by
biological variables.

Conduct disorders, as the name implies, include behavior tendencies
involving violations of the rules of society: addiction to alcohol or drugs,
sex deviations, delinquency, etc. Those who exhibit such behaviors are usually described as impetuous, weak, and unrepentant; they are unable to
inhibit forbidden responses in the absence of a punitive agent.

There is overlap among the four kinds of psychopathology, especially
among neuroses, psychoses, and psychosomatic disorders. Such overlap raises
two issues. The first concerns whether an individual can move from one
kind of disorder to another. Is there a continuous sequence of psychopathology based on severity, or are the various disorders discontinuous? The second
issue concerns classification. If the various disorders are not mutually exclusive, is there a value in classification?

CONTINUITY VERSUS DISCONTINUITY

The continuity-discontinuity issue concerns only neuroses and psychoses.
The emphasis on neuroses and psychoses, which occurs throughout this book,
reflects their importance in the study of psychopathology. While all four
groups are important, neuroses and psychoses constitute the majority of cases
seen by clinicians, and their longer history and more intensive study has
yielded more extensive knowledge and a larger number of theories.

The Continuity Position

The continuity position assumes a simple continuum of psychopathology:

normal—neurotic—psychotic.

The neurotic is presumably more deviant than the normal and less so than
the psychotic. In severity of psychopathology, the normal and the psychotic
occupy opposite poles, with the neurotic between them.

Consider the practical criterion of abnormality, inefficiency. By definition, the normal is at least moderately successful in everyday tasks. The
neurotic's performance is impaired by anxiety or self-defeating behaviors,
but he can get the job done; he may be tardy or inefficient, but he meets

the low standards of a tolerant society. The psychotic is periodically or chronically so incapable of managing his own affairs that he must be hospitalized. Thus inefficiency increases continuously from normality to neuroses to psychoses.

The continuity position assumes a similar continuum of bizarreness, another criterion of abnormality. By definition the normal manifests no symptoms or only trivial, transient symptoms. The neurotic displays more serious and enduring symptoms: phobias, excessive rituals, obsessive thoughts, etc. The psychotic shows more weird and incomprehensible symptoms: hallucinations, fantastic delusions, delirious excitement, deep melancholy, etc. Neurotic symptoms, being less bizarre, differ only slightly from normality; psychotic symptoms, being more bizarre, are regarded as considerably deviant from normality. Thus strangeness or incomprehensibility is also continuous through normality, neuroses, and psychoses.

The basic continuity assumption concerns how psychopathology develops over time. A psychosis is presumed to develop slowly and continuously. The normal does not leap from normality to psychosis but progresses first to neurosis and then to psychosis. The first step is to a mild neurosis; then the neurosis becomes more severe; finally, when the neurotic can no longer cope with his problems using neurotic mechanisms, he has a psychotic breakdown. The crux of the argument is that a psychosis represents the failure of neurotic attempts to master anxiety. When the neurotic cannot cope with frightening reality, he gives up reality and becomes psychotic. Presumably a normal would never surrender reality without first adopting neurotic mechanisms in an attempt to reduce anxiety. Thus increasing severity of psychopathology represents successive attempts to avoid anxiety. In the face of increasing anxiety, the normal becomes neurotic and the neurotic, psychotic.

The continuity position suggests that recovery from a psychotic episode consists of a retracing of the progression. The psychotic again establishes contact with reality, using neurotic mechanisms to cope with the threatening aspects of reality. Subsequently, he may remain neurotic, or he may be helped to discard neurotic mechanisms for more adaptive responses that comprise normal adjustment. Presumably a psychotic cannot span the gap directly to normality; he must pass through a neurosis on his way to normality. In brief, whether an individual is moving toward or away from normal adjustment, the sequence is: normality—neuroses—psychoses.

Continuity Models

In seeking the causes of symptoms, we may divide the etiological variables into two broad classes—psychological and biological. All models of psychopathology employ these two classes either singly or jointly, and one's stand on the continuity position leads to two models.

Psychological Variables Only. This model assumes that neuroses and psychoses share a common etiology: excessive stresses and strains of everyday living. Faulty parental training, lack of affection, disappointments, failures, and numerous painful events ostensibly produce neurotic symptoms or a psychotic breakdown.

Assuming a psychological cause, there are two basic approaches to psychopathology, learning and psychoanalytic. The learning approach focuses on behavior: inability to develop adaptive and mature responses, to resolve conflicting habits, to avoid excessive anxiety, to extinguish childish fears, etc. The psychoanalytic approach focuses on underlying personality conflicts: ego versus id, or ego versus superego. In psychoanalytic terms both neuroses and psychoses evolve from intrapsychic conflicts, which in turn result from painful experiences or faulty development at particular psychosexual stages. Fixation during a childhood stage of development initiates latent conflicts which may not become manifest until adulthood; then the stresses and demands of adult life may force a retreat to an earlier level of development. Adult responsibility gives way to childish dependence; adult reality gives way to childish fantasy. The tendency to retreat is determined mainly by the earlier fixation: the greater the fixation during childhood, the greater the tendency to regress in adulthood.

Psychoanalytic theory specifies the fixation points that eventually lead to neuroses and psychoses. Neurotics are fixated at the later psychosexual stages of childhood, psychotics at the earlier stages; normals are not strongly fixated at any childhood stage of development. Thus there is a continuum of the points of fixation (and therefore of regression): normal—neurotic—psychotic. The earlier the fixation, the greater the regression; the greater the regression, the more severe the psychopathology. The continuity of psychopathology—milder regression equals neuroses and severer regression equals psychoses—parallels the continuity of development. Normal development represents moving forward through successive psychosexual stages; psychopathology represents moving backward through these stages.

Psychological and Biological Variables. This model assumes that there are two causes of neuroses and psychoses: biological predisposition and psychological stress. The biological predisposition renders the individual weak, inadequate, or overanxious. A physiological or neural defect prevents him from making normal, adjustive responses to fear stimuli or to painful experiences. He tends to respond with neurotic mechanisms, avoiding rather than facing problems. The biological predisposition sets the stage for psychological variables to act. Consider the continuum: normal—neurotic—psychotic. Biological variables might predispose the individual toward the middle (neurotic) part of the continuum; psychological stress might then move him to the psychotic end. Thus both biological and psychological variables tend to move the individual toward severer psychopathology.

Presumably biological variables alone would not lead to psychopathology; the individual's life experiences might be so benign as to prevent any conflicts or pathogenic strains. Psychological variables alone would not lead to psychopathology because the individual would have the resources, derived from a benign biological predisposition, to cope with disappointments, failures, and similar painful events. In the context of this model, psychopathology requires both the necessary condition of biological prediposition and the sufficient condition of psychological stress.

The Discontinuity Position

The discontinuity position assumes that neuroses and psychoses are qualitatively different, not continuous. Neuroses and psychoses are regarded as different kinds of psychopathology, different ways of deviating from normality. It is conceded that normals, neurotics, and psychotics may be aligned in some respects; for example, the three line up in increasing order of inefficiency. Nevertheless, the different kinds of psychopathology are considered discontinuous with respect to all the important variables.

Consider bizarreness. Continuity theorists suggest that psychotic symptoms are more bizarre than neurotic symptoms. Discontinuity theorists reply that the two kinds of symptoms are *qualitatively* different. Weird neurotic symptoms consist of either motor dysfunction (tics, rituals, or paralysis) or sensory dysfunction (blindness, deafness, or anesthesia). Weird psychotic symptoms are mainly cognitive (hallucinations, delusions, and incoherent speech). The neurotic may engage in peculiar behavior, but he remains in contact with reality, whereas the psychotic is out of contact with reality. In brief, discontinuity theorists agree that psychotic symptoms are more bizarre than neurotic symptoms, but they insist that the fundamental difference is qualitative and therefore discontinuous.

The third criterion of abnormality, discomfort, does not distinguish neurotics from psychotics; both are miserable. This is not an argument for discontinuity, but it is not entirely consistent with the continuity position. If psychoses are severer disturbances than neuroses, there should be greater discomfort among psychotics. So far as is known, neurotics and psychotics do not differ in this respect.

The basic assumption of the discontinuity position is that over time normals become *either* neurotic or psychotic; some may become a combination of the two:

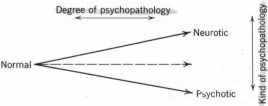

Note that the diagram contains two dimensions. The first is a continuous dimension of psychopathology, which varies from normality to severe psychopathology (from left to right). The other (vertical) dimension refers to qualitative differences in psychopathology, that is, psychotics are no more deviant from normals than are neurotics.

This position assumes that a normal may become psychotic without first becoming neurotic; or if a normal becomes neurotic, he will *not* subsequently become psychotic. With increasing psychopathology, normality divides into *either* neuroses or psychoses. The only exception is a combination of neurotic and psychotic features, indicated by the horizontal dotted line in the diagram.

When a psychotic recovers, he moves toward normality without first becoming neurotic. When a neurotic-psychotic (dotted line) recovers, he loses both his neurotic and psychotic tendencies. Thus normality is regarded as a common starting point for psychopathology. Deviance from normality occurs along one of two tracks; one leads to neuroses, the other to psychoses. In the process of recovery both neurotics and psychotics move toward normality.

Discontinuity Models

As might be expected from the presence of two dimensions (deviance and neurotic versus psychotic), the discontinuity position generates complex models.

Psychological Variables Only. This model, which assumes that both neuroses and psychoses are caused by psychological variables, is different from the comparable continuity model that employs only psychological variables. The discontinuity position requires an explanation of both deviance from normality and the presence of neuroses or psychoses. Consequently the model must be more complex than the comparable continuity model. The problem is solved by distinguishing between two aspects of the psychological stresses that ostensibly cause psychopathology: kind and amount. Harmful experiences may be divided into rejection, loss, failure, isolation, etc. Presumably certain kinds of noxious experiences lead to neuroses and others to psychoses. The *amount* of psychological stress refers to a combination of intensity, number, and chronicity of painful experiences; it is not specified how these three are added together, but painfulness, frequency, and duration are all thought to be important. The amount of stress determines the extent of deviance from normality: the more stress there is, the severer the neurosis *or* psychosis.

The two aspects of psychopathology are matched by two aspects of psychological variables. The discontinuity position specifies a qualitative aspect (neuroses versus psychoses) and a quantitative one (deviance); the model specifies a qualitative aspect (kind of psychological stress) and a quantitative one (amount of psychological stress). The causal aspects precisely match the psychopathological aspects:

> kind of psychological stress → kind of psychopathology (neuroses or psychoses)
> amount of psychological stress → extent of deviance from normality.

Psychological and Biological Variables. The combination of psychological and biological variables yields two etiological models of psychopathology. The first assumes that psychological variables determine the *extent* of deviance from normality. No distinction is made between kind and amount of psychological stress; presumably, they combine to produce deviance. Biological variables determine the *kind* of deviance, yielding this scheme:

> biological variables → kind of psychopathology (neuroses or psychoses)
> psychological variables → extent of deviance from normality.

This model offers two possibilities through which biological variables lead to neuroses or psychoses. One possibility is that one biological disposition leads to neuroses and another to psychoses. This is essentially the theory espoused by Eysenck (1955), who suggests separate factors of Neuroticism and Psychoticism. Another possibility is that biological variables are present in psychoses and absent in neuroses. This position assumes that the cause of neuroses is solely psychological: painful and faulty life experiences. The neurotic is biologically intact, but he has learned maladaptive modes of behaving.

The etiology of psychoses is assumed to be essentially biological; genetic or constitutional variables predispose the individual to psychoses. Life events may facilitate the occurrence of psychosis, but the basic cause is a biological predisposition. Viewed in this light, a psychosis is analogous to a faulty heart valve. The disposition to heart failure is present, and whether it occurs depends on both the severity of the condition and the severity of the strains placed on the heart. Similarly, the psychotic is assumed to have a biological defect. Searching his life history is of little use because the explanation lies in his heredity and bodily (especially brain) processes. In this variant of the model, psychoses are regarded as diseases, with genetic, constitutional, and biochemical variables bearing the major explanatory burden; psychological variables play the minor role of precipitating events. In contrast, neuroses are regarded as learned, inappropriate ways of coping with everyday situations, and consequently psychological variables bear the sole burden of explanation.

The second model assumes that psychological variables determine the kind of psychopathology, and biological variables determine the extent of deviance:

psychological variables → kind of psychopathology
            A   → neuroses
            B   → psychoses
biological variables → extent of deviance from normality.

Certain kinds of harmful experiences (*A*) lead to neuroses, and other kinds (*B*) to psychoses. These psychological variables operate jointly with biological variables, which dispose the individual to greater or lesser psychopathology. The worse the biological disposition is, the greater the deviance. The *amount* of psychological stress is unimportant in this model, but the *kind* is of crucial importance because it determines which track will be followed—toward neuroses or toward psychoses.

Comments

It is difficult to evaluate the continuity and discontinuity positions because of a lack of evidence, although the little evidence available favors the discontinuity approach. S. B. G. Eysenck (1956) and H. J. Eysenck (1955) administered batteries of perceptual, motor, and association tasks to diverse psychiatric groups. The tasks were correlated, and a factor analysis yielded two factors. The Neuroticism factor consisted of tasks differentiating normals from neurotics, and the Psychoticism factor consisted of tasks differentiating normals from psychotics. Using a clinical approach, Trouton and Maxwell (1956) had psychiatrists complete checklists of their patients' symptoms and histories. The items were correlated, and a factor analysis yielded two unrelated factors, again Neuroticism and Psychoticism.

These studies strengthen the discontinuity position, but they do not touch the crucial issue, which is whether an individual must be neurotic before he becomes psychotic. On this basic question there is no reliable evidence, only clinical impressions. Clinicians agree that most neurotics do not become psychotic and that some psychotics have neurotic symptoms.

These clinical opinions, if accepted as factual, are open to two interpretations. The continuity theorist asserts that whereas most neurotics do not break down and become psychotic, some of them do; during their psychotic episodes they continue to manifest symptoms of their previous neurotic state. The discontinuity theorist replies that neurotics do not break down and become psychotic. Rather, such "neurotics" are misclassified and have really been mildly psychotic all along. The presence of neurotic symptoms is explained by the diagram shown earlier:

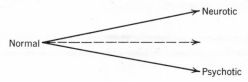

Whereas most patients follow either the neurotic or the psychotic track, some follow the dotted line in the middle; they have both neurotic and psychotic symptoms, and because a diagnosis always consists of the severest pathology, they are diagnosed psychotic. Both the continuity and discontinuity interpretations explain the sequence of psychopathology over time, and there is no factual basis for choosing either of them.

The treatment of neurotics and psychotics in clinics and hospitals is related to continuity-discontinuity. Although the continuity position does not demand that neurotics and psychotics be treated identically, similar treatment is consistent with the position. The discontinuity position suggests that neurotics be treated differently from psychotics. In practice psychotics tend to be hospitalized, neurotics not. Psychotics tend to receive biological therapy (drugs or coma-inducing procedures), whereas neurotics tend to receive psychotherapy as the treatment of choice. Thus in professional practice, neurotics and psychotics are treated as though there were a qualitative difference between them. This does not mean that the discontinuity position is necessarily correct, only that its consequences are the ones acted on by clinicians.

CLASSIFICATION

The grouping of observations is fundamental to progress in any area because it is impossible to make any sense out of a collection of unassorted facts. There is a bewildering array of symptoms in psychopathology, and they must be sorted into some kind of classification. The most prominent classification system in this country is that of the American Psychiatric Association (1952). It is a revision of previous systems, most of which derive from Kraepelin's pioneering work (1909).

Any system of classification has an immediate application: diagnosis. Assigning a diagnostic label requires a system or taxonomy in which individuals or objects are ordered into classes:

Diagnosis involves the gathering of observations, an act of judgment whereby the object is placed in a category or class, and then the drawing of inferences. (Caveny et al., 1955, p. 368)

Note that after observations have been made, there are two separate processes: placing in a category and drawing inferences. In recent years psychiatric diagnosis has been severely criticized as being unreliable and useless. Reliability and utility correspond precisely to the two processes just mentioned.

Reliability

There appears to be a belief among clinicians that psychiatric diagnoses are unreliable; psychiatrists presumably cannot agree on the labels they assign to patients. This belief seems to be sustained largely through earlier studies, which reported low reliability. Ash (1949) compared the diagnoses of pairs of psychiatrists and found that agreement on specific diagnoses varied from 34 to 44%, but these diagnoses were so specific (for example, conduct disorder, schizoid type versus conduct disorder, paranoid type) that *any* agreement is surprising. On major categories (psychosis, conduct disorder, etc.) the agreement ranged from 58 to 67%, which is fairly respectable. Ash himself cautioned that the number of cases, 52, was too small and that many kinds of psychopathology were not represented. There were only a few psychotics and neurotics, and most of the patients (outpatients) had only minor adjustment difficulties. It is well known that the fewer the symptoms, the milder the disturbance is; the closer to normality, the more difficult it is to diagnose. This holds for *any* patients, psychiatric or medical.

Another study often cited as evidence of unreliability is Mehlman's report (1952) on the frequencies of diagnoses made by psychiatrists in the same hospital. The incidence of diagnoses varied significantly among psychiatrists, but Kreitman (1961) has estimated that the average discrepancy was only 20%. In any event, Mehlman used psychiatrists of greatly different skill and experience, and during the study the diagnostic manual was changed.

Kreitman (1961) and Beck (1962) reviewed these earlier studies and found so many flaws as to negate the findings. Beck listed six defects:

(1) differences in clinicians' experience
(2) extraneous considerations in classifying patients
(3) unequal amounts of information on various patients
(4) a long time between first and second diagnoses
(5) lack of independent judgment
(6) poorly defined, overlapping categories

Of these, only the last is a defect of the classification system; the first five refer to faulty research techniques.

Later studies have corrected most of these faults and have reported better agreement. As might be expected, the reliability of broad categories (psychoses versus neuroses) is better than for specific categories (schizophrenia versus psychotic depression). Thus Kreitman et al. (1961) reported 78% agreement for generic diagnoses and 63% agreement for specific diagnoses; for Schmidt and Fonda (1956) the corresponding figures were 84 and 55%; for Norris (1959) they were 84 and 55%.

The *kind* of psychopathology also affects agreement, psychoses being diagnosed more reliably than neuroses. Kreitman et al. (1961) found 71% agreement on the generic label psychoses and 52% for neuroses. Concerning *specific* diagnoses the agreement was 61% for psychoses and only 28% for neuroses. In a more recent report Sandifer, Pettus, and Quade (1964) obtained 74% agreement for schizophrenia and 56% for neuroses. The one inconsistent finding is that of Beck et al. (1962), who reported 53% agreement for schizophrenia and 55 to 63% for specific neuroses; but their sample consisted of outpatients, in whom schizophrenia might be expected to be milder and therefore more difficult to identify.

Several conclusions emerge from this array of percentages. First, the later, better controlled studies yield greater reliability of diagnosis than the earlier studies. Disagreement is inevitable when the psychiatrists used in such research are untrained or trained to proceed differently. Ward et al. (1962) showed that individual interviewers used different techniques, elicited different information, and made different interpretations of what they observed; these differences led to serious disagreements in diagnoses.

When these and other sources of disagreement are controlled, reliability increases. Wilson and Meyer (1962) compared the incidence of diagnoses by psychiatrists of approximately equal training who used the same diagnostic criteria on patients all drawn from one segment of the city. The incidence of various diagnoses for two 2-year periods was essentially the same, suggesting considerable consistency. Compare this indication of reliability with Mehlman's (1952) finding of unreliability; the difference lies in the control of extraneous variables by Meyer and Wilson.

The second conclusion is that not all diagnoses are made with the same reliability; it is necessary to specify what is being diagnosed. Psychoses are usually diagnosed more reliably than neuroses. In fact, there is so much unreliability in diagnosing neuroses that we must question the value of such labeling. We may speculate that the problem is a basic lack of agreement as to what a neurosis is. Specifically, there is considerable debate as to whether neuroses are clusters of symptoms or certain personality traits, as we shall see in Chapter 4.

The more generic the category is, the more reliable the diagnosis; the more specific the category is, the worse the diagnosis. This relationship is not surprising, for finer discriminations commonly lead to greater error. The implication is clear that diagnostic labels more specific than *psychosis, neurosis*, etc. require discriminations that are too fine to be made reliably, and any classification in need of this will be unreliable.

Summarizing, we may conclude that psychoses, taken generically, can be diagnosed with considerable reliability. There is some evidence that one psychosis, schizophrenia, can be diagnosed reliably (74% agreement reported by Sandifer et al., 1964). Thus the commonly held belief in the unreliability of psychiatric diagnoses is incorrect or at best only partly correct. Specific diagnoses and diagnoses of the milder forms of psychopathology tend to be unreliable. Nevertheless, the more serious kinds of deviance can be diagnosed with consistency, which is reassuring because these kinds of psychopathology require the most immediate attention and the greatest care. But this does not mean that present classifications are without faults. They tend to demand excessively fine discriminations, and they are vague in their descriptions. These defects, which lead to unreliability, are less serious than those concerning utility.

Utility

Classification is useful in professional practice. The law demands that a defendant be legally sane and therefore responsible for his acts before he is tried in court. A diagnosis of psychosis is equivalent to legal insanity; other diagnoses mean that the client is responsible and may be tried. Classification is also helpful to hospital authorities in determining assignment to wards and to the armed services in screening potential military personnel. Diagnostic labels are also needed in compiling statistics on hospitals, frequency and distribution of psychopathology, etc.

Aside from practical utility, what do present classifications offer? We saw earlier that a diagnosis involves assigning individuals to classes and drawing inferences from class membership. Assignment to classes concerns reliability; drawing inferences concerns validity (the utility of the classification). When a patient has been diagnosed, we are interested in drawing inferences about etiology and prognosis. In a perfect classification each diagnostic category would have a single etiology and a single prognosis. The patient's diagnosis would tell us without error both the cause of his condition and the eventual outcome. No diagnosis attains such perfection, but some approach it. The diagnosis of appendicitis, together with an evaluation of how close the appendix is to bursting, indicates both the cause and the prognosis; most medical and psychiatric diagnoses permit fewer inferences.

Clinicians disagree about the inferential value of present classifications. Meehl takes the strong position that:

. . . there is a sufficient amount of etiological and prognostic homogeneity among patients belonging to a given diagnostic group, so that the assignment of a patient to this group has probability implications which it is clinically unsound to ignore. (1959, p. 103)

The differential prognoses of schizophrenics and psychotic depressives (see Chapter 9) support Meehl's position. Nevertheless, present classifications offer little information on etiology; schizophrenia, for example, appears to have many different causes. Furthermore, most of the diagnostic categories offer little information about prognosis.

Consider the American Psychiatric Association classification (1952), which appears to have all the virtues and faults of previous systems. It is a conglomeration of syndromes without an overall principle to guide the diagnostician. As Zigler and Phillips (1961) and Lorr, Klett, and McNair

(1963) have pointed out, the system is based on several different principles.

Most of the diagnostic categories are defined by clusters of symptoms, but some are defined by etiology. Schizophrenia consists of patients with certain clusters of symptoms, and its etiology is left unstated; but chronic brain-disorders include diverse symptoms whose only bond is that they are caused by damage to the brain. Thus some categories are defined by the joint occurrence of symptoms, others by a common etiology. There are also categories determined on the basis of prognosis or social conformity.

This classification also wanders back and forth between syndrome and type concepts. A syndrome is a group of *symptoms* that occur together, whereas a type is a group of *persons* with certain common characteristics. Measles is a disease; redheads are a type. In the American Psychiatric Association classification most of the psychotic categories refer to types (groups of persons), but the psychosomatic categories refer to syndromes (clusters of symptoms), such as neurodermatoses and respiratory disorders.

The classification also employs a mixture of class and trait concepts. A *class* consists of objects, events, or people that meet the criteria of class membership. Both types and syndromes are class concepts, which are discontinuous. One is either a member of a type or one is not; one either has the syndrome or one does not; there are no gradations. A *trait* is a continuous variable, some aspect of behavior which varies from one person to the next. Traits are by definition present to a greater or lesser extent in everyone, for example, anxiousness, which varies from panicky apprehensiveness to phlegmatic unconcern.

The problem with the class concept in diagnosis is that it assumes that a disease is either present or absent. It is true that some diseases fit this model, and in the American Psychiatric Association classification psychoses are defined in terms of a class (type) concept. Nevertheless, most diseases do not fit the class concept because they vary in degree over a range from mild to severe, from few symptoms to many. In psychiatric classification neuroses are defined in terms of traits; for example, *anxiety reaction* varies from mild tension to panic, from diffuse anxiety to specific fears. Anxiety varies continuously from the low level of normals to the high level of severe neurotics; it is present in everyone but in differing degrees. In contrast, the classification regards a psychosis as being present or absent.

Thus the American Psychiatric Association classification suffers from three inconsistencies in its organization of psychopathology. It classifies on the bases of both manifest symptoms and etiology, both clusters of symptoms and groups of persons, and both class and trait concepts. It has yielded little information about etiology or prognosis, although such information may yet emerge from further research.

Nevertheless, classification is necessary in order to grasp the diverse facts of psychopathology. Some clinicians insist on using the complex and detailed American Psychiatric Association system with all its faults because of its administrative and legal utility. Others, citing the defects of the various classifications, refuse to use any of them. We shall take the position that some classification is needed, at least as a shorthand means of describing symptom clusters.

Whatever disagreements exist about using present classification systems, there is universal agreement that the goals of diagnosis are to discover etiology and prognosis. Cause and outcome are not necessarily related; it is possible for a classification to include etiology but not prognosis, or prognosis but not etiology. Discovering prognosis is an easier task because it can be purely empirical: it consists of determining relationships between symptoms and outcome. Discovering etiology is a harder task because it involves not only finding the facts but also explaining the origins of symptoms. At present there is considerable speculation about the etiology of psychoses but a paucity of reliable facts; in contrast, much is known about prognosis of psychoses (see Chapter 10).

Typically, etiology is the last aspect of psychopathology to be discovered (Zigler & Phillips, 1961). While some investigators recommend that the description of symptoms be given up in favor of a concentrated search for causes, others reply that we need more, not less, research involving description and classification:

. . . The process of moving from an empirical orientation to an etiological one is, of necessity, inferential and therefore susceptible to the myriad dangers of premature inference. We propose that the greatest safeguard against such prematurity is not to be found in the scrapping of an empirical descriptive approach, but in an accelerated program of empirical research. What is needed at this time is a systematic, empirical attack on the problem of mental disorders. Inherent in this program is the employment of symptoms, broadly defined as meaningful and discernible behaviors, as the basis of a classificatory system. Rather than an abstract search for etiologies, it would appear more currently fruitful to investigate such empirical correlates of symptomatology as reactions to specific forms of treatment, outcome in the disorders, case history phenomena, etc. (Zigler & Phillips, 1961, p. 616)

REFERENCES

American Psychiatric Association. *Diagnostic and statistical manual, mental disorders.* Washington, D.C.: Author, 1952.

Ash, P. The reliability of psychiatric diagnosis. *Journal of Abnormal and Social Psychology,* 1949, 44, 272–277.

Beck, A. T. Reliability of psychiatric diagnoses: 1. A critique of systematic studies. *American Journal of Psychiatry,* 1962, 119, 210–216.

Beck, A. T., Ward, C. H., Mendelson, M., Mock, J. E., & Erbaugh, J. K. Reliability of psychiatric diagnoses: 2. A study of consistency of clinical judgments and ratings. *American Journal of Psychiatry,* 1962, **119,** 351–357.

Caveny, E. L., Wittson, C. L., Hunt, W. A., & Herrman, R. S. Psychiatric diagnosis, its nature and function. *Journal of Nervous and Mental Disease,* 1955, **121,** 367–380.

Eysenck, H. J. Psychiatric diagnosis as a psychological and statistical problem. *Psychological Reports,* 1955, **1,** 3–17.

Eysenck, S. B. G. Neurosis and psychosis: an experimental analysis. *Journal of Mental Science,* 1956, **102,** 517–529.

Kraepelin, E. *Psychiatry.* Leipzig: Barth, 1909.

Kreitman, N. The reliability of psychiatric diagnosis. *Journal of Mental Science,* 1961, **107,** 876–886.

Kreitman, N., Sainsbury, P., Morrissey, J., Towers, J., & Scrivener, J. The reliability of psychiatric assessment: An analysis. *Journal of Mental Science,* 1961, **107,** 887–908.

Lorr, M., Klett, C. J., & McNair, D. M. *Syndromes of psychosis.* New York: Mac-Millan, 1963.

Meehl, P. E. Some ruminations on the validation of clinical procedures. *Canadian Journal of Psychology,* 1959, **13,** 102–128.

Mehlman, B. The reliability of psychiatric diagnosis. *Journal of Abnormal and Social Psychology,* 1952, **47,** 577–578.

Norris, V. *Mental illness in London.* London: Chapman & Hall, 1959.

Sandifer, M. G., Jr., Pettus, C., & Quade, D. A study of psychiatric diagnosis. *Journal of Nervous and Mental Disease,* 1964, **139,** 350–356.

Schmidt, H. O., & Fonda, C. P. The reliability of psychiatric diagnosis: A new look. *Journal of Abnormal and Social Psychology,* 1956, **52,** 262–267.

Trouton, D. S., & Maxwell, A. E. The relation between neurosis and psychosis. *Journal of Mental Science,* 1956, **102,** 1–21.

Ward, C. H., Beck, A. T., Mendelson, M., Mock, J. E., & Erbaugh, J. K. The psychiatric nomenclature. *Archives of General Psychiatry,* 1962, **7,** 198–205.

Wilson, M. S., & Meyer. E. Diagnostic consistency in a psychiatric liaison service. *American Journal of Psychiatry,* 1962, **119,** 207–209.

Zigler, E., & Phillips, L. Psychiatric diagnosis: a critique. *Journal of Abnormal and Social Psychology,* 1961, **63,** 607–618.

CHAPTER 4

Neurotic Symptoms

A neurotic symptom is an observed reaction or a complaint that does not consitute a clean break with reality, for example, worry, pain, inability to concentrate, recurrent thoughts, and phobias. Any of these might occur occasionally in normal individuals faced with temporary stress; when the stress is over, the transient reaction disappears. Neurotic symptoms are more enduring. They exist continuously or recur periodically over extended periods of time, and may not disappear when stress is eliminated.

Concerning the criteria of abnormality, most neurotic symptoms involve either discomfort or inefficiency; only rarely are neurotic symptoms bizarre. Many neurotic symptoms are uncomfortable by their very nature: pain, obsessional impulses to kill, and fatigue. The individual is extremely tense, perhaps even ill, and he seeks immediate relief. Other symptoms lead to misery only indirectly. Neither phobias nor compulsive rituals cause immediate discomfort; the phobic person can avoid anxiety so long as he circumvents the objects of his fears, and the compulsive person need not be concerned so long as he completes the entire sequence of his rituals. Unfortunately, it is difficult to avoid all objects of one's fears, and the person who fears elevators, airplanes, and crowded places cannot cope with modern urban life. Similarly, no one has time for long and involved rituals, and the person who must cease all other activity to engage in compulsive behavior surely cannot hold a job or manage a home efficiently. Thus phobias and compulsions, while not necessarily uncomfortable in themselves, cause misery by their disruption of the behavior sequences needed for everyday adjustment.

Symptoms may be classified on the basis of their joint occurrence, and as we saw earlier a cluster of symptoms that tend to go together is called

46

a *syndrome*. We shall follow traditional usage and delineate five syndromes of neurosis. Before describing these, however, we shall introduce another classification system, which should help the exposition of neurotic syndromes.

REACTION SYSTEMS

Consider the following behavior sequence: an individual plans revenge against his enemy, confronts him, becomes enraged, fights, is beaten, and slinks away depressed. This sequence involves all four reaction systems of behavior: cognitive (planning and imagining), somatic (the autonomic components of the emotion of rage), motor (fighting, or any instrumental act), and affective (depression). These four reaction systems may be used to classify both normal and abnormal behavior; our focus in this chapter will be on neurotic symptoms, although the classification will also be used in the description of psychotic symptoms (Chapter 9).

Somatic

The somatic reaction system has two aspects, both involving physiological reactivity. The first consists of the reaction of the autonomic nervous system to emotional stimuli. The bodily response to strong fear or anger stimuli is sweating, flushing, breathing disturbance, heart pounding, etc. Neurotics tend not to express their anger in the form of aggression, but they do have the massive autonomic reaction that constitutes preparation for aggression. They tend to suffer from excessive and prolonged anxiety reactions, which have a strong somatic component. It has been suggested that neurotics have over-reactive autonomic nervous systems, which would explain their inability to cope with fear stimuli and the enduring effects of these stimuli.

The second aspect of the somatic reaction system consists of the residuals of physiological tension. Autonomic arousal may persist over time, and when temporary, emergency mechanisms endure too long, symptoms are produced. For example, the elevated blood pressure that is part of fear or anger may eventually cause a headache. Fear sometimes causes involuntary muscular contractions, which in time can lead to aches and pains. Some of these residuals of tension concern specific organ systems and produce symptoms identical to those seen in medical illness; these psychosomatic symptoms will be discussed in Chapter 16. The remainder are nonspecific complaints of pain, vague bodily distress (for example, "butterflies" in the stomach, cramps), and fatigue; these complaints are seen in several of the syndromes of neurosis.

Cognitive

The cognitive reaction system also has two aspects. The first consists of the various implicit and covert activities that many authorities believe

are largely restricted to man: thinking, planning, imagining, inventing, remembering, dreaming, and labeling. These activities fall under the heading
of *thought processes,* which are essentially intact in neurosis. The only exception is remembering, which may show a large deficit, especially in hysteria. The other thought processes are not aberrant in neurosis, although
the *content* of the thoughts may be deviant. For example, an anxious
neurotic tends to worry excessively, the content of his imagination consisting
of catastrophes, dreadful possibilities, or perhaps even nightmares. This distinction between process and content of thought processes is important.
Thought *processes* are disturbed only in psychosis, whereas thought *contents*
are disturbed in both neurosis and psychosis.

The second aspect involves the functioning of the senses of vision, hearing, touch, taste, and smell. The operation of sense organs is obviously a
bodily process, which means that sensory behavior might be classified as
part of the somatic reaction system. On the other hand, perception involves
the reception and integration of stimulus inputs, and it is therefore linked
with thought processes. Thus perception might be classed as somatic or cognitive, depending on which properties one chooses to emphasize. We have
classed perception under the cognitive reaction systems, emphasizing
stimulus input properties rather than anatomical properties of the senses.

Some neurotics do show an inability to see, hear, or feel, although
this is rare. Such sensory symptoms may be confused with the symptoms
of medical illness, especially damage to the central nervous system; but
psychological symptoms can be distinguished from medical symptoms by the
absence of anatomical change, the sequence over time, and the possibility
of "miraculous cures" (for example, a return of function under hypnosis).

Motor

The motor reaction system includes all muscular responses, both skeletal
and vocal, that interact with the environment. These responses fall under
the heading of instrumental behavior, the term *instrumental* meaning that
they move the individual closer to or farther from rewards or punishments.
Such responses have consequences, and a major aspect of adjustment is
making responses that lead to desirable, enduring consequences.

Motor reactions may be divided into two types, depending on the nature of the environment they affect. One type is *social,* involving the behavior of one or more persons. Social responses are of great importance
in adjustment because the most potent rewards and punishments come from
persons, and most of the rules that regulate behavior concern other persons.
The other type of motor reaction is *nonsocial,* involving objects and events
but not persons. Such responses are made in relation to the environments
of job, school, and play. Although they are of lesser importance in adjustment, they are not trivial.

Neurotics display several kinds of motor symptoms. One kind concerns faulty learning, the behavior either failing to lead to desirable consequences or only temporarily avoiding undesirable consequences. For example, a compulsive ritual momentarily reduces or avoids the neurotic's anxiety, but the response is superstitious in that it does not affect the source of the anxiety, which then reappears.

The second kind of motor symptom is a failure in modulation. This may be seen in the restlessness of an anxious neurotic, who shifts in his chair, drums on the table, paces up and down, has muscular tics or twitches, or perhaps even manifests tremors. Such motor symptoms may be regarded as an overflow of tension, which keeps the neurotic continually in motion. The end point of tremors represents action of opposing muscles (agonists and antagonists), the individual failing to inhibit one set of muscles when the opposite set is contracting. In addition to symptoms of an overflow of tension, there are symptoms of insufficient tension. Some hysterics are temporarily crippled by partial or complete paralysis of hands, legs, or vocal chords. Here the failure of modulation is in the direction of underactivity.

Affective

The term *affect,* which has many connotations, is used here as a synonym of *mood.* The major dimension of affect is bipolar, ranging from elation to depression. The variations are illustrated in this list of scaled adjectives (Buss & Gerjuoy, 1957):

euphoric	serious
elated	solemn
frivolous	mirthless
buoyant	grave
gay	gloomy
jovial	brooding
lighthearted	dejected
cheerful	disconsolate
placid	despondent
sober	hopeless

Note that the adjectives start at the happy end of the dimension, proceed through a middle range of little affect (*placid*), and finish at the unhappy end. The extremes of mood are at both ends of this bipolar dimension. Neurotics tend to occupy the depressed segment (right-hand column of adjectives) of the continuum. They may be mildly depressed (*solemn*) or intensely depressed (*despondent*), but they are rarely on the happy side (*cheerful or gay*).

Two other dimensions are usually associated with elation-depression:

anxiety and irritability. Both are unipolar, as indicated by scaled adjectives:

Anxiety	*Irritability*
nonchalant	civil
calm	grudging
composed	petulant
uneasy	grouchy
fretful	irritable
tense	resentful
apprehensive	provocative
tremulous	surly
agitated	quarrelsome
panicky	embittered
terrified	malicious

Anxiety and irritability may be regarded as *negative affects* in that they refer to aversive states of the individual; anxiety is aversive to the experiencing person and irritability to others. Similarly, the depressed end of elation-depression is aversive to the experiencing individual. It is these aversive states that we are concerned with in neurosis, and they are especially intense in *anxiety reaction* and *neurotic depression*.

TRADITIONAL SYNDROMES

Chapter 3 delineated three kinds of neurotic symptoms: excessive fear, maladaptive attempts to escape from or avoid anxiety, and psychological residuals of tension. These three kinds of symptoms include the five syndromes we shall discuss:

excessive fear—anxiety reaction
escaping anxiety—hysteria, obsession-compulsion
psychological residuals—depression, fatigue-hypochondriasis

Anxiety reaction, hysteria, and obsession-compulsion are present in every list of neuroses. Depression and fatigue-hypochondriasis are included in some lists and not in others; they are included here in the belief that they are as well-defined as the first three syndromes.

Anxiety Reaction

This syndrome traditionally refers to *free-floating* anxiety, in which the fear stimuli are unknown. Phobias are usually distinguished from free-floating anxiety, largely because of the Freudian label for phobia, *anxiety hysteria*. This latter term is no longer used, and there appears to be no important reason for separating phobias from free-floating anxiety. The only difference between the two is in the specificity of the fear stimuli: unknown

TABLE 4.1   SYMPTOMS OF FREE-FLOATING ANXIETY

Somatic	*Cognitive*
flushing	worry
sweating	dread
dry mouth	inattention
shallow breathing	distractibility
chest oppression	forgetfulness
heart palpitation	nightmares
pounding pulse	*Motor*
increased blood pressure	muscular tightness
headache	tremors
feeling of weakness	startle reaction
intestinal distress	incoordination
Affective	"freezing"
agitation	
panic	
depression	
irritability	

and generalized in free-floating anxiety versus known and specific in phobia. Therefore both are included under anxiety reaction.

Free-Floating Anxiety. There is mild, chronic anxiety, interspersed with occasional panic. Symptoms may occur in all four reaction systems, as shown in Table 4.1.

The *somatic* symptoms largely reflect overactivity of the autonomic nervous system, the major changes being in the cardiovascular and respiratory systems. This autonomic reaction is part of the response to fear stimuli, the only difference being that the individual cannot identify these fear stimuli. Not all anxiety neurotics display the full range of somatic symptoms. As Lacey (1950) has demonstrated, there are individual differences in the *pattern* of autonomic reactivity. Thus in one individual, anxiety is seen mainly in sweating and a dry mouth; in another person the major somatic symptoms are heart palpitation and chest oppression.

In addition to these symptoms of autonomic arousal, there are symptoms of residual physiological tension. Prolonged anxiety has concomitants of muscular tightness, gastric upset, and elevated blood pressure and pulse. Over-reactivity in these various physiological systems leads to the end products of aches, cramps, intestinal distress, headache, and weakness; these are residual or secondary somatic symptoms of anxiety.

In the *cognitive* sphere, the major symptoms involve an apprehensiveness that varies from mild worry to dread. The anxiety neurotic often has a feeling of impending disaster without any idea of the source of the threat.

Preoccupation and concern over unknown danger tend to make him inattentive to immediate stimuli and forgetful of past events. His vague fears distract him from the task at hand and weaken his memory.

The major *affective* symptom is a feeling of tense excitement which varies from mild upset to panic. There may be a feeling of impending doom, which lends a depressive tone to the neurotic's mood. It is like sitting on a metaphorical time bomb, a situation that understandably leads to despondence. There may also be irritability as an adjunct to the tension. The restless, jumpy anxiety neurotic often has difficulty in sleeping; the lack of sleep tends to make him grouchy and sour.

Motor symptoms are the easiest to observe. There is random movement, from a fine tremor through unsteadiness to the larger, skeletal shakes of the panic state. Many anxiety neurotics reveal their tension by restlessness, excessive pacing, squirming in chairs, and lip biting. Facial tics, excessive eye blinking, and grimacing may also be present. Another kind of motor symptom is the overquick reaction of the anxiety neurotic, who may be "jumpy," responding too quickly and too intensely to sudden noises or sights. In his tension state he is primed to react, and sudden stimuli may elicit responses of an intensity disproportionate to the intensity of the stimuli.

Presumably the anxiety neurotic's tension spills over into excessive muscular movement because of the association between fear and flight. Fear (anxiety) is an emotional reaction to threatening stimuli; it is usually followed by an escape response. Thus the rapid, intense exertion of skeletal muscles is the common concomitant of anxiety, the escape response serving to reduce anxiety by removing the individual from the presence of the threatening stimulus. Since the anxiety neurotic cannot specify what he fears, he does not know which way to run. He cannot make the escape re sponse that would at least temporarily reduce anxiety. Because of the close association between anxiety and escape responses, the presence of anxiety usually initiates preparation for rapid escape. The anxiety neurotic makes all the preparations for massive skeletal movement but does not make the instrumental response of escaping. In the absence of an escape response, the physiological tension seems to spill over into random movements and tics.

There are individual differences in the total pattern of anxiety symptoms. Anxiety neurotics may manifest symptoms in one, two, three, or (rarely) four reaction systems. The fact that some persons show symptoms in more than one reaction system precludes the possibility of there being four kinds of anxiety neurotics, each with symptoms in a single reaction system. Nevertheless, there may be types of anxiety neurotics based on *combinations* of reaction systems. Two studies have offered information on this issue. In one study, Hamilton (1959) interviewed anxiety neurotics and rated their symptoms. A factor analysis of the correlations among the ratings yielded a bipolar factor:

muscular tension		gastrointestinal complaints
fears		genito-urinary complaints
insomnia	*versus*	respiratory complaints
apprehension		cardiovascular complaints
difficulty in concentrating		

The two ends of the bipolar factor show a pattern. At one end are motor symptoms (muscular tension and perhaps insomina) and cognitive symptoms (fears, apprehension, and difficulty in concentrating). At the other end are somatic symptoms in four organ systems. Affective symptoms are absent, probably because they are not evaluated in such research. Thus there appear to be two patterns of anxiety neurosis: somatic symptoms versus a combination of motor and cognitive symptoms.

The second study confirmed this separation of somatic components of anxiety from skeletal-motor and ideational components in psychiatric patients of varying diagnoses (Buss, 1962). Patients were interviewed, and their reported and observed symptoms were rated. The correlations among symptoms yielded two factors:

	Factor 1	*Factor 2*
combined rating	sweating flushing shallow breathing excessive swallowing heart palpitations subjective discomfort aches and pains distractibility	restlessness worry muscular tension

The first factor consists of symptoms in the somatic reaction system, both primary autonomic and secondary residual symptoms. The exception is distractibility, which was assessed by efficiency on a task (subtracting sevens) and is therefore suspect—it was not observed and rated directly, as were the other symptoms. The second factor consists of symptoms of the cognitive and motor spheres. These findings are thus parallel to those of Hamilton.

Eysenck (1961) has suggested that there are two components of anxiety. The first is autonomic over-reactivity, which corresponds to somatic symptoms; the second is conditioned anxiety, which corresponds to cognitive and motor symptoms. The results of both the Hamilton and Buss studies seem to confirm his hypothesis. There appear to be two types of anxiety reactions: one characterized by somatic symptoms and the other by cognitive and motor symptoms. Affective symptoms, which were not investigated, may be present in both types of anxiety.

Phobias. Certain objects or events are recognized by everyone as being dangerous. High-tension wires are avoided by all except technicians trained to handle them; fear of high-tension wires is *consensually* appropriate because of potential danger. What distinguishes phobias is that the fears are unrealistic and disproportionate. The phobic individual fears and avoids objects, places, and events that are not inherently and consensually dangerous, giving wide berth to stimuli that are innocuous to the rest of us. The commonest stimuli for phobias are:

animals	high places
crowds	poison
dark	shut-in places
germs	storms

These various stimuli cause little anxiety for most persons, but a phobic person may react with intense anxiety in their presence. He can verbalize precisely what he fears, and so long as he can avoid the source of his fears, he may not become anxious. Thus the sphere of symptom formation is *motor;* the phobic *avoids* or *escapes from* stimuli that are innocuous to most others.

If the phobia is sufficiently circumscribed, it may not interfere with everyday adjustments. Unfortunately, many phobias concern common stimuli. In the list mentioned above, only high places and poison would be easy to avoid; the other stimuli are abundantly present in everyday life. The phobic who fears crowds, for example, cannot help but cripple his adjustment if he succeeds in avoiding the object of his fear.

The number of possible phobias is very large, although the ones listed above account for most of what is seen in clinical practice. Is there any clustering of phobias? Dixon et al., (1957) attempted to answer this question by administering an inventory to clinic patients. There were 26 phobia items, and a factor analysis yielded two factors:

Fear of Separation	*Fear of Harm*
being left alone	surgery
crossing a bridge	hospitals
open spaces	being hurt
water, drowning	bearing pain
train journey	dentist
dark	

This statistical grouping makes psychological sense. Fears of separation stem from anxiety about interpersonal relations, especially those with parental figures, for example, the childish fear of darkness and of being alone. They are common in children who rely heavily on adult care, attention, and love. They are uncommon in normal adults, who have matured beyond the need for parental nurturance. Such separation fears appear in neurotics, many of whom still desperately need assurance that they are loved and who therefore continually fear rejection and loneliness.

Fears of harm are common in both children and adults, and it is not strange that they occur in neurotics. These phobias are "normal" in that they are widespread in the population. When they are the only symptoms seen in a neurotic, the focus must be on the intensity of the fear response. Whereas most normal individuals fear pain, dentistry, and surgery, they will undergo the unpleasant experiences, if necessary. The neurotic, however, reacts so intensely that he cannot face what he must. His "normal" phobia is so strong that he tries to avoid the necessary surgery or dentistry. Thus what distinguishes neurotic from normal fear of harm is the intensity of reaction to the fear stimulus.

Hysteria

Symptoms. Hysteria includes a large variety of symptoms all having one common characteristic: they superficially resemble those present in organic disease, but there is no organic basis for the symptoms. Hysterical paralysis of the hand does not conform to the innervation of the hand and is therefore clearly distinguishable from paralysis caused by neural damage to motor tracts. On the other hand, vague hysterical pains in the intestinal area are difficult to distinguish from pain caused by intestinal disease or malfunction. Nevertheless, most hysterical symptoms are sufficiently flamboyant to be distinguished from organic symptoms, and the hysteric is sufficiently naive to give himself away under close examination. As may be seen in Table 4.2, hysteria includes every sphere of symptom formation, but the individual hysteric usually has symptoms in only one or two spheres.

TABLE 4.2 SYMPTOMS OF HYSTERIA

Somatic	*Cognitive*
pain	loss of hearing
weakness	loss of vision
pseudo-organic illness	loss of touch
fainting	loss of memory
Affective	somnambulism
indifference	*Motor*
	loss of speech
	loss of locomotion
	muscular cramps
	tics
	seizures

The number of possible *somatic* symptoms is very large. The hysteric is known for his recital of multiple aches and pains. Going beyond pain, the hysteric often describes symptom pictures that mimic syndromes seen in organic disease. The complaints involve bodily ills; autonomic symptoms, such as occur in anxiety, are usually absent. Since the hysteric seems to be extremely suggestible, the organic symptoms may resemble those of a previous illness, those seen in others, or those encountered in media of mass communication. When a hysteric is hospitalized, he often acquires many of the complaints of other patients.

The major *cognitive* symptoms in hysteria concern memory and the senses. The hysteric may show a selective memory loss, which sometimes mimics that seen in patients with organic brain damage. However, the hysteric's memory disturbance is related to anxiety-laden stimuli whereas the brain-damaged patient does not have the same kind of *selective* memory loss. Hysterical loss of memory has been labeled *overexclusion* by Cameron (1947). The extreme and most dramatic kind of overexclusion is seen in the rare instances of *multiple personality,* in which the patient excludes one set of memories, attitudes, and dispositions, while remembering and living out another. Less bizarre but still unusual is somnambulism or sleepwalking.

In some hysterics sensitivity to touch is greatly diminished, occasionally reaching the point of complete anesthesia of part of the body. The affected area never corresponds to the pattern of sensory innervation of the body region. Rather the individual has no sensation on half his body, or the area covered by a glove or by a stocking. In addition to touch and pain, sight and hearing are often affected. The hysterical impairment of vision may be only partial, as in *tunnel vision,* or complete, as in hysterical blindness. Hysterical deafness may also be partial or complete. Impairment of vision and hearing, while more dramatic than other hysterical sensory symptoms, are less common.

There is a single *affective* symptom in hysteria. A minority of hysterics seem to be inappropriately unconcerned with their symptoms. In the face of memory loss, anesthesia, or partial paralysis, they are blithely optimistic. Certain that their problems are of medical origin, they are paradoxically nonchalant about the symptoms. This unconcern, called *la belle indifference,* has been suggested by some authorities as a hallmark of hysteria.

Symptoms in the *motor* sphere are of two kinds: inactivity and overactivity. Inactivity may be seen in partial or complete paralysis of the hands, arms, legs, or voice. Overactivity is seen in tremors and convulsive movements, as well as in tics and cramps. The cramp, due to fatiguing muscle tenseness, is often related to the patient's vocation—writer's cramp, telegrapher's cramp, etc. Disablement of the muscle system may prevent the patient from working, especially where the work situation is associated with intense anxiety. The end point of muscular overactivity, a convulsive seizure, is a rarity.

Diagnostic Issues. (1) *Conversion versus Dissociation.* The cognitive symptoms of memory loss, split personality, and somnambulism are not always included under the heading of hysteria; some authorities place them in a separate category, dissociative reactions. The reasoning is as follows. The somatic and motor symptoms of hysteria represent a conversion of psychic tension to physical tension, of psychic pain to physical pain. Alternatively, the bodily symptoms are a kind of symbolic *somatic language* used by the hysteric to communicate his underlying personality conflicts. In dissociative reactions there is no conversion to physical symptoms and no somatic language. Since the underlying mechanisms are different, the argument runs, conversion hysteria and dissociative reactions should be kept separate.

If one accepts this line of reasoning, the two should not be included under one heading. However, including dissociative reactions under the heading of hysteria does not necessarily imply a rejection of the above approach. It is simply a more neutral position to adhere to the traditional cluster known as hysteria. The grouping is on the basis of symptoms, not a dynamic theory of the origin of the symptoms. Amnesia and other bizarre cognitive symptoms superficially resemble symptoms seen in some neurological conditions. Therefore, they are labeled hysterical, just as are other symptoms that mimic organic disease. Since there is disagreement on this point, it seems best to stay close to observables, that is, the symptoms themselves. There is likely to be more agreement on symptoms than on the cause of symptoms.

(2) *Pain and Indifference.* It has been suggested that the most prominent features of hysteria are pain and an indifference to discomfort, a paradoxical combination. It is difficult to check out this suggestion because statistics on neurotic symptoms are not kept in the same way as they are on psychotic symptoms. Nevertheless, there have been reports on series of hysteric patients. The consensus is that pain is present in one-half to two-thirds of hysterics (Chodoff & Lyons, 1958; Purtell et al., 1951; Stephens & Kamp, 1962; Ziegler et al., 1960).

An attitude of unconcern about symptoms is observed in approximately one-third of hysterics (Stephens & Kamp, 1962; Ziegler et al., 1960). Unfortunately, these studies do not state whether the hysterics with pain were those who were concerned over their condition, but it is a reasonable hypothesis. The patient with a partial paralysis or blindness cannot function, but he is not necessarily uncomfortable. The patient with pain is so uncomfortable that it is difficult to believe that he is unconcerned. Furthermore, Stephens and Kamp (1962) report depression in more than one-third of their hysteric patients, which suggests a more intense reaction than mere concern over symptoms. In brief, it appears that pain is the most prominent feature of hysteria, whereas *la belle indifference* occurs in a minority of cases.

(3) *Incidence.* It is a common belief that the incidence of hysteria has greatly diminished during the last 60 years. The most popular explanation is that there is greater sophistication today, less naivete, and less need to repress (repression presumably leading to hysteria). Regardless of the acceptability of the explanation, there is a real question of fact. Let us assume that the diagnosis of hysteria is applied less today than 60 years ago. There are several hypotheses that explain away this "fact." First, 60 years ago practitioners might have misdiagnosed, using the label of hysteria where it was inappropriate. Second, clinicians today may use a narrower concept of hysteria, eliminating psychosomatic patients who once might have been called hysterics. Third, hysterics may now bring their problems to a general practitioner, who fails to recognize hysteria, rather than to a psychiatrist.

Statistics concerning neurotics are rare, but Stephens and Kamp (1962) compared diagnoses at an outpatient clinic for two eras, 1913–1919 and 1945–1960. For both eras the incidence of hysteria was 2%. It is possible that all the other diagnoses also diminished in incidence, thus concealing a real drop in the incidence of hysteria, but this highly speculative supposition is not supported by incidence figures from clinics. Furthermore, the two samples of hysterics were roughly comparable in age, social class, and similar variables. One study is not conclusive, but it is better than the casual and perhaps unreliable observations of clinicans. Thus there are no reliable data to sustain the belief that the incidence of hysteria has declined.

(4) *Sex Difference.* It is widely believed that hysteria is a "female syndrome." Most early reports, dating back to the last century, were of women patients, but in both World Wars large numbers of male hysterics were reported. Thus there has been disagreement about whether there is a sex difference. The statistical consensus is that virtually all hysterics are women (Purtell et al., 1951; Noyes, 1953; Ziegler et al., 1960; Stephens & Kamp, 1962; and Guze & Perley, 1963). Chodoff and Lyons (1958) report a predominance of men in their sample, but these may have been compensation cases. When pensions or other payments for disability are involved, it is difficult to distinguish among hysteria, fatigue-hypochondriasis, and malingering. Guze and Perley (1963) suggest that hysteria is a women's syndrome and that, except for an occasional feminine man, men are diagnosed as hysteric only through a misuse of the term. This raises the issue of how to define hysteria.

(5) *Definition.* Guze and Perley (1963) argue that if hysteria is defined properly it should prove to be a valid diagnostic category. By validity, they mean, ". . . demonstrating that patients with a particular diagnosis

have a fairly uniform course . . . ." (p. 960). Accordingly, in their research they adopted the description of hysteria outlined by Purtell et al., (1963):

clinical picture starts early in life
mainly in women
recurrent symptoms in many organ systems
dramatically described symptoms
many and varied pains
menstrual disorder
sexual maladjustment
headache
anxiety symptoms
excessive hospitalization and surgery

They selected a sample of women hysterics and followed them up after a six- to eight-year interval. Roughly 90% had the same diagnosis, hysteria, on follow-up. The majority had not had a symptom-free year in the interval, had been hospitalized (nonpregnancy), had menstrual troubles, had sexual maladjustment, and had seen physicians repeatedly. About half reported conversion symptoms, such as loss of voice and blindness. Guze and Perley conclude that hysteria is a women's syndrome that starts before the age of 20, has multiple symptoms, and that its most striking features are:

excessive hospitalization and surgery
many and varied pains
menstrual and sexual problems
long history of ill health
conversion symptoms

They insist on distinguishing between hysteria and conversion reactions. Hysteria is a circumscribed syndrome with stable features which, with one exception, are not seen in other syndromes. The exception is conversion symptoms, which are seen in a variety of syndromes, including psychoses, and in men as well as women. If their point of view is accepted, it is possible that the instability of the diagnosis of hysteria and the dispute over sex differences are caused by faulty definition. Perhaps their description of hysteria will establish a more reliable diagnosis of the syndrome.

Obsessive-Compulsive Reaction

Obsessions and compulsions are traditionally treated together, ostensibly because they tend to occur in the same patients. Authorities disagree on which of the two predominates, some using the term *obsessional neurosis* and others *compulsion neurosis*. There does not appear to be any basis for settling this dispute. Some patients are primarily obsessive, manifesting no compulsive behavior; others have elaborate compulsive rituals but do not engage in obsessive doubting.

Obsessions. An obsession is an excessive preoccupation with certain topics to the exclusion of all others. The sole area of symptom formation is ideation, and the symptoms are of two kinds.

(1) *Obsessive Doubting.* The individual is in a perpetual state of indecision. His conflict may be approach-approach, in which two alternatives appear equally desirable; approach-avoidance, in which a course of action has both rewarding and punishing consequences; or avoidance-avoidance, in which two alternatives are equally undesirable. Ordinarily, the implicit weighing of alternatives precedes a choice response. The obsessive makes all the preparations for action but does not act. The deliberations that should lead to action are prolonged indefinitely, and the obsessive doubter does not get around to making a choice.

Doubting is not limited to future choices; the obsessive may brood about past behavior. Anyone may occasionally question whether he has left a door unlocked, but the obsessive doubter is continually involved in such uncertainties. Did he turn out the light, turn off the gas, stamp the envelope? He cannot depend on his memory and is usually forced to check on previous actions, sometimes having to check and recheck interminably.

(2) *Obsessive Thoughts.* Obsessive thoughts may involve prohibited actions or temptations. The forbidden desires are commonly aggressive or sexual, for example, torture, murder, rape, incest. Such impulses are regarded with horror and repulsion by the obsessive individual, who believes they are foreign, intruding from the outside. He is at a loss to explain how he, a respectable citizen, could think such thoughts or have such impulses. Surely, he believes, they are like a tune that runs through one's head: an outside stimulus that somehow intrudes itself upon one's thoughts. The impulses and images may be so repugnant to the obsessive that he must deny responsibility for them.

The content of the obsession is not necessarily a forbidden impulse. It may be a thought or series of associations bearing no affective component; the obsessive individual is indifferent to the ideas, but cannot escape them. Often the recurrent thoughts constitute an avoidance response in that they prevent the individual from thinking about painful or unpleasant topics. One way to ignore or otherwise avoid thinking or planning because of the associated anxiety is to occupy oneself with other matters. The anxiety-laden topics are avoided by preoccupation with incompatible thoughts, and the escape from anxiety may lead to an overpowering tendency to think about trivial or indifferent subjects.

Compulsions. Compulsions are behavior sequences that the individual feels impelled to carry out; if he does not or cannot perform the ritual, he becomes anxious. Initially the compulsive person may resist his irresistible urge, but the ensuing tension and discomfort soon force him to give up the fight. Thereafter he indulges in the ritual and tends to avoid becoming anxious.

Two common compulsions concern repetition and symmetry. In the former the individual repeats a behavior sequence over and over. Evidently, the end of the sequence becomes a signal for anxiety, leading to repetition of the sequence. Usually the compulsive person is not sure he has performed the ritual well enough and in sufficient detail. In symmetry compulsions the last part of a behavior sequence balances out the first part. For example, the left shoe must be lined up exactly with the right shoe. It is as if the compulsive individual must prove that he is neutral; he cannot take sides or leave matters unbalanced. Both repetition and symmetry compulsions are counterparts of obsessive doubting. In one instance the compulsive person doubts that he performed the act correctly, and therefore, repeats it; in the other instance, he cannot take sides and must balance every plus with a minus.

Other compulsions reflect fussiness and exaggerated attention to details, as in serial compulsions. Serial compulsions with special numbers and magical compulsions illustrate the superstitious nature of compulsions. In his attempt to avoid anxiety, the compulsive individual seizes on gestures or behavior sequences that have accidently coincided with relief from anxiety. He resorts to the primitive logic that performance of rites will ward off evil (anxiety).

Characteristics of Obsessive-Compulsives. Obsessive-compulsive persons have not received as much attention as hysterics, and this is especially true of their nonsymptom characteristics. Only a few investigators have compiled enough cases to sustain generalizations. The most recent study is by Ingram (1961a), who reports the following composite picture of the majority of his sample of 89 obsessive-compulsive individuals, a picture in accord with clinical reports. The incidence of obsessive-compulsive neurosis is low, probably the lowest of the neuroses. Onset occurs relatively early, the mean age being approximately 25 years. These patients are more intelligent than any other neurotics and tend to be of higher social class status. They tend not to marry and are less incapacitated in relation to their work than are most neurotics.

Neurotic Depression

Depression is one of the two neurotic syndromes falling under the heading of *psychological residuals of tension.* This label indicates that neurotic depression may be viewed as a reaction to failure or loss: failure to solve important life problems, failure to cope with conflict, or loss of an important relationship. These issues will be discussed in the next two chapters. They are mentioned here because of their relevance to the nature of symptoms

TABLE 4.3   SYMPTOMS OF NEUROTIC DEPRESSION

Affective	*Motor*
melancholy	slowness of speech
pessimism	slowness of movement
self-depreciation	
apathy	

that appear. The symptoms represent a kind of surrender, whereas in hysteria and obsessive-compulsive neurosis the symptoms represent attempts to avoid or escape from anxiety. Consequently, the symptoms of depression tend to be vague and diffuse, whereas the symptoms of hysteria and obsessive-compulsive neurosis tend to be more circumscribed and clear.

Symptoms appear in two reaction systems, as shown in Table 4.3. *Affective* symptoms are prominent: the neurotic depressive shows excessive and prolonged mourning. The expected reaction to a personal loss is grief, but the depth of grief in depressives is excessive and the period of mourning, overlong. There are dejection and sadness, together with self-depreciation and a profound pessimism about the future. This prevailing mood often leads to apathy, which is manifested in both listlessness and a dull, mask-like facial expression. There is a profound feeling of loss and an inability to cope with everyday situations.

Motor symptoms match the solemn mood. Speech and body movements are slow, and there is a failure to initiate new activities. This inability to "get moving" helps to sustain the depression because there are no new stimuli to divert attention from mourning. Thus the affective and motor symptoms augment each other: melancholy slows action, and failure to act preserves the dark mood.

Melancholy is the major symptom in both neurotic and psychotic depression, which may make it difficult to distinguish between the two. They are qualitatively different in only one respect: the presence or absence of psychotic symptoms. In psychotic depression, as in any psychosis, there are usually such cognitive symptoms as hallucinations, delusions, or gross distortions of reality. The neurotic maintains an adequate perception of reality and does not manifest such bizarre symptoms.

Otherwise, neurotic and psychotic depression may be placed on a continuum of severity. In psychotic depression the depth of melancholy is greater, the degree of hopelessness is greater, and the strength of suicidal tendencies is stronger than in neurotic depression. Psychotic depressives are extremely guilty, and their past history reveals cyclical alterations in mood. Neurotic depressives usually show only mild guilt, there are no previous mood swings, and there is usually a clear precipitating incident. The differences between neurotic and psychotic depression will be discussed in more detail in Chapter 9.

Fatigue-Hypochondriasis

This hyphenated syndrome combines two kinds of symptoms which are sometimes kept separate: weariness and overconcern with health. They show sufficient overlap to be included in the same class. Symptoms occur in two spheres, as shown in Table 4.4. The somatic symptoms are of two kinds. One kind reflects the individual's excessive attention to his body processes. He is oversensitive to minor changes in body temperature, in the appearance of the skin, and in digestive regularity. He is overalert to internal noises, his pulse, minor pains, and headaches. The morbid focusing on vegetative function is facilitated by the patent medicine industry, which strives continually to make people aware of "conditions" that need treatment.

The second kind of somatic symptom is tiredness. This weariness appears similar to that seen in some nutritional deficiencies or debilitating diseases. However, in fatigue-hypochondriasis neither aches and pains nor absence of energy can be attributed to an underlying medical problem. These symptoms occur in the absence of organic pathology and therefore are labeled *residuals of psychological tension.*

The major *affective* symptom is boredom, which is analogous to the motor symptom of fatigue. The feeling of weakness and tiredness extends across symptom spheres, with mood more or less matching bodily weakness. In some patients there are irritability and resentment over lack of what they deem adequate care, but these attitudes are not frequent or intense.

Syndromes and Symptom Spheres

The symptoms constituting the five syndromes have been ordered to four different spheres. In comparing syndromes it is helpful to see in which spheres the symptoms occur, as in Table 4.5.

Let us examine the columns of this table. The somatic column includes anxiety reaction, hysteria, and fatigue-hypochondriasis. The somatic symptoms of anxiety reaction are largely autonomic, whereas in hysteria and fatigue-hypochondriasis they are usually nonautonomic (aches and pains). Hysterical somatic symptoms usually relate to muscle systems under voluntary control; somatic fatigue-hypochondriasis symptoms usually relate to in-

TABLE 4.4 SYMPTOMS OF FATIGUE HYPOCHONDRIASIS

Somatic	*Affective*
aches and pains	boredom
no energy	irritability

TABLE 4.5   PRESENCE OF SYMPTOMS IN THE FOUR SPHERES

	Somatic	Cognitive	Affective	Motor
anxiety reaction	✓	✓	✓	✓
hysteria	✓	✓		✓
obsessive-compulsive reaction		✓		✓
depression			✓	✓
fatigue-hypochondriasis	✓		✓	

voluntary, vegetative systems. These differences help in differential diagnosis.

The *cognitive* column includes three syndromes, and again the symptoms are different in each. The anxiety neurotic worries, the hysteric forgets, and the obsessive person cannot stop himself from remembering and mulling.

While the *affective* column includes three syndromes, affective symptoms are important in only two. Anxiety neurotics are often panicky, and depressives are of course melancholy. In fatigue-hypochondriasis affect is of less importance, including only boredom and irritability.

Motor symptoms may be divided into underactivity and overactivity. In depression there is slowing of speech and movement; in hysteria there may be partial or complete paralysis. Both represent underactivity. Overactivity is seen in anxiety and obsessive-compulsive neuroses. In anxiety reactions excess tension spills over into muscular activity, leading to tremors and jumpiness. In obsessive-compulsive neurosis the activity is less random and more purposive: the completion of a ritual that avoids the onset of anxiety.

DIFFERENTIAL DIAGNOSIS

In discussing the various neurotic syndromes it was implicitly assumed that the symptoms cluster on the basis of joint occurrence. It would follow that the presence of one group of symptoms precludes the presence of symptoms occurring in other syndromes. This is a property of an ideal classification, but it is not true of any classification, including the one just discussed. There is considerable overlap of symptoms, which makes differential diagnosis difficult. In many instances the problem is minor. The most important symptoms in a cluster are present, and other symptoms are minor. For example, intense obsessive thoughts may be accompanied by one or two mild phobias. Since phobias are common and in this instance they are slight, they may safely be ignored.

There are mixtures of symptoms, however, that cause more serious problems. Occasionally one sees a combination of compulsive rituals and hysterical pain. Such combinations occur often enough for some clinicians to use the designation *mixed neurosis*. When symptoms of different syndromes occur together, it is useless to try to impress a specific diagnostic label on them. Such a label would be important only if it indicated a specific etiology or treatment. For example, it is of great importance for a physician to decide whether vague intestinal pain and constriction are due to gastrointestinal upset or to heart condition, but in diagnosing neurotic symptoms the situation is different. Whether the label is anxiety reaction or hysteria tells us little about differential etiology or treatment. The emphasis here must be on the word *little*. *Some* etiological or treatment possibilities may derive from a psychological diagnosis, but they are not of the same information value as most medical diagnoses.

FACTOR ANALYSIS

The five neurotic syndromes consist of clusters of symptoms. These clusters have been observed by clinicians, who have made subjective judgments about the joint occurrence of symptoms. An alternative to this procedure is to obtain correlations among symptoms and factor-analyze the correlations. This alternative does not remove subjectivity from the observations, but it does relieve the observer of the difficult task of judging joint occurrence (covariation). Covariation can be determined objectively by means of correlation and factor analysis.

Factor analyses of symptoms have yielded evidence that the five syndromes accepted by clinicians are statistically meaningful. The clusters of symptoms have varied from one study to the next, and they are not always in complete agreement with those listed earlier. Furthermore, some syndromes have been reported in factor analytic studies oftener than others. The results of these studies are presented below, with the symptoms found in each study listed separately.

1. Anxiety Reaction
   O'Connor (1953)—anxiety, apprenhension, breathing difficulties, feeling of weakness, tremors;
   Lorr et al. (1953)—anxiety, tension, irritability, low frustration tolerance, sleeping difficulty;
   Lorr and Rubenstein (1955, 1956)—tense, irritable, disrupted by anxiety.
2. Hysteria
   Wittenborn (1951), Wittenborn and Holzberg (1951)—using physical symptoms, no organic basis for complaints, organic pathology with an emotional basis, no concern over physical handicaps;

Lorr et al. (1953)—gastric and intestinal complaints, headache, conversion symptoms, drinking.
3. Obsessive-Compulsive Neurosis
   O'Connor (1953)—compulsive behavior, fears, ruminative thinking, self-consciousness, guilt;
   Lorr et al. (1953)—compulsions, obsessive thinking, skin symptoms;
   Lorr and Rubenstein (1956)—highly deliberate, over-acceptance of responsibility, painstaking with tasks, strong concern with orderliness.
4. Depression
   O'Connor (1953)—depression, suicidal thoughts, phobias, crying spells, apprehension, withdrawal.
5. Fatigue-Hypochondriasis
   O'Connor (1953)—fatigue, dislike of crowds.

The differences in clusters from one study to the next may be attributed to three possible causes. First, different phrases were used, and some of the differences between studies are more apparent than real. Second, the studies were conducted in different settings. In settings involving compensation (such as Veteran's Administration clinics) the patients and professional staff tend to focus on physical symptoms more than in other settings. Third, the samples used in different studies may have differed considerably in such variables as age, sex, and chronicity. Chronicity is an especially important variable because it is possible that symptom clusters change as the neurosis continues over time. Clinicians have observed that individuals diagnosed as anxiety reaction at one time may be diagnosed as obsessive-compulsive neurosis at a later date. Also obsessive-compulsive persons occasionally show clear signs of depression as the years pass. Thus chronicity may alter the pattern seen, and it is an important determinant of diagnosis.

Despite these flaws and discrepancies, factor analyses have in the main substantiated the five clinical syndromes of neurosis. Other clusters (factors) have been discovered, but most of them vary from one study to the next. Two factors were reported by Lorr et al., (1953) which are of more than passing interest: hostility and sex conflict. These factors refer to personality characteristics rather than symptoms.

PERSONALITY AND NEUROSIS

Neurosis has been discussed in terms of symptoms, but it can also be viewed in terms of personality. For example, psychoanalytic theory assumes that obsessive-compulsive neurotics are fixated at the *anal* stage of development, the "anal personality" consisting of the traits of excessive neatness, hoarding, perfectionism, etc. It is implicitly assumed that this set of traits is the real neurosis and that symptoms are merely superficial manifestations of it. In this framework the individual is always "sick" because the neurosis *is* his abnormal personality. Symptoms represent a flare-up or exacerbation of underlying personality tendencies that have been present all along. An analogous medical model is malaria. Once contracted, this disease is more or less permanent, manifesting itself in periodic fever and other symptoms. When the symptoms subside, the person is still sick in the sense of having a chronic disease which may flare up at any time. Similarly, the view that neurosis is a personality disturbance assumes that certain personality features carry the seeds of neurotic symptoms. Whereas symptoms may wax and wane, the *personality* is always neurotic.

Neurotic Symptoms and Personality Traits

Personality traits are simply habitual ways of responding in frequently occurring situations. They are universal. All of us are more or less aggressive, more or less sociable, more or less ambitious, etc. Traits are the attributes by which we recognize one another, the enduring aspects of our behavior. As such, they are not important in the context of abnormal behavior. They begin to assume importance when they are extreme or intense. When an individual is excessively aggressive, sociable, or ambitious, the trait stands out as a deviation from normal. The deviation is abnormal not in the sense of psychopathology but in the sense of being uncommon.

Extreme traits render the individual more rigid. The normally aggressive person can move in the direction of greater or lesser aggressiveness; the intensely aggressive person is near the ceiling of aggressiveness and can move only toward lesser aggressiveness. Extreme traits probably have two sources. The first is temperament. As has been discussed elsewhere (Buss, 1961), the temperamental characteristics of quickness of responding, over-intensity of responding, and high activity level all tend to produce the trait of high aggressiveness. The second source is repeated environmental demands for extreme behavior. The bank clerk is required to be precise, punctual, orderly, and formal; these attributes, demanded over a period of years by the person's vocation, can freeze his personality into a mold of fussy, punctilious formality. Many vocations and social groups make similar demands for behavior which may eventually become solidified into an unchanging pattern of extreme traits.

Symptoms are more *transient* than traits. Although symptoms may persist over a period of years, usually they wax and wane; traits are always present. Symptoms are *uncommon;* few persons manifest panic, obsessive thoughts, hysterical blindness, or any of the neurotic symptoms described earlier. Symptoms have an *overdriven* character: the neurotic individual appears to be pushed into the reaction by forces beyond his control. He must make the response, or else suffer dreaded, unknown consequences. This *insatiable* quality applies mainly to the symptoms of obsessive-compulsion and anxiety reactions and, to a lesser extent, hysteria. The symptoms of depression and fatigue-hypochondriasis are residuals of tension; they represent surrender and resignation, rather than attempts to cope. It is only when the neurotic actively struggles with his problems that his symptoms have a rigid, intense, overdriven character.

Neurotic symptoms tend to be irrational: childish fears of separation, obsessive impulses, or hysterical paralysis. They make no sense to the neutral observer or to the neurotic. Traits are rational in that they are appropriate responses to oft-repeated situations. In the example mentioned earlier, the fussy, punctilious person will probably succeed as a bank clerk. Thus traits tend to facilitate adjustment; symptoms tend to hinder adjustment. Symptoms render the neurotic uncomfortable, inefficient, or both.

Although traits and symptoms clearly differ in a number of properties, the personality approach to neurosis assumes that they are on a continuum, personality traits predisposing toward the development of symptoms. Coleman (1964) suggests this sequence of the development of neurotic symptoms:

(1) faulty personality, which leads to specific weakness in personality structure
(2) over-reaction to common stresses, which causes severe anxiety
(3) defenses against anxiety
(4) cycles of inefficiency and secondary symptoms of fatigue and dissatisfaction.

Unfortunately, the term *personality* has several meanings. We have been using it to denote a cluster of traits, but Coleman's list of "personality characteristics of neurotics" includes:

(1) inadequacy and low stress tolerance
(2) egocentricity and disturbed interpersonal relationships
(3) lack of insight and rigidity
(4) dissatisfaction and unhappiness
(5) anxiety and fearfulness
(6) persistent nonintegrative behavior
(7) psychological and somatic symptoms
(8) tension and irritability.

The first four items on the list might be considered personality characteristics, whereas the last four concern not personality but neurotic symptoms. If symptoms and personality traits are not kept separate, there can be no meaningful discussion of the relationship between the two.

The basic assumption of the personality view is that faulty or extreme personality traits lead to neurotic symptoms. This view is relevant only to hysteria and obsessive-compulsive neurosis because only for these two syndromes has a specific set of traits been stated.

Hysterical Personality. Chodoff and Lyons (1958), after reviewing the work of a number of authorities, compiled this list of features constituting the hysterical personality:

(1) egoism, vanity, self-indulgence
(2) exhibitionism, dramatization, histrionic behavior, lying
(3) labile affect, emotional outbursts
(4) emotional shallowness
(5) lasciviousness, coquetry
(6) sexual frigidity
(7) dependency.

There are some apparent paradoxes on the list. *Emotional outbursts* would not seem to go with *emotional shallowness*. The problem lies with the word *emotional,* which is one of the most abused terms in psychopathology. Emotional outbursts are due to a lack of control, an inability to modulate one's behavior. Emotional shallowness refers to a lack of empathy, feeling for others, loyalty, and altruism. Similarly, *lasciviousness* and *sexual frigidity* do not appear to belong together, but they do occur in the same individual. The hysterical personality is marked by teasing, flirtatiousness, and all of the preliminary responses that mark the beginning of sexual interaction, but there is no interest in, and in fact an aversion to, actual sexual behavior, that is, frigidity. The entire pattern is one of immaturity: a childish manipulation of others, lack of emotional control, and little capacity for adult social and sexual interaction.

The personality view assumes that a particular personality leads to a specific set of symptoms. In this instance, a hysterical personality should be associated with hysterical symptoms. Four studies bear on this issue. Foulds and Caine (1959) found that most of their sample of hysterics had a hysterical personality, but that roughly half of a group of dysthymics (anxiety neurotics and obsessive-compulsives) also had a hysterical personality. These positive but equivocal findings are opposed by the results of three studies, all reporting that a minority of hysterics have a hysterical personality (Chodoff & Lyons, 1958; Ziegler et al., 1960; and Stephens & Kamp, 1962). Only the Stephens and Kamp study used hysterics as subjects; the other two used patients diagnosed as conversion reaction. As Guze and Perley (1963) note, conversion reactions occur in a variety of syndromes and cannot be equated with hysteria. Therefore only the Stephens and Kamp findings can be regarded as unequivocally negative.

Thus of the four studies, only two are clearly relevant. Foulds and Caine report mixed positive findings, and Stephens and Kamp report clearly negative findings. This issue must remain in doubt until it is clarified by further research. Nevertheless, the following reasoning does account for all the data. It is possible that a hysterical personality does facilitate the development of hysterical symptoms rather than any other kind of neurotic symptoms. Hysterical personalities should always develop hysterical symptoms, but hysterical symptoms may also occur in the absence of a hysterical personality. Thus the hysterical personality is not a necessary condition of hysteria but may lead to it.

Compulsive Personality. The best picture of the compulsive personality has been supplied by Sandler and Hazari (1960). They factor-analyzed the inventory responses of 100 neurotics attending an outpatient clinic and extracted two correlated factors. The first may be labeled *compulsive personality:*

(1) systematic, thorough, well-ordered
(2) strong aversion to dirt, fussy, punctual
(3) overconscientious
(4) attentive to details, minutiae, petty formalities
(5) traits are accepted and are a source of self-esteem.

Note that these traits all involve compulsiveness and a tight, orderly existence; there is no mention of the cognitive components that might be labeled *obsessional personality*. The fifth item is important because it shows that the individual accepts his extreme traits as part of adjustment to everyday situations. This acceptance is in marked contrast to the neurotic's aversive response to his own symptoms, of which he wants to rid himself.

The second factor is a straightforward description of obsessive-compulsive symptoms:

(1) unwanted thoughts
(2) worrying, brooding
(3) inability to make up mind, resistance to starting work
(4) compulsion to engage in rituals, to memorize twice, to count.

Sandler and Hazari commented that elements of this second factor probably existed in mild form in most neurotics but in severe form only in obsessive compulsives. Note that the symptoms are *unwanted* cognitive or motor responses, which the individual disowns and fights against; in contrast, compulsive personality traits are not only accepted but are perhaps also a source of pride.

There is equivocal evidence linking the traits to the symptoms. Ingram (1961b) had obsessive-compulsive neurotics rated for the presence of seven compulsive personality traits: excessive cleanliness, orderliness, pedantry, conscientiousness, uncertainty, and inconclusiveness in thinking and acting.

Of 77 patients, 12 had none of the traits, 41 had two to four traits, and 24 had five to seven traits. Thus a large majority of the sample had at least two of the traits. Unfortunately, there was no control group, which renders interpretation difficult. We do not know how prevalent these traits are among other neurotics or among normal persons, and it is possible that possessing two compulsive traits is common. Furthermore, there is no basis for linking *compulsive* traits with *obsessive* symptoms. No one has described the obsessive personality that should lead to obsessive symptoms, and until this is done, there is no theoretical rationale to link the two.

Speculation. The results of several studies offer no clear answer to the question of personality traits and neurotic symptoms. It seems best, therefore, to go along with clinical opinion, which suggests a moderate relationship. It follows that hysterics should tend to have a hysterical personality, and compulsives a compulsive personality. Nevertheless, there is no one-to-one relationship between personality and neurosis; there are three reasons for this.

First, traits and symptoms are linked for only two syndromes, hysteria and compulsion neurosis. There is no specific personality pattern associated with obsessive neurosis, anxiety reaction, depression, or fatigue-hypochondriasis. Second, the traits may simply be well-learned, *appropriate* responses to oft-recurring situations; for example, teachers are pedantic, athletes competitive. Such traits are useful, contributing to good adjustment. As such, they are accepted and may even be valued by the individual. Sandler and Hazari (1960) showed that compulsive traits were a source of pride, whereas compulsive symptoms were a source of concern. The point is that even extreme traits may serve an adjustive purpose, helping to prevent rather than to facilitate the development of neurotic symptoms. Third, symptoms may occur in the absence of traits. A noncompulsive person may try a compulsive response when confronted by a sudden stress; if the response helps him to escape from the stress, it may become part of his repertoire. Subsequently, he will tend to make the compulsive response whenever he is anxious; he will have a neurotic symptom—a compulsion—in the absence of the corresponding personality traits.

Personal Relations

The term *personality* includes not only traits but also personal relations, the interaction of an individual with the significant figures in his life. It has been argued that the crux of neurosis is impaired personal relations, neurotic symptoms being a superficial and trivial manifestation of the deeper interpersonal problem. Before discussing this issue it is necessary to clarify the nature of the disturbance, for it varies with different kinds of psychopathology. The psychotic patient tends to run away from others, avoiding relationships he sees as painful and threatening. The patient with a conduct disorder tends to manipulate others for immediate gain, equating persons with commodities that can be bought, sold, or used for one's own advantage. The neurotic patient may attempt to manipulate others, but he fails. He is ambivalent, demanding, and anxious in his dealings with others; he may seek help, only to despise the person who supplies it. In general, his personal relations are marked by inconsistency, insecurity, and dissatisfaction.

There are many ways to classify personal relations, but the one adopted here aligns them in a developmental sequence from earliest to latest: dependency, aggression, and sexuality.

Dependency is regarded as a continuum ranging from complete dependence on an adult during infancy to relatively complete independence during adulthood. The infant, being biologically helpless, is immediately cast into a "baby role." He is allowed to maintain this role throughout childhood, but early in childhood he must also begin to respond as a peer to playmates. During adolescence he is expected to surrender any remaining components of the baby role, although he is still in a subordinate position to his parents and other authority figures. Finally, in adulthood he is expected to add the role of authority to his repertoire, as a parent or a superior (boss, teacher, etc.).

The neurotic may have trouble with any or all of these three roles. He may persist too long in childish ways or at any given period insist on too much parental care and affection. He may respond as though he has been deprived of parental attention and love, and he may seek these insatiably. He may be unable to develop peer relations because of an inability to engage in the give-and-take of such situations; his strong needs for nurturance may prevent him from interacting easily with age-mates because they are not sufficiently giving of affection and parental-type care. Lastly, he may be able to be a peer but unable to assume superior status. This is a less serious problem than inability to be a peer, but it is seen occasionally in the form of "promotion neurosis": promotion to a position of authority triggers an intense anxiety reaction, together with inferiority feelings and occasional guilt.

The socializing of *aggressive* tendencies is a major issue in childhood. Children are taught to inhibit and control their anger and to channelize their aggressive behavior. Less attention is paid to hostility (dislike and hatred) because it tends to be covert. If there is excessive emphasis on inhibiting and controlling aggression, the child may become underaggressive. Some minimum of attacking behavior (verbal or physical) is necessary in order to maintain one's sense of identity, to assert oneself, and to defend oneself. Neurotics typically are unable to aggress appropriately and directly. Thus they are prevented from asserting themselves or defending themselves adequately when such actions are necessary. Situations calling for aggression or eliciting anger may elicit anxiety or guilt instead. A related tendency is the neurotic's intense hostility: he hates those whom he sees as threatening and those on whom he must depend.

During childhood and especially during adolescence there is an emphasis on channelizing *sexual* urges and sharply defining one's sex role. The ability to engage in adult heterosexual behavior presupposes good peer relations, and a relative lack of anxiety or guilt about sex. However, it is just these prerequisites that are often lacking in the neurotic, who tends to be childish, anxious, or guilty. Thus the area of sexual behavior may be the focus of the neurotic's symptoms, the area that elicits so much guilt or anxiety that one or more of the three kinds of neurotic symptoms develop: anxiety, attempts to escape from or avoid anxiety, and psychological residuals of tension.

It is clear that neurotics do have problems with dependency, aggression, and sexuality, but this does not mean that the interpersonal view is correct. Two considerations make it questionable. First, personal relations are important for everyone. In everyday life, especially in industrialized society, we are almost constantly surrounded by other persons, who constitute the most salient stimuli in the environment. The pleasures and pains of life are derived from others and are enjoyed or endured in competition or in concert with others. In this context it is not surprising that most normal individuals have *some* difficulty in personal relations.

It is a cliché among clinicians that any particular patient has some anxiety, guilt, or problem of modulation about dependency, aggression, or sexuality. If both normal persons and neurotics have difficulty in personal relations, this aspect of adjustment cannot be the crux of neurosis. One answer to this argument is that neurotics have worse personal relations than normal persons. This is undoubtedly true, but perhaps it is because of their neurotic *symptoms*. An excessively fearful, compulsive, hysterical, or depressed individual will necessarily find it hard to get along with others. His symptoms force him to be dependent, to inhibit his aggression, and in general to be deficient in the normal give-and-take of social interaction. Thus the neurotic's personality difficulties, insofar as they are worse than those of normal individuals, may be due to his symptoms.

Second, the interpersonal view assumes that neurotics have difficulties in *interpersonal* situations but not in *impersonal* situations. Do personal relations play this special role in neurosis or are they merely one of several important areas of adjustment? It is difficult to answer this question. The case histories of neurotics are usually filled with examples of disturbed personal relations, but such histories are not appreciably different from those of normal persons. Moreover, case histories focus on social aspects of adjustment, making it difficult to decide whether personal relations are truly crucial or merely noticed more.

Neurotics do have difficulties with impersonal stimuli. Anxiety neurotics are fearful of bridges, the dark, and heights; compulsives engage in rituals of counting or of arranging objects, with no one else present; and obsessives have persistent thoughts that often involve no other persons. Thus the *symtoms* of neurosis seem to be impersonal as well as interpersonal. Perhaps neurotics with impersonal symptoms are in the minority, most neurotics manifesting interpersonal symptoms. We do not know, and only an extensive survey would resolve the issue. In the absence of clear evidence to the contrary, the position taken here is that neurotic symptoms are not exclusively interpersonal and that it is best to *begin* the study of neuroses by focusing on symptoms, not merely on one aspect of symptoms. In brief, there are no compelling arguments that lead us to substitute personality traits or personal relations for symptoms as the events to be studied in neurosis.

COMMENT

The role of personality (traits or personal relations) raises the question of whether the character of neurosis has changed during the last five or six decades. It has been argued that the classical symptoms and syndromes of neurosis did occur once but are no longer seen, at least in appreciable numbers. They have been replaced by character problems, identity problems, or both. *Character problems* consist of ingrained personality traits of the kind discussed above. These traits—tendencies toward compulsiveness, toward histrionics and overemotionality, and toward passive or active rebellion—are believed to be the true neuroses of modern life. *Identity problems* center on roles and self-concepts: feelings of inferiority and rootlessness, lack of a stable sense of belonging or of relating to others, lack of a role or set of roles in society—in brief, a sense of alienation.

It is difficult to evaluate these arguments because, as with a similar issue concerning hysterical symptoms, data that would resolve the issue are missing and there are other plausible explanations. One possibility, suggested by Schofield (1964), is that the mental health movement has focused attention on abnormality, and the increased awareness has led to a greater number of persons seeking help. Most of those now seeking help do not have the serious and traditional symptoms characteristic of patients of an earlier era. The new patients have the minor problems that affect all of us, problems relating to identity, unhappiness, one's role in life, etc. Thus it is possible that neurosis has not changed at all during the last sixty years, but the problems brought to clinics may be milder and concerned with life problems common to all persons.

Another explanation emphasizes modes or fashions in the complaints brought to clinics and practitioners. A fair proportion of patients are literate and aware of trends in the social sciences. They read the works of social philosophers, whose access to mass media has made common such concepts as *inner directed versus other directed, existential reality,* and *alienation.* When a person verbalizes his problems, he does so in terms and concepts in current usage. Sixty years ago he might have stated his difficulties in terms of anxiety and depression; today he might reveal feelings of not belonging and of not having clear aims in life. Perhaps the verbal descriptions represent real change in neurotic symptoms compared to what symptoms were sixty years ago, but it is equally possible that the new verbalizations overlay symptoms that have not altered over the years. The issue is further confused by the clinician's susceptibility to the same media of mass communication. The notion of modes and fashions in diagnosing neurosis is certainly not farfetched, and the patient's complaints may fit nicely into precisely the kind of symptoms the clinician has been led to expect from his own reading of the works of social philosophers.

Fashions in clinical practice offer two other explanations. First, character and identity problems may have been present in neurotics in previous eras, but they were overlooked by clinicians who were not trained to observe them. Second, today's preoccupation with personality and personal relations may blind clinicians to the classical neurotic symptoms that still occur in their patients. In brief, it is not clear whether the historical changes in neurotic symptoms are real or apparent; if they are real, they may be due to differences in the sample of patients now being seen or they may be due to changes in the social environment.

Let us consider the last possibility—real changes due to alterations in the social environment. If this notion is correct, it follows that the nature of symptoms is determined exclusively or principally by *culture* (social environment). We must distinguish two aspects of such environmental influences on behavior. The first is *process:* the specific procedures used in training children to be part of society. These procedures consist of the way rewards and punishments are delivered, the schedules (such as feeding) children are put on, and the *modes* of learning that are fostered. The second aspect is *content:* the signs and rules important in everyday life, the accent and pattern of speech, the preference for verbal over physical aggression, the need to delay gratification, etc.

It seems likely that most of the cultural changes occurring during the last sixty years have altered the *content* rather than the *process* of our social environment. If this is true and if there have been changes in the nature of neurotic symptoms, it follows that content, not process, is the essential determinant of the nature of symptoms. This position assumes that *what* children are taught, not *how* they are taught, determines their symptoms.

Our final comment concerns the reliability of diagnosis. We noted in the last chapter that neuroses are diagnosed less reliably than psychoses. One cause of the lower reliability may be the personality versus symptoms issue. The personality-oriented clinician seeks information about aggressiveness, sexuality, guilt, and the personality mechanisms designed to cope with conflicts in these areas. The symptom-oriented clinician seeks information about specific abnormal responses and is less concerned with personality tendencies and traits. The two clinicians would perceive and report quite different aspects of a client's behavior, and we should not be surprised if they disagreed on diagnosis.

Reliability of diagnosis is one aspect of the larger issue of what constitutes a neurosis. There is an unfortunate tendency to define neurotic behavior within the context of one's own theory. This parochialism has interfered with the development of a set of universally accepted terms to describe the observable behavior that is labeled neurotic. As we mentioned in the preface, a scientific approach demands the separation of data from explanations of data. This requirement underlies our insistence on defining neurosis in terms of observables (symptoms) rather than in terms of explanatory concepts (defensive systems or underlying traits). The latter, which are part of theory, are discussed in the next four chapters.

REFERENCES

Buss, A. H. *The psychology of aggression.* New York: Wiley, 1961.
Buss, A. H. Two anxiety factors in psychiatric patients. *Journal of Abnormal and Social Psychology,* 1962, **65**, 426–427.
Buss, A. H., & Gerjuoy, H. The scaling of adjectives descriptive of personality. *Journal of Consulting Psychology,* 1957, **21**, 366–371.
Cameron, N. A. *The psychology of behavior disorders.* Boston: Houghton Mifflin, 1947.
Chodoff, P., & Lyons, H. Hysteria, the hysterical personality and hysterical conversion. *American Journal of Psychiatry,* 1958, **114**, 734–740.
Coleman, J. C. *Abnormal psychology and modern life.* Chicago: Scott, Foresman, 1964.
Dixon, J. J., deMonchaux, Cecily, & Sandler, J. Patterns of anxiety: The phobias. *British Journal of Medical Psychology,* 1957, **30**, 34–40
Eysenck, H. J. Classification and the problems of diagnosis. In H. J. Eysenck (Ed.) *Handbook of abnormal psychology.* New York: Basic Books, 1961.
Foulds, G. A., & Caine, T. M. Symptom clusters and personality types among psychoneurotic men compared with women. *Journal of Mental Science,* 1959, **105**, 469–475.
Guze, S. B., & Perley, M. J. Observations on the natural history of hysteria. *American Journal of Psychiatry,* 1963, **119**, 960–965.
Hamilton, M. The assessment of anxiety states by rating. *British Journal of Medical Psychology,* 1959, **32**, 50–59.
Ingram, I. M. Obsessional illness in mental hospital patients. *Journal of Mental Science,* 1961, **107**, 382–402 (a).
Ingram, I. M. The obsessional personality and obsessional illness. *American Journal of Psychiatry,* 1961, **117**, 1016–1019 (b).
Lacey, J. I. Individual differences in somatic response patterns. *Journal of Comparative and Physiological Psychology,* 1950, **43**, 338–350.

Lorr, M., Rubenstein, E. A., & Jenkins, R. L. A factor analysis of personality ratings of outpatients in psychotherapy. *Journal of Abnormal and Social Psychology,* 1953, **48,** 511–514.

Lorr, M., & Rubenstein, E. A. Factors descriptive of psychiatric patients. *Journal of Abnormal and Social Psychology,* 1955, **51,** 514–522.

Lorr, M., & Rubenstein, E. A. Personality patterns of neurotic adults in psychotherapy. *Journal of Consulting Psychology,* 1956, **20,** 257–263.

Noyes, A. P. *Modern clinical psychiatry.* 4th Edition. Philadelphia: Saunders, 1953.

O'Connor, J. P. A statistical test of psychoneurotic syndromes. *Journal of Abnormal and Social Psychology,* 1953, **48,** 581–584.

Purtell, J. J., Robins, E., & Cohen, M. E. Observations on the clinical aspects of hysteria. A quantitative study of 50 hysteria patients and 156 control subjects. *Journal of the American Medical Association,* 1951, **146,** 902–909.

Sandler, J., & Hazari, A. The "obsessional": On the psychological classification of obsessional character traits and symptoms. *British Journal of Medical Psychology,* 1960, **33,** 113–122.

Schofield, W. *Psychotherapy: the purchase of friendship.* Englewood Cliffs, New Jersey: Prentice-Hall, 1964.

Stephens, J. H., & Kamp, M. On some aspects of hysteria: A clinical study. *Journal of Nervous and Mental Disease,* 1962, **134,** 305–315.

Wittenborn, J. R. Symptom patterns in a group of mental hospital patients. *Journal of Consulting Psychology,* 1951, **15,** 290–302.

Wittenborn, J. R., & Holzberg, J. C. The generality of psychiatric syndromes. *Journal of Consulting Psychology,* 1951, **15,** 372–380.

Ziegler, F. J., Imboden, J. B., & Meyer, E. Contemporary conversion reactions: A clinical study. *American Journal of Psychiatry,* 1960, **116,** 901–910.

CHAPTER 5

The Psychoanalytic Approach
to Neurosis

The approach to be described here may be called *classical psychoanalytic*. This is the orthodox Freudian view, which differs from the views of Adler and Jung, as well as the more modern concepts of Fromm, Horney, and Hartmann. The orthodox view has gained wider acceptance than any of the others and has been the most influential. Expositions of its variants may be found in Blum (1953) and Munroe (1955). They will enter here only insofar as they have been accepted as part of traditional doctrine. When in doubt, Fenichel's interpretation (1945) will be accepted as orthodox.

GENERAL THEORY OF NEUROSIS

A basic assumption is that instinctual urges strive for discharge, that is, to be expressed in manifest behavior. Such discharge is consistent with the "conservative" nature of instincts: tension states must be dispelled. The homeostatic balance point is some low ebb of tension; impulses or excitation above this point will strive vigorously for discharge.

Society does not allow all impulses to be expressed in behavior. Many urges are punished when they appear in behavior, and subsequently they arouse anxiety. The normal ego regulates the flow of impulses so that most of them are expressed in one form or another and with a minimum of anxiety.

Anxiety

Anxiety itself originates in the undifferentiated excitement that occurs when the organism is flooded with excitation. This flooding may be regarded as the original trauma, the "primal anxiety." All later anxiety represents a repetition of this early, undifferentiated state of painful tension.

As the ego develops and assumes new functions, it "tames" anxiety. When the organism is threatened with a future danger, the ego uses part of the tension as a signal. This signal serves as a warning, allowing the organism to take protective action. Thus the ego can master small quantities of excitation and use them for its own purposes.

The problem arises when the excitation is more than the ego can handle. Then the anxiety is not merely a signal but the trigger for a full-scale panic. It is as if someone shouts "Fire" in a crowded theater: the signal results in a wild stampede.

Developmentally, the first and most basic anxiety is an unconscious fear of the recurrence of traumatic or panic states. This is followed by a fear of separation, that is, loss of the love of the omnipotent parent. Still later in the developmental sequence fear of physical punishment (castration anxiety) occurs. All three anxieties are present in everyone, but they are more intense in neurotics.

Psychoanalytic theory distinguishes between fear and anxiety. Fear is realistic or objective apprehension about a clear threat from the environment. In the face of fear stimuli the ego may use some of the "excitement" as a signal of impending danger; or the signal may set off a panic state. Anxiety, or neurotic anxiety, is a fear of the consequences of expressing one's own impulses or instincts. Thus the son's erotic impulse toward his mother (Oedipal feeling) arouses anxiety because a likely consequence will be punishment by his father. The difference, then, between fear and anxiety (or, as it has been stated, between objective and neurotic anxiety) is in responsibility for the threat. In fear (real anxiety) the individual is a passive victim of a potentially dangerous environment. In anxiety (neurotic anxiety) the individual can bring on the danger by expressing his impulses or prevent the danger by inhibiting them. It is fear of external stimuli (fear) versus fear of internal stimuli (anxiety).

Repression

Freud defined repression as a mechanism that rejects impulses from consciousness and keeps them unconscious. This definition is deceptively simple. There is disagreement among psychoanalysts on precisely what is repressed and where it came from originally. Freud himself expressed different ideas about repression, and his theoretical shifts have caused confusion. The present account follows Freud and includes both his earlier and his later theories of repression.

The term *repression* has two referents. The first is the preventing of an idea (the mental representation of an instinct) from attaining consciousness. The second is the expelling of ideas already in consciousness. The second referent is the one commonly used, and it has been called *repression proper*.

The only ideas that must be banished from consciousness are those associated with anxiety. When the ego is threatened with psychic pain (anxiety), it responds with defense mechanisms. The most fundamental and primitive mechanism is repression, which protects the ego by expelling ideas from awareness. The motivation for this defensive maneuver is anxiety.

The repressed material (ideas, associations, and impulses) retains its psychic energy, which continually attempts to attain consciousness. Repression may be likened to clamping a lid on a steaming pot and preventing the steam from escaping. The repressed material that is trapped in the unconscious exerts strong pressure to escape. This pressure requires unceasing counterpressure in order to prevent entry into consciousness. Thus repression must occur again and again, with no surcease so long as ideas are denied awareness. Since energy can be countered only with energy, the conflict between repressed ideas and the counterforce of repression requires considerable psychic energy. The more repression there is, the more psychic energy is bound in intrapsychic conflict. Such conflict removes psychic energy needed for other, more adjustive purposes and leads to psychological fatigue.

Repressed material seeks to attain consciousness not only by overcoming repression but also by circumventing it. The unconscious, repressed ideas and associations attract other associations to themselves, the links being symbolic and largely unconscious. These new ideas and impulses are derivations of the original, unacceptable ones. If the derivations are sufficiently dissimilar to the original repressed ideas, they may escape the repressive forces of the ego and enter consciousness. Such escape is facilitated by ego weakness. An everyday example is dreams. While the ego is less alert during sleep, disguised derivations of the repressed ideas become manifest in the weird images of dreams. If the disguise is successful, the dream is remembered; if the disguise fails, the dream itself cannot be recalled. This inability to recall or think of derivatives is called *secondary repression*. It occurs when the associated or symbolic ideas are too similar to the original, repressed material to be allowed consciousness.

So far the discussion has dwelt on ideas and impulses that are excluded from consciousness.

. . . beside the idea there is something else, another presentation of the instinct to be considered, and that this other element undergoes a repression which may be quite different from that of the idea. We have adopted the term *charge of affect* for this other element in the mental presentation . . . . (Freud, 1950, p. 91)

Freud suggested that when the affective component of an instinct is suppressed, it may be transformed into anxiety. Thus if a sexual urge is unacceptable and therefore repressed, part of its affect may be converted to anxiety. Since the idea (the mental representation of committing a sexual act) is also repressed, the person is unaware of the impulse. Despite this unawareness, he may become anxious without knowing why: part of the unconscious sexual affect has been transformed into anxiety. Thus a neurotic may be terrified without knowing the cause of his fear; the cause is kept unconscious.

Repression of ideas and repression of affects are analogous. Repressed ideas strive for consciousness directly, by overthrowing repression, or indirectly, by forming derivatives that escape detection by the ego's censor. Repressed affects strive for consciousness directly, by overthrowing repression and being discharged (a temper tantrum or sexual excitement), or indirectly, by being transformed into anxiety, part of which becomes conscious.

Anxiety plays a paradoxical role in the process of repression. Anxiety is the motivating force behind repression. Anxiety-laden thoughts or ideas are unbearable and must be ejected from consciousness. The purpose of repression is to protect the ego from the anxiety associated with particular impulses and associations. However, the repressed material retains its psychic energy, part of which is transformed into anxiety. This, then, is the paradox: the repressed material, which is kept unconscious because awareness would cause anxiety, still causes anxiety through the transformation of unconscious affect into anxiety. Thus repression cannot be entirely successful because part of the anxiety that initially motivates repression filters through in the form of transformed affect. This outcome follows logically from the assumption that repressed impulses retain their psychic energy.

Repression may suffice to prevent impulses from attaining consciousness or discharge. The price is a drain on psychic energy and a weakened ego. On the other hand, the impulses may be so strong that repression alone cannot contain them within the unconscious. Other defenses must be thrown up; other counterforces must help contain the repressed material striving for consciousness and discharge. The interplay of the instincts seeking expression and the defensive forces preventing it constitute the dynamics of neurosis. If another defense succeeds in preventing discharge, repression may become unnecessary. Fenichel uses the illustration of obsessive thoughts of murder; the obsessive person uses the mechanism of *isolation* to guarantee that no action will occur and is then able to allow the murderous thoughts to become conscious. This illustration also demonstrates another principle: the ultimate aim of repression, as of all defense mechanisms, is to prevent repressed impulses from being expressed in behavior.

Repression establishes a tension state, instincts being opposed by counterforces. It is especially frequent in childhood, probably because the childish ego cannot cope with infantile sexuality and Oedipal longings. Repression isolates and fixates ideas, which cannot develop and mature because they are kept unconscious. This "deep freeze" of ideas and impulses sets the stage for neurosis after puberty. Biological maturation at puberty intensifies instinctual urges, especially sexual impulses. The increased strength of instincts destroys the equilibrium formerly in effect between impulses and defenses. Now defenses other than repression are demanded; now compromises are needed between instincts and defenses. These compromises represent a partial discharge of the original impulse, now distorted by the defending forces; these are the symptoms of neurosis. Thus neurotic symptoms in adults are caused by unconscious conflict between impulses and defenses (repression or others); the unconscious conflict always has its roots in the repression of impulses during childhood. In brief, the etiology of neurosis must be sought in the inner, unconscious conflict that occurs when infantile sexuality is not handled adequately.

The Development of Neurosis

Neurosis consists of sudden, involuntary expressions of emotion (affect) as a result of failure of ego control. Such failure is always the result of excessive tension, the excitation overwhelming any attempts at control. Excessive excitation occurs in two ways. First, a normal individual may find himself flooded with fear, as in the traumatic neuroses seen especially in war. Second, the previous damming up of tension may make the individual so high-strung that normal stimulation has the same effect as trauma.

All ego defenses are designed to reduce anxiety. When instinctual urges are denied expression, it is only because they have become associated with anxiety. The motivation for all neurotic mechanisms is anxiety, and the way in which anxiety is reduced determines the form of the neurosis.

The psychoanalytic model of neurosis may be stated briefly. An instinctual urge strives for expression, but because it is anxiety-arousing, it is repressed. The repressed impulse continually presses for discharge and a return to consciousness, but the defending forces of the ego strive just as tenaciously to prevent these. This neurotic conflict results in a state of tension, irritability, fatigue, and even pain; these are symptoms both of ego-insufficiency (no energy left to initiate other activities) and the conflict between instincts and defenses (irritability, tension, pain). At this juncture the label *actual-neurosis* is appropriate: a state of being dammed up, in the absence of direct expressions of the defending forces in the form of specific symptoms. Anxiety reaction (free-floating), depression, and fatigue-hypochondriasis are all actual-neuroses.

So far the only defense mechanism to be mentioned has been repression, which is the only defense present in actual-neuroses. When other defenses (reaction formation, compulsiveness, etc.) are elaborated in the attempt to reduce anxiety, we have a *psychoneurosis*. A psychoneurotic symptom represents a compromise between the original impulse and the defense against it. In such a compromise the impulse is distorted sufficiently for it to be expressed with only minimal anxiety. With some of the neurotic tension relieved, there is less pressure for discharge of impulses, and the defensive forces can do their job better. The simplest compromise is that seen in phobias, in which the urge (anxiety) is admitted but the real reason for it is repressed.

ACTUAL-NEUROSIS

The three actual-neuroses—anxiety reaction, fatigue-hypochondriasis, and reactive depression—are all the result of the dammed-up state that is the outcome of neurotic conflict. Except for repression, there are no clear-cut defense mechanisms or symptoms that are rich in symbolism and ripe for interpretation. Because of these features, psychoanalysts have paid less attention to actual-neuroses, and theoretical accounts are meager.

Anxiety Reaction

Anxiety neurotics are tense and irritable, and they have periodic attacks of acute panic. Acute panic represents the breaking through of excitement, breaching the inhibiting defense of repression by the uncontrollable surge of the affect. The discharge is involuntary, being due to a temporary loss of control. After such attacks there is less tension, and the ego is able to inhibit further discharges, at least temporarily.

The chronic tension and restlessness of the anxiety neurotic reveal his inner excitement. The source of his anxiety is not some external danger but the terrifying possibility that inner impulses will become manifest in behavior. The greater the pressure of impulses for discharge, the stronger must be the defense against such expression; thus the waxing and waning of restlessness, exhaustion, and panic. Throughout all the inner turmoil and conflict the individual does not know what it is that he fears. He cannot know because the reason for his anxiety lies in the possibility of expressing and becoming aware of impulses that must be repressed. These impulses are usually sexual or aggressive.

The sole defense mechanism in anxiety reaction is repression. The ego cannot allow forbidden impulses to be expressed because of the punishment that would inevitably follow. The affect associated with the unacceptable urges (sexual excitement or rage) is partially transformed into anxiety. Thus the act of repression may itself generate unconscious anxiety, some of which reaches consciousness. The ideas associated with the impulses never reach awareness, so that the person is vaguely apprehensive without knowing why.

Fear itself may be repressed. In a situation calling for bravery in the face of danger, there is usually a strong impulse to escape. Cowardly flight is incompatible with masculinity, and men must occasionally repress the fear impulse. The repression of specific cowardly impulses may then lead to free-floating anxiety. The man has protected himself from the terrifying knowledge of his own cowardice at the expense of vague apprehension and a fear of unseen terrors. Sometimes it is best not to know the source of one's fears.

The conflicts just described—between expressing impulses and fear of punishment for such expression—are common in both neurotics and normals. Neurotics differ from normals quantitatively: more intense conflicts, more repression, and a greater tendency to use earlier, more primitive modes for handling anxiety. Anxiety reactions represent regression to the phallic stage, with Oedipal conflicts prominent. It is believed that repression is ordinarily used as a defense against sexual impulses rather than aggressive impulses. Such sexual urges undoubtedly have Oedipal associations and must therefore be kept unconscious and latent.

The attacks of panic that occur in anxiety reaction are periodic. After the panic subsides there is a tense equilibrium between instincts and repression. This tenuous balance can be upset by an upsurge of instinctual energy or a weakening of the ego, as in fatigue or illness. At such times repression partially fails and impulses come close to awareness and discharge. The anxiety component (transformed affect) breaks through to consciousness or is expressed physiologically through the autonomic nervous system, or both. The state of being dammed up disintegrates into a flood of anxiety that contains elements of the excitement of the unacceptable instinctual urges. The autonomic excitement of sex or rage has components in common with the autonomic excitement of panic. This partial catharsis of affect may help the panic attack to subside, at least temporarily.

Neurotic Depression

In the actual-neuroses the ego's energies are bound up with the task of defending against instinctual urges. Repression is the main defense, and other defenses, if present, are not important in keeping instinctual urges unconscious. The contest between instincts and counterforces leaves little energy available for initiating new activities, and the neurotic depressive feels tired and apathetic.

He is vaguely aware of his ego's incapacity and dimly perceives that he lacks the interest and motivation (psychic energy) to achieve and to live with zest. This knowledge is one source of inferiority feelings. A second source of self-depreciation is his failure to resolve the Oedipal complex; the implicit assumption is that because his infantile sexuality was a failure, he will always be a failure. These two sources of inferiority feelings inevitably lead to a dark, melancholic view of life.

The neurotic depressive is not only forlorn and self-abasing but also guilty. Remember that the neurotic conflict always consists of instinctual urges and defending forces. The impulses must be unacceptable, else they would enter consciousness and be discharged. In *anxiety neurosis* the impulses are unacceptable to others; if the impulses attained consciousness and behavioral expression, they would be punished by *external* authority. In *neurotic depression* the impulses are unacceptable to the superego; if the impulses attained consciousness and behavioral expression, they would be punished by internal authority. Repression prevents awareness of the impulses, but as we know neurosis occurs only when defenses fail. The partial failure of repression results in a partial awareness of the unacceptable urges. The superego, on becoming aware of the immoral impulses, attacks the ego, and this attack is, of course, guilt.

Note that the failure of repression is relative; the depressive person becomes only partially and vaguely aware of his unacceptable urges. His situation is analogous to that of the anxiety neurotic. The anxiety neurotic has vague fears, but the source of the anxiety is kept from consciousness; the neurotic depressive has vague guilt, but the source of the guilt is kept from consciousness.

Feelings of guilt and inferiority sharply diminish the neurotic depressive's self-esteem, and he desperately attempts to acquire narcissistic supplies for his needy ego. He requires attention and affection to restore his depleted ego, and these are available only from parental figures. His forlorn and melancholic behavior help him to obtain sympathy, which demonstrates to him that he is at least partially worthwhile. The attempt to obtain love is only halfhearted because he is not sure he deserves it. Guilt makes him ambivalent about his own attempts to restore self-esteem.

So far we have discussed neurotic depression as an enduring, chronic problem. It may also be episodic, set in motion by a real loss. The neurotic depressive reacts to loss (death, desertion, etc.) with more profound and longer-lasting mourning than does the normal. The loss represents a sudden cutting off of a necessary source of narcissistic supplies (love and attention).

The over-reaction to loss is primed by the previous equilibrium between instincts and counterforces. The impulses are usually hostile, and their expression would elicit guilt. The loss weakens the ego, weakening the repressive defense. The underlying hostility begins to become conscious, thereby arousing vague feelings of guilt. Part of the hostility is turned inward against the ego, attacking and lowering self-esteem. Thus the superego may turn instinctual aggression against the ego.

The strong need for love and the dependence on others for self-esteem suggest that the depressive individual is fixated at the oral stage. This is certainly true of psychotic depressives, but whether it is also true of neurotic depressives is a moot point. The absence of psychotic features and the relative intactness of the ego suggest that the major regression is to a later stage, probably the anal-sadistic stage. This would account for the strong unconscious hostility that motivates repression.

Thus the issues of fixation and regression are not entirely clear in neu-rotic depression. They are clearer in psychotic depression, in which the re-gression is unquestionably to the oral stage. It may well be that psychotic and neurotic depression lie on a dimension of depth of regression: the greater the regression to the oral stage, the closer the individual is to psy-chotic depression.

Fatigue-hypochondriasis

This syndrome, consisting of complaints of vague aches and pains and of being worn-out, was at one time called *neurasthenia.* Psychoanalytic ac-counts of it are sketchy. Freud attributed it to excessive masturbation, but Fenichel had a broader view. He believed that the syndrome results from any excess of sexual tension, the crucial failure being insufficient orgasm. The person who cannot discharge his sexual excitement is in a state of tension from the conflict between the urges and the defending forces and also from the sexual urges themselves. Consequently, he is tense, tired, ir-ritable, and he tends to develop vague bodily complaints. The character of these complaints may be retentive (muscular tightness, constipation) or expulsive (diarrhea, tremors), depending on which aspect of the conflict predominates.

Sexual impulses are not the only ones to underlie fatigue-hypochon-driasis. In some patients there are intense aggressive urges that must be repressed. Being tired and playing the sick role both represent attempts to aid repression. The patient says in effect, "I am not sufficiently energetic or healthy to act aggressively or sexually." This is an attempt to disarm not only potential punishing agents in the environment but also a potentially punishing superego.

The boredom and apathy so prominent in fatigue-hypochondriasis ap-pear to be end products of repression. The interests most people have in the world around them are always tinged with aggressive elements (as in ambition and competition) or erotic elements (as in painting, dancing, and other arts). Repression tends to keep aggressive and sexual components deeply unconscious, thereby removing the basic motivation for taking initia-tive. The individual eventually learns to avoid interests tinged with hostile or erotic impulses. Since there is little in life that avoids these connotations, a profound feeling of boredom is inevitable.

The *regression* in fatigue-hypochondriasis is to primary narcissism, an intense interest in one's own body. The regression is only partial, and there is still a strong interest in others. As in neurotic depression, there is a reaching out to others for narcissistic supplies, and what could be better than the sick role? Bodily aches and pains mark the person as one who needs and deserves tender care and affection. In fatigue-hypochondriasis this "second-ary gain" of love and attention is more transparent than in neurotic depression. Another distinguishing feature is the relative absence of guilt, which suggests less maturity in fatigue-hypochondriasis than in neurotic depression.

This account of the actual-neuroses points up both their differences and similarities. The differences are mainly in emphasis: vague fears in anxiety reaction; brooding, inferiority feelings and guilt in depression; and bodily complaints in fatigue-hypochondriasis. Underlying all three syndromes is the basic state of being damned-up: the conflict between anxiety-arousing instinctual urges and the mechanism of repression. Given this state of tension, the precise syndrome that develops is a matter of the constitution and particular history of the individual.

PSYCHONEUROSES

In the genesis of psychopathology, the state of being dammed-up (actual-neuroses) is a prelude to the breakthrough of impulses in compromise form (psychoneurosis). The precise nature of psychoneurotic symptoms depends on both the impulses seeking gratification and the defending forces. The simplest compromise occurs in phobia, and the more complex and entrenched defense mechanisms occur in hysteria and obsessive-compulsive reaction.

Phobia

The psychoanalytic name for phobia is *anxiety hysteria,* a term implying neurotic conflicts similar in some ways to those seen in conversion hysteria. Phobia begins with a basic conflict between instincts (sexual or aggressive) and repression. This conflict renders the individual tense and filled with suppressed excitement. When such a person is confronted with a stimulus that symbolizes his basic conflict (that is, represents in some way the urges being repressed), there is mild anxiety. The normal ego would utilize this mild anxiety as a warning of impending danger; but when the warning stimulus impinges on a tense, conflict-ridden ego, it triggers a massive anxiety attack. The warning is reacted to as if it were the ultimate danger itself. The confusion between the warning signal and the danger itself occurs partly because the weakened ego loses some of its capacity to judge correctly and partly because the manifest warning stimulus symbolizes the latent, unconscious anxiety stimulus.

The intense anxiety becomes attached to the relatively innocuous warning stimulus. The person is able to identify the source of his fear as a situation that objectively should elicit little fear; it is a fear stimulus for him only because of what it symbolizes. Once the manifest fear stimulus is identified, the underlying, free-floating anxiety becomes bound. It is this binding of anxiety to a specific content that is the process of psychoneurotic symptom formation; it is this elaboration beyond repression that differentiates phobia (and the other psychoneuroses) from actual-neuroses.

Displacement. The major defense mechanism in phobia (beyond repression) is displacement. Some phobias, such as the fears concerning stimuli directly related to the unconscious impulses, involve little or no displacement. For example, a timid person who has difficulty in aggressing may develop a fear of situations that would arouse anger in a normal individual; thus he might develop a phobia concerning weapons. Such a phobia involves virtually no displacement of either his temptation to be aggressive or his fear of doing so. On the other hand, a phobia may represent punishment for instinctual urges rather than the temptation itself. Thus, a fear of knives might represent castration anxiety for forbidden wishes. Whether the phobia represents temptation or punishment, so long as the feared object or situation is directly related to such temptation or punishment, there is little or no displacement; these phobias are in the minority.

Phobias involving considerable displacement are more frequent: the feared object is related only indirectly and symbolically to the unconscious conflict. Unlike the simple phobia in which there is little or no displacement, in this more complex type the unconscious conflict cannot be deduced from knowledge of the fear stimulus. The connection between the object of the phobia and the instinctual urge is concealed; the object of fear represents the unconscious conflict only in terms of the distorted symbols and associations of the dreamworld. Thus a fear of open places symbolizes opportunity for sexual adventure or a place to be caught and punished. This example is typical of complex phobias; the feared situation does not elicit anxiety in normal persons, and it is remote from the basic conflict (sexual temptation or punishment for such impulses). Since the feared situation is sufficiently distant from the real conflict, it need not be repressed; in fact, it serves as a substitute for the original repressed idea.

Phobias involving considerable displacement have two advantages. First, the original impulse or idea is allowed to return from the repressed in such distorted form that it is not recognized as such and therefore cannot cause further anxiety. Second, the displaced object or situation may be such that it can be avoided. If an individual hates and fears his mother, it is to his advantage to displace the fear to a distant object, say cows. A cow may symbolize *mother,* and therefore fear of one is unconsciously equal to fear of the other; but cows can be avoided, and one can admit to consciousness the fear of cows, whereas fear of one's mother is inadmissible. This kind of displacement is typical of children's phobias, in which an animal is simply substituted for a familial figure. The process is facilitated by the stereotypes of animals that are learned during childhood (foxes are sly, cows are maternal, kittens are childlike, etc.).

Projection. Children's phobias, such as the type just described, do not involve the mechanism of projection, but projection is often present in adult phobias. The person with a sexual or aggressive impulse that cannot be expressed tends to experience it as an inner feeling or compulsion to take action. This inner impulse may be projected onto another person or object; for example, one might say in effect, "I do not wish to attack him, but he wants to harm me." Then there is anxiety concerning this other person, and a phobia develops.

Usually, the aggressive impulse is not projected to another person but rather to an animal or to a situation. When aggression or hostility is projected to another person, paranoid tendencies come to the fore, rather than phobic responses. In phobia the dominant mechanism is displacement; paranoiac responses represent a development beyond fear of an avoidance of someone else. Paranoia always involves projection of negative impulses to other people, whereas in phobia it is rare for the feared object to be another person.

Regression. Like all neurotic phenomena, phobia involves a regression to childhood, especially to the phallic stage of psychosexual development. By displacing the danger and clearly labeling it, the child (or the childlike adult) attempts to gain protection and help from others. Many phobics are not fearful so long as they are accompanied by another person, preferably an adult. There is the further gain of playing the sick role, in that the phobic cannot be expected to handle any situation that concerns his phobia. For example, a person who fears closed places is not expected to work or reside in closed places; thus he has an excuse for not assuming adult responsibilities in the home or on the job unless his special conditions are met.

The point is that the real danger is inner and instinctual: the return of the repressed to consciousness and the expression of forbidden wishes. Since the basic regression is to the phallic stage, the primary temptation is sexual, involving the Oedipal complex. The excitement of sexual impulses toward the opposite-sexed parent must be displaced to external objects such as fast-moving vehicles, which are then feared. Pregenital temptations may also occur. These are almost exclusively aggressive (and also retribution for aggressive impulses), and they usually lead to phobias involving harm to the individual by means of weapons (no displacement) or to distorted, symbolic representations such as stage fright (excessive displacement), in which being seen means one will be recognized as aggressive and therefore be killed.

Two Aspects of Anxiety. In the development of a phobia the original anxiety attack is a warning that the stimulus is somehow associated with forbidden desires and therefore dangerous. Although this attempt to warn the ego fails, it is clear that the anxiety represents a defense, that is, an attempt to ward off more serious danger. Subsequently, the phobic person becomes anxious in the presence of the displaced stimulus, and this anxiety is no longer a warning but a discharge of tension. What happens is that the warning so panics the ego that it loses control and is overwhelmed by the danger. In a phobia, anxiety is not only a defense (a warning of impending danger) but also an involuntary discharge of affect.

Hysteria

The psychoanalytic label for this syndrome is *conversion hysteria,* which emphasizes the basic mechanism of the neurosis: the conversion of psychic impulses that had previously been repressed into physical symptoms. The physical symptoms of hysteria are analogous to the physical symptoms that occur during an anxiety attack; in both instances the ego is temporarily overwhelmed with tension which must be discharged. The difference is that a panic reaction is more or less the same for all human beings, being determined by properties of the autonomic nervous system, whereas conversion symptoms are specific, symbolic representatives of repressed thoughts, ideas, or impulses.

Sexual Impulses. The impulses are usually sexual, with the symptoms expressing sexual excitement in a concealed form. The basis for somatic expression of sexual excitement is in hysterical thinking, the daydreaming kind of fantasying dominated by the pleasure principle. In the face of harsh reality the hysteric turns to his daydreams, but because some of these fantasies involve dangerous impulses, they must be repressed. It is these repressed fantasies that return as somatic symptoms. Thus the process proceeds from action to fantasy, then to the removal of fantasy from consciousness, and finally to the reappearance of the repressed material in the form of bodily symptoms that express the underlying sexual conflict.

As with all neurotic symptoms, conversion symptoms are a compromise between the instinctual forces seeking expression and the defending forces of the ego. In some symptoms the balance is tipped toward the impulses being expressed, and there is something akin to the substitute gratification of sexual urges; but the presence of defense mechanisms may be seen in the fact that the individual can experience no pleasure from such gratification, only pain or discomfort. Other conversion symptoms represent more of the defensive side of the conflict, for example, sensory dysfunction, which prevents the person from perceiving stimuli related to the unconscious sexual conflict.

In hysteria, more than any other neurosis, the Oedipal complex is the core problem. It is not surprising, then, that many male hysterics are tied to their mothers' apron strings and that many female hysterics have an excessively strong tie to their fathers. The problem is one of overgeneralization: all sexuality has Oedipal overtones and is therefore strictly prohibited. Thus both ends of the conflict are intense. On the one hand, there are strong incestuous wishes toward a parental figure with whom a close bond exists and, on the other hand, there is the need to repress all sexual urges. The impulses are so evil that repression is inevitable, and action is surrendered for fantasy. If the fantasy approaches the basic sexual conflict, it, too, will have to be repressed. The repressed sexual impulses cause the hysteric to be continually preoccupied with sexual matters, but repressive mechanisms force him to be entirely naive concerning sex. The sexual excitement itself can be expressed only in the form of bodily symptoms that represent in distorted form the repressed instinctual urges.

Regression to the Phallic Stage. Although the Oedipus complex is crucial to hysteria, as in all neuroses, there is regression to earlier stages. There is little regression to pregenital stages (oral, anal) because the fixated stage in hysteria is the phallic stage. Regression to the phallic stage accounts for the infantile character of the hysteric's sexuality: the failure to distinguish between incestuous love and love oriented toward peers. The importance of phallic fixation is also seen in the intense conflict concerning masturbation that underlies many hysterical symptoms; tics, spasms, and uncontrollable muscular contractions are often masturbatory equivalents.

Hysterical Pain. The importance of infantile sexuality may be seen in one kind of hysterical pain. A child may confuse the bodily sensations of illness (pain and fever) with those of infantile sexual excitement; in adulthood this person may develop the same pains when the childhood conflicts concerning infantile sexuality are rearoused. In childhood there is often an association between pain arising from physical illness and special attention and affection from a parent. The additional parental love may throw the child into an intense conflict because of incestuous longings. Later, in adulthood, the pain comes to represent both the excitement stimulated by parental affection and a warning anxiety that such impulses will be severely punished.

There is a second kind of hysterical pain in which the person has not experienced pain previously but copies it from another. Hysterics are notorious mimics and tend to imitate the symptoms of those around them. The dynamic basis of such imitation is a childlike identification in which the hysteric attempts to be like an admired love-object (usually parental) or a rival. The pain or illness is taken over, just as the latest clothing fad is copied by fashion-conscious women.

Motor Symptoms. Hysterical motor symptoms are of two kinds: paralysis or muscular spasms. The difference, dynamically, is more apparent than real because in paralysis the muscles are usually tense; thus in both kinds there is muscular contraction. Motor paralysis and spasms both represent defensive forces which seek to prevent action because of an unconscious association with infantile sexuality. The muscular contraction serves not only as a defense against action but also as a distorted, substitute gratification for the sexual excitement. The generalized increase in muscular tension that occurs in hysterical motor symptoms is merely the physical aspect of repression; the person holds on tight lest he let go and lose control. Thus increased muscle tonus may be regarded as the converted physical form of the psychic energy used in repression.

Motor symptoms represent an attempt to hold back action, but they require perception for action to be initiated, and the defensive forces may act directly upon perception. This is precisely what occurs in hysterical blindness, deafness, or numbness. In blindness, for example, the hysteric represses his impulse to look (ostensibly at sexually exciting stimuli) or is punished by blindness for daring to want to look, or both. The same is true of disturbances in other sensory modalities: the hysteric prevents himself from perceiving "dangerous" stimuli, and his affliction is also punishment for wanting to perceive.

Determinants of Body Symptoms. Conversion symptoms occur in any part of the body, in any organ or organ system. Fenichel lists four determinants of the site of the symptoms. The first is the *stage of fixation.* All hysterics are primarily fixated at the phallic stage, but there are secondary fixations at pregenital stages, just as there are minor pregenital fixations in normal persons who have attained genitality. Fixation at the oral stage results in symptoms related to the mouth and the digestive tract; fixation at the anal stage leads to "anal" symptoms, etc. The second determinant is the *presence of a weak organ or organ system,* one that is more susceptible to dysfunction and therefore more likely to succumb. The third determinant is *timing:* body parts that were most active during the crucial conflict and ensuing repression are likely to manifest hysterical symptoms at a later date. The fourth determinant concerns *symbolism.* Some organs are well suited to express in symbolic form the unconscious conflict underlying the symptom. Thus convex organs such as the nose may symbolize the penis; or incorporative tendencies may be represented by the mouth.

Success of the Defenses. Now that the various dynamics of hysteria have been described, it is necessary to comment on the success of the defensive forces against anxiety. In some hysterics the conversion of psychic impulses into somatic equivalents is not sufficient to discharge all tension, and there is anxiety lest the instinctual urges break through to consciousness. However, these hysterics are in the minority. Most hysterics are indifferent to their aches, pains, paralysis, or sensory dysfunction; they are blandly optimistic about the outcome and never doubt the medical nature of their ills. They are free to play the sick role and achieve the appropriate secondary gains: attention, affection, and an excuse for not facing problems. The blandness illustrates how neatly the ego can separate repressed impulses (expressed in physical form) from the main stream of consciousness.

Dissociative Reactions

Dissociative reactions have received little attention from psychoanalysts, but it is not clear why this is so. Perhaps it is because they occur so rarely, or perhaps because there are so few neurotic derivatives of the unconscious conflict. In any event, the account here is necessarily brief because there has been little theorizing.

The sole defense mechanism is repression, which is more massive and pervasive than in any other neurosis. As in all neuroses, infantile sexual urges are the principal ones being repressed, and since this is one form of hysteria, the crucial regression is to the Oedipal phase. The background features of dissociation consist of strong Oedipal longings that are ruthlessly repressed, little or no possibility of sublimating these urges, and a tendency to regress to the primary process of wish-fulfilling fantasy.

These features set the stage for dissociation in adulthood. For whatever reason, the Oedipal longings increase in strength, placing an intolerable burden on the defensive forces of the ego. Then there is a breakthrough into consciousness and motility: the sexual urges are expressed, usually in some wanton outburst of sexual behavior. Now it is too late to attempt the ordinary kind of repression; what is needed is a repression pervasive enough to render the entire event unconscious, and this is precisely what occurs. The person splits off from awareness an entire segment of his personality. Thoughts, memories, and behaviors are thrust from consciousness, and, in fact, part of the person's identity is split off and in effect surrendered. In this state, called *fugue*, unconscious wishes are expressed in isolation from the main body of the personality. When the episode has been completed, there is a sudden return to the usual personality with no memory of what has occurred. There is no conscious awareness of what transpired during a few hours or a few days.

This massive repression is more primitive than that seen in other neuroses. It is similar to the infant's assigning of "good" to himself (his own ego) and of "evil" to others (nonego). Thus part of the self is in effect disowned, a repression more infantile and pervasive than the usual repression (which merely pushes from consciousness particular instincts and their derivatives).

Obsession and Compulsion

Obsessions and compulsions are regarded as essentially similar. The only difference is that obsessions are ideas and thoughts (derivatives of repressed material) and compulsions are impulses to act. As in any neurosis, the basic formula is: instinctual forces in their attempt to attain consciousness and discharge are blocked by defending forces. The instincts are sexual or aggressive, but the latter predominate. In hysteria, by way of contrast, sexual urges are paramount and aggressive impulses play a minor role. In obsession-compulsion hostility must be controlled, and sexual urges are of minor importance.

Instincts versus Defenses. The symptoms generated by the conflict between instincts and defenses tend to reflect one side or the other of the conflict, or a fairly equal compromise. For example, when there are obsessive thoughts of killing, the instinctual side predominates, but when the obsessive thought concerns danger to oneself, the defensive forces predominate. The second possibility is more frequent, and this is another difference between obsession-compulsion and hysteria. In hysteria it is the instinctual forces that usually find greater representation in symptoms, whereas in obsession-compulsion it is the defensive forces, especially those of the superego.

In some kinds of obsessive doubting both sides of the conflict are represented, with the person caught between temptation and morality. This is a straightforward approach-avoidance conflict: the opportunity for immediate reward on one side and pangs of guilt on the other. It is also seen in certain compulsions in which the neurotic first makes a response and then undoes it, or yields to temptation and then punishes himself.

Defenses. There are four major defense mechanisms in obsession-compulsion: reaction-formation, isolation, displacement, and undoing. They make complete repression unnecessary because they allow expression of repressed impulses in distorted form. Whereas repression is directed primarily against genital sexual urges, these four mechanisms are directed against pregenital (oral, anal, and aggressive) urges.

Reaction formation involves a change of personality so that the individual need not throw up a defense each time instinctual urges threaten him. He develops attitudes or behavior patterns diametrically opposed to his instinctual demands. Thus the person with strong aggressive urges becomes compulsively kind and gentle; the compulsive, fixated at the anal stage, reacts against his basic urge to soil and becomes rigidly neat and orderly. Engaging in opposite behavior serves to convince and reassure the individual that he need not fear his instinctual urges, and because the energy of these urges is partially taken over when the opposite behavior occurs, there is less need for repression.

Reaction formation is one of the hallmarks of compulsive behavior; it is what makes the orderliness and punctuality of the compulsive so rigid and enduring. To be messy or late for appointments can be terrifying because of the breakthrough of the instinctual urges symbolized by these "anal" responses. However, breakthroughs do occur, and many compulsive persons can bind the ensuing anxiety by limiting the scope of their compulsions. The compulsive individual may insist on keeping his office neat, while allowing his home to be messy. There is a childish, magical quality about his rules and fine distinctions, but the rules allow the breakthrough of part of the basic urge (messiness) without causing anxiety. Thus there are two qualities evident in behavior dominated by the mechanism of reaction formation: rigidity and occasional breakthroughs of the instinct being defended against.

The mechanism of *isolation,* rather than repressing anxiety-arousing material, breaks the association between such material and its affective qualities. Thus the obsessive person may have continual thoughts of murder or rape in the absence of appropriate affective reactions to these thoughts. He is not angry or sexually aroused, and the thoughts, isolated from all else, appear to be alien and external. This isolation of affect has its counterpart in normal thinking, in which calm reflection leads to objectivity. However, in obsession the elimination of the affective components of thoughts is accomplished, not for objectivity, but for the purpose of allowing the impulse to become conscious without the anxiety that would ordinarily be attached to it. Such isolation renders obsessive persons unemotional, detached, and somewhat aloof. There may be breakthroughs, but emotional outbursts occur only when the stimulus is sufficiently displaced from the forbidden impulse. For example, the usually calm, compulsive individual may have a temper tantrum if the arrangement of books in his bookshelf is slightly disturbed.

When the defense is successful, the original impulse is completely neutralized. Thus an obsessive idea of killing may be so far removed from possible action that it can be admitted to consciousness. When the defense is unsuccessful, the impulse rarely appears in its original form; there must be some distance in space, time, or associations between the impulse and its mode of expression. Thus there is *displacement* in both hysteria and obsession-compulsion. In hysteria the displacement is from the psychological to the physiological sphere; in obsession-compulsion the displacement is entirely psychological, from near to remote associations.

Undoing is the next step beyond reaction formation. In reaction formation the behavior is opposite to that associated with the forbidden instinctual urges. In undoing, the behavior represents a magical attempt to restore conditions to what they were before the occurrence of the forbidden thought or action. In a sense all attempts at penance are attempts to undo the original sinful action. Undoing may be seen in several kinds of compulsive symptoms. A compulsive individual may go through a sequence of two responses that cancel out each other; the ritual might be opening and then closing a door or making a threatening gesture, followed by a supplicating gesture. In each instance the second response magically expunges the evil in the first response (the one connected with forbidden urges). Symmetry compulsions are based on the undoing mechanism, the one side balancing (and undoing) the other side.

Regression. As in hysteria, what must be defended against in obsession-compulsion are urges associated with the Oedipal complex, but in both neuroses there are pre-Oedipal elements, the character of which is determined by the major fixation. In obsession-compulsion, unlike hysteria, the major fixation is pregenital—the anal-sadistic phase. In addition to this fixation, there must also be weakness of the phallic phase and a general weakness of the ego in order for the crucial regression to occur. The ego of the obsessive-compulsive person is a peculiar mixture of strength and weakness, of precocity and immaturity. It is strong enough to fight instinctual urges but too weak to use mature methods in the battle. It develops the capacity for preparatory thinking and for criticism early in life but the modes of thinking are immature and primitive, such as the magical thinking involved in superstitious rituals and undoing compulsions.

Ego regression in obsession-compulsion occurs in two stages. First, there is opposition to Oedipal urges, which are replaced with anal-sadistic urges. Second, the anal-sadistic impulses, being no more acceptable, are also opposed. It is these anal-sadistic tendencies that motivate the four defense mechanisms described above; moreover, these tendencies furnish the basic personality features of the obsessive-compulsive individual (frugality, orderliness, punctuality, cruelty, etc.).

In comparing hysteria with obsession-compulsion there is an apparent paradox. Hysterics are closer to full genitality than are obsessive-compulsives, but the latter have more defense mechanisms and a stronger superego. The paradox may be resolved as follows. Obsession-compulsion develops later but involves a greater regression than hysteria. The later development of obsession-compulsion means that the superego has had more time to develop, along with more complex defense mechanisms. Although hysterics use less mature defense mechanisms, they regress only to the phallic phase, whereas obsessive-compulsives regress to the anal phase. The concept of *differential regression* solves the paradox.

Guilt and Ambivalence. Guilt plays a much larger role in obsession-compulsion than in hysteria. The superego of the obsessive-compulsive person is well-developed and is a potent determinant of the outcome of neurotic conflicts; most of the symptoms represent punishment for forbidden urges, rather than the urges themselves. While the superego is well-developed, it is also primitive because of the decisive regression. The regression to anal-sadism affects not only the id but also the superego; there are not only more aggressive urges, but the superego returns to the talion principle of an eye for an eye. Whenever there are concessions to instinctual demands, whether in thought or action, the harsh superego demands atonement. This gives rise to the symmetry compulsions mentioned earlier, in which self-punishment is expiation for evil (and symbolically, up balances down, right balances left).

The presence of a tyrannical superego means that the ego must battle two enemies. The first is the id, whose urges must be held in check or at least modified; the second is the superego, whose punitive demands are as threatening to the ego as the instinctual urges of the id. Thus in obsession-compulsion there is a double conflict: id versus ego, and ego versus superego.

The struggle between the urges of the id and the punishments of the superego over the battleground of the ego is only one aspect of the ambivalence that occurs in obsession-compulsion. The second aspect concerns sexual identification, for with all his doubts, the obsessive-compulsive person is also torn between masculinity and femininity. The third aspect concerns aggression and hostility, the core problems of the anal-sadistic phase; the obsessive-compulsive individual is torn between love and hate. Thus in verbal form these three conflicts are basic:

> "May I be bad or must I be good?"
> "Am I a man or a woman?"
> "May I destroy others, or must I love them?"

COMMENT

It is clear that psychoanalytic theory adopts a completely environmentalistic approach. Although Freud and other theorists have nodded in the direction of genetics and biology, they have largely ignored everything but the individual's developmental history. Presumably, each child proceeds through a fixed sequence of stages. His basic personality depends upon what happens at each stage. If he is deprived of love during the oral stage, he will subsequently "hunger" for affection and attention. If his toilet training is premature and harsh, he will subsequently be "anal"—frugal, orderly, punctual, and fussy.

Thus the child's experience at each stage of development determines how he will subsequently approach the world. It also determines the area of greatest conflict: dependency, aggression, or sexuality—in that developmental sequence. In addition, his experience at each stage determines in large part his defenses against anxiety. In summary, the stage at which painful events occur (and cause fixation) is what determines the *kind* of neuroses. As we noted earlier, each neurosis represents fixation at a specific stage.

Painful experiences always involve anxiety, which stems from either threat (of punishment or of rejection) or excessive instinctual excitement. Psychoanalytic theory assumes that the "mental apparatus" of a child can tolerate only moderate amounts of psychic energy. An excess of psychic energy—owing to threat, to sexual stimulation, or to aggressive urges—renders the child anxious and automatically activates the "safety valve" of repression.

Repression seals off part of the personality, preventing it from participating in growth experiences. Most of the self continues to develop and to acquire the controls and mechanisms required for adult adjustment. A smaller part, isolated by repression, does not take part in growth experiences and remains childlike. This is the psychoanalytic explanation of the paradoxical coexistence of adult and childish tendencies in the neurotic adult.

The severer the repression is, the larger the part of the self that is isolated and the more complete is its isolation. The larger the isolated part of the self is, the severer is the neurosis. We have noted that the severity of repression is determined by the painfulness of life experiences. It follows, then, that the severity of the neurosis is determined by the intensity of the painful experiences, the sequence being:

painful experiences → repression → isolation
from psychological maturation (fixation) → childish
trends persist to adulthood → neurosis

In the exposition we have been following psychoanalytic usage, stating the theory as if it were describing the *inner personality*. Of course, psychoanalytic theory does not refer to *observables*. It *assumes* the presence of a hypothetical personality structure, and it describes this *conceptual personality*. This distinction between fact and theory—between observations and theoretical constructions—is occasionally forgotten, especially in the psychoanalytic literature. It is assumed that the personality is like an iceberg, with only a small part being above the surface. Presumably, the hidden parts can be "observed" with such techniques as dream analysis, free association, and analysis of Freudian slips. Note, however, that these techniques yield *inferences* about a hypothetical personality structure, not *facts* about observable personality features. In summary, we must be careful to distinguish between observations and inferences. This care is especially necessary because psychoanalytic terms lend themselves to such confusion.

REFERENCES

Blum, G. S. *Psychoanalytic theories of personality.* New York: McGraw-Hill, 1953.
Fenichel, O. *The psychoanalytic theory of neuroses.* New York: Norton, 1945.
Freud, S. *Collected papers.* London, Hogarth Press, 1950, vol. 4.
Munroe, Ruth. *Schools of psychoanalytic thought.* New York: Drydon Press, 1955.

CHAPTER 6

Learning Approaches
to Neurosis

Unlike orthodox psychoanalytic theory there is no comparable orthodox learning theory that represents *the* learning approach to neurosis. There are only theories of greater or lesser popularity. This chapter discusses the most prominent of these learning positions, which may be arranged according to their acceptance of psychoanalytic theory.

One theory fully accepts the psychoanalytic position, acknowledging that the psychoanalytic approach to neurotic symptoms is the best one available. Admittedly, psychoanalytic concepts and language lack precision and hence must be translated into analogous learning concepts and language. For example, the psychoanalytic concept of displacement is explained by the learning concept of stimulus generalization. A second theory also translates psychoanalytic theory into learning terms but accepts only part of the translation. Finally, several theories categorically reject psychoanalytic theory, denying its value in either the original form or the translations.

FULL ACCEPTANCE

Dollard and Miller (1950) fully accept psychoanalytic theory and translate it into their own modification of Hull's learning theory. They do not specifically accept all psychoanalytic concepts; they would probably not endorse the constructs of psychic energy, a structural unconscious, and related *mentalistic* notions. Nevertheless, in their 1950 book they concern themselves only with adapting Freud's theory to a learning framework, and nowhere do they criticize or reject any aspect of the theory. Thus they appear to take a position of full acceptance of the classical psychoanalytic approach to neurosis.

Basic Concepts

Dollard and Miller specify four fundamentals of learning: drive, cue, response, and reinforcement. A *drive* is any stimulus strong enough to impel action. Pangs of hunger strong enough to initiate food-seeking responses are drive stimuli; smells (say a skunk's odor) strong enough to initiate escape responses are drive stimuli. Note that internal, physiological stimuli are not differentiated from external stimuli with respect to drive; the source of stimuli is unimportant, but their intensity is crucial. The stronger the stimulus, the greater is the drive.

Certain drives are closely tied to physiological processes and to survival of the organism. Hunger and thirst are straightforward examples of such drives; pain is more complex. Hunger and thirst are internal, pain either internal or external; all three drives are associated with the physical well-being of the organism. They innately impel the organism to action and hence are called *primary drives*.

Although there are only a few primary or innate drives, there are many *secondary* or *acquired* drives; these must be learned.

When, as the result of learning, previously neutral cues gain the capacity to play the same functional role in the learning and performance of new responses as do primary drives, such as hunger and thirst, these cues are said to have learned-drive value. (Dollard & Miller, 1950, p. 78)

Hunger is a primary drive, but an appetite for candy is an acquired one. Pain is a primary drive, but fear is an acquired one. The acquired or secondary drive is learned by association with the primary drive. When an individual receives pain in a particular room, the room becomes a fear stimulus. The sight of the room comes to elicit the acquired drive of fear through the association of the room with pain; witness the common fear of dentists' offices.

Drives energize behavior but do not direct it. Guidance is provided by *cues,* which determine the time, location, and direction of behavior, as well as which response will occur. Only the intensity of a stimulus is related to its drive function, but *any* aspect of a stimulus can serve as a cue: intensity, quality, duration, and patterning. The cue value of stimuli depends upon their distinctiveness, the drive value upon their intensity.

The response is what is learned, what is measured, and what is the focus of attention in psychopathology. In the framework of a learning approach, many neurotic symptoms are merely maladaptive responses. Responses may be arranged into a hierarchy of strength or probability of occurrence, from the most likely to the least likely to occur. Prior to learning there is an *initial* hierarchy and after learning, a *resultant* hierarchy. Other things being equal, the tendency of a response to occur depends on its place in the hierarchy, that is, its relative *habit strength*. Strong habits are difficult to break (extinguish) and yield frequently occurring responses.

The fourth fundamental is *reinforcement*, which is more or less synonymous with reward. It is defined as an event that strengthens the tendency of a response to occur. Dollard and Miller believe that all such events involve a sudden reduction in drive; reinforcement equals drive-reduction.

Drive, cue, response, and reinforcement are the four fundamentals of learning for Dollard and Miller, but two auxilliary topics are also important: stimulus generalization and higher mental processes. *Stimulus generalization* refers to the spread or transfer of a response to stimuli other than the stimulus to which the response is conditioned. Learning results in a bond between a stimulus and a response; once the bond is established the stimulus elicits the response. But the response may also be elicited by stimuli similar to the original or conditioned stimulus. The more similar the stimulus is to the original one, the greater is the tendency of the response to occur. A graph of response strength (frequency, amplitude, or latency) on the ordinate (vertical axis) against stimulus similarity on the abscissa (horizontal axis) yields a gradient of decreasing response strength with distance from the original stimulus. This is called the gradient of stimulus generalization. The similarity among stimuli may be physical: brightness, loudness, size, etc. The spread of a response to stimuli similar in physical dimensions is called *primary* stimulus generalization. Stimuli may be linked by nonphysical attributes such as beauty, aggressiveness, and anxiety; here stimulus similarity is mediated by words or similar internal (response-produced) cues. The spread of a response to stimuli of *mediated* similarity is called *secondary* generalization.

The notion of response-produced cues is part of what Dollard and Miller label *higher* mental processes. They distinguish between instrumental responses, which produce a change in the environment, and cue-producing responses, which produce a cue that leads to another response. The prime example of a cue-producing response is language. Words, spoken or subvocal, serve as cues for instrumental response, or initiate a series of cue-producing responses that fall under the headings of reasoning, planning, imagining, labeling, etc. These higher mental processes provide effective short-cuts to action because the individual can engage in *implicit* trial-and-error instead of *overt, instrumental* trial-and-error. *Labeling* is especially helpful in making discriminations among stimuli and in facilitating secondary generalization.

These, then, are the basic concepts of this learning translation of Freud. Note that Dollard and Miller do not postulate a *structure* of personality, as does Freud. Nevertheless, they do have concepts analogous to id, ego, and superego. The id corresponds to primary drives; hunger, aggression, and sex are directly analogous to Freudian instincts (with the same names) which originate in the id. The ego is equivalent to higher mental processes: reasoning, planning, organizing, synthesizing, labeling, discriminating, etc. The superego is analogous to certain acquired drives, namely guilt and shame. In brief, the following identities seem to be part of the Dollard and Miller approach:

id   = primary drives
ego   = higher mental processes
superego = certain acquired drives

Causes of Neurosis

Conflict. Neurosis, according to Dollard and Miller, is caused by conflict, and all conflict consists of the opposition of two or more drives. As we saw earlier, there are primary drives (hunger, sex, thirst, pain) and acquired drives (fear, guilt, shame, disgust). All drives are noxious to the individual, who attempts to reduce their strength; drive reduction is reinforcing.

The simplest conflicts involve only two drives. When an individual has a strong drive, he makes responses directed at the goal or target of the drive; these responses lead to satiation (drive reduction). Where punishment occurs, a secondary drive (fear) is conditioned to the primary drive (pain). The secondary drive opposes the original drive, blocking the responses that would ordinarily reduce the original drive.

One kind of conflict consists of anger versus fear. When a person is angered, his high drive leads him to attempt aggressive responses against the target of his wrath. Aggression would reduce the anger drive, but let us assume that in the past there has been punishment for aggressive behavior. Now the presence of the stimulus for aggression (the target) also elicits fear. If the fear drive is stronger than the anger drive, the aggressive response will be inhibited. Such avoidance of a response associated with pain leads to a sharp reduction in fear, and this drive reduction, being reinforcing, produces a strong avoidance habit.

The original drive remains high because the goal response that would ordinarily reduce it is prevented from occurring. The residual anger drive makes the individual tense and uncomfortable. So long as both the original drive and the fear are present, the conflict remains. The conflict itself produces drive stimuli and is itself another source of tension and misery.

Chronic high drive leads to two kinds of symptoms. The first kind consists of the excessive physiological reactions that accompany any high drive, for example, the anxiety syndrome. The second kind consists of responses that are maladaptive in the long run but that temporarily reduce anxiety. Thus someone who is both angry and frightened of expressing his aggression might develop a ritual of counting numbers. Counting numbers serves to prevent him from thinking about aggressing and from worrying about its consequences. Since such counting is followed by a drop in drive, it is strongly reinforced. Subsequently, the person may develop a counting compulsion whose sole value is a temporary relief from anxiety. Since the ritual does not cope with the real problem (the conflict between the drives of anger and fear), the chronic high drive state persists.

Repression. Since the concept of repression is crucial in psychoanalytic thinking, Dollard and Miller present a detailed learning account of it. They compare it with inhibition. In deference to a host, we do not tell him that we did not enjoy our visit; we inhibit the verbal response. Just as we can shut our mouths, we can inhibit our thoughts. Thus repression is an inhibition of thought that is strongly motivated, automatic (nonvoluntary), and unverbalized. This *not-thinking response* prevents us from solving problems, and the ensuing "stupidity" may lead to maladaptive behavior.

There are three kinds of repression, all deriving from conflict. First, the drive is present, but the individual is unaware of it. He may be angry and look angry but would be surprised if asked what he is angry about. The drive is present in full force, but the *not-thinking* response prevents it from being observed and labeled by the individual. Thus there may be unconscious motivation for the development of symptoms.

Second, one drive is inhibited by a stronger, incompatible drive. Thus a woman's sex drive might be suppressed by fear of pregnancy. The conflict is strongest in this type of repression because the original drive is usually strongly motivated and persistent.

Third, the mediating responses that produce the drive are inhibited. For example, an individual simply does not recognize the presence of a sexual or aggressive stimulus. If he is not aware of the stimulus, he is protected from making responses that might be punished.

The second kind of repression, the conflict of one drive with another, involves no cognitive or language components and therefore could occur in animals as well as humans. The first and third kinds of repression do involve language components and hence are limited to humans. Dollard and Miller emphasize the importance of language and awareness in making both the discriminations and generalizations required by society. Much of problem solving is mediated by language, and the person who is unaware of the important stimuli in his environment or who cannot label them properly is likely to develop maladaptive behavior. By implication the first and third kinds of repression (not being aware of one's own impulses or of the crucial stimuli in the environment) are more important in this formulation than is the second kind. This emphasis on lack of insight as a major feature of neurosis is consistent with the psychoanalytic emphasis on repression as the keystone of neurosis.

Displacement. Dollard and Miller convert the psychoanalytic mechanism of displacement ("psychic energy is displaceable") into the learning mechanism of generalization. Let us assume there is a drive oriented toward a particular goal or stimulus, say anger toward an authority figure. When the anger drive is opposed by a stronger anxiety drive (fear of retaliation), the aggressive response against the authority figure is inhibited. The anger is displaced to a target similar to the original target, that is, stimulus generalization occurs. If this displaced target were too similar to the original one, the anxiety drive might still be sufficiently strong to inhibit the aggressive response, and the aggressive response would be made to a more dissimilar target. Thus aggression would be most likely to occur when the target is similar enough to express anger against but not similar enough to elicit strong anxiety.

If the responding individual were to become angrier, the increase in drive level might be enough to overcome the inhibiting effects of anxiety. If this occurred, he would aggress against a target more similar to the original or even against the original target (the authority figure). But if the threat of retaliation were to increase, the increase in anxiety level would lead to an attack against a target more dissimilar to the original target. Thus the effect of an increase in anger drive is to *reduce* displacement, and the effect of an increase in anxiety drive is to *increase* displacement. In brief, the three variables determining this kind of displacement are the strength of the original drive (anger), the strength of the opposing drive (anxiety), and the similarity of the stimuli to the original stimulus (target).

Another kind of displacement is *response generalization*. When a drive is inhibited by a stronger, opposing drive, the original response does not occur. An alternate response may occur, one that is in some way similar to the original response. For example, if the original response of physical aggression (punching) were inhibited by fear of retaliation, the alternative might be verbal aggression (cursing). As in stimulus generalization, three variables determine the extent of response generalization: strengths of the original and of the opposing drives and similarity of response.

Thus the psychoanalytic notion of displacement may be translated into the learning concepts of stimulus and response generalization. Of course, mere translation from one vocabulary to another serves little purpose. The real gain accrues when the new concepts lead to more knowledge or greater explanation. In the present instance the possibilities of new knowledge are considerable, assuming the stimulus generalization paradigm of the laboratory can be made to work in situations involving personality dimensions of similarity.

Neurotic Symptoms

Like Freud, Dollard and Miller suggest that the principal cause of neurotic symptoms is the blocking of forbidden drives. When children are severely punished for responses that reduce primary drives, they inhibit the overt responses to these drives. In adolescence there is an intensification of drives, and the old fears return. The neurotic adult represses drives because of fear or guilt. He is oversocialized and overinhibited, his primary drives being blocked by the acquired (socialized) drives of fear, guilt, shame, and disgust. Problem solving behavior is hampered by the repression (not-thinking) of primary drives and by the chronic high level of these blocked drives.

These conflicts produce three kinds of neurotic phenomena: stupidity, misery, and symptoms. The neurotic is "stupid" because both repression and the presence of strong drives (tension) prevent him from thinking about certain topics and confuse his thinking. He is miserable because much of his behavior does not cope with the environment, and he does not attain the goals he seeks. He has symptoms either of the physiological kind (components of anxiety or other drive states) or of the behavioral kind (obsessions, compulsions, phobias, and other anxiety-reducing mechanisms).

Phobia. A phobia, as we saw earlier, is an unreasonable fear. Following Freud, Dollard and Miller assume that the origin of the fear is unknown because it is to be found in childhood conflicts over sex and aggression. Of course, the phobia itself may have no obvious relation to sex or aggression. The gap between the original fear and the overt phobia is bridged by the principle of stimulus generalization. The generalization may be primary (stimuli physically similar to the original one come to be feared) or secondary (words or symbols transfer the fear).

For example, a young man may have fear attached to cues produced by the first incipient responses of sexual excitement. Then if a previously indifferent girl is labeled "sexy," she may arouse incipient responses of sexual excitement which in turn elicit fear. (Dollard & Miller, 1950, pp. 161–162)

It is assumed that intense anxiety leads to a higher gradient of generalization, that is, to a spread of the fear response to a greater number of stimuli. In the face of the fear stimulus the individual runs away, and this avoidance is reinforced by the subsequent drop in anxiety. With such potent reinforcement, it is not surprising that phobias are extremely resistant to extinction.

Compulsion. The analysis of compulsions is similar to that of phobias, except that in compulsions the emphasis is on the response. In the face of anxiety, a motor response somehow reduces the fear drive. The contingency may be quite accidental, for example, the relationship between knocking wood and not having an accident. The response that constitutes the compulsion may be a generalized one that has been well learned in childhood. For example, washing one's hands is a well-learned response for removing dirt. If dirt is equated with evil or fear or guilt, then washing one's hands may reduce the anxiety associated with these states.

The compulsion reduces anxiety only temporarily. Since the response does not cope with the real threat, the source of the anxiety remains. It is still necessary to cope with the anxiety, for which the only recourse is to repeat the compulsions that have in the past provided a temporary drop in drive level. The compulsive response may be complex, requiring concentration on the part of the responder. This has the added advantage of distracting him from the object of his fear.

Hysteria. Dollard and Miller suggest two possible sources of hysterical symptoms. The first is organic, the individual having suffered in the past from a set of symptoms associated with a medical disease, for example, intestinal distress due to appendicitis. The second is a model, whose symptoms are copied. They also note that the origin of many hysterical symptoms is unknown, arising from the murky conflicts of childhood.

Whatever its source, once the symptom occurs, it sharply reduces anxiety and is thereby strongly reinforced. Usually the symptom occurs in situations that call for responsibility and facing up to unpleasant reality. The symptom, which resembles those seen in medical illness, excuses the individual from action. Since he is "sick," he cannot be held responsible for making decisions and must be excused from normal activities. Thus he escapes from adult responsibility and anxiety-laden decisions, and the reduction in drive level reinforces the hysterical symptoms.

The drop in anxiety also produces the indifference to symptoms often seen in hysterics. The reduction in anxiety level may be so great that the hysteric has a feeling of relief and well-being despite his "sick" symptoms, that is, *la belle indifference.*

The Neurotic Paradox. If a response is maladaptive in that it does not deal with the environment, why does it persist and predominate over adaptive behavior? Dollard and Miller suggest two explanations. The first involves the temporal sequence between a response and its consequences. An escape response tends to reduce anxiety immediately, although subsequently it may lead to punishment of other bad consequences. A more adaptive response usually requires the individual to remain in the situation and tolerate anxiety, rather than have the drive reduced. Since the maladaptive escape response is followed *immediately* by drive reduction, it overpowers competing adaptive responses that reduce drive at some later time.

The second explanation involves self-punishment. The neurotic who anticipates punishment because he is anxious, guilty or both, is often willing to punish himself rather than receive punishment from others. He prefers a known punishment to an unknown punishment because he is certain that the self-punishment is milder than that delivered by others. It is as if he were pleading guilty to a minor offense in order to escape being charged with a major offense.

PARTIAL ACCEPTANCE

The psychoanalytic approach to neurosis has been partially accepted by Mowrer (1950, 1953). He fully agrees with the pleasure principle, reality principle, normal and neurotic anxiety, and repression, and with intrapsychic conflict as the underlying cause of neurosis. But he rejects the idea that neurotics are oversocialized, nor can he accept regression as being directed against id impulses. If this were the sum of Mowrer's approach, he would be classified as a neo-Freudian. However, like Dollard and Miller, he recasts psychoanalysis into learning terms; his special contribution is a two-factor learning theory.[1]

Two Kinds of Learning

Mowrer was not the only learning theorist to suggest a two-factor theory of learning, nor was he the first; but he has emphasized it so strongly and applied it so forcefully to neurotic phenomena that his name is the one most closely associated with it.

The first kind of learning is *instrumental conditioning:* a response occurs (for whatever reason), followed by a reward or the cessation of punishment. The individual learns by a process of trial and error which responses lead to positive goals or to escape from negative consequences, that is, he acquires responses that lead to pleasure and avoid pain. He learns what he must *do* in order to attain his goals, and what he does has some effect on his environment. This means that he must use his effector mechanisms: the skeletal and vocal muscles that serve to interact with the environment. This behavior is voluntary and under the control of the central nervous system, especially the cerebral cortex.

The crucial time relation in instrumental conditioning is that between the response and the (rewarding) consequences that follow it. The sooner the reward follows the response, the more entrenched the habit becomes. Similarly, the better the reward and the oftener it occurs, the stronger the habit. Thus the responses learned best are those that lead most quickly and consistently to the best rewards. Which responses will do this is discovered by trial and error.

The second kind of learning is *classical conditioning.* Initially, an unconditioned stimulus elicits a response, for example, a puff of air elicits an eyeblink. When neutral stimuli are paired with the unconditioned stimulus, they eventually come to elicit the response. These new, conditioned stimuli thus substitute for or symbolize the original, unconditioned stimuli. The individual learns the important "signs" in his environment, which has prompted Mowrer to label this *sign learning.*

Most of the reflexes involved in classical conditioning concern response to noxious or unpleasant stimuli. The reflex usually protects the person from the stimulus, for example, finger withdrawal from a hot stove. Thus sign

[1] Mowrer has subsequently revised his two-factor learning theory. The revision does not deal with neurosis, and therefore the text includes only the initial version of his theory.

learning has a clear survival value. The issue is not of obtaining pleasure but of behaving realistically in a potentially dangerous world.

The two types of learning may be compared directly:

Instrumental Conditioning	*Classical Conditioning*
solution learning	sign learning
pleasure	realism
trial and error	indoctrination
teaching	training
skeletal and vocal muscles	smooth muscles and glands
behavioral	physiological
central nervous system	autonomic nervous system

Instrumental conditioning concerns situations that require a *solution to a problem.* The individual must compute his income tax, use a map to reach a new location, sell a product, etc. He must be able to make the response that will solve the problem and lead him to the goal. His instrumental behavior leads him to *pleasure.* He may learn the correct solutions through *trial and error,* correct responses being followed by pleasure and incorrect ones by no pleasure. He may also be *taught* how to solve problems (how to read a map, how to sell a product).

Classical conditioning concerns potentially dangerous situations. Avoiding pain and injury requires a knowledge of the *signs* of imminent threat. Many of the symbols that must be learned for survival are social because so much of adjustment occurs in interpersonal settings. The individual must learn the signs of social danger, for example, parental punishment or rejection by a peer group. After such classical conditioning, the signs of danger elicit at least mild anxiety or pessimism. The goal of classically conditioned responses is not pleasure but *realism,* the avoidance of danger. The learning must begin early in life, at the start of socialization. The young child must be *indoctrinated* with knowledge about the signs and rules of his society; he must be *trained* to respond reflexively to certain crucial, symbolic stimuli. Rather than actively solve problems, he passively learns to obey rules and recognize signals. He is trained to respond reflexively and automatically, not to obtain pleasure but to survive.

Instrumental conditioning involves *behavioral* responses, those initiated by *skeletal and vocal muscles* and hence having an impact on the environment. These behavioral reactions are under the control of the *central nervous system,* notably the cerebral cortex. As such, they are *voluntary,* flexible, and specific. Classical conditioning involves *physiological responses,* those initiated by *smooth muscles and glands.* They are under the control of the *autonomic nervous system* and hence are *involuntary,* automatic, inflexible, and diffuse.

These distinctions between instrumental and classical conditioning provide the cornerstone for Mowrer's theory of neurosis. Maladaptive instrumental conditioning results in defensive behavior, whereby anxiety (fear) is avoided but the source of the anxiety remains untouched; it is problem-solving gone wrong. Maladaptive classical conditioning results in excessive anxiety.

Causes of Neurosis

Like Dollard and Miller, Mowrer recasts psychoanalytic theory into a learning framework, but his translation is different. We start with these identities:

id = primary drives
ego = solution learning
superego = a product of sign learning (the rules of society)

The development of a neurosis is a two-stage process, the first being covert and the second, overt. The first stage begins with severe parental disciplining. The child's sign learning is traumatic, and the classical conditioning process, so important for socialization, becomes associated with considerable anxiety. Anxiety and other secondary drives conflict with primary (id) drives. This conflict causes the primary drives to be repressed and denied discharge. Such repression temporarily solves the conflict, and problem-solving (instrumental conditioning) can then be used in coping with secondary drives. Solution learning is used in order to obtain rewards and escape punishment from the parents and later from the superego. These developments constitute the first or covert stage of neurosis.

The second stage starts when the instrumental, defensive habits (especially repression) are weakened. Old conflicts are intensified, and primary drives threaten discharge and consciousness. This crisis calls for new and more elaborate defensive measures (problem-solving) in order to hold down primary drives. These habits or instrumental behaviors are the symptoms that constitute neurosis.

Freud saw repression as being directed against primary drives. Repression and other defenses are examples of problem-solving. It is the superego that opposes primary drives, and the superego is a product of sign learning. Thus sign learning and solution learning would operate together to defend against the primary drives of the id: sign learning sounds the alert and problem-solving defends against the danger of the primary drives being expressed.

Mowrer's major objection to the Freudian approach concerns its emphasis on repression of id impulses. He believes that repression and other defensive solution learning are used in the interests of the id, against the superego. The primary (id) drives use problem-solving in the fight against the secondary drives of anxiety and guilt. Mowrer postulates four developmental stages.

First, there is only the pleasure principle. By a process of trial and error the infant learns to attain pleasure and avoid pain. The only learning consists of instrumental conditioning (solution learning).

Second, socialization begins: cleanliness training, inhibition and modulation of behavior, and responses to other persons. The parents socially condition the child, indoctrinating him into society. This sign learning (classical conditioning) consists mainly of punishment for forbidden behavior. The child is required to learn the signs of danger.

Third, there is also indoctrination of moral precepts and a strong push to be honest. However, in the face of parental punishment, the child does not inhibit the forbidden behavior. Instead he restricts it and becomes deceitful and secretive, engaging in the taboo behavior furtively. This is the stage of resistance to socialization, and criminals never outgrow it. When there is strong training for honesty, the child may be caught in a bind. Engaging in forbidden behavior is pleasurable, but fear of discovery and knowledge of guilt are painful. The anxiety and guilt may lead to confession, followed by punishment and atonement; or it may lead to attempts to cope with the strong superego. Guilt feelings can be avoided if they can be repressed.

This leads to the fouth stage. Parental values and commands have been introjected, and the superego is harsh and demanding. This marks the difference between the criminal and the neurotic. The criminal resists socialization, using problem-solving to cheat and deceive those around him. The neurotic internalizes the world (now his conscience) and uses problem-solving to cheat and deceive his superego. The problem-solving may be conscious, as in rationalization; or it may be unconscious, as in repression. The neurotic continues his childhood resistance to socialization, but now the battle is intrapsychic. Repression is directed against the superego, not the id.

Thus problem-solving represents the mechanisms of defense, the ego's attempts to attain pleasure and avoid pain. It is used against sign learning, which represents the attempts by the ego and superego to deal realistically with the world. The neurotic is not oversocialized but undersocialized; he is dominated by the pleasure principle at the expense of the reality principle. He wishes only to escape from anxiety and to avoid guilt, and he uses solution learning to accomplish these ends without coping with the real problem. Mowrer suggests that the neurotic would react to an air raid siren by stopping up his ears or by shooting it down. He reduces anxiety by tuning out the signal but does not cope with the source of the anxiety.

The neurotic ends up with a learning deficit because he uses solution learning as a defensive, protective device. He uses it first to resist social conditioning and later to resist the force of his conscience. This rebellion serves to maintain an immature ego, one that tends to be asocial and dominated by the id. There is constant anxiety that his immaturity will be exposed and his deceit revealed. These are the processes that cause neurotics to be immature:

> To say that an individual is neurotic is not to say that there is anything deficient about his problem-solving ability. Indeed, it is the very fact that he has been skillful in parrying the early attempts of his elders, and later of his conscience, to socialize him that has kept him neurotic. The essence of the difficulty is precisely that, through problem-solving learning or the primitive pleasure principle he has learned how to keep from learning in the sense of being conditioned, i.e., changed emotionally and attitudinally. To put this matter somewhat paradoxically but succinctly, the neurotic is an individual *who has learned how not to learn.* (1950, p. 526)

REJECTION

Dollard and Miller freely accept psychoanalytic theory, adding a number of learning variables and translating the theory into learning terms, for example, instinct becomes drive. Mowrer accepts much of psychoanalytic theory but rejects the notion of the neurotic as being oversocialized and dominated by a tyrannical superego. Other learning theorists categorically reject psychoanalytic theory in general and the assumptions of unconscious conflicts and regression to psychosexual stages in particular. Such theorists may be divided into three groups on the basis of their learning models of neurosis: experimental neurosis, temperament and conditioning, and imitation learning.

Experimental Neurosis

There are many explanations of the neurotic-like behavior produced in animals in the laboratory. Our interest here is in the variables that produce such behavior and especially in their relation to human neurosis. The most comprehensive attempt to relate the animal data to human neurosis is Wolpe's theory (1958).

He assumes that in both animals and humans, neurosis is produced by situations that elicit intense anxiety. The most obvious anxiety-provoking situation is the administration of noxious stimuli such as electric shock. Pavlov (1927) conditioned an alimentary reaction to weak electric shock by pairing it with food. The current was gradually strengthened until it was intense; then it was applied to different parts of the dog's body. Eventually, the conditioned response disappeared, and the dog became violent. Other animals showed similar "neurotic" reactions. Intense noxious stimuli have also been used by Solomon and Wynne (1954) and Masserman (1943) to produce neurotic-like behavior in animals. Liddell (1944) produced deviant behavior in various animals by means of mild electric shock in a withdrawal-conditioning situation.

The other class of situations that leads to experimental neurosis is *con-*

flict, which, according to Wolpe, produces anxiety indirectly. Again Pavlov (1927) first demonstrated the effect. A circle was paired with food until a conditioned alimentary response was well trained to the circle. Then an ellipse was introduced, but it was not paired with food. The ellipse was gradually made more circular until the discrimination between circle and ellipse was extremely difficult. Eventually, the experimental animals became violent and displayed a variety of emotional reactions. Gantt (1944) reported similar findings with pairs of tones, again the emotional behavior occurring only after repeated difficult discriminations.

Thus there are two kinds of situations that produce experimental neurosis. The first is noxious stimuli (a few intense ones or many weak ones), and the second is conflict such as occurs in difficult discriminations. Wolpe points out that the animal must be confined within a harness or a cage. This spatial restriction is necessary in order to prevent the animal from escaping from the situation, thereby reducing anxiety with an appropriate (escape) response. Keeping the animal confined forces it to maintain contact with the noxious situation, which in turn produces better conditioning of anxiety responses and a higher level of emotional (autonomic) reactivity.

The confinement variable is ordinarily not present in the development of human neurosis, at least not in the physical sense. Nevertheless, humans are kept in the anxiety-provoking situation by psychological pressures. There may be strong approach tendencies or there may be intense aversive consequences to escape responses. For example, some students suffer severe anxiety when confronted with examination questions, but they cannot escape from the examination room because the consequences of such escape are more frightening than the questions.

So far, Wolpe's formulation accounts for anxiety reactions: the individual has learned an enduring anxiety response in situations involving noxious stimuli or conflict. What needs to be explained are the neurotic symptoms of hysteria and obsession-compulsion, which reveal no overt signs of anxiety.

Wolpe starts by dividing reactions to noxious or conflict situations into two types: anxiety reactions involving the autonomic nervous system and nonanxiety reactions involving the sensory, motor, and cognitive reaction systems of the individual. He assumes that in hysteria the latter reactions predominate:

The central feature of hysterical reactions is the conditioning, in situations of stress, of neurotic reactions other than anxiety, although anxiety is often conditioned as well. It is necessary to ask what determines this. There are two possible answers. One is that these reactions are conditioned when they happen to be evoked in addition to anxiety. The other is that although such reactions may be evoked by stress in all subjects, they become the neurotic responses conditioned only in those in whom some special factor is present that gives preference to nonanxiety conditioning. Since, in fact, the immediate response to neurotigenic stimulation always seems to implicate all response systems, the latter possibility is the more likely to be relevant. (1958, p. 87)

He goes on to assume that hysterics show only a low-intensity anxiety reaction in stress situations, which makes other, nonanxiety neurotic reactions more likely. These reactions, which may be accidental or incidental, become conditioned like any conditioned response. What distinguishes hysterical responses is their specificity and unchanging nature: the inhibition of particular sensory, motor, or cognitive responses.

Obsessional symptoms, on the other hand, are more complex, elaborate, and organized. Wolpe distinguishes between anxiety-elevating and anxiety-reducing obsessions.

Anxiety-elevating obsessions are simply part of the anxiety reaction to the stressful situation. Ostensibly, the anxiety neurotic with strong ideational tendencies would tend to develop such obsessions: continual worry and apprehension about feared objects, loss of control of one's own dangerous tendencies, or both.

Anxiety-reducing obsessions are responses to anxiety itself, and they are strengthened because they diminish anxiety. The obsessional tendency to count or to think of a particular tune or poem has the effect of preventing one from thinking about anxiety-provoking situations.

Wolpe's distinction between these two types of obsession would be fully accepted by Mowrer. In fact, they appear to demonstrate the two kinds of learning that Mowrer insists are different. Anxiety-elevating obsessions are obviously an example of classical conditioning: responses conditioned in an emotional situation and involving sign learning. Anxiety-reducing obsessions tend to be instrumental responses that solve the problem of a noxious state of affairs by means of psychological escape. Mowrer would consider only the anxiety-reducing obsessions as neurotic because they are the only ones to meet his definition of neurotic behavior as problem-solving directed against sign learning.

Temperament and Conditioning

Psychoanalytic theory is more comprehensive than most learning theories in that it attempts to describe the *personality predispositions* to neurosis. Thus the person with anal personality features is likely to become obsessive-compulsive, and those fixated at other psychosexual stages are predisposed to develop hysterical, depressive, or other neurotic symptoms. Virtually all learning theories concentrate on the *mechanisms* crucial to neurotic symptoms rather than on the background personality features; they do not attempt to predict *which* neurosis will develop.

The exception among learning theories is Eysenck's combination of

Pavlov, Hull, and factor analysis (1957). In the course of factor analyzing laboratory and clinical data, he has isolated three factors important in the realm of psychopathology: neuroticism, psychoticism and introversion-extraversion. Only the neuroticism and introversion-extraversion factors are relevant here.

Neuroticism. The neuroticism factor is made up of several components, but the most important one appears to be emotionality or autonomic lability. Eysenck assumes that the tendency of the autonomic nervous system to be easily aroused and over-reactive is inherited. This tendency to be overemotional (specifically, to be oversusceptible to anxiety-provoking stimuli) is a major determinant of neurosis.

Thus a major aspect of neuroticism is an inherited autonomic lability; this is one kind of anxiety. The second kind of anxiety is conditioned; it depends on both the number of noxious stimuli delivered and the conditionability of the individual. As we saw in Chapter 4, two studies have verified the presence of these two kinds of anxiety. Both Hamilton (1959) and Buss (1962) found one factor in which autonomic reactions predominated and one in which the motor and cognitive aspects of anxiety were paramount. Thus there is some empirical support for Eysenck's assumptions about neuroticism.

Introversion-Extraversion. Eysenck has adopted the traditional dichotomy between those, on the one hand, who are less sociable, more solitary, more inhibited, more contemplative and deliberative and those who are more gregarious, less inhibited, less thoughtful, more impulsive and restless. However, he has not been content to use these as part of a descriptive typology. Rather, he has demonstrated their presence as factors emerging from the analysis of laboratory tasks, and he has related them to basic learning variables.

He assumes that extraverts condition slowly and build up reactive inhibition quickly. They need more time to learn, but they cannot be kept in learning situations too long because of the rapid buildup of resistance to conditioning (reactive inhibition). Furthermore, reactive inhibition is assumed to dissipate slowly in extraverts, which means that more time is required for the individual to return to a state of conditionability. Thus the extravert suffers from a triple learning deficit: he is slow to learn, quick to develop psychological "fatigue," and slow to dissipate this fatigue.

Introverts, on the other hand, are assumed to condition rapidly, requiring fewer trials to learn. They develop reactive inhibition slowly and dissipate it quickly, which means that they are conditionable longer and need less rest and time out from learning.

Eysenck specifies other differences between extraverts and introverts, and he couches them in such Pavlovian and Hullian terms as *excitatory potential* and *cortical inhibition.* However, in the present context only his basic assumption of learning differences, the so-called *typological postulate,* need concern us here.

Application to Neurosis. One more assumption is needed to apply the theory to neurosis, namely, that the different neurotic syndromes vary along the dimension of introversion-extraversion. Eysenck has done just that, placing hysteria at one end and dysthymia (anxiety reaction, obsession-compulsion, and depression) at the other end. Hysterics are assumed to be extraverted and dysthymics, introverted. There is evidence for this assumption, especially in the way neurotics perform on laboratory tasks.

Now it is possible to combine the learning and temperament hypothesis into a theory of neurosis. Eysenck accepts Mowrer's contention that socialization occurs by means of conditioning, but Eysenck does not differentiate between classical and instrumental conditioning. The extravert is slow to condition and quick to build up reactive inhibition, which does not dissipate easily. He is slow to learn the rules of society and is therefore undersocialized. He fails to learn the inhibitions and modulations of behavior that society deems important, and as a result he is childish and impulsive.

If the extravert is low on neuroticism, he will remain an immature but essentially normal person. However, if he is high on neuroticism, he will tend to over-react to stressful situations. He will be unable to develop adequate means of coping with threatening stimuli and will fall back on childish, impulsive modes of responding. This is the pattern seen in hysteria: a combination of neuroticism and extraversion.

The introvert follows a different path. He is quick to condition and slow to build up reactive inhibition, which dissipates easily. He learns the rules of society, in fact, learns them too well. He becomes oversocialized, inhibited by the complex rules and restrictions of society. His conscience is too strict, and he tends to deliberate excessively.

Add to this personality picture of the introvert a labile autonomic nervous system (high neuroticism). The introvert is susceptible to more anxiety-provoking stimuli, and he over-reacts to them. Furthermore, because the introvert conditions so quickly, he develops an excess of conditioned fear responses, especially to stimuli that are only incidentally associated with the original fear stimuli. Since he is oversocialized and inhibited, the neurotic introvert cannot resort to the childish, impulsive behavior seen in hysteria. He can follow one of three paths: (1) he can remain in a chronic state of anxiety (anxiety reaction); (2) he can become morbidly concerned and guilty over his actions and impulses (neurotic depression); or (3) he can develop elaborate rituals in thought or action which may temporarily reduce anxiety (obsession-compulsion). These patterns are labeled dysthymia: a combination of neuroticism and introversion.

Eysenck was quick to see that his theory might resolve Mowrer's dispute with Dollard and Miller. Dollard and Miller insist that the neurotic is guilt-ridden and driven by a hard conscience to repress basic drives. Mowrer suggests that the neurotic is driven by his basic urges to repress the warnings of his conscience. Eysenck contends that there are two kinds of neurotics, each corresponding to those described by Dollard and Miller and by Mowrer, respectively. The dysthymic is oversocialized, a· ixious, and guilt-ridden because of his quick conditioning. He has learned trict ethical standards and has high aspirations. He is unsociable, being introverted, and also fearful of social contacts, being neurotic. The hysteric is undersocialized, impulse-ridden, and has few conditioned fears. He has a conflict about social contacts, being extraverted and therefore drawn toward others, but also being neurotic and therefore afraid of others. Eysenck suggested that Dollard and Miller meant *dysthymic* when they said *neurotic,* whereas Mowrer meant *hysteric.*

Comment. Eysenck's theory, as noted earlier, is the only learning approach that attempts to explain why one neurosis rather than another develops. Psychoanalysis attempts to do this by means of the concepts of fixation and regression, the implicit assumption being that the personality patterns that predispose a person to one or another neurosis are laid down during psychosexual development. Eysenck, in contrast, assumes that one inherited tendency predisposes an individual to *any* neurosis, namely being high on neuroticism. He further assumes that inherited personality *dispositions,* namely, one's place on the introversion-extraversion scale, predispose an individual toward the hysteric or dysthymic ends of the neurotic spectrum.

Thus Eysenck's postulation of temperament variables is not the only issue that distinguishes his theory from other learning theories of neurosis. Another is his insistence on hereditary dispositions, a notion that is contrary to the heavy environmentalist bias of virtually all learning theories. The last difference between this theory and other learning approaches is its deductive nature. Eysenck has attempted to deduce clinical symptoms, learning curves, and such physiological variables as sedation threshold from a few basic postulates. It would be tangential to attempt an evaluation of how well this deductive approach has fared in the laboratory, especially in light of the considerable controversy surrounding this issue. However, we may note in passing that Eysenck's is one of the rare theories in this area that is stated with sufficient precision to be capable of disproof. This is an unusual feature of theories not only of neurosis but of behavior in general.

Imitation Learning

Imitation learning has been neglected by most learning theorists. Miller and Dollard (1941) opened up the area for psychology but there was little followup for 20 years. Bandura and Walters (1963) formulated an imitation learning theory in terms amenable to personality development and psychopathology.

They list three effects of a model upon an observer. The first is called the *modeling effect:* the observer copies responses that he had not made heretofore. This effect is responsible for the acquisition of new behavior, which may be entirely novel responses or new, complex ones consisting of components already in the observer's repertoire. Another possibility is that old responses occur to new stimuli. Regardless of the pattern, what is important in the modeling effect is that the behavior is novel in some way, either the stimulus or the response aspect.

The second kind of effect is inhibitory or disinhibitory. The observer, imitating the model, tends *not* to make a response that he might ordinarily make—the inhibitory effect. On the other hand, after imitation the observer may tend to make a response that has previously been inhibited by punishment—the disinhibitory effect.

The third kind is the eliciting effect. Here the observer, after imitation, makes responses that are already in his repertoire but that have not been inhibited by punishment.

Bandura and Walters have suggested several variables that determine the extent of imitation. The more salient the cues offered by the model, the better is the imitation by the observer. Reinforcement of the model for his behavior facilitates copying by the observer. Interestingly, Bandura and Walters do not include reinforcement of the observer's copying behavior as an important determinant of imitation. They believe that the acquisition of an imitative response occurs by means of contiguity (closeness in space and time), whereas the *performance* of imitative behavior is affected by reinforcements to the model (Bandura, Ross, & Ross, 1963). They present clear evidence for these assertions, and it may well be that imitative behavior is sustained in the absence of subsequent rewards for its occurrence.

Bandura and Walters have applied their formulation to the development of aggressive behavior, but it may also be applied to psychopathology. The modeling effect may lead to deviant responses which were not previously in the repertoire of the observer. Such imitation can occur very easily in childhood, the child copying the disturbed attitudes, mechanisms, or even symptoms of a parental model. Thus a particular symptom may be acquired, not as an unadaptive compromise to a conflict situation, but as a matched response that is copied from a neurotic model.

The inhibitory effect may lead to the suppression of adaptive responses necessary for everyday adjustment. For example, a child might copy his parent's tendency to withdraw from stressful situations, thereby inhibiting the child's own tendency to continue in the situation until there is some resolution of it. Contrariwise, a parental model might serve to disinhibit socially disapproved behavior, thereby increasing the child's adjustment difficulties. For example, the parent may engage in such childish behavior as temper tantrums, which may release the child's previously punished tantrums from their inhibition.

The parental model may also serve to elicit responses that are present in the child's repertoire but not frequently made. For example, the parent might use somatic complaints to escape from anxiety-laden situations. The child may have engaged in similar behavior but only rarely. The presence of a parental model may tend to increase the frequency of this neurotic behavior.

Self-reward has been shown to be an important determiner of learning (Kanfer & Marston, 1963), and patterns of self-reward may be learned by imitation. Bandura and Kupers (1964) showed that children followed the self-rewarding and self-disapproving behavior of models, regardless of whether the models had high or low standards of performance. It follows that children might learn by imitation to reward themselves only for superlative performance and to disapprove of themselves for lesser performance. Children who are incapable of living up to their own standards (acquired by imitation) might eventually develop feelings of shame and inferiority. Clients with such problems do appear in clinics:

These clients experience a great deal of self-generated aversive stimulation and self-imposed denial of positive reinforcers stemming from their excessively high contingencies of self-reinforcement, often supported by comparisons with historical or living models noted for their extraordinary achievements. This process frequently gives rise to depressive reactions, a lessened disposition to perform because of the unfavorable work to self-reinforcement ratio, and efforts to escape the self-generated aversive stimulation through alcohol, grandiose ideation, and other modes of avoidant behavior. (Bandura & Kupers, 1964, p. 9)

Thus imitation may account for many of the deviant behavior patterns seen in neurosis. We cannot ignore the subsequent fate of responses that have been acquired or elicited by imitation. Such responses may subsequently be rewarded or punished, continuously or periodically. Previous learning theories (for example, Dollard & Miller) have shown how reduction of anxiety can serve as a powerful reward for neurotic responses. Once a response occurs, it may then serve to reduce anxiety, which in turn serves to maintain the response.

COMMENT

Various learning theories of neurosis have been reviewed, each taking some position with respect to psychoanalysis: acceptance, partial acceptance, and rejection. Each theory has emphasized a particular kind of learning, a particular kind of concept (for example, drive), or a particular model for neurosis (for example, experimental neurosis). Acceptance of any single theory depends upon one's attitude toward psychoanalytic theory, as well as one's predilection for specific concepts such as drive, two-factor learning, and temperament variables. However, adopting a learning approach to neurosis does not require accepting any particular theory. It is possible to be neutral concerning the specific theories and still espouse a general learning approach. This neutral position does not preclude the identification of learning variables in neurosis, and, in fact, there are two broad classes: noxious stimuli and faulty learning.

Noxious Stimuli

The presentation of noxious or painful stimuli to the individual sets in motion a number of response tendencies or states of the organism that tend to lead to neurotic symptoms. A direct effect may be intense, chronic anxiety. This effect has been demonstrated in the laboratory: animals given massive electric shock develop bizarre responses which have been labeled *experimental neurosis*. There have been no similar laboratory demonstrations of *chronic* anxiety with human subjects, but the histories of anxiety neurotics are replete with instances of intense punishment, painful misfortune, or both. Thus the most direct effect of noxious stimuli may be to produce a chronic anxiety reaction.

Punishing stimuli may also produce conflict. In the terms used by Dollard and Miller, such stimuli set up an avoidance drive in conflict with an approach drive. Such conflict prevents the original drive from being reduced, and the conflict itself is a source of drive stimuli; these two sources of tension produce both physiological symptoms of distress and maladaptive responses that temporarily reduce tension.

The maladaptive responses are of two kinds: escape and avoidance. An individual exposed to too much punishment may develop such strong escape or avoidance responses that he cannot cope with his environment. The avoidance response may take the form of a phobia, the person steering clear of situations associated with anxiety. It may take the form of repression: not thinking about present life situations or forgetting important ones from the past. Such avoidance responses protect the person from intense anxiety but only at the expense of excluding a significant part of his world.

Excessive escape tendencies are equally neurotic. All of us are required to deal with situations that are at times painful (for example, an examination or the dentist's chair), and one response that must be learned is to remain in the situation long enough to make appropriate instrumental responses. Such responses, whether they consist merely of waiting or involve action against the source of the noxious stimuli, will in the long run deal effectively with the painful situation. The person who has learned to escape at the first sign of anxiety does not remain in the situation long enough to make adjustive, coping responses. Like the avoider, the escaper cripples his adjustment in order to effect a temporary reduction in anxiety.

Faulty Learning

There are several kinds of faulty learning, all having their maximal effect during childhood and adolescence. The child may be required to learn a discrimination that is too difficult. Analogizing from laboratory work with animals, this contingency may establish a neurosis. So far there is no good evidence for the analogy, but this may be because of the ethical and practical difficulties of investigating experimental neurosis in humans. However, there is no doubt that overtaxing a child's discriminative abilities often leads to both excessive emotionality and a breakdown of previously learned discriminations. The excessive use of rewards may lead to such resistance to extinction that an individual cannot give up outmoded response patterns for newer and more appropriate ones. In a psychoanalytic context this has been labeled *fixation*. During the developmental sequence, responses that are appropriate during one phase may have to be modulated or inhibited at a later phase. For example, crying is appropriate in an infant but must be toned down and partially inhibited as a child grows older. Young children who have been rewarded for crying, may have great difficulty in inhibiting this response. Furthermore, it will be more difficult to acquire the more mature responses required by society.

Lawrence and Festinger (1962) have identified a paradoxical property of rewards: goals that must be struggled for are valued more than goals attained easily. This principle may account for the paradoxical attachment of some neurotics to goals that appear to have little intrinsic worth. Once an individual has committed himself to attaining a goal and expends considerable effort in achieving it, he may be extremely reluctant to relinquish it. During the developmental sequence children are continually called upon to surrender childish goals for more mature ones. Thus children are taught to surrender personal victories for team victories, immediate gratification for delayed gratification, etc. A child who has experienced much difficulty in reaching an early, immature goal may be expected to value it beyond the appropriate developmental stage and to have difficulty in substituting more mature and more socially appropriate goals.

Finally, the deficiency may consist of insufficient learning. The first two decades of life mainly train individuals in the ways of their society, and in this context, it is not surprising that many people do not complete their education. Everyone must learn certain discriminations, that is, to recognize crucial differences in both physical and social situations. In a communication framework, this means that we must all learn the "signs" that society deems important and the "rules" of behavior (Szasz, 1961). The individual may have the appropriate responses in his repertoire, but unless he recognizes the stimuli that call for one set rather than another set of responses, his behavior is likely to be maladaptive. Thus a person with strong needs for achievement may fail to achieve his goals because of failure to learn new rules and cues as he moves from one stratum to another within the social structure. What is appropriate for a bright young man just out of college is usually not appropriate behavior for a man ten years older and part way up the ladder of success.

The insufficient learning may involve the response repertoire itself. A model may not be available for copying, or parents and teachers may fail to teach the child the important social responses required for adjustment in a complex society. For example, as adolescents become involved in hetero-sexual relationships, it becomes important that the boy or girl acquire such responses as dancing, "what to talk about on a date," various appropriate sexual responses (whatever the subculture allows), etc. Some neurotic diffi-culties may be explained in terms of a failure to acquire an appropriate and varied set of responses necessary for social intercourse.

The last kind of insufficient learning concerns the ability to tolerate tension and inhibit emotional response. This is only one of many responses that must be learned as an individual heads toward maturity, but it is a crucial one. Young children can tolerate little tension. They cannot wait quietly and they cannot suppress emotional reactions. Adults are required to be patient and to modulate or inhibit most emotional reactions, such as violent rage, weeping, and wailing. Tolerance for tension must be learned slowly, by successive approximations. Children must be rewarded for wait-ing, for not bursting into tears, and for restraining their tempers. There must be a payoff for the child who is willing to forsake an immediate goal (either reward or relief of tension) for a more distant one. If a child is not rewarded for self-restraint or if he is rewarded for temper tantrums, he will not develop the necessary "no-response" behavior required of adults. He will tend to respond too quickly and with excessive emotion, and the end result may be a hysterical disorder.

REFERENCES

Bandura, A., Ross, Dorothea, & Ross, Sheila A. A comparative test of the status envy, social power and secondary reinforcement theories of identificatory learn-ing. *Journal of Abnormal and Social Psychology,* 1963, **67,** 527–534.

Bandura, A., & Walters, R. H. *Social learning and personality development.* New York: Holt, Rinehart & Winston, 1963.

Bandura, A., & Kupers, Carol J. Transmission of patterns of self-reinforcement through modeling. *Journal of Abnormal and Social Psychology,* 1964, **69,** 1–9.

Buss, A. H. Two anxiety factors in psychiatric patients. *Journal of Abnormal and Social Psychology,* 1962, **65,** 426–427.

Dollard, J., & Miller, N. E. *Personality and psychotherapy.* New York: McGraw-Hill, 1950.

Eysenck, H. J. *Dynamics of anxiety and hysteria.* London: Routledge & Kegan Paul, 1957.

Gantt, W. H. *Experimental basis for neurotic behavior.* New York: Hoeber, 1944.

Hamilton, M. The assessment of anxiety states by rating. *British Journal of Medical Psychology,* 1959, **32,** 50–59.

Kanfer, F. H., & Marston, A. R. Determinants of self-reinforcement in human learn-ing. *Journal of Experimental Psychology,* 1963, **66,** 245–254.

Lawrence, D. H., & Festinger, L. *Deterrents and reinforcement: The psychology of insufficient reward.* Stanford: Stanford University Press, 1962.

Liddell, H. S. Conditioned reflex method and experimental neurosis. In J. McV. Hunt (Ed.) *Personality and the behavior disorders.* New York: Ronald, 1944.

Masserman, J. H. *Behavior and neurosis.* Chicago: University of Chicago Press, 1943.

Miller, N. E., & Dollard, J. *Social learning and imitation.* New Haven: Yale University Press, 1941.

Mowrer, O. H. *Learning theory and personality dynamics.* New York: Ronald, 1950.

Mowrer, O. H. *Psychotherapy: Theory and research.* New York: Ronald, 1953.

Pavlov, I. P. *Conditioned reflexes: An investigation of the physiological activity of the cerebral cortex.* London: Oxford University Press, 1927.

Solomon, R. L., & Wynne, L. C. Traumatic avoidance learning: the principles of anxiety conservation and partial irreversibility. *Psychological Review,* 1954, **61,** 353–385.

Szasz, T. S. *The myth of mental illness.* New York: Hoeber-Harper, 1961.

Wolpe, J. *Psychotherapy by reciprocal inhibition.* Stanford: Stanford University Press, 1958.

CHAPTER 7

Comparison of Psychoanalytic
and Learning Approaches

This chapter compares psychoanalytic and learning approaches[1] to neurosis without any attempt at evaluation. Both approaches extend well beyond neurosis or even psychopathology as a whole, and a critique would carry us too far afield. Furthermore, it is difficult enough to attempt an objective exposition of the theories without adding the perils of evaluation. These approaches are accepted or rejected because one or the other fits comfortably into the psychologist's system of professional values. One theory is experimental, academic, and quantitative; the other is clinical, applied, and qualitative. One leans toward statistics and group trends, the other toward case study and the uniqueness of the individual. If we substitute *statistical* for *learning* and *clinical* for *psychoanalytic*, the following quotation is apt:

It is customary to apply honorific adjectives to the method referred, and to refer pejoratively to the other method. For instance, the statistical method is often called operational, communicable, verifiable, public, objective, reliable, behavioral, testable, rigorous, scientific, precise, careful, trustworthy, experimental, quantitative, down-to-earth, hardheaded, empirical, mathematical, and sound. Those who dislike the method consider it mechanical, atomistic, additive, cut and dried, artificial, unreal, arbitrary, incomplete, dead, pedantic, fractionated, trivial, forced, static, superficial, rigid, sterile, academic, oversimplified, pseudoscientific, and blind. The clinical method, on the other hand is labeled by its proponents as dynamic, global, meaningful, holistic, subtle, sympathetic, configural, patterned, organized, rich, deep, genuine, sensitive, sophisticated, real, living, concrete, natural,

---

[1] Although there are several learning approaches to neurosis, for expositional purposes we shall combine them into a single, overall approach.

true to life, and understanding. The critics of the clinical method are likely to view it as mystical, transcendent, metaphysical, supermundane, vague, hazy, subjective, unscientific, unreliable, crude, private, unverifiable, qualitative, primitive, prescientific, sloppy, uncontrolled, careless, verbalistic, intuitive, and muddleheaded. (Meehl, 1954, p. 4)

The opposition between the two approaches is not surprising when we consider their different origins. Psychoanalysis is essentially a European theory, arising from a background of nineteenth century Victorian society, Darwinian evolutionary theory, and phenomenology. It is a clinical theory, originating in experiences with disturbed persons and attempting to provide a rational account of irrational behavior. Learning theory is of more recent vintage, and, with a bow to Pavlov, it is essentially American. It stems from an empirical, functional background of research primarily with animals, and it nurtures strong attitudes concerning objective measurement, operational definition, and experimental verification. Learning theory starts in the laboratory and attempts to explain neurosis by extending principles discovered with normal subjects to disturbed persons. These different vantage points explain the divergent positions taken on issues related to neurosis. We shall discuss the five most relevant issues: surface versus depth, the unconscious, mechanisms, and shame and guilt.

SURFACE VERSUS DEPTH

The Psychoanalytic Approach

Psychoanalysis is a *depth* theory in that it focuses on the "deep," underlying tendencies of persons rather than on superficial, overt behavior. Neurotic symptoms are believed to be caused by nonobservable, unconscious intrapsychic conflict—ego versus id or ego versus superego. The psychoanalyst is interested in impulses, not in how the impulses are expressed in behavior. The *affects* are important, not their surface manifestations. For example, the psychoanalyst considers it trivial whether rage is expressed as a violent verbal attack or as a physical assault; he is concerned mainly with the affect of rage itself, together with the *impulse* to aggress and the *feeling* of hostility.

Thus psychoanalysis is clearly a *phenomenological* theory, one that emphasizes the individual's impulses, thoughts, feelings, ideas, and dreams—in brief, his *inner world*. Surface behavior is seen as merely a superficial manifestation of the really important psychic events hidden from view Associations, dreams, slips of the tongue, and sudden forgetfulness provide clues about the inner life, the *phenomenological reality* that is going on beneath the surface.

Symbolism is of crucial importance in this theoretical framework. Psychoanalysts distinguish between manifest and latent content. *Manifest content* is simply the overt and observable property of the response; *latent content* is the symbolic meaning of the response, a meaning that is kept hidden or disguised by the forces of repression. The manifest content of dreams is weird and illogical; it represents a distortion of the true, unconscious, symbolic meaning that is too anxiety-laden to be allowed into consciousness. Associations *manifestly* have a strangely illogical quality, but they make good sense to the psychoanalyst who is armed with the translating code—a knowledge of universal symbolism. Similarly, neurotic symptoms make no sense in their overt, observable form, but the psychoanalyst can demonstrate that *symbolically* they make good psychological sense. A phobia about knives represents castration anxiety, and a hand-washing compulsion represents an attempt to expiate guilt (cleansing of the hands equals cleansing of the soul).

The Learning Approach

Learning theory, on the other hand, is a *surface* theory in that it focuses on observable behavior. The underlying causes of neurotic symptoms are sought, but the causes are not assumed to be in some hypothetical *inside* of the individual. There are nonobservable theoretical constructs such as habit strength, but they are no "deeper" than the physical construct of gravity. For the learning theorist, the ultimate reality is behavior, not phenomenology.

Interest centers on easily observed, quantifiable aspects of behavior:

(1) Frequency—the number of times a response occurs;
(2) Rate—frequency of response per minute, hour, or day;
(3) Amplitude—the force or intensity of the response;
(4) Latency—the time required to initiate the response, as measured by the interval between stimulus and response;
(5) Duration—the time taken to complete the response or the time period during which the response is maintained.

These surface details are of no interest to the psychoanalyst. He takes a case history that encompasses many years of the client's life. His explanations of the generalized tendencies of, say, a decade emphasize broad developmental variables and such instincts as sex and aggression. The psychoanalytic approach, emerging from such clinical material, naturally favors broad, *deep* explanations.

The learning approach, emerging from a mass of data on specific responses in a controlled laboratory situation, naturally emphasizes precise, detailed, *surface* explanations. The learning theorist's account of neurotic symptoms specifies details of reward, punishment, and time relations between stimuli and responses. In extrapolating to clinically relevant behavior, he assumes that such details are as important as they are for laboratory behavior. He assumes that the generalized tendencies reported in the clinic consist of and perhaps even conceal a multitude of specific stimulus-response connections. He demands that descriptions be detailed and precise: the precise stimuli that elicit an anxiety reaction; the precise response made in escaping from threatening stimuli; the precise time relations between stimuli, between stimuli and responses and between responses and rewards; the precise schedules of reward and punishment, and the precise rewards and punishments that follow responses. In brief, the learning approach emphasizes the surface details of stimuli and responses, in contrast to the psychoanalytic approach, which emphasizes deep, inner explanations and accounts for neurotic symptoms in more generalized terms.

THE UNCONSCIOUS

The Psychoanalytic Approach

In his book, *The Unconscious Before Freud,* Whyte (1960) points out that the notion of unconscious mind antedated Freud by several hundred years and was very much in vogue when Freud began his professional career. Nevertheless, there was also a strong tradition of regarding man as bascially a rational creature, whose behavior is determined mainly by *will* or the seeking of conscious goals in a conscious manner. Furthermore, Herbart's view—that unconscious ideas were weaker ideas that had been pushed from consciousness by stronger ones—was also well accepted. Freud reacted strongly against both the rational view and the view that the unconscious consists of weak ideas. He insisted on the primacy and strength of the unconscious and that the only way to understand neurosis is by means of exploring unconscious motivations, impulses, and conflicts.

Freud brought to fruition the notions of unconscious that had been developing since Descartes and, more than those before him, brought conscious and unconscious into sharp opposition. The unconscious is essentially irrational, dominated by primary process (hallucinatory fantasy), wish fulfillment, and the pleasure principle. It has no sense of time and contains ideas and motivations that may be mutually incompatible but that nevertheless are not in conflict; there is no conflict in the unconscious. The conscious is essentially rational, dominated by secondary process (imagination in the service of planning) and the reality principle. There is a well-developed sense of time and an acute awareness of conflicting needs; ideas must be socially acceptable.

In the normal person there are relations between the conscious and the unconscious. Ideas usually originate in the unconscious and gradually become conscious, unless there is resistance to them. (The notion of preconscious, something between conscious and unconscious, will not be discussed here because it is not central to the concepts being discussed.) On the other hand, perceptions that arise from stimuli in the external world may travel from the conscious to the unconscious.

In the neurotic there is an isolation of conscious from unconscious material, which occurs because of the mechanism of repression. An unconscious idea can become conscious only when it is attached to words. Repression, which breaks the association between the idea and the words, renders the idea unconscious; it also prevents the transforming of an unconscious urge into affective expression. Consequently, ideas cannot be brought into consciousness because their associations are broken, affect cannot be expressed directly because it is isolated from its origin (the instinctual impulse), and impulses cannot be translated directly into behavioral expression. Repression can be initiated and maintained only by means of an *anti-cathexis,* a force that opposes and blocks the unacceptable idea or impulse. The mental energy of anti-cathexes is derived from the instincts themselves, and in neurotics the consumption of this energy in keeping ideas unconscious often leads to exhaustion.

Repression serves to prevent *direct* expression of ideas and impulses in behavior or awareness, but the *derivatives* of unconscious ideas succeed in breaking through to consciousness. Repression does not rob the unacceptable ideas of their mental energy, and they continue to press toward consciousness and motility. When the ideas can assume a symbolic form that is sufficiently different from their original form, they can circumvent censorship and be admitted to consciousness; but since the altered, now-conscious ideas still represent forbidden, unconscious wishes, the ego regards them as alien.

In brief, the manifest symptoms of neuroses can be understood only in terms of the unconscious: ". . . the conflict, its history, and the significance of the symptoms are unconscious" (Fenichel, 1945, p. 20). The neurotic has symptoms because he has repressed ideas and impulses, because he cannot cope directly with his basic conflicts, since they are unconscious, and because he is using excessive psychic energy in attempting to deal with unconscious conflicts.

The Learning Approach

Whereas Freud downgraded consciousness by asserting the crucial role of the unconscious, Watson completely ignored consciousness. He maintained that thinking, which he regarded as nothing more than subvocal speech, was unimportant in behavior. The early behaviorists denied that consciousness was an acceptable area of study for psychologists, but most modern learning theorists have more moderate views. Consciousness is seen as one of several reaction systems of the human organism. In addition to the skeletal-instrumental system and the autonomic-emotional system, there is a cognitive system that includes sensory processes, attending, labeling, thinking, and planning. There is no opposition implied between these reaction systems. Sometimes they interact, and other times they act independently.

In learning terms, consciousness is nothing more than awareness, that is, attention to external stimuli or to mediated stimuli (thoughts or internal stimuli). There is no entity called the *unconscious*, although there may be many aspects of behavior of which one is unaware. Whether one is aware of the background of his responses or of the motivation for them may make a difference in how or whether the responses occur, but it may not. The learning theorist, although not ignoring the issue of awareness, insists that it is part of only one reaction system of the organism. The neurotic may be aware of his self-defeating tendencies but is powerless to alter them, not because they are unconscious but because they are the products of strong conditioning.

Repression is regarded as a fact, not as the major mechanism of neurosis. It is an escape or avoidance response. In the face of an anxiety-provoking situation, an individual may escape by running away. Excessive arousal of the autonomic reaction system (anxiety) may thus interact with the skeletal reaction system (escape). When the anxiety-provoking stimuli are thoughts or memories, the instrumental response of escape is useless. The person can escape only by inhibition of the cognitive system; he represses the idea or thought—the *not-think* response suggested by Dollard and Miller. The learning theorist does not suppose that the memory then becomes unconscious in the sense that there *is* an unconscious. The question "Where do repressed memories go?" makes sense only in a theoretical framework that has a psychic anatomy; otherwise it is meaningless.

In this context, repression is an escape or avoidance response comparable to similar responses that might be made to any anxiety-provoking stimulus, but repression is not necessary for neurotic behavior. The phobic person may attempt to avoid or escape from the objects of his phobia without repressing what he is afraid of; his response is *skeletal* rather than *cognitive* (repression). This view is in sharp contrast to the psychoanalytic position, which maintains that the neurotic fears a phobic stimulus only because it is a symbolic representative of *unconscious* fears that have been repressed.

In brief, the learning theorist takes the position that the conscious-unconscious issue is essentially irrelevant in neurosis. Neurosis is a problem of faulty learning: strong but incompatible habits, failure of extinction, excessive use of avoidance or escape responses, excessive autonomic lability, failure to learn appropriate discriminations or the learning of incorrect discriminations, the imitation of self-defeating behavior, and the direct imitation of neurotic symptoms. Faulty learning can occur with or without awareness, as can adjustive learning. Lack of awareness (unconsciousness) does not guarantee neurotic symptoms any more than awareness (consciousness) guarantees adjustive behavior.

MECHANISMS

Both psychoanalysis and learning theory state the *processes* that underlie both normal adjustment and neurotic symptoms. These processes or *mechanisms* differ considerably because of the basically different models used by the two theories.

The Psychoanalytic Approach

Psychoanalytic theory employs two kinds of mechanisms: those used as part of normal development and those that lead to neurotic symptoms. *Normal mechanisms* are necessary for the proper proliferation and functioning of the ego. The ego must develop means of "binding" mental energy to prevent "flooding" and the consequent feeling of basic anxiety. This means that instinctual urges must be delayed or altered in their expression in behavior. All ego mechanisms that allow the expression of id-impulses or ideas in an altered and socially acceptable form fall under the heading of *sublimation*. Another kind of mechanism, *introjection,* facilitates the development of the superego. The positive attributes of parents and other authority figures are "taken in" and form the basis of the ego-ideal. The ego-ideal is the part of the superego used to evaluate the positive striving aspects of the ego's activity.

Psychoanalytic theory has much more to say about *neurotic defense mechanisms,* which have been studied intensively during therapeutic psychoanalyses. These mechanisms directly oppose id-impulses, blocking any discharge of urges or affects. As we have seen, repressed material keeps its mental energy and continually presses for discharge and consciousness. Neurotic mechanisms are only partly successful in warding off the tabooed strivings, which eventually come to the surface in the derivative and compromise form called symptoms.

Lists of neurotic defenses resemble lists of instincts in that the number varies with the compiler's predilection for brevity or expansiveness. In Chapter 5 we mentioned these defense mechanisms: denial, displacement, isolation, projection, reaction-formation, repression, and undoing. The reader who is interested in a more complete list has only to consult a psychoanalytic tract or a textbook on adjustment or abnormal psychology. Regardless of the variety of mechanisms, they all have one function in common: protecting the ego from being flooded with anxiety-laden, primitive urges. Since these urges are unconscious, the mechanisms must operate unconsciously. It follows that part of the ego is unconscious. This part of the ego (comprising defense mechanisms) attempts to protect the other part from the paralyzing effects of anxiety. We may analogize to the bodyguard of an important figure: the protectors defend the potential victim without his knowing it. Thus the conscious ego, which organizes and synthesizes the various activities of everyday living, is protected from disruptive urges by the unconscious ego.

These defense mechanisms are *learned* ways of coping with deeper, more unconscious material. They are closer to the surface, and the increased attention they have received in the past few decades reflects a tendency to focus on less instinctual, more ego-oriented, and less deep aspects of the personality. In this context it is not surprising that defense mechanisms have been accepted by psychologists who reject other aspects of psychoanalytic theory. This *process* aspect of the theory has found some measure of acceptance among learning theorists, who have translated psychoanalytic mechanisms into learning mechanisms (for example, displacement into stimulus generalization).

The Learning Approach

The mechanisms of learning theory are the *principles underlying learning*. Learning may occur through classical conditioning, instrumental conditioning, or imitation. The residuals of learning consist of tendencies to make certain responses to particular stimuli; these residuals are called habits. Presumably, all neurotic symptoms are learned and therefore consist of habits (for example, compulsions) or the residuals of habits (for example, depression).

In the last chapter we mentioned several learning mechanisms: stimulus generalization, response generalization, extinction, interval between response and reward, and modeling. These are the principles that determine the important features of responses: when, where, which, how much, how quickly, and how long. Another principle is schedule of rewards. In everyday life a reward does not follow every instrumental response but occurs after a group of responses or after an interval of time, for example, a weekly or monthly payday. The schedule of rewards—regular, irregular, high percentage, low percentage—has been found to be an important determinant of the frequency or rate of responses. Schedules are of great importance during extinction (absence of reward). For example a low percentage of reward leads to slower extinction (greater persistence in responding) than a high percentage of reward (Ferster & Skinner, 1958). Extinction is an important adaptive mechanism, for when responses are no longer rewarded, they should be replaced by responses that are rewarded. One problem manifested by neurotics is an inability to stop making a response when it is no longer rewarded. One determinant of such excessive persistence is the schedule of reward that occurs during learning.

In addition to the standard principles of learning that have emerged from the laboratory, there are translations of psychoanalytic mechanisms. Dollard and Miller (1950), as we have seen, explain displacement in terms of stimulus generalization, and repression in terms of a *not-thinking* response. Let us examine the details of two other translations to facilitate the comparison of psychoanalytic and learning theories.

The psychoanalytic mechanism of *identification* is part of the normal process of development. The most primitive kind of identification consists of oral incorporation: the infant puts objects in the mouth, thereby becoming one with them. Oral introjection and imitation are closely linked, both involving a kind of "incorporation":

> The concept of a primary identification denotes that actually 'putting into the mouth' and 'imitation for perception's sake' are one and the same and represent the first relation to objects . . . It is all one: the first (oral) object love, the first motor reaction to external stimuli, and the first perception. (Fenichel, 1945, p. 37)

The growth of the ego depends on the availability of benign personalities to serve as models. The ego introjects various aspects of persons around it, thereby attaining both stable structure and means of solving problems. Of course, the process of introjection does not involve a literal incorporation of objects and of others' personalities, but the infantile oral component underlies all subsequent *psychological incorporation,* as revealed by the regressive fantasies of psychotics.

Learning theory rejects this kind of analogizing, replacing it with the notion of imitation learning. The child does not merely make random responses to random stimuli but systematically copies certain salient aspects of his environment. Adults constitute the most salient part of a child's world, which probably accounts for their being more effective models than peers (Bandura & Kupers, 1964). The modeling effect—imitation of others' responses—would seem to depend upon an innate tendency (or a tendency learned very early in life) to mimic. Presumably, instrumental responses are profoundly affected by cognitions; witness the inability of deaf persons to learn speech. In brief, the learning approach emphasizes cognitive variables as being crucial for imitation, which in turn underlies identification. In contrast the psychoanalytic approach emphasizes oral incorporation as the basic component of identification.

The psychoanalytic mechanism of *regression* is not part of normal development but is basic to all psychopathology. Psychoanalysis specifies a fixed sequence of psychosexual stages in early childhood, each stage having particular problems associated with it:

oral—dependence and affection
anal—independence and hostility
phallic—aggression and sexuality

Normal adjustment requires that a child pass though each stage with a minimum of trauma so that fixations do not develop. Fixation at a particular stage results in a tendency to regress back to it under the pressures of adolescent and adult adjustment. Regression is what determines psychopathology, and the particular stage regressed to determines the specific kind of psychopathology. Thus hysterics regress mainly to the phallic phase, obsessive-compulsives mainly to the anal phase, and psychotics mainly to the oral phase.

In brief, the various syndromes are ordered in a hierarchy of depth of regression. This ordering assumes that psychopathology represents a backtracking down the road of normal development, which has a fixed sequence. The greater the regression, the more severe is the psychopathology. It is assumed that each stage has its own problems and its own defense mechanisms. Therefore the depth of the regression specifies not only the severity of the psychopathology but also the precise nature of the symptoms. Note that the depth of regression and the presence of particular mechanisms are *inferred* from the symptoms manifested by the neurotic. Psychoanalytic theory attempts to explain the symptoms that occur, but it does not *predict* which ones will occur.

Learning theory rejects the notion of a fixed developmental sequence and replaces the concept of regression with that of a *habit hierarchy*. Let us assume there are three responses—A, B, and C—arranged in decreasing order of habit strength. In a situation that might elicit any of them, A is most likely to occur, B next most likely, and C least likely. If A is not rewarded, its habit strength will eventually drop below that of B and perhaps even that of C; then B would be most likely to occur.

Which response occurs is a function solely of the habit hierarchy, not *when* the response was learned. An old response might have a greater habit strength than a new one. For example, in the initial hierarchy A might be the newest response, C next, and B the oldest. Note that it is possible for B to be stronger than C although B is older. Thus if A were not rewarded, its eventual replacement would be B, not C. This position holds that it is not the *time* of learning but relative *habit strength* that determines the occurrence of a response. When a response weakens or cannot be made, its replacement is not the most recently learned response but the response next on the habit hierarchy.

In brief, learning theory runs counter to psychoanalysis, which assumes that the developmental sequence is the crucial variable. A mature response is replaced by the next most mature response, and successive replacements occur on the basis of recency in the time sequence—from most recent to earliest. Learning theory states that the time of learning is of no importance in itself but only in its influence on the number of learning trials, that is, the earlier a response is learned, the more opportunity for practice and reinforcement. What the learning theorist must demonstrate is that a response learned earlier can be of greater habit strength than a response learned later and that replacement depends on habit strength, not on the time of learning. These have yet to be demonstrated, and the issue remains unresolved.

GUILT AND SHAME

Many neurotics are guilt-ridden. Some are self-punitive and feel sinful; and others are so inhibited by their conscience that they are unable to engage in the sexual and aggressive behaviors that are important in everyday adjustment; still others are excessively involved with mechanisms for avoiding or escaping guilt. In addition some neurotics are overwhelmed with a pervasive sense of inferiority; they are full of shame concerning their own achievements and believe it impossible to do anything worthwhile.

There are many approaches to the problems of guilt and shame, but only three will be discussed here. The first is classical psychoanalytic theory; the second, a modification of psychoanalytic theory incorporating some historical perspective; and the third, a learning approach.

Classical Psychoanalytic Theory

Freud combined both conscience and ego-ideal into the single concept of superego, believing that the two were so intertwined as to be inseparable. The superego develops from the ego, just as previously the ego developed from the id. The first step is the projection of the child's omnipotence onto his mother. Since the mother is all-powerful, the child's greatest fear is losing her affection; so long as he stays on good terms with her, he is secure. Loss of mother's love is catastrophic in that it raises the threat of annihilation. When a child is punished by his mother, he learns not to make the punished response.

The next step occurs when the child learns to inhibit the forbidden response even when the mother is absent. The mother's prohibitions are introjected, and part of the ego becomes a watchdog, warning that certain responses will be followed by loss of love. Since it is now the ego that warns, the parent need not be present. This development within the ego foreshadows the later development of conscience. The warning function parallels another ego function: anxiety as a warning of impending punishment. However, the ego function that leads to a superego consists of parental inhibitions that have been internalized, and the danger that must be warded off is the loss of parental love and affection.

The superego itself is established only as a consequence of the Oedipus complex. The child, unable to compete with the same-sexed parent for the love of the opposite-sexed parent, temporarily gives up his Oedipal longings. He identifies with the same-sexed parent to attain the latter's power, to avoid castration anxiety, and to usurp his place. Thus there is a second introjection, this time a borrowing of parental strength that helps the child to fight off his Oedipal strivings. The combination of the previously introjected parental inhibitions and the new, positive parental identification constitutes the superego.

Thus the superego may be divided in two ways. First, there are the *negative* aspects, which consist of parental commands and prohibitions that have been introjected, and the *positive* aspects or ego-ideal, which consists of introjected parental characteristics and ideals. Second, the negative aspects may be divided into (1) an early primitive, unvoiced, unconscious part that is rigid and tyrannical ("an eye for an eye"), and (2) a later voice of conscience that is more rational, flexible, and compassionate.

Prior to the establishment of the superego, the child depends on his parents for love and esteem. He must guard against the danger of the withdrawal of parental affection and must seek parental approval. The superego takes over these functions. Now the ego must obtain approval and avoid punishment from the superego; the danger is no longer from without but from within.

Guilt feelings are the ego's anxiety concerning the superego's disapproval. The experience of guilt is the withdrawal of affection by the superego, which is comparable to the withdrawal of affection by a parent. The child initially requires love from a parent because he projects his feelings of omnipotence to his parents; if these all-powerful figures love him, he is secure. Later, if his superego approves of him, he is secure; if his superego disapproves, he is threatened with annihilation. Thus in guilt the superego robs the ego of some of its self-esteem. The superego functions normally by warning the ego that a particular action will be followed by a loss of self-esteem. If this warning is heeded and the impulse inhibited, self-esteem is maintained. However, if the warning fails and the action occurs, the superego attacks the ego by withdrawing affection; the person experiences guilt.

There are basically three kinds of superego pathology. In the first kind the superego is dominated by the introjection of parental inhibitions. These "early" introjects are extremely demanding, often irrational and excessively rigid. The rules of conduct may be so unrealistic that the ego is prevented from carrying on the normal activities required for everyday adjustment. The superego's demands, being irrational, are perceived by the ego as being alien; thus the ego may be caught between instinctual demands and superego prohibitions, both of which are alien and unrealistic. The compromise effected by the ego may be seen in various neurotic symptoms, especially the obsessive and compulsive varieties.

The second kind of superego pathology parallels an anxiety attack. In an anxiety attack the warning of impending danger throws the ego into a panic; instead of being a signal, the warning is a trauma. The same process may occur with a guilt warning: instead of informing the ego that a future action will result in loss of self-esteem, the warning triggers the loss of self-esteem itself. This can occur only in the context of an ego already low in self-esteem and a rigid, punitive superego: the warning guilt turns into the panic of melancholy. This kind of superego pathology leads to a depression.

The third type of superego problem is an underdeveloped conscience. Because of faulty identification with parents, insufficient love from parents, or faulty resolution of the Oedipal complex, the superego may be weak. When the ego has little to fear from the superego, it becomes dominated by the pleasure principle. Uninhibited by superego commands, the ego is relatively free to express id impulses without regard for the moral consequences. This kind of problem is seen in *conduct disorders:* alcoholics, drug addicts, asocial and antisocial personalities.

A Modified Psychoanalytic Position

Piers and Singer (1953) have modified the classical Freudian position, giving a larger role to shame. They make a sharper differentiation between the two components of the superego, ego-ideal and conscience. The ego-ideal represents parental identifications, feelings of omnipotence, and, to a lesser extent, identification with peers. Conflict between the ego and the ego-ideal results in shame, not guilt. The ego-ideal presents goals for the ego to attain, and when these goals are not reached, the ego-ideal makes the ego aware of this discrepancy. What the ego fears from the ego-ideal is contempt, followed by abandonment. Piers and Singer suggest that shame is different from inferiority feelings in that the latter arise only in relation to peers, whereas shame arises in relation to the ego-ideal. If the parents emphasize the child's stupidity, clumsiness, and general inability to achieve, the child may learn to think of himself as unworthy. He may become shame-driven, dedicating himself to achieving grandiose goals in order to convince the ego-ideal that he is truly worthwhile.

Guilt arises out of parental punishment and hostility. The conscience consists of introjected parental inhibitions, and when the ego is in conflict with the conscience, the consequence is guilt—a fear of hatred from within. The Law of Talion (an eye for and eye) operates in guilt, the conscience demanding that the ego suffer for its transgressions of the moral code. In contrast to shame (fear of abandonment), guilt consists of a fear of castration from within. The guilt-ridden person attempts to atone for his sins; he has not failed to act but has acted wrongly and must expiate guilt.

Piers and Singer point out that in the history of Western culture, guilt came before shame. As part of the early, Catholic emphasis on guilt, it was presumed that everyone was sinful and should therefore be guilty. The only source of salvation was humiliation, the penitent atoning for his sins by submitting to authority. Since everyone was regarded as sinful, there was no element of shame.

The Reformation changed all this by emphasizing personal responsibility and internalization of guilt. Subsequently, rapid development in technology led to a work ethic: competition with others, personal achievement, and aggressiveness with a minimum of guilt. Failure to compete became wrong and was punished by shame.

In comparing the operation of shame and guilt in society, Piers and Singer write:

Guilt transfers the demands of society through early primitive parental images. Social conformity achieved through guilt will be essentially one of *submission*. Shame can be brought to the individual more readily in the process of comparing and competing with peers (siblings, schoolmates, gang, etc.). Social conformity achieved through shame will be essentially one of identification. (1953, p. 36)

This view is similar to one presented by Lynd (1958), who links guilt with anxiety, and shame with inferiority. She notes that guilt concerns specific acts (violations of social codes), and surmounting guilt leads to self-righteousness. Shame is concerned with more general behaviors (one's ability to achieve), and overcoming shame leads to identity and freedom.

Both these modifications of the classical psychoanalytic position give more emphasis to shame than Freud did. For Freud, shame is somewhere between a child's anxiety and an adult's bad conscience. It concerns being looked at and being found out and therefore despised. It is closer to embarrassment than to guilt, and it does not occupy the same prominent place in neurotic symptom formation as guilt does.

The modifications of Freud's position thus upgrade shame, giving it a more important place in the genesis of neurotic behavior. These modifications probably reflect a change that has occurred since Freud's first theories were formulated. In Freud's early days, at the turn of the century, there was more emphasis on sin and more inhibition of sexual behavior and even of talk about sex. There were more tabooed areas of behavior and a larger number of transgressions to be avoided. Today there is less emphasis on sin and more on "doing one's share." In brief, the historical developments described by Piers and Singer have also been occurring during the last 60 years, and if Freud were theorizing today, he might assign a larger role to shame.

The Learning Approach

The learning approach begins by rejecting the notions of inner psychic structures such as the superego and of immutable developmental phases such as the psychosexual stages and the Oedipal complex. These sweeping and generalized constructs are replaced with detailed concepts of stimulus, response, timing, reward, punishment, and various kinds of learning.

The first step is to separate shame and guilt from self-control. Psychoanalytic theory adopts the commonsense view that guilt and, to a lesser extent, shame, are the major determinants of self-control; an individual restrains himself from engaging in tabooed behavior because of the feelings of guilt that would follow. The learning approach assumes that although guilt may deter tabooed behavior, it is a minor determinant of self-control: in fact, self-control is usually learned in the absence of guilt.

Self-Control. Self-control is defined as the inhibition of socially prohibited behavior in absence of a punishing agent. Bandura and Walters (1963) offer three different methods of obtaining self-control: punishment, imitation, and reward.

(1) *Punishment.* One way of weakening behavior, in this instance tabooed behavior, is by failing to reward it. However, some responses are strongly motivated and intrinsically rewarding, that is, the individual rewards himself in the absence of external rewards; masturbation is an example. Thus mere absence of reward may not suffice, but punishment often does. The individual learns not to make the punished response so long as the punishing agent is present.

How is behavior inhibited when the punishing agent is absent? Hill (1960) suggests several answers. First, the punishment may be so severe that the avoidance response never extinguishes, as in traumatic avoidance conditioning. The intensity of punishment evidently guarantees that the response will not be repeated even though the punishment is never again applied. Second, the individual may learn that the punisher is, in a sense, ubiquitous. If parents are good detectives, they can surmise that their offspring have transgressed from available evidence (cookie crumbs, dirt smudges, etc.); the child may eventually believe that his parents are equipped with all-seeing eyes. In this event, the punisher is always "present" in that transgressions are virtually always discovered and punished. Another possibility is the belief that God is always watching us and will punish us immediately or wait until the final Judgment Day. A literal belief in Hell also helps to sustain the view that there is never a safe time for transgression.

The timing of punishment is also important (Mowrer, 1960). A response may be divided into an early, preparatory phase and a late, consummatory phase. When punishment occurs early in the sequence, its emotional effects (fear) are linked with the *initiation* of the response. This means that on subsequent occasions, starting to make the response will elicit a fear reaction. This fear reaction tends to inhibit the previously punished response, thus leading to self-control. Late in the response sequence, the individual attains his goal or is about to attain the goal. When punishment occurs late in the sequence, its negative effects are opposed by the positive effects of the reward or stimuli associated with the reward. Furthermore, what is being punished is the *completion* of the response, not its *initiation*. This means that there is no fear reaction when the individual *starts* to make the tabooed response, only when he *completes* it. Thus punishment late in the sequence does not stop the response from occurring. Late punishment allows the response to occur and then elicits anxiety; there is no self-control.

(2) *Imitation.* Just as children acquire their regional speech accents by imitation, they also imitate the immediately prevailing behavior patterns with respect to self-control. Middle-class children, for example, are in frequent contact with adult models who usually demonstrate self-denial and waiting behavior. Middle-class adults marry later than lower-class adults, and middle-class adults are often willing to deny present pleasures for future gain and to work for a distant goal. The middle-class child has appropriate models available and has only to imitate their behavior.

Note that guilt need not be involved. The child imitates waiting, self-denial, and rejection of socially prohibited conduct. Such modeling has been demonstrated in a number of experimental situations, and Bandura and Walters (1963) specifically report research on self-control. Children obeyed a verbal prohibition when the model did and violated the prohibition when the model did. Such modeling presumably occurs in everyday life, where parental and peer models are probably more powerful and certainly more available. The point here is that the concept of guilt is not needed to explain the children's self-control. The self-control, acquired through imitation in the absence of specific moral training, is fully explained by the mechanism of modeling.

(3) *Reward.* Self-control is acquired not only by imitation but also by rewarding it when it occurs. Parents and teachers tend to reward children for waiting, for being honest, and for resisting temptation. Unfortunately, as the term temptation implies, the prohibited response itself is usually rewarding. Cheating may lead to a better grade, lying may avoid punishment, and stealing may increase one's income or property. These clear and extrinsic rewards must be opposed not only by punishment but also by rewards for incompatible, *prosocial* behavior. Bandura and Walters (1963) suggest that rewarding the desired behavior is the most effective way to achieve self-control:

This technique primarily emphasizes the production of prosocial behavior, involves actively teaching the child what he should do, and focuses relatively little on the deviant or erroneous response . . . . the relative ineffectiveness of much social training is probably due to its focusing on the modification of deviant responses as they occur, instead of concentrating on the eliciting and rewarding of prosocial behavior. (p. 199)

This quotation implies that rewarding behavior that is beneficial to society is a more effective way of achieving self-control than training in anxiety or guilt over the consequences of making prohibited responses. While this may or may not be true, it is clear that self-control can be developed in the absence of guilt.

Shame. Shame involves a sense of embarrassment such as one experiences in the classical dream of being caught naked in public. It is anxiety, not of being harmed, but of being seen publicly in a situation that should be private. In fact shame may be described as *social anxiety:* the situation is aversive only because others are present.

Since everyone is taught to discriminate what is allowed in public versus what is allowed in private, we have all encountered shame situations. What concerns us here is the individual who has an excessive tendency to feel shame. This tendency may take the form of excessive personal modesty, an unusual need for privacy, or aloofness. It may also take the form of anxiety in *any* social situation: a readiness to believe that one is clumsy, ugly, or in some way the object of scorn. In brief, the shame seen in neurotics consists of repeatedly labeling oneself as awkward, inept, unattractive, or disgusting.

One advantage claimed for the learning approach is that it specifies the details of the development of such responses as shame. In the present context this task may be framed as an answer to the question: if we deliberately set out to produce shame in an individual, how would it be done?

As a prologue to describing how to produce shame, we shall first discuss the reward systems used by parents because they are important in the development of shame and guilt. The major reward a parent can bestow on a child is his attention and affection, and these can be given unconditionally or conditionally. The earliest common parental response, especially by the mother, is to love the child unconditionally—not for what the child *does* but simply because he *is*. To the extent that the child imitates the parent, the child learns that he is worthwhile regardless of what he does or fails to do. Later, when training begins, conditional love is necessary, the parent bestowing affection only if the child is good or if he achieves. If conditional love is begun too early or is too pervasive, the child will learn by imitation that he is not intrinsically worthwhile but of value only for what he does. His esteem will always depend on being good or on achieving the goals set by parents. Thus to the extent that conditional love predominates, the child will be predisposed to develop excessive guilt and shame.

Therefore, in the production of shame, the first step is to institute a regime of conditional love as early as possible. The child is taught that his parents' affection depends on what the child does: precocity in motor development, obeying rules, toilet training, etc. This should make the child dependent on parental support to maintain his self-esteem; later his self-esteem will depend on what he achieves. He will have little intrinsic self-esteem and will have to achieve and obey rules or suffer from a lack of worth.

Second, the parents set lofty goals for the child, goals difficult to attain but possible of attainment at least part of the time. This means the child is placed on a schedule of low percentage of reward for achieving the parental goals, a schedule that helps resist extinction. He learns that the goals are within his reach and that reaching them is the major avenue of parental affection, and later, of self-esteem. Similarly, the parents establish a strict code of social conventions, with many restrictions and complex rules to follow. Third, failure to achieve and failure to be socially correct are punished by withdrawal of affection and by ridicule. The ridicule is essential because the child must learn that the parent not only temporarily does not love him but is also disgusted with him. The child is held up to scorn, and his disgrace is observed by others; he learns that failure to achieve or a breach of conduct leads to scorn and debasement. If the standards are so high that they cannot always be obeyed, then the child cannot conform to parental expectations. Therefore there will be many occasions on which he is labeled *inept, dirty, stupid,* or *clumsy,* and he will feel shame. So long as the child is held in the parental bind (needing love for self-esteem and later needing to fulfill parental goals taken over as his own), he cannot escape a pervasive feeling of shame. He must continually doubt his own worth and feel that he does not measure up to his (his parents') standards.

This description includes three learning variables. The first is reward: the parents start early to reward instrumental responses with affection and approval rather than delivering generalized, unconditional love. The second is punishment, specifically rejection in the form of verbal labels indicating contempt and disgust. The third is imitation: the child models himself after the parents, adopting both their standards and their negative labels directed against himself.

Guilt. Guilt involves a sense of one's own evil, the labeling of oneself as bad. It is private, not public, and it cannot be avoided by escaping from the presence of others. Unlike shame, it is not a kind of anxiety but a variety of hostility. Hostility consists of feelings and verbalizations of ill will and aversiveness toward others (Buss, 1961); guilt consists of hostility toward oneself. Like shame, guilt can be conditioned to a variety of situations, but the usual ones are those involving transgressions of a generalized moral code. Anyone may feel guilty occasionally, but our concern is with the neurotic tendency to suffer excessively strong and frequent guilt. The development of this tendency is similar to the development of neurotic shame: conditional love, a strict code, punishment, imitation, and reward.

Conditional love is instituted very early, and the child, who needs parental affection in order to maintain self-esteem, learns that he will receive it only if he is good. He need not achieve, but he must not engage in forbidden behavior. Next, he is taught a moral code so strict that it must be broken in the course of everyday living. Optimally, the set of rules prohibits behaviors strongly motivated in children and adolescents, especially sexual and aggressive behaviors. These are labeled *bad,* and when the child engages in such behaviors, he is labeled *evil.* The child learns to respond to himself as his parents do; whenever he transgresses, he labels himself sinful. Since violations must occur with some frequency because of the strict moral code, the child finds himself making negative self-labels fairly often. Copying negative parental attitudes is not the only imitation that can lead to guilt. The parents themselves may act guilty when they transgress, thus serving as models for the child. If the modeling effect occurs, the child will respond to his own transgressions with a reaction of guilt, just as his parents do. Thus imitation of either parental attitudes or parental guilt reactions can lead to a pervasive sense of guilt and evil.

The type of punishment used by the parents is crucial. Physical punishment should never be attempted; instead parental affection should be withdrawn. Hill (1960) has pointed out that withdrawal of parental affection usually lasts until the child has made an expiatory response. As soon as the child admits his errors and asks forgiveness, parental love is reinstated. When parental punishment is physical, the noxious stimuli are delivered and then end. The punishment is transitory and does not endure until the child makes an expiatory response. Therefore physical punishment is less likely to lead to guilt. Thus the crucial difference between psychological discipline and physical punishment may be how long they last. Since the withdrawal of love continues until the child makes a guiltlike response, this kind of punishment is best for the induction of guilt. However, it might be possible to devise a mild physical punishment that continued until the child admitted his error. Such punishment would endure just as long as deprivation of affection, and according to Hill's hypothesis, should lead to as much guilt as deprivation of affection.

There is another difference between the withdrawal of love and physical punishment: the child's immediate reaction. Withdrawal of love is a form of rejection, the parent saying in effect, "You are bad and therefore undeserving of my love." The child is thus cast out of the circle of parental nurturance and at the same time labeled as aversive. The child's immediate reaction is likely to be dejection because he is temporarily unloved. In physical punishment the element of rejection is either absent or minor, and the child's immediate reaction to the adult's "aggression" is likely to be anxiety, anger, or both. Fear of painful stimuli and anger at being hurt are both incompatible with guilt feelings. The child is likely to become more secretive in engaging in the forbidden behavior, as well as truculent in his approach to his parents, but he is unlikely to punish himself for having transgressed. Thus, the crucial difference between physical punishment and withdrawal of love may be not how long they last but their immediate consequences. Physical punishment tends to provoke anger, imitation of parental aggression, and anxiety rather than guilt; withdrawal of love tends to induce dejection and self-blaming responses.

Inducing guilt in the child is facilitated by the parent's behaving as though he were hurt. If the parent can convince the child that the child's transgressions have in some way harmed the parent (disappointment, sorrow, illness, etc.), this will enhance the negative labels. The child would then learn that his transgressions cause harm to a beloved person. To the extent that the child loves and identifies with the parent, he cannot help but attack himself. If another person caused harm to the parent, the child would become angry and perhaps attempt to attack the other person. When the child learns that it is he who is causing the harm, he has no recourse but self-recrimination.

Finally, the reward of parental forgiveness is made contingent upon the child's admission of guilt and an appropriate penance, with the parent insuring that the admission and the penance are not perfunctory. Note that guilt need not involve embarrassment. The child learns that he is evil whether or not anyone else discovers his transgressions. In guilt the child attacks himself for being evil (sometimes for "harming" the parent), whereas in shame the child is ridiculed by others.

One of the major differences between the development of guilt and shame is the kind of label used by the parents. If the parents brand the child as inept or disgusting, the child becomes ashamed; if the parents brand the child as evil, the child becomes guilty. These distinctions may be blurred during the developmental sequence. If parents use both kinds of labels and if they react to the child's behavior by being both disgusted and hurt, then both shame and guilt will occur and be difficult to distinguish. However, in most homes probably one or the other predominates. If the parents are religious, the moral aspect and evil will be emphasized, and guilt will develop. If the parents are upwardly mobile and relatively nonreligious, then their emphasis on attaining goals and conforming to social conventions (together with scorn for failure or clumsiness) will lead to shame.

COMMENT

In the last few decades psychoanalytic theory has moved from an emphasis on the id and its instincts to an emphasis on the ego and its mechanisms. Learning theory has moved toward a consideration of some of the motivational variables considered important by psychoanalysts. Thus the two approaches are not as far apart as they once were. Nevertheless, there is still little overlap, in spite of attempts at reconciliation (Dollard & Miller, 1950). The two approaches stem from fundamentally different views of behavior, and it is doubtful that they will ever be reconciled.

Does it make a difference? Are the differences merely of intellectual interest, or are these consequences for those who study psychopathology? There are certainly consequences for research. The psychoanalyst insists that the best way to acquire new knowledge is to place an individual (normal or neurotic) on a couch and probe his unconscious. The individual's verbalizations can be examined for hints about his underlying conflicts, mechanisms, and motivations. There is considerable emphasis on observing "the whole person" and a horror of "atomistic." There is a willingness to forego the refinements and precision of laboratory techniques for the opportunity to study real-life situations in all their complexity. The focus is on the *content* of behavior rather than on how it is acquired.

The learning theorist insists that the best way to acquire knowledge is to study the individual in the laboratory. He is not only unconcerned about fragmentation but welcomes it, believing that only by analysis of constituent parts will he understand the integrated whole. His criteria of good research are precision and control, and he gladly accepts the artificiality of the laboratory to achieve them. The focus is on *how* behavior is acquired rather than on what is acquired.

There are also consequences for therapy. The psychoanalyst, viewing neurosis in terms of inner conflict, attempts to purge the client of his unconscious problems. He seeks an alteration of the personality that will obviate the need for symptoms. The learning theorist, viewing neurosis in terms of faulty learning, attempts to rehabilitate the client by altering his habits. He seeks a change that is analogous to remedial reading—the replacement of bad habits with good ones. These contrasting approaches to therapy are discussed in detail in the next chapter.

REFERENCES

Bandura, A., & Walters, R. H. *Social learning and personality development.* New York: Holt, Rinehart & Winston, 1963.

Bandura, A., & Kupers, Carol J. Transmission of patterns of self-reinforcement through modeling. *Journal of Abnormal and Social Psychology,* 1964, 69, 1–9.

Buss, A. H. *The psychology of aggression.* New York: Wiley, 1961.

Dollard, J., & Miller, N. E. *Personality and psychotherapy.* New York: McGraw-Hill, 1950.

Fenichel, O. *The psychoanalytic theory of neuroses.* New York: Norton, 1945.

Ferster, C. B., & Skinner, B. F. *Schedules of reinforcement.* New York: Appleton-Century-Crofts, 1958.

Freud, S. *Collected papers.* London: Hogarth Press, 1950, vol. 4.

Hill, W.F. Learning theory and the acquisition of values. *Psychological Review,* 1960, 67, 317–331.

Lynd, Helen M. *On shame and the search for identity.* New York: Harcourt, Brace, 1958.

Meehl, P. E. *Clinical versus statistical prediction.* Minneapolis: University of Minnesota Press, 1954.

Mowrer, O. H. *Learning theory and behavior.* New York: Wiley, 1960.

Piers, G., & Singer, M. B. *Shame and guilt.* Springfield, Illinois: Thomas, 1953.

Whyte, L. L. *The unconscious before Freud.* New York: Basic Books, 1960.

CHAPTER 8

Psychotherapy

The two kinds of psychotherapy to be discussed here are part of a larger list. Virtually all psychotherapies use a "talking cure," in which the therapist converses with the client in an attempt to remove or minimize neurotic symptoms. Almost all psychotherapies are therefore variants of psychoanalytic therapy, with its emphasis on the relationship between therapist and client. White (1964) has listed five processes that occur in all of the standard forms of psychotherapy:

(1) therapeutic relationship—a unique and close tie between a professional person and his client;

(2) expression of feelings—the client is encouraged to verbalize his fears, loves, hates, tensions, and attitudes;

(3) pointing out his feelings—the therapist helps the client to recognize his feelings, and, in many psychotherapies, interprets these feelings;

(4) transference—the client responds to the therapist as he has to significant figures from his past;

(5) new behavior—the client starts to develop new and more adaptive ways of responding.

These five features are present in psychoanalysis and all psychotherapies employing a "talking cure." Since psychoanalysis has a comprehensive theory of neurosis that leads directly to certain techniques of psychotherapy, we shall discuss only psychoanalytic therapy and ignore the other therapies that rely solely on conversation between therapist and client.

The learning approach has led to an entirely different kind of therapy—behavior therapy. The emphasis is on only one of the five processes listed by White, new behavior; the other four—therapeutic relationship, expression and interpretation of feelings, pointing out of feelings, and transference—are ignored. Talking is part of the therapy but only a small part, for behavior therapy is essentially a "nontalking cure."

PSYCHOANALYTIC THERAPY

Orthodox or standard psychoanalytic therapy requires a large number of therapy hours—50 minutes a day for four to five days per week, lasting two to seven years. One reason for this huge expenditure of time is that psychoanalysis is historical in its orientation. It delves into the childhood events, attitudes, and feelings that lay the foundation for the neurotic symptoms of adulthood. A second reason is the assumption that the processes of therapy cannot be hurried. Symptoms cannot be attacked directly because they are merely surface manifestations of underlying conflicts. These unconscious conflicts must slowly be brought to the surface, and then the client must be helped to recognize them and work them through. The intrapsychic conflicts underlying symptoms develop slowly over a period of years, and therefore it is not surprising that it requires years to reverse the process.

The basic goal of psychoanalytic therapy is to make the unconscious conscious. Actually, not *all* of the unconscious needs to be conscious, only the material that has been repressed. Repression consists of blocking the associations of unconscious ideas and isolating them from affective expression, and the various neurotic defense mechanisms help to prevent associations and impulses from attaining consciousness. Therapy consists of reinstating the associations, bringing together idea and affect, and in general diminishing the strength of neurotic defense mechanisms.

Free Association and Dreams

The two basic techniques designed to accomplish these goals are free association and the reporting of dreams. The client is instructed to say whatever comes into his head, whether or not it seems foolish. He is to be a passive reporter of his thoughts, with no attempt at control or censorship. These instructions obviously do not remove conscious control over what is said, but they weaken it. Slightly repressed material near consciousness can now be verbalized. The effect is slight but significant, for it leads to a mild, temporary drop in defensiveness and allows weakly-repressed material to become conscious.

The associations themselves are important because they symbolize deeper and more unconscious conflicts. The *manifest content* (what the client verbalizes) is sufficiently neutral to escape censorship and achieve consciousness. The *latent content* is what the manifest content symbolizes: the underlying impulses that are too anxiety-laden to escape repression. The deep, unconscious urges are distorted and linked associatively to other, less painful associations, and it is these more neutral associations that are reported by the client. In the course of verbalizing these associations, the client is led by the bonds between associations to deeper, more painful material. At this point repression becomes stronger, and the associations abruptly stop. The client cannot continue in the same associative vein, a phenomenon called *blocking*. The analyst is of course aware of the reason for the blocking and recognizes that the client's verbalizations are coming too close to his basic, anxiety-laden conflicts.

Dreams, like free associations, symbolize in distorted form the basic unconscious conflicts. Dreams do not follow logical sequences and are often a jumble of seemingly unconnected events and feelings. The reported dream is the manifest content that has undergone drastic change because of the defensive forces of the ego. The manifest dream represents in distorted form the latent content that gave rise to the dream. Psychoanalysts believe that dreams occur only when the dreamer is anxious. The dream allows some of the repressed impulses to be expressed in a form that is sufficiently disguised to avoid anxiety. The dream allows the dreamer to continue sleeping because some of the tension of the unconscious conflict is discharged. Since the ego is weaker during sleep, deeper and more unconscious material is allowed to become conscious, always in symbolic and disguised form. The analyst, knowing the latent content of the manifest dream symbols, can link the apparently meaningless materials to ideas which in their original state are too unacceptable to be allowed into awareness.

Interpretation

The analyst is not merely a passive observer and recorder of the client's associations and dreams. He attempts to interpret to the client what he is really saying and how it relates to unconscious material near the surface. Initially, the interpretations are not deep because the client cannot accept explanations of strongly repressed material. Even the analyst's superficial interpretations may be rejected by the client, either because he is still too defensive or because the timing is not appropriate.

In the early phases of therapy, the free associations reveal more about defenses than they do about repressed material, and the analyst's interpretations must deal mainly with these defenses. He attempts to show the client that he is avoiding certain topics and that every time his associations come close to these topics, there is blocking or other defenses. When the interpretation is timed correctly, there is an immediate therapeutic gain. The client can then recognize his defensiveness, as well as the impulse previously repressed. In the relaxed and accepting atmosphere of the therapy room he may be able to realize that the impulse is not necessarily frightening. This leads to a small reduction in defenses which in turn results in a relaxation of tension—less pressure for expression and less counter-pressure to contain the impulse. Occasionally, the client remembers for the first time a remote, painful event. When he can "relive" the event—link the memory with the appropriate angry, anxious, or sexual affect—he attains emotional insight (*corrective emotional experience*). These occurrences labeled *catharsis* because of the eruption of material that had previously been kept unconscious, are crucial to cure; they must occur if psychoanalytic therapy is to be more then merely an intellectual exercise.

As therapy proceeds, there is a gradual relaxation of defenses. The path is not smooth, and resistances thought to have been overcome often reappear. Each time the client manifests resistance (blocking of associations, etc.) the therapist must *work through* the problem. The process is slow because a given impulse or unconscious conflict may have many associative links. Repressed material retains its mental energy and attracts derivative associations. Therefore each time a conflict comes to the surface (consciousness), it must be integrated with the client's knowledge of and emotional experience with other aspects of the conflict.

Progress in therapy may be measured by three concurrent processes. First, what had previously been repressed gradually becomes conscious so that manifest behavior comes to be less dominated by unconscious forces. The client gradually moves toward greater freedom to deal with his problems rationally and has less need to repress. Second, the energy formerly needed to keep ideas and impulses unconscious is no longer needed in large amounts, and it becomes available for use in everyday adjustment, for example, tolerating frustration and sublimating impulses. Third, the personality is less *dammed up* by unacceptable urges and is therefore less tense and less susceptible to panic and defensiveness.

Transference Neurosis

The analyst attempts to remain a neutral figure throughout therapy, going so far as to sit behind the client's couch, out of sight. Nevertheless, in standard psychoanalytic therapy, the client inevitably develops a strong attachment to the therapist. The feelings are a curious mixture of strong affection, admiration, respect, resentment, hostility, and guilt. It is assumed that these are the feelings that the client has toward one or more major figures in his life, usually one or both parents. Ostensibly these attitudes, which arose during the client's childhood and adolescence and which persist into adulthood, are transferred to the analyst. Hence the name *transference neurosis*—the client's ambivalence, guilt, and anxiety occur *as though* the therapist were a close and crucial figure in the client's everyday life.

The occurrence of the transference neurosis is a major event in psychoanalytic therapy. Instead of reporting thoughts and feelings concerning the crucial figures of his past, the client now begins to direct these attitudes and impulses to the analyst. There is a partial shift from the *real* neurosis to the *unreal* transference neurosis, and this occasionally leads to a pseudocure. The client may surrender neurotic patterns to please the analyst or to prove to him that he is really not neurotic. Whatever the client's motivation, this kind of "cure" ostensibly cannot endure because as soon as analysis is terminated, the client loses his motivation to suppress neurotic symptoms, which then return in full force.

What is required for a real cure is the working through of the transference neurosis, and this is the most important part of standard psychoanalytic therapy. The basic technique is again interpretation: the pointing out of defenses, resistance, barely-repressed feelings, and ambivalences. The analyst gently confronts the client with discrepancies between his emotional responses and the neutral stance of the analyst. The latter remains constantly neutral, yet the client responds to him with anxiety, rage, guilt, and sexual urges. Moreover, the client's manner or behavior is often childish and immature, as he regresses to earlier patterns in the context of the transference neurosis.

The fact that the patient continues to act and feel according to outdated earlier patterns whereas the therapist's reactions conform to the actual therapeutic situation makes the transference behavior a kind of *one-sided shadowboxing*. He has the opportunity not only to understand his neurotic patterns, but at the same time to experience intensively the irrationality of his own emotional reactions . . . . As soon as the old neurotic patterns are revived and brought into the realm of consciousness, the ego has the opportunity to readjust them to the changed external and internal conditions. This is the essence of the corrective influence of those series of experiences which constitute the transference. (Alexander, 1956, p. 75)

Gradually the client is helped to recognize the disparity between his view of the therapist as a parental figure and the therapist as he really is, between feelings carried over from childhood and feelings appropriate to adult situations, and between his childish needs for nurturance and his adult needs for affection. The client can learn to accept these distinctions because part of his ego is reasonable. It is the *reasonable ego* to which the analyst directs his interpretations and it is the reasonable ego that gradually comes to dominate the unreasonable part of the ego which maintains defensive operations against unconscious urges. The reasonable ego is the adult part of the personality; the unreasonable ego, together with the id, constitutes the childlike part of the personality. As defensiveness decreases and repression lifts, the rational part of the ego has more psychic energy at its disposal for the everyday adult problems that require sublimation and controlled discharge of impulses. This part of the ego can identify with the analyst in an attempt to understand the basic forces motivating behavior and how they must be channelized.

The *working through* occurs in the context of the transference neurosis, which allows virtually all conflicts to be directed toward the therapist. Once the conflicts are worked through with the therapist, they are permanently changed and no longer occur in outside, everyday contexts. When the transference neurosis is resolved, the real neurosis is thereby resolved; this represents psychoanalytic cure. The unconscious has been made conscious, and corrective emotional experiences have occurred. Repression and allied defense mechanisms are no longer necessary, and psychic energy need not be dammed up. In brief, the psychoanalytic position is that a lasting cure can be effected only by making the ego deal with the unconscious conflicts it has previously warded off, and this can be accomplished only by analysis of the transference neurosis.

Some psychologists have offered a different interpretation of the transference relationship. They argue that the analyst is not the neutral figure presented by psychoanalytic theorists but a dominant, controlling figure. It is the analyst who states the basic rule ("say anything that comes to mind") and who interprets resistances and underlying feelings. It is the analyst who lays bare the client's childishness and unacceptable impulses, as well as his attempts to conceal these immaturities. It is also the analyst who reassures the client and offers him hope for the future. When confronted with such an all-powerful figure, with his potential for great good or harm, it is not surprising that the client responds to the analyst as a child would to a parent. The psychoanalytic rebuttal is that the analyst attempts to be as neutral as he can. His job is not to dominate and control but to guide the client to a better understanding of himself. His role is more of a teacher than an omnipotent parent.

It has also been argued that the analyst selectively rewards the verbalization of certain material, which has the effect of increasing its frequency of occurrence. For example, during analysis there is usually a period when sexual dreams are reported with increasing frequency. Critics suggest that this is because the analyst is especially attentive to sexual dreams, and his manner is generally more receptive when listening to them. Attention and positive regard could serve as rewards, strengthening the tendency to talk about selected topics. The psychoanalytic rebuttal is that the analyst does not direct or control free associations or dreams. He is a passive observer and recorder who does nothing more than help the client to see relationships and unconscious motivations. The material that emerges from the upper levels of unconsciousness is forced out by the pressure of psychic energy, which strives for discharge.

Ideally, the therapist is a neutral figure who neither dominates the client nor selectively elicits certain kinds of material (sexual or aggressive) from the client. However, psychoanalysts readily admit that this ideal can only be approximated, and they have given the name *counter-transference* to the therapist's *personal* attitudes (both positive and negative) toward the client. Presumably, the therapist will recognize these counter-transference attitudes and both make allowances for them and struggle to overcome them. Professional psychoanalytic recognition of this problem has made it mandatory for all recognized psychoanalysts to have undergone psychoanalysis themselves. This experience, it is believed, renders the therapist less susceptible to counter-transference and more alert to its occurrence.

Symptom Substitution

Psychoanalytic theory emphasizes that symptoms cannot be treated directly because they are caused by underlying unconscious conflicts. Freud once tried hypnosis in an attempt to suppress symptoms but found that it was not effective. Another possibility is waking suggestion, in which the client follows the therapist's recommendations in every detail. This may allow a compulsive neurotic to substitute such a *therapeutic ritual* for his everyday rituals and compulsions. This kind of substitution may lead to a temporary relief from anxiety, which lasts only so long as the client has faith in the therapist and is allowed to continue in therapy. The substitute symptom is effective in reducing tension only if it fulfills the same function as the original symptom, that is, only if it is symbolically a derivative of the basic conflict and sufficiently removed from the unconscious conflict so as not to cause anxiety.

In any event, the substitution of one symptom for another is not the purpose of psychoanalytic therapy, and it does not constitute a psychoanalytic cure. A cure requires treating the underlying cause of the symptoms. The implicit analogue is to an infectious disease accompanied by fever. If only the symptom of fever is treated, the patient may feel more comfortable, and perhaps the infection will abate. However, unless the underlying cause of the fever is treated, the symptom cure will only be temporary. Sooner or later other manifestations of the infection will appear. The psychoanalytic position is even stronger: the suppression of one symptom makes inevitable the appearance of another to replace it. Thus if the unconscious conflict is expressed in a particular compromise symptom and this symptom is removed, the conflict must be represented by a new compromise symptom.

The only way to effect an enduring cure is to treat the disease itself, which in neurosis consists of unconscious conflicts. These must be made conscious by lessening the defenses against them:

Although in analysis all methods available are used to induce the patient to lessen his production of defenses, the desired effect is more lastingly and efficaciously obtained, the more the analyst succeeds in using no other means of eliminating resistances than the confronting of the patient's reasonable ego with the fact of his resistance and the history of its origin. This confronting, bringing to the

patient the unconscious part of his resistance, also renders the resistance superfluous. (Fenichel, 1945, p. 571)

The notion of a *reasonable ego* is basic to psychoanalytic therapy. This
is the conscious, rational part of the personality that seeks adjustment of
unconscious needs to environmental pressures. When the conscious ego
understands that some of the personality's behavior is irrational, it can replace this behavior with more rational behavior. The solution to unconscious
conflicts is to make them conscious. Since the unconscious conflicts have a
history, the therapy must be historical. The childhood anxieties and guilt
must be traced back to their source, together with the repressed incidents and
associations of the childhood era. Unless this is done, any symptom relief
must be temporary.

LEARNING THEORY

The learning position is that all symptoms are learned. There is no
inner etiology corresponding to an infection because the symptom *is* the
disease. This does not mean that there are no medical models for the learning theorist. He might choose, for example, certain anomalies of the eye
that result in one eye's being better than the other, for example, the person
relies too much on his good eye and does not use the other sufficiently.
This condition is corrected both by a lens for the poor eye and by covering
up the good eye. Since the poor eye must be used, the condition is corrected
and the patch over the other eye may be removed. The symptom is nonuse
of the poorer eye, and the person is cured when this symptom is alleviated.
The therapy is remedial, and there is no need to cure an "underlying disease
process." This medical model fits the learning approach, as contrasted with
the infectious disease model which fits the psychoanalytic approach.

Moreover, the learning approach emphasizes present behavior, and the
treatment might be called *ahistorical behavior therapy*. There is no attempt
to trace back the historical roots of the neurotic symptoms for therapeutic
reasons. Of course a history is taken to determine the nature of the problem,
how it was learned, how long it has persisted, etc. This history-taking is
for diagnostic purposes only, and the behavior therapist neither probes
deeply into childhood events and attitudes nor attempts to interpret them.
The history of the neurotic symptom helps him to understand how it came
about and how it might be treated, but unlike the psychoanalyst, he does
not retrace the developmental sequence as part of therapy.

Psychoanalytic and learning therapies also differ in the specificity of
the techniques to be used with varying problems. Psychoanalytic therapy
is fundamentally the same whether the client has obsessive-compulsive or
hysteric symptoms. There are of course minor variations in the timing of
interpretations and on the emphasis given to material related to the various

psychosexual stages, but in general the basic techniques are always the same: free association, dream interpretation, and working through the transference neurosis.

Behavior therapy employs a variety of techniques that vary from one patient to the next, depending upon the nature of the problem. Three kinds of problems may be distinguished in neurotics: excessive anxiety and inhibition, incorrect or inadequate responses, and absence of responses.

Excessive Anxiety and Inhibition

Anxiety neurotics, whether they have free-floating anxiety or specific phobias, tend to be fearful in situations others can tolerate calmly. They often have histories of many painful incidents which involve the conditioning of fear to a variety of stimuli. There are two aspects to their problems. First, they suffer from the discomfort of intense anxiety: apprehension, autonomic disturbance, restlessness, and tremors. Second, their fears prevent them from making adjustive responses that would lead to the rewards and satisfactions that make life worthwhile. The goals of therapy must reflect these twin issues: to reduce anxiety and to overcome the inhibitions against appropriate responses. These goals are accomplished by conditioning a response incompatible with anxiety. The assumption is that the stronger the incompatible response, the more the anxiety response is inhibited. If the therapy is successful, the stimuli that had originally evoked an anxiety response now elicit an adaptive, non-anxiety response. This kind of therapy is called *reciprocal inhibition*.

Reciprocal inhibition therapy was devised by Wolpe (1958), one of the first and most prominent behavior therapists. The general principle underlying this kind of therapy is:

If a response antagonistic to anxiety can be made to occur in the presence of anxiety-evoking stimuli so that it is accompanied by a complete or partial suppression of the anxiety responses, the bond between these stimuli and the anxiety responses will be weakened. (Wolpe, 1958, p. 71)

This principle is a simple one: when one response precludes another, only one of the responses can be made, for example, the right arm can be raised or lowered, but not both simultaneously. The basic idea in therapy is to substitute an adaptive response that precludes the occurrence of an anxiety response.

Anxiety responses always include muscular tension. The experiencing individual usually reports being tense, and there is often a *spilling over* of tension which is seen in the form of restlessness, motor incoordination, or muscular spasms. Relaxation is a good response for therapy because it is impossible to be tense and relaxed simultaneously.

Therapy starts with the presenting situation: certain stimuli elicit an anxiety response. The process of therapy consists of conditioning a relaxation response to the anxiety-provoking stimuli, the goal being to replace mal-adaptive fear responses with adaptive relaxation responses. While this pro-cedure is simple in principle, the technique is complex in operation, requir-ing considerable skill in timing and management. The learning therapist focuses on the *details* of discrete stimulus-response relationships, and he must exercise care in controlling the strength and frequency of anxiety-provoking stimuli.

Wolpe and others have used the relaxation technique, called *systematic desensitization,* in the treatment of phobias. There are three steps in the procedure. First, a complete list of the phobic stimuli is obtained, and they are arranged on a hierarchy of intensity of anxiety. (In practice there may be several such lists but for clarity of exposition we shall discuss only the simplest case.) Second, the client is trained to relax. Third, relaxation re-sponses are conditioned to the stimuli on the anxiety hierarchy.

Wolpe (1958) has furnished this example of an anxiety hierarchy of stimuli related to fear of death, in order of decreasing intensity:

(1) first husband in his coffin
(2) at a burial
(3) seeing a burial assemblage from afar
(4) obituary notice of young person dead of heart attack
(5) driving past a cemetery
(6) seeing a funeral
(7) passing a funeral home
(8) obituary notice of old person
(9) inside a hospital
(10) seeing a hospital
(11) seeing an ambulance

This list, like all anxiety hierarchies, was derived from interviews with a client.

The most concise description of the rest of the procedure may be found in a study by Lang and Lazovik on snake phobias:

The subject is then trained in deep muscle relaxation, following the method presented by Jacobson (1938). He is further instructed to practice relaxation 10–15 minutes per day at home. In the final phase of the training period the subject is introduced to hypnosis, and an effort is made to teach him to visualize vividly hypnotic scenes.

Following training, there are 11 45-minute sessions of systematic desensitiza-tion. In this, the subject learns to respond with relaxation to stimuli that originally evoked anxiety. At the beginning of the first session the subject is hypnotized and instructed to relax deeply. He is then told to imagine the hierarchy item which he previously rated as least distressing—the smallest "dose" of anxiety. If relaxation is undisturbed by this experience, the subsequent item is presented. Items which induce small amounts of anxiety are repeated, followed by deep relaxation, until the subject reports he is undisturbed by the scene. In this way successive items are presented from session to session. The goal of treatment is the presentation of the item originally ranked as most frightening without impairing the individual's calm state. At this point a new response (relaxation) has been attached to the imagined representative of the fear inducing stimulus, and clinicans working with the method assume that it will readily transfer to actual life situations. (1963, p. 520)

Systematic desensitization, then, consists of neutralizing the anxiety-provoking stimuli by counter-conditioning a relaxation response to these stimuli. It is assumed that the client can tolerate small amounts of anxiety, an assumption common to all psychotherapies. It is further assumed that as the client learns to relax to a given stimulus, there is a weakening of the anxiety response to the more intense stimuli or the hierarchy. This assumption is based on the familiar principle of stimulus generalization. When a relaxation response is conditioned to a particular stimulus on the hierarchy, it should generalize to neighboring stimuli. Thus in the fear of death hierarchy mentioned above, relaxation conditioned to *seeing a hospital* should generalize at least to the adjacent stimuli, *inside a hospital* and *seeing an ambulance*. Any strengthening of the relaxation response weakens the anxiety response because they are incompatible.

The process of therapy consists of moving slowly up the hierarchy, weakening the anxiety response to a particular stimulus directly by conditioning and to more intense stimuli indirectly by stimulus generalization. Ultimately the client should be able to relax and therefore be nonanxious even in the presence of the most intense stimulus on the hierarchy. The actual fear stimulus need not be present. It has been found that imagining it is equivalent to seeing or touching it. Hypnosis helps to make the imagined stimuli more salient, but it is not essential.

These theoretical assumptions have been shown to work in the laboratory by Lang and Lazovik (1963), who used college students as subjects. Theirs is the only *experimental* study, complete with control subjects. They reported:

The results of the present experiment demonstrate that the experimental analogue of desensitization therapy effectively reduces phobic behavior. Both subjective ratings of fear and overt avoidance behavior were modified, and gains were maintained or increased at the six-month follow-up. The results of objective measures were in turn supported by intensive interview material. Close questioning could not persuade any of the experimental subjects that a desire to please the experimenter had been a significant factor in their change. Furthermore, in none of these interviews was there any evidence that other symptoms appeared to replace the phobic behavior. (1963, p. 524)

The conditioning of relaxation to anxiety-laden stimuli is the preferred technique when the stimuli are impersonal, but when the stimuli are interpersonal it is not sufficient to train the client to relax. He must also learn to make adaptive, interpersonal responses. The two classes of behavior most inhibited by anxiety are assertive and sexual responses. In treating inhibited assertive or sexual responses, the principles are the same as for relaxation responses. The main difference is that the hierarchy of anxiety pertains to responses rather than stimuli. Consider assertive responses. The client must be encouraged to make these responses, rather than giving way to his anxiety and inhibiting them. Initially, the therapist exhorts the client to make very mild assertive responses and suggests practicing them outside the therapy situation. When the client begins to feel comfortable as he behaves assertively, progressively more assertive responses are encouraged. Gradually, the approach (assertive) responses should replace the avoidance (inhibition) responses, and the client is free to assert himself with relatively little or no anxiety.

What holds for assertive responses also applies to sexual responses. Of course there must be appropriate modifications because of the nature of the response, especially since there can be no practicing in the therapy situation. However, engaging in sexual responses is more likely to be followed by immediate and significant rewards than the making of assertive responses. In any event, the basic procedure is the same: the making of weak responses associated with little anxiety, followed by stronger and stronger responses associated with much anxiety. The client faces only small doses of anxiety any time he initiates the appropriate behavior, and, with the support of the therapist, he is able to tolerate such small doses.

Incorrect Responses

Neurotics carry a heavy load of excess baggage in the form of incorrect and unwanted responses. Obsessive-compulsive persons may be plagued by complex rituals, muscular tics, or frightening obsessive thoughts. Anxiety neurotics and hysterics may suffer from an overflow of tensions such as seen in writer's cramp. These various responses seriously interfere with adjustment. Punishment, if applied judiciously and timed correctly, is one means of getting rid of them.

Wolpe (1954) used punishment to eliminate a food obsession in a neurotic woman who was required to maintain a restricted diet. The client was told to visualize a desirable food and raise her hand when she did so. She was then given a very strong electric shock, which was maintained until she signalled that it was no longer bearable. This avoidance conditioning was repeated at the rate of 10 shocks per session for five sessions. At that point the thought of delicious but tabooed foods filled her with revulsion, and she tended to think less about all kinds of food.

When avoidance conditioning is attempted, modifications are necessary for the various kinds of responses to be eliminated. Liversedge and Sylvester (1955) used punishment in treating writer's cramp—spasms and tremors of the hand that prevent the person from writing legibly, if at all.

> The patient was required to insert a metal stylo, held as a pen is held, into these holes, working from larger to smaller as each size was successfully negotiated. Electrical circuits were arranged so that, whenever the stylo touched the side of the holes, the patient received a shock passing from palm to dorsum of the *left* hand. (1955, p. 1148)

Two other kinds of training were employed. In one, the client was required to make movements with the stylus that are similar to handwriting movements, and he was shocked for deviating from the patterns. The other procedure used electric shock whenever there was excessive thumb pressure on a specially wired pen. These various techniques were successful in alleviating writer's cramp and restoring normal writing.

Another way to get rid of maladaptive, surplus responses is to perform them repeatedly, which presumably builds up a strong inhibition against making the response. It is assumed that the response is already at peak strength, and therefore further practice cannot increase its habit strength. Consider a tic, which is a simple, unadaptive muscular movement such as rapid eyeblinking, neck squirming, or nose twitching. Yates (1958a) has outlined the learning approach to treatment:

> According to the model, then, the tic may be treated as a simple learned habit which has attained its maximum habit strength. In terms of the theory, it should be possible, therefore, to extinguish the habit by building up a negative or incompatible habit of "not performing the tic." If the subject is given massed practice in the tic, then reactive inhibition (I_R) should build up rapidly. When I_R reaches a certain critical point, the patient will be forced to "rest" or not perform the tic. This habit ($_sI_R$) of not performing the tic will be associated with drive-reduction due to the dissipation of I_R and hence will be reinforced. With repeated massed practice, therefore, a negative habit ("not doing the tic") will be built up, incompatible with the positive habit of doing the tic. Furthermore, the repeated voluntary evocation of the tic should *not* serve to increase the habit strength of the tic, since it is already asymptotic [at a maximal level] and consequently not subject to strengthening by massed practice. (1958a, pp. 237–238)

Yates tried the technique and discovered that the best combination was prolonged massed practice followed by prolonged rest. This procedure was effective in diminishing and eliminating tics not only in the clinic but in everyday situations.

It might be argued that a tic is a minor symptom of neurosis, one that is prevalent in otherwise normal individuals, and therefore its cure by learning methods is of little importance. This argument assumes that a tic is such a *superficial* symptom that it is easy to cure. The assumption is difficult to check, but it may be noted that many of Yates' clients had been treated unsuccessfully by standard psychotherapeutic techniques, including psychoanalysis. Moreover, we cannot readily accept the idea that so-called superficial symptoms are necessarily easy to eliminate. Many non-organic speech defects are no *deeper* than tics and yet are difficult to alleviate.

Lack of Response

Hysterics are known for their tendency to stop responding; they may be unable to respond because of defects in the sensory apparatus or because of paralysis of muscles. The hysteric who "cannot see" obviously cannot be expected to respond to visual stimuli; the hysteric who "cannot move his arm" obviously cannot engage in behavior requiring the use of the arm. The therapeutic problem is to get the client to make a response that employs the sensory or motor aspect that is nonfunctional. The "blind" neurotic has to be manipulated so as to respond to visual cues, the "paralyzed" neurotic so as to respond with the "unusable" muscles. One technique for accomplishing these goals is operant conditioning. Operant conditioning consists of getting the subject to make a simple response and then rewarding him until he maintains a high rate of responding. It has been used therapeutically primarily with psychotics (for example, Ayllon, 1963), but it has also been tried successfully with neurotics.

Brady and Lind (1961) used operant conditioning as therapy for hysterical blindness, traditional psychotherapies having failed. The "blind" man's hand was placed on a button, and he was instructed to push the button every 18 to 21 seconds. If his time discrimination response was correct (in the 18 to 21 second interval), a buzzer sounded; otherwise the apparatus merely reset itself. The sessions were one half hour each, five days per week. The client was praised for good performance, criticized for poor performance. Similarly, various hospital privileges were manipulated in relation to his performance.

There were five phases in the therapy, each involving one to three weeks. *In the first phase* the client learned the time discrimination, making approximately two-thirds correct responses. *In the second phase* a dim bulb was lighted during the 18 to 21 second interval. Initially, the client became anxious, although he did not report seeing it. His performance deteriorated at first and then returned to its previous level. *In the third phase* the light was made very bright and placed directly in front of the client, who was told it would help him. Again he became anxious and his performance deteriorated. Soon he improved beyond his previous performance but still failed to "see" the light, explaining that its heat helped him. *In the fourth phase* the light was dimmed, and the client was told he would no longer feel its heat. His performance steadily improved, and he reported seeing the light. *In the fifth phase* patterns of lights were introduced, and their brightness was kept very low. The client continued to improve his time discrimination performance, and his vision outside the experimental situation began to improve. He was soon sent home from the hospital with his sight restored, and he maintained it thereafter.

Note that this procedure is analogous to systematic desensitization in that it presents a graded series of stimuli while the client continues to make a well-learned response. It differs in that no attempt is made to desensitize or minimize the client's fear of certain stimuli. The cause of the symptom is completely ignored, and the focus is entirely on removing the symptom, in this instance, hysterical blindness.

Extinction as a General Technique

Extinction of fear responses have been proposed by Dollard and Miller (1950) as a major aspect of therapy. They also proposed that other techniques were important in therapy, but we shall focus here on extinction. We must remember that they were translating psychoanalytic therapy into learning terms, which means that their major emphasis was necessarily on the client's verbalization and repression of ideas.

> By encouraging the patient to talk and consistently failing to punish him, the therapist creates a social situation that is exactly the opposite of the original one responsible for attaching strong fears to talking and thinking. The patient talks about frightening topics. Since he is not punished, his fears are extinguished. The extinction generalizes and weakens the motivation to repress other related topics that were originally too frightening for the patient to discuss or even to contemplate. (Dollard & Miller, 1950, p. 230)

The hypothesized sequence is as follows. Usually, whenever the client thinks or verbalizes certain tabooed thoughts, he becomes terrified because the thoughts have been associated with punishment. In therapy, when he verbalizes the thoughts, punishment does *not* follow. When punishment is no longer a consequence of these responses, he is free to make them without anxiety, that is, the anxiety response extinguishes.

It follows from this formulation that anxiety is a response that is not difficult to extinguish. All that is needed is to allow the instrumental response (in this instance, talking about certain topics) to occur without any ensuing punishment. After a few trials of response-without-punishment, the fear response weakens considerably. Nevertheless, as Dollard and Miller themselves have noted, fear extinguishes very slowly, if at all:

> Fear is so resistant to extinction that it is sometimes difficult to determine whether the curve of extinction will eventually reach zero or flatten off at some

constant level above zero. Sometimes it is even difficult to be certain that any extinction at all is taking place. (1950, pp. 72–73)

At first glance it appears that Dollard and Miller have contradicted themselves, but the paradox may be more apparent than real. The fear responses of humans and animals are extremely resistant to extinction, as has been shown in a variety of punishment experiments (Solomon, 1964). In these experiments an instrumental response is followed by severe punishment, and the subject learns to avoid making the response. Subsequently, the punishment is omitted, but the subject still does not make the response that has now been closely linked to fear (of punishment). The instrumental response always involves *doing something,* not *talking about doing something.* Thus what is resistant to extinction is fear associated with an instrumental, nonverbal response.

Perhaps fear associated with verbal responses is not difficult to extinguish. Reporting an impulse is obviously different from carrying out the impulse, for example, verbalizing anger versus striking another person. Thus neurotics can usually talk about their phobias but cannot make the instrumental response of approaching the feared stimulus. It follows that the fear of talking about tabooed topics is mild and can be extinguished. Psychoanalysts insist that the fear of thinking and verbalizing certain topics is so great as to induce repression. Learning theorists downgrade the importance of repression, arguing that the fear of thinking about certain ideas and memories is a mild anxiety. What really frightens people is the punishment associated with *doing,* not with *talking about doing.*

If learning theorists minimize repression and the importance of verbalizing, why do Dollard and Miller emphasize them? The answer lies in their purpose: to translate psychoanalytic theory into learning terms. They must accept the tenets of psychoanalytic therapy and therefore insist on the importance of ideas, impulses, and talk. Their immediate goals in therapy are to allow the client first to verbalize freely and then to think freely. Eventually, the client is helped to make more adaptive responses in the outside everyday world; but they insist that the client is not free to attempt such responses until the anxiety associated with talking and thinking is extinguished: "Without relief from repression and practice on the higher mental processes, the patient *cannot* try" (1950, p. 349). This is the orthodox psychoanalytic position, which insists that the goal of therapy is to make the unconscious conscious.

In light of the foregoing, what can we conclude about extinction of anxiety as a therapeutic technique? First, extinction may help clients to verbalize ideas and thoughts they are fearful of expressing; but such verbalization may be facilitated more by the therapist's urging and encouragement than by the absence of punishment. Second, extinction does not help in dealing with instrumental (nonverbal) avoidance responses such as phobias. All learning theorists agree that an individual should not be forced to approach a feared stimulus because he would panic. The anxiety would be too intense, and there would be no opportunity to perceive the lack of punishment. This notion is borne out by experimental evidence showing that fears and avoidance responses are extremely resistant to extinction. Even if there is some extinction of fears, the process is too slow to be useful in therapy. This point has not been lost on behavior therapists, none of whom use straightforward extinction as a technique of therapy. They prefer the faster and more active techniques of punishing or mass-practicing incorrect responses and conditioning of incompatible responses.

Controversial Issues

Behavior therapy contrasts sharply with psychoanalytic therapy and its derivatives. The principles and techniques of behavior therapy are not accepted by advocates of personal-interpretive therapy, and the dispute revolves around five controversial issues; the therapist-client relationship, the effectiveness of behavior therapy with "complex neuroses," the permanence of cure, symptom substitution, and the goals of therapy.

The Therapist-Client Relationship. Behavior therapists tend to deny the importance of the therapist-client relationship. This denial strongly opposes the view of virtually all psychotherapists, who insist that this relationship is essential to successful treatment. If a relationship is an essential part of therapy, it follows that what works in behavior therapy is the therapist-client relationship. This point has been made by White in referring to behavior therapy:

The therapist communicates confidence in his methods. His history-taking conveys his interest in the patient's problems, and his techniques for producing relaxation tend to strengthen a sense of trustful alliance. (1964, p. 333)

White's implication is that the relationship is crucial in therapy, and the behavorial techniques are not as important as behavior therapists believe. If this hypothesis is true, it follows that: (1) progress should be made only in the context of the relationship; and (2) the absence of conditioning procedures would be unimportant so long as the relationship were present.

Concerning the first prediction, Wolpe (1962) offered some contrary evidence in his treatment of a single case. All desensitization sessions were conducted in a mechanical manner and although the relationship was essentially ignored, progress was made. The lessening of anxiety continued when a medical student replaced Wolpe as therapist for one week and also when the sessions were held in a room filled with an audience of students. Concerning the second point, Lang, Lazovik, and Reynolds (1966) in their research on desensitization of snake phobia, employed a control group that received no desensitization. This group constructed an anxiety hierarchy, was given a *dynamic* explanation of the phobia, and was encouraged to talk about *emotional problems*. These procedures insured that there was at least as much of a relationship as in the experimental group, which in addition received desensitization treatment. The desensitization group manifested significant improvement in anxiety about snakes, but the control group remained unchanged. This well-controlled study indicates that in behavior therapy the relationship is at best a minor aspect of treatment.

  Effectiveness with Complex Neuroses. Traditional psychotherapists maintain that behavior therapy is superficial and is therefore effective only with *simple* or monosymptomatic neuroses. They suggest that only relationship therapy, in which problems are talked out, can successfully treat the complex neuroses marked by multiple and deeply entrenched symptoms; behavior therapy is not sufficiently "deep" to cope with the problems underlying such neuroses. Wolpe (1964) has suggested two reasons for these beliefs. First, behavior therapy has had outstanding success with phobias, and this has been publicized. Phobias are simpler neurotic symptoms in the sense that anxiety is clearly present and complex, indirect avoidance responses are absent. Second, behavioral analysis of cases tends to make all neurotic problems resemble phobias because of the delineation of anxiety stimuli and consequent avoidance responses. Traditional psychotherapists insist that the development of neurotic symptoms is more complicated than the simpler schemes suggested by stimulus-response analysis. One answer is that a stimulus-response analysis makes cases appear simple because it makes salient what traditional theoretical approaches tend to obscure or complicate unnecessarily.

  In any event, an empirical question remains: does behavior therapy work only with simple neuroses? Wolpe (1962) attempted to answer this question by separating his cases into simple and complex neuroses. He listed six features that render a neurosis complex:

  (1) Multiple families of hierarchies may be conditioned to neurotic reactions.
  (2) The reactions may involve unadaptiveness in important areas of social behavior ("character neuroses").
  (3) The neurosis may involve obsessional behavior.
  (4) The neurosis may have somatic consequences.
  (5) There may be continuous anxiety in addition to that which is associated with specific stimuli.
  (6) Essential stimulus antecedents of the neurotic reactions may be obscured by conditioned inhibition of associations. (1962, p. 29)

Using these criteria, Wolpe separated 86 therapy cases into 65 complex and 21 simple neuroses. His criterion of cure was improvement on at least four of the following: symptoms, stress tolerance, and adjustment at work, sex, and social relationships. Both complex and simple neuroses showed the

same rate of improvement after behavior therapy—89%. The only difference was a greater number of therapy sessions with the complex cases, which
is expected because of the greater number of symptoms. Thus Wolpe's results suggest that behavior therapy is as good for complex neuroses as it
is for simple neuroses. This conclusion is subject to the usual reservations
about the results of any study conducted by a partisan and lacking control
groups.

Permanence of Cure. If behavior therapy is superficial and does not
get at the underlying causes of neurotic symptoms, it follows that the cure
will be only temporary and relapses inevitable. The issue is whether symptoms, after having been treated successfully with behavior therapy, will reappear after a lapse of time. Although this is an empirical question, it is
not easy to answer. A number of behavior therapists have reported that
their clients have maintained their therapeutic gains for long periods after
the termination of therapy, but such reports are difficult to evaluate. The
cases are not representative, there are no controls, and the evaluation of
symptom status is obviously not objective. The only investigators to use
rigorous followup procedures were Lang and Lazovik (1963), who evaluated both therapy subjects and controls after a six-month interval. The therapy group showed a slight reduction in phobic behavior after six months,
and they were still significantly less phobic than the untreated controls. This
is only a single piece of evidence and the followup was only six months;
it is possible that a longer followup might have yielded different results.
Nevertheless, the evidence suggests that behavior therapy leads to lasting
changes. Parenthetically, the issue of permanency of cure is important for
all therapies, and the evidence concerning traditional therapies is both weak
and inconclusive.

Can the learning approach say anything specific about the reasons for
relapse? Eysenck (1963), answering in the affirmative, suggests that the
probability of relapse depends on the type of neurotic symptom and the
type of therapy. He separates symptoms into two types. The first consists
of anxiety reactions, which involve (loosely speaking) sympathetic nervous
system reactions. Phobias, for example, are classically conditioned fears: a
neutral stimulus is linked with a fear stimulus, and after conditioning the
previously neutral stimulus comes to elicit a fear reaction. The therapy of
choice for conditioned fear responses is systematic desensitization. The fear
response is extinguished, and an incompatible relaxation response is learned.
We may expect some extinction of the original fear response to occur in
every day life because occasionally the conditioned stimulus occurs in the
absence of the unconditioned fear stimulus. To the extent that there is any
extinction of the conditioned fear response, it helps therapy, which is working in the same direction. Thus the random events of everyday life should
lead to extinction that *facilitates* therapy. It follows that relapses should

be rare when the problem is an anxiety reaction and the technique is systematic desensitization. This hypothesis is borne out by reports of behavior therapists, insofar as these reports can be accepted as evidence: relapses are rare and seem to occur only when there is new fear conditioning (this of course cannot be helped because therapy cannot protect clients from all future painful events in everyday life).

The second type of symptom consists of responses that are either unconditioned (for example, bedwetting) or unwanted (for example, tics, compulsions, and obsessions). The responses in this class of symptoms are reinforced, often by a relief from tension. The preferred treatment is aversive conditioning, in which a punishment is delivered after the response is made. The therapist must exercise care in the timing of the punishment: as soon after the response as possible and before any rewarding consequences occur. Aversive conditioning is opposite to desensitization therapy, and in fact it is analogous to fear conditioning. What the client must learn is to avoid making the response because of the noxious consequences. Consider what happens after therapy has been successful. Suppose in the course of everyday life the client makes the punished response. Now there is no immediate punishment, and therefore there is some extinction of the conditioned avoidance response. Here extinction works *against the effects of therapy,* which consists of conditioning an avoidance response. It follows that relapses should be relatively frequent when the problem is an unwanted (but perhaps rewarded) response, and the therapy is aversive conditioning.

Eysenck suggests that extinction is more likely because learning stops when conditioning has barely been achieved. Let us recall the client who had obsessive thoughts of food. During therapy, whenever she thought of food, a painful shock was delivered. Once she stopped thinking of food, there was no more punishment. The conditioning lasted only until the response was suppressed, and there could be no opportunity for overlearning. This situation favors extinction.

What can be done to retard extinction and thereby prevent relapses? Eysenck suggests four techniques. The first is scheduling punishments at less than 100%. Instead of punishing every unwanted response, the therapist could punish two-thirds of them. Such scheduling has been found to slow down extinction, and it is a well-established principle. Lovibond (1963) confirmed this hypothesis with behavior therapy for bedwetting. The second technique is to avoid massed practice, which facilitates extinction: trials should be spaced over time. Third, the conditioning should be overlearned. The unwanted response must somehow be elicited and punished beyond the point where avoidance conditioning has barely been achieved. Finally, the client should return to the therapist periodically for *supportive conditioning* designed to retard the extinction process.

Whether these particular techniques are found to be successful in preventing relapses, they constitute good arguments for the learning approach to therapy. Behavior therapists maintain that their approach is better than traditional psychotherapeutic approaches because it specifies in detail the techniques to be used in alleviating symptoms. The therapy procedures, they argue, are derived from basic learning theory, which has been established and tested under the rigorous conditions of laboratory experimentation. Eysenck's application of learning principles is precisely what behavior therapists are talking about: extrapolation from the basic science of the laboratory to the applied methods of the clinic.

Symptom Substitution. The *traditional point of view* was stated earlier in the section on psychoanalytic therapy. This view assumes that neurotic symptoms are superficial manifestations of underlying intrapsychic conflicts. Treating the symptoms alone, it is argued, is like trying to cure an infection by reducing fever: it cannot succeed because the underlying cause of the symptom remains untouched. *Behavior therapy* assumes that there is no underlying disease. The symptom, which is a learned response, *is* the disease. When the symptom is removed, the disease is cured.

These two positions lead to exactly opposite predictions about the final outcome of behavior therapy. The traditional view holds that when a symptom is removed or suppressed, the conflicts underlying the symptom will produce substitute symptoms. In the end there can be no real therapeutic gain because one symptom is merely given up for an alternate symptom of the underlying neurosis (disease process). *There is no reliable evidence that this is true.* Psychoanalytic theory predicts this outcome, but psychoanalysts have not produced facts to verify the prediction. In fact, there has been a dearth of clinical reports concerning symptom substitution, and at present the notion is apparently accepted merely on faith.

The learning view holds that when a symptom is removed by means of behavior therapy, the occurrence of new symptoms is unlikely. Moreover, successful treatment of the symptom tends to set up a benign cycle: the client is no longer preoccupied with the annoying response, he tends to be calmer (at least in the presence of the stimulus situations that have been desensitized), and he is more self-assured because of a success in coping with an adjustment problem.

Behavior therapists, because they are sensitive to the charge that their "superficial therapy" necessarily leads to symptom substitution, have been especially attentive to the problem. Yates (1958b) and Rachman (1963), reviewing reports concerning the outcome of behavior therapy, concluded that there is no evidence for symptom substitution. Obviously, such clinical reports by behavior therapists are not objective, but they constitute the only evidence available. Since it is traditional therapists who insist that compensatory symptoms must occur, the burden of proof is on them. At present, such proof is lacking.

Whereas behavior therapists believe that the appearance of substitute symptoms is unlikely, they cannot deny the possibility. What would the therapist do if faced with such a symptom? Rachman (1963) has considered this eventuality:

The therapist after having desensitized the patient to the original noxious stimulus situations, if confronted with a so-called "substitute symptom" would proceed to desensitize this new symptom in turn. When this treatment has been successfully completed, the probability of recurrence is slight. It will be agreed that all neurotic symptoms in the patient have some degree of interdependence and that the weakening or extinction of any one symptom is likely to affect all the others in like manner. The symptom which is treated first is usually the most resistant. Behavior patterns treated subsequently are more easily modified. If a new symptom arises it can be expected to be of rather weaker strength and hence readily amenable to inhibition or extinction. (1963, p. 12)

Goals of Therapy. The final area of difference between behavior therapy and traditional psychotherapy concerns the goals of treatment. Neurosis, in learning terms, consists of excessive fear reactions and inappropriate responses—either because of excessive and only temporary avoidance of anxiety stimuli or because of inefficiency. Thus behavior therapy has two goals: (1) to extinguish excessive anxiety reactions and replace them with adjustive, nonanxious alternatives, and (2) to remove maladaptive instrumental responses, and, if necessary, to replace them with socially approved responses that lead to the customary rewards of everyday life.

Neurosis, in psychoanalytic terms, consists of surface symptoms that represent a compromise between opposing forces engaged in unconscious conflict. The problem is that the client is too anxious to deal with certain thoughts, and they are repressed.

Thus, the goal of analysis is to reduce the negative affect which maintains the avoidance of the ideas (repression). When this is accomplished, the thoughts will return to awareness automatically. . . . the purpose is to extend his self-awareness so that he recognizes his psychologically determined wishes, his self-evaluative thoughts, and the demands of reality, and is able to apply the power and logic of his conscious thought to the choice of an effective course of action. (Ford & Urban, 1963, pp. 161–162)

Since the lifting of repression is a basic goal, it is clear why psychoanalytic therapy must be verbal. The client is encouraged to verbalize conscious thoughts so that gradually he can become aware of and verbalize thoughts that were previously unconscious. He must be freed from repression in order to discover the *real,* unconscious bases of his conscious thoughts and actions. In the context of this formulation, it is easy to see why behavior therapy does not suffice. Such therapy does not get at the unconscious motivations that cause symptoms. Only a verbal therapy that explores the historical background of conscious feelings, beliefs, and attitudes can hope to root out and cure the basic cause of neurotic symptoms, which is unconscious conflict.

Behavior therapists reject the entire psychoanalytic formulation, and since their goals are nonverbal, their therapy is essentially nonverbal. The focus is on maladaptive instrumental responses and on the various manifestations of anxiety (motor, autonomic, and cognitive). Ideas, beliefs, attitudes, and relationship with the therapist are all secondary and kept in the background. The goal is the alteration of discrete nonverbal responses, and in this context a "talking cure" makes no sense. Thus one reason for the dispute over psychoanalytic versus behavior therapy is a difference in goals. The aims are different, and therefore the methods are different. The real bone of contention is which kind of therapy leads to *enduring* relief from neurotic symptoms. Psychoanalysts maintain that an enduring cure depends upon the lifting of repression by slow and painstaking procedures, whereas behavior therapists (believing that the symptom *is* the disease) maintain that an enduring cure depends solely on the removal or suppression of symptoms.

This issue is related to a similar one discussed in Chapter 4: the relationship between personality and neurosis. Neurosis may be defined as patterns of symptoms or as patterns of personality traits. The learning approach assumes the former definition, regarding neurotic symptoms as unnecessary behaviors which interfere with adjustment or cause discomfort. The psychoanalytic approach assumes that neurosis consists of personality faults, with symptoms being exaggerations of personality faults. Thus the psychoanalyst regards compulsions as being exaggerations of the traits that constitute the compulsive personality; the symptoms are merely superficial aspects of the "true" neurosis—the compulsive personality.

These opposing views of neurosis lead to divergent goals of psychotherapy. The learning theorist, believing the symptoms to be the neurosis, attempts to alleviate or abolish them. His goal is the disappearance of symptoms, and he is convinced that there will be no subsequent substitution of symptoms. The psychoanalyst, believing the personality deviation to be the neurosis, attempts to alter the personality. His goal is the replacement of immature personality features with mature ones. He seeks to substitute mature modes of sublimation for immature defense mechanisms. There is no attempt to treat the symptoms directly. It is the "disease" of personality disturbance that is treated, not the superficial aspects of the disease (symptoms). When the personality problem is cleared up, the symptoms should disappear because their presence is no longer motivated.

This discussion points up the importance of the model of psychopathology chosen by the clinician. The *field* model leads to direct treatment of symptoms, the goal being their removal. The *inner* model leads to indirect treatment of symptoms through treatment of personality problems, the goal being alteration of the personality.

COMMENT

The two therapeutic approaches we have been discussing represent only a fraction of the list of therapies. For example, Ford and Urban (1963) compare ten different systems of therapy, only three of which have been mentioned here—those of Freud, Wolpe, and Miller and Dollard. Thus the comparison between psychoanalytic and learning therapies cannot do justice to the variety of psychotherapies currently practiced. This is inevitable in a book of this nature, but a brief account of a phenomenological approach to psychotherapy may help to fill the gap.

One of the most popular psychotherapies today is the *client-centered* approach of Rogers (1942, 1961). He focuses on the *self,* assuming that the client's view of himself and of the world is central to adjustment. Maladjustment consists of distortions in the way events are perceived and denials of one's own experience. Rogers assumes that the need to value oneself positively is paramount. Experiences that run counter to positive self-regard lead to defensiveness and the distortions of experience that constitute maladjustment. It is painful events and experiences involving inferiority that render an individual maladjusted. If left to oneself, there is a basic tendency to *grow* and *self-actualize.*

Psychotherapy is viewed as a process of restoring experiences to awareness and of correcting distortions. Rogers insists that these changes must be undertaken by the client; the role of the therapist is relatively passive. The therapist has two functions: (1) to accept the client as he is, thereby showing *positive regard* for him, and (2) to reflect the underlying *feelings* of the client's verbalizations. These therapist behaviors are presumably sufficient to allow the client to solve his underlying problem. The basic problem is the same for all maladjusted persons: a disparity between experience and awareness, or stated another way, an excessive disparity between one's self-concept and ideal concept.

Like Freud's therapy, Roger's therapy emphasizes the client-therapist relationship, but there are differences. The client-centered approach, in common with other phenomenological and existential approaches, focuses on *identity* as the basic concept in adjustment. Rogers is unconcerned with intrapsychic conflicts, with specific neurotic symptoms, or with learning faults. The issue is not what the individual *does* but what he feels (his attitudes, thoughts, and inner experiences). Internal cognitive processes are central; all else is peripheral. Thus it is the client who must initiate change and who is responsible for what occurs in therapy. The role of the therapist is reduced to that of a passive "good person." In fact, client-centered therapy has obvious similarities to the pastoral counseling practiced by the clergy. The therapist-client relationship is important, but transference aspects are minimized.

Client-centered, psychoanalytic, and learning therapies may be considered a representative sample of the various approaches used with adults. They differ so much that we must consider the possibility that they were designed for different kinds of clients. This notion deserves consideration in light of the origins of the three theories.

Psychoanalytic therapy was first attempted with hysterics. It grew out of Freud's attempts to cope with dramatic symptoms that followed sudden, painful experiences. Freud's first clients tended to have a history of a sudden traumatic episode being followed by a sudden loss of function such as paralysis. Typically, the client could not remember the episode, which clearly indicates repression. Perhaps when a therapist is confronted with a clear instance of repression of one or several traumatic events, together with a sudden hysterical symptom, psychoanalytic therapy should be the treatment of choice. This therapy focuses on repressed thoughts and associations, and it is reasonable to assume that making the unconscious conscious should alleviate the symptoms.

Learning therapy has arisen in the context of specific complaints, especially phobias. The typical client has specific fears that need to be extinguished, and reciprocal inhibition would appear to be the treatment of choice. Similarly, unwanted responses can be eliminated by massed practice (reactive inhibition) or avoidance conditioning. Thus when the complaint is specific and circumscribed, learning therapy might be the best approach.

Client-centered therapy emerged from a college counseling clinic whose clients were predominantly young people uncertain of vocation, of life, of current relationships—in brief, uncertain of their own identities. Rogerian therapy would seem to be just right for such problems. The client is encouraged to talk about his aspirations, attitudes, self-concepts, relationships with others, and above all his uncertainties. In matters of life goals, self-concept, and vocation, the client probably should take the major responsibility. Thus, when the presenting complaint concerns identity, perhaps the treatment of choice should be client-centered therapy.

Of course proponents of each approach do not agree that their techniques are limited to certain kinds of clients. Each technique has been applied to all problems. The psychoanalyst would argue that all neurotic symptoms may be traced to intrapsychic conflict. Learning faults are superficial manifestations of underlying unconscious conflicts, and identity problems are merely reflections of disharmony between the ego and the superego. The learning theorist would argue that all neurotic symptoms consist of anxiety responses or faulty habits. This includes not only instrumental behavior but self-reactions (which can be learned by imitation). The client-centered therapist would argue that so-called neurotic symptoms and learning faults are irrelevant; the basic problem is always the same—the identity problem of a confused or distorted self-concept.

REFERENCES

Alexander, F. *Psychoanalysis and psychotherapy.* New York: Norton, 1956.

Ayllon, T. Intensive treatment of psychotic behavior by stimulus satiation and food reinforcement. *Behavior Research and Therapy,* 1963, **1**, 53–61.

Brady, J. P., & Lind, D. L. Experimental analysis of hysterical blindness. *Archives of General Psychiatry,* 1961, **4**, 331–339.

Dollard, J., & Miller, N. E. *Personality and psychotherapy.* New York: McGraw-Hill, 1950.

Eysenck, H. J. Behavior therapy, extinction and relapse in neurosis. *British Journal of Psychiatry,* 1963, **109**, 12–18.

Fenichel, O. *The psychoanalytic theory of neuroses.* New York: Norton, 1945.

Ford, D. H., & Urban, H. B. *Systems of psychotherapy.* New York: Wiley, 1963.

Jacobson, E. *Progressive relaxation.* Chicago: University of Chicago Press, 1938.

Lang, P. J., & Lazovik, A. D. Experimental desensitization of a phobia. *Journal of Abnormal and Social Psychology,* 1963, **66**, 519–525.

Lang, P. J., Lazovik, A. D., & Reynolds, D. J. Desensitization, suggestibility and pseudotherapy. *Journal of Abnormal Psychology,* 1966 (in press).

Liversedge, L. A., & Sylvester, J. D. Conditioning techniques in the treatment of writer's cramp. *Lancet,* 1955, *June,* 1147–1149.

Lovibond, S. H. Intermittent reinforcement in behavior therapy. *Behavior Research and Therapy,* 1963, **1**, 127–132.

Rachman, S. Introduction to behavior therapy. *Behavior Research and Therapy,* 1963, **1**, 3–16.

Rogers, C. R. *Counseling and psychotherapy.* Boston: Houghton Mifflin, 1942.

Rogers, C. R. *On becoming a person.* Boston: Houghton Mifflin, 1961.

Solomon, R. L. Punishment. *American Psychologist,* 1964, **19**, 239–253.

White, R. W. *The abnormal personality.* New York: Ronald Press, 1964.

Wolpe, J. Reciprocal inhibition as the main basis of psychotherapeutic effects. *Archives of Neurology and Psychiatry,* 1954, **72**, 205–226.

Wolpe, J. *Psychotherapy by reciprocal inhibition.* Stanford: Stanford University Press, 1958.

Wolpe, J. Isolation of a conditioning procedure as the crucial therapeutic factor: A case study. *Journal of Nervous and Mental Disease,* 1962, **134**, 316–329.

Wolpe, J. Behavior therapy in complex neurotic states. *British Journal of Psychiatry,* 1964, **110**, 28–34.

Yates, A. J. The application of learning theory to the treatment of tics. *Journal of Abnormal and Social Psychology,* 1958, **56**, 175–182. (a)

Yates, A. J. Symptoms and symptom substitution. *Psychological Review,* 1958, **65**, 371–374. (b)

CHAPTER 9

Symptoms of Psychosis

At first glance it would appear easy merely to list and discuss the symptoms of psychosis, but the issues involved are not simple at all. Some authorities, especially European psychiatrists delineate a large number of psychoses; for example, schizophrenia is fragmented into four, five, or six discrete and ostensibly different syndromes. Others insist that the overlap between psychoses, however few are listed, is so great as to render useless any division. They argue that it is best to think of psychosis as a unity because there are no stable and meaningful symptom clusters within psychosis.

We shall pursue a middle course, adopting the common convention of listing two psychoses: schizophrenia and affective psychosis. This decision does not solve the problem of overlap because, as we shall see, there are symptoms common to both psychoses and there is a symptom cluster falling between them. These considerations suggest that there should be good reasons for rejecting the notion of a single psychosis in favor of two; more of this later.

The listing of symptoms under particular diagnostic labels is also complicated by changes that occur during the course of psychosis. A psychosis resembles a chronic medical illness in that its duration may be measured in years and perhaps even in decades. As the psychosis runs its course, the symptom picture may be expected to change, just as the symptoms of a chronic medical illness may change. Symptoms may wax and wane; new symptoms may appear and old ones disappear; if the psychosis is prolonged, progressive deterioration may lead to new symptoms not present in the early stages of the psychosis. When "deteriorative symptoms" appear, there may be a problem in deciding their origin. Do they originate in general deterioration of psychological functions or are they due to prolonged hospitalization and the debilitation of incarceration?

Another important consideration in listing the symptoms of psychosis is that they are not all of equal importance. Recognizing this issue, Bleuler (1950) made two distinctions. The first is between fundamental and accessory symptoms. Fundamental symptoms are those that characterize the psychosis: they should be present in every case of the disorder and absent in other disorders. Accessory symptoms may be present in the particular psychosis, but they are not limited to it; they may be present in other psychoses as well. The second distinction is between primary and secondary symptoms. Primary symptoms are those thought to be basic to the psychosis; they occur early and constitute the essence of the particular psychotic reaction. Secondary symptoms are part of the individual's reaction to his psychosis; they develop because he attempts to come to terms with his changed behavior. Stated another way, after the psychotic break with reality, the individual may attempt to regain his sense of reality or at least to cope with a changed reality. Thus secondary symptoms may be regarded as restitutional, that is, attempts to restore a balance between self and environment.

Unfortunately, symptoms occur in the context of such a profusion of complicating variables (precipitating events, family background, social variables, speed of recognition of symptoms, duration of hospitalization, chronicity of psychosis) that it is difficult to decide which symptoms are fundamental and which are accessory. We can say that certain symptoms best characterize a psychosis but must then hedge by noting exceptions. Bleuler's two distinctions are worthwhile but difficult to apply in the present state of diagnostic knowledge.

THE AFFECTIVE PSYCHOSES

The affective psychoses include syndromes in which mood symptoms predominate. The major division is between mania and depression, which are included under the same heading for several reasons. First, there are patients who alternate between manic episodes and depressive episodes. They are rare, but their existence argues for a single diagnostic category. Second, both mania and depression are *mood disorders,* differing only in that they are at opposite ends of the elation-depression dimension. Third, manic behavior often appears to be a last-ditch effort to stave off depression. If depression underlies many manic episodes, then mania and depression would seem to belong together.

Mania is rare, and clinical reports suggest it is diminishing in frequency. Psychotic depression is more frequent and therefore of greater practical importance; it is also more important theoretically because of its relationships to neurotic depression and schizophrenia.

Mania

The most important symptoms of mania are in the affective and motor spheres. These two symptom spheres are almost by definition closely related in any affective disorder; one aspect of mood is the associated activity level that varies from excess energy in elation to motor retardation in melancholy.

Affective. The manic's mood is jovial, and his elation spills over into all his activities. He sees himself as the center of the universe and has a multitude of plans and schemes for bettering his own state of being and that of everyone else. There is a buoyant optimism that knows no bounds and is reflected in grandiose and pretentious projects to be started immediately.

Self-esteem is up, self-insight is down. The manic does not realize that to others he is self-exalting, pompous, conceited, boastful, and vain Yet he may be the best of fellows: gregarious, convivial, and companionable. Unfortunately, his sociability is usually carried to excess, like all else, and he becomes meddlesome and intrusive.

His sense of humor is endearing, at least for short intervals. He may be witty, his speech filled with puns and rhymes; he may be gay and mischievous, full of playful, innocuous tricks; but he may also be provocative, silly to the point of annoyance, and harmful in his playfulness. In brief, the manic would be pleasant company if he could restrain his excessive good spirits, but this annoying excess is one of the essential characteristics of mania.

Motor. The other essential characteristic is the spilling over of the euphoria into motor activity. Restlessness and excessive physical movement are so great as to exhaust the onlooker and eventually the manic himself. Everyday activities are imbued with an excitement and lack of inhibition that clearly indicate a lack of normal, adult control. The manic appears to be making a 100-yard dash through life. He is hasty and abrupt, rash and reckless, impulsive and impetuous, and, above all, excited and excitable. Activity is incessant and unending, whether it is talking, walking, singing, dancing, or exercising.

There appears to be little need for sleep, and energy supplies seem inexhaustible. Many activities are started but few finished, as the manic rushes madly through the day. In some instances there is a danger of violent behavior (aggressive or sexual) because of the lack of inhibitions and the sheer push of activity. This excess of energy is precisely the problem: it is as if the idler has been set too high, and the engine races on wildly to an overdue exhaustion.

Cognitive. The remaining symptoms, all cognitive, derive from the fundamental elation and overactivity. The manic's mad dash through everyday events is reflected in his speech and thought processes. There is a flight of ideas, the patient leaping from one topic to the next without pause and often without apparent connection. Attention is intense but brief and fleeting; it falters in the face of a continued push to move on to new stimuli. Train of thought shows the same rapidity and distractibility.

Associations may be tangential, but there is no real deterioration of thought processes as there is in schizophrenia. Rather, it is more like a phonograph record revolving too rapidly: the excessive speed makes some of it sound like nonsense. In addition, the manic is evidently under such pressure to produce rapid speech that he mouths ideas and thoughts that he might otherwise inhibit. Normals have bizarre and tangential associations as well as occasional weird thoughts and illogical ideas, but experience has taught caution in communicating them to others. We think twice about our private, idiosyncratic ideas when confronted with social reality. However, if a normal person were required to talk rapidly and incessantly, he would probably sound as bizarre as manics do.

Social reality presents an important barrier to the manic. His conceit and grandiosity lead him to make dictatorial demands, which are not obeyed by an uncooperative environment. In the face of such "stubbornness" the manic may develop delusions of grandeur in an attempt to overcome obstacles through egocentric fantasy; or he may develop delusions of persecution, seeking reasons for the "lack of cooperation." The former are commoner, and in general the delusions appear to be relatively free of hostility: plans for a new world order, for ridding the world of sin, or for inventions that will revolutionize industry.

Delusions, when present, do not have the same sharp quality as they do in schizophrenia. In fact, it is often difficult to establish a boundary between magnificent, boastful lies and outright delusions. Hallucinations are absent in mania.

Depression

Depression is more complex than mania. Like anxiety, it is not only a diagnostic label but also a symptom. In addition, some authorities distinguish subtypes of depression: simple depression, agitated depression, involutional melancholia, and postpartum depression. Others insist that neurotic and psychotic depression are continuous and difficult to distinguish in practice. Before discussing these issues, we shall explore the symptoms of depression, which occur in all four symptom spheres.

The most important symptoms of depression are in the affective and motor spheres. The symptoms are mirror images of those seen in mania: the depressive's gloom and listlessness contrast with the manic's buoyant optimism and overactivity.

Affective. The depressive's melancholia casts a dark shadow on all aspects of behavior. His facial expression is unsmiling and drawn, and the haggard look is relieved only by disconsolate weeping. Past, present, and future are reviewed through a haze of despondency. Preoccupation with former actions and feelings generates attitudes of remorse, regret, and self-blame. The everyday events of the present have no interest for the depressive; he cannot muster any enthusiam for activities and interests that now leave him bored and disinterested. His mood is blackest when he considers the future. There is no hope, only despair. His life stretches out before him like a yawning abyss of darkness, and his reactions vary from a resigned, helpless pessimism to a gloomy despair. In brief, there is no joy or color in life—past, present or future—only despondency and blackness. Whatever is experienced is painful.

Motor. The motor sphere may be regarded as simply another aspect of the affective sphere in depression. The brooding melancholy merely carries over into general activity, resulting in a sluggish, lethargic indolence. Posture is slumped, work remains undone, friends are avoided or shunned, and initiative drops to zero. In extreme cases the patient may remain motionless for several hours and appear to be stuporous. However, this extreme, like other extremes of psychosis, is rare in the present era of prompt recognition of psychopathology and the presence of energizing and tranquilizing drugs.

The only activity likely to be initiated by the retarded depressive is an attempt at self-harm. This may take various forms: tearing of the hair and clothes, self-mutilation, or suicide. Suicide, of course, occurs more frequently in psychotic depression than in any other kind of psychopathology. The most dangerous time is after a temporary lifting of melancholy and especially during the first few weeks after leaving the hospital.

This description of low activity does not apply to a group of patients labeled *agitated depressives,* who manifest many of the usual symptoms of anxiety. They frown apprehensively, wring their hands, and pace restlessly. Mood is definitely despondent, but the accompanying anxiety elevates activity level from the usual depressive retardation to the diffuse excitement of an anxiety state.

As a group, depressives have a low activity level. The agitated depressive may be tense and excited, but he does not initiate meaningful sequences of instrumental behavior. The retarded depressive appears to be too immersed in grief to initiate activity. The key word is *initiate.* Depressives can be induced to engage in meaningful activities under external pressure. Friedman (1964) reports that psychotic depressives scored as high as matched normals on the majority of a group of cognitive tasks. The patients protested that they were inadequate, hopeless, and simply too tired to take the tests; but they did take the tests. Some of the patients, while performing adequately, complained that they could not do it. Thus the depressive's deficit appears to be in self-initiated activity. If pressured, he may show no motor retardation, although his self-evaluation of his capabilities may continue to reflect his melancholy mood.

Somatic. Paralleling the diminished activity level of depression is a slowing down of body processes, especially gastro-intestinal functioning. There is a drop in gastric acidity, and both digestive tonus and motility are low. There is a loss of appetite and a consequent loss of weight. Complaints about somatic troubles are various: constipation, heaviness of the limbs, pressure in the head or chest, and feelings of energy depletion and being tired and run down. Finally, there is a severe insomnia, which includes both inability to fall asleep and waking after a few hours to remain restlessly awake for the remainder of the night.

Cognitive. There is no formal thought disorder: associations are normal, and memory, attention, and perception are intact. The commonest cognitive symptom is *depersonalization*: an awareness of a drastic change in oneself. The depressive recognizes his inability to feel, to love, and to experience pleasure, and this recognition is interpreted as a change in personality. He is not really incorrect in recognizing that a profound change has occurred, and therefore the depersonalization is mild compared to that seen in schizophrenia.

Delusions are less common, and they are restricted to three kinds. The first concerns guilt: past and present events are interpreted in such a manner that the depressive can shoulder a full burden of self-blame. He claims responsibility for all accidents, losses, hurts, and grievances; his interpretation is so distorted as to attain delusional proportions.

The second kind of delusion concerns body processes. Vague internal stimuli may be interpreted as meaning the body is disintegrating or melting away. Some patients construe a realistic digestive symptom as punishment, which of course they believe to be richly deserved. However, neither somatic nor guilt delusions occur frequently in depressives.

The last kind of delusion seen in depression is nihilistic: the patient himself or the entire world is headed for destruction and nothingness. The end is near, and there is no way to escape doom. Such gloomy predictions are consistent with the patient's despondency, and they lack the ideas of reference or complex plots that characterize paranoid delusions.

Hallucinations are rare and difficult to distinguish from normal perceptual distortions. If they occur, it is usually at night, when many normals misinterpret unusual noises or visual stimuli. Some patients see horrible faces or hear screams or accusations, but again these occur rarely in depression.

Involutional Melancholia. The label involutional melancholia has a long history. As might be guessed from the name, it refers to depression occurring during the involutional period, especially the era of menopause (change of life in women). It was originally thought to be related to the biological changes occurring during menopause. However, because research failed to provide evidence for this view, it has been discarded. Now the problems of aging that occur in the fourth and fifth decades of life are regarded as precipitating variables in neuroses and psychoses.

With the demise of the biological view of involutional melancholia, there remained the problem of assigning a place to this syndrome. There are two opposing views. One suggests that it must be differentiated from a simple psychotic depression. The other view maintains that there is no need for a separate diagnostic label and that the patients called involutional are in reality psychotic depressives.

Regarding involutional melancholia as a separate entity is a traditional position, espoused by clinicians who tend to go along with classical diagnostic practices (for example, Mayer-Gross, Slater, & Roth, 1955; Mendelson, 1959; and Gregory, 1961). The diagnosis is made on the basis of four variables:

(a) age—in the forties for women and the fifties for men.
(b) symptoms—presence of anxiety and agitation, as well as delusions, especially nihilistic delusions.
(c) prepsychotic personality—rigid, moralistic, compulsive, guarded, and hostile.
(d) history—no previous depressive episodes.

The first and last features, age and no previous breakdowns, are holdovers from the earlier views on involutional melancholia, that is, that the depression is caused by endocrine changes that occur only during the change of life. As Cameron (1963) has pointed out, the age criterion has an unfortunate flexibility. Women diagnosed as involutional depressives range in age from 35 years ("approaching the menopause") to 60 years ("delayed effects of menopause"). Men in this category range in age from 40 to 65 years, and in men there is no way of marking precisely the change of life, as there is in women. Thus the age range of involutional psychosis begins in the late thirties and ends in the middle sixties. This includes the vast majority of psychotic depressives, which are infrequent before the age of 35.

The lack of previous episodes is an important feature for clinicians in deciding on a diagnosis. However, this may be a mistake, held over from an earlier era. That an individual has not had a psychotic episode might simply mean the stresses of life were not sufficient or his resistance to them was sufficient. With increasing age, there are often severer stresses (death of friends and members of the family, business reverses, etc.), as well as a decreasing capacity (certainly physically) to cope with the environment. These two changes, in environment and in ability to adjust, begin to make themselves felt after the age of 40. It is not surprising that there is an increase in the frequency of depression beyond this age. The stresses present in the forties are also present in the fifties and sixties, decades which have their share of first episodes of depression. Insofar as these facts and arguments are correct, there is little justification for a separate entity of involutional melancholia.

The presence of a compulsive personality prior to the depressive episode is also a weak criterion. Such personalities are found in individuals labeled psychotic depressive, but not in all of those called involutional. We should not be surprised to discover that a depressive attack has been preceded by years of maladjustment. The compulsive approach to everyday life is merely one of several maladjustive patterns that might be (and no doubt are) present in a person who later has a psychotic depression.

The remaining criterion, symptoms, offers the only hope of resolving the controversy. Involutional depressives are characterized as being apprehensive, agitated, panicky, and delusional. They are contrasted with retarded depressives, who are characterized as sluggish, lethargic, unanxious, and without delusions. We saw earlier that psychotic depressives do have variable symptoms in the motor sphere (agitation or listlessness) and the cognitive sphere (delusions or no delusions). Those who insist on separating involutional melancholia from psychotic depression suggest that they approximate syndromes of agitated depression and retarded depression, respectively.

Those who do not agree with this separation (for example, Cameron, 1963) refuse to equate involutional melancholia with agitated depression. They suggest that agitation and delusions are present in patients classified as psychotic depressives and that lethargy and absence of delusions occur in patients classified as involutional melancholics.

Here the matter rests: clinical judgment against clinical judgment. However, the issue is resolvable, and there are two promising research possibilities. The first is to attempt an objective study of symptoms, using clinicians who do not take a stand on this matter, as was done by the Public Health Service in the cigarettes-cancer controversy. Patients diagnosed as involutional and as psychotic depressive could be compared for incidence of agitation and delusions. The second possibility is to employ tests, especially self-report devices, to check on differences between the two ostensibly different groups. The debate will be settled only by means of objective evidence and not by pitting clinical judgments against each other.

One other point needs to be made about involutional melancholia. Depression is not the only symptom manifested by patients having their first psychotic episode during the forties or fifties. Another prominent syndrome is that resembling paranoid schizophrenia; such delusional patients resemble schizophrenics not only in manifest symptoms but also in course and prognosis of the psychosis. These two symptom patterns may not exhaust the possibilities. For example, Wittenborn and Bailey (1952) factor-analyzed symptoms of a group of involutional psychotics and derived five different clusters of symptoms, two of which include such neurotic features as hysteria and anxiety.

Clearly, then, the involutional period of life can precipitate forms of psychosis other than depression. If involutional paranoids really do not differ from other schizophrenics, the involutional period would seem to be merely the beginning of an era of increasing stress. Under the impact of the physical and psychological changes accompanying aging, the individual would tend to succumb to any psychosis to which he had previously been disposed. Thus he might become depressed or schizophrenic. Insofar as this line of reasoning is accepted, it is an argument against separating involutional melancholia from psychotic depression.

Postpartum Depression. The depressions that occur during the months immediately following childbirth (postpartum) are in some ways similar to involutional depressions. Both involve a precipitating event related to a change in reproductive functions; both involve women, involutional depression being more frequent in women and postpartum depression, of course, being limited to women; both have been challenged as separate entities; and both are only one aspect of the psychosis that may occur, the other aspect resembling schizophrenia. Thus there are involutional psychosis with depression and involutional psychosis with paranoid features, postpartum psychosis with depression and postpartum psychosis with schizophrenic features.

As Seager (1960) has pointed out, there are three possibilities concerning the effects of childbirth: (1) no relationship to psychosis; (2) a causal relationship, with a pattern of symptoms occurring only in women and only during the postpartum period; and (3) a relationship as a stressor, which precipitates symptom patterns that might occur at any time in women or men. Seager reviewed the evidence concerning these three hypotheses and concluded that the research was either too poorly conceived (faulty design, too few subjects, no controls, etc.) or too contradictory to establish any of them. His own research yielded a definite conclusion. He matched women with postpartum psychosis and women whose psychosis did not follow childbirth. The two kinds of patients manifested essentially similar symptoms, familial background, and personalities, all of which were different from those seen in normal controls (pregnant and postpartum women). This evidence leads directly to two conclusions: (a) postpartum psychosis is no different from any other psychosis, and (b) the third hypothesis is correct, that is, childbirth acts as a stress that may precipitate a psychosis. The second conclusion is strengthened by Ryle's (1961) study of depression in an unselected sample of deliveries. He found that during the postpartum year (first year after childbirth) neurotic depressions were at one-fifth of normal frequency and psychotic depressions occurred at five times the normal rate for the age group. In brief, the psychotic depressions that occur after childbirth are no different from other psychotic depressions, and there is no need for a separate entity called postpartum psychosis.

NEUROTIC VERSUS PSYCHOTIC DEPRESSION

Neurotic and psychotic depressions are traditionally differentiated by whether there is a precipitating event. The neurotic presumably becomes depressed because of a loss, a rejection, or, paradoxically, a success (the so-called promotion neurosis) ; hence, neurotic depression is also called *reactive depression.* On the other hand, psychotic depression presumably occurs in cycles, without a clear precipitating event. The individual becomes melancholy, either gradually or suddenly—hence psychotic depression is also called *endogeneous depression.*

This distinction has been challenged by some clinicians, who claim the two kinds of depression are really not different. The issue is related to the continuity-discontinuity of neurosis and psychosis, which goes beyond the presence or absence of a precipitating event. It is the recurring question of whether neurosis and psychosis differ quantitatively or qualitatively. Concerning depression, discontinuity adherents claim four areas of qualitative difference between neurotic and psychotic depression: precipitating event, symptoms, response to treatment, and sedation threshold.

(1) *Precipitating Event.* The discontinuity position assumes that a precipitating event is present in neurotic depression but absent in psychotic depression. The implicit model being used here is: psychological cause for neurosis, biological cause for psychosis. According to this model, neurotic depression represents an over-reaction to a traumatic event. The neurosis, being determined by psychological variables, should be triggered by psychological trauma. On the other hand, psychotic depression is presumably determined by biological variables (biochemical, genetic, physiological, etc.). The depression is set in motion by cyclical biological activity, and no psychological event is needed to precipitate it.

The continuity position assumes that neurotic and psychotic depression are both caused by psychological determinants. These determinants might be stronger in psychotic depression, but both kinds of depression require a precipitating event. Therefore, the presence of such an event would not distinguish between neurotic and psychotic depression.

Clinicians are divided into continuity and discontinuity adherents, and the literature reflects this divergence. Regardless of theory, there is a practical problem: can the precipitating event be identified? Such identification requires both an excellent case history and a highly trained clinician. We may assume that most clinicians possess sufficient skill to make a reliable judgment, but case histories are notoriously unreliable. The case history is based on information from the patient or the patient's relatives, and neither source is reliable. Past events are forgotten or distorted, or were perhaps unnoticed when they occurred. These considerations suggest that the differentiation of reactive from endogenous depression solely on the basis of a precipitating event tends to be unreliable.

Perhaps in some psychiatric hospitals, those who take histories are able to surmount the difficulties just mentioned, but in most hospitals case histories are unreliable. This point is illustrated in a study by Winokur and Pitts (1964). They selected 75 patients with an admission diagnosis of reactive depression. On discharge only 12 of these patients were diagnosed as reactive depressives; 45 were labeled endogenous depressives, and the remaining 18 received a variety of diagnoses. One interpretation of these findings is that identification of precipitating events is unreliable, and therefore the reactive-endogenous dichotomy is meaningless. An alternate interpretation is that the psychiatrists making the final (discharge) diagnoses took into account not only the presence of a precipitating event but also the nature of the symptoms, the course of the illness, and the outcome of therapy.

Thus we must fall back on clinical opinion. Some clinicians insist that the reactive-endogenous distinction can be made on the basis of the presence or absence of a precipitating event, but others deny it. In research to be cited below, patients have been separated into reactive and endogenous depressives, which suggests that the distinction can be made. However, it can be argued that some of the reactive patients might have been psychotic and some of the endogenous patients, neurotic. Thus two questions need to be answered in a controlled study: can the reactive-endogenous distinction be made reliably, and if so, is it parallel to the neurotic-psychotic dichotomy?

(2) *Symptoms.* Continuity adherents state that a psychotic depression is merely a more severe neurotic depression. Discontinuity adherents, admitting the quantitative difference in depth of depression, claim that psychotic melancholy has a bizarre quality, whereas neurotic depression is essentially the same as normal mourning. This emphasis on *qualitative* differences is typical of the discontinuity position, which also stresses the presence-absence dichotomy. For example, Roth (1959) suggests that neurotic depression has a strong anxiety component that is usually missing in psychotic depression. Gregory (1961) and Kiloh and Garside (1963) have compiled lists of features that differentiate the two kinds of depression, and a composite list is shown in Table 9.1.

In discussing this table, we must bear in mind that neurotic behavior is usually understandable and not very different from normal behavior, whereas psychotic behavior is often bizarre and incomprehensible. In neurotic depression the melancholy is appropriate to the event being mourned; there are no delusions, diurnal variations, or guilt; concentration is intact;

TABLE 9.1.   CLINICAL FEATURES OF NEUROTIC VERSUS PSYCHOTIC
DEPRESSION

Feature	Neurotic Depression	Psychotic Depression
1. quality of depression	normal despondency	abnormal melancholy
2. variability of depression	much	little or none
3. delusions	absent	sometimes present
4. depersonalization	absent	present
5. anxiety component	strong	weak
6. neurotic components (hysteria, obsessive compulsiveness, etc.)	strong	weak
7. diurnal variation	none	worse in morning or evening
8. concentration	intact	poor
9. guilt	none or insincere	intense remorse
10. reaction to self	pity	pitiless
11. weight loss	variable	invariable
12. constipation	variable	invariable
13. health	usually poor	good except during episode
14. precipitating event	clear and strong	absent or weak
15. family history of depression	absent	present

the individual feels sorry for himself; there are often other neurotic symptoms; and while health is poor, there is no marked change in eating habits or digestion. The table suggests that there are neither feelings of depersonalization nor an anxiety component. However, as we shall see later in the chapter, feelings of depersonalization do occur in neurotics. Furthermore, anxiety is part of the clinical picture seen in agitated depression. Thus depersonalization and anxiety are not differentiating features of neurotic versus psychotic depression.

In psychotic depression the melancholy is so profound as to be bizarre, and its depth varies only slightly, being worse in the morning or evening[1]; delusions are present, and there is a loss of concentration; intense guilt is accompanied by pitiless hostility toward the self; health, which is usually good, becomes poor; appetite is poor, digestion is impaired, and weight loss is invariable.

Although some of the differences in Table 9.1 are quantitative, taken together they establish *patterns* that dichotomize depression into neurotic

---

[1] Hall et al. (1964) found that more than half of a sample of psychotic depressives were worse either in the morning or in the evening, but treatment eliminated these diurnal variations.

and psychotic forms. This conclusion is not accepted by some clinicians (for example, Ascher, 1952) who insist that the ostensible differentiating features do not work in psychiatric practice.

(3) *Response to Treatment.* The continuity argument is as follows. If psychotic (endogenous) depression and neurotic (reactive) depression are on a continuum, it is obvious that the former is severer. If psychotic depression is severer, it follows that treatment should be less successful in psychotic depression than in neurotic depression. In brief, the effects of treatment should be continuous, not discontinuous.

There have been three kinds of treatment for depression. The most popular and most successful has been electroconvulsive shock therapy, although there is no good or widely accepted explanation for its success. Roth (1959) divided a patient sample into reactive and endogenous depressions on the basis of presence versus absence of a precipitating event. The response to shock therapy was significantly better for the endogenous patients, as may be seen in Table 9.2. These results are supported by similar findings reported by Roberts (1959a) and Rose (1963). Roth (1960), in discussing these differential effects of shock therapy, pointed out that they were incompatible with the continuity position. If neurotic depression were merely a milder form of psychotic depression, why should the prognosis with shock treatment be worse?

One possible answer is that neurotic depressives are helped less by treatment. However, this possibility involves a paradox that is difficult to accept, namely that there is a better prognosis for psychosis than for neurosis. Moreover, there is evidence that other kinds of treatment are beneficial to neurotic depressives. Psychotherapy is known to be moderately effective with reactive depressives but totally ineffective with endogenous depressives. Furthermore, antidepressant drugs have differential effects. It would take us too far afield to discuss pharmacological treatment of depression, but one study will illustrate the point. Roberts (1959b) administered *methyl amphetamine,* an energizing drug, to neurotic and psychotic depressives. The symptoms of most of the neurotics were markedly improved, but those of virtually all the psychotics intensified. These results are in the opposite direc-

TABLE 9.2.   RESPONSE TO ELECTROCONVULSIVE THERAPY
(From Roth, 1959)

	Total	Symptom Free	Marked Improvement	Slight Improvement
endogenous depression	64	45	12	7
reactive depression	21	3	9	9

tion to those found with shock therapy, but both the drugs and the electric shock results have one point in common: qualitative, not quantitative differences between endogenous and reactive depressives.

Response to treatment does seem to differentiate two groups of depressives. Perhaps the reactive-endogenous issue is less important in this context than some investigators believe. It is possible that the presence of precipitating factors does not distinguish neurotic from psychotic depression but that the two forms of depression are discontinuous. Forrest et al. (1965) have shown that endogenous and reactive depressives (classified by the criteria of Kiloh & Garside, 1963) do not differ in either previous depressive episodes or adverse social factors prior to illness. Yet, on the basis of their clinical experience, these authors suggested:

. . . there is a group of depressive illnesses characterized by clinical severity, advancing years, the presence of guilt and retardation, and a satisfactory response to imipramine. (Forrest et al., 1965, p. 251)

This description appears to fit psychotic depressives, and, as such, it supports research previously mentioned. Thus the evidence concerning response to treatment indicates that there is a dichotomy between neurotic and psychotic depression, not a continuity.

(4) *Sedation Threshold.* Shagass and his co-workers have devised a technique of measuring the threshold of sleep induced by sedation (Shagass & Naiman, 1956; Shagass & Jones, 1958). Sodium amytal is administered until the subject's speech becomes slurred or his electroencephalograph (EEG) pattern changes to a sleep pattern. The dependent variable is the amount of drug per body weight required to induce sleep. A small amount of drug indicates a low sleep threshold; a large amount indicates a high threshold.

Normals were found to have a low threshold, and the threshold increases with increasing anxiety through the following neuroses:

hysteria
mixed neurosis
phobia
obsessive-compulsive neurosis
neurotic depression
anxiety state

Thus the more severe the neurosis is (in terms of increasing anxiety), the higher the sleep threshold. However, psychotic depressives were found to have a *lower* threshold, and, in fact, all psychotics had an average threshold roughly the same as that of normals. Shagass and Jones (1958) reported that a distribution of the thresholds of neurotics depressives showed virtually no overlap with the distribution of the thresholds of psychotic depressives.

These findings have been questioned by Martin and Davis (1962, 1965). They had considerable difficulty in deciding when a subject's speech was sufficiently slurred to indicate sleep, and they found no differences in thresholds among normals, reactive depressives, and endogenous depressives. Ackner and Pampiglione (1959) also encountered difficulties in determining sleep thresholds by means of speech slurring or brain wave patterns. They too failed to replicate Shagass' findings.

Boudreau (1958) also had difficulty in determining sleep thresholds, but he replicated Shagass' findings with depressives. Perez-Reyes et al. (1962) had little difficulty in determining thresholds by means of both EEG patterns and galvanic skin response (GSR). They found significantly higher thresholds in neurotic depressives than in psychotic depressives, as did Perris and Brattemo (1963) with the EEG sedation threshold.

These discrepant results yield no clear conclusion. It is possible that some investigators are more skilled with the technique, and they can determine thresholds reliably enough to discover real differences between neurotic and psychotic depressives. Another possibility is that the technique is fundamentally unreliable, and some investigators, without being aware of it, are allowing their knowledge of the subject's status to influence their assessment of his sleep threshold.

If the positive findings are sustained by further research, they constitute evidence for the discontinuity position. Consider the relationship between severity of neurosis (intensity of anxiety) and threshold: the severer the neurosis is, the higher the threshold. If there is a continuity between neurosis and psychosis, with the latter being more severe, it follows that the threshold should be higher in psychoses. The findings are precisely opposite: psychotic depressives and psychotics generally have *lower* sedation thresholds. If the data are reliable, this break in continuity supports the discontinuity position.

FACTOR ANALYTIC STUDIES

It is appropriate to end this section on depression on a research note, and we shall examine three large scale studies. Wittenborn (1964) has been examining a population of depressed women whose upper age limit is prior to the change of life. His battery includes a number of tests and experimental tasks, but our interest here is limited to clinical ratings and self-reports, on the basis of which he has extracted seven factors:

(1) no interest in appearance, pleasure, or friends
(2) obsessive, anxious, hopelessness
(3) retardation in interpersonal situations

(4) despondency and negative self-evaluation
(5) a combination of manic and depressive symptoms
(6) somatic complaints
(7) impaired appetite

These factors, which include the symptoms mentioned earlier, are independent,[2] that is, they do not cluster to form a syndrome such as agitated depression (which would be a combination of numbers 2, 4, and 6). However, the presence of so many independent dimensions may be due to the relative youth of these female patients. The peak frequencies of depression are in the forties and fifties, whereas most of Wittenborn's patients, being premenopausal, must be in their thirties or early forties. What is obviously needed to clear up this issue is a study that compares symptoms in depressives of different ages.

The other two research programs were conducted in Chicago (Grinker, Miller, Sabshin, Nunn, & Nunnally, 1961) and in Philadelphia (Friedman, Cowitz, Cohen, & Granick, 1963). Grinker et al. studies an unselected group of neurotic and psychotic depressives. Their factor analysis yielded four patterns:

(1) dismal hopelessness, loss of self-esteem, slight guilt feelings, isolation, withdrawal, apathy, slowed speech and thinking
(2) hopelessness, low self-esteem, much guilt, high anxiety, agitation, clinging demands for attention
(3) feelings of abandonment and loss of love, agitation, demands for attention, hypochondria
(4) gloom, hopelessness, anxiety, demands for attention, anger, and provocativeness.

The first two factors contain familiar clusters of symptoms, the first being retarded depression and the second, agitated depression. The third factor appears to be a possible combination of psychotic depression (hopelessness, gloom) and neurotic features (demands for attention, hypochondria). The fourth factor is an unusual combination of some of the symptoms in the first and third factors, and the pattern may be specific for the particular sample of patients.

The Friedman et al. (1963) research involved a more homogeneous group: age range 37 to 79 years, with no neurotic or schizophrenic features. They had so few patients under 45 years that they were led to suggest that psychotic depression is an illness of middle and old age.

They extracted four factors from ratings on 22 variables:

[2] Wittenborn used an *orthogonal* solution deriving factors. An *oblique* solution would have yielded correlated factors which might have clustered together to yield such a syndrome as agitated depression.

(1) retarded, withdrawn, apathetic
(2) guilty, loss of self-esteem, self-doubting, and psychological internalizing
(3) loss of appetite, sleep disturbance, constipated, work inhibition, loss of satisfaction
(4) hypochondriacal, self-preoccupied, demanding, complaining, and irritable.

Again the first two factors are recognizable as retarded and agitated depression, respectively. The third factor consists of the various secondary effects of melancholy that are present in most psychotic depressives. The fourth factor corresponds to the whining, complaining syndrome found by Grinker et al. Since the patients of Friedman et al. were all psychotics, this hypochondriacal-irritable syndrome cannot be attributed to a mixture of neurotic and psychotic features. Rather, it may be a third pattern of psychotic depression, which should be sought after by clinicians. Thus there may be three separate syndromes within psychotic depression:

retarded
agitated
complaining - hypochondriacal

SCHIZOPHRENIA

The number of symptoms that have been labeled schizophrenic is so large as to bewilder the student. Fortunately, there is fair agreement on the major symptoms, although no two authorities list identical symptoms as being fundamental. Bleuler (1950) believed that there were four fundamental symptoms: association, affect, autism, and ambivalence. The last two are rejected as being fundamental by most authorities, and there is some doubt about the first two. Should we attempt to specify fundamental symptoms? Mayer-Gross, Slater, and Roth deny the value:

It is demanding too much to hope to find one fundamental psychological disturbance underlying all symptoms, especially if there is doubt whether the present concept of schizophrenia does not comprise several diseases. At the present state of our knowledge all that can be done is to group the *essential psychological abnormalities* as they affect the different mental functions. . . . (1955, p. 231)

Cognitive

The most important and the most salient symptoms of schizophrenia are those in the cognitive sphere, and there are five varieties: disturbances of language and thought, disturbances of the self, autism, hallucinations, and delusions.

Disturbances of Language and Thought. Most schizophrenics show a basic disturbance in their manipulation of symbols and as a result their verbalizations deviate from those of normals. Part of the problem is perceptual; they do not perceive stimuli in the same way as the rest of us. This is especially evident in performance on the Rorschach Ink Blots. When a response is determined by the form (shape) of the ink blot, it is possible to compare it with norms for a good response. Schizophrenics tend to make a relatively large number of poor form responses, that is, the responses do not correspond well to the form of the ink blot. In other words, schizophrenics tend to have perceptual distortions of the stimuli around them.

Concerning the thinking process itself, Bleuler, using association theory, has provided us with an excellent description:

In the normal thinking process, the numerous actual and latent images combine to determine each association. In schizophrenia, however, single images or whole combinations may be rendered ineffective, in an apparently haphazard fashion. Instead, thinking operates with ideas and concepts which have no, or a completely insufficient, connection with the main idea and should therefore be excluded from the thought-process. The result is that thinking becomes confused, bizarre, incorrect, abrupt. Sometimes all the associative threads fail and the thought chain is totally interrupted; after such "blocking," ideas may emerge which have no recognizable connection with preceding ones. (1950, p. 22)

The blocking referred to by Bleuler is responsible for the gaps and jumps in schizophrenic speech. The speech would be understandable if we were supplied with the missing associations, but these associations are simply not available. Bleuler suggested that they are "split off," and this splitting is the basis for the name he gave to the condition, *schizophrenia.*

Associative disturbances are widespread in schizophrenia, resulting in speech patterns that are strikingly deviant. For example, there are clang associations, in which word sequence is determined solely by rhyme (hole-mole, red-bed, hang-sang). In normals there is some control or inhibition of such associative sequences, so that thought and speech are determined mainly by grammatical and logical requirements. In schizophrenics there is at least a partial loss of this control, leading to the intrusion of bizarre and illogical associations into thought and speech. Thus thoughts unconnected except that they occur simultaneously may be expressed together or in immediate sequence. With logical control lost or damaged, it is as if the associations proceeded down paths of their own, unfettered by the requirements of logic or the need to communicate with the listener. It is not so much that the schizophrenic can understand the speech and thoughts that we cannot but that he is unable to restrain the direction of this association. The combination of bizarre associations and blocking of associations thus produces schizophrenic speech, which ranges from slight peculiarity at best to *word salad* at worst.

Disturbances of the Self. Everyone develops a sense of his own body in relation to the surrounding world. The infant learns during the first year of life to distinguish between "me" and "not me." Beyond this gross differentiation, there develops a sense of one's own body: the inner noises, the kinesthetic feedback of muscles contracting, the size of the limbs and trunk, and a feeling of one's own weight. These various phenomena have been grouped under the heading of *body image,* and a disturbance of body image is one of the frequent manifestations of schizophrenia.

The schizophrenic may feel too light or too heavy. Objects around him may appear too close or too distant, or they may seem to be part of him rather than distinct from him. There may be sensations of numbness or of special sensitivity and tingling. Body parts may seem too large or too small, together with difficulty in attaining coordination, especially in sequential movements. Angyal (1936) described five kinds of body image disturbances which he believed were due to kinesthetic (muscle sense) dysfunction and a general loss of self-awareness:

(1) Impairment of the unity of the body—
    body does not seem to stay together
    falling apart
    head and neck do not connect
(2) Continuity of the body-self impaired—
    body is continuous in space
    body is empty, only a frame
    food falls into a vacuum
    sensations of emptiness
(3) Reduction of body dimensions—
    chest and back touch each other
    feeling of flatness
(4) Displacement of parts—
    arms creeping into chest
    head sinking into body
(5) Parts not alive—
    skin papery
    parts of body are wood

He noted that these symptoms occurred only infrequently among schizophrenics and then mainly in the more severe and deteriorated schizophrenics (hebephrenics and catatonics).

Schizophrenics generally show deficit in sensorimotor functioning. The kinesthetic disturbances just mentioned are only part of a larger malfunction of perception and coordinated movement, which will be described in more detail in a later chapter. However, one perceptual anomaly should be noted in passing: changes in the sense of smell. Schizophrenics reported that their own body odor is more noticeable and more unpleasant, that other people smell stronger, and that food and objects smell funny (Hoffer & Osmond, 1962). These olfactory symptoms, which are not hallucinations but distortions of smells that are present, are part of the changed self of the schizophrenic, and they must seem as bizarre to him as the kinesthetic changes.

Bruch (1962) ascribes distorted body concepts to contradictory and inappropriate responses to stimuli originating within the child.

If failure of confirmation of child-initiated behavior is severe and extends to many areas, to body sensations as well as to higher mental functions, the outcome will be an individual who lives chiefly by responding to stimuli coming from others, without awareness of and reliance on his processes. Bodily sensations, thoughts, feelings are experienced as originating in the outside. Such an individual will have a defective sense of self-effectiveness and will be lacking in initiative and spontaneity. This deficit in self-experience is a prerequisite for later schizophrenic development. (1962, p. 24)

In brief, many schizophrenics experience a distortion of body image, the precise symptoms varying from one patient to the next. These distortions, which must be experienced as weird and inexplicable changes in the most basic aspects of the self, are frightening, and it is not surprising that many schizophrenics are panicky and apprehensive for reasons that escape the unaware observer.

The changes in body image may be responsible for the other aspect of disturbances of the self, *depersonalization*. This is a cognitive symptom like delusions but involving body image and perception of self rather than beliefs or explanations. Most normal persons have had the experience at some time of feeling strange and different. These are transitory phenomena in normals, who accept their rare occurrence as being due to such variables as lack of sleep, a hangover, excessive eating, or illness. The schizophrenic finds it difficult to accept the sensations of change so easily, perhaps because the change is more intense and more bizarre. The few autobiographies of schizophrenics that are available reveal that suddenly the patient's entire world seems changed. Everyday events appear in a new light, everyday objects seem strange, and one's own body does not feel the same anymore.

Bleuler attributes the sudden change to changes in the pathways of associations: the old familiar associations no longer occur with their usual regularity and are replaced with novel and unusual associations. Many schizophrenics assume that they have lost their former selves and have taken on a new identity. In fact they may change their names and reconstruct a new history for themselves; some patients believe that they are now someone else and attempt to assume the name and characteristics of the other person.

In the face of depersonalization, the schizophrenic may react in two different ways. The first method was just described: an attempt to adjust to the change by altering behavior patterns and accepting the new perceptions. A second mode of reaction is not to accept the change but to fight it. This latter mode is associated with a better prognosis; the patient has a better chance of making at least a minimal social adjustment if he struggles to maintain his identity in the face of the perceived changes in his body and environment.

Some authorities believe that depersonalization and distortions of body image are crucial signs of schizophrenia. This belief is reasonable because of the apparent bizarreness of the symptoms. Reality starts with the self, and if the patient's contact with reality is so tenuous that his own person seems unreal or distorted, then surely he must be schizophrenic. This view is merely an extension of the traditional clinical approach to these deviant symptoms. This approach implicitly assumes that disturbances of the self are absent in normals, neurotics, and perhaps even all nonschizophrenics. This assumption can be checked empirically, but only in the last few years has the necessary evidence been collected. A number of investigators have questioned the traditional clinical view and have sustained their doubts with data.

Sedman and McKenna (1963) found that only six out of a sample of 54 schizophrenics manifested depersonalization. Depersonalization is a prominent symptom in depressives with compulsive personalities but not in manics or depressives with "normal personalities" (Sedman & Reed, 1963). Dixon (1963) reports that nearly half of a sample of college students have depersonalization experiences of the following types: self-estrangement, persons or objects appearing unreal, feelings of body change or distortion, self-detachment, and feelings of change in self-identity. Roberts (1960) reports similar findings: depersonalization in 23 of 59 college students.

Concerning body image, schizophrenics have been found both to *overestimate* the size of body parts (Cleveland, Fisher, Reitman, & Rothaus, 1962) and underestimate body parts (Fisher & Seidner, 1963). The latter authors failed to find reliable differences in body image distortions between neurotics and schizophrenics:

. . . not even sensations of depersonalization, which have long been thought to have serious portent, distinguish the disturbed from the nondisturbed. (1963, pp. 256–257)

Fisher (1964) continued his investigation, this time using a Body Experience Questionnaire consisting of nine kinds of items:

(1) body too large
(2) body too small
(3) loss of body boundaries
(4) body dirty or contaminated
(5) body openings blocked
(6) unusual skin sensations
(7) depersonalization
(8) body change
(9) miscellaneous

Schizophrenics were compared with their normal relatives and with severe neurotics. Neurotics and schizophrenics did not differ significantly on any of the items or on the overall score, but both groups of patients showed significantly more body image disturbance than normals. Schizophrenics and neurotics failed to show more deviance on several items, including depersonalization, which led Fisher to conclude:

> There is now good support for asserting that depersonalization experiences are not more common in psychotic patients than in normal subjects who are undergoing unusual stress. This is indeed a surprising finding. It stands in contradiction to the anecdotal literature. (1964, p. 526)

This recent research echoes Angyal's thirty year-old statement (1935) that disturbances in body image occur in only a small minority of schizophrenics, usually those with the severest symptoms. The next step is to discover precisely *which* schizophrenics have a disturbed body image. This should be done by means of objective laboratory techniques rather than subjective techniques (interviews and questionnaires).

Three laboratory techniques are available. Bennett (1956) used the Rod and Frame task, which assesses perception of the vertical. The rod is inside the frame, and both are tilted. The subject is asked to adjust the rod to a vertical position in the absence of other cues (the room is darkened). Bennett found that schizophrenics without body image disturbance performed similarly to normals; psychotics (mainly schizophrenics) with body image disturbance were markedly different from normals, manifesting deviations in perception of the vertical. This task appears to be an excellent technique for obtaining objective data on body image.

The other techniques are more recent. Traub and Orbach (1964) have devised an adjustable mirror which can be distorted to produce bizarre reflections. The subject stands seven feet from the mirror and adjusts its surface (by using control knobs) until he sees an accurate reflection of himself. The amount and pattern of distortion can be measured in physical terms, yielding an objective measure of body image distortion.

Arnhoff and Damianopoulos (1964) presented male subjects with seven photographs of bodies, with no clothing, facial, or situational clues. One of the photographs was the subject's own body, and he was asked to pick it out. All 21 college students made correct identifications, but only 9 of 24 schizophrenics made correct identifications. As the authors point out, the technique will have to be used with nonschizophrenic patients to determine whether body image disturbances are severer in schizophrenia.

Research with objective techniques should validate or refute the following hypotheses. First, perceptual changes in the "body sense" may occur in certain kinds of schizophrenics and not in others, for example, in catatonics and hebephrenics but not in paranoids. Second, depersonalization may be the individual's response to *any* sudden change in his environment. Perhaps schizophrenics perceive more changes in their environment and therefore feel more changed than normals. This leads to the third hypothesis, that schizophrenics may experience the same distortions as normals but more frequently. A fourth possibility is that there are qualitative differences, schizophrenics having different *kinds* of body image changes than normals. Finally, the difference may reside in the individual's reaction to depersonalization: does he regard it as a transient and unimportant change in himself (normal) or a fundamental, permanent change in himself and the environment (schizophrenic)? These are issues for future research to decide.

Autism. Autism refers to a retreat or detachment from reality, together with an overvaluation of one's own thoughts and fantasies. It is basic to normality that the individual maintain a clear separation between his interpretations of events and a social consensus concerning these events. In other words, normal persons realize that there may be a discrepancy between their wish-fulfilling fantasies and the world as it is (that is, as it is defined by the appropriate reference group). Not only is the discrepancy recognized, but the normal suits his actions to reality, no matter how distasteful reality may be. The schizophrenic, on the other hand, only vaguely perceives a discrepancy between his fantasies and reality. Insofar as the two are in conflict, he avoids reality and predicates his actions on his own idiosyncratic, private thoughts and ideas.

The rejection of reality in favor of one's own fantasy varies from one schizophrenic to the next, and patients may be placed along a continuum of contact with reality. For some patients there are two "realities": socially defined reality and their own fantasies and misinterpretations. Such patients usually have difficulty in distinguishing between the two and may, for example, believe that a hallucinated person really exists. Other patients can maintain the separation more clearly but tend to give more credence to their autistic "reality" than to the reality recognized by normals.

Hallucinations. Hallucinations are responses to sensory inputs where the sensory inputs are absent. The patient behaves as though there were visual objects, sounds, smells, and tastes, but actually these stimuli are not present. What the patient is usually responding to is his own fantasy, the demands of his imagination superseding his real sensory inputs. Thus patients do not usually hallucinate meaningless patterns of stimuli, as often occurs with *illusions*. They see other people, animals, or familiar objects; they hear voices or music; they feel prickly or burning sensations; they smell sweet or distasteful odors. In brief, whereas illusions are based on mistakes of the sensory apparatus, hallucinations are based on the *confusion* of fantasied stimuli with stimuli that ordinarily impinge on sense receptors. Since the contents of fantasy are usually meaningful and personal it is not surprising that hallucinations are usually both meaningful and intensely personal. For example, a common hallucination is that of hearing condemning voices, shouting out the patient's guilt for real or imagined sins.

Auditory hallucinations are the commonest type in schizophrenia, which might be expected because thinking is so closely related to speech. Small children often talk aloud while thinking, but gradually they learn to inhibit the vocal components of thought. The inhibition is rarely complete, and most adults at one time or another "talk to themselves." For example, a tennis player may instruct himself to throw the ball higher when serving, and the instruction is often not only thought but mumbled. At a more covert level, the employee about to ask his boss for a raise usually rehearses "in his head" the speech he is about to make. One way of verbalizing guilt is to report the demands of "the small, still voice of conscience."

The normal individual thus operates so as to make auditory hallucinations likely were he to become psychotic; but the normal knows that the voices are not only in his head but also that they are imaginary. The mild psychotic realizes that the voices are in his head but believes they are real; he hears them. The severe psychotic not only knows that the voices are real but attributes them to other people, real or imagined. In brief, the clarity of the hallucination is a clue to the severity of the psychosis.

Another common type of hallucination is visual, but the frequency depends upon the kind of schizophrenic. Among patients who are in good contact with reality, who know where they are, and what time it is, visual hallucinations are rare. But in confused patients who are at least mildly disoriented, visual hallucinations are fairly common (Bleuler, 1950). Hallucinations of taste, smell, and touch are rarer. This order of decreasing frequency parallels a decreasing degree of interpersonal involvement of the senses. The commonest type of interchange between people is by means of speech; next is interchange by observing each other; the other senses are relatively unimportant in social interaction. Thus the more the sense modality is used in dealing with others, the more likely it is that a hallucination will occur in its sphere.

One of the more unusual cognitive symptoms of schizophrenia is the "Lilliputian hallucination" (Lewis, 1961). The patient sees or hears miniature persons or objects. The persons may be clearly defined and engaging in group activity; they may be vague, indistinct, and localized inside the body; or they may be clearly defined single individuals comparable to the imaginary companions of normal children.

Delusions. A delusion is an unshakable personal belief that is obviously mistaken or unreal, a belief which directs a significant aspect of the individual's behavior. The belief is an attempt to explain events or interpersonal relations of importance to the individual, but it is incorrect on both logical and realistic grounds. The explanation fits an already held distorted view of self and others. Thus when a patient believes he has considerable talents, failure of the world to recognize them is attributed to persecution by specified or unspecified persons. Since the mistaken belief is rooted in such a strong cognitive system as the self-image, it cannot be shaken by mere logic or a consensus about the nature of reality. Delusions do not occur in normals because they retain a firm grasp of reality, but schizophrenics have definite autistic tendencies, which lead them to favor their own fantasy over distasteful reality. Thus one basis of delusions is autism.

The definition of a delusion as a *personal* belief excludes group, professional, or religious beliefs that persist in the face of logic or contrary evidence. There are some religious sects who take the Bible literally and maintain that the earth was formed in six ordinary days; there have been scientists whose belief in the *ether* as a propagator of light and sound waves was unshakable. Such explanations cannot be labeled delusions without running the risk of branding every incorrect explanation as delusional. Therefore a persistent misinterpretation must tend to be unique rather than shared by a group, if it is to be called delusional.

Finally, the belief must have some consequences for the individual's behavior. Most people have their "dreams of glory" along the lines suggested by Thurber in his Walter Mitty story, but we cannot accuse most of the population of being delusional because they have wish-fulfilling fantasies. Normals can distinguish fantasy from reality and therefore do not act on the basis of fantasy. The delusional patient acts on his fantasied beliefs and misinterpretations: he tries to escape from his fantasied pursuers or carry out his grandiose schemes. Thus a mistaken belief becomes a delusion only when it organizes and directs a significant portion of the individual's behavior.

Delusions may be classified into types on the basis of content. The most recent attempt to discover the relative frequency of the various types of delusions is that of Lucas, Sansbury, and Collins (1962). Of a sample of 405 schizophrenics of both sexes, 71% were found to be delusional. *Of the remaining patients,* 35% had such serious thought disorder that it was impossible to tell whether they had delusions or not, and 16% were mute. Thus the overwhelming majority of schizophrenics were delusional.

The relative frequencies of delusions were as follows:

paranoid	71%
grandiose	44
sexual	44
religious	21
hypochondriacal	20
inferiority	12

Note that a given patient might have more than one type of delusion, and the percentages add up to considerably more than 100%. The most popular delusions are paranoid, a label that includes delusions of persecution, reference ("the television messages are being directed at me, personally"), and influence ("my behavior is being controlled by another person's thought waves"). Almost three out of four patients with delusions had paranoid delusions. If the presence of paranoid ideas means that the patient is a paranoid schizophrenic, then approximately three out of four patients with delusions should have been so diagnosed. Some clinicians classify patients in just this fashion, which probably accounts for the predominance of paranoid schizophrenia over the other three types (catatonic, hebephrenic, and simple). However, many clinicians, noting that paranoid delusions may occur together with other symptoms (for example the silly giggling typical of hebephrenics), are reluctant to use the paranoid schizophrenia label solely because paranoid delusions are manifest.

Grandiose and sexual delusions were the next most frequent, reflecting the importance of self-esteem and sexual impulses in adjustment and maladjustment. Religious delusions occurred in only one out of five patients. It may be speculated that this relatively small incidence is a manifestation of the waning importance of religion in the training of children and in everyday life, a diminution that has been noted by many observers of recent history in Western culture.

Lucas et al. also related the presence of different types of delusions to age, sex, marital status, and social class. Religious or supernatural delusions were more frequent in patients of higher social status and in single, rather than married, patients. Grandiose delusions were more frequent in patients of higher social class, and delusions of inferiority were more frequent in patients of lower social class. Paranoid delusions varied with age of onset: the later the psychosis occurred, the more frequent were paranoid ideas. Sexual delusions occurred more frequently in women than in men and more frequently in married than in single patients.

Affective

As noted in an earlier chapter, there is confusion about the meaning of *affect,* and it is necessary to specify what kind of affect is meant in listing it as a symptom sphere. In manic and depressive psychoses the affect dimension is elation to depression, and in anxiety neurosis it is panic to apathy. Some theorists have also included rage as an affect. Concerning the latter two, anxiety and rage, the schizophrenic often has both. He may be extremely fearful, and his irritability may reach the proportions of rage. What is peculiar about these emotional states in schizophrenia is that they are inappropriate. The patient may be fearful of someone attempting to help him or enraged at someone who is merely in the same room. The emotional states are not related to realistic situations but to fantasies, hallucinations, and misinterpretations.

The major dimension of affect is the one that ranges from elation to depression, and it is here that the schizophrenic suffers a basic inadequacy. There is a relative absence of joy or sadness that is called "blunting of affect." A schizophrenic may describe harrowing life experiences or the details of a somatic delusion ("my insides are rotting away") without displaying signs of worry or melancholy. This emotional apathy is seen most clearly in the later stages of schizophrenia. In the early stages of the psychosis, the schizophrenic may still have some emotional involvement, some degree of appropriate affective response to the ups and downs of everyday life. The early schizophrenic can still experience some joy over good fortune, some sadness over misfortune, but gradually these mood reactions disappear. Eventually, affects such as these are severely blunted or entirely wiped out.

Even in the early stages of the psychosis there may be an affective disturbance. The early schizophrenic is capable of becoming anxious or even of panicking, but there is often a relative inability to enjoy the rewards of everyday existence. It is not so much that life depresses the schizophrenic but that it leaves him apathetic, and it is believed that this emotional dullness is present from the very beginning in schizophrenia. Some authorities believe this deficiency in affective response may be a basic component in schizophrenia, leading to progressive withdrawal from others. When an individual is indifferent or unable to respond emotionally to the rewards of social interaction, he might as well avoid social contacts, which have negative as well as positive aspects.

Motor

Symptoms in the motor sphere are among the most bizarre that occur in schizophrenia, and there are three kinds. The first kind includes a variety of silly behaviors: giggling, wild laughter, facial grimaces, and stereotyped postures. The schizophrenic with these symptoms conforms to the popular notion of what an insane person is: wild, unpredictable, incoherent, out of contact with reality, nonsensical, and in brief, "crazy." In some instances there is loss of control of elimination and inability to eat unaided.

The second kind of motor symptoms varies in activity level, with only the polar extremes being manifested. There may be great excitement, wild flailing, and an expenditure of energy comparable to that seen in mania; the difference is that schizophrenic excitement is seemingly unrelated to reality and makes no sense to the observer. The manic-like behavior has no apparent source in preceding events and is unaccompanied by joy or optimism; it is often dangerous, resulting in destruction and harm.

At the other extreme of activity level is immobility. The patient may stubbornly resist the impact of any stimuli, remaining mute and apparently uncomprehending of his environment. Often this negativistic withdrawal resembles an unconscious stupor, except that the patient is obviously awake although unable or unwilling to interact at all with the people or objects around him.

The third kind of motor symptom is social withdrawal. The schizophrenic tends to avoid interpersonal situations, evidently preferring to remain isolated. This "shut in" tendency often characterizes the schizophrenic's adjustment long before the appearance of other (especially cognitive) symptoms. He appears to fear social situations because of a fear of harm, either to himself or by himself.

Types of Schizophrenia

Four types of schizophrenia are traditionally delineated: simple, hebephrenic, catatonic, and paranoid. The symptoms of *simple* schizophrenia are insidious withdrawal from social interaction, poverty of thought (no hallucinations or delusions), and a profound apathy and lack of emotional reponsiveness.

The *hebephrenic type* is marked by one of the three kinds of motor symptoms described above: silliness, giggling, and generally childish and foolish behavior. There is also a pervasive deterioration of thought processes which is manifested in incoherent speech, neologisms (made-up words), and bizarre associations. Hallucinations are a prominent symptom, and delusions may also occur.

The *catatonic* label applies mainly to patients manifesting the second kind of motor symptoms: the extremes of activity level. Catatonics are either mute and stuporous or dangerously excited and manic. They share the hebephrenic's propensity for hallucinations and, to a lesser extent, delusions.

The *paranoid* type, which is more homogeneous than the other three, includes only cognitive symptoms. Paranoid schizophrenia is defined by the presence of delusions, which vary in clarity, organization, and comprehensiveness. Some patients have only vague ideas of reference; others have a crystallized misinterpretation of life around them. Some patients spin delusions limited to themselves or their bodies; others generate themes of great inclusiveness, for example, world destruction fantasies. In addition to delusions, hallucinations may also be present. However, paranoids rarely manifest the deterioration of thought and behavior seen in the other three types. This marks paranoid schizophrenia as a somewhat different type, a point to which we shall return in the next chapter.

At one time the prevalent view was that these four types constituted separate disease entities, and there are some today, mainly European psychiatrists, who maintain this view. However, it has long been recognized that the types show considerable overlap even in their definition. Besides, patients may shift symptom patterns from one type to another during the course of schizophrenia. Because of both the overlap and the change in symptoms with time, it is acknowledged that the various types cannot be clearly and consistently separated. As we shall see in the next chapter, there are better ways of classifying the heterogenous patients diagnosed as schizophrenic.

The Course of Schizophrenia

Arieti (1955) has distinguished four successive stages that merge into one another. The first stage, *anxiety*, starts with panic, the patient being perplexed and frightened. This is followed by psychotic insight and an attempted resolution of new perceptions and bizarre sensations. The resolution results in the proliferation of new symptoms. For example, the patient may decide that he has lost his identity because he is being controlled by the thought waves of another person.

Arieti calls the second stage *advanced*. Now the patient has accepted his disorder and has become apathetic. Affect becomes blunted and there is a massive withdrawal from social interaction. Many patients remain at this stage for the rest of their lives. In the third stage, *preterminal*, there is a fading of symptoms, and it is difficult to distinguish the subtypes of schizophrenia. Regressive habits, such as the hoarding of food or worthless objects, begin to appear. In the fourth, *terminal*, stage the patient's behavior is completely dominated by primitive habits. He grabs at food and tends to place objects in his mouth; eventually there may be partial anesthesia.

It is necessary to add that many patients who start to follow this sequence do not complete it but remain at the second stage or vacillate between schizophrenic episodes and relatively symptom free periods. Furthermore, in these days of more prompt recognition of schizophrenia and various drug therapies, patients tend to be discharged from mental hospitals more quickly. It is widely recognized that the environment of the typical "back ward" of a mental hospital is conducive to a generalized withdrawal from ordinary social activities, together with a deterioration of thought and behavior. With quicker recognition and drug treatment of schizophrenia, the sequence described by Arieti is becoming rarer.

As schizophrenia runs its course, the symptom patterns often change, as they do in any illness, and this is one of the great difficulties in diagnosis. For example, the childhood disease of measles has obvious and classical symptoms: red spots on the body, face, and in the mouth, together with fever and feelings of discomfort. Once these clear-cut symptoms appear, the diagnosis is easy, but there are two kinds of complications. First, some children have only a mild case of measles, the intensity and clarity of all the symptoms being diminished. In these instances the diagnosis is based as much on known exposure to carriers of measles and the presence of measles in the immediate geographic area as on the presence of a specific symptom pattern. Second, and more important in the present context, in the early stages of measles the symptoms are usually mild and diffuse. The child may simply feel unwell and have a mild fever but not show the crucial red spots. Diagnosis is difficult until the disease proceeds further in its course, and the classical signs become manifest.

The problems in schizophrenia are similar. First, some schizophrenics show only minimal symptoms, and it is possible that they have only a mild form of the disease. They present diagnostic difficulties because the classic signs are either absent or so slight that they are difficult to detect.

Second, and more important, symptoms usually change during the course of schizophrenia. It requires only a few days for the classical symptoms of measles to become manifest because the course of the disease is measured in days; it may require months or years for the classical symptoms of schizophrenia to become manifest because the course of the disease is measured in months and years. Furthermore, as in any disease, there are wide individual differences in the symptom picture, not only in severity of symptoms but also in their manifest pattern.

In brief, the changes in symptoms that occur in schizophrenia with the passage of time are analogous to changes that occur in many diseases. This does not render the concept of schizophrenia less useful or the classification unreliable. Physicians find the diagnostic concept of *cancer* useful, although it includes a variety of symptom patterns; certainly schizophrenia is no more diffuse a concept than is cancer. The point to remember is that the clearest diagnostic signs typically appear only when a disease has run at least part of its course. The classical signs are often absent in the early stages, which creates serious diagnostic difficulties. Those who advocate discarding schizophrenia as a diagnostic term fail to see that the points first mentioned apply as well to most physical diseases, whose diagnostic labels are unquestioned, as they do to schizophrenia.

Schizophrenia versus Mania and Depression

There are similarities and areas of overlap between schizophrenia and the affective psychoses, and consequently there are problems of differential diagnosis. Some schizophrenics are depressed, others excited; some manics and some depressives have delusions or hallucinations. The various mixtures of symptoms of schizophrenia and the affective psychoses have led some authorities to suggest abandoning any attempt at diagnosis. This position is extreme, and it ignores the values (especially prognostic) of diagnosis, whatever the faults of the diagnostic classification. The problem that confronts us here is to delineate differences where superficial similarities appear.

Affective. The schizophrenic typically has one of two kinds of affective symptoms. He may be apathetic, detached, unresponsive, and in general devoid of the joys or sorrows that most people have; or he may respond with inappropriate affect: extremely abrupt mood swings within hours and for no apparent reason, or silly giggling and gesturing.

In contrast, the depressive shows a consistent melancholic mood that is the opposite of emotional apathy. He is deeply despondent and usually preoccupied with apprehension and misery. The manic is consistently elated, optimistic, and grandiose. Thus while there are mood symptoms in both schizophrenia and the affective psychoses, it is usually possible to distinguish between them.

Excitement. Catatonic excitement and mania are superficially similar. However, catatonic excitement is periodic, blindly impulsive, and without the elation and ideational content of mania. In fact, in catatonia there is a poverty of ideas and speech is repetitious. In mania there is verbal productivity, at least some planfulness, and a verbal content of speech that indicates some ideational activity. Manic excitement is more prolonged and is associated with a happier mood and with fewer hallucinations than catatonic excitement.

Cognitive. In schizophrenia the major symptoms are cognitive: incoherence, hallucinations, delusions, ideas of reference and loose associations. In the affective psychoses, however, cognitive symptoms are minor and secondary. Delusions are infrequent and hallucinations are rare. The manic may resemble the schizophrenic during a period of flight of ideas, but his accompanying excitement, rapid speech, and joviality clearly identify him. An important source of diagnostic confusion is the presence of delusions (especially somatic delusions) in both schizophrenia and psychotic depression. In some instances the delusions are so pronounced or other cognitive features are so clear that the patient must be labeled "schizo-affective."

Prognosis. It is obvious from the foregoing exposition that there are diagnostic problems in differentiating between schizophrenia and the affective psychoses, especially depression. The presence of a borderline group, called schizo-affective psychosis, further attests to flaws in the classification scheme. Since it is troublesome in some instances to maintain the separation, we may ask if it is worth the effort. The answer is that the effort would be worthwhile if there were meaningful differences in prognosis.

It is a long-standing clinical belief that the prognosis is relatively good in psychotic depression and relatively poor in schizophrenia. Clark and

TABLE 9.3   CLINICAL STATE DURING FOLLOW-UP OF THREE
KINDS OF PSYCHOTIC PATIENTS
(From Clark & Mallett, 1963)

	Schizophrenic	*Schizo-affective*	*Depressive*
symptom-free	11%	18%	34%
admitted to hospital	72	53	20

Mallett (1963) report evidence consistent with this belief. They followed up psychotics for three years after discharge from a mental hospital. The majority were diagnosed schizophrenic or depressive, the minority schizo-affective. The results are shown in Table 9.3.

This table demonstrates markedly different prognoses for schizophrenia and psychotic depression. A greater percentage of depressives than schizo-phrenics were symptom free, and a smaller percentage of depressives had to be readmitted to a mental hospital. For both variables the schizo-affective group occupied an intermediate position.

The follow-up diagnoses were also interesting. After three years 96% of those originally diagnosed schizophrenic were again diagnosed schizo-phrenic. Of the original depressives, 67% were again diagnosed as depres-sive and 27% as schizophrenic. Of the original schizo-affectives, 56% were diagnosed as schizophrenic, 22% as depressives, and 22% as schizo-affective.

Thus the results of this study indicate that the diagnoses of schizo-phrenia and psychotic depression are meaningful. The presence of schizo-phrenic symptoms means that the prognosis is poor, and the presence of depressive symptoms means that the prognosis is relatively good. When both kinds of symptoms are present (schizo-affective psychosis), the prognosis is intermediate. Furthermore, the presence of affective symptoms evidently complicates the formulation of a reliable diagnosis. When depressive symp-toms are absent, as in the diagnosis of schizophrenia, patients are rediag-nosed after three years with 93% consistency. When depressive symptoms are present, this consistency drops to 67%. The schizo-affective label, being a mixture, has the least consistency over a three-year period.

Involutional and Postpartum Psychoses

Earlier in the chapter we discussed the relationship of psychotic de-pression to both involutional depression and postpartum depression. Some authorities regard involutional depression as being different from depressions occurring earlier in life, but the arguments for similarity of the two appear to be stronger. Concerning postpartum depression, there seems to be no doubt that it is no different from any other kind of depression.

Involutional and postpartum psychoses are of course not limited to de-

TABLE 9.4   CONDITION ON FOLLOW-UP OF 83 POSTPARTUM
PSYCHOTICS
(From Brew & Seidenberg, 1950)

	Schizophrenics	*Psychotic Depressives*
committed to hospital	67%	39%
home against advice	14	9
much improved or recovered	19	52

pressions; they also include schizophrenic symptoms, especially delusions.
Thus the same question arises for schizophrenia that arose for psychotic
depression: are the symptoms occurring in involutional and postpartum
psychoses sufficiently different to warrant a separate diagnostic category?
The answer here is more clear-cut than it is for depressions. There is no
valid reason for distinguishing among schizophrenia, involutional psychosis,
and postpartum psychosis when there are frankly psychotic symptoms of
a nondepressive nature. The symptom patterns are not different, nor is the
prognosis.

A study by Brew and Seidenberg (1950) supports these conclusions.
They followed up 83 women who were diagnosed as postpartum schizophrenics or psychotic depressives. The results are shown in Table 9.4. The
figures correspond to known differences in recovery rates for schizophrenics
and psychotic depressives. As we saw in Table 9.3, depressives have a
better prognosis. The onset of a psychosis just before or after childbirth
evidently does not affect prognosis. Postpartum schizophrenics have the
same symptom patterns and prognosis as other schizophrenics; postpartum
depressives have the same symptom patterns and prognosis as other psychotic
depressives.

COMMENT

As we indicated early in the chapter, merely listing the symptoms of
psychosis raises several complex issues. Concerning neurotic and psychotic
depression, there is controversy over whether they are continuous or discontinuous. The disagreement centers on evidence from four areas: precipitating event, pattern of symptoms, response to treatment, and sedation
threshold. Continuity adherents view the evidence in these areas as indicating only minor differences between neurotic and psychotic depression;
the slight differences are seen as quantitative, not qualitative. Discontinuity
adherents interpret the evidence as indicating clear and qualitative differences between neurotic and psychotic depression. The strongest continuity
evidence concerns the presence of a precipitating event; there appears to
be little or no difference between neurotic and psychotic depression in
whether an incident triggered the symptoms. The strongest discontinuity

evidence concerns response to treatment; neurotics and psychotics respond differentially to various methods, the difference being qualitative. Thus the controversy remains deadlocked, and we can only hope that research on prognosis, treatment, and laboratory techniques (such as sedation threshold) will resolve it.

A complicating variable is time. Like any other event, depression progresses from inception to termination. Patients may start with an acute phase, move to a chronic phase, and then change to a recovery phase. The *depth* of the depression may be the same at the beginning as at the end, but other variables might be different. Thus sedation threshold and pattern of (nondepressive) symptoms might be different in the acute phase from the recovery phase. Diagnosis is usually static, being based on brief observation of a patient, together with a report (history) of the complaint. We know that patients change over time, and perhaps this change is a source of disagreement among investigators. One sample of depressives might consist of predominantly recent admissions who are acute cases, perhaps having their first episodes; another sample might consist of predominantly longer-stay cases, perhaps having their third or fourth episode or being in the more chronic phase of depression. Thus different investigators may be comparing depressives who differ markedly on a number of dimensions because of differences in the phase of depression. The time variable should certainly be investigated or at least controlled.

The issue of time is also important in schizophrenia. As Arieti has pointed out, there are sharp differences between a schizophrenic in the acute or *anxiety* stage and one in the chronic or *advanced* stage. The acute stage presents a special problem for diagnosis. Many schizophrenics are morbidly fearful when they first recognize their own bizarre cognitive symptoms. This morbid anxiety—a fear of going or being crazy, of being hospitalized, or of dying—may be confused with depression. These patients subsequently lose their intense anxiety, and the more typically schizophrenic symptoms become manifest; the diagnosis is then easy. Thus a small proportion of schizophrenics are diagnosed as depressive psychotics on their first admission to a hospital, only to be correctly diagnosed on subsequent admissions.

Time also affects delusions. Many schizophrenics show only rudimentary and vague delusions early in the psychosis, but as time passes the delusion may crystallize into a definite form that remains unchanging for years. Disturbances of thought also proliferate over time, the chronic patient usually manifesting severer symptoms than the acute patient.

Thus the symptoms of psychosis tell only part of the story. There are several dimensions of considerable importance in understanding psychosis. Some of them are dimensions of symptoms and some are not. They will be discussed in the next chapter.

REFERENCES

Ackner, B., & Pampiglione G. An evaluation of the sedation threshold test. *Journal of Psychosomatic Research,* 1959, **3**, 271–281.

Angyal, A. The experience of the body-self in schizophrenia. *Archives of Neurology and Psychiatry,* 1936, **35**, 1029–1053.

Arieti, S. *Interpretation of Schizophrenia.* New York: Brunner, 1955.

Arnhoff, F. N., & Damianopoulos, E. N. Self-body recognition and schizophrenia. *Journal of Genetic Psychology,* 1964, **70**, 353–361.

Ascher, E. A criticism of the concept of neurotic depression. *American Journal of Psychiatry,* 1952, **108**, 901–908.

Bennett, D. H. Perception of the upright in relation to body-image. *Journal of Mental Science,* 1956, **102**, 487–506.

Bleuler, E. *Dementia praecox or the group of schizophrenias.* New York: International University Press, 1950.

Boudreau, D. Evaluation of the sedation threshold test. *Archives of Neurology and Psychiatry,* 1958, **80**, 771–775.

Brew, Mary F., & Seidenberg, R. Psychotic reactions associated with pregnancy and childbirth. *Journal of Nervous and Mental Disease,* 1950, **111**, 408–423.

Bruch, Hilde. Falsification of bodily needs and body concept in schizophrenia. *Archives of General Psychiatry,* 1962, **6**, 18–24.

Cameron, N. *Personality development and psychopathology.* Boston: Houghton Mifflin, 1963.

Clark, J. A., & Mallett, B. L. A follow-up study of schizophrenia and depression in young adults. *British Journal of Psychiatry,* 1963, **109**, 491–499.

Cleveland, S. E., Fisher, S., Reitman, E. E., & Rothaus, P. Perception of body size in schizophrenia. *Archives of General Psychiatry,* 1962, **7**, 277–285.

Dixon, J. C. Depersonalization phenomena in a sample population of college students. *British Journal of Psychiatry,* 1963, **109**, 371–375.

Fisher, S. Body image and psychopathology. *Archives of General Psychiatry,* 1964, **10**, 519–529.

Fisher, S., & Seidner, R. Body experiences of schizophrenic, neurotic and normal women. *Journal of Nervous and Mental Disease,* 1963, **137**, 252–257.

Forrest, A. D., Fraser, R. H., & Priest, R. G. Environmental factors in depressive illness. *British Journal of Psychiatry,* 1965, **111**, 243–253.

Friedman, A. S. Minimal effects of severe depression on cognitive functioning. *Journal of Abnormal and Social Psychology,* 1964, **69**, 237–243.

Friedman, A. S., Cowitz, B., Cohen, H. W., & Granick, S. Syndromes and themes of psychotic depression. *Archives of General Psychiatry,* 1963, **9**, 504–512.

Gregory, I. *Psychiatry.* New York. W. B. Saunders, 1961.

Grinker, R. R., Miller, J., Sabshin, M., Nunn, R., & Nunnally, J. C. *The phenomena of depressions.* New York: Hoeber, 1961.

Hall, P., Spear, F. G., & Stirland, D. Diurnal variation of subjective mood in depressive states. *Psychiatric Quarterly,* 1964, **38**, 529–536.

Hoffer, A., & Osmond, H. Olfactory changes in schizophrenia. *American Journal of Psychiatry,* 1962, **119**, 72–75.

Kiloh, L. G., & Garside, R. F. The independence of neurotic depression and endogenous depression. *British Journal of Psychiatry,* 1963, **109**, 451–463.

Lewis, D. J. Lilliputian hallucinations in the functional psychoses. *Canadian Psychiatric Association Journal,* 1961, **6**, 177–201.

Lucas, C. J., Sansbury, P., & Collins, Joyce G. A social and clinical study of delusions in schizophrenia. *Journal of Mental Science,* 1962, **108**, 747–758.

Martin, Irene, & Davis, B. M. Sleep thresholds in depression. *Journal of Mental Science,* 1962, **108**, 466–473.

Martin, Irene, & Davis, B. M. The effect of sodium amytal on autonomic and muscle activity in patients with depressive illness. *British Journal of Psychiatry,* 1965, **11**, 168–175.

Mayer-Gross, W., Slater, E., & Roth, M. *Clinical Psychiatry.* Baltimore: Williams & Wilkins, 1955.

Mendelson, M. Depression: The use and meaning of the term. *British Journal of Medical Psychology,* 1959, **32**, 183–192.

Perez-Reyes, M., Shands, H. C., & Johnson, G. Galvanic skin reflex inhibition threshold: a new psychophysiologic technique. *Psychosomatic Medicine,* 1962, **24**, 274–277.

Perris, C., & Brattemo, C. E. The sedation threshold as a method of evaluating anti-depressive treatments. *Acta Psychiatrica Scandinaivca,* 1963, **39**, Supplementum 169, 111–119.

Roberts, J. M. Prognostic factors in the electroshock treatment of depressive states. I. Clinical features from history and examination. *Journal of Mental Science,* 1959, **105**, 693–702. (a)

Roberts, J. M. Prognostic factors in the electroshock treatment of depressive states. II. The application of specific tests. *Journal of Mental Science,* 1959, **105**, 703–713. (b)

Roberts, W. W. Normal and abnormal depersonalization. *Journal of Mental Science,* 1960, **106**, 478–493.

Rose, J. T. Reactive and endogenous depressions—response to E. C. T. *British Journal of Psychiatry,* 1963, **109**, 213–217.

Roth, M. The phenomenology of depressive states. *Canadian Psychiatric Association Journal,* 1959, **4**, S32–S54.

Roth, M. Depressive states and their borderlands: classification, diagnosis and treatment. *Comprehensive Psychiatry,* 1960, **1**, 135–155.

Ryle, A. The psychological disturbances associated with 345 pregnancies in 137 women. *Journal of Mental Science,* 1961, **107**, 279–286.

Seager, C. P. A controlled study of post-partum mental illness. *Journal of Mental Science,* 1960, **106**, 214–230.

Sedman, G., & McKenna, J. C. Depersonalization and mood changes in schizophrenia. *British Journal of Psychiatry,* 1963, **109**, 669–673.

Sedman, G., & Reed, G. F. Depersonalization phenomena in obsessional personalities and in depression. *British Journal of Psychiatry,* 1963, **109**, 376–379.

Shagass, C., & Naiman, J. The sedation threshold as an objective index of manifest anxiety in psychoneurosis. *Journal of Psychosomatic Research,* 1956, **1**, 49–57.

Shagass, C., & Jones, A. L. A neurophysiological test for psychiatric diagnosis: results in 750 patients. *American Journal of Psychiatry,* 1958, **114**, 1002–1010.

Traub, A. C., & Orbach, J. Psychophysical studies of body image. I. The adjustable body-distorting mirror. *Archives of General Psychiatry,* 1964, **11**, 53–66.

Winokur, G., & Pitts, F. N., Jr. Affective disorder: I. Is reactive depression an entity. *Journal of Nervous and Mental Disease,* 1964, **138**, 541–547.

Wittenborn, J. R. Depression. In B. Wolman (Ed.) *Handbook of clinical psychology.* New York: McGraw-Hill, 1965.

Wittenborn, J. R., & Bailey, C. The symptoms of involutional psychosis. *Journal of Consulting Psychology,* 1952, **16**, 13–17.

CHAPTER 10

Dimensions of Psychosis

The last chapter described the symptoms of psychosis and discussed diagnostic issues that have divided clinicians who have attempted to group the symptoms into clusters or syndromes. The present chapter looks at psychotic symptoms and behaviors from a different vantage point. Now the search is for dimensions along which symptoms, psychotic patients, or both can be aligned.

The exposition includes two kinds of dimensions. The first are those derived from factor analysis, which is a statistical tool of potentially great power in the discovery of how symptoms and behaviors cluster. The second are dimensions believed to be associated with prognosis, and these cut across both diagnostic groupings and dimensions derived from factor analysis. Onset is one such dimension. Two patients may have the same cluster of symptoms and therefore be included in the same diagnostic class, but because of differences in the onset of psychosis, their prognoses may differ markedly. Thus a discussion of factorial and prognostic dimensions is needed to round out our understanding of the symptoms of psychosis.

FACTOR ANALYTIC RESEARCH

Factor analysis of psychotic symptoms has a short history, virtually all the research having been conducted since 1950. Wittenborn (1964b) whose factor analysis of depressive symptoms was mentioned in the last chapter, has been an active investigator. He has demonstrated that although male and female patients have similar symptom clusters, there are some sex differences. A number of other factor analysts deserve mention, but the scope of our review is necessarily limited to a series of studies by one group of investigators.

This section is based on a book, *Syndromes of Psychosis,* by Lorr, Klett, and McNair (1963), who reviewed most of the previous factor analytic research and added major contributions of their own. Building on their own and others' previously defined factors, Lorr et al. identified ten factors of psychotic symptoms and demonstrated meaningful relationships among them. Then they used statistical similarity indices to delineate six patient types and identified the dimensions underlying these types by further statistical procedures.

Ten Psychotic Factors

Lorr et al. (1963) identified ten factors (or syndromes) that emerged from their own work and were consistent with the research of other investigators.[1] Each of the factors appeared in at least three or more studies. This cross-identification indicates stability of symptom clusters, and we may anticipate that some of the clusters (factors) will be similar to those mentioned in the last chapter.

Hostile Belligerence.[2] The patient verbalizes resentment and hostility. He is irritable, annoyed easily, and given to complaining. He is suspicious, disdainful, and critical of others.

This factor, which emerged from interviews and observations of psychotics, is not specific to psychosis, for it has been identified in research with normals. The Hostile Belligerence factor is virtually identical to a Hostility factor identified in a factor analysis of college students' responses to the Buss-Durkee Inventory (1957). The Hostility factor included the Resentment and Suspicion scales, whose items are highly similar to the characteristics of Hostile Belligerence.

The fact that there is a hostile component in the behavior of normals does not lessen the importance of this component in the behavior of psychotics, who are undoubtedly more hostile than normals. It does follow that there should be no *isolated* symptom pattern that consists solely of hostility, that is, recognizable and repeated clusters of psychotic symptoms will always include hostility *plus* another factor, never hostility alone.

Paranoid Projection. The patient has delusional beliefs in general and the following in particular: people are influencing, persecuting, conspiring against, and talking about him. Lorr et al. believe that this syndrome evolves from Hostile Belligerence, the resentment and suspicion developing into delusions that others are attempting harm.

---

[1] Bostian, Smith, Lasky, Hover, and Ging (1959); Degan (1952); Guertin (1952, 1961); Lorr, Jenkins, and O'Connor (1955); Lorr, O'Connor, and Stafford (1957); Lorr, McNair, and Klett (1962); Raskin and Clyde, 1963; Wittenborn (1951, 1962); and Wittenborn and Holzberg (1951).

[2] The names of the factors are those of Lorr et al. (1963).

Lorr (1964) attempted to test this sequence of hostility—blaming others—delusions. He reasoned that if the sequence did occur, then a patient with late symptoms (delusions) would also show early symptoms (hostility). It was necessary to demonstrate a "simplex" model: stages of increasing complexity, each state including symptoms present in earlier, simpler stages. Using statistical means too technical to describe here, Lorr showed that the following eight items lined up in order of increasing severity (from early to late in the sequence) :

hostile attitude
verbalized hostility
resentment
blames others
persecuted
conspired against
controlled by people
controlled by forces

Grandiose Expansiveness. The patient has marked feelings of superiority and hears voices praising him. There are beliefs of special abilities and a divine mission. Lorr et al. hypothesize that some paranoids resolve their delusions of persecution by assuming special powers or a special mission, and their "enemies" are either jealous or opposed to the mission. However true this may be, it is obvious that this factor also includes the symptoms of mania: self-exaltation, inventions or plans to save the world, and an optimistic manifest destiny.

Excitement. The patient is overactive, and his speech is loud, boisterous, hurried, and excessive. Elated mood and little or no emotional restraint are accompanied by superiority feelings and attention-seeking behavior. These characteristics appear to be the emotional and motor counterparts of the cognitive symptoms that define Grandiose Expansiveness. A combination of the Excitement and Grandiose Expansiveness corresponds well to the description of mania given in the last chapter.

Anxious Intropunitiveness. This factor is a combination of anxiety and depression, which fits the typical symptom picture of agitated depression. The patient has vague fears and specific worries. He tends to blame himself, lacks self-esteem, and feels sinful and guilty. Although he has insight into his problems, he is depressed and upset by recurring thoughts.

Retardation and Apathy. The patient's speech is slow, his voice is low, and he is unresponsive to questions. His movements are slow, and motor activity as a whole is at a low ebb. He appears lethargic and indifferent to his surroundings, and his facial expression is bland and unchanging. This pattern applies to the symptoms seen in two diagnostic categories: retarded depression and catatonic schizophrenia. We must remember that these factors cut across the classical diagnostic entities. There is no reason to expect that the factor syndromes will necessarily be the same as the diagnostic syndromes arrived at by clinicians.

Perceptual Distortion. This factor includes only hallucinations. The disturbance may be in the various sense modalities (vision, touch, taste, smell), but it is manifested especially as voices that accuse, threaten, or urge the patient. It is surprising to discover that there is a factor so narrow that it includes only hallucinations, but evidently the pattern is sufficiently clear to emerge on statistical analysis. The symptoms included are seen mainly in schizophrenics, although, as we saw in the last chapter, some depressives also have mild or borderline hallucinations.

Disorientation. This is also a narrow factor, encompassing a small class of symptoms. The patient is disoriented as to time and place. He does not know the month, the year, or his own age, and he does not know where he is or where the hospital is located.

Motor Disturbances. There are bizarre postures and movements, as well as facial grimaces, silly smiling, and laughing. This is of course the pattern seen in hebephrenic schizophrenia.

Conceptual Disorganization. This factor includes incoherent speech, rambling discourses, irrelevant answers, and repetitious words or phrases. These are symptoms that define *formal thinking disorder.*

When we add together these last four factors (Perceptual Distortion, Disorientation, Motor Disturbances, and Conceptual Disorganization), the pattern is that of classical schizophrenia. As we shall see later, three of these factors do indeed define a patient type that is clearly schizophrenic.

The Syndrome Circle

Lorr et al. correlated each of the ten factors (syndromes) with every other one, and the resulting matrix of correlations met the statistical criterion[3] for a circular arrangement of the syndromes. Two factors did not meet this criterion: Hostile Belligerence and Perceptual Distortion. The remaining eight are shown in Figure 10.1.

In this figure, adjacent syndromes are positively correlated, and syndromes distant from one another have either low or negative correlations. This statistically-derived arrangement makes good clinical sense. A patient showing symptoms of Grandiose Expansiveness is likely to manifest some of the symptoms of either Excitement or Paranoid Projection, or both. The patient showing symptoms of Motor Disturbances is likely to manifest symptoms of Conceptual Disorganization or Disorientation, or both.

[3] The statistical details are beyond the scope of this book. Briefly, correlations are arranged in a matrix, and the criterion for circular order is that correlations are highest next to the principal diagonal, decrease in size with distance from this diagonal, and then increase again. Thus the arrangement has no beginning or end, that is, it is circular.

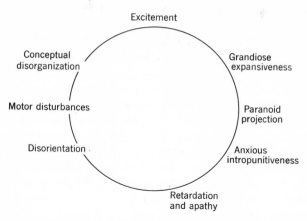

Figure 10.1. The Psychotic Syndrome Circle (Lorr et al., 1963).

Lorr et al. noted other links between adjacent syndromes. The factors Anxious Intropunitiveness and Retardation and Apathy may share a common turning inward of hostility and blame. Extreme social withdrawal could result in the symptoms of Motor Disturbances and Disorientation; patients with this combination may vacillate between symptoms of Retardation and Apathy (for example, catatonic stupor) and Conceptual Disorganization and Excitement (for example, thought disorder and catatonic excitement).

Finally, the circle is consistent with diagnostic problems that occasionall arise in clinical practice. Apathy is sometimes mistaken for retarded depression, and thought disorder may be confused with a manicky flight of ideas. The more adjacent the syndromes in the circle, the more the symptoms overlap and tend to cause diagnostic difficulties.

Patient Types

In using the ten psychotic factors to derive six types of patients, Lorr et al. made the scores of patients comparable by conversion to standard scores. They then prepared a profile for each patient, which they examined for similarities to the profiles of other patients. This examination yielded six groups of patients whose profiles were similar, marked by elevations of one or more of the ten factors (syndromes). These groups were: *Excited-Grandiose, Excited-Hostile, Intropunitive, Retardation, Hostile Paranoid, and Schizophrenic Disorganization*[4]

The Excited-Grandiose type, defined by the Excited and Grandiose Ex-

[4] McNair et al. (1964) succeeded in replicating these six types with patients of both sexes drawn from a variety of private and state hospitals and clinics. They also extracted three new types which need not concern us here.

pansiveness factors, approximates the pattern found in mania. The *Excited-Hostile* type, defined by Excitement and Hostile Belligerence, would seem to include symptoms of both mania and catatonic excitement. Thus excitement may be associated with either hostile irritability or with elation and grandiosity.

The *Intropunitive* type of patient scores high only on the Anxious Intropunitiveness factor. Such patients are anxious depressives who may manifest a slowing of motor activity but who rarely display thinking or motor disturbances.

The *Retarded* type of patient scores high only on the Retardation and Apathy factor, which appears to include both depressives and apathetic schizophrenics. As we noted above, retarded depression may be confused with apathetic schizophrenia.

The *Hostile-Paranoid* type is defined by Paranoid Projection and Hostile Belligerence. Hallucinations are absent, and there is no thought disorder. This is the picture of an *intact* paranoid schizophrenic—a delusional, hostile patient who manifests none of the other cognitive symptoms of schizophrenia. This type has relevance for the paranoid-nonparanoid dimension, which is discussed later in the chapter.

The last type, *Schizophrenic Disorganization,* scores high on Retardation and Apathy, Motor Disturbances, Disorientation, and Conceptual Disorganization. These factors, taken together, are essentially the pattern for a nonparanoid schizophrenic: emotional dulling, bizarre motor responses, disorientation, and formal thought disorder.

Dimensions of Type Differences

To determine the dimensions differentiating the six patient types Lorr et al. used a statistical technique called *multiple discriminant analysis.* This yielded four variables or dimensions of difference. The first three are the major dimensions in that they account for virtually all the differences among types.

Loss of Contact with Reality. On this continuum the Disorganized type scores highest and the Retarded type next; both are significantly higher than the remaining four types. Since these are the two groups most divorced from reality, the name of the dimension, Contact with Reality, seems appropriate.

The way the factors line up sustains this conclusion. Hostile Belligerence, Grandiose Expansiveness, and Anxious Intropunitiveness are at one end, opposed by Retardation and Apathy, Motor Disturbances, and Disorientation. Note that the latter three constitute three-fourths of the Schizophrenic Disorganization type. Thus the dimension contrasts relatively adequate communication and reality orientation with social withdrawal, retreat from reality, and little response to the environment.

Degree of Self-Expansiveness. The poles of this dimension are occupied by the Excited-Grandiose and Intropunitiveness types; the remaining types are intermediate. At one end are overactivity, assertiveness, blaming of others, and feelings of superiority; at the other end are worry, guilt, low self-esteem, and blaming of self. Thus the dimension corresponds to one aspect of the manic-depressive bipolarity.

Self-Directed Hostility versus Other-Directed Hostility. Again the intropunitive type lines up at one end of a dimension, but this time the Paranoid and Excited-Hostile types occupy the other end. The Excited-Grandiose and Retarded types are relatively close to the Intropunitive type. These three all tend to inhibit hostility, whereas the opposite groups express hostility against others; thus the name of the dimension.

Degree of Affect or Emotionality. This minor variable is defined by the Retarded type at one pole and by the Intropunitive, Excited-Hostile, and Disorganized types at the other pole. The name was derived as follows: the Retarded type is apathetic, whereas the other types exhibit various kinds of affect (anxiety, hostility, etc.).

DIMENSIONS OF SCHIZOPHRENIA

The factors just mentioned and the symptom dimensions included in the last chapter do not exhaust the dimensions of psychosis. There are a number of other dimensions of considerable importance, especially in schizophrenia. These are variables thought to be related to prognosis. As we saw in the last chapter, the outlook for recovery is very good in the affective psychoses, one of the salient characteristics of these syndromes being a good prognosis. In schizophrenia the prognosis is worse, although there is considerable variation in recovery potential from one patient to the next. Thus the dimensions we shall consider not only round out the clinical picture of schizophrenia but also bear some relationship to prognosis.

Affect

In the present context affect refers to depression. The prognosis in psychotic depression is good; patients sooner or later cast off their despondency and are able to resume existence without special care—at least until a subsequent episode. Evidently there is something about depression that bodes well for recovery. When depressive symptoms are present in schizophrenia, prognosis is relatively good.

Clinical lore has for many years emphasized affect as a positive prognostic sign, and this notion has been substantiated by research. If we accept depression as a good sign, it follows that the more prominent the depression, the better the outlook for recovery. This is precisely what Clark and Mallet (1963) found. They compared the recovery rates of psychotic schizophrenics, schizo-affectives, and psychotic depressives, groups that line up in increasing order of the prominence of depression. On followup, the schizophrenics had the lowest recovery rate and the greatest number of symptoms, the schizo-affectives were next, and the depressives had the best recovery rate and the fewest symptoms remaining. Other studies dealing solely with schizophrenics will be reviewed below, but we may note here that they corroborate the hypothesis that the presence of affect is a good prognostic sign.

Severity

The manifest symptoms of schizophrenia are exhibited in different degrees in various patients. Delusions vary from misinterpretations of social interactions to bizarre and incomprehensible fantasies. The latter range from the insides of the body to persecutory plots that include the entire universe. Thought disturbances vary from slight blocking of speech and unusual associations to clang associations, "word salad," and similar gibberish.

Severity of symptoms is more difficult to deal with in practice partly because it is a quantitative concept. Affect may be dichotomized into categories of presence versus absence, and this is a relatively easy judgment; but severity requires a quantitative estimate, which means that symptoms must be ordered for increasing degree of psychopathology. Such ordering may best be accomplished by means of psychological scaling procedures, but unfortunately such scaling has not been attempted. We must be content with a substitute: rating scales of symptoms (Lorr, 1954). These measures offer some hope that eventually we shall be able to evaluate severity of symptoms in a quantitative fashion.

Lorr (1964) has shown that the task may not be too difficult. He had clinicians rank paranoid symptoms for severity and the following sequence of increasing severity emerged:

> hostile attitude
> verbally expressed feelings of hostility
> feelings of resentment
> blaming others for difficulties
> suspicion of people's motives
> delusions of persecution
> delusions of conspiracy
> ideas of reference
> ideas of control by people
> ideas of control by forces
> ideas of grandeur
> ideas of divine mission
> voices extoll

This sequence is essentially the same as the one that emerged from a statistical ordering of correlations, the "simplex" model discussed earlier under the heading of the Paranoid Projection factor. These findings support the view that paranoid delusions represent the projection of hatred: the patient is initially hostile toward others, then suspicious, and finally paranoid (others are hostile toward him).

Severity is complex not only because it requires quantification but also because it refers to a property of symptoms, *intensity*, not a class of symptoms. Any symptom can vary in severity, and what makes one symptom severer than the next varies from one class of symptoms to the next. Thus when considering mania, the *greater* the activity level, the severer the symptom; but when considering schizophrenic withdrawal, the *lower* the activity level, the severer the symptom.

Severity is not only complex, but it is not consistently related to prognosis. In some instances the milder the symptom is, the better the prognosis, for example, social withdrawal. In other instances the severer the psychotic symptom is, the better the prognosis, for example, depressive affect.

Confusion

During the course of schizophrenia some patients become confused, perplexed, and disoriented. They cannot furnish an accurate account of the time, the date, or the location. In their turmoil state, they are lost and bewildered. These symptoms which resemble those seen in toxic states (overuse of drugs or alcohol) usually occur during the acute phase of schizophrenia. They are rarely seen in chronic schizophrenics. The acute phase of schizophrenia is the first one, and the confusion is usually part of a catastrophic break with reality. Thus turmoil and disorientation are associated with sudden rather than insidious onset.

Confusion is also associated with a good prognosis. This clinical observation is more than a hundred years old (Vaillant, (1964a), and it has been sustained by research (for example, Vaillant, 1962). It is not clear whether confusion is a good prognostic sign in itself or because of its joint occurrence with acute onset, which is also a good prognostic sign. This issue needs empirical clarification.

Onset

As just noted, sudden onset is linked with subsequent recovery. There is considerable variation in time of onset. In some instances the patient has been leading an apparently normal life (although this superficial picture seldom stands close inspection), when suddenly there is a flowering of bizarre, psychotic behavior. In other instances onset is insidious, the individual almost imperceptibly withdrawing from others and only gradually developing the deviant patterns that are the hallmark of a full-blown psychosis; the process may take years. The slower the onset, the worse is the prognosis.

Onset is associated with another prognostic variable: presence or absence of precipitating factors. When the psychosis develops slowly over a period of years, it makes little sense to look for a clear precipitating incident in the life history; but when onset is sudden, we would be surprised not to discover a painful event such as death of someone close, rejection, or failure. This is not to say that a sudden psychotic episode can occur only when triggered by a precipitating event. There are puzzling and unexplained instances of quick onset in the absence of a precipitant, but these are rare, and quick onset is usually associated with a painful life situation.

Chronicity

As we have seen, confusion and disorientation usually occur during an acute schizophrenic episode. After such an episode, the patient may start to make a recovery or slip into a stable pattern of social withdrawal and psychotic symptoms. Thus schizophrenics may be divided into acute and chronic patients. The acute psychotic is usually struggling with his problems and is perplexed, anxious, and intensely upset. The chronic psychotic is likely to be more apathetic; he is not struggling with immediate problems and is less upset and concerned. The acute psychotic is usually still struggling with the immediate crisis. He has some motivation to seek help, and there is ordinarily a large residue of adjustive, nonpsychotic components in his behavior. The chronic psychotic has usually made his peace with the way he is; he has settled for a more or less psychotic existence and is less oriented toward social conformity and social validation of reality.

Acute schizophrenics often are agitated, depressed, and bewildered. Typically, there has been a strong precipitating event, and onset has been sudden. In contrast, chronic schizophrenics tend to show little affect, anxiety, or confusion. Onset has typically been insidious and in the absence of a precipitating event. Thus the acute-chronic dimension interacts with several previous ones. The acute patient, because he is often depressed and confused and because he has often had a rapid onset in the context of a painful life event, has a better prognosis than the chronic schizophrenic, who occupies the opposite pole of these various prognostically related dimensions.

Chronicity refers to duration of symptoms. No patient has chronic symptoms to begin with; he becomes chronic through a sequence of events over time. These events may occur within a psychiatric hospital. Sommer and Witney (1961) have described the process of becoming chronic as a chain of events, as shown in Table 10.1. These investigators found that

TABLE 10.1   THE PROCESS OF BECOMING CHRONIC
(From Sommer & Witney, 1961)

Chain of Chronicity	Other Alternatives

Person becomes ill

Peculiar behavior noticed
by family and friends →

Peculiar behavior unnoticed
and eventually disappears

↓

Peculiar behavior brought
to the attention of clinic,
physician, police, etc. →

Peculiar behavior accepted
by family and friends

↓

Referral or commitment to
a mental hospital →

Treatment as an outpatient

↓

Treatment on admission
ward with minimal
improvement →

Treatment on admission ward,
rapid improvement, and prompt
discharge

↓

Transfer to continued
treatment ward →

Remains on admission ward, continues to receive psychotherapy
and individual attention

↓

Regular employment at
hospital job, loss of contact
with family and outside,
acquisition of institutional
values →

Remains in individual or group
psychotherapy, retains contact
with family and friends, frequent
visits outside, no hospital
employment

---

most of the patients who became chronic were simple, catatonic, or undifferentiated schizophrenics. Twice as many paranoid schizophrenics were discharged as any other kind of schizophrenic.

Process-Reactive

Another dimension, although some would call it a dichotomy, is that
of process-reactive. At one end of the dimension is the schizophrenic with
poor heredity, insidious onset, and a poor prognosis. At the other end is
the patient with good heredity, sudden onset, and a good prognosis for
recovery. Obviously, this process-reactive dimension includes most of the
previous five dimensions. It also includes several others and is of considerable theoretical importance.

Criteria. The most complete list of criteria for deciding whether a patient is process or reactive is that of Kantor, Wallner, and Winder (1953),

TABLE 10.2   ITEMS DEFINING FRAME OF REFERENCE FOR CASE
HISTORY JUDGMENTS
(Kantor, Wallner, & Winder, 1953)

Process Schizophrenia	Reactive Schizophrenia

Birth to the fifth year

(a) Early psychological trauma	(a) Good psychological history
(b) Physical illness—severe or long	(b) Good physical health
(c) Odd member of family	(c) Normal member of family

Fifth year to adolescence

(a) Difficulties at school	(a) Well adjusted at school
(b) Family troubles paralleled with sudden changes in patient's behavior	(b) Domestic troubles accompanied by behavior disruptions. Patient "had what it took."
(c) Introverted behavior trends and interests	(c) Extroverted behavior trends and interests
(d) History of breakdown of social, physical, mental functioning	(d) History of adequate social, physical, mental functioning
(e) Pathological siblings	(e) Normal siblings
(f) Overprotective or rejecting mother. "Momism"	(f) Normally protective, accepting mother
(g) Rejecting father	(g) Accepting father

Adolescence to adulthood

(a) Lack of heterosexuality	(a) Heterosexual behavior
(b) Insidious, gradual onset of psychosis without pertinent stress	(b) Sudden onset of psychosis; stress present and pertinent. Later onset
(c) Physical aggression	(c) Verbal aggression
(d) Poor response to treatment	(d) Good response to treatment
(e) Lengthy stay in hospital	(e) Short course in hospital

Adulthood

(a) Massive paranoia	(a) Minor paranoid trends
(b) Little capacity for alcohol	(b) Much capacity for alcohol
(c) No manic-depressive component	(c) Presence of manic-depressive component
(d) Failure under adversity	(d) Success despite adversity
(e) Discrepancy between ability and achievement	(e) Harmony between ability and achievement
(f) Awareness of change in self	(f) No sensation of change
(g) Somatic delusions	(g) Absence of somatic delusions
(h) Clash between culture and environment	(h) Harmony between culture and environment
(i) Loss of decency (nudity, public masturbation, etc.)	(i) Retention of decency

as shown in Table 10.2. This dual list includes examples from four of the five dimensions just discussed:

affect—presence of manic-depressive components
severity—massive paranoid trends, loss of decency
onset—sudden onset of psychosis
chronicity—length of stay in hospital

In addition there are two dimensions that have not been mentioned: premorbid personality (or adjustment) and family history. The premorbid (pre-illness) personality of schizophrenics varies from a shut-in, introverted, asexual kind of adjustment to a gregarious, extraverted, heterosexual kind of adjustment. Family history ranges from poor (overprotecting or rejecting parents) to good (accepting, loving parents and siblings). Examination of these two dimensions, as well as the others on the Kantor et al. list, makes us wonder why a patient labeled reactive would become schizophrenic. Certainly, his history would be as benign as that of the best-adjusted normal person.

Theory. The process-reactive distinction has a long history, being linked with the theoretical issue of the definition of schizophrenia. Kraepelin (1909) asserted that schizophrenia is a deteriorative incurable disease. Adopting this view, it follows that when a psychosis resembles schizophrenia in its manifest symptoms but is curable, it cannot be schizophrenia. Bleuler (1950), who was not as pessimistic about schizophrenia as Kraepelin was, indicated that a minority of schizophrenics do have a good prognosis.

Nevertheless, it has been Kraepelin's view that has persisted: if a patient recovers, he does not have *true* schizophrenia but a schizophrenic-like or schizophreniform psychosis. Vaillant (1964a) has traced the history of this distinction back to 1849, pointing out the features common to most definitions of schizophrenic-like psychosis:

recovery
acute picture resembles schizophrenia
good premorbid adjustment
psychologically understandable symptoms
precipitating cause
symptoms of psychotic depression
acute onset
confusion
concern with dying

Those who accept a *dichotomy* of process and reactive schizophrenics adopt the following theoretical position. Schizophrenia is an inherited, organic disease which proceeds inexorably through successive stages of deterioration. The major manifest symptom, formal thought disorder, is present

in every case. Onset is insidious, the psychosis developing gradually throughout adolescence and becoming manifest by the twenty-fifth year of life. Prognosis is universally poor, and treatment is virtually useless. Impairment of
intellectual functions is inevitable, as is a gradual deterioration of social
behavior. Such patients, the true schizophrenics, are regarded as qualitatively different from patients with similar symptoms but acute onset, good
premorbid history, and a good prognosis. The latter are distinguished by
the labels *schizophreniform, schizophrenoid,* or *reactive schizophrenic*—in
contrast to the *true, nuclear,* or *process* schizophrenic.

Bellak (1947), agreeing with this point of view, has suggested another
terminology.

> One wonders then, if it would not be profitable to consider this emerging
> group as an entity by itself—a syndrome rightfully to be separated from the again
> rather well-circumscribed group with the complementary characteristics. After all,
> one of the most important tasks of a diagnostic category is to afford a good prog-
> nostic concept.
> Another justification of separating this particular group from classic dementia
> praecox is that it differs from the disease to which Kraepelin gave that name.
> The prepsychotic personality is atypical; its onset is not insidious; it does not
> take place in the presence of a clear sensorium; there is often a precipitory factor;
> many of the phenomena can be understood and dealt with in terms of psychological
> dynamics; and the outcome is relatively good.
> We believe that the criteria outlined above for the favorable prognostic group
> should be diagnostic for the nosological entity of schizophrenia, while its counter-
> part should be designated more properly as dementia praecox. (p. 404)

This dichotomy has been welcomed by many clinicians. It is especially
helpful to those who have adopted the Kraepelinian view that schizophrenia
is a morbid condition, marked by a downhill course through successive stages
of deterioration. It is also a source of comfort for those who take a biological
approach to schizophrenia; they are able to assert that the only evidence
contrary to their position (that schizophrenia is an inherited, organic defect)
comes from patients mistakenly diagnosed as dementia praecox. Such patients only superficially resemble the true or process schizophrenic, but they
are different in onset and in prognosis. The true or process schizophrenic
has an inherited, organic defect, and his disease is incurable; whereas the
schizophrenic-like reactive schizophrenic has a temporary (and therefore
possibly curable) psychosis precipitated by an unkind environment.

The process-reactive question has some bearing on the continuity-discontinuity issue concerning neurosis and psychosis. Those who espouse the
continuity of neurosis and psychosis are embarrassed by the qualitative
differences between the two. By taking the position that process and reactive
form a dichotomy, they can escape their predicament as follows.

Assume that process schizophrenia has an etiology consisting mainly of genetic and biological components. It is a disease qualitatively different from other kinds of psychopathology, and it is marked by a poor prognosis. Reactive schizophrenia, in contrast, has a psychological etiology: it is caused by traumatic experiences in everyday life. Thus it has the same etiology as neurosis; in fact, neurotics under severe stress break down and become reactive schizophrenics. The prognosis for reactive schizophrenia is good, and such patients may be expected to return to their prepsychotic state, neurosis. Thus there is continuity between neurosis and reactive schizophrenia (which is not "true" schizophrenia) and discontinuity between neurosis and true schizophrenia.

This position is a compromise. Its adherents are willing to admit that process schizophrenia is qualitatively different. This admission rids them of such embarrassing issues as the poor prognosis of process schizophrenics and the biological components in the etiology of process schizophrenia. Reactive schizophrenia has a better prognosis and ostensibly strong psychological components in its etiology. Hence those who believe in the continuity of neurosis and psychosis tend to find the process-reactive *dichotomy* quite acceptable.

Dichotomy versus Continuity. If process schizophrenia is an organic disease, perhaps it is similar to organic brain disease. Brackbill and Fine (1956) compared the Rorschach response of patients with organic brain damage, process schizophrenia, and reactive schizophrenia. Rorschach signs of organicity revealed organic and process patients to be similar and to be different from reactive patients. However, these results cannot be accepted at face value because of the dubious character of the Rorschach signs of organicity. As Herron (1962) has pointed out, they have not been cross-validated and are probably inadequate as signs of brain damage. Therefore the Brackbill and Fine conclusion that there is a dichotomy (organic versus nonorganic) between process and reactive schizophrenia is of doubtful validity. Furthermore, no research has shown any *neurological similarity* between brain-damaged and process or reactive schizophrenics, although there has been considerable speculation.

A technique known to have validity in detection of brain damage is the Critical Flicker Fusion (CFF) task, which requires the subject to report when a flickering light becomes steady. McDonough (1960) used the CFF with normals, organics, and process and reactive schizophrenics. The CFF clearly distinguished between normals and organics, offering further evidence of its validity. It also differentiated organics from both process and reactive schizophrenics, with these last two groups not differing from each other. These results oppose the hypothesis that process schizophrenics and brain-damaged patients are similar.

A number of studies, to be reported below, have found differences between process and reactive schizophrenics. These positive findings have been interpreted by some psychologists as evidence for a process-reactive dichotomy. For example, Meadow et al. (1953) found a relationship between abstraction ability on a proverbs task and physiological response (blood pressure) in schizophrenics. They concluded:

> It is possible therefore to think now in terms of two polar types of schizophrenia: one with poor abstraction, personality and thinking disorganization, low physiological reactivity following mecholyl injection, and poor prognosis; and another with good abstraction, good organization of personality and thought, high physiological reactivity following mecholyl injection, and good prognosis (particularly with electric shock). Patients in the first group belong to the 'process' schizophrenia or schizophrenia with ominous outcome in the sense implied by Kraepelin. (p. 337)

These conclusions were premature because the findings underlying them have been rendered suspect by two subsequent studies. Zuckerman and Grosz (1959) reported that the blood pressure response to mecholyl is so unreliable that it varies from one arm to the other, and from one testing to another. Judson and Katahn (1963) could not replicate the findings of Meadow et al.; they found no relationship between the autonomic response to mecholyl and performance of the proverbs task.

Although the Meadow et al. results have not been replicated, other differences between process and reactive schizophrenics are known to be reliable. The basic problem is one of inference, not reliability of findings. The conclusions of Meadow et al. and those of like-minded investigators rest on two logical steps. First, patients are separated into the dichotomous classes of process and reactive schizophrenics; second, the two classes of patients are shown to be different on psychological tasks.

If there is any fault with this inferential sequence, it lies in the first step. In virtually all research on process and reactive schizophrenics, the patients are *not* assigned to qualitatively different categories but to different points on a single dimension. Meadow et al. used blood pressure response, which varies continuously over a wide range. Other investigators have used the Kantor et al. (1953) criteria, the Elgin Prognostic Scale (Wittman, 1941), and the Phillips Premorbid Adjustment Scale (1953). These all yield continuous distributions of scores, from which process and reactive groups are selected. If process and reactive represent two qualitatively different kinds of schizophrenics, then the distribution of scores on the instruments just mentioned should be bimodal. The process patients should cluster in one range of scores and the reactive patients in another range, with essentially no overlap between groups. At present there is no evidence of bimodality in the distributions of schizophrenics on the instruments used to divide them into process and reactive groups.

The selection is made by carving up a continuous distribution of scores, as follows. The distribution is divided into three parts—high, middle, and low. The high scores are labeled say, process; the low scores are labeled reactive; and the middle scores are omitted. This procedure insures a clear difference in scores between process and reactive patients, but it yields groups that are *quantitatively* different. A high scoring group of patients cannot be called *qualitatively* different from a low scoring group merely because the middle scoring group has been omitted. An analogous mistake would be to divide men into tall, medium and short groups, discard the medium height group, and then claim that there were two qualitatively different kinds of men—tall and short. Neither the labeling of a particular range of scores nor the omission of a middle group constitutes a meaningful definition of a dichotomy. This is as true for the process-reactive issue as for the height illustration.

Virtually all the studies on process and reactive schizophrenics have used one of the instruments mentioned above; the two groups have differed along a continuous dimension of scores. Since the selection has been quantitative, the findings cannot be used as evidence of a dichotomy. Evidence for a dichotomy must come from studies that separate patients into two different *types*, that is, the selection must be made on the basis of qualitative differences.

One possibility is to adopt a system of classification that distinguishes among symptom clusters within schizophrenia. Leonhard (1961) has such a system, and Stephens and Astrup (1963) have used it to divide schizophrenics into process and nonprocess groups. The results of a 5 to 13 year followup may be seen in Table 10.3. As the table shows, the recovery and improvement rates are markedly different. Those who are process patients have a considerably poorer prognosis. Note that there are two *types* of patients because the selection was based on presence versus absence of certain clinical features. When Stephens and Astrup examined the case folders of the patients, they discovered that among the signs present in nonprocess patients and absent in process patients were the following familiar ones: acute onset, nonschizoid premorbid personality, precipitating factors, confusion, and depression. These are precisely the variables found by Vaillant (1964b)

TABLE 10.3   FOLLOW-UP OF PROCESS AND NONPROCESS
SCHIZOPHRENICS
(From Stephens & Astrup, 1963)

	Process	*Nonprocess*
recovered	10%	38%
improved	41	59
unimproved	49	3

to be present in schizophrenics who recovered and absent in those who did not.

The selection procedure of Stephens and Astrup offers one means of testing whether process-reactive is a dichotomy or a continuity. Another possibility is evidence that the two groups form bimodal distributions along such dimensions as acuteness of onset, immaturity, and physiological responsivity. A final possibility is that the process-reactive distinction is continuous at a descriptive level (signs, symptoms, and other observable features) but dichotomous at an explanatory level. Thus the two groups might be qualitatively different genetically, biologically, or psychologically (for example, different kinds of psychological stress or different kinds of family constellations). At present the data are too sparse to decide whether the process-reactive distinction is dichotomous or continuous.

Research with Process and Reactive Patients. Three measures have been used to select process and reactive patients. The first is the dual list of Kantor et al. (1953), which is presented in Table 10.2 (see page 218). This list is comprehensive, including life history data, symptoms, and a variety of dimensions of psychosis. It is rarely used because it requires more information than is usually available on psychiatric patients and because a number of the items are vague and qualitative.

The Elgin Prognostic Scale (Wittman, 1941) is a check list of items that correlate with outcome, the items referring to life history data and symptoms. It is less inclusive than the Kantor et al. criteria and is easier to use.

The most popular measure is the Phillips Scale (1953). It includes no symptoms, consisting wholly of life history items. These items refer to sexual, social, and vocational areas of everyday life, and the scale has been referred to as a measure of *premorbid competence*. Some of the items overlap those of the Elgin Scale, and the two measures appear to be tapping the same aspects of premorbid adjustment. The correlation between them is .87 (Solomon & Zlotowski, 1964), which, in light of the reliability of each instrument, is so high as to render them interchangeable.

These three measures have been used to discover differences between process and reactive patients in a number of areas (Higgins, 1964). The three areas that concern us here are prognosis, maturity, and attitudes toward parents.

(1) *Prognosis.* The process-reactive distinction arose in the context of prognosis: schizophrenics, who were thought to be incurable, did recover—at least in some instances. It follows from this *theoretical* distinction that there should be *empirical* differences in the prognosis of process and reactive patients.

Wittman and Steinberg (1944) followed up psychotic patients who underwent electroconvulsive shock therapy. The Elgin Scale correctly predicted the outcome of treatment in better than 80% of the cases. Chapman, Day, and Burstein (1961) administered the Elgin Scale to patients on admission to a mental hospital. The scale correlated .38 with the outcome of hospitalization (discharge versus remaining).

Four studies have demonstrated similar relationships with the Phillips Scale. Farina and Webb (1956) found that discharged patients had significantly higher scores (better premorbid adjustment) than patients who remained hospitalized. Seidel (1960) followed up male schizophrenics and found a correlation of .46 between the Phillips Scale and recovery versus hospitalization. Nonrecovered female schizophrenics have been shown to have poorer levels of premorbid adjustment (Phillips Scale) than recovered patients (Farina, Garmezy, Zalusky, & Becker, 1962). Finally, Farina, Garmezy, and Barry (1963) obtained significant correlations between Phillips Scale scores and recovery.

These various studies demonstrate a clear relationship between the process-reactive dimension and prognosis, but the strength of the relationships is not encouraging. The correlations do not reach .50, and differences in scores on the Phillips Scale are sometimes quite small, although statistically significant. These facts lend weight to the argument that process and reactive are points on a continuum rather than qualitatively different *types* of patients. If the latter were true, there should be clearer and stronger differences in prognosis and less overlap in scores.

(2) *Maturity.* Maturity is a much used concept in psychopathology, but it is particularly elusive to assess. None of the research to be reported utilized direct measures or ratings of maturity. Friedman (1953) developed a method of scoring Rorschach responses for *genetic level* (maturity) and found that the severer the psychopathology, the lower is the genetic level of Rorschach responses. *Genetically low* responses appear to be precisely those that clinicians have been using as Rorschach indicators of severe psychopathology. Thus what Friedman really demonstrated is that Rorschach indicators of psychopathology are correlated with behavioral indicators of psychopathology. Nevertheless, a number of investigators have adopted Friedman's scoring system as a means of assessing maturity, and for expository purposes we shall go along with this assumption.

Becker (1956) compared the Rorschach responses of process and reactive patients selected by the Elgin Scale. The process patients showed significantly greater "perceptual immaturity" or genetically lower responses than the reactive patients. A later study (Steffy & Becker, 1961) obtained similar results using the Holtzman Ink Blots instead of the Rorschach. Zimet and Fine (1959) duplicated these findings with the Rorschach and the Kantor et al. criteria for process-reactive. In a subsequent study (1965) process patients showed more primary process (less mature) thinking than reactive patients.

Phillips and his colleagues used an entirely different approach in assessing maturity. Phillips and Rabinovitch (1958) searched the files of a state hospital and listed 39 symptoms that appeared with at least a moderate frequency in the records of over 600 patients. Symptoms were paired to discover whether they occurred together, and three clusters of symptoms emerged from the analysis. Their classification, which has been slightly rearranged to make it consistent with the four symptom spheres used throughout this book, is presented in Table 10.4.

The first cluster was labeled by Phillips and Rabinovitch as *Avoidance of Others*. This heading makes sense when we look at the symptoms of withdrawal and apathy, but the cognitive symptoms do not fit it as well. The second cluster was called *Self-Indulgence and Turning Against Others,* which fits well the antisocial nature of these behaviors. The bottom cluster was called *Self-Deprivation and Turning Against the Self*.

These three clusters were then ordered as a sequence of psychological development. Phillips and Rabinovitch, using Werner's developmental

TABLE 10.4   CLUSTERS OF SYMPTOMS FOUND BY PHILLIPS
AND RABINOVITCH (1958)

	Cognitive	Affective	Motor	Somatic
No. 1.	suspiciousness hallucinations bizarre ideas feels perverted sexual preoccupation perplexed	apathetic	withdrawn	
No. 2.			threatens assault assaultive emotional outbursts drinking robbery rape perversions irresponsible behavior	
No. 3.	suicidal ideas self-depreciation	depression tense-nervous	suicidal attempt compulsions doesn't eat	bodily complaints insomnia headaches

theory, suggested that the three groups of symptoms represented increasing maturity:

. . . a genetically early period in which the boundaries between the self and the world are relatively diffuse; a subsequent period of selfcenteredness in which a separation of self and world has occurred but with little recognition of the rights of others; and a final phase in which self identity is maintained, but in which relationships on the basis of reciprocity also take place. In this last stage of development, a recognition and acceptance of the social mores has been internalized. (1958, p. 185)

This is an ambitious attempt to classify symptoms on the basis of their implied maturity level. Acceptance of it depends upon how closely it fits what is known about development and whether it can be established that psychopathology represents regression to earlier developmental modes. These issues will be discussed in Chapter 11.

Let us accept the three symptom clusters as indicators of increasing maturity: avoidance of others, self-indulgence and turning against others, and self-deprivation and turning against self. Zigler and Phillips (1962) used the Phillips Scale to divide patients into three groups varying in social competence: process patients, a middle group, and reactive patients. The process patients had more symptoms in the Avoidance of Others cluster, the reactive patients had more in the Turning Against the Self cluster, and the middle group had intermediate symptoms. Thus if we assume that the symptom clusters indicate level of maturity, process patients were immaturer than reactive patients.

This finding, in conjunction with the earlier finding that both schizophrenic and nonschizophrenic patients with high social competence scores have a better prognosis than those with low scores . . . calls into question the heuristic value of the process-reactive distinction in schizophrenia. The implication here is that the process-reactive distinction is reducible to the social competence dimension, which is continuous in nature, and which is applicable not only to schizophrenia but to all of psychopathology. (Zigler & Phillips, 1962, p. 220)

(3) *Relations with Parents.* The parent-child relationships of process and reactive schizophrenics have been studied almost exclusively by Rodnick and Garmezy and their students. In a preliminary study Rodnick and Garmezy (1957) used the Phillips Scale to select good premorbid (reactive) and poor premorbid (process) schizophrenic men. The patients were asked about their parents' child-rearing practices.

In general, the roles played by mothers and fathers of goods and poors appeared to be reversed. Whereas the mothers of the poor premorbid patients were perceived as having been more dominating, restrictive, and powerful and the fathers as more easy-going and ineffectual, the pattern was clearly reversed in good premorbids. These patients reported that their fathers were more tyrannical, harsh, and oppressive in their behavior toward them, whereas the mothers tended to be more easy-going and more warm and loving. (1957, p. 154)

These findings were extended and confirmed by Garmezy, Clarke, and Stockner (1961), who also noted that poor premorbid patients reported more deviant parental attitudes than good premorbid patients. Baxter and Becker (1962) presented pictures of mother-son and father-son relationships and had patients make up stories about the pictures. The stories were scored for anxiety, and the results were in the expected direction: good premorbid patients showed more anxiety with the father-son picture than poor premorbid patients with either the father-son or the mother-son picture.

Three studies of psychological deficit (impaired performance) are consistent with the pattern. Dunham (1959) presented slides showing a father scolding a child and a mother scolding a child, and the task was to detect minor variations in the scenes. The good premorbid patients showed deficit only on the father-censure scene, and the poor premorbids showed deficit only on the mother-censure scene. Kreinik (1959) found supporting evidence on a conceptual task, although her results were not as clear-cut. The strongest evidence has been provided by Goodman (1964). He had subjects perform in a digit symbol task, then listen to a record of paternal or maternal censure or approval, and finally repeat the digit symbol task. Although the interpolated recordings of parental censure or approval did not affect normal subjects, they profoundly affected schizophrenic subjects. Paternal censure deteriorated the performance of good premorbid patients, and maternal censure deteriorated the performance of poor premorbid patients. Good premorbid patients were unaffected by maternal censure, and poor premorbid patients were unaffected by paternal censure.

Analogous findings have been reported by Donovan (1963), who investigated recognition thresholds of the human voice. Poor premorbid schizophrenics had higher thresholds (had more difficulty in recognizing the spoken words) when the voice was female than when it was male. Also the poor premorbid schizophrenics' threshold for recognizing words spoken by a woman was higher than those of good premorbid schizophrenics and normal controls.

All these investigations used patients as subjects. The only one to study *parents* of schizophrenics was Farina (1960), who matched parents of good and poor premorbid schizophrenics with normal controls. The mother and father of each patient were studied as they interacted in attempting to solve hypothetical child-rearing problems. Observations of parental behavior in this laboratory setting revealed the following significant facts. For good premorbid patients, the father tended to be assertive and dominant and the mother weaker and more submissive. For poor premorbid patients, the pattern was reversed; the mother was dominant, and the father weak and submissive. For normal controls, authority was more or less shared, with the balance tipping very slightly toward maternal dominance.

All this laboratory research on parent-child relationships in schizophrenia has yielded two clear-cut patterns. First, poor premorbid (process) patients have dominant mothers, and good premorbid (reactive) patients have dominant fathers. Second, censure from fathers has a disastrous effect on the performance of reactive patients, and censure from mothers negatively affects the performance of process patients. All the studies mentioned previously employed only men as subjects. However, Stoller (1964) compared male and female process and reactive patients and found no sex differences in reactions to maternal censure. Thus whatever it is about parent-child relationships that differentiates process from reactive patients, the sex of the patient is not crucial. This issue will be pursued further within the broader context of interpersonal aspects of psychosis (Chapter 15).

Paranoid-Nonparanoid

The paranoid-nonparanoid dimension has a long history. There has been disagreement for more than a hundred years over the issue of including paranoids as schizophrenics versus keeping them as a separate class of psychotics. There is general agreement about the dimension itself. It is defined by three points: paranoid schizophrenia, paranoid reaction (also called paraphrenia and paranoid state), and paranoia.

The schizophrenic end of the dimension was described in the last chapter: the usual schizophrenic symptoms of language and thought, disturbances of self, autism, hallucinations, and in addition, *delusions*. The other end of the continuum, paranoia, is so rare that it is usually grouped with paranoid reaction. These two (paranoid reaction and paranoia) have been characterized by Foulds and Owen (1963) as follows:

a. Massive, well-ingrained delusions of persecution or grandiosity, which are highly systematized.
b. Long-standing traits of suspiciousness and projection of blame.
c. Late onset, characterized by problems different from those seen in psychotics with earlier onset.
d. Relative absence of thought disorder, psychological deficit, and deterioration.
e. Greater resistance to change but greater probability of making at least a marginal adjustment outside a mental hospital.

Kraepelin maintained a clear separation among the three types mentioned above. He considered paranoia as a kind of involutional or old-age reaction to failure in life, rather than as a psychosis. He believed paranoid schizophrenics have hallucinations as well as delusions, and, like all schizophrenics, their prognosis is poor. The middle group, paranoid reactions, were seen as having systematized delusions but no hallucinations or deterioration of thought; their prognosis would therefore be better than that of paranoid schizophrenics.

Bleuler adopted a different view, as follows. Paranoia is so rare that a separate category is unnecessary. The transitional forms (paraphrenia or paranoid reaction) occur so frequently, in such variety, and with sufficient associative disturbance to warrant classifying all of them as schizophrenics.

These two positions, Bleuler's and Kraepelin's, are unresolved to this day. Many textbooks include paranoids under the heading of schizophrenia, but a sizable number have a separate category called paranoid reactions or paranoid states.

Some clinicians believe that it is not possible to make a reliable distinction between paranoid schizophrenics and the other subtypes. This belief was refuted by Orgel (1957), who devised a detailed set of criteria. Two judges rated case histories using these criteria. Their ratings correlated better than .95, which indicates excellent reliability in distinguishing paranoid from other schizophrenics.

Paranoids differ from nonparanoids not only in symptom patterns but also in the degree of psychological deficit shown on a variety of experimental tasks. Raush (1952) showed that paranoids manifested overconstancy compared to nonparanoids and normals on a task assessing size constancy. Similar findings were obtained by Hartman (1962) for size changes in afterimages. This kind of perceptual distortion—a failure to adjust to changes in stimuli and a rigid persistence in nonappropriate perceptual responses—is precisely what we should expect from paranoids.

Payne and Hewlett (1960) found that paranoids were less impaired than nonparanoid schizophrenics on several perceptual and conceptual tests. Johannsen et al. (1963) reviewed experiments demonstrating the superiority of paranoids over nonparanoids on such diverse tasks as tapping speed, hand steadiness, Rorschach genetic level, double alternation learning, and conditioning.

The Johannsen et al. research is particularly interesting because the paranoid-nonparanoid dimension was found to be unrelated to the process-reactive and acute-chronic dimensions. In recent years the process-reactive dimension has been the focus of attention, and a growing body of research attests to this interest. The paranoid-nonparanoid dimension appears to be just as significant in dividing schizophrenics into meaningful and potentially homogeneous subgroups. Like reactive patients, paranoids are more intact intellectually, perform better in a variety of tasks, and have a higher level of maturity (defined by Rorschach responses).

The problem that persists, however, is whether paranoids should be regarded as schizophrenics or as an independent group of psychotics. Foulds and Owen (1963) attempted to solve the problem by studying the inventory responses of paranoid and nonparanoid psychotics. Dividing their subjects into the usual groups that define this dimension (paranoid schizophrenics, paranoids, and paranoiacs), they discovered that the paranoids were more similar to the paranoiacs than to the paranoid schizophrenics. They concluded:

The Paranoids who have schizophrenic symptoms can be distinguished from those who do not by virtue of a different problem, a different short-term and, probably, a different long-term course. It is, therefore, suggested that a profitable differentiation can be made along the paranoid continuum at a point further removed from "pure" Paranoia than has recently been customary. In other words, it looks as though the acute variety of Kraepelin's Paraphrenics have aligned themselves with the Paranoids rather than with the schizophrenic group. (1963, p. 678)

More research of this kind is needed. Are paranoids different from nonparanoids not only in symptoms but also in onset and prognosis? If the differences are as pronounced as Foulds and Owen believe, then paranoids should certainly be assigned to a class of psychotics different from schizophrenics. At the present time there is insufficient evidence to accept or reject this decision.

COMMENT

We have considered various dimensions of psychosis, both factorial and nonfactorial. The factorial dimensions emerge from an empirical procedure—the analysis of correlations among symptoms. The empirical analysis can be carried a step further to derive higher order factors, as we noted in the first section of the chapter. An alternate procedure is to attempt an integration of nonfactorial dimensions through a simplifying hypothesis. The purpose of the hypothesis is to supply a theoretical framework for the various dimensions discussed in the second section of the chapter.

Let us define schizophrenia as a psychosis with classical symptoms (thought disorder, hallucinations, social withdrawal, etc.) and a poor prognosis. This corresponds to the definition of nuclear or process schizophrenia. There is a strong hereditary predisposition, insidious onset, absence of confusion, chronicity of symptoms, and intellectual deficit (as shown in a variety of laboratory tasks—see Chapters 12 and 13).

Schizophrenia, so defined, is one of four kinds of functional (nonorganic) psychoses, the remaining ones being psychotic depression, atypical psychoses, and paranoia. Schizophrenia is related to each of the other three psychoses in that there are patients who display a mixture of symptoms of schizophrenia plus one of the other psychoses. The two dimensions under-

Worse ← PROGNOSIS → Better

More ← INTELLECTUAL DEFICIT → Less

$$
\text{SCHIZOPHRENIA} \left\}\begin{array}{l} \leftrightarrow \text{Psychotic Depression} \\ \leftrightarrow \text{Atypical Psychoses } (reactive) \\ \leftrightarrow \text{Paranoia} \end{array}\right.
$$

Figure 10.2. Relationship of Schizophrenia to the Other Psychoses.

lying the relationships are prognosis and intellectual deficit, as shown in Figure 10.2.

The relationship between schizophrenia and psychotic depression was examined in Chapter 9. We saw that schizophrenics have a poorer prognosis than depressives and that there is a mixture of symptoms called *schizo-affective psychosis.* Depressives show little intellecutal deficit, schizophrenics a considerable amount. Thus the first dimension consists of schizophrenia at one end (poor prognosis, much intellectual deficit) and psychotic depression at the other (good prognosis, little intellectual deficit). Patients with a mixture of symptoms occupy the middle range of the dimension (guarded prognosis, some intellectual deficit).

Atypical psychoses consist of the schizophreniform, and cyclic psychoses discussed under the heading of *reactive.* These include cyclic psychoses (Leonhard, 1961), nonprocess psychoses (Stephens & Astrup, 1963), and pseudoneurotic schizophrenia (Hoch & Pollatin, 1949). This group of patients is marked by sudden onset, acuteness of symptoms, confusion, little or no hereditary taint, good prognosis, and little intellectual deficit. Again there are patients with features of both schizophrenia and atypical psychoses—in the terms used previously, with features of both process and reactive schizophrenia, or both schizophrenia and schizophreniform psychosis.

Paranoia was discussed briefly in the last section. As we saw, patients who tend more toward the paranoid end of the dimension show less intellectual deficit and have a better prognosis than those who tend toward the schizophrenic end. We can mark four points on the dimension, moving from least to most intellectual deficit: paranoia, paranoid reaction, paranoid schizophrenia, and nonparanoid (nuclear, process) schizophrenia.

This framework places the various manifestations of psychosis (onset and prognosis, as well as symptoms) on three dimensions, each bounded at one end by nuclear or process schizophrenia. It assumes that the dimensions are distinct and unrelated. So far the only evidence on this point is the Johannsen et al. (1963) report that the paranoid-nonparanoid dimension is unrelated to both the acute-chronic and process-reactive dimensions. However, the real value of the hypothesis is that it attempts to boil down the heterogeneity of schizophrenia and of psychosis to three basic dimensions.

REFERENCES

Baxter, J. C., & Becker, J. Anxiety and avoidance behavior in schizophrenics in response to parental figures. *Journal of Abnormal and Social Psychology,* 1962, **64**, 432–437.

Becker, W. C. A genetic approach to the interpretation and evaluation of the process-reactive distinction in schizophrenia. *Journal of Abnormal and Social Psychology,* 1956, **53**, 229–236.

Bellak, L. *Dementia praecox.* New York: Grune & Stratton, 1947.

Bleuler, E. *Dementia praecox or the group of schizophrenias.* New York: International Universities Press, 1950.

Bostian, D. W., Smith, P. A., Lasky, J. J., Hover, R. J., and Ging, Rosalie J. Empirical observations on mental-status examination. *Archives of General Psychiatry,* 1959, **1**, 253–262.

Brackbill, G., & Fine, H. Schizophrenia and central nervous system pathology. *Journal of Abnormal and Social Psychology,* 1956, **52**, 310–313.

Buss, A. H., & Durkee, Ann. An inventory for assessing different kinds of hostility. *Journal of Consulting Psychology,* 1957, **21**, 343–349.

Chapman, L. J., Day, Dorothy, & Burstein, A. The process-reactive distinction and prognosis in schizophrenia. *Journal of Nervous and Mental Disease,* 1961, **133**, 383–391.

Clark, J. A., & Mallett, B. L. A follow-up study of schizophrenia and depression in young adults. *British Journal of Psychiatry,* 1963, **109**, 491–499.

Degan, J. W. Dimensions of functional psychosis. *Psychometric Monographs,* 1952, No. 6.

Donovan, M. J. Meaning dimensions and sexual aspects of premorbid adjustment in schizophrenia. Unpublished doctoral dissertation, Vanderbilt University, 1963.

Dunham, R. M. Sensitivity of schizophrenics to parental censure. Unpublished doctoral dissertation, Duke University, 1959.

Farina, A. Patterns of role dominance and conflict in parents of schizophrenic patients. *Journal of Abnormal and Social Psychology,* 1960, **61**, 31–38.

Farina, A., & Webb, W. W. Premorbid adjustment and subsequent discharge. *Journal of Nervous and Mental Disease,* 1956, **124**, 612–613.

Farina, A., Garmezy, N., Zalusky, Marian, & Becker, J. Premorbid behavior and prognosis in female schizophrenic patients. *Journal of Consulting Psychology,* 1962, **26**, 56–60.

Farina, A., Garmezy, N., & Barry, H., III. Relationship of marital status to incidence and prognosis of schizophrenia. *Journal of Abnormal and Social Psychology,* 1963, **67**, 624–630.

Foulds, G. A., & Owén, Anna. Are paranoids schizophrenics? *British Journal of Psychiatry,* 1963, **109**, 674–679.

Friedman, H. Perceptual regression in the use of the Rorschach test. *Journal of Projective Techniques,* 1953, **17**, 171–185.

Garmezy, N., & Rodnick, E. H. Premorbid adjustment and performance in schizophrenia: Implications for interpreting heterogeneity in schizophrenia. *Journal of Nervous and Mental Disease,* 1959, **129,** 450–466.

Garmezy, N., Clarke, A. R., & Stockner, Carol. Child rearing attitudes of mothers and fathers as reported by schizophrenic and normal patients. *Journal of Abnormal and Social Psychology,* 1961, **63,** 176–182.

Goodman, D. Performance of good and poor premorbid male schizophrenics as a function of paternal versus maternal censure. *Journal of Abnormal and Social Psychology,* 1964, **69,** 550–555.

Guertin, W. H. A factor-analytic study of schizophrenic symptoms. *Journal of Consulting Psychology,* 1952, **16,** 308–312.

Guertin, W. H. Empirical syndrome groupings of schizophrenic hospital admissions. *Journal of Clinical Psychology,* 1961, **17,** 268–275.

Hartman, A. M. The apparent size of after-images in delusional and nondelusional schizophrenics. *American Journal of Psychology,* 1962, **75,** 587–595.

Herron, W. G. The process-reactive classification of schizophrenia. *Psychological Bulletin,* 1962, **59,** 329–343.

Higgins, J. The concept of process-reactive schizophrenia: criteria and related research. *Journal of Nervous and Mental Disease,* 1964, **138,** 9–25.

Hoch, P., & Polatin, P. Pseudoneurotic forms of schizophrenia. *Psychiatric Quarterly,* 1949, **23,** 248–276.

Johannsen, W. J., Friedman, S. H., Leitschuh, T. H., & Ammons, Helen. A study of certain schizophrenic dimensions and their relationship to double alternation learning. *Journal of Consulting Psychology,* 1963, **27,** 375–382.

Judson, A. J., & Katahn, M. The relationship of autonomic responsiveness to process-reactive schizophrenia and abstract thinking. *Psychiatric Quarterly,* 1963, **37,** 19–24.

Kantor, R., Wallner, J., & Winder, C. Process and reactive schizophrenia. *Journal of Consulting Psychology,* 1953, **17,** 157–162.

Kraepelin, E. *Psychiatry.* Leipzig: Barth, 1909.

Kreinik, Phyllis S. Parent-child themas and concept attainment in schizophrenia. Unpublished doctoral dissertation, Duke University, 1959.

Leonhard, K. Cycloid psychoses—endogenous psychoses which are neither schizophrenic nor manic-depressive. *Journal of Mental Science,* 1961, **107,** 633–648.

Lorr, M. Rating scales and check lists for the evaluation of psychopathology. *Psychological Bulletin,* 1954, **51,** 119–127.

Lorr, M. The Wittenborn psychiatric syndromes: an oblique rotation. *Journal of Consulting Psychology,* 1957, **21,** 439–444.

Lorr, M. A simplex of paranoid projection. *Journal of Consulting Psychology,* 1964, **28,** 378–380.

Lorr, M., Jenkins, R. L., & O'Connor, J. P. Factors descriptive of psychopathology and behavior of hospitalized psychotics. *Journal of Abnormal and Social Psychology,* 1955, **50,** 78–86.

Lorr, M., O'Connor, J. P., & Stafford, J. W. Confirmation of nine psychotic symptom patterns. *Journal of Clinical Psychology,* 1957, **13,** 252–257.

Lorr, M. McNair, D. M., Klett, C. J., & Lasky, J. J. Evidence of ten psychotic syndromes. *Journal of Consulting Psychology,* 1962, **26,** 185–189.

Lorr, M., Klett, C. J., & McNair, D. M. *Syndromes of psychosis.* New York: MacMillan, 1963.

McDonough, J. M. Critical flicker frequency and the spiral after-effect with process and reactive schizophrenics. *Journal of Consulting Psychology,* 1960, **24,** 150–155.

McNair, D. M., Lorr, M., & Hemingway, P. Further evidence for syndrome-based psychotic types. *Archives of General Psychiatry,* 1964, **11,** 368–376.

Meadow, A., Greenblatt, M., Funkenstein, D. H., & Solomon, H. C. Relationship between capacity for abstraction in schizophrenia and physiologic response to autonomic drugs. *Journal of Nervous and Mental Disease,* 1953, **118,** 332–338.

Orgel, S. A. Differential classification of hebephrenic and paranoid schizophrenics from case material. *Journal of Clinical Psychology,* 1957, **13,** 159–161.

Payne, R. W., & Hewlett, J. H. G. Thought disorder in psychotic patients. In H. J. Eysenck (Ed.) *Experiments in personality.* London: Routledge & Kegan Paul, 1960, Vol. II, pp. 3–104.

Phillips, L. Case history data and prognosis in schizophrenia. *Journal of Nervous and Mental Disease,* 1953, **117,** 515–525.

Phillips, L., & Rabinovitch, M. S. Social role and patterns of symptomatic behaviors. *Journal of Abnormal and Social Psychology,* 1958, **57,** 181–186.

Raskin, A., & Clyde, D. J. Factors of psychopathology in the ward behavior of acute schizophrenics. *Journal of Consulting Psychology,* 1963, **27,** 420–425.

Raush, H. L. Perceptual constancy in schizophrenia. *Journal of Personality,* 1952, **21,** 176–187.

Rodnick, E. H., & Garmezy, N. An experimental approach to the study of motivation in schizophrenia. In M. R. Jones (Ed.) *Nebraska symposium on motivation.* Lincoln: University of Nebraska Press, 1957, pp. 109–183.

Seidel, Claudene. The relationship between Klopfer's Rorschach Prognostic Rating Scale and Phillips' Case History Prognostic Rating Scale. *Journal of Consulting Psychology,* 1960, **24,** 46–49.

Solomon, L., & Zlotowski, M. The relationship between the Elgin and the Phillips measures of process-reactive schizophrenia. *Journal of Nervous and Mental Disease,* 1964, **138,** 32–37.

Sommer, R., & Witney, Gwyneth. The chain of chronicity. *American Journal of Psychiatry,* 1961, **118,** 111–117.

Steffy, R. A., & Becker, W. C. Measurement of severity of disorder in schizophrenia by means of the Holtzman Ink Blot Test. *Journal of Consulting Psychology,* 1961, **25,** 555.

Stephens, J. H., & Astrup, C. Prognosis in "process" and "non-process" schizophrenia. *American Journal of Psychiatry,* 1963, **119,** 945–953.

Stoller, F. H. The effect of maternal evaluation on schizophrenics and their siblings. Unpublished doctoral dissertation, University of California, Los Angeles, 1964.

Vaillant, G. E. The prediction of recovery in schizophrenia. *Journal of Nervous and Mental Disease,* 1962, **135,** 534–543.

Vaillant, G. E. An historical review of the remitting schizophrenias. *Journal of Nervous and Mental Disease,* 1964, **138,** 48–56. (a)

Vaillant, G. E. Prospective prediction of schizophrenic remission. *Archives of General Psychiatry,* 1964, **11,** 509–518. (b)

Wittenborn, J. R. Symptom patterns in a group of mental hospital patients. *Journal of Consulting Psychology,* 1951, **15,** 290–302.

Wittenborn, J. R. The dimensions of psychosis. *Journal of Nervous and Mental Disease,* 1962, **134,** 117–128.

Wittenborn, J. R. Distinctions within psychotic dimensions—A principal components analysis. *Journal of Nervous and Mental Disease,* 1964, **137,** 543–547. (a)

Wittenborn, J. R. Psychotic dimensions in male and female hospital patients: Principal components analysis. *Journal of Nervous and Mental Disease,* 1964, **138,** 460–467. (b)

Wittenborn, J. R., & Holzberg, J. D. The generality of psychiatric syndromes. *Journal of Consulting Psychology,* 1951, **15,** 372–380.

Wittman, Phyllis. A scale for measuring prognosis in schizophrenic patients. *Elgin State Hospital Papers,* 1941, **4,** 20–33.

Wittman, Phyllis, & Steinberg, D. L. Follow-up of an objective evaluation of prognosis in dementia praecox and manic depressive psychoses. *Elgin State Hospital Papers,* 1944, **5,** 216–227.

Zigler, E., & Phillips, L. Social competence and the process-reactive distinction in psychopathology. *Journal of Abnormal and Social Psychology,* 1962, **65,** 215–222.

Zimet, C. N., & Fine, H. J. Perceptual differentiation and two dimensions of schizophrenia. *Journal of Nervous and Mental Disease,* 1959, **129,** 435–441.

Zimet, C. N., & Fine, H. J. Primary and secondary process thinking in two types of schizophrenia. *Journal of Projective Techniques and Personality Assessment,* 1965, **29,** 93–99.

Zuckerman, M., & Grosz, H. J. Contradictory results using the mecholyl test to differentiate process and reactive schizophrenia. *Journal of Abnormal and Social Psychology,* 1959, **59,** 145–146.

CHAPTER 11

Regression Theories of Psychosis

The regression approach to psychosis assumes that psychopathology reverses the normal course of development from childhood to adulthood. Regression may be defined as a return to tendencies or responses appropriate to an earlier period of development. This concept is a crucial one in the psychoanalytic theory of neurosis (see Chapter 5). Psychoanalytically, conversion hysteria represents regression to the phallic psychosexual stage; obsessive-compulsive neurosis represents regression to the anal stage.

As used in psychoanalytic and other theories, the concept of regression assumes a fixed developmental sequence. In the progression from infancy to adulthood, earlier stages blend into later ones in an immutable sequence. An adult is normal to the extent that he manifests mature behaviors, the tendencies that occur late in the developmental sequence. Psychopathology represents a return to earlier, childlike moods of responding. Obviously, the more that early, childish patterns are retained by the developing individual, the more he will be susceptible to psychopathology when he reaches adulthood. The retention of early, childish patterns is called *fixation*, which is necessarily closely linked with regression:

. . . in mental development the progress to a higher level never takes place completely; instead characteristics of the earlier level persist alongside of or behind the new level to some extent. Disturbances of development may occur not only in the form of a total arresting of development but also in the form of retaining more characteristics of earlier stages than is normal. When a new development meets with difficulties, there may be backward movements in which the development recedes to earlier stages that were more successfully experienced. Fixation and regression are complementary to each other. (Fenichel, 1945, p. 65)

237

Cameron relates fixation and regression to the genesis of psychosis:

Special vulnerability to psychosis originates in an early fixation. The ground is laid by a failure in infancy or childhood to resolve some of the basic conflicts. The child represses or otherwise defends against recognition of his conflicts, and proceeds to mature while keeping them out of his preconscious and conscious organization. If in adulthood he is exposed to extreme or prolonged stress, which he cannot withstand, he will suffer a sweeping subtotal regression to the general area of his unresolved conflicts. The subtotal, psychotic regression then lays bare the early fixations. (1963, p. 216)

Thus the concept of regression requires the assumption of a fixed developmental sequence that suffers some kind of defect or interference. It is the task of a regression theory to furnish the details of psychological development and to demonstrate that each kind of pathology represents a return to a previously fixated developmental stage. Since there are a number of dimensions of psychological development, it is not surprising to find different regression theories, each emphasizing different aspects. The theories to be discussed are psychoanalysis, a modified Sullivanian approach, Arieti's teleological regression theory, and applications of Werner's developmental theory.

PSYCHOANALYTIC THEORY

Psychoanalytic theory assumes that psychopathology represents a partial return to defenses and problems appropriate to pregenital (pre-Oedipal) stages of psychosexual development. The psychoses are the severest kinds of psychopathology, and therefore regression must be the deepest. Whereas the crucial regression in neuroses is never earlier than the anal period, in psychoses it goes back to the oral period; this is true for psychotic depression, mania, and schizophrenia.

Depression

Psychotic depression represents a decisive loss of self-esteem. The normal person has a healthy love for himself and is only partially dependent on others for attention, affection, and praise; the potentially depressive person has little self-love and requires the affection of someone else in order to maintain his self-esteem. The predisposition to a loss of self-esteem is laid down during infancy.

The Developmental Sequence. During infancy there are alternate periods of hunger and satisfaction (being fed). When the infant is hungry, he tries to abolish this state and achieve a return to satisfaction by believing that he is omnipotent; to the extent that he is all-powerful, his needs must be served. However, the infant learns that he is not omnipotent, that hunger is abolished only when a parent appears. The self-omnipotence is therefore projected onto the parents. The problem then becomes one of abolishing the state of being alone rather than of being hungry; now being without the omnipotent parent is akin to a sense of annihilation. The presence and affection of the parent becomes the same as being comfortable and well-fed, the unconscious equation being: food equals love.

In this early period when the ego is just starting to form, the child's self-esteem is entirely dependent on the affection of the parents. If the parents disappoint or reject the child, that is, if they do not consistently love him, the child cannot develop a sense of being worthwhile. He will always require the attention and good opinion of others in order to feel self-worth.

When development is normal, the self-esteem sequence is as follows. Omnipotence is succeeded by its projection to the parents and then an attempt to share it first by identification with the parents and later by receiving attention and affection from them. Finally, self-esteem is determined by the self, specifically by that portion of the ego that differentiates into the superego. When fixation occurs at the earlier stages, there is a predisposition toward depression. This consists of attempting to achieve omnipotence by identifying with the parents; symbolically, this means orally incorporating them.

Fixation at the oral phase also affects the person's identifications and relations with others. The sequence starts with an absence of external figures before the ego has separated from the id. This is followed by incorporation (*primitive identification*), then by ambivalent love relationships, and finally by mature love. If the infant is frustrated very early in life, there is fixation at the first stage (*primary narcissism*). Such fixation prevents him from having adequate and strong bonds with others and renders him susceptible to deep regression. It is precisely this fixation that predisposes toward depression; ambivalent feelings toward others are given up first for primitive identification and then for primary narcissism.

Consistent with the depressive's oral fixation is his major defense mechanism, *introjection*. Introjection is the psychological analogue of the act of eating (oral incorporation), and as we noted earlier, food equals love. The specific problem for the potentially depressive child is that he must somehow avoid the terrifying feeling of annihilation which accompanies rejection or desertion by his mother. He solves this problem by absolute compliance to his mother's wishes, which is achieved by psychologically taking in his mother as a part of himself. Therefore this "internalized figure" represents and in part substitutes for the mother, making demands and doling out approval. This *introject* is the primitive forerunner of the superego, which is the major source of problems for the psychotic depressive.

The Development of Psychosis. Two kinds of events may precipitate a psychotic depression. The first includes failure to live up to expectations and transgressions of the moral code, although the latter are rare. The second consists of the rejection or isolation of the person by loved ones, for example, through death or desertion. In the first instance there is guilt, and in the second there is a loss of external love and affection, both causing a marked drop in self-esteem. The immediate reaction may be a feeling that the person is unloved and that the world is a barren place, but oftener the depressive person verbalizes self-hatred (superego attacking ego).

The similarity between depression and mourning was pointed out by Freud long ago, but two differences are important. First, in normal grief the loss is conscious, whereas in depression the loss is unconscious. Second, in normal grief there is no loss of self-esteem, whereas in depression the ego is attacked and impoverished.

Faced with a loss of self-esteem, the depressive attempts to regain at least some measure of love and affection in order to diminish his feeling of annihilation. He attempts to undo the loss by introjecting the lost love object—parent or parent-substitute. This introjection is crucial to psychotic depression and is what sets it off from both neurotic depression and normal grief. Both the neurotic and the normal person, after losing the affection of a parental figure, attempt to establish a similar relationship with another figure, but the psychotic depressive individual reacts to his loss by a symbolic oral incorporation of the lost figure, whereby he identifies the figure with his own ego.

Introjection of the loved person reveals the depressive's ambivalence toward this figure. The depressive person craves nurturance from the loved person but at the same time resents being in a subordinate position and also the frustration of not receiving sufficient love. Once the figure has been introjected and is part of the ego, it can be attacked through an attack on the ego. Thus when the depressive says, "I hate myself," he is in part attacking the loved figure who abandoned him and was subsequently taken into the ego. The "I" is the superego, and the "myself" the ego, which now includes the introjected loved person.

The individual who is predisposed toward a psychotic depression has marked ambivalence in his relations with others, but can reveal only his affection, not his hostility. After the loss of the loved one and the subsequent introjection, it is possible to express the latent hatred by means of the superego's attacking the ego. Now all the sadistic impulses originally directed against the loved person can be directed against the ego. The superego is in command of the personality, and the ego is merely a whipping boy.

Despite constant attacks by the superego, the ego somehow attempts to undo the loss, to placate the superego. By bearing the self-reproach without protest, the ego attempts to impress its basic worth on the superego. This effort initially fails because it is impossible to stop the torrent of sadism loosed by the regression to oral sadism; but eventually the sadism of the superego lessens, and the ego begins to regain a measure of self-esteem. Sooner or later the superego exhausts itself in its attacks on the ego, and gradually the depression lifts. Summarizing, the ego reacts to the loss of a loved person by introjecting this figure, the introjection marking a regression to oral sadism and primary narcissism. The ego attempts to placate a strict, punitive superego, which attacks the ego not only because the superego has taken over the sadism of the oral-sadistic phase but also because the loved-hated person is now part of the ego. As long as the depression lasts, the superego is in command of the personality, and it acts like a vengeful God toward the ego.

Mania

In mania there is an enormous increase in self-esteem and a corresponding decrease in the demands of conscience. The manic achieves what the depressive desires but cannot realize: an overwhelming feeling of self-worth and a magical belief in his own omnipotence. The superego is somehow defeated or neutralized, and all the psychic tension that went into the battle with the superego is released, to be disposed of by the ego. This accounts for the unrestrained mood and energy of the manic, who in effect celebrates his "victory."

This is not to say that the superego ceases to operate. The victory is temporary, just one battle in a war. The ego must resort to defense mechanisms in order to deny the presence of the superego, which hovers in the background. The typical mechanisms are denial, reaction formation, and overcompensation. In fact, some of the manic's mirth may be interpreted as a reaction formation to the depression threatened by the superego. The presence of defense mechanisms also helps to explain the rigidity and "driven" character of the manic's feelings of omnipotence, euphoria, and energy level.

In accounting for the cycles of mania and depression seen in some patients, it is necessary to go back to the cycles of hunger and satiation which occur in infancy. These lead to pain-pleasure cycles: the infant learns that pleasure follows pain and pain follows pleasure. This cycle may be indelibly imprinted in the psychic structure of the potential cyclothymic. Later, when he becomes depressed, the cycle is set in motion. First, the superego persecutes the ego (depression); this gives way to triumph by the ego over the superego (mania), which in turn, is succeeded by a return to the predominance of the superego.

Schizophrenia

In schizophrenia, as in affective psychoses, there is a break with reality, which is manifested in the bizarre symptoms described earlier. And in schizophrenia, as in any psychopathology, the psychoanalytic explanation emphasizes the nature and depth of the regression. Both affective psychoses and schizophrenia are similar in that the patient has regressed to primary narcissism. In schizophrenia the regression is seen more clearly, partly because it is to an even earlier stage (early oral, as opposed to the late oral or oral-sadistic stage in affective psychoses) and partly because the superego plays a minor role.

During early infancy the ego has not yet differentiated from the id; there is no awareness either of self or of reality as something separate from self. Gradually, the infant learns to distinguish between inside the body and outside, between self and other; the "outside" and the "other" are reality. This distinction is the basis of the ego, whose major function is reality testing. Schizophrenia is viewed in terms of a regression to this primitive stage, to an era before the ego became differentiated from the id or during its emergence. The schizophrenic, like the infant, cannot test reality adequately; unlike the developing infant, the schizophrenic rejects reality.

There are two immediate causes of the break with reality. The first is an increase in id demands, especially of infantile sexual impulses (homosexual, anal erotic, etc.). The second is an increase in guilt or anxiety revolving around forbidden impulses. The ego may react to these precipitating events by siding with the id against reality. However, only in a minority of psychotics does the ego turn away from reality in order to indulge in id impulses. Generally, the ego seeks not a gain of pleasure through the expression of id impulses but an escape from the temptation to express such impulses. Thus reality is rejected because it is so tempting that the psychotic person fears that he cannot hold back his infantile sexual and aggressive urges.

These precipitating events will not lead to a psychotic break unless there is a predisposition to reject reality. This predisposition is rooted in fixation at the early oral stage of development, before the development of the ego. Psychoanalysts admit that the tendency to develop such a fixation may be due to unspecified biological variables, but emphasize only the developmental variables that can induce a fixation at any phase: traumatic incidents and frustration.

Schizophrenia starts with a break with reality, and then the sequence consists of initial regressive symptoms followed by later restitutional symptoms. *Regressive symptoms* are appropriate to the loss of identity and the vegetative existence characteristic of infancy; they occur because the ego no longer functions adequately, denying or rejecting reality. *Restitutional symptoms* are part of the ego's attempt to deal with both reality and the pressure of id impulses; the result is symptoms analogous to the compromise symptoms of neurosis but representing greater regression.

Regressive Symptoms. (1) *Feelings of Depersonalization and Loss.* When the ego is developing during infancy, there is a growing awareness of one's own body and the development of a body image which does not necessarily correspond to what the body is like. When the schizophrenic regresses to primary narcissism, he returns to a state of extreme awareness of his body. The regression exposes concern about body image, which is the core of the ego. Since the schizophrenic's reality testing mechanism no longer functions, he may develop bizarre ideas about his body. In any event, the regression to primary narcissism leads him to an excessive interest and concern about his own body, which makes the schizophrenic feel strange. The ego defends against this interest by means of repression. The patient is aware of a change in himself, his body image having been altered by the regression, but because of repression he is only aware that certain internal perceptions or sensations are missing. The altered body image, together with a sense that something is missing, tends to perplex the schizophrenic. He knows that something has changed but does not know precisely what. This is depersonalization.

Depersonalization is one aspect of the larger process of retreating from the external world. When the ego sinks into the id, the schizophrenic's awareness of this makes him sensitive to the changes that are occurring. Once he rejects reality, the world may seem like a dead or empty place. He may feel dead himself or believe that the world has come to an end. Thus, when the regression to primary narcissism occurs, the schizophrenic's awareness of the loss of contact with the world may manifest itself in feelings of depersonalization or fantasies of the world's being destroyed. Underlying both is a withdrawal of interest in and relationships with people and events in the world of reality.

(2) *Grandiosity*. The decisive regression to primary narcissism may not lead to feelings of strangeness. The psychotic may simply regress to the stage of infantile omnipotence, denying a frustrating reality and asserting his own magic power. The reality testing function of the ego ordinarily prevents the widespread use of the mechanism of denial, but when the ego abandons this function, there is no longer any inhibiting of the mechanism. The patient simply denies that the world can hurt him by dismissing its existence. He is magically all-powerful and more lovable than any other person could possibly be. This leads to "secondary narcissism," wherein the patient responds to himself as he would to another person. Thus he loves himself as he would another and may even have sexual fantasies about himself as a love object. These possibilities may be ascribed to the upsurge of self-love that occurs in the schizophrenic regression to primary narcissism, a stage of infancy when there is no outside world and the infant is omnipotent. The further possibility of delusions of grandeur occurs only as part of attempts at restitution, to be discussed shortly.

(3) *Passivity*. The decisive regression in schizophrenia may go back to the earliest days of life, during which the infant is passive and orally

receptive. The schizophrenic who regresses this far gives up trying to deal with harsh reality and maintains only a vegetative existence. He recognizes no world outside of himself, and he must be attended to and fed. In extreme cases he may assume positions similar to those of a fetus.

If the regression is not quite so extreme, the schizophrenic may return to the era during which the infant is fascinated by the stimuli around him and tends to imitate them. He may echo the sounds he hears, imitate the gestures he sees, or engage in infantile movements which have no value in terms of communication or impact on the environment. The schizophrenic may regress so far as to manifest behavior similar to that seen in nursing infants.

(4) *Archaic Thinking.* The last aspect of the decisive regression involves going from logical to prelogical thinking, from *secondary process* to *primary process.* Secondary process thinking concerns itself with what might happen, thus allowing the ego to respond appropriately. Primary process thinking concerns itself with what is desirable, regardless of reality. The schizophrenic retreats from thinking with words to thinking pictorially, just as the child does before the advent of speech. In the prespeech era of early childhood, ideas are largely concerned with wish fulfillment, and it is this era to which the schizophrenic regresses. Such thinking (primary process) is unorganized and contains contradictory ideas. It is magical; the idea of a thing and the thing itself are equated. Since the ego has sunk into the id and there is no distinction between the ego and the world, events that happen to things in the world may be experienced as happening to the ego. Thinking is also symbolic, with the symbol of a thing and the thing itself being equated. Thus for a schizophrenic the penis and a snake are the same, and he may react to a snake with all the affect connected with the penis. There are none of the restraints and censorship of thinking that occur when the ego is functioning properly, and the regressed schizophrenic may express Oedipal thoughts directly. The decisive regression renders the schizophrenic's thinking primitive and prelogical, and it can be understood only in terms of the thinking of a young child who has not begun to speak or is just learning words.

Restitutional Symptoms. The schizophrenic breakdown consists of a rejection of reality, as the ego sinks into the id and is no longer able to carry out the function of reality testing. Regressive symptoms are manifestations of this return to primitive, infantile modes of thinking, perceiving, and feeling. However, the end point of regression is not merely a static state analogous to early infancy. The schizophrenic, having surrendered reality, makes desperate attempts either to recapture it or to substitute for it. These attempts result in *restitutional symptoms.*

(1) *Bizarre Language.* One way for the schizophrenic to get back to reality is to re-establish relations with external stimuli, but his attempt to

do this cannot wholly succeed. Usually he succeeds only in recapturing the symbols of external stimuli, the words that represent external objects. Because his thinking is dominated by primary process, he cannot distinguish between a word and the object or events it represents. In equating the word with what it represents, the schizophrenic renders his speech incomprehensible to a normal listener.

Freud stated that the conscious idea of an external stimulus could be divided into the idea of the word and the idea of the concrete object, whereas the unconscious idea was only the idea of the concrete object itself, without the idea of the word. Repression consists of splitting off the idea of the word from the idea of the concrete object, but the kind of repression occurring in schizophrenia is not quite the same as that occurring in neuroses. The schizophrenic may seize on the verbal idea as a substitute for the idea of the object because it is as close as he can get to reality. He tries first to attain reality with words and is stopped from proceeding to the external reality represented by the words. This is what gives schizophrenic speech its bizarre, elaborate character.

(2) *Hallucinations.* In the normal person contact with reality involves perceiving the stimuli of the outer world and the memories of them, which together constitute the "inner world" of the ego. When a schizophrenic psychosis occurs, outer reality is rejected, and there is little or no perception of external stimuli. This condition is analogous to dreaming, when the sensory apparatus is functioning only minimally. Just as dreams are dominated by the illogical wish fulfillment of primary process, the perceptions of schizophrenics are dominated by the same process. Just as anxiety creeps into dreams, anxiety enters the hallucinations of schizophrenics.

Thus hallucinations may be expected to occur whenever perceptions of the external world are cut off: in sleep (dreaming), in sensory isolation, and in schizophrenic psychosis. The schizophrenic first rejects the external world, regressing to a stage prior to the separation of ego from id. In the relative absence of external perceptions, he creates a new "reality," that of hallucinations. For some schizophrenics the hallucinations represent simple wish fulfillment, instinctual urges thus being discharged without the obstacles and encumbrances of reality. However, for most schizophrenics the hallucinations have frightening elements, which represent the return of part of the rejected reality. Hallucinations thus include not only elements of an escape from reality and reversion to the wish fulfillment of primary process but also elements of anxiety and guilt connected with instinctual urges. Since the superego is a kind of "voice from within," it is not surprising that many auditory hallucinations are heavily laden with guilt, the schizophrenic hearing voices accusing him of terrible thoughts and deeds.

Insofar as hallucinations represent a return to primary process thinking, they are regressive symptoms. However, hallucinations are also perceptions that replace those lost when reality is given up or rejected. They occur in response to the breakdown of reality testing and represent an attempt to cope with reality and the instinctual urges demanding discharge. As such, they must be regarded primarily as restitutional symptoms rather than as regressive symptoms of schizophrenia.

(3) *Delusions.* The major mechanism underlying delusions is projection, whereby impulses and ideas unacceptable to the ego are cast out and attributed to other people, events, or objects. Projection is one of the most primitive mechanisms, being based on the infant's spitting out or "projecting" the evil within himself. Since the infantile definition of evil is anything that causes pain or discomfort, the primitive projection lays the groundwork for the later casting out of *any* "inner badness."

Because delusions are the most prominent symptom in paranoid schizophrenia, it is in paranoids that delusions have been the focus of study. The Freudian approach to paranoid delusions was initiated by Freud's analysis of the case of Schreber (1950, vol. 3). Initially, Freud conjectured that the attribution of delusions to homosexuality might be limited to men, but subsequently women were included also. Nevertheless, as the theory has been stated, it applies mainly to men. The main conflict in paranoid delusions is the inability of the patient to accept his homosexual impulses, and this conflict initiates one of three kinds of delusions.

The first is the common delusion of persecution, the dynamic sequence of which is as follows. The homosexual impulses are denied by the mechanism of reaction formation: "I do not love him, I hate him." This denial assuages guilt concerning homosexuality, but it leads to guilt concerning hostility. Therefore the hostility is projected: "I do not hate him, he hates me." This formula places all the blame on the other person and accounts for anxiety in his presence. Thus the original homosexual impulse is concealed and the hostility is rationalized.

Such projection can occur only in an individual who is extremely ambivalent in his relations with others. It is as though the person resembled an infant who wished to incorporate (orally) his entire environment, and who had then to spit out the evil that he had taken in. The paranoid has strong love and hate tendencies. Insofar as the love tendencies are unacceptable to the rigid superego because of their homosexual nature, they must be cast out. Insofar as the hate tendencies are unacceptable, they too must be cast out. The love tendencies are denied by means of reaction formation: "I do not love him, I hate him." The hate tendencies are projected onto the formerly loved person.

The nature of the delusion is determined mainly by the reaction formation to the homosexual impulses. In delusions of persecution, love tendencies are denied altogether. If the object of the love is altered, the outcome is erotomania: "I do not love him, I love *her*." This formula is then changed to, "I love her because she loves me," and the sequence of reaction formation and projection is complete. Because his heterosexual impulses are tinged with homosexuality, the paranoid cannot even accept the normal urge to love a woman; he must rationalize his love for her in terms of her love for him.

The other possible outcome of homosexual urges is jealousy: "It is not I who loves him but she." It follows that the woman must be suspected of infidelity. If the paranoid is persistent enough, he may drive the woman into the arms of another man, thus validating his jealous delusion.

The second kind of delusion consists of ideas of *reference,* in which the patient feels controlled by others, receives messages for himself alone over mass media of communication, or hears voices accusing him of evil. Such delusions involve projection of his own superego. The superego of paranoids is harsh and rigid, being based on the early, frightening commands of parents. When the ego has a well-developed mechanism of projection, it is only natural that it should try to escape from such a punitive superego by projecting it to the outside world. The projection succeeds only in externalizing the guilt. The patient no longer has to fear his own conscience or be controlled by it, but he must fear attack and control from the whole world around him. The evil is no longer "within"; it surrounds him.

The superego is also projected in delusions concerning the law. The litigious kind of paranoid insists that his legal rights have been flouted, and he seeks redress through the courts. He feels that he has been wronged and demands that his innocence be asserted. The sequence is as follows. The ego cannot deal with the harsh punitive superego and therefore projects it to the environment, specifically to authority. Now legal authority is equated with the superego, and the ego can attempt to establish its innocence, and thereby deny any possible guilt, by the "rational" procedures of the courtroom.

The last kind of delusion involves *world reconstruction fantasies.* Just as in the regressive stage of schizophrenia, the patient loses the world or sees it as an empty place, so in the restitutional phase he attempts to build it up again and attribute meaning to it. The commonest type is the religious delusion, in which the patient is a messiah or savior.

Mixed Symptoms. Some symptoms may be either regressive or restitutional. When the decisive regression occurs, the schizophrenic returns to the primitive modes of thinking, feeling, and acting which characterize early infancy. However, his entire personality does not necessarily regress all the way. Parts of his personality may regress only some of the way, to phases more mature than the early oral phase. Thus some of the symptoms manifested in schizophrenia may be attributed to this partial regression.

On the other hand, anal, phallic, or Oedipal symptoms may represent the schizophrenic's attempt to fight off the regression and make a partial return to a higher phase of psychosexual development. For example, when a schizophrenic suddenly engages in sexual behavior or in anal erotic behavior (for example, smearing or incontinence), it is not clear whether it is because he has regressed or because he is attempting to fight the decisive regression. Thus there are symptoms that cannot be classified as *either* regressive or restitutional.

A MODIFIED SULLIVANIAN APPROACH

Harry Stack Sullivan made assumptions similar to those of classical psychoanalysis; he stressed the crucial importance of the first two years in determining psychosis and saw psychotic symptoms as regressions to particular developmental stages. However, his approach emphasized slightly different aspects of early development, and, as elaborated by Kantor and Winder (1959), dealt only with schizophrenia.

Kantor and Winder (1959) construe the process-reactive dimension in terms of the depth of regression that occurs in schizophrenia: the severer the regression, the more the picture is one of process schizophrenia. They adopt Sullivan's five developmental stages in relating schizophrenic symptoms to depth of regression: empathic, prototaxic, parataxic, autistic, and syntaxic.

The Empathic Stage

At the earliest time of infancy the mother may not furnish enough love and attention. Such failure or a rejection by the crucial adult figure usually results in panic on the part of the infant. The anxiety may be severe enough to cause biological dysfunction. The helpless infant, unable to cope with his massive fear, may retreat to detachment from all human figures. This kind of withdrawal should lead to process schizophrenia: gradual onset, deterioration of thought processes and personality, and delusions.

The Prototaxic Stage

The young child has not yet discriminated between himself and others and maintains his infantile omnipotence. Rejection or an absence of love tends to fixate him at this stage, which leads to severe thinking disorder, grandiose delusions, and hallucinations later, when schizophrenia occurs. There is also withdrawal from others but to a lesser extent than when the fixation occurs at the empathic stage.

The Parataxic Stage

The ego is forming and the self is being differentiated from the external world. The young child begins to perceive relations between himself and others, especially those involving approval and disapproval. Approval elicits satisfaction and rudimentary self-esteem; disapproval elicits anxiety. Fixation at this stage leads to the following schizophrenic symptoms: fear of one's inner processes and of world disaster, dissociated ideas that appear to come from "outside," panic, perplexity, and delusions that everything is deteriorating to nothingness. All of these symptoms are attempts to deny a lack of self-worth, by projecting "inner" troubles to the "outer world." As such, they represent restitutional, rather than regressive, symptoms.

The Autistic Stage

The young child is learning language and other symbols. Fantasy is being put to use in the rehearsal of roles, but both symbolization and fantasy have not yet been restrained by reality, and the child must learn to check his ideas and perceptions against a social consensus. Fixation here leads to paranoid suspiciousness, incorrect interpretation of reality, and systematic delusions. A schizophrenic with these symptoms cannot separate his personal, private symbols and his fantasy from a reality that is shared and agreed on by others. Nevertheless, he can discriminate between self and others, and there is little of the confusion and panic of the schizophrenic fixated at the parataxic stage. The autistic schizophrenic *knows* the solution to the puzzle and has elaborated a set of delusions around this basic assumption of a "plot" whose center is himself. He does not withdraw from others but attempts to convince them of the correctness of his interpretation of reality.

The Syntaxic Stage

The child learns normal role-taking and the need for consensual validation of one's perceptions and interpretations. He learns to feel sympathy for others, and the rudiments of understanding of others. The person who has progressed this far is essentially a normal personality. If he becomes schizophrenic, it can only be a temporary, appropriate reaction to an impossible situation. Onset is sudden, the precipitating incident severe, and the episode temporary.

The five stages of regression in schizophrenia are thus related to severity of symptoms, to immaturity, and to prognosis. Kantor and Winder suggested this extension of Sullivan's thinking as the theoretical basis for the process-reactive continuum. Process schizophrenics are represented by the severer symptoms accompanying regression to the earlier stages (empathic and parataxic), whereas reactives are represented by the maturer symptoms accompanying regression to the later stages (prototaxic and syntaxic).

THE TELEOLOGICAL REGRESSION HYPOTHESIS

Arieti (1955) has proposed a regression hypothesis that has neural analogues. He borrows from the neural theorizing of Jackson, who assumed that higher nervous centers (late in the evolutionary sequence) control lower centers by means of inhibition. When higher centers are knocked out, lower centers take over, the organism functioning at a lower level of organization.

Arieti hypothesized the following sequence:

1. Anxiety leads to a "functional paralysis" of the higher mental processes.

2. This impairment of higher processes results in a release of lower levels from inhibition.

3. The individual now re-adjusts to a new organization of mental activity at a lower level of functioning; this lower level entails less anxiety and conflict, which makes the regression to it *teleological* or purposive.

4. The schizophrenic cannot attain equilibrium or integration at the lower, regressed level of functioning because it is too deviant from normal functioning (from what the organism is "built for").

5. Therefore there is usually further regression, and the individual goes through successive stages of mental deterioration; the complete term used by Arieti is *progressive teleological regression*.

Arieti uses this hypothesis to explain schizophrenic thinking. He adopts the distinction, stated by von Domarus, between Aristotelian logic and paleologic. Aristotelian logic is the higher and more mature form, which is used by normal individuals. A normal person reaches a conclusion rationally, that is, on the basis of a logical deduction from a premise. This is illustrated by the well-known, "all men are mortal; Socrates is a man; therefore Socrates is mortal." This is Aristotelian logic, with identity based on identical subjects.

A schizophrenic uses paleologic, in which identity is based on identical predicates: "I am in this institution; that doctor is in this institution; therefore I am a doctor." This kind of reasoning, together with the confusion of both connotation and symbolic representation with denotation (proper definition), can lead to bizarre delusions and weird behavior. The use of paleologic represents a regression by the schizophrenic in the face of severe anxiety. When the anxiety impairs his higher level of functioning, he reverts to this lower, primitive kind of thinking.

THE COMPARATIVE-DEVELOPMENTAL APPROACH

The developmental views of Heinz Werner (1948) emphasize the maturation of *process* through sequential stages from infancy to adulthood. In contrast to the orthodox psychoanalytic approach to development, Werner's approach focuses on *formal structure* rather than *content: how* rather than *what,* cognition rather than impulses.

The basic assumption is that *development involves increasing differen-*

tiation and organization. When an infant is stimulated, he can respond in only a generalized, undifferentiated manner—with his entire body. As maturation proceeds, there is an increasing differentiation of cognition and activity. The response becomes more focused, less diffuse, and less stimulus-bound. As the child progresses toward adulthood, the increasingly differentiated processes become organized into levels. The earlier, more primitive processes are subordinated to later, more complex processes. The final mature organization of the psychic apparatus represents an integration of the various sequential stages, with later, differentiated processes predominating earlier, diffuse ones.

The end point of development is maturity and normality. Psychopathology represents a return to earlier, more primitive processes. As it stands, this regression hypothesis is too broad to be useful in explaining psychosis. It does not specify the details of regression: the depth of the regression and the particular behaviors to be expected because of the regression. Goldman (1962) attempted to remedy this defect by applying the theory specifically to schizophrenia. He attempted to show how schizophrenia represents a reversal of developmental patterns in the areas of emotional behavior, social behavior, learning, perception, thinking, and language.

In each of these areas Goldman stated the normal developmental sequence and then reviewed evidence of schizophrenics' regression to early, primitive phases. Since Goldman was strongly in favor of comparative-developmental theory, his evaluation of the evidence was not without bias. In order to correct for this bias and obtain a more balanced view, the evidence will be reevaluated. In each of the areas we shall first present the developmental view and the accompanying interpretation of the evidence, followed by an independent evaluation of the evidence.

Emotional Behavior

Developmental View. Throughout childhood emotional behavior matures along three dimensions. First, it is initially overt and uncontrolled, the young child manifesting directly and immediately every passing emotion. Gradually, emotional expression is modulated and becomes less manifest; for example, boys learn not to cry even when they are hurt or sad. Second, the primitive, diffuse excitement of infancy differentiates with increasing age into a variety of emotions, each with subtleties and nuances of feeling. Third, the young child's emotional states are unstable and changing, but as he matures, they become stable and enduring.

In schizophrenia there is a reversal of these maturational changes, and the patient's emotionality resembles that of a young child. The acute schizophrenic is excited, anxious, and generally uncontrolled in his emotional expression. In both acute and chronic schizophrenics emotions become diffuse and undifferentiated; sexual and aggressive feelings are likely to combine, as are love and hate. Finally, emotional expression tends to be unstable, as the schizophrenic rapidly shifts from one affective state to another for no apparent reason.

Evaluation. The developmental sequence seen in children fits the three dimensions proposed by Goldman, but the assertions about schizophrenics seem doubtful. Only a minority of acute schizophrenics are excited and confused; the majority manifest a variety of emotional behaviors, such as quiet withdrawal, "rational" attempts to convince others of the truth of delusions, passive resignation, or indifference. The tendency to cry readily in the face of frustration or rebuff, seen in most young children, appears in only a minority of schizophrenics, acute or chronic. Most schizophrenics are *not* emotionally labile. Their emotional behavior may be unpredictable, but generally it is marked by a *lack* of outbursts, in contrast to the frequent emotional upheavals of children.

The issue of fusion of emotions is an open one. It is difficult to say that the emotional experiences of a given schizophrenic are more undifferentiated than those of an adult. Love-hate ambivalance exists in everyone, normal persons as well as psychotics. Schizophrenics express this ambivalance more openly and with less control, but this may occur because of failure to deal adequately with social reality. Normal adults know that it is not socially acceptable to admit negative feelings toward a "loved one" such as a husband, wife, or parent. Schizophrenics tend to be bound less by such social conventions. In brief, it is not known whether the emotions of schizophrenics are less differentiated than those of normal adults.

The emotional behavior of schizophrenics is different from that of normal adults, but the sole element of difference appears to be predictability. It is difficult for an observer to understand or explain the anxiety or anger that a schizophrenic may manifest in the absence of an appropriate stimulus. This kind of unpredictability is not seen in children, whose emotional behavior can usually be easily explained. Although the emotional behavior of many schizophrenics is deviant, it is not childlike. The regression hypothesis appears to lack support in this area.

Social Behavior

Developmental View. At first the infant does not distinguish between himself and others but learns to do so gradually. Then he begins to play alone, and this solitary play gives way to side-by-side play in which there is no interaction. The last stage is reciprocal play, in which children give and take with and against one another, abiding by or breaking the rules of a variety of games.

All three stages are seen in schizophrenia, the most regressed patients manifesting the most primitive social behavior. Paranoids, the most mature patients, often seek the company of others, if only to spin out the details of their delusions. Hallucinating schizophrenics may engage in a kind of "parallel play" with other patients: they are present but preoccupied with their own fantasy world. Last, the most regressed schizophrenics tend to withdraw completely, avoiding even minimal contact with others.

Evaluation. The foregoing hypotheses are based on the assumption that suspicious, hallucinating, and isolated schizophrenics may be placed on a continuum of increasing severity of symptoms. This assumption is reasonable: one index of severity of psychosis is the extent to which the patient withdraws from others. The key word here is *withdraws.* The more severely disturbed schizophrenics tend to be frightened of others and avoid social contacts because they are anxiety laden.

Young children engage in solitary play for an entirely different reason. They do not fear others but simply have not become sufficiently aware of others as social objects. Severely regressed schizophrenics, in contrast, are aware of others as social objects but fear them. Thus the superficial similarity between the social behavior of young children and that of regressed schizophrenics does not stand up to scrutiny; the behaviors are really quite different.

Similarly, the parallel between hallucinating schizophrenics and children in side-by-side play, and the parallel between paranoids and socially interacting children are tenuous and superficial. Hallucinating schizophrenics become lost in fantasy whether or not others are present, whereas children in parallel play do affect one another's behavior. Paranoids interact with others only to involve them in their delusional schemes, whereas children who can interact in play situations are capable of deeper and more enduring involvement with other children. Although the social behavior of schizophrenics is different from that of normal adults, it is not really similar to the social behavior of children. It follows that the social behavior of schizophrenics does not constitute a regression to more primitive developmental modes of responding.

Learning

Developmental View. Goldman distinguished three kinds of learning and arranged them in a developmental sequence from primitive to mature. The first kind of learning is *classical conditioning,* in which the learner passively acquires associations between unconditioned and conditioned stimuli presented to him in pairs. Classical conditioning is characteristic of infants and young children, who are at the mercy of an environment that presents paired stimuli.

The second kind is *instrumental conditioning,* in which the learner is more active but still learns by rote. He does not conceptualize, generalize, or check out hypotheses. Such learning is typical of young children.

The third kind is *problem solving,* in which the learner is most active. He develops hypotheses and tests them: he looks for regularities and sequences; and he generalizes beyond present stimuli so that solutions are not dependent upon rote learning. This learning is characteristic of older children and adults.

This developmental hierarchy of learning processes has testable consequences. First, young children should classically condition faster than older children or adults, and there is evidence for this in studies of early conditioning. Second, stimulus generalization, which represents a lack of differentiation, should decrease with age; there is positive evidence on this point also.

Concerning schizophrenics, it is assumed that their learning processes resemble those of young children. They should condition faster and generalize more than normal persons but perform more poorly on complex, problem-solving tasks. There is evidence for both of these deductions.

Evaluation. The hierarchy of types of learning is an interesting and novel idea. It is beyond the scope of this book to evaluate this developmental hypothesis, and we shall concentrate on the research on learning in schizophrenics and normal individuals.

First, it is questionable whether schizophrenics condition faster than normal persons. Two studies report positive findings (Pfaffman & Schlosberg, 1936; Spence & Taylor, 1953). However, six studies report negative findings (Shipley, 1934; Franks, 1954; Peters & Murphree, 1954; Howe, 1958; O'Connor & Rawnsley, 1959; and Pishkin & Hershiser, 1963). Thus, the weight of evidence suggests that schizophrenics do not condition faster.

Second, the belief that schizophrenics overgeneralize in comparison to normals may be attributed to a paper by Mednick (1958), who mentions four ostensibly supporting studies. Lang and Buss (1965) reviewed the four studies and showed that the results were either equivocal or did not support the hypothesis. The most recent research (Daniell, 1964) found no differences between schizophrenics and normal controls in stimulus generalization. Thus the only clear evidence fails to support the notion that schizophrenics tend to overgeneralize.

Third, it is true that schizophrenics generally perform more poorly than normal persons on complex tasks. However, it is also true that schizophrenics perform worse on simple tasks such as reaction time. The research relevant to this issue will be discussed in the next two chapters, but it may be summarized here. Schizophrenics tend to have worse performance than normal individuals on *both* simple and complex tasks, and therefore the developmental hypothesis is not supported.

Perception

Developmental View. It is in the area of perception that the sequence from diffuseness to differentiation to hierarchic organization may be seen most clearly.

Figure and ground, contours, patterns of light and shadow, movement, all merge into an undifferentiated and perceptual mass . . . From this globality emerges stages of increasingly differentiated perception. Here visual patterns acquire object-properties, with definitive contours and localized in three-dimensional space. This development then terminates in a stage in which these differentiated aspects of the perceptual field are integrated, or synthesized into a single meaningful percept. (Goldman, 1962, p. 60)

Supporting evidence comes from performance on the Rorschach test. The regression hypothesis asserts that there is a parallel between the development of perception during childhood and the changes in perception that occur in proceeding from psychopathology to normality. Two kinds of evidence are required. First, it must be shown that there is a progression of successive stages of perception in childhood. Second, it must be demonstrated that the severer the psychopathology, the more perception is developmentally early, or, stated another way, the more perception resembles that of young children.

The system for scoring developmentally early and late Rorschach responses was devised by Friedman (1952). Briefly, Friedman attempts to score responses on the basis of such dichotomies as labile-stable, diffuse-discrete, fragmented-integrated, and rigid-flexible. An important consideration is goodness of form: the degree to which the response fits the actual form of the inkblot.

Hemmendinger (1953, 1960) used this scoring system in comparing the responses of 3, 4, 5, 6, 7, 8, 9, and 10 year old children, to those of adults. He concluded that the children's data revealed clear trends.

With increasing age there is a decrease of the undifferentiated, diffuse whole and detail responses, an increase of the highly articulated, well-integrated whole and detail responses, and an interesting shift from the early whole responses toward small details between the ages of six and eight years, then declining in favor of the integrated whole responses later on. (1960, p. 64)

Thus the first kind of evidence has apparently been obtained.

The second kind of evidence requires a demonstration of perceptual regression in psychopathology. Friedman (1952) compared schizophrenics, normals, and children in the three-to-five-year range on Rorschach responses, scored developmentally.

On the whole the results would suggest that the perceptual functioning of the schizophrenic, in its structural aspects is intimately related to that of the child. . . . its characteristics may be understood as those of a primitive globality, syncretism, lability, diffuseness, and rigidity. In the capacity for differentiation and hierarchic integration which marks the normal adult group, the schizophrenic seems to suffer considerable impairment. Although there is this similarity to children, certain aspects of higher level functioning are identifiable. (1952, p. 184)

Siegel (1953), in a similar study, compared the Rorschach performance of children of three to ten with that of different kinds of schizophrenics. Hebephrenic and catatonic schizophrenics were considered to be more severely disturbed and less mature than paranoid schizophrenics. He found the following general similarities in developmental level of perception: hebephrenic-catatonics and three-to-five-year-olds, and paranoids and six-to-ten-year-olds. Thus there appears to be a relationship between severity of psychopathology and depth of regression.

Evaluation. Developmental theorists, following Werner's approach, seem to have made a strong case for the regression hypothesis on the basis of Rorschach results. However, these researchers have chosen certain Rorschach indicators as crucial and neglected others. For example, the total number of responses, and the percentages of whole, large detail, and small detail responses are all part of the formal, structural approach to the Rorschach. Although Hemmendinger reports these data for children and adults, he accords them little importance. On the basis of these indicators, we find the following:

(1) total number of responses—normal adults resemble six-year-olds.
(2) percentage of whole responses—normal adults resemble six-year-olds.
(3) percentage of large detail responses—normal adults resemble eight-year-olds.
(4) percentage of small detail responses—normal adults resemble four-year-olds.

The data for these responses suggest that the normal adult shows as much regression as does the schizophrenic. Admittedly, it is not fair to select only those data that prove one's point; but this admonition applies also to developmental theorists. Thus while there are data that clearly support the regression hypothesis, there are also data inconsistent with it.

Now it may be argued that normal adults are not entirely free from regression, and in fact this is the position of developmental theorists; but this places them in a definitional bind. Regression must be defined as a deviation from adulthood toward childhood; thus by definition the normative data of healthy adults cannot be described as being partially regressive. The adult norms are the base against which regression (similarity to children's behavior) is computed. Therefore, if it can be shown that the performance of adults is in some ways similar to children, the regression hypothesis is weakened.

Two consequences of the regression hypothesis need to be examined empirically. First, we must determine whether the regression hypothesis works with color responses on the Rorschach. There is some evidence that the following developmental sequence occurs from early to late childhood: pure color responses to color dominant over form, to form dominant over color. It follows from the regression hypothesis that the severer the psychopathology, the more color dominates over form or the more color is used without form. It is generally believed that psychotics have more pure color and color-dominant-over-form responses than do normal persons, but conclusive data are lacking. What is needed is a study like Siegel's (1953), in which groups differing in severity of psychopathology are compared, using Rorschach color indicators.

The second consequence stems from the assumption that the potentially disturbed adult has gone through the usual stages of childhood, developing new modes of response along the way. In the face of severe life stress, his adult level of functioning is disrupted, and he returns to modes of functioning that were adaptive at earlier stages. When this regression occurs, his approach to the environment, say his perceptual functioning, becomes more diffuse and less organized. He may still retain some aspects of adult functioning side-by-side with the earlier, childlike modes that are the consequence of regression. On the basis of this formulation, it follows that there should be changes in perceptual functioning on the Rorschach from prepsychosis to psychosis to postpsychosis, assuming remission occurs. The prepsychotic should respond at nearly the same developmental level as a normal adult; the psychotic should regress to a childlike level; and the psychotic who is now recovered should respond at a higher level, again approximating that of a normal adult. The predicted sequence is a direct consequence of the regression hypothesis, and a demonstration of its validity would considerably strengthen the hypothesis.

Thinking

Developmental View. Three dimensions are believed to be important in the development of thinking in children. First, the child's concepts and ideas are at first personal and idiosyncratic, and they gradually become more public and commoner in a consensual sense. Second, early concepts are labile and shifting, whereas later ones are more stable. Third, early concepts are more concrete and tied to the stimuli and events that form their context, but later concepts are more abstract and relatively independent of the objects or events with which they were originally associated.

The thinking of schizophrenics is regressed along all three dimensions, manifesting the properties of idiosyncrasy, lability, and concreteness. There is clear evidence that the associations of schizophrenics are deviant and idiosyncratic (Moran, 1953; Sommer et al. 1960, 1962; and Johnson, Weiss, & Zelhart, 1964).

Concerning instability of concepts, there is some positive evidence (Goldman, 1960). Concerning concreteness, a number of investigators have reported that schizophrenics are more concrete than normal individuals in their concepts (Cameron, 1938; Kasanin, 1946) and in their definitions of words (Feifel, 1949; Choderkoff & Mussen, 1952; Harrington & Ehrmann, 1954; and Flavell, 1956).

Evaluation. It is clear from past research that the verbalizations of schizophrenics are deviant, idiosyncratic, nonconsensual, variable, and difficult to understand. However, the basic issue is whether this deviance from adult normals is in the same direction as children's deviance from adults. Children's and schizophrenics' thinking and language are alike in that they are both different from the language and thinking of normal adults. This gross similarity is not enough to sustain the regression hypothesis. What must be demonstrated is that the thinking and language of schizophrenics is similar and directly comparable to the thinking and language of children and that the more regressed the schizophrenic, the more primitive (in developmental terms) is his thinking. Clinicians have reported such similarities, but there is no positive evidence from formal experiments. Thus the evidence neither sustains nor rejects the regression hypothesis.

The issue of concreteness would seem to be clearer because a body of evidence points to excessive concreteness in schizophrenics. However, these were all earlier studies, and more recent research has forced a revision of earlier conclusions. Schizophrenics are capable of responding with abstract concepts, and the only reason they were thought to be concrete is that their deviant and unusual concepts, which were nevertheless abstract, were scored as concrete (Fey, 1951; McGaughran & Moran, 1956, 1957; Chapman & Taylor, 1957; and Lothrop, 1960). Thus the problem with schizophrenics is not that they are abnormally concrete but that their concepts are eccentric and therefore difficult for normal persons to understand.

Concerning general similarities between children's and schizophrenics' thinking, there is some positive evidence. Children and schizophrenics have been found to define words similarly (Feifel, 1949), use different parts of speech similarly (Ellsworth, 1951), and equate antonyms with synonyms to a greater extent than normal adults (Burstein, 1959, 1961). However, an earlier study (Cameron, 1938) found that children's concepts of causality were different from those of schizophrenics.

Chapman et al. (1961) note that some investigators might have inadvertently "stacked the dice" in favor of finding similarities between children and schizophrenics. They point out that there were restrictions on the responses available or the number of categories used in scoring, so that there were too few ways in which responses *could* deviate from those of normal adults. The restrictions on responses thus enhanced the likelihood of finding similarities between children and schizophrenics. These investigators compared children, schizophrenics, and brain-damaged patients on two thinking tasks. On one task the children resembled schizophrenics but not brain-damaged patients, and on the other task the children resembled brain-damaged patients but not schizophrenics. They concluded:

> There is no blanket similarity between the error patterns of children and of either schizophrenics or brain-damaged patients, and the use of the term "regression" to imply such a blanket similarity is not justified. (Chapman et al. 1961, p. 545)

Thus the evidence for regression of thought in schizophrenics is equivocal. There are both positive and negative findings, and the positive findings may be due to experimental flaws. Thus we must regard the regression hypothesis as unproved in the area of thinking.

Overall Evaluation

The foregoing review of evidence bearing on developmental theory and schizophrenia covered five areas. In the areas of motivational and social behavior there is little support for the theory, and in the areas of learning and thinking the theory may be regarded as unproved. Only in the area of perception, specifically research with the Rorschach Test, is there positive evidence. In defense of the approach, it is ambitious in its scope, and no large-scale theory should be expected to be correct in all of its details. Moreover, it is the only one of the regression theories to generate hypotheses that can be tested in controlled situations, and we must give credit to any theory of psychopathology that is precise enough to be proven right or wrong. With these considerations in mind, it is perhaps best to regard the theory as lacking in supporting evidence but perhaps potentially useful. A more definitive evaluation must await the development of better techniques of measuring behavior in the five areas covered by the theory.

COMMENTS

The four regression theories (psychoanalysis, modified Sullivan, teleological regression, and Werner's developmental theory) all share three basic assumptions: (1) there are progressive stages of development that every child must pass through in a rigid, unchanging sequence; (2) psychopathology represents a retracing of these developmental sequences and a return to more primitive modes; and (3) the greater the regression, the severer is the psychopathology. All four theories share these assumptions, but otherwise they differ considerably.

The first two theories—psychoanalysis and modified Sullivan—are phenomenological theories. Their developmental assumptions deal with the *inner world* of the infant and young child. They are concerned with how the individual views the world, specifically with how the infant learns to separate self from others. The last two theories—teleological regression and developmental theory—do not inquire into the child's inner world. Their emphasis is on *structure,* that is, on the formal mechanisms of cognition. Arieti's approach emphasizes thinking and symbolization, and the analogy is to neural functioning, namely, higher functions are knocked out, releasing lower, more primitive functions. Werner's approach emphasizes perception, and the analogue is maturation of function: the basic law is increasing differentiation, ending in a hierarchy of functions. Developmental theory is the most specific of the four in that it suggests a number of dimensions along which maturation occurs (rigid-flexible, diffuse-specific, etc.).

All four theories provide an explanation for psychopathology in terms of a backward retracing of developmental sequences. They may differ in the models they take as analogues, but they do offer a rationale for severity of psychopathology. If we reject all of them, that is, reject the regression hypothesis, is there an alternate explanation of psychopathology?

No explanation of psychopathology can deny that early difficulties often lead to later maladjustment. More specifically, to the extent that early maladjustments are not resolved they *cause* later adjustment problems. Nevertheless, it is not necessary to assume that the disturbed adult necessarily becomes more childlike. An alternate assumption is that there are a number of dimensions of deviance. Although it is possible to deviate from adult normality in the direction of childhood, it is also possible to deviate in non-normal but adult ways. For example, during Vincent van Gogh's psychotic episodes his paintings often reflected his turmoil and deviance. Yet these paintings were no more childlike than those of his nonpsychotic periods. The psychotic's behavior, perceptions, and thought processes may thus be different from those of a normal adult without being childlike.

The difference between this approach and the regression hypothesis may be stated briefly. This alternate approach assumes that the dimension of maturation is only one of a number of dimensions along which a psychotic may differ from normal adults; deviance is not equated with childishness. The regression hypothesis assumes that the only dimension of deviance is developmental, and therefore deviance equals childishness. Regression theorists admit that not all psychotic behavior resembles that of children, but they insist that the crucial aspects of psychotic behavior represent a return to childhood.

The alternate approach does not reject the *fact* of regression, only regression as the explanation of *all* psychopathology. Thus Cameron and Magaret defined regression as,

. . . the recurrence, or new occurrence, of behavior which is considered biosocially immature, in terms of the cultural norms accepted in a given individual's society for persons of his age, sex and status. (1951, p. 221)

The individual need not repeat earlier, outgrown modes; he may simply act in a fashion that is judged immature in his culture. Such regression is a fact; it is seen in psychotics, among others. However, in this alternate approach it does not *explain* psychopathology but is merely one aspect of it. We shall return to the issue of immaturity in Chapter 15.

REFERENCES

Arieti, S. *Interpretation of schizophrenia.* New York: Bruner, 1955.

Burstein, A. G. Primary process in children as a function of age. *Journal of Abnormal and Social Psychology,* 1959, **59**, 284–286.

Burstein, A. G. Some verbal aspects of primary process thought in schizophrenia. *Journal of Abnormal and Social Psychology,* 1961, **62**, 155–157.

Cameron, N. *Personality development and psychopathology.* Boston: Houghton Mifflin, 1963.

Cameron, N. S. Reasoning, regression and communication in schizophrenics. *Psychological Monographs,* 1938, **50**, No. 1 (Whole No. 221).

Cameron, N., & Magaret, Ann. *Behavior pathology.* Boston: Houghton Mifflin, 1951.

Chapman, L. J., Burstein, A. G., Day, Dorothy, & Verdone, P. Regression and disorders of thought. *Journal of Abnormal and Social Psychology,* 1961, **63**, 540–545.

Chapman, L. J., & Taylor, Janet A. The breadth of deviate concepts used by schizophrenics. *Journal of Abnormal and Social Psychology,* 1957, **54**, 118–123.

Choderkoff, B., & Mussen, P. Qualitative aspects of the vocabulary responses of normals and schizophrenics. *Journal of Consulting Psychology,* 1952, **16**, 43–48.

Daniell, Edna F. Stimulus generalization in relation to schizophrenia, paranoid-nonparanoid dichotomy, and drug states. Unpublished master's thesis, University of Pittsburgh, 1964.

Dunn, W. L. Visual discrimination of schizophrenic subjects as a function of stimulus meaning. *Journal of Personality,* 1954, **23**, 48–64.

Ellsworth, R. B. The regression of schizophrenic language. *Journal of Consulting Psychology,* 1951, **15**, 378–391.

Feifel, H. Qualitative differences in the vocabulary response of normals and abnormals. *Genetic Psychology Monographs,* 1949, **39**, 151–204.

Fenichel, O. *The psychoanalytic theory of neurosis.* New York: Norton, 1945.

Fey, Elizabeth T. The performance of young schizophrenics on the Wisconsin Card Sorting Test. *Journal of Consulting Psychology,* 1951, **15**, 311–319.

Flavell, J. H. Abstract thinking and social behavior in schizophrenia. *Journal of Abnormal and Social Psychology,* 1956, **52**, 208–211.

Franks, C. M. An experimental study of conditioning as related to mental abnormality. Unpublished doctoral dissertation, University of London, 1954.

Freud, S. *Collected Papers.* London: Hogarth Press, 1950, vol. 4.

Friedman, H. Perceptual regression in schizophrenia: an hypothesis suggested by the use of the Rorschach Test. *Journal of Genetic Psychology,* 1952, **81**, 63–98.

Garmezy, N. Stimulus differentiation by schizophrenic and normal subjects under conditions of reward and punishment. *Journal of Personality,* 1952, **21,** 253–276.

Goldman, A. E. Symbolic representation in schizophrenia. *Journal of Personality,* 1960, **28,** 293–316.

Goldman, A. E. A comparative-developmental approach to schizophrenia. *Psychological Bulletin,* 1962, **59,** 57–69.

Harrington, R., & Ehrmann, J. C. Complexity of response as a factor in the vocabulary performance of schizophrenics. *Journal of Abnormal and Social Psychology,* 1954, **49,** 362–364.

Hemmendinger, L. Perceptual organization and development as reflected in the structure of the Rorschach Test response. *Journal of Projective Techniques,* 1953, **17,** 162–170.

Hemmendinger, L. Developmental theory and the Rorschach method. In Maria A. Rickers-Ovsiankina (Ed.) *Rorschach psychology.* New York: Wiley, 1960.

Howe, E. S. GSR conditioning in anxiety states, normals, and chronic functional schizophrenic subjects. *Journal of Abnormal and Social Psychology,* 1958, **56,** 183–189.

Johnson, R. C., Weiss, R. L., & Zelhart, P. F. Similarities and differences between normal and psychotic subjects in response to verbal stimuli. *Journal of Abnormal and Social Psychology,* 1964, **68,** 221–226.

Kantor, R. E., & Winder, C. L. The process-reactive continuum: A theoretical proposal. *Journal of Nervous and Mental Disease,* 1959, **129,** 429–434.

Kasanin, J. S. The disturbance of conceptual thinking in schizophrenia. In J. S. Kasanin (Ed.) *Language and thought in schizophrenia.* Berkeley: University of California Press, 1946, pp. 41–49.

Lang, P. J., & Buss, A. H. Psychological deficit in schizophrenia. II. Interference and activation. *Journal of Abnormal Psychology,* 1965, **70,** 77–106.

Lothrop, W. W. Psychological test covariates of conceptual deficit in schizophrenia. *Journal of Consulting Psychology,* 1960, **24,** 496–499.

McGaughran, L. C., & Moran, L. J. "Conceptual level" vs. "conceptual area" analysis of object sorting behavior of schizophrenic and nonpsychiatric groups. *Journal of Abnormal and Social Psychology,* 1956, **52,** 43–50.

McGaughran, L. S., & Moran, L. J. Differences between schizophrenic and brain-damaged groups in conceptual aspects of object sorting. *Journal of Abnormal and Social Psychology,* 1957, **54,** 44–49.

Mednick, S. A. Distortions in the gradient of stimulus generalization related to cortical brain damage and schizophrenia. *Journal of Abnormal and Social Psychology,* 1955, **51,** 536–542.

Mednick, S. A. A learning theory approach to research in schizophrenia. *Psychological Bulletin,* 1958, **55,** 316–327.

Moran, L. J. Vocabulary knowledge and usage among normal and schizophrenic subjects. *Psychological Monographs,* 1953, **67,** No. 20 (Whole No. 370).

O'Connor, N., & Rawnsley, K. Two types of conditioning in psychotics and normals. *Journal of Abnormal and Social Psychology,* 1959, **58,** 157–161.

Peters, H. N., & Murphree, O. D. The conditioned reflex in the chronic schizophrenic. *Journal of Clinical Psychology,* 1954, **10,** 126–130.

Pfaffman, C., & Schlosberg, H. The conditioned knee jerk in psychotic and normal individuals. *Journal of Psychology,* 1936, **1,** 201–206.

Pishkin, V., & Hershiser, D. Respiration and GSR as functions of white sound in schizophrenia. *Journal of Consulting Psychology,* 1963, **27,** 330–337.

Shipley, W. C. Studies of catatonia. VI. Further investigation of the perseverative tendency. *Psychiatric Quarterly,* 1934, **8,** 736–744.

Siegel, E. L. Genetic parallels of perceptual structuralization in paranoid schizophrenia: An analysis by means of the Rorschach test. *Journal of Projective Techniques,* 1953, **17,** 151–161.

Sommer, R., Dewar, R., & Osmond, H. Is there a schizophrenic language? *Archives of General Psychiatry,* 1960, **3,** 665–673.

Sommer, R., Witney, Gwynneth, & Osmond, H. Teaching common associations to schizophrenics. *Journal of Abnormal and Social Psychology,* 1962, **65,** 58–61.

Spence, K. W., & Taylor, Janet A. The relation of conditioned response strength to anxiety in normal, neurotic, and psychotic subjects. *Journal of Experimental Psychology,* 1953, **45,** 265–277.

Werner, H. *Comparative psychology of mental development.* Chicago: Follett, 1948.

CHAPTER 12

Motivational Theories
of Schizophrenia

Most clinicians agree that the outstanding symptoms of schizophrenia are in the cognitive and motor areas. The cognitive symptoms include disturbances of language and thought, distortions of the body image, a retreat from reality, hallucinations, and delusions. The motor symptoms consist mainly of aspects of *social withdrawal:* fear of others, isolation from others, and avoidance of close contact or any contact at all. Is one kind of symptom more fundamental than the other? Does the presence of one kind serve as a basis for understanding the other? Two approaches answer in the affirmative. The cognitive approach assumes that cognitive symptoms occur first and then lead to social withdrawal. We shall discuss this approach in the next chapter. The motivational approach assumes that motivational variables (rewards, punishments, and drives) account for the subsequent development of cognitive symptoms. We shall discuss the relevant theories in this chapter.

It is difficult to evaluate the opposing approaches to schizophrenia. One way is to investigate the inefficiency of schizophrenics. Clinicians agree that most schizophrenics are so inefficient in managing their affairs that they must be hospitalized. The male schizophrenic tends to be too disorganized to maintain an acceptable output of work; the female schizophrenic tends to be too disorganized to manage a home, children, or both. Such inefficiency may be due to the interference of cognitive symptoms or to a problem of motivation, for example, social withdrawal. Unfortunately, it is difficult to decide whether the cause is cognitive or motivational, and case histories lack the rigor required of scientific method.

The problem is to devise a means of testing the theories in a less complex and equivocal context than everyday life. Inefficiency cannot be assessed precisely in everyday life because of both variations in the demands placed on different individuals and inability to measure efficiency quantitatively. Furthermore, many everyday tasks require teamwork, which renders it difficult to evaluate *individual* efficiency.

The solution is to investigate inefficiency in the laboratory. The task requirements are known, and the subject's performance can be measured precisely and quantitatively. This solution has been widely adopted, and there are now hundreds of studies. A recent review (Buss & Lang, 1965; Lang & Buss, 1965) included almost 400 references. The usual experiment compares the performance of schizophrenics with that of normals. On most tasks schizophrenics perform worse than normals; this decrement has been labeled *psychological deficit* (Hunt & Cofer, 1944).

There are two motivational approaches to psychological deficit. The first assumes that the schizophrenic *lacks motivation*. He is withdrawn, isolated, and apathetic. There is simply no interest or involvement in immediate situations or in the larger social environment. There has been ". . . an extinction of standards for performance and of thought skills that have been socially rewarded" (Hunt & Cofer, 1944, p. 1023). Thus the cause of the apathy and isolation is an insusceptibility to the usual rewards of everyday life. This lack of motivation would seem to account for his inefficiency. In the absence of a reward for efficient behavior, the schizophrenic does not exert himself and therefore cannot adjust to the tasks of the laboratory or the requirements of everyday life.

The second approach assumes that the schizophrenic is *overmotivated;* he is extremely sensitive to rebuff or rejection, over-reactive to stimuli connoting affect, and excessively anxious. He is easily threatened and sees the world around him as dangerous and potentially destructive. His reaction to a wide range of situations, especially social situations, is to avoid them if he can or to escape from them if already involved.

LACK OF MOTIVATION

The theory of insufficient motivation uses the schizophrenic's disinterest in social contacts to explain his psychological deficit. Unlike the normal subject who tries to please the experimenter and who therefore perseveres at boring or meaningless tasks, the schizophrenic lacks the motivation to do well. The schizophrenic presumably tends to be uncooperative, disinterested, and unmoved by the usual rewards given in the laboratory or by pleasing the experimenter. Thus Slechta et al. (1963) showed that schizophrenics show less verbal conditioning than normal subjects when the reinforcer was the experimenter's saying "mmm-hm" or nodding his head. Cohen and Cohen (1960) found that although neurotics verbally conditioned when the experimenter said "good," schizophrenics did not. Leventhal (1959) also found that schizophrenics show no evidence of verbal conditioning when the reinforcer is "good."

If the schizophrenic is undermotivated, his efficiency should be greatly improved by increasing his motivation. It is implicitly assumed that the schizophrenic suffers no real loss in ability to learn, to think, or to solve problems. Rather, his inability consists of apathy; he simply does not care whether the problem is solved or not. This position generates an experimentally testable hypothesis, as follows:

> If impaired motivation is a significant determinant of the performance deficit shown by schizophrenics, then an experimentally produced increase in motivation should improve performance. In normal subjects, however, relatively little improvement can be expected with experimentally increased motivation . . . [because] they work near their limit of proficiency under ordinary testing conditions, leaving relatively little room for improvement with experimentally increased motivation.
>
> [It follows that] . . . an experimentally induced increase in motivation will occasion greater improvement in the performance of schizophrenics than in normal individuals. (Cohen, 1956, p. 186)

Motivation can be increased in one of two ways. The individual can be urged to do better, the experimenter's exhortations increasing the subject's incentive to do well. The alternative is to apply noxious stimuli such as verbal punishment, electric shock, or annoying noise, producing a motivation to learn or solve the problem in order to escape from the punishing stimuli.

Urging

The theory of undermotivation suggests that schizophrenics should improve their performance more than normal persons when both are urged to do better. A variety of tasks has attempted to test this hypothesis; a typical one is that used by D'Alessio and Spence:

> The apparatus consisted of a board, 8×21 inches, containing 11 rows of 60 holes. The subjects' task was to place small brass pins into the holes as rapidly as possible. The task was selected for two reasons: pilot work indicated that it is predominantly a performance task, subjects exhibiting little improvement over trials, thus performance differences between control and experimental groups could be expected to be minimally contaminated by possible differences in rate of learning; it can easily be performed by chronic schizophrenics, thus minimizing fear of failure. (1963, pp. 390–391)

The urging consisted of using phrases like "That's very good," "That's the fastest I've seen," and "That's still fine. See if you can't do even faster the next time" immediately after each trial.

Eight studies examined the hypothesis that encouragement facilitated the performance of schizophrenics more than that of normal persons. Only one of these unequivocally supported the hypothesis. Olson (1958) told his subjects that they were doing very well, better than most men of their age and background. This encouragement improved the performance of the schizophrenics but not of the normal subjects.

Another experiment produced mixed results. Stotsky (1957) had psychotherapists encourage their schizophrenics during an interval between tasks, whereas he encouraged normal subjects. There were two tasks—simple and complex reaction time. The encouragement yielded greater improvement for the schizophrenics on the former but greater improvement for the normal subjects on the latter.

In one experiment (Ladd, 1960) encouragement had no effect on schizophrenics' performance. In the remaining five studies, praise and encouragement were found to enhance the performance of schizophrenics and normal subjects *equally* (Benton, Jentch, & Wahler, 1960; D'Alessio & Spence, 1963; Goodstein, Guertin, & Blackburn, 1961; Johannsen, 1962).

Thus only one experiment clearly corroborated the hypothesis, one experiment yielded equivocal results, and five experiments yielded negative results. The weight of evidence indicates that the performance of schizophrenics is *not* helped more than that of normal persons by urging and encouragement. These findings weaken the theory that schizophrenics are undermotivated.

Noxious Stimuli

Noxious stimuli may be administered in two ways. The subject may be punished verbally for making incorrect responses, or he may be subjected to noxious stimuli, from which he can escape by making correct responses. Thus two kinds of variables bear on this aspect of undermotivation theory: verbal punishment and annoying stimuli ("biological motivation").

Verbal Punishment. The tasks employed have varied widely but the punishers have been restricted to a few verbal comments such as "Wrong" and "Not so good." The hypothesis is that schizophrenics, being undermotivated, will show a greater improvement than normal persons when incorrect responses are punished. Verbal punishment presumably supplies the motivation the schizophrenic lacks.

Two experiments sustain the hypothesis. Losen (1961) censured both normal persons and schizophrenics for incorrect responses on digit span and arithmetic tasks. Censure improved the schizophrenics' performance on both tasks but not the normal subjects'. Losen suggested that the normal individuals were already operating at maximal efficiency and therefore could not improve their performance. Atkinson and Robinson (1961) found that saving "Wrong" after incorrect responses improved the rote learning of schizophrenics but not of normal persons.

The preponderance of evidence indicates no difference between schizophrenics and normal subjects in the effects of verbal punishment: it helps both to learn faster. Buss and Buss (1956), compared the conceptual performance of student nurses and a mixed group of psychiatric patients, approximately two-thirds of whom were schizophrenic, and found that verbal punishment ("Wrong") facilitated the learning of both. Leventhal (1959) obtained similar findings on a verbal conditioning task. Smock and Vancini (1962) and Maginley (1956) reported similar results in learning situations: verbal censure does *not* affect the performance of normals and schizophrenics any differently. Brooker's (1962) findings were mixed. When the verbal punishment ("Wrong") was relevant to a conceptual task, both learned better; but when the punishment was irrelevant to the task, schizophrenics performed *worse* and normal persons were unaffected.

Note that verbal punishment should *better* performance if the schizophrenic is undermotivated; if it *worsens* performance, this opposes the theory. In addition to Brooker, two other investigators reported that verbal censure leads to poorer performance in schizophrenics: Garmezy (1952) with a stimulus generalization task and Bleke (1955) with a memory task.

Thus two experiments support undermotivation theory and seven oppose it. Again the weight of evidence is against the theory. *The performance of schizophrenics may be facilitated by verbal punishment but no more so than the performance of normal individuals.*

"*Biological Motivation.*" One way of motivating a subject is to expose him to noxious physical stimuli such as a "white noise" (which sounds like radio static) or electric shock. The subject can escape from the aversive stimuli by responding quickly or correctly. Presumably normal persons already have sufficient motivation, and therefore their performance will be affected slightly, if at all. Schizophrenics, who presumably lack motivation, should benefit greatly from the increase in motivation —in this instance a strong tendency to escape from the noxious stimuli.

Most of the experiments in this area have involved reaction time, and all support the hypothesis. Comparing normal subjects' and schizophrenics' complex reaction times, Pascal and Swensen (1952) found that in a control condition the normals were much faster. However, when white noise was delivered through earphones and could be turned off only by a correct response, the schizophrenics' improvement was so much better than that of the normal subjects that there were no differences in reaction time between the two groups. These results—that reaction times of schizophrenics improve significantly more than those of normal subjects when white noise is administered—have been corroborated by four subsequent experiments (Grisell & Rosenbaum, 1963; King, 1962; Lang, 1959; and Rosenbaum, Grisell, & Mackavey, 1957).

Further support comes from two concept learning studies in which white noise was employed. Cavanaugh (1958) found that the conceptual performance of schizophrenics improved more with "biological motivation" than did the performance of normal individuals, and Brown (1961) essentially reproduced these findings. Finally, Cohen (1956) used electric shock as the noxious stimulus. Subjects learned to make a motor response to visual stimuli, a correct response terminating the shock. The electric shock helped schizophrenics but not normal subjects.

All eight experiments demonstrated that physical, noxious stimuli motivated schizophrenics to perform better and that their improvement exceeded the improvement of normal subjects. These results constitute strong evidence for the theory that schizophrenics are undermotivated.

Evaluation

Undermotivation theory is both opposed and supported by experimental evidence. When subjects are urged or encouraged, *both* schizophrenics and normal persons tend to improve their performance. If schizophrenics benefitted *more* than normal individuals, it would corroborate the hypothesis that schizophrenics are undermotivated and need additional incentive. If schizophrenics benefitted *less,* it might be argued that they are so withdrawn as to be unaffected by social motivation (the experimenter exhorts them to do better). Thus, if schizophrenics were *differentially* affected by social motivation such as encouragement, whether more *or* less than normal persons, the results could be squared with undermotivation theory. However, if the theory were correct, schizophrenics and normal subjects should not be *equally* affected by social motivation, and this is precisely the trend of the experimental findings.

The theory is also weakened by the results of experiments using verbal punishment. Again the trend is for schizophrenics and normal subjects to be affected equally by social motivation, this time "negative motivation." This is the one finding that the theory cannot handle because schizophrenics should either benefit more from the added motivation or benefit less because they are too withdrawn to be affected by it. That normal persons and schizophrenics benefit equally from verbal punishment argues against a motivational deficit in schizophrenia.

On the other hand, the theory is strongly supported by the results of experiments using biological motivation such as white noise and electric shock. As predicted by the theory, schizophrenics benefit more from these noxious stimuli than do normal persons. Can these results be integrated with the results based on social motivation (urging and verbal punishment) in such a way as to be consistent with the theory?

One possibility is to assume that biological motivation is more potent than social motivation. Presumably the schizophrenic lacks motivation and needs strong stimuli to overcome his apathy and withdrawal. Stimuli such as urging and verbal punishment help in overcoming his lack of involvement, but they are so weak that they help him no more than the normal person. Normal subjects can also benefit from additional motivation, but since they are not basically undermotivated, they do not need as *strong* a dosage. Schizophrenics need potent doses of motivation, and when supplied with it in the form of biological motivation, they benefit more than normal individuals.

The amended theory states that schizophrenics are so undermotivated that they require a strong motivator to shake them from their apathy and increase their efficiency. The motivators used in the laboratory may be arranged in increasing order of strength:

verbal reward
urging
verbal punishment
physical punishment

Verbal reward has virtually no effect on schizophrenics, although it can motivate normal individuals. Urging helps schizophrenics but no more than normals. Verbal punishment usually helps schizophrenics no more than normals, but in some instances schizophrenics benefit more (Losen, 1961; Atkinson & Robinson, 1961). Physical punishment generally helps schizophrenics more than normal individuals. Thus in the progression from weak to strong motivators, schizophrenics are first not helped at all, then helped no more than normal subjects, and finally helped more than normal subjects. This progression, which is one way of viewing the research discussed previously, is consistent with undermotivation theory.

Thus the results can be squared with undermotivation theory but only at the cost of adding new assumptions. Most theories can be stretched to fit apparently inconsistent evidence in just this fashion—by adding new assumptions. The problem is to decide when a theory becomes too cumbersome because of such additional, after-the-fact assumptions.

EXCESSIVE MOTIVATION

This second approach assumes that the schizophrenic is excessively anxious. There are two theories, each emphasizing a different aspect of anxiety. The first theory focuses on *content,* that is, on what the schizophrenic fears: affect-laden situations and stimuli. The second theory focuses on process, that is, on anxiety as a drive state.

Censure and Affective Stimuli

The general assumptions underlying this theory are that affective stimuli and situations are painful to the schizophrenic, and that his heightened fear renders him inefficient. The theory has two variants. The first specifies a particular kind of stimulus, *social censure,* as the traumatic event. The second is more general and includes *all* affective stimuli.

Social Censure. The social censure hypothesis was originally formulated by Rodnick and Garmezy:

> . . . clinical psychiatric reports stress the sensitivity of the schizophrenic patient to the threat of criticism or rebuff inherent in almost any social situation. If such criticism does accentuate the patient's difficulty in differentiating cues in his environment, then it would follow that the experimental introduction of censure should produce greater discrimination decrements in schizophrenic patients than in normal individuals. (1957, p. 118)

This hypothesis generates two testable predictions. First, the performance of schizophrenics should be poorer with censure or criticism than it is with praise, verbal rewards, or a control condition. Second, when criticism is administered, the performance of schizophrenics should suffer more than the performance of normal persons. Rodnick and Garmezy attempted to confirm these predictions in research conducted largely by their students.

Garmezy (1952) showed that schizophrenics had flatter generalization gradients with censure ("Wrong") than with praise ("Right"), whereas normal subjects had steeper generalization gradients with consure than with praise. Webb (1955) found that failure led to poorer conceptual performance, while a control group improved performance; all subjects were schizophrenics, and the effect of failure on normal persons could not be assessed.

Bleke (1955) compared normal persons with good and poor premorbid schizophrenics on a memory task. Both praise ("Right") and censure ("Wrong") were used during learning. The poor premorbid schizophrenics showed better reminiscence and relearning than did good premorbid schizophrenics or normal subjects. This result was interpreted as stemming from the effects of censure: criticism interfered with the original learning of the poor premorbids, but on the later testing for recall (reminiscence) in the absence of censure they improved. In addition to assumptions about the learning process, this interpretation requires the assumption that poor premorbid schizophrenics are, for unknown reasons, more sensitive to censure than are good premorbid schizophrenics.

Bleke's experiment was followed up (Smock & Vancini, 1962), using a similar task and not separating schizophrenics into good and poor premorbid groups. There were no differences between normal persons and schizophrenics or between praised and censured subjects in original learning. Nevertheless, the censured schizophrenics showed *less* reminiscence than both the praised schizophrenics and the normal subjects. This experiment is not identical to Bleke's but it is sufficiently similar to make us question the reliability of his results.

Alvarez (1957) praised or censured subjects' judgments about pictures and later assessed their preferences. Poor premorbid schizophrenics showed a greater decline in preference for pictures associated with censure than did good premorbid schizophrenics or normal persons. Similar results were reported by Neiditch (1963); schizophrenics manifested a greater falling off of preference for tasks that followed failure than did normal subjects. Note that in neither study was censure shown to produce a decrement in *performance;* its only effect was a differential change in *preference.*

Zahn (1959) asked subjects to estimate the size of pictures involving censure or praise. Good premorbid schizophrenics tended to *overestimate* size with censured pictures, whereas normal persons and poor premorbid schizophrenics did not. Normal persons and *poor* premorbids were similar in this experiment, in contrast to the Bleke study in which normals and *good* premorbids were similar.

This inconsistency seems to characterize the evidence collected by Rodnick and Garmezy and their students. They have interpreted their results as supporting the social censure hypothesis, but a more balanced appraisal suggests that the evidence is weak and somewhat equivocal. This conclusion refers to the research done mainly by their students. Research conducted in other settings has been predominantly negative.

Earlier in the chapter we saw that results involving verbal punishment (censure) were predominantly negative. One experiment had mixed findings (Brooker, 1962); two studies found that censure *improved* schizophrenics' performance (Atkinson & Robinson, 1961; Losen, 1961), and four observed no difference between schizophrenics and normal persons in the effects of censure. In general, however, censure (being told "Wrong" after an incorrect response) *facilitates* the performance of schizophrenics (Buss, Braden, Orgel, & Buss, 1956; Buss & Buss, 1956; Leventhal, 1959; and Fischer, 1963). This finding is opposite to what should occur if the social censure hypothesis were correct: there are some situations in which censure deteriorates the performance of schizophrenics, but in most situations censure helps. The original social censure hypothesis clearly does not account for the inefficiency of schizophrenics on laboratory tasks. Evidence for it is weak, whereas evidence against it is strong.

Garmezy (1965) has admitted that the original censure theory is not tenable. He has amended it to conform with research findings, adopting a position similar to one first espoused by Cohen (1959). The new theory specifies the conditions under which censure deteriorates or improves efficiency.

Censure leads to psychological deficit, Garmezy contends, when it is irrelevant to the task and the subject cannot avoid it. Thus when a subject is criticized generally for failing, and there is no response that "turns off" the criticism, the performance of schizophrenics should worsen. Furthermore the deterioration in performance should be greater than that of normals.

Censure should lead to an improvement in performance when: (a) it is relevant to performance, (b) it follows an incorrect response, and (c) improved performance "turns off" the censure. The assumption is that schizophrenics are so sensitive to censure that they will improve their performance to avoid it, that is, the threat of censure motivates better performance. A corollary is that censure improves the performance of schizophrenics more than that of normal subjects.

This amended censure theory is certainly more consistent with the data than the original one. It retains the original assumption that schizophrenics are abnormally sensitive to censure but assumes that the threat of criticism can lead to either better or worse performance. This new assumption—that censure can better *or* worsen performance—means that the theory must be used with care lest it be insusceptible to disproof. This is a danger with any theory that predicts diametrically opposed results.

The amended theory is not wholly consistent with research findings. It assumes that schizophrenics are so sensitive to censure that the threat of it serves to motivate better performance. This leads to the prediction that when the censure can be avoided and it is relevant to the response, schizophrenics should show greater improvement than normals. However, as we saw earlier, only two studies sustain this prediction, whereas five studies found that schizophrenics and normal subjects improved *equally* with censure. Thus the weight of evidence is against the hypothesis that avoidance of censure differentially improves the performance of schizophrenics. Note that a *differential* change is required by the theory. Whether censure produces deficit or improvement, its effects must be greater with schizophrenics than with normal individuals.

The amended theory is also inconsistent with Garmezy's own doctoral dissertation, the study that initiated research on censure (1952). Garmezy reported that censure after incorrect responses led to poorer performance (flatter generalization gradients) than reward without censure; but the amended theory predicts better performance when censure can be avoided and it follows an incorrect response.

A recent study (Berkowitz, 1964) also clearly contradicts the theory. Schizophrenics and normals were tested for reaction time after an interview with the experimenter. There were two experimental conditions and a control. In one condition the experimenter rebuffed the subjects during the interview; he remained aloof and generally silent but answered direct questions briefly and in a flat tone of voice. The implied rebuff was clear to anyone with any social sensitivity and should have been clear to schizophrenics, who presumably are abnormally sensitive to rejection. In the second condition the experimenter was warm, friendly, and complimentary (when this was possible in the interview context). In the control condition there was no interview. The reaction time trials followed immediately. For normal subjects the rebuff and warmth conditions at first led to slower reaction times than the control condition, but later there were no differences among the three conditions. For schizophrenics rebuff and control conditions led to *faster* reactive times than warmth. Thus rebuff resulted not in deficit but in relative improvement. Note that the theory predicts that when censure or rejection is irrelevant to the task and unavoidable (the situation in Berkowitz's experiment) the outcome should be *psychological deficit*. That rejection in these circumstances led to relative *improvement* is strong evidence against the theory.

Thus the amended theory is consistent with some findings but inconsistent with others. It is an interesting attempt to maintain the basic assumption that the schizophrenic is oversensitive to criticism, in the face of contrary data. Obviously more research is needed, but the theory's exponents must answer a fundamental criticism. If the schizophrenic is abnormally sensitive to censure, then the presence of censure should make him so emotional that his performance is seriously disturbed. Yet the theory insists that the threat of censure can lead to improved performance. One way out of this dilemma is to assume that the schizophrenic's emotional arousal in the face of censure is intense enough to motivate better performance but not intense enough to disrupt ongoing performance. Many psychologists would find it difficult to accept the plausibility of this assumption. Here is another theory that can be squared with research findings but only at the cost of adding new assumptions whose plausibility is doubtful. Again the issue is whether to retain a theory that requires after-the-fact assumptions or to discard it for a theory with fewer encumbering assumptions.

Affective Stimuli. It is no simple matter to define "affective stimuli," and this problem prevents clear interpretation of results. Let us delay discussing it until after considering the research findings.

One kind of affective stimulus concerns social censure, which gives rise to a variant of the social censure hypothesis: schizophrenics are oversensitive to stimuli connoting parental censure, and these stimuli disrupt their performance. This hypothesis has been tested mainly by students of Rodnick and Garmezy.

Dunn (1954) showed schizophrenics and normal subjects pictures of scolding, whipping, feeding, and neutral objects. They were to judge whether a standard picture was different in each case from one of five variations. The schizophrenics judged more of the variations of the scolding scene as being the same than did the normal subjects, but the other scenes yielded no differences. These results were partially corroborated by Turbiner (1961), who used neutral, scolding, and affectionate pictures. The schizophrenics' judgments were the same as the normal persons' for neutral pictures, and poorer for the scolding pictures *and* the affectionate pictures.

Garmezy and Rodnick (1959) modified their original proposal, specifying that good premorbid schizophrenics were disrupted by *paternal* censure

and poor premorbid schizophrenics by *maternal* censure. This more specific
hypothesis was subsequently verified by two of their students (Dunham,
1959; and Kreinik, 1959), although their results are open to several interpretations. Baxter and Becker (1962) also supplied supporting evidence:
poor premorbid schizophrenics showed more anxiety in response to mother-
son pictures, and good premorbid schizophrenics showed more anxiety in
response to a father-son picture.

Harris (1957) found that good premorbids *underestimated* the size of
mother-son pictures, but Zahn (1959) in a similar situation found *over-
estimation*. Moriarty and Kates (1962) reported that the conceptual performance of both good and poor premorbid schizophrenics was disrupted by
both approval and disapproval stimuli. Furthermore, the normal subjects
were as affected by censure stimuli as were the schizophrenics. Finally,
Lebow and Epstein had schizophrenics and normal persons respond to pictures of nurturant, rejecting, and ambiguous situations. They concluded:

Thus, if anything, the schizophrenics find nurturant as well as rejecting cues disruptive, and the former more so. Rather than a specific censure-cue deficit, the
schizophrenic exhibits a general deficit for cues associated with emotional involvement, whether of a positive or a negative nature. (1963, p. 32)

This conclusion is sound. Some of the evidence does support the hypothesis that schizophrenics are disturbed by stimuli connoting censure.
However, in addition to conflicting evidence, other research has made it
clear that schizophrenics are also disrupted by affective stimuli unrelated
to censure. That stimuli connoting affection and nurturance disturb schizophrenics means that the censure hypothesis is at best too restrictive. On
balance, the hypothesis clearly cannot account for the research findings.

The more general hypothesis—that schizophrenics are oversensitive to
and disturbed by *any* affective stimulus—has been strongly supported. In
addition to the evidence just mentioned, a number of studies have shown
schizophrenics to be upset by a variety of affective stimuli. In each experiment performance with affective stimuli is contrasted with performance with
neutral stimuli. The following dichotomies of affective versus neutral stimuli
have been used:

(1) mother versus square (Culver, 1962)
(2) symbolic (cigar) versus neutral (overcoat button) (Raush, 1956)
(3) drawings of heterosexual, affiliative, and autonomous interactions
    versus geometric figures (Ehrenworth, 1960)
(4) patient-figure versus psychiatric aide-figure (Pishkin, Smith, &
    Leibowitz, 1962)
(5) human versus nonhuman (Davis & Harrington, 1957; Brodsky,
    1961; and Marx, 1962)

(6) social versus nonsocial (Whiteman, 1954)
(7) sexual versus nonsexual (Arey, 1960)
(8) unpleasant versus neutral (Silverman, 1963)

In every instance the affective stimuli were found to upset schizophrenics, disrupting their performance in comparison to their performance with neutral stimuli. There are also experiments in which no differences between affective and neutral stimuli were found (Feldstein, 1962; Nelson & Caldwell, 1962), but these are only a small minority. In general, the evidence is clear that schizophrenics are sensitive to and disrupted by a variety of affective stimuli.

The problem in interpreting all this evidence is that so many stimuli have been disruptive that the term *affective* no longer has a precise definition. The underlying assumption of this variant of overmotivation theory is that past events in the lives of schizophrenics have rendered them abnormally sensitive to stimuli related to painful situations and anxiety-laden interpersonal relationships. Although some of the affective stimuli mentioned pertain to such special areas of maladjustment, most of them do not.

Thus we are faced with a theoretical dilemma. If the term *affective* is loosely defined, the theory can account for the evidence, but it lacks precision. If the term *affective* is defined precisely, the more restricted definition means that some of the results do not fit the theory; nonaffective stimuli, as well as affective stimuli, disrupt performance. Thus overmotivation does not suffice as an explanation of the available data.

An alternate approach is to assume that affective stimuli, however defined, elicit a greater number of associations. It seems reasonable that human, sexual, symbolic, and social stimuli are likelier to set off a train of personal and idiosyncratic associations than are neutral and impersonal stimuli. This assumption has been checked by Deering (1963), who had subjects associate to affective (pleasant and unpleasant) and neutral stimuli. Although schizophrenics did not differ from normal subjects with neutral words, they gave significantly more associations to affective words. Presumably, the more associations, the more the responder is distracted and the more his performance suffers. This association theory will be discussed in the next chapter.

Anxiety as a Drive

Anxiety plays a major role in psychopathology, and schizophrenia is construed by many clinicians as a rejection or retreat from terrifying reality. In the Hull-Spence learning framework, anxiety may be regarded as a drive state that is one determinant of conditioning and generalization. Mednick (1958) has attempted to explain the associative disturbance and thinking disorder of schizophrenics in terms of this drive approach.

Mednick's Theory. Mednick assumes that the preschizophrenic individual is intensely anxious. A high level of anxiety means a high level of drive. Drive is presumably related to generalization: the higher the drive is, the greater the amount of stimulus generalization. The excessive generalization leads to more stimuli becoming linked to anxiety and therefore capable of invoking fear. As more fear-arousing stimuli are added to the list, the level of anxiety mounts. The higher drive level not only intensifies previously present fear responses but initiates still greater stimulus generalization. Thus intense anxiety leads to excessive stimulus generalization, which in turn intensifies anxiety. Mednick suggests that this vicious spiral continues until the anxiety is no longer bearable or further generalization is impossible.

> Long before this point is reached, however, the behavior of the individual will become noticeably unusual. His drive level will keep thoughts racing through his mind. Many of these thoughts will be out of context or silly. (1958, p. 322)

The individual tends to think of remote associations or thoughts because they are distant from anxiety-laden thoughts or associations. Silly or out-of-context thoughts occur because of excessive stimulus generalization:

> As the spiral of anxiety and generalization mounts, his drive level may increase to an almost insupportable degree. As this is taking place, his ability to discriminate is almost totally eclipsed by his generalization tendencies. Any unit of a thought sequence might call up still another remote associate. Clang associates based on stimulus-response generalization may be frequent . . . His speech may resemble a "word salad." He will be an acute schizophrenic with a full-blown thinking disorder. (Mednick, 1958, p. 322)

Mednick recognized that, in contrast to acute schizophrenics, chronic schizophrenics tend not to give overt evidence of intense anxiety. Therefore he proposed a transition from acute to chronic schizophrenia. The excessive generalization of the high drive (anxiety) state may lead to a "highly generalized, remote, irrelevant, tangential associate." A remote association diverts the individual's attention from anxiety-provoking stimuli, and the resulting drive (anxiety) reduction is reinforcing. Continued repetition of the strongly reinforced tendency to escape anxiety through remote associations leads to deviant, disorganized thinking. Thinking irrelevant thoughts proves to be so effective in reducing anxiety that the schizophrenic may appear emotionally phlegmatic. Now the well-learned tendency toward remote and tangential associations is maintained even in the absence of a high anxiety level. In deriving his theory Mednick made four assumptions.

(1) *Schizophrenics acquire classically conditioned responses faster than normal persons*. Two studies support this assumption. Pfaffman and Schlosberg (1936) demonstrated more frequent conditioned patellar tendon reflexes in schizophrenics than in normal persons. Spence and Taylor (1953) reported similar results for eyelid conditioning.

On the other hand, six studies have shown that normal persons condition at least as well as, or better than schizophrenics. Shipley (1934) and Pishkin and Hershiser (1963) found better conditioning for normal persons with the galvanic skin response (GSR), and Howe (1958), also using GSR conditioning, failed to obtain significant differences between the two. Franks (1954), Peters and Murphree (1954), and O'Connor and Rawnsley (1959) also found that schizophrenics failed to learn faster or better than normal persons on a variety of conditioning tasks. Thus the weight of evidence is against the assumption, which receives little support from the studies just cited.

(2) *In more complex situations schizophrenics learn slower*. This assumption is linked to the first one in an attempt to apply drive theory to two types of learning situations. In simple situations (for example, classical conditioning) high drive leads to faster learning; in complex situations high drive enhances irrelevant and incorrect responses, causing a decrease in learning. Schizophrenics, having greater anxiety and therefore higher drive, should learn faster in simple situations and slower in complex situations. The second part of this statement is true: schizophrenics do learn slower in complex situations. However, the first part is probably untrue. Except for classical conditioning, where the evidence is admittedly equivocal, schizophrenics learn *slower* than normal persons in simple situations (Buss & Lang, 1965; Lang & Buss, 1965).

(3) *Schizophrenics overgeneralize in comparison to normal persons.* Mednick cited four experiments that ostensibly found elevated generalization gradients in schizophrenics. The first is a study by Bender and Schilder (1930), who presented data that were difficult to interpret in terms of generalization gradients and who did not employ normal controls. The second is Garmezy's study (1952), which is open to several interpretations, (Buss & Lang, 1965). The third is Mednick's doctoral dissertation, in which he wrote:

With respect to the hypothesis that schizophrenics would display a more elevated GSG [gradient of stimulus generalization] than normals, the results are not conclusive. While the C [normal] and S [schizophrenic] groups differ, the differences occur both in the predicted direction and counter to it. (1955, p. 540)

The fourth study is that of Dunn (1954), who found an elevated generalization gradient in schizophrenics in one experimental condition and no differences between the gradients of schizophrenics and normal subjects in three other conditions. The most neutral comment to be made about these four studies is that they do not offer support for this third assumption.

There is considerable evidence that schizophrenics tend to be overinclusive, including more stimuli in their vocabulary definitions and conceptual sortings than normal persons (Buss & Lang, 1965).

Phenomena of this sort might tempt one to describe schizophrenia as being characterized by a heightened and flattened gradient of semantic generalization, since in one variety of semantic generalization a subject gives a response to a word which he has previously learned to a different word of similar meaning. However, the more direct evidence concerning semantic generalization in schizophrenia contradicts this interpretation. At least three different investigators have compared schizophrenics and normals on tasks which are usually thought of as measuring semantic generalization. These three studies uniformly obtained negative results, that is, they found no difference between schizophrenics and normals on degree of semantic generalization. (Chapman & Chapman, 1965, p. 136)

Chapman went on to report an experiment demonstrating that schizophrenics were *less* inclusive than normal individuals.

Finally, Daniell (1964) compared the stimulus generalization gradients of schizophrenics and normal controls, taking care to control for heterogeneity (paranoids versus nonparanoids) and treatment status (on drugs versus off drugs). This careful study yielded no differences between schizophrenics and normal persons in either the height or the slope of their generalization gradients. Taken together with previous research, this study suggests that schizophrenics do *not* generalize more than normal persons.

(4) *High anxiety leads to overgeneralization.* This assumption has been the subject of considerable debate. We cannot review all of the relevant research because it is too remote from our topic, schizophrenia. In summary, the positive evidence has been equivocal and the negative evidence, unequivocal. Only Rosenbaum (1956) has demonstrated that anxiety leads to overgeneralization, and his results are open to question because of possible artifacts in procedure. Mednick himself (1957) was surprised to find that middle anxious psychiatric patients had flatter generalization gradients than either high or low anxious patients, that is, there was no consistent relationship between anxiety and generalization.

The relevant literature has been reviewed by Murray (1965), who concludes that there is virtually no evidence for the widely held belief that anxiety causes overgeneralization. Murray's own carefully controlled study (1965) shows no differences in generalization gradients in relation to either chronic or acute anxiety. Thus this fourth assumption appears to lack sustaining evidence.

Evaluation. Examination of Mednick's four assumptions indicates that supporting evidence is either equivocal or lacking and that there is negative evidence. Thus none of the assumptions is sustained by research findings.

The theory places all its eggs in one basket in that it accounts for schizophrenia solely in terms of anxiety. The difficulty is, that with anxiety so prevalent, it is necessary to explain why schizophrenia is still relatively rare in the population. Mednick was aware of this issue of "over-explanation":

Why doesn't everybody proceed to schizophrenia after an extremely anxiety provoking event? The answer lies in three factors: the individual's original drive level, his rate of recovery from anxiety states, and the number of stimuli that elicit anxiety responses from the individual.

. . . high drive, slow recovery rate, and the number of fear arousing stimuli are highly correlated factors. (1958, p. 323)

Only those with all three factors tend to become schizophrenic, but Mednick himself admitted that *the three factors are all highly correlated.* Thus an extremely anxious individual, being high on all three factors, should become schizophrenic. Clearly, Mednick has not answered his own question. We may guess that he cannot answer it because he identifies anxiety as the sole cause of the thinking disorder in schizophrenia. This explanation will not be acceptable to the majority of psychologists. It is evident that many individuals with extremely high levels of anxiety never become schizophrenic, whereas Mednick's drive theory clearly implies that they should.

What appears to be wrong with the theory is its identification of anxiety as the crucial drive that leads to schizophrenia. Although many schizophrenics do appear anxious, this could be a reaction to incapacity rather than a cause of it. Moreover, many acute schizophrenics are not anxious but apathetic or depressed. The theory is further embarrassed because the predictions from anxiety theory are not supported. The fault, then, seems to lie in placing an excessive burden of explanation on anxiety. It is possible that schizophrenics suffer from excessive drive, but limiting the drive to anxiety is simply not consistent with the evidence.

COMMENTS

We have reviewed the evidence bearing on two social-motivational theories of schizophrenia. The theory that schizophrenics lack motivation has received some support, but it requires the after-the-fact assumption that schizophrenics are helped only by the strongest external motivation, that is, their performance is *differentially* facilitated only when they are confronted with "biologically" noxious stimuli. Thus despite some negative evidence, the theory is still viable.

The theory that schizophrenics are overmotivated has received little research support. Mednick's anxiety theory not only lacks positive evidence but has clear evidence opposing it. Furthermore, it suffers from "overexplanation" in that it cannot explain why all intensely anxious individuals do not become schizophrenic.

The theory that schizophrenics are inordinately sensitive to criticism or rebuff is also weak. The original theory—that censure always leads to deficit—has been abandoned. The revised theory—that censure leads to either deficit or improvement—is equivocally supported by research findings.

Some experiments support it; others negate it. It, too, suffers from internal difficulties. It assumes that a schizophrenic, being abnormally sensitive to elements of rejection in his environment, becomes anxious and disorganized when he is criticized. However, the theory also insists that this fear-ridden, disorganized individual actually *benefits* from censure in that his performance improves when he can escape it. Exponents of the theory have yet to specify why a state of turmoil should lead to improved performance, especially in tasks requiring close attention or memorization of details.

None of the theories discussed in this chapter is, strictly speaking, an etiological theory of schizophrenia. Each attempts to specify the essential element in schizophrenia—lack of or excessive motivation—but none of them states the cause of the motivational difficulty. The cause is not explicitly stated, but the motivational approach implies that it resides in early social relations, especially within the family. Garmezy (1965) has speculated about the effects of early parental training and how certain patterns of reward and punishment might lead to an excessive sensitivity to censure. These and related issues will be discussed in Chapter 15, which deals with interpersonal and social factors as causes of psychosis.

Finally, we may inquire whether motivational theories of schizophrenia are related to any of the dimensions discussed in Chapter 10: acute-chronic, process-reactive, paranoid-nonparanoid, etc. The only relevant dimension would seem to be acute-chronic, as may be seen from the following speculations.

Acute schizophrenia, as we saw in Chapter 10, is marked by sudden onset, confusion, turmoil, anxiety, and disorganization. This fits the picture of an excessively sensitive, *overmotivated* individual who is bewildered by perceived changes in the environment. The acute patient is tense, fearful, and prepared for the worst. His oversensitivity to those around him, and perhaps especially to rejection or criticism, not only disorganizes his behavior but drives him to the solace of isolation from others.

Chronic schizophrenia is marked by apathy, insensitivity to others, and social withdrawal. The patient is uninvolved with those around him and seems unresponsive to the usual social and impersonal rewards and goals of everyday life. This fits the picture of an *undermotivated* individual who no longer responds to the usual values and standards of adult existence.

These speculations suggest that the two basic motivational theories refer to different kinds of schizophrenics or, stated another way, to schizophrenics at different stages in the progression of the psychosis. Perhaps the acute schizophrenic is overmotivated and the chronic schizophrenic, undermotivated. If this is true, there is no need to choose between the two theories because both might be correct. On the other hand, there may be more fruitful ways of approaching schizophrenia than motivational theories. Next we examine an alternate approach, cognitive theories.

REFERENCES

Alvarez, R. R. A comparison of the preferences of schizophrenic and normal subjects for rewarded and punished stimuli. Unpublished doctoral dissertation, Duke University, 1957.

Arey, L. B. The indirect representation of sexual stimuli by schizophrenic and normal subjects. *Journal of Abnormal and Social Psychology*, 1960, **61**, 424–431.

Atkinson, Rita L., & Robinson, Nancy M. Paired-associate learning by schizophrenic and normal subjects under conditions of personal and impersonal reward and punishment. *Journal of Abnormal and Social Psychology*, 1961, **62**, 322–326.

Baxter, J. C., & Becker, J. Anxiety and avoidance behavior in schizophrenics in response to parental figures. *Journal of Abnormal and Social Psychology*, 1962, **64**, 432–437.

Bender, Lauretta, & Schilder, P. Unconditioned and conditioned reactions to pain in schizophrenia. *American Journal of Psychiatry*, 1930, **87**, 365–384.

Benton, A. L., Jentsch, R. C., & Wahler, H. J. Effects of motivating instructions on reaction time in schizophrenia. *Journal of Nervous and Mental Disease*, 1960, **130**, 26–29.

Berkowitz, H. Effects of prior experimenter-subject relationships on reinforced reaction time of schizophrenics and normals. *Journal of Abnormal and Social Psychology*, 1964, **69**, 522–530.

Bleke, R. C. Reward and punishment as determiners of reminiscence effects in schizophrenic and normal subjects. *Journal of Personality*, 1955, **23**, 479–498.

Brodsky, M. J. Interpersonal stimuli as interference in a sorting task. *Dissertation Abstracts*, 1961, **22**, 2068.

Brooker, H. The effects of differential verbal reinforcement on schizophrenic and non-schizophrenic hospital patients. Unpublished doctoral dissertation, Indiana University, 1962.

Brown, R. L. The effects of aversive stimulation on certain conceptual error responses of schizophrenics. *Dissertation Abstracts*, 1961, **22**, 629.

Buss, A. H., Braden, W., Orgel, A., & Buss, Edith H. Acquisition and extinction with different verbal reinforcement combinations. *Journal of Experimental Psychology*, 1956, **52**, 288–295.

Buss, A. H., & Buss, Edith H. The effect of verbal reinforcement combinations on conceptual learning. *Journal of Experimental Psychology*, 1956, **52**, 283–287.

Buss, A. H., & Lang, P. J. Psychological deficit in schizophrenia I: Affect, reinforcement, and concept attainment. *Journal of Abnormal Psychology*, 1965, **70**, 2–24.

Cavanaugh, D. Improvement in the performance of schizophrenics on concept formation tasks as a function of motivational change. *Journal of Abnormal and Social Psychology*, 1958, **57**, 8–12.

Chapman, L. J., & Chapman, Jean P. Interpretation of words in schizophrenia. *Journal of Personality and Social Psychology*, 1965, **1**, 135–146.

Cohen, B. D. Motivation and performance in schizophrenia. *Journal of Abnormal and Social Psychology*, 1956, **52**, 186–190.

Cohen, B. D. Verbal reinforcement, punishment and motivational level in schizophrenia. Unpublished paper delivered at the Midwestern Psychological Association meetings, Chicago, 1959.

Cohen, E., & Cohen, B. D. Verbal reinforcement in schizophrenia. *Journal of Abnormal and Social Psychology*, 1960, **60**, 443–446.

Culver, C. M. The effect of cue value on size estimation in schizophrenic subjects. *Dissertation Abstracts,* 1962, **22,** 4405.

D'Alessio, G. R., & Spence, Janet T. Schizophrenic deficit and its relation to social motivation. *Journal of Abnormal and Social Psychology,* 1963, **66,** 390–393.

Daniell, Edna F. Stimulus generalization in relation to schizophrenia, paranoid-nonparanoid dichotomy, and drug status. Unpublished master's thesis, University of Pittsburgh, 1964.

Davis, R. H., & Harrington, R. W. The effect of stimulus class on the problem solving behavior of schizophrenics and normals. *Journal of Abnormal and Social Psychology,* 1957, **54,** 126–128.

Deering, Gayle. Affective stimuli and disturbance of thought processes. *Journal of Consulting Psychology,* 1963, **27,** 338–343.

Dunham, R. M. Sensitivity of schizophrenics to parental censure. Unpublished doctoral dissertation, Duke University, 1959.

Dunn, W. L. Visual discrimination of schizophrenic subjects as a function of stimulus meaning. *Journal of Personality,* 1954, **23,** 48–64.

Ehrenworth, J. The differential responses to affective and neutral stimuli in the visual-motor performance of schizophrenics and normals. Unpublished doctoral dissertation, Boston University, 1960.

Feldstein, S. The relationship of interpersonal involvement and affectiveness of content to the verbal communication of schizophrenic patients. *Journal of Abnormal and Social Psychology,* 1962, **64,** 39–45.

Fischer, E. H. Task performance of chronic schizophrenics as a function of verbal evaluation and social proximity. *Journal of Clinical Psychology,* 1963, **19,** 176–178.

Franks, C. M. An experimental study of conditioning as related to mental abnormality. Unpublished doctoral dissertation, University of London, 1954.

Garmezy, N. Stimulus differentiation by schizophrenic and normal subjects under conditions of reward and punishment. *Journal of Personality,* 1952, **21,** 253–276.

Garmezy, N. The prediction of performance in schizophrenia. In P. H. Hoch, & J. Zubin (Eds.) *Schizophrenia,* New York: Grune & Stratton, 1965.

Garmezy, N., & Rodnick, E. H. Premorbid adjustment and performance in schizophrenia: Implications for interpreting heterogeneity in schizophrenia. *Journal of Nervous and Mental Disease,* 1959, **129,** 450–466.

Goodstein, L. D., Guertin, W. H., & Blackburn, H. L. Effects of social motivational variables on choice reaction time in schizophrenics. *Journal of Abnormal and Social Psychology,* 1961, **62,** 24–27.

Grisell, J. L., & Rosenbaum, G. Effects of auditory intensity on schizophrenic reaction time. *American Psychologist,* 1963, **18,** 394.

Harris, A. Sensory deprivation and schizophrenia. *Journal of Mental Science,* 1959, **105,** 235–237.

Harris, J. G., Jr. Size estimation of pictures as a function of thematic content for schizophrenic and normal subjects. *Journal of Personality,* 1957, **25,** 651–671.

Howe, E. S. GSR conditioning in anxiety states, normals, and chronic functional schizophrenic subjects. *Journal of Abnormal and Social Psychology,* 1958, **56,** 183-189.

Hunt, J. McV., & Cofer, C. Psychological deficit in schizophrenia. In J. McV. Hunt (Ed.) *Personality and the behavior disorders.* Vol. 2. New York: Ronald Press, 1944, pp. 971–1032.

Johannsen, W. J. Responsiveness of chronic schizophrenics and normals to social and nonsocial feedback. *Journal of Abnormal and Social Psychology*, 1962, **18**, 204–207.

King, H. E. Anticipatory behavior: Temporal matching by normal and psychotic subjects. *Journal of Psychology*, 1962, **54**, 299–307.

Kreinik, Phyllis S. Parent-child themas and concept attainment in schizophrenia. Unpublished doctoral dissertation, Duke University, 1959.

Ladd, C. E. The digit symbol performance of schizophrenic and nonpsychiatric patients as a function of motivational instructions and task difficulty. Unpublished doctoral dissertation, State University of Iowa, 1960.

Lang, P. J. The effect of aversive stimuli on reaction time in schizophrenia. *Journal of Abnormal and Social Psychology*, 1959, **59**, 263–268.

Lang, P. J., & Buss, A. H. Psychological deficit in schizophrenia II: Interference and activation. *Journal of Abnormal Psychology*, 1965, **70**, 77–106.

Lebow, K. E., & Epstein, S. Thematic and cognitive responses of good premorbid schizophrenics to cues of nurturance and rejection. *Journal of Consulting Psychology*, 1963, **27**, 24–33.

Leventhal, A. M. The effects of diagnostic category and reinforcer on learning without awareness. *Journal of Abnormal and Social Psychology*, 1959, **59**, 162–166.

Losen, S. M. The differential effect of censure on the problem solving behavior of schizophrenics and normal subjects. *Journal of Personality*, 1961, **29**, 258–272.

Maginley, H. J. The effect of "threats" of failure upon the conceptual learning performance of hospitalized mental patients. Unpublished doctoral dissertation, University of Pittsburgh, 1956.

Marx, A. The effect of interpersonal content on conceptual task performance of schizophrenics. Unpublished doctoral dissertation, University of Oklahoma, 1962.

Mednick, S. A. Distortions in the gradient of stimulus generalization related to cortical brain damage and schizophrenia. *Journal of Abnormal and Social Psychology*, 1955, **51**, 536–542.

Mednick, S. A. Generalization as a function of manifest anxiety and adaptation to psychological experiments. *Journal of Consulting Psychology*, 1957, **21**, 491–494.

Mednick, S. A. A learning theory approach to research in schizophrenia. *Psychological Bulletin*, 1958, **55**, 316–327.

Moriarty, D., & Kates, S. L. Concept attainment on materials involving social approval and disapproval. *Journal of Abnormal and Social Psychology*, 1962, **65**, 355–364.

Murray, E. N. Stimulus generalization in relation to anxiety. Unpublished doctoral dissertation, University of Pittsburgh, 1965.

Neiditch, S. J. Differential response to failure in hospital and nonhospital groups. *Journal of Abnormal and Social Psychology*, 1963, **66**, 449–453.

Nelson, Sandra, & Caldwell, W. E. Perception of affective stimuli by normal and schizophrenic subjects in a depth perception task. *Journal of General Psychology*, 1962, **67**, 323–335.

O'Connor, N., & Rawnsley, K. Two types of conditioning in psychotics and normals. *Journal of Abnormal and Social Psychology*, 1959, **58**, 157–161.

Olson, G. W. Failure and subsequent performance of schizophrenics. *Journal of Abnormal and Social Psychology*, 1958, **57**, 310–314.

Pascal, C., & Swensen, G. Learning in mentally ill patients under unusual motivation. *Journal of Personality*, 1952, 240–249.

Peters, H. N., & Murphree, O. D. The conditioned reflex in the chronic schizophrenic. *Journal of Clinical Psychology*, 1954, **10**, 126–130.

Pfaffman, C., & Schlosberg, H. The conditioned knee jerk in psychotic and normal individuals. *Journal of Psychology,* 1936, **1**, 201–206.

Pishkin, V., & Hershiser, D. Respiration and GSR as functions of white sound in schizophrenia. *Journal of Consulting Psychology,* 1963, **27**, 330–337.

Pishkin, V., Smith, T. E., & Leibowitz, H. W. The influence of symbolic stimulus value on perceived size in chronic schizophrenia. *Journal of Consulting Psychology,* 1962, **26**, 323–330.

Raush, H. L. Object constancy in schizophrenia. The enhancement of symbolic objects and conceptual stability. *Journal of Abnormal and Social Psychology,* 1956, **52**, 231–234.

Rodnick, E. H., & Garmezy, N. An experimental approach to the study of motivation in schizophrenia. In M. R. Jones (Ed.) *Nebraska symposium on motivation:* Lincoln: University of Nebraska Press, 1957, pp. 109–184.

Rosenbaum, G. Stimulus generalization as a function of clinical anxiety. *Journal of Abnormal and Social Psychology,* 1956, **53**, 281–285.

Rosenbaum G., Grisell, J. L., & Mackavey, W. R. Effects of biological and social motivation on schizophrenic reaction time. *Journal of Abnormal and Social Psychology,* 1957, **54**, 364–368.

Shipley, W. C. Studies of catatonia: VI. Further investigation of the perseverative tendency. *Psychiatric Quarterly,* 1934, **8**, 736–744.

Silverman, J. Noxious cue sensitivity in schizophrenia. Paper presented at the American Psychological Association, Philadelphia, August, 1963.

Slechta, Joan, Gwynn, W., & Peoples, C. Verbal conditioning of schizophrenics and normals in a situation resembling psychotherapy. *Journal of Consulting Psychology,* 1963, **27**, 223–227.

Smock, C. D., & Vancini, J. Dissipation rate of the effects of social censure in schizophrenics. *Psychological Reports,* 1962, **10**, 531–536.

Spence, K. W., & Taylor, Janet A. The relation of conditioned response strength to anxiety in normal, neurotic, and psychotic subjects. *Journal of Experimental Psychology,* 1953, **45**, 265–277.

Stotsky, B. Motivation and task complexity as factors in the psychomotor responses of schizophrenics. *Journal of Personality,* 1957, **25**, 327–343.

Taylor, Janet A., & Spence, K. W. Conditioning level in the behavior disorders. *Journal of Abnormal and Social Psychology,* 1954, **49**, 497–502.

Turbiner, M. Choice discrimination in schizophrenic and normal subjects for positive, negative, and neutral affective stimuli. *Journal of Consulting Psychology,* 1961, **25**, 92.

Webb, W. W. Conceptual ability of schizophrenics as a function of threat of failure. *Journal of Abnormal and Social Psychology,* 1955, **50**, 221–224.

Whiteman, M. The performance of schizophrenics on social concepts. *Journal of Abnormal and Social Psychology,* 1954, **49**, 266–271.

Zahn, T. P. Acquired and symbolic affective value as determinants of size estimation in schizophrenic and normal subjects. *Journal of Abnormal and Social Psychology,* 1959, **58**, 39–47.

CHAPTER 13

Cognitive Theories
of Schizophrenia

The last chapter considered motivational theories of schizophrenia. All motivational theories are based on a *social model,* in which interpersonal variables are paramount. The crucial aspects of adjustment are believed to involve relations between the self and others. The two fundamental variants of motivation theory are that the schizophrenic is either too apathetic and withdrawn from others (insufficient motivation) or that he is too fearful of rebuff, failure, or affectively-toned stimuli (excessive motivation).

The present chapter considers cognitive theories, which are based on an *impersonal model. All* cognitions are important, not merely those involving others. The fundamental defect is believed to lie in the schizophrenic's perceptions, associations, and concepts. The emphasis is on the *structural* aspects of cognition—its normal and abnormal functioning—rather than on the *content.* This distinction will become clearer as the exposition proceeds.

The cognitive approach to psychopathology is less familiar than the motivational approach. Most persons readily accept the motivational approach because they have been taught that motivation explains behavior. The notion that fear can lead to severe psychopathology makes sense not only because there is evidence for it (see the chapters on neurosis), but also because we tend to construe our everyday behavior in such terms. Similarly, it is widely believed that personal interactions constitute the core of adjustment; in fact, many individuals equate psychopathology with interpersonal difficulties. All this emphasis on social motivation makes it appear reasonable and understandable.

The cognitive approach is less familiar and therefore less understandable. At first glance it may be difficult to grasp the connection between

286

problems in attending to stimuli and psychosis, or between conceptual performance and psychopathology. There are two reasons for the difficulty. First, whereas the familiar social motivational approach focuses on interpersonal situations, the cognitive approach is impersonal in that it makes no distinction between personal and nonpersonal (social and nonsocial) contexts. Second, whereas the social motivational approach focuses on content (aggression, sexuality, guilt, achievement, etc.), the cognitive approach ignores content and focuses on the *process* of cognition (attention, information processing, etc.).

Cognition may be divided into perception, association, and conceptual thinking. Perception includes all the information that comes from the senses; this includes the senses attuned to internal environment, for example, stretch receptors that constitute "muscle sense," as well as the senses attuned to the external environment, for example, eyes, ears, skin, nose, and tongue. Perception also includes the selective function of central neural mechanisms. The organism cannot attend to every stimulus that impinges on its sense organs. It must select, organize, and process incoming information, and these aspects of perception will be the focus of our exposition.

Association includes the implicit verbal stimuli called ideas, simple thoughts, and memories. Here, too, there is a selective function; the individual must choose certain associations and exclude others, or else he would be at the mercy of every association he ever acquired.

Conceptual thinking includes the sorting of ideas, thoughts, and stimuli into appropriate categories. It is involved in the "mapping" of an individual's psychological world: the marking off of boundaries and of establishing basic similarities among stimuli. Note that the three aspects of cognition (perception—association—conceptual thinking) constitute a sequence from lower to higher complexity, from more concrete to more abstract, or from immediate contact with explicit stimuli to mediated contact with implicit, ideational stimuli.

There are cognitive theories of schizophrenia for each of the three areas. In perception, the focus is on disturbances in attention, especially as they affect psychomotor performance on such simple tasks as reaction time and tracking of targets. In association, the focus is on free associations and the conditioning of associations. In conceptual thinking, several theories compete in attempting to explain verbal concepts and sorting behavior. One theory attempts to encompass all three aspects: interference theory.

INTERFERENCE THEORY

The leading exponent of interference theory is David Shakow, who has been conducting laboratory research on schizophrenia for three decades. Interference theory regards the organism as a system that processes information. It assumes that the individual selects and responds only to relevant aspects of his environment and ignores extraneous, irrelevant aspects. In its most general form, it suggests the presence of "noise" in the system, which adversely affects all areas of behavior and leads to both the cognitive and the motor symptoms of schizophrenia.

> . . . proper adaptation calls for two kinds of response: (1) high arousal focused on the relevant aspects of the situation with minimum attention paid to the omnipresent multitude of irrelevant aspects; and (2) reduced arousal quality of the focal stimulus as the situation is repeated, as it becomes familiar. The second quality could in part be thought of as a corollary of the first, for old stimuli to some extent, must, if one is to maintain a high level of adaptation take on the low attention-cathexis of irrelevant stimuli, in competition with the new actual or potential stimuli.
>
> The schizophrenic falls down in each respect. He has difficulty in focusing on the relevant aspects of the defined situation, while being more susceptible to the influence of the peripheral. He does not habituate readily . . . . (Shakow, 1962, p. 10)

> If we were to try to epitomize the schizophrenic person's system in the most simple language, we might say that he has two major difficulties: first, he reacts to old situations as if they were new ones (he fails to habituate), and to new situations as if they were recently past ones (he perseverates); and second, he overresponds when the stimulus is relatively small, and he does not respond enough when the stimulus is great. (Shakow, 1963, p. 303)

This approach suggests that schizophrenics lack an efficient "filter mechanism" (Broadbent, 1958) and fail to shift readily to the changing environment around them. In contrast, normals filter out trivial aspects of the environment, focus properly on crucial aspects, and are able to shift their attention with changing requirements of the situation. The normal person is thus an efficient information-processing machine, capable of adapting to his environment through proper attention to relevant stimuli and owing to a relative absence of "noise" in the system.

We may speculate that infants are poor information-processing organisms. How does the process develop so that the normal adult attains efficiency? McGhie and Chapman (1961) have offered an explanation. They assume that early in development the infant passively takes in sensory inputs and that perception changes with each shift in the environment. As the child matures, he becomes more active and begins to integrate sense impressions with previous experience. Gradually, the individual imposes order on his environment, attaining some degree of perceptual constancy despite changes in sensory inputs. The incoming stimuli, which early in development are chaotic bits of information, are later organized into the stable and meaningful categories we recognize as reality. The adult thus imposes a structure on his environment and achieves stability. He can focus on particular stimuli and neglect others; he can relate new stimuli to categories of information already present because of prior experience; and he can respond automatically to stimuli that have appeared repeatedly over an extended period, leaving attention free for new and possibly important aspects of the environment.

McGhie and Chapman attempt to relate these issues of consciousness to schizophrenia. When the attentional process breaks down, there is a failure to select from incoming stimuli. A chaotic mass of sensory messages bombards the individual, who cannot sort them or impose order on them. Perception is now passive, marked by a flood of unconnected sensory impressions as well as internal, mediated thoughts and associations. The stable structure of reality is swept away, sometimes followed by a frightening loss of identity. Some schizophrenics report being passive victims of their environment, unable to initiate action.

The loss of spontaneity in behavior which they describe would seem to be a natural consequence of their conscious attention being invaded by the volitional impulses and stimuli from the effectors which normally function autonomously outside of the range of awareness. The patient now has consciously to initiate and control his bodily movements, every one of which involves a decision. Activities which were before self-regulative are now experienced as uncertain and requiring deliberate coordination. It is small wonder that the patient speaks of a split between his mind and body, and feels that he is in danger of losing control over his own actions.

The patient finds difficulty in ordering, not only his movements, but also his thoughts. Like his movements the patient's thoughts are non-volitional, uncoordinated, and subject to sudden stops. The disturbance of thinking again reflects the fundamental loss of the normal mechanism of selective-inhibitory control of attention. (McGhie & Chapman, 1961, p. 112)

Like Shakow, McGhie and Chapman believe that the fundamental defect in schizophrenia is an inability to select, attend to, and regulate the stimuli that impinge on the organism. This breakdown in information processing is assumed to underlie all the other symptoms: bizarre language, feelings of change and depersonalization, difficulty in reality-testing, and especially inefficiency in performance.

The schizophrenic's inability to concentrate on relevant stimuli and to shift the focus when necessary is assumed to cause him to be deficient in a number of areas. He should show a performance deficit not only in more complex situations such as concept attainment and the generating of associations but also in simpler situations such as reaction time and similar psychomotor tasks.

Note that interference theory emphasizes *cognition* and neglects *motivation*. Although it is acknowledged that lack of interest may cause inefficiency in performance, the basic trouble is believed to be an *inadequacy*, not a lack of motivation. The schizophrenic simply does not possess the cognitive ability required to process information efficiently. This defect should affect the entire range of cognitive behavior, from simple to complex: perception, association, and conceptual thinking.

PERCEPTION

Perception is too broad a topic to discuss here, even when it is limited to research relevant to schizophrenia. Research on size constancy, figure-ground relationships, and allied phenomena have been reviewed by Silverman (1964b) and Lang and Buss (1965). We shall concentrate on the perceptual aspects of psychomotor tasks.

The simplest psychomotor task is the reaction time situation. The subject is required to process incoming stimuli and respond as quickly as possible. There are many variations in procedure, but they all require the subject to maintain a readiness to respond quickly and efficiently. This readiness to respond has been called a *major set* (Shakow, 1962). The stimulus may be specific or general, presented singly or as part of a series of stimuli, and it may involve awareness or not. Whatever the situation, the subject must be able to keep the major set and disregard any intruding minor sets. It is precisely here that the schizophrenic has difficulty. This hypothesis leads to three deductions.

1. *Schizophrenics should have slower reaction times than normals.* This deduction follows directly from the set hypothesis. In the reaction time task the sequence is: warning signal—preparatory interval—the signal to respond—the response. During the preparatory interval the subject must maintain a state of readiness for the oncoming stimulus (signal to respond). Normals can do this efficiently; schizophrenics cannot.

There is abundant evidence confirming the prediction that schizophrenics have slower reaction time, the studies stretching out over a period of three decades (Huston, Shakow, & Riggs, 1937; Rodnick & Shakow, 1940; King, 1954; Tizard & Venables, 1956; Goodstein, Guertin, & Blackburn, 1961; Zahn, Rosenthal, & Shakow, 1961, 1963; and Shakow & McCormick, 1965). Moreover, it has been found that the faster the reaction times, the better the mental health rating among psychiatric patients (Rosenthal, Lawlor, Zahn, & Shakow, 1960; King, 1954, 1961).

2. *Variations in stimuli or procedures should adversely affect schizophrenics more than normals.* When the preparatory interval is irregular, the subject finds it more difficult to maintain the set, and his reaction time is slower. An inability to maintain a set is presumably what is wrong with schizophrenics; hence such variations should affect them more than they affect normals.

All the evidence supports the prediction. When the preparatory interval is lengthened, the reaction times of schizophrenics increase disproportionately (Huston, Shakow, & Riggs, 1937; Rodnick & Shakow, 1940). When the preparatory intervals are irregular (vary randomly from short to long), normals are adversely affected but schizophrenics' reaction times are again disproportionately longer in comparison to normals' (Zahn, Rosenthal, & Shakow, 1961; Zahn & Rosenthal, 1964). These studies found schizophrenics to be especially hampered by a long preparatory interval *on the preceding trial*. Zahn et al. speculated that the schizophrenics, confronted with puzzling variations in stimulus inputs, simplified the situation. Rather than attempt to cope with a complex environment, they paid excessive attention to the previous preparatory interval. If it was long, they were prepared for another long one. Consequently, when a short interval occurred on the next trial, they were unprepared and had long reaction times. Such attempts at guessing the forthcoming interval would not only slow reaction time but also lead to considerable variability from one trial to the next; such variability is characteristic of schizophrenics. The point is that attending to the interval on the previous trial constitutes a *minor, irrelevant set*, which detracts from the *major set* of attending to the present, oncoming stimulus. Interference of the major set by minor sets is precisely what Shakow postulates in schizophrenia.

In addition to reaction time, schizophrenics have difficulty in attending to relevant aspects of a variety of psychomotor tasks. Chapman and McGhie (1962) showed that on several motor tasks schizophrenics were especially disturbed by distractions and unable to inhibit attention to extraneous stimuli. For example, one task was tracking a visual target (similar to "shooting" airplanes in a penny arcade). A sporadic, high-pitched noise caused a greater increase in errors for schizophrenics than for either normals or non-schizophrenic psychiatric patients. Schizophrenics also proved especially susceptible to distracting visual cues when the relevant stimuli were auditory. These findings support those with serial reaction time (Sutton et al. 1961); a shift from visual to auditory stimuli or *vice versa* deteriorated schizophrenics' performance more than normals'.

Two further experiments by McGhie et al. (1965) have helped to pinpoint the difficulty in attending. Schizophrenics were again found to perform worse than normals, depressives, and paranoids. However, on tasks involving only motor speed, distraction did not differentially worsen the performance of schizophrenics. The Punch Board illustrates the nature of the task: the subject was required to punch a stylus through a series of holes. Note that the task requires motor speed and involves little perception. On this and similar tasks, distraction was not a special problem for schizophrenics.

The second kind of task involved perception but not motor speed. Consider the Auditory-Visual Integration Test:

> The subject was asked to perceive and report sequences of six letters or numbers, the individual items of which were presented alternately in the auditory or visual channels. This task thus demanded the integration of information derived from two sensory channels. (McGhie et al., 1965, p. 385)

On this and similar tasks, distraction seriously deteriorated the performance of the schizophrenics but not of the control subjects. Thus schizophrenics, although not especially susceptible to distraction on simple motor tasks, are differentially affected on tasks requiring processing of information. Two hypotheses can account for these findings.

Shakow (1962) has suggested that the problem may be one of pacing, the schizophrenic needing to move at his own pace and the normal being able to adjust to a tempo set by an experimenter. On a simple tapping task in which the subject sets his own tempo, schizophrenics perform as well as normal persons. In the reaction time setting, it is the experimenter who determines the timing of the stimuli, and here schizophrenics show a performance deficit.

The alternate hypothesis emphasizes information processing and a deficient filter mechanism.

> . . . schizophrenic patients have a marked inability to attend selectively to stimuli in such a way that only relevant information is processed. This inability on the part of the schizophrenic to filter out irrelevant data tends to lead to an overloading of the limited information processing and storing mechanism available to him. (McGhie et al., 1965, p. 397)

This explanation accounts for differences between tasks involving mainly motor responses and those involving mainly perception of stimuli. Attention is crucial only in the latter tasks and only in these is distraction a special problem for schizophrenics.

Thus the evidence unequivocally supports the prediction that schizophrenics are especially disturbed by the variations that constitute distractions. The variations may involve pacing (tempo) or intruding stimuli from a secondary sense modality (for example, auditory stimuli interfering with attention to visual stimuli). Whatever the source, such irrelevant aspects of the situation render it difficult to maintain the major set. The schizophrenic has a special problem in maintaining the major set, and consequently his performance suffers.

3. *Conditions that enhance maintaining the major set will improve the performance of schizophrenics more than that of normals and may eliminate schizophrenic deficit.* Evidence relevant to this prediction has come largely from experiments designed to test the theory that schizophrenics are under-

motivated. As we saw in the last chapter, aversive stimuli (usually white noise) have been used in an attempt to increase schizophrenics' motivation and thereby improve performance. All the evidence indicates that aversive stimuli do indeed lead to better performance, the increment being greater in schizophrenics than in normals. However, these results may also be explained in terms of an enhancement of the stimuli, which should help to maintain set.

Consider the reaction time task. After a preparatory interval, the stimulus comes on. The subject's speed of response depends in large part on how closely he attends to this stimulus. Normals attend very well, schizophrenics poorly. If this stimulus can be emphasized so as to facilitate attention to it, schizophrenics should benefit more than normals. This is what has happened in the "motivation" studies. The white noise starts simultaneously with the onset of the stimulus, thereby helping to define and emphasize the stimulus. The accompanying aversive stimulation, being in phase with the stimulus, facilitates the subject's attending to it. This is precisely the help schizophrenics need, and under these conditions their reaction times approximate those of normals.

Of course these results are also consistent with motivation theory. It has been suggested that the schizophrenic performs better in order to escape from or avoid the noxious stimuli, the additional motivation being necessary because schizophrenics are undermotivated. However, Lang (1959) showed that an avoidance condition did not necessarily lead to better performance; giving the subjects information about their performance proved to yield the most enduring improvement in reaction time. Furthermore, when the accompanying stimuli were of low intensity and therefore not aversive, they still sped up reaction time. Thus it is the *presence* of accompanying stimuli rather than their motivational properties that enhances performance. This means that such stimuli must improve performance by helping to maintain set rather than by adding to motivation.

Wienckowski's research on reaction time (1959) strongly supports this conclusion. He showed that when there was a large change in the total stimulus complex (two stimuli going off and one going on) schizophrenics improved their performance more than normal subjects. The stimuli were not noxious and therefore their beneficial effect cannot be ascribed to motivational properties. Rather, the improvement of the schizophrenics may be ascribed to their better attention to the ready signal, which was enhanced and emphasized by the addition of two collateral stimuli.

The three deductions from Shakow's set hypothesis have all been verified. Schizophrenics have slower reaction times than normals; they are affected more adversely than normals by conditions that distract attention; and they benefit more than normals by conditions that help focus attention. Moreover, the set hypothesis accounts for results previously explained by motivation theory, in addition to results that cannot be explained by assuming that schizophrenics are undermotivated. In brief, the research on psychomotor tasks corroborates interference theory.

ASSOCIATIVE INTERFERENCE

Bleuler was the first exponent of the theory that disturbed associations are the crucial issue in schizophrenia. Although his writings date back many decades, the English translation of his major work is more recent (1950). The primary disturbance in association may be seen in bizarre ideas, loose associations, fragmented thinking, and the blocking of the usual chains of associations and ideas. This primary disturbance ostensibly gives rise to such secondary elaborations as hallucinations and delusions.

Disturbed associations handicap the schizophrenic in his attempts to cope with the environment. Stimuli that are seen as being neutral by normal subjects may be provocative for schizophrenics, who perceive them in idiosyncratic ways. Moreover, the schizophrenic is unable to filter out bizarre ideas and associations, which tend to intrude on consciousness and distract him from the task at hand. Thus the idiosyncratic associations of the schizophrenic distract him and cause performance deficits. This theory has two testable deductions.

1. *The associations of schizophrenics are uncommon.* In addition to clinical reports, there are research findings to support this hypothesis. Moran (1953) found that the word associations of schizophrenics were less related to the stimulus words than those of normal subjects. Johnson et al. (1964) reported that schizophrenics produced more idiosyncratic word associations than normal subjects. Sommer et al. (1960) obtained the same results with the Kent-Rosanoff word association task. In a follow up experiment, Sommer et al. (1962) attempted to condition common associations to words. Alcoholic controls conditioned rapidly, but schizophrenics showed little evidence of conditioning. However, Ullman et al. (1964) managed to condition common associations, although the speed and level of learning were both low.

Wynne (1963) found that the free associations of acute schizophrenics differed little from those of normals. However, when instructed to give the associations "most people do," normals gave more common associations but schizophrenics did not. Maltzman, Seymore, and Licht (1962) attempted to condition normal subjects to give common or uncommon associations. They learned to give more common associations but did not learn to give more uncommon associations. Maltzman, Cohen, and Belloni (1963) found that schizophrenic children give more uncommon associations than normal children.

Taken together, these studies suggest that schizophrenics tend to give uncommon associations and have difficulty in learning common ones, whereas normal subjects tend to give common associations and have difficulty in learning uncommon ones. Thus the deduction is supported.

2. *Intrusive associations worsen the performance of schizophrenics more than of normal subjects.* The evidence concerning this hypothesis comes from a variety of sources. Chapman (1958) presented subjects with a stimulus word and had them choose from three response words; the task was to choose a word in the same conceptual class. For example, when *hat* was the stimulus word, the three response words were *head* (incorrect association), *cap* (correct response in the same conceptual class), and *garage* (irrelevant word). Schizophrenics had more associative intrusions— incorrect associations as responses—than normal subjects. Furthermore, the greater the associative strength of the distracting incorrect response, the greater was the schizophrenics' decrement in performance.

Donahoe et al. (1961) taught subjects associations between nonsense syllables. These built-in intrusive associations produced an equal decrement in the learning of schizophrenics and normal subjects. Evidently, *meaningless* associations such as nonsense syllables do not differentially distract schizophrenics. Downing et al. (1963) varied the type of distractor words in a conceptual task similar to Chapman's. They found that associatively linked words led to more errors than contiguity or clang distractors. Note that associative distractors have meaning, whereas contiguity distractors are based on spatial nearness and clang distractors on similar sounds. These findings, taken together with the negative results of Donahoe et al. and the positive results of Chapman, suggest that schizophrenics are not differentially distracted by *all* types of irrelevant associations but only by *meaningful* associations.

Further evidence comes from an experiment by Lang and Luoto (1962). They found that although schizophrenic's mediational processes were not different from normal subjects', schizophrenics made different kinds of errors. They persisted in giving previously correct responses in a new learning situation, the old responses interfering with subsequent learning. Spence and Lair (1964) also found that the error patterns of schizophrenics were different from those of normal subjects. Normals produced more errors of omission, whereas schizophrenics gave more inappropriate responses that were borrowed from other learning lists. Evidently the schizophrenics were unable to prevent the intrusion of irrelevant associations. A follow up study (1965) showed that normal subjects and partially recovered schizophrenics manifested less associative interference than unrecovered patients.

Two more memory studies offer positive evidence. Kausler et al. (1964) report that associative interference affects schizophrenics more than normals in a negative transfer situation (previous learning retards subsequent learning). Lauro (1962) found that although normal subjects and schizophrenics did not differ in recall, schizophrenics tended to bring up more irrelevant words than normals.

There should be more associative interference when words have several meanings than when they have only one meaning. Faibish (1961) had normals and schizophrenics define and free associate to words with either one meaning or multiple meanings. Both normals and schizophrenics showed poorer word association and vocabulary performance with the multiple meaning words, but the schizophrenics' decrement was greater than the normals'. The schizophrenics were disrupted by the multiple meanings, and Faibish concluded that ". . . the majority of the results can be understood in terms of interference effects." (1961, p. 423)

Finally, Lester (1960) studied restricted associations in normals, hebephrenic and paranoid schizophrenics, and epileptics. The patient groups showed more interference than the normals in the selection of associates, the interference occurring because of the intrusion of extraneous associations. The interference was greatest for epileptics, followed by hebephrenics, paranoids, and normals, in decreasing order.

All this evidence supports the theory of associative interference. Schizophrenics have relatively unique, nonshared associations, which, like external distractors, serve to deteriorate performance because they are intrusive. As with external distractors, the internal distractors—associations—evidently cannot be filtered out by schizophrenics.

CONCEPTUAL THINKING

There are three theories of impaired conceptual thinking in schizophrenia. The first holds that schizophrenics are incapable of abstract thinking or attaining concepts. The second assumes an inability to communicate concepts but no inherent loss of conceptual ability. The third is interference theory, as applied to conceptual thinking.

Loss of Abstractness

The term *abstract* is usually defined in conjunction with its opposite, *concrete*. Concreteness refers to being stimulus bound; the individual classifies stimuli on the basis of physical properties or sensory attributes such as *sound, red,* and *pointed.* Abstractness refers to nonphysical attributes such as *beauty* or *fright,* and also to concepts involving complex, multiple functions or properties. For example, *weapons* is an abstract concept because it refers to a complex of properties and includes a variety of concrete objects.

Goldstein (1946) defined "the abstract attitude" in broader terms than our definition of abstractness, but the two definitions are basically similar.

Goldstein had conducted much research with brain-damaged patients, whom he found to be abnormally concrete. His investigations of schizophrenics revealed similar concreteness, and he suggested that the fundamental thinking disorder in schizophrenia is an inability to form abstract concepts. Goldstein was careful not to conclude that schizophrenia is the same as brain damage, but he did attribute the poor performance of schizophrenics on conceptual tasks to a loss of function similar to that seen in neurological disorders.

Goldstein cited as evidence for his theory the poor performance of schizophrenics on tasks requiring conceptual ability, flexibility of thinking, and abstract thinking (Bolles & Goldstein, 1938; Goldstein & Scheerer, 1941). In addition to his own observations, there was corroborating evidence from Hanfmann and Kasanin, (1942), Benjamin (1946), and Kasanin (1946). Unfortunately, it is difficult to interpret this body of data. The early techniques were largely qualitative and depended upon subjective evaluations of abstractness or concreteness. Most of the research used small numbers of subjects and failed to employ adequate control groups. Thus those early findings must be judged as inconclusive.

Later work with better, quantitative tasks and adequate control groups has reversed the initial verdict: schizophrenics are capable of conceptual thinking. Of course, the conceptual performance of schizophrenics is impaired in comparison to that of normal subjects, just as their performance on a variety of tasks is impaired, but there is no loss of the ability to think conceptually (Lothrop, 1961). After reviewing a large number of studies using conceptual tasks, Payne (1961) concluded:

> These studies then suggest that schizophrenics as a group are probably not abnormally concrete in the sense of being unable to form a new concept. They are, however, abnormal in the *type* of concepts they form. Their concepts tend to be unusual and often eccentric. They are able to learn normal concepts, but tend to have difficulty in adhering to them when asked to employ them over a period of time. (p. 243)

The evidence behind these conclusions was obtained in research with a variety of tasks, for example, vocabulary tests, verbal conceptual tasks, sorting tasks, and interpretation of proverbs. It is clear that although schizophrenics have a conceptual deficit, it is not due to a loss of abstractness or to an excessive concreteness. Thus Goldstein's formulation is not sustained by research findings. Schizophrenics are not more concrete, nor do they closely resemble brain-damaged patients in their conceptual performance.

According to Payne (1961) the problem with schizophrenics is their tendency to verbalize deviant concepts, which normal individuals cannot comprehend. It is only a short step to assume an inability to communicate with others.

Loss of Communication

This theory emphasizes social feedback. It assumes that the basic problem is an inability not to form concepts but to communicate them. The first one to advance this approach was Sullivan (1946), who stressed language problems:

> The peculiarities of language behavior in the schizophrenic arise from his extreme need of a feeling of personal security. The schizophrenic, early convinced that since it is unobtainable, satisfaction is not the prime consideration in life, uses language exclusively and more or less knowingly in the pursuit of durable security. (p. 7)

What the schizophrenic lacks is consensual validation or feedback from others about his perception of reality. Everyone depends on social feedback to verify perceptions and conceptions; this is the way to learn what is acceptable, permissible, and desirable, and also what reality is.

Sullivan assumes that the schizophrenic, expecting no gain from social give-and-take, wishes only to protect himself from anxiety. He retreats from others and cuts off the social feedback that might correct private, eccentric, bizarre notions. His thinking and language become peculiar because he does not use them to communicate.

This approach was adopted and further developed by Cameron (1938, 1951), who emphasized role-taking and fantasy. He regarded the schizophrenic as an isolated person who cannot share other's perspectives; nor could others share his perspective:

> Social communication is gradually crowded out by fantasy; and fantasy itself, because of its nonparticipation in and relation to action, becomes in turn less and less influenced by social patterns. The result is a progressive loss of organized thinking. . . . (1946, pp. 51–52)

Unfortunately, this theory lacks precision. It does not distinguish clearly between two alternatives: (1) schizophrenics have bizarre, deviant concepts, which implies that their conceptual thinking is *different* from that of normal individuals; and (2) the sole problem is an inability to communicate essentially normal and correct concepts, which implies that schizophrenics' conceptual thinking is the *same* as that of normal individuals. There is no doubt that many schizophrenics have difficulty in communicating their thoughts. However, as we shall demonstrate later, this is probably due to the eccentricity and bizarreness of the concepts, which anyone would have difficulty in communicating, rather than an inability to communicate.

Interference Theory

There are two variants of interference theory. The first one emphasizes the tendency of schizophrenics to include irrelevancies in their concepts;

this tendency is called *overinclusion.* In his early work, Cameron (1938) found that schizophrenics had difficulty in maintaining boundaries. If the task was sorting objects, the patient might include not only the task objects but also the experimenter's desk, chair, pen, etc. Cameron also pointed out that personal and idiosyncratic themes would intrude into a schizophrenic's speech and concepts, a phenomenon labeled *interpenetration.*

Cameron coined the term *overinclusion* and developed the notion as follows:

Extravagant *overinclusion* is characteristic of schizophrenic disorganization. A patient's unstable behavior organization does not limit the number and kind of simultaneously effective excitants to a relatively few coherent ones. In consequence, his reactions are not sufficiently restricted in range for him to deal with even the ordinary situations of daily living. Schizophrenic patients often complain of the way everything seems jumbled up and crowding in on them, but it is actually their own behavior disorganization that makes the situation seem impossibly unrestricted and confused. (1947, p. 59)

Cameron and Magaret (1951) and more recently Payne (1961) have pointed out that *exclusion* is necessary for success on a given task. At first the subject attends to too many aspects of the situation. Gradually his attention becomes focused on only the crucial aspects of the situation; nonessentials are ignored. Schizophrenics, however, have difficulty in excluding distracting irrelevancies, and their overinclusiveness impairs conceptual performance.

Overinclusiveness has been investigated with both verbal and nonverbal tasks. Epstein (1953) constructed an Inclusion Test consisting of items like the following:

MAN   arms   shoes   hat   toes   head   none.

The key word is *man,* and there are five response words plus the word *none.* The subject is instructed to underline all the response words that fall under the heading of the key word. In this example the correct response words are *arms, toes,* and *head.* Overinclusiveness is manifested by underlining nonessential or unrelated response words. Using this test, Epstein found that schizophrenics were significantly more overinclusive than normals matched for age and vocabulary level. This finding was corroborated by Payne, Matussek, and George (1959) who showed that schizophrenics were significantly more overinclusive on the Inclusion Test than matched neurotics.

A similar instrument was devised by Moran (1953), who used eight response words. Schizophrenics underlined more distant words than did matched normals, and when asked to free associate to the key words, schizophrenics gave more distant associations. These results were confirmed in every respect by Seth and Beloff (1959).

The nonverbal tasks have consisted of sorting objects on the basis of their properties or functions. For example the three objects *desk, chair,* and *notebook* might be sorted on the basis of studying (desk and notebook) or on the basis of furniture (desk and chair). The early sorting tests yielded only qualitative scores and were therefore little better than clinical observation. Nevertheless, the test stimuli and the notion of a sorting test were worthwhile, and it remained for McGaughran (1954) to demonstrate that with modification they were useful.

He postulated two dimensions that underlie sorting behavior: open-closed and public-private. The open-closed dimension is a translation and modification of the Goldstein and Scheerer (1941) abstract—concrete dichotomy. Closed concepts are restricted and limited to narrow groups, whereas open concepts are unrestricted and include a great number of stimuli. Thus openness equals overinclusiveness.

The public-private dimension concerns reality testing and consensual bases of sorting as opposed to personal and idiosyncratic bases. Schizophrenics, being overinclusive and idiosyncratic, should produce concepts that are both open and private.

McGaughran and Moran (1956) found that schizophrenics' concepts were indeed both more open and more open-private than the concepts of normal subjects. However, the differences were of borderline statistical significance, and they have been challenged by Sturm (1964) who failed to replicate them. One possibility for the discrepancy in findings is different kinds of schizophrenics in the two experiments. As we have seen, the acute-chronic, process-reactive, and paranoid-nonparanoid dimensions are all important, and they might account for differences between two samples of schizophrenics. We shall return to this issue later.

The sorting of objects as a means of investigating concepts has been popular in research on schizophrenic thinking, the method of scoring varying from one study to the next. Regardless of how the task is scored, the results have been essentially similar: the concepts of schizophrenics are significantly more inclusive than those of normals or neurotics (Lovibond, 1954; Payne, Matussek, & George, 1959; and Payne & Hewlett, 1960). The Payne and Hewlett study is especially interesting because overinclusiveness was found to be limited to schizophrenics; it did not appear in depressives or neurotics. In summary, most of the studies with both sorting and vocabulary tasks have found that schizophrenics are overinclusive.

In a series of experiments Chapman demonstrated both overinclusiveness and a special sensitivity to distracting stimuli in schizophrenics. He modified the sorting procedure to attain greater control, using standard cards and response cards containing drawings of objects (1956). Some of the objects on the response cards were incorrect but shared a common property with objects on the standard card. These were the distracters, and the number of distracters varied. Schizophrenics tended to ~~the~~ use incorrect, distractor commonalities as a basis for sorting but normals tended not to; the more distracters there were the greater was the discrepancy between schizophrenic and normal performance. Ostensibly, the schizophrenics were too overinclusive to ignore the distracting elements.

The next study employed words instead of drawings as the stimuli to be sorted (Chapman & Taylor, 1957). Schizophrenics were again significantly more inclusive than normals in their conceptual sorting. Of incidental interest was the finding that schizophrenics are slightly more overexclusive than normals, but the large majority of schizophrenic errors was due to overinclusiveness.

Chapman's findings bring us to the second variant of interference theory, this one emphasizing attention. This variation explains disturbances in conceptual thinking on the same basis as it explains all schizophrenic deficit—in terms of the interference of irrelevant cognitive elements that can be filtered out by normal individuals but not by schizophrenics. The theory was stated explicitly by two groups of British investigators.

All purposeful behavior depends for its success on the fact that some stimuli are 'attended to' and some other stimuli are ignored. It is a well-known fact that when concentrating on one task, normal people are quite unaware of most stimuli irrelevant to the task. It is as if some 'filter mechanism' cuts out or inhibits the stimuli, both internal and external, which are irrelevant to the task at hand, to allow the most efficient 'processing' of incoming information. Overinclusive thinking might be only one aspect of a general breakdown of this 'filter mechanism.' (Payne, Matussek, & George, 1959, p. 631)

Both disorders of perception and thinking in schizophrenia are secondary to a disorder of the span of attention, which can be too broad or too narrow, or may alternate between the two. Constancy of perception . . . depends on the ability to perceive a thing in its context, or to take into account all the 'cues' existing in the whole perceptual field. Thus it is related to 'broadness of attention.' 'Overinclusiveness' or wide span of schizophrenic concepts is related also to 'overbroadness' of their attention, which makes them incapable of excluding irrelevant stimuli. (Weckowicz & Blewitt, 1959, p. 914)

Note that the second quotation, which appeared two years before Chapman's (1961) findings, contains a hypothesis that explains these findings. Excessively broad attention should lead to overinclusive concepts and excessively narrow attention to overexclusive concepts; alternating between excessively broad and excessively narrow attention should lead to both overinclusive and overexclusive concepts such as Chapman found in his schizophrenic subjects.

Weckowicz and Blewitt (1959) were able to test one implication of their theory. A faulty filter mechanism should affect both *conceptual* and *perceptual* performance. They found high correlations (larger than .50) between abstraction scores on a sorting task (conceptual) and a size constancy task (perceptual), thereby strengthening their theory.

The second variation of interference theory is broader than the first. It assumes that schizophrenics, although predominantly overinclusive, may also be overexclusive. It also assumes that faulty attention, not overinclusion, is the fundamental cognitive defect in schizophrenia. Thus it makes contact with the mass of data on psychomotor deficit and deviant associations in schizophrenia. Both variations are consistent with previous research, but the second one is to be preferred because of its comprehensiveness.

Heterogeneity among Schizophrenics

Earlier we mentioned the possibility that not all schizophrenics are overinclusive. This notion is reinforced by the presence of wide differences in the extent of overinclusive tendencies among schizophrenics. If these differences are meaningful, they are likely to be related to the three dimensions noted earlier: paranoid-nonparanoid, acute-chronic, and process-reactive.

Payne and his colleagues have conducted a series of studies on overinclusion. Payne and Hewlett (1960) factor-analyzed a large number of tasks and discovered those with the highest loadings on a factor of overinclusion. The schizophrenics in their study split into two groups that performed quite differently on the experimental tasks. One group performed slowly and was not overinclusive; the other group performed at an adequate speed but was markedly overinclusive. Payne and Hewlett speculated that the first group was probably catatonics who showed symptoms of motor retardation and inappropriate affect, whereas the second group probably comprised paranoids with delusions and ideas of reference.

The factors of overinclusion and retardation were replicated in a study by Craig (1965), who found it necessary to distinguish between paranoid and delusional patients:

Three groups emerge from overinclusion and retardation: (a) those with disorders of thinking but not generally slowed, being retarded only on tests involving conceptual processes; (b) those with general retardation, which shows up on tests of conceptual processes, but whose thinking is only slowed, not disordered; (c) those with both disordered thinking and general retardation . . . The first group might be paranoids, the second depressed, and the third the delusional and thought-disordered patients. (p. 544)

These speculations differ from those of Payne. Payne links retardation to catatonia, Craig to depression; Payne links delusions to paranoid patients, Craig to nonparanoid patients. Obviously, further research will be needed to disentangle the nature of these patients. Until then it seems best to go along with Payne, whose views are backed by a substantial body of research.

Payne developed a rationale linking overinclusion with delusions. Overinclusion means that any generalization will be excessively broad, the patient failing to screen out irrelevant features.

Thus, for example, a patient may genuinely (and normally) believe that a certain individual dislikes him. However, his overinclusive 'concept' (cerebral representation) of this individual may extend to other similar people (for example, all foreigners, all dark men) so that he may develop the same negative emotional reactions to this entire category of people, being incapable of the necessary discrimination which normally circumscribes fairly precisely the stimuli which will evoke the particular response. This could partly explain how it is that delusions so frequently come to include a broad category of people as they develop. (Payne, Caird & Laverty, 1964, p. 563)

This hypothesis is a reasonable account of how overinclusiveness might lead to delusions, but the empirical question remains as to whether delusional schizophrenics are in fact more inclusive than nondelusional schizophrenics. Payne et al. (1964) compared delusional schizophrenics, nondelusional schizophrenics, and nonschizophrenics (a combination of neurotics, depressives, and character disorders). Two-thirds of the delusional patients were found to be overinclusive, as opposed to one-fifth of the nondelusional patients. Since delusions are what characterize paranoids, it would seem that the paranoid-nonparanoid dimension offers one explanation for the heterogeneity of schizophrenics with reference to overinclusiveness.

Nevertheless, the explanation is incomplete. Evidently, some paranoid (delusional) patients are not overinclusive, and a theory is needed to explain why. Cameron's (1951) formulation of how delusions develop offers an explanation. In the initial stage the patient is overinclusive. He is seeking "the explanation" and is attentive to a broad range of stimuli. In his search for a solution to his problem he cannot afford to eliminate any possibilities. His hypotheses are vague and unformed, and his concepts tend to be unstructured and overinclusive. Eventually, he arrives at a scheme (the delusion) that makes sense to him. This scheme integrates all the vague, disturbing, amorphous "facts" of his existence. Once the delusion is fixed, it becomes rigid and airtight. The paranoid will consider no stimuli that do not fit his scheme. He is hyperattentive only to facts that fit his theory, but he ignores all other stimuli. Consequently, his span of attention and the breadth of his concepts become narrow, and he may progress all the way to overexclusiveness in his conceptual thinking.

Silverman (1964a) reports data consistent with Cameron's explanation. He found that chronic paranoid patients tended to use narrower categories than acute paranoid patients. Relating this finding to Cameron's formulation, he concluded:

Things and events either fit the paranoid schizophrenic's delusional system or they do not exist. Under these conditions, a state of information overload—a state which appears to characterize certain other schizophrenics—is not possible. For there are only two kinds of information to be processed—that which is congruent with one's delusional system and that which is not. (Silverman, 1964a, p. 392)

Silverman's study demonstrates the importance of the acute-chronic dimension in accounting for differences in inclusiveness among schizophrenics. Corroborating evidence has been reported by Payne (1962). He had subjects sort blocks that varied in a number of properties (shape, color, size, material, etc.) and derived an overinclusiveness score. Only acute schizophrenics were more inclusive than normals; chronic schizophrenics and depressives were no more inclusive than normals. These results were replicated in a subsequent study with two sorting tasks (Payne et al., 1963). Acute schizophrenics were more inclusive and chronic schizophrenics were less inclusive than nonpsychotic controls. Since acute patients have a better prognosis, the authors speculated that overinclusiveness is associated with a better prognosis.

In one study the acute-chronic dimension was found to be highly correlated with the good premorbid-poor premorbid dimension (Johannsen et al., 1963). If these two are related, it follows that good premorbid schizophrenics should be overinclusive and poor premorbid schizophrenics, underinclusive. Tutko and Spence (1962) compared the performance of good and poor premorbid patients on a sorting task. The measure of interest in the present context is the number of "expansive errors" because these are essentially errors of overinclusion. The good premorbid schizophrenics were significantly higher in expansive errors than the normals, while the poor premorbids were lower than the normals.

We noted earlier that overinclusiveness is seen almost exclusively in schizophrenics (Payne et al., 1964). The evidence just presented suggests that overinclusiveness occurs only in some schizophrenics, namely those with delusions, an acute or recent onset of psychosis, or a good premorbid history—all these are either not more overinclusive than normals or are less overinclusive than normals. These facts suggest that overinclusiveness is a relatively benign kind of thinking disorder. We know that the performance deficit seen in schizophrenia appears to be caused by some kind of interference in proper focusing on the relevant stimuli. Perhaps the *kind* of interference is as important as the fact of interference itself, that is, overinclusiveness may be a good prognostic sign and other kinds of cognitive dysfunction, a poor prognostic sign.

We have established that a tendency toward overinclusiveness, which is characteristic of certain kinds of schizophrenics, underlies the relatively poor performance of schizophrenics in conceptual tasks. This leaves us with the problem of accounting for conceptual deficit in schizophrenics who are not overinclusive. Why are their concepts deficient?

The answer would seem to lie in the nature of their associations. It has been established that schizophrenics tend to have deviant and bizarre associations. These associations might easily intrude into the concept attainment process. Whereas a normal person would give a common and consensual basis for sorting, a schizophrenic would be expected to give an uncommon, eccentric basis. Thus there appear to be two kinds of thought disturbance underlying the conceptual deficit of schizophrenics. The first kind, overinclusiveness, was described at length earlier. The second kind, bizarreness has been discussed by Payne:

> There is considerable evidence that some schizophrenics form unusual and even eccentric concepts, and that this abnormality is related to their low scores on intelligence tests. It is also associated with severity of illness, and with a lack of sociability, perhaps because it makes communication with others difficult. (1961, p. 250)

When these remarks are placed in the context of heterogeneity among schizophrenics, an interesting hypothesis emerges. Let us assume that there are two kinds of schizophrenics, each with a different type of conceptual deficit. The first kind is characterized by delusions, recent onset of psychosis, and a good premorbid history; their thought disorder consists of overinclusiveness, their concepts being too broad and contaminated by irrelevancies. The second kind is characterized by an absence of delusions, chronicity of psychosis, and a poor premorbid history; their thought disorder consists of bizarre associations, their concepts being too deviant and eccentric to be understood by normal persons.

This dichotomy corresponds roughly to the one suggested by Wynne and Singer (1963) in their attempt to classify thought disorder. One type of schizophrenic thinking was labeled *fragmented,* and patients of this type manifest fairly clear and differentiated attention, perception, and communication. They suffer from an intrusion of fantasies and wishes into their logical thought, and they tend to split off ideas, impulses, and emotions. They are often delusional and hallucinatory, and they may be overemotional. Their premorbid history is good.

The second type, labeled *amorphous,* consists of indefinite thought that lacks ideas. Schizophrenics showing this kind of disturbance are not delusional or hallucinatory, but their perceptions are uncertain and blurred. Their efforts at communication are characterized by blocking and vague approximations in place of precise terms. They lack affect and appear apathetic; their premorbid history is poor.

The evidence is consistent with this dichotomous classification. Overinclusiveness is associated with the more benign forms of schizophrenia: acuteness, delusions, communicability, affect, and a good premorbid history. Deviance and eccentricity are associated with the more ominous forms of schizophrenia: chronicity, no delusions, lack of communicability, apathy, and a poor premorbid history. It will be interesting to see whether future research sustains this dichotomy.

The foregoing speculations and evidence point up the importance of dimensions *within* schizophrenia. It no longer suffices to compare a schizophrenic sample with a normal sample. There must be specification of the premorbid history, the presence or absence of delusions, and the chronicity of the psychosis.

All three of these dimensions have been incorporated into a cognitive theory by Silverman (1964b). The theory uses such concepts as *field-articulation* and *scanning,* and it becomes involved in rather technical details of perception and cognition. An adequate exposition of the theory is therefore beyond the scope of this book, but we may note that the theory is consistent with much of the previous exposition. Thus Silverman finds it important to distinguish between paranoid and nonparanoid, process and reactive, and acute and chronic patients in explaining problems of attention and cognition in schizophrenia.

COMMENT

Interference theory emphasizes the difficulties schizophrenics have in dealing with stimulus imputs, both external and internal. The theory is supported by an array of facts concerning cognitive functioning. Schizophrenics have difficulty in focusing on relevant stimuli and excluding irrelevant stimuli, in maintaining a set over time, in shifting a set when necessary, in pacing themselves, and generally in performing efficiently.

Interference theory is, of course, not the only approach that explains the performance deficit of schizophrenics. Chapter 12 reviewed several motivational theories that also offer explanations of schizophrenics' inefficiency. If interference theory is to be accepted as a general explanation of schizophrenic deficit, it must include alternate hypotheses to the motivational theories (sensitivity to affective stimuli, social censure, and insufficient motivation).

Concerning affective stimuli, we saw in the last chapter that the term *affective* has so many referents that it cannot be defined precisely. Interference theory approaches this issue by assuming that so-called affective stimuli are those that elicit more associations. Deering (1963) demonstrated that schizophrenics give more associations to affective stimuli than do normals, but the two groups do not differ in number of associations to neutral stimuli. Earlier we saw that schizophrenics have deviant and eccentric associations, which serve as distractors. Thus the poor performance of schizophrenics with affective stimuli can be explained as follows: such stimuli set off personal, idiosyncratic associations which intrude into the schizophrenic's field of attention, and the resultant distraction renders his performance inefficient.

Concerning punishment and the theory of insufficient motivation, interference theory offers the following possibilities. Verbal punishment often helps the schizophrenic to overcome some of his inefficiency but no more so than information about his responses. Unlike normals, schizophrenics fail to make statements during tasks that suggest self-guidance, for example, "I got that one wrong." Thus it seems likely that external cues (saying *Wrong* to the subject) serve a directive purpose for the schizophrenic which the normal accomplishes for himself.

The evidence concerning social censure indicates that the theory is incorrect or at best does not account for all the facts. Schizophrenics do not show a personal reaction to social censure, at least not any more than do normals. In fact, verbal punishment, as we have seen, seems to assist schizophrenics by breaking up perseverative tendencies, which means that the informational aspects of such punishment are crucial.

Some of these arguments also apply to physical punishment. The theory of insufficient motivation receives its greatest support from the data on physical punishment, which has been shown to facilitate the performance of schizophrenics more than of normals. The interference view is that physical punishment is an excellent source of information about errors, breaking up incorrect sets and guiding responding. The importance of the cue value of punishing stimuli has been demonstrated in studies of normal subjects, whose performance is improved when electric shock follows *correct* responses. Furthermore, when intense stimuli, punishing or otherwise, coincide with important discriminative stimuli (for example, in reaction time), the discriminative stimuli are emphasized and more clearly separated from irrelevant stimuli.

Interference theory can account for the data that have been offered in support of the various motivational theories of schizophrenia. Beyond this, the theory explains a variety of cognitive deficits in schizophrenia, including psychomotor inefficiency, associative disturbance, and conceptual inadequacy. As a broad explanation of schizophrenic deficit, interference theory has clearly been supported by research findings and appears to be the only theory comprehensive enough to account for what is known.

Interference theory is not an etiological theory of schizophrenia. It attempts to specify the essential element in schizophrenia—an inability to inhibit or filter out irrelevant stimuli—but it does not state the cause of this cognitive difficulty. The cause is not explicitly stated, but presumably the cognitive difficulty is inherent in schizophrenics. Perhaps schizophrenics are "built that way," and the explanatory variables reside in heredity or early development. Cognitive theories can remain neutral about etiology because their concern is with the *essence* of schizophrenia, not its cause. Let us note that interference theory is more consistent with a biological orientation toward etiology than with a personal-social or dynamic orientation. Nevertheless, interference theory can be squared with theories of early development (see Silverman, 1964b).

Having pointed out that the theories considered in this and the previous chapter are not theories of the cause of psychosis, let us proceed to theories of etiology. There are two main possibilities, biological and personal-social, and they will be discussed in turn.

REFERENCES

Benjamin, J. D. A method for distinguishing and evaluating formal thought disorders in schizophrenia. In J. S. Kasanin (Ed.) *Language and thought in schizophrenia.* Berkeley: University of California Press, 1946, pp. 55–90.

Bleuler, E. *Dementia praecox or the group of schizophrenias.* New York: International Universities Press, 1950.

Bolles, Marjorie, & Goldstein, K. A study of schizophrenic patients. *Psychiatric Quarterly,* 1938, **12,** 42–65.

Broadbent, D. E. *Perception and communication.* London: Pergamon Press, 1958.

Cameron, N. S. Reasoning, regression and communication in schizophrenics. *Psychological Monographs,* 1938, **50,** 1 (Whole No. 221).

Cameron, N. S. Experimental analysis of schizophrenic thinking. In J. S. Kasanin (Ed.), *Language and thought in schizophrenia.* Berkeley: University of California Press, 1946, pp. 50–64.

Cameron, N. S., & Magaret, Ann. *Behavior pathology.* Boston: Houghton Mifflin, 1947.

Cameron, N. S. Perceptual organization and behavior pathology. In Blake, R. R., & Ramsey, G. V. (Eds.) *Perception: An approach to personality.* New York: Ronald, 1951, pp. 283–306.

Cameron, N. S., & Magaret, Ann. *Behavior pathology.* Boston: Houghton Mifflin, 1951.

Chapman, J., & McGhie, A. A comparative study of disordered attention in schizophrenia. *Journal of Mental Science,* 1962, **108,** 487–500.

Chapman, L. J. Distractibility in the conceptual performance of schizophrenics. *Journal of Abnormal and Social Psychology,* 1956, **53,** 286–291.

Chapman, L. J. Intrusion of associative responses into schizophrenic conceptual performance. *Journal of Abnormal and Social Psychology,* 1958, **56,** 374–379.

Chapman, L. J. A reinterpretation of some pathological disturbances in conceptual breadth. *Journal of Abnormal and Social Psychology,* 1961, **62,** 514–519.

Chapman, L. J., & Taylor, Janet A. The breadth of deviate concepts used by schizophrenics. *Journal of Abnormal and Social Psychology,* 1957, **54,** 118–123.

Chapman, L. J., & Chapman, Jean. Interpretation of words in schizophrenia. *Journal of Personality and Social Psychology,* 1965, **1,** 135–146.

Craig, W. J. Objective measures of thinking integrated with psychiatric symptoms. *Psychological Reports,* 1965, **16,** 539–546.

Deering, Gayle, Affective stimuli and disturbance of thought processes. *Journal of Consulting Psychology,* 1963, **27,** 338–343.

Donahoe, J. W., Curtin, Mary E., & Lipton, L. Interference effects with schizophrenic subjects in the acquisition and retention of verbal material. *Journal of Abnormal and Social Psychology,* 1961, **62,** 553–558.

Downing, R. W., Ebert, J. N., & Shubrooks, S. J. Effects of phenothiazines on the thinking of acute schizophrenics. *Perceptual and Motor Skills*, 1963, **17**, 511–520.

Epstein, S. Overinclusive thinking in a schizophrenic and a control group. *Journal of Consulting Psychology*, 1953, **17**, 384–388.

Faibish, G. M. Schizophrenic response to words of multiple meaning. *Journal of Personality*, 1961, **29**, 414–427.

Goldstein, K. Methodological approach to the study of schizophrenic thought disorder. In J. S. Kasanin (Ed.) *Language and thought in schizophrenia*. Berkeley: University of California Press, 1946, pp. 17–40.

Goldstein, K., & Scheerer, M. Abstract and concrete behavior: An experimental study with special tests. *Psychological Monographs*, 1941, **53**, 2 (Whole No. 239).

Goodstein, L. D., Guertin, W. H., & Blackburn, H. L. Effects of social motivational variables on choice reaction time of schizophrenics. *Journal of Abnormal and Social Psychology*, 1961, **62**, 24–27.

Hanfmann, Eugenia, & Kasanin, J. S. Conceptual thinking in schizophrenia. *Nervous and Mental Disease Monographs*, 1942, No. 67.

Huston, P. E., Shakow, D., & Riggs, L. A. Studies of motor function in schizophrenia: II. Reaction time. *Journal of General Psychology*, 1937, **16**, 39–82.

Johannsen, W. J., Friedman, S. H., Leitschuh, T. H., & Ammons, Helen. A study of certain schizophrenic dimensions and their relationship to double alternation learning. *Journal of Consulting Psychology*, 1963, **27**, 375–382.

Johnson, R. C., Weiss, R. L., & Zelhart, P. F. Similarities and differences between normal and psychotic subjects in response to verbal stimuli. *Journal of Abnormal and Social Psychology*, 1964, **68**, 221–226.

Kasanin, J. S. The disturbance of conceptual thinking in schizophrenia. In J. S. Kasanin (Ed.) *Language and thought in schizophrenia*. Berkeley: University of California Press, 1946, pp. 41–49.

Kausler, D. H., Lair, C. V., & Matsumoto, R. Interference transfer paradigms and the performance of schizophrenics and controls. *Journal of Abnormal and Social Psychology*, 1964, **69**, 584–587.

King, H. E. *Psychomotor aspects of mental disease*. Cambridge: Harvard University Press, 1954.

King, H. E. Some explorations in psychomotility. *Psychiatric Research Reports*, 1961, **14**, 62–86.

Lang, P. J. The effect of aversive stimuli on reaction time in schizophrenia. *Journal of Abnormal and Social Psychology*, 1959, **59**, 263–268.

Lang, P. J., & Luoto, K. Mediation and associative facilitation in neurotic, psychotic, and normal subjects. *Journal of Abnormal and Social Psychology*, 1962, **64**, 113–120.

Lang, P. J., & Buss, A. H. Psychological deficit in schizophrenia: II. Interference and activation. *Journal of Abnormal Psychology*, 1965, **70**, 77–106.

Lauro, L. P. Recall of nouns varying in clustering tendency by normals and schizophrenics. Unpublished doctoral dissertation, New York University, 1962.

Lester, J. R. Production of associative sequences in schizophrenia and chronic brain syndrome. *Journal of Abnormal and Social Psychology*, 1960, **60**, 225–233.

Lothrop, W. W. A critical review of research on the conceptual thinking of schizophrenics. *Journal of Nervous and Mental Disease*, 1961, **132**, 118–126.

Lovibond, S. H. The Object Sorting Test and conceptual deficit in schizophrenia. *Australian Journal of Psychology*, 1954, **6**, 52–70.

Maltzman, I., Cohen, S., & Belloni, Marigold. Associative behavior in normal and schizophrenic children. Technical Report No. 11, 1963, University of California, Los Angeles, Contract Nonr. 233 (50).

Maltzman, I., Seymore, S., & Licht, L. Verbal conditioning of common and uncommon word associations. *Psychological Reports,* 1962, **10**, 363–369.

McGaughran, L. S. Predicting language behavior from object sorting. *Journal of Abnormal and Social Psychology,* 1954, **49**, 183–195.

McGaughran, L. S., & Moran, L. J. "Conceptual level" vs. "conceptual area" analysis of object sorting behavior of schizophrenic and nonpsychotic groups. *Journal of Abnormal and Social Psychology,* 1956, **52**, 43–50.

McGhie, A., & Chapman, J. Disorders of attention and perception in early schizophrenia. *British Journal of Medical Psychology,* 1961, **34**, 103–116.

McGhie, A., Chapman, J., & Lawson, J. S. Effect of distraction on schizophrenic performance. (1) Perception and immediate memory. (2) Psychomotor ability. *British Journal of Psychiatry,* 1965, **111**, 383–398.

Moran, L. J. Vocabulary knowledge and usage among normal and schizophrenic subjects. *Psychological Monographs,* 1953, **67**, No. 20 (Whole No. 370).

Payne, R. W. Cognitive abnormalities. In H. J. Eysenck (Ed.) *Handbook of abnormal psychology.* New York: Basic Books, 1961, pp. 193–261.

Payne, R. W. An object classification test as a measure of overinclusive thinking in schizophrenics. *British Journal of Social and Clinical Psychology,* 1962, **1**, 213–221.

Payne, R. W., Caird, W. K., & Laverty, S. G. Overinclusive thinking and delusions in schizophrenic patients. *Journal of Abnormal and Social Psychology,* 1964, **68**, 562–566.

Payne, R. W., Friedlander, D., Laverty, S. G., & Haden, P. Overinclusive thought disorder in chronic schizophrenics and its response to "Proketazine." *British Journal of Psychiatry,* 1963, **109**, 523–530.

Payne, R. W., & Hewlett, J. H. G. Thought disorder in psychotic patients. In H. J. Eysenck (Ed.) *Experiments in personality.* Vol. II. London: Routledge & Kegan Paul, 1960, pp. 3–104.

Payne, R. W., Mattussek, P., & George, E. I. An experimental study of schizophrenic thought disorder. *Journal of Mental Science,* 1959, **195**, 627–652.

Rodnick, E. H., & Shakow, D. Set in the schizophrenic as measured by a composite reaction time index. *American Journal of Psychiatry,* 1940, **97**, 214–225.

Rosenthal, D., Lawlor, W. G., Zahn, T. P., & Shakow, D. The relationship of some aspects of mental set to degree of schizophrenic disorganization. *Journal of Personality,* 1960, **28**, 26–38.

Seth, G., & Beloff, Halla. Language impairment in a group of schizophrenics. *British Journal of Medical Psychology,* 1959, **32**, 288–293.

Shakow, D. Segmental set: A theory of the formal psychological deficit in schizophrenia. *Archives of General Psychiatry,* 1962, **6**, 17–33.

Shakow, D. Psychological deficit in schizophrenia. *Behavioral Science,* 1963, **8**, 275–305.

Shakow, D., & McCormick, M. Y. Mental set in schizophrenia studied in a discrimination reaction setting. *Journal of Personality and Social Psychology,* 1965, **1**, 88–94.

Silverman, J. Scanning-control mechanism and "cognitive filtering" in paranoid and nonparanoid schizophrenia. *Journal of Consulting Psychology,* 1964, **28**, 385–393 (a).

Silverman, J. The problem of attention in research and theory on schizophrenia. *Psychological Review,* 1964, **71**, 352–379 (b).

Silverman, L. H., & Silverman, Doris K. Ego impairment in schizophrenia as reflected in the Object Sorting Test. *Journal of Abnormal and Social Psychology,* 1962, **64,** 381–385.

Sommer, R., Dewar, R., & Osmond, H. Is there a schizophrenic language? *Archives of General Psychiatry,* 1960, **3,** 665–673.

Sommer, R., Witney, G., & Osmond, H. Teaching common associations to schizophrenics. *Journal of Abnormal and Social Psychology,* 1962, **65,** 58–61.

Spence, Janet T., & Lair, C. V. Associative interference in the verbal learning performance of schizophrenics and normals. *Journal of Abnormal and Social Psychology,* 1964, **68,** 204–209.

Spence, Janet T., & Lair, C. V. Associative interference in the paired-associate learning of remitted and nonremitted schizophrenics. *Journal of Abnormal Psychology,* 1965, **70,** 119–122.

Sturm, I. E. "Conceptual area" among pathological groups: A failure to replicate. *Journal of Abnormal and Social Psychology,* 1964, **69,** 216–223.

Sullivan, H. S. The language of schizophrenia. In J. S. Kasanin (Ed.) *Language and thought in schizophrenia.* Berkeley: University of California Press, 1946, pp. 4–16.

Sutton, S., Hakerem, G., Zubin, J., & Portnoy, M. The effect of shift of sensory modality on serial reaction-time: A comparison of schizophrenics and normals. *American Journal of Psychology,* 1961, **74,** 224–232.

Tizard, J., & Venables, P. H. Reaction time responses by schizophrenics, mental defectives, and normal adults. *American Journal of Psychiatry,* 1956, **112,** 803–807.

Tutko, T. A., & Spence, Janet T. The performance of process and reactive schizophrenics and brain-damaged subjects on a conceptual task. *Journal of Abnormal and Social Psychology,* 1962, **65,** 387–394.

Ullmann, L. P., Krasner, L., & Edinger, R. L. Verbal conditioning of common associations in long-term schizophrenics. *Behavior Research and Therapy,* 1964, **2,** 15–18.

Weckowicz, T. E., & Blewitt, D. B. Size constancy and abstract thinking in schizophrenic patients. *Journal of Mental Science,* 1959, **105,** 909–934.

Wienckowski, L. A. Stimulus factors influencing the disjunctive reaction time of schizophrenic and "normal" subjects. Unpublished doctoral dissertation, University of Buffalo, 1959.

Wynne, L. C., & Singer, Margaret T. Thought disorder and family relations in schizophrenia. II. A classification of forms of thinking. *Archives of General Psychiatry,* 1963, **9,** 199–206.

Wynne, R. D. Can schizophrenics give the associations that "most people" do? Paper read at Eastern Psychological Association, New York, April, 1963.

Zahn, T. P., Rosenthal, D., & Shakow, D. Reaction time in schizophrenic and normal subjects in relation to the sequence of series of regular preparatory intervals. *Journal of Abnormal and Social Psychology,* 1961, **63,** 161–168.

Zahn, T. P., Rosenthal, D., & Shakow, D. Effects of irregular preparatory intervals on reaction time in schizophrenia. *Journal of Abnormal and Social Psychology,* 1963, **67,** 44–52.

Zahn, T. P., & Rosenthal, D. Preparatory sets in acute schizophrenia. *American Psychologist,* 1964, **19,** 495 (abstract).

CHAPTER 14

Biological Approaches to Psychosis

Seen biologically, psychosis is like a systemic disease. The organism fails in some way to cope physiologically with the demands of its environment. In the medical area there is hypertension, in which elevated blood pressure (whose origin may be obscure) places a great strain on the heart, eventually leading to severe cardiovascular complaints. Like hypertension, psychosis is assumed to result from an inherited predisposition. The term *predisposition* is of crucial importance because what is inherited is a *tendency* to become psychotic, not the psychosis itself. This is in contrast to the inheritance of physical traits such as eye color; here the anatomical trait is the direct outcome of genetic transmission. In the inheritance of psychosis, on the other hand, what the individual inherits are processes that lead to psychosis. The inherited tendency is a necessary but not a sufficient condition for psychosis; what is usually needed in addition is a detrimental environment.

What is the nature of the inherited predisposition? It may consist of a particular constitution (body build); it may consist of biochemical defects in the substances used in transmitting impulses in the central nervous system; or it may consist of an imbalance in the autonomic nervous system. These three possibilities, together with the genetics of psychosis, constitute the major biological approaches to psychosis. We shall discuss first the genetics of psychosis and then what is inherited.

THE GENETICS OF PSYCHOSIS

The inheritance of psychosis is as controversial a topic as there is in psychopathology. Opinion ranges from an unequivocal assertion that he-

312

redity is *the* determinant of psychosis to an equally unequivocal assertion that psychosis is completely determined by life events. In this section we shall review briefly some of the evidence bearing on this issue, noting in advance that the evidence may either be accepted as it stands or be challenged on methodological grounds. A cursory review of genetics principles and methods will precede the exposition of theory and evidence.

Some Fundamentals of Genetics

The *gene* is the basic unit of heredity. The simplest kind of inheritance is that in which a trait appearing in the offspring is determined by a pair of genes, one from each parent. The trait as it is manifested in the individual is called a *phenotype*, which is a product of both genetic endowment and environment (environment including all nongenetic influences, both inside and outside of the body). The *genotype* is simply the organism's genetic makeup, which may or may not become manifest in the phenotype.

Single Major Genes. The genotype of many traits is determined by a single pair of genes. One member of the pair may be dominant and the other, recessive. The recessive trait appears only if both members of the gene pair are recessive (for example, blue eyes), whereas the dominant trait (for example, brown eyes) appears even when its gene is paired with a recessive gene. If both parents have brown eyes (phenotype), their genotype might be either a brown-brown or a brown-blue combination. The actual genotype could be ascertained by the proportions of brown and blue eyes in their children.

Inheritance is not always as simple as dominant versus recessive genes. Some traits are sex-linked, that is, their inheritance is associated with the genes that determine the sex of the offspring. An example of this in humans is color blindness, which is many times more prevalent among men than among women.

Inheritance by single major genes is an all-or-none affair when the genes are clearly dominant or recessive, but some genes are neither one nor the other, which results in quantitative variations. Thus a white chicken mated to a black chicken yields grey offspring. It is believed that few abnormalities are inherited by intermediate genes.

Penetrance and Expressivity. A genotype may or may not produce a given trait. One reason was just given: one member of the gene pair is recessive, which means that it does not become manifest because it is subordinate to the dominant trait. When a genotype fails to produce a given trait for nongenetic reasons, it is because of *lowered penetrance*. For example both parents might have a recessive trait, say blue eyes. If we examined a series of families in which the parents were blue-eyed and found that less than 100% of the children were blue-eyed, we would assume a lowered penetrance.

In this simple example it would be easy to establish a degree of penetrance, but in other instances it might be difficult. Some inherited traits do not appear until maturity or old age, and the individual might die before manifesting them, for example, baldness or circulatory weakness.

Expressivity refers to the degree to which the trait is manifested. Thus color blindness varies from mild color weakness in one person to total absence of color vision in another. The genotype may be expressed fully, the trait appearing in full measure, or it might be given lesser expression, the trait barely appearing.

Penetrance and expressivity are not properties of the genes but the result of the interaction of the individual pair of genes, other genes, and the environment in its broadest sense.

Penetrance and expressivity as consequences of developmental events in gene action are interrelated. Many genes with a low degree of penetrance express themselves weakly when they are penetrant, and high penetrance and strong expressivity often go together. (Stern, 1960, p. 300)

In order to establish penetrance as an explanatory variable, it is necessary to demonstrate that there is a percentage of individuals showing the expected trait caused by the gene in question. Thus if lowered penetrance is assumed, its degree should be verified by subsequent research. Otherwise, penetrance (and to some extent, expressivity) might be used as a catch-all explanation for all departures from genetic predictions.

Of course penetrance need not be used as a catch-all explanation. Consider an inherited allergy such as hay fever. The affected individuals have a disposition to over-react to say, ragweed. Some of these predisposed persons may live in an area that has no ragweed, and they will show no symptoms of allergy. Thus a benign environment can prevent the genotype from showing up as a phenotype, a condition that shows up as lowered penetrance.

Other inherited defects may lead to more complex organism-environment interactions. Burch (1964a,b) notes that certain systemic diseases (for example, rheumatoid arthritis) may be caused by a combination of an inherited predisposition plus such environmentally-caused events as infection. Infection, or perhaps random mutations in the genes of body cells, which are not concerned with reproduction, may lead to an *autoimmune* reaction: the body reacts to certain of its cells as if they were not its own but foreign.

Burch has applied these ideas to affective psychoses and schizophrenia. His mathematical and medical theorizing are too technical for this book, but we may note a novel aspect of his approach. He assumes that two kinds of abnormal conditions need to be met for a psychosis to develop. First, in common with other biological theorists, he assumes a genetic predisposition. Second, he suggests the presence of random mutations in body genes, such that the genetic pattern *is copied incorrectly.* Such incorrect copying presumably leads to an autoimmune disease, and Burch regards psychoses as such diseases. Note that incorrect copying of the inherited pattern is different from the process of genetic selection that occurs in reproduction. Thus some persons with the disposition to have a defect will have the random mutations and develop the autoimmune disease; others will not have the random mutations and therefore not develop the disease. Thus random somatic fluctuations may account for lowered penetrance. The notion of lowered penetrance, as it applies to the autoimmune hypothesis, is certainly not a catch-all explanation, for it leads both to specific predictions about incidence of disease and to specific causes of the disease.

Multiple Minor Genes. Many inherited traits are normal, and they vary in graded fashion, for example, height. When their frequencies in the population are plotted, they fall into a bell-shaped or normal distribution. It is difficult to reconcile gradations in traits having a continuous, normal distribution with single gene inheritance, and it becomes necessary to add nongenetic constructs such as penetrance and expressivity.

However, inheritance through multiple minor genes offers a straightforward explanation. Assume that a number of genes all affect the same trait. If the number of genes is large and they are relatively independent in their action, the outcome should be a continuous, normal distribution of the trait. The problem with using multiple gene inheritance as an explanation is that it is difficult to generate easily tested, quantitative predictions. If the number of minor genes is assumed to be large, then it would be a simple matter to account for many different trait distributions *after the fact.* It is not surprising, therefore, that in the genetics of psychosis most researchers have avoided theories involving polygenic inheritance.

Methods. There is no truly experimental method in human genetics, but, like astronomers, geneticists have accumulated reliable evidence. The basic method is to observe the appearance of traits in individuals of differing degrees of blood relationship. A determination of the incidence of the trait in the general population is followed by rating its incidence in aunts-uncles-cousins, parents, siblings, and twins. The logic is straightforward. In order to conclude that a trait is inherited it must be shown that: (1) the trait occurs significantly more often in blood relatives than in the general population, and (2) environmental variables are not sufficient to account for the increased frequency.

In the study of blood relatives, twins occupy a special place. One-celled or monozygotic twins have the same heredity. Two-celled or dizygotic twins have similar but not identical heredities, that is, they are no more alike genetically than siblings born at different times. A comparison of monozygotic with dizygotic twins tends to eliminate or at least minimize the effects of environment. Therefore, when a trait occurs significantly more often in both monozygotic twins than it does in both dizygotic twins, it is likely that the trait is inherited.[1] One measure of relative incidence is the rate of *concordance*. When both twins have a trait or do not have it, there is concordance; when one twin has the trait and the other does not, there is discordance.

Affective Psychoses

The inheritance of affective psychoses has received less attention than the inheritance of schizophrenia. Consequently, there are fewer studies, and the number of cases in these studies is not large. Nevertheless, there is sufficient evidence to indicate that heredity is one determinant of affective psychoses.

Table 14.1 summarizes a number of studies and reviews (Kallmann, 1953; Planansky, 1955; Fuller & Thompson, 1960; Gregory, 1960; Shields & Slater, 1961; and Stern, 1960), giving the expectancy rates for affective psychoses in both the general population and in relatives of patients. Note that in each category there is a considerable range in the percentages. This lack of agreement is probably due to a combination of three factors: (1) different criteria for diagnosis, leading to greater or lesser numbers of cases identified as affective psychoses; (2) real differences in the frequencies from one sample to the next, perhaps because of such variables as age, social class, rural-urban differences; and (3) random errors such as occur in all research projects when a series of samples are drawn from one or more populations.

Despite the disparities among studies, there are still trends in the data. The expectancy rate (rate of occurrence) in the general population is very low, and a number of investigators agree on a figure of approximately 1 in 200 (0.5%). The rates for parents, children, and siblings overlap one

TABLE 14.1   RATES OF OCCURRENCE OF AFFECTIVE PSYCHOSES

	Range (in %)
general population	0.2–0.8
parents	2–24
children	13–39
siblings	4–29
dizygotic twins	16–24
monozygotic twins	67–94

[1] This statement ignores exceptions involving problems of method that are too complex to discuss here.

another and so does the rate for dizygotic twins. If there is truly no difference in the expectancy rate between siblings and dizygotic twins, then the
effect of environment is probably small. All these similarities in rates are
overshadowed by the extremely high rate for monozygotic twins, which is
so much higher than the rate for dizygotic twins that it is obvious that
there is a strong hereditary component in affective psychoses.

In addition to rates of occurrence in relatives of patients, there are
concordance rates for both kinds of twins. Stern (1960) averaged the concordance rates found in a number of studies and arrived at the following
means:

monozygotic twins	77%
dizygotic twins	19%

These results establish a hereditary basis for affective psychoses, but what
is the mode of inheritance? The most favored hypothesis is that of a single,
dominant gene, and there are four kinds of evidence cited in support of
it:

(1) When the families of patients are examined, there is a bimodal
distribution of melancholy versus normal affect (Shields & Slater, 1961).
Some members of the family tend to be moody or depressed; others show
no affective disturbance at all. This is the same kind of distribution found
with eye color; family members are either brown-eyed or blue-eyed. The
implication is that inheritance is due to a single dominant gene, which is
known to produce such distributions.

(2) Presumably a patient has the gene combination of Psychotic-
normal $(P - n)$; since the psychotic gene is assumed to be dominant, the
patient shows this trait. If he marries a normal (by definition $n - n$, else
the person would not be normal), half the children should be psychotic
and half, nonpsychotic:

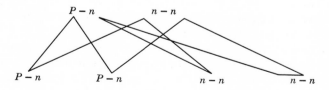

Figure 14.1

When the definition of affective psychoses is broadened to include individuals with severe mood problems who may not be clinically psychotic,
the ratio of affected to unaffected children is nearly 1:1, which is the

ratio predicted if a single dominant gene is present (Fuller & Thompson, 1960).

(3) As we saw in Table 14.1, the incidence of affective psychoses is roughly the same in siblings, parents, and children of patients. This is precisely what should occur if the mode of hereditary is a single, dominant gene. If the gene were recessive, siblings would have a higher incidence of psychosis than parents or children.

(4) The relative incidence among parents, aunts-uncles, and cousins is in the relation 4:2:1 (Slater, 1936). These represent precisely the diminishing rates expected if the inheritance involves a single, dominant gene.

These four lines of evidence all support the hypothesis that a single dominant gene is involved in the inheritance of affective psychoses. The major stumbling block for the hypothesis is the low rate of incidence for all relatives of patients. The presence of a dominant gene requires a rather high rate of occurrence in blood relatives of patients because only one member of the gene pair need be present for the trait to manifest itself.

Proponents of the hypothesis have two kinds of answers. First, they point out that the diagnosis of an affective psychosis may be too restrictive, investigators omitting doubtful cases or being too stringent in applying diagnostic criteria. Furthermore, the birth rate for patients is known to be lower than that of the general population, which could result in a lower incidence than would be expected from the operation of a single, dominant gene.

Second, proponents suggest that there is low penetrance of the gene. This means that hereditary predisposition to affective psychoses is a necessary but not a sufficient condition for its occurrence. Consistent with this notion is the belief that affective psychoses occur with greater frequency among endomorphs (those with rounded body build) and those afflicted with gout and cardiovascular diseases. Thus it is possible that incidence of the psychosis is lowered by the absence of certain constitutional and biochemical variables. The psychosis would become manifest only in those who possessed both the inherited predisposition (through a dominant gene) and the proper constitutional-biochemical conditions.

Some investigators are not willing to accept these interpretations of the genetic data. They rightfully point out that the number of cases is small, the clinical diagnoses are often uncertain, and the variability from one study to the next is sometimes large. In brief, the genetic data do not unequivocally support the hypothesis that a single dominant gene underlies the predisposition toward affective psychoses. However, while the precise genetic mechanism is controversial, the evidence clearly indicates a hereditary component in such psychoses. That environmental variables are also important is suggested by the low rates of incidence in relatives of patients and the lowered penetrance assumed to be operating.

Schizophrenia

There has been considerably more research on the genetics of schizophrenia, and consequently the evidence is more detailed. The expectancy rates for schizophrenia, derived from the same studies mentioned earlier (Kallmann, 1953; Planansky, 1955; Fuller & Thompson, 1960; Gregory, 1960; Shields & Slater, 1961; Stern, 1960), are presented in Table 14.2. The expectancy rate of schizophrenia in the general population is 1%, a widely accepted figure. As the relationship between schizophrenic patients and their relatives becomes closer, the expectancy rate goes up. It is between 3% and 4% for distant relatives, between 4% and 14% for close relatives, and between 3% and 17% for dizygotic (fraternal) twins. There are much higher rates for both children of two schizophrenic parents and monozygotic (identical) twins. These rates are consistent with a genetic theory of schizophrenia.

It might be argued that the rates are also consistent with an environmental theory of schizophrenia. A schizophrenic parent might pass on schizophrenia to his child through faulty child rearing rather than through faulty genes; two schizophrenic parents would surely provide a stressful environment, which might lead to schizophrenia in the offspring. Also identical twins might be treated more alike than fraternal twins, which would account for the higher rate of schizophrenia in the former.

This environmental approach faces two obstacles. First, it cannot account for the fact that the rates for fraternal twins are approximately the same as for siblings. Fraternal twins often look alike and are therefore treated alike. Even when they do not look alike, their simultaneous birth means that they undergo highly similar life experiences. Thus the environ-

TABLE 14.2   RATES OF OCCURRENCE OF SCHIZOPHRENIA

general population	1%
grandparents	4
grandchildren	4
nephews and nieces	4
cousins	3
parents	4–10
half-siblings	7
siblings	5–14
children	
one schizophrenic parent	16
two schizophrenic parents	39–68
dizygotic twins	3–17
monozygotic twins	67–86

ment of fraternal twins is considerably more similar than that of children who are born one or more years apart. The environmental approach would therefore predict a higher expectancy rate for fraternal twins than for siblings. The fact that the rates are similar argues against environmental theory.

Second, the expectancy rate for identical twins has been reported as being at least four times larger than the rate for fraternal twins. The environmentalist argument suggests that identical twins are treated more alike than fraternal twins. Although this is probably true, it does not account for the fourfold increase in the expectancy rate. If the environmentalist hypothesis were correct, the rate for fraternal twins would be much higher than that for siblings and only slightly lower than that for identical twins. Thus the relatively low expectancy rate for fraternal twins favors the hereditary position.

Recent reports, however, have mentioned evidence contrary to the genetic approach. Tienari (1963) surveyed more than 200 identical twins and found 16 pairs of which at least one twin was schizophrenic. In every instance the other twin was not schizophrenic—a concordance rate of 0%! Although this finding is surprising, Tienari noted two other studies of Northern Europeans that yielded concordance rates of zero in identical twins.

It is difficult to reconcile these findings with the data presented in Table 14.2. Tienari suggested several reasons for the discrepancy. First, when a study examines only chronic inmates of psychiatric hospitals, the concordance rate is higher. Second, the concordance rate is higher in female than in male identical twins. In previous research the subjects were predominantly females in psychiatric hospitals. Third, some investigators define schizophrenia broadly, including schizoid traits and "psychotic tendencies." Tienari reported that several of the nonpsychotic identical twins had schizoid features; these might have been included as schizophrenics by other investigators, thereby elevating the concordance rate.

These considerations do not resolve the basic discrepancy in findings. The safest conclusion at present is that the concordance rate for schizophrenia in identical twins is somewhat lower than was previously believed. Research in this area is now more sophisticated and precise than in earlier decades, and perhaps a large-scale, careful study will resolve the issue. The recent research does suggest that ". . . heredity does not account for as much of the variance with respect to what is called schizophrenia as some have alleged" (Rosenthal, 1962, p. 132).

Note that a weakening of genetic theory does not necessarily mean a strengthening of environmental theory. The latter still has difficulty in accounting for low expectancy rates in fraternal twins and in brothers and sisters of schizophrenics. If the family environment is sufficiently vicious to induce schizophrenia in one child, surely it must produce serious psychological disturbance in other children in the family. We shall return to this question in the next chapter.

Although genetic theory has been weakened by recent findings, it is still consistent with most of the facts. If there is at least a partial hereditary basis for schizophrenia, what is the mechanism of inheritance? There are two principal theories, one emphasizing a recessive major gene and the other, a dominant major gene.

Recessive Gene. Kallmann (1953) is the leading proponent of the recessive gene hypothesis. The gene is believed to produce an enzyme or metabolic deficiency, which in turn has a disastrous effect on general psychological adjustment. Thus the defect is biological, and the affected individual is predisposed to a generalized inability to handle life stress. He tends to develop schizophrenia, with the particular pattern of symptoms being determined by specific life events.

The problem this theory must face is that empirical frequencies do not match those expected by the theory. Thus when both parents are schizophrenic, the recessive trait should show up in 100% of the offspring; the actual figure is somewhere between 39% and 68%. The concordance rate for monozygotic twins should also be 100%, but it is not. Finally, a recessive trait should be manifest in 25% of the siblings, but the empirical rate is between 5% and 14%.

To account for these diminished rates, Kallmann postulates a lowered penetrance, owing to the action of multiple minor genes. He argues that these minor genes determine the individual's constitution and that constitution is a partial determinant of schizophrenia. The presence of endomorphic (fatty, rounded) or mesomorphic (muscular) components in body build serves as a kind of defense against schizophrenia, thus lowering the rate that would be expected on the basis of genetic factors alone. Ectomorphs (thin, slight individuals) show the greatest tendency to develop schizophrenia, a hypothesis that receives partial confirmation from the work of Kline and Tenney (1950). This theory is plausible, but at present it is too flexible to be put to a crucial test.

Dominant Gene. The leading alternate hypothesis suggests that the mode of inheritance is a major dominant gene (Böök, 1953). Again the expectancy rates are lower than those predicted by the theory, and again a lowered penetrance is invoked to account for these lowered rates. The problem with assuming lowered penetrance is that one can easily account for *any* results by raising or lowering the presumed degree of penetrance. However, once a quantitative figure is specified, the hypothesis of lowered penetrance becomes testable; it can be shown to be in agreement or disagreement with observed rates of occurrence.

Böök rendered his hypothesis testable by making the following assumptions: (1) when both members of the gene pair are for schizophrenia (homozygotes), the penetrance rate is 100%; (2) when one member of the gene pair is for schizophrenia and the other for normality (heterozygotes), the penetrance rate is 26%. These assumptions make sense in that if penetrance is lowered at all, it should be lowered when the members of the gene pair represent different traits.

The two assumptions yield theoretical rates of occurrrence that may be compared with the observed rates. The comparison is presented in Table 14.3. The results are in close agreement with the theory, which is strongly supported. It also predicts that 70% of those with an inherited predisposition to schizophrenia will not become schizophrenic, which leaves considerable latitude for the action of the environment.

Data consistent with the dominant gene theory have come from an unexpected source. McConaghy (1959) selected schizophrenics who showed evidence of thought disorder on an object sorting task. Then he tested both parents of the schizophrenics on the sorting task and compared their performance with that of normal controls (hospital employees). Significantly more parents of schizophrenics than controls showed evidence of thought disorder, a finding that has been replicated by Lidz, Wild, Schafer, Roseman, and Fleck (1962).

These findings may be explained in environmental terms. A parent may transmit irrationality either by teaching it to his child or by serving as a model. The findings may also be explained in genetic terms; the tendency to think irrationally might be passed on through the genes, in a fashion analogous to the inheritance of intelligence. In this chapter on biological approaches we shall tentatively go along with the latter interpretation.

Of special importance for the dominant gene theory is the fact that in McConaghy's study at least one parent of each schizophrenic patient showed thought disorder, and it was rare for two parents to show thought disorder. If the gene for schizophrenia is dominant, schizophrenia will show up in the offspring whether the gene pair is homozygous (both genes schizophrenic) or heterozygous (one gene schizophrenic, the other normal). Thus two facts are consistent with Böök's theory: (1) every schizophrenic with

TABLE 14.3   THEORETICAL AND EXPECTED RATES RELATING TO
BÖÖK'S HYPOTHESIS
(From Shields & Slater, 1961)

	Theoretical	Observed
siblings	14	14
children of one schizophrenic parent	14	16
children of two schizophrenic parents	40	40
children of cousins	1	1

thought disorder had at least one parent with thought disorder on the sorting task; and (2) only rarely did two parents show thought disorder. Of course caution is needed here. As we noted above, an environmental basis for these results cannot be ruled out.

Thus on the basis of two sets of data, the theory of a dominant gene with lowered penetrance appears to be better than the theory of a recessive gene with reduced penetrance. However, both theories require the assumption of a drastically reduced penetrance in heterozygotes, and geneticists usually avoid hypotheses that assume a very low degree of penetrance because the concept tends to become too flexible. Specifying a quantitative degree of penetrance would appear to answer this argument, and the dominance model does appear to be testable. At present there are insufficient data to choose between the two theories, but further research should confirm or reject the dominant gene theory, which makes quantitative predictions on the basis of a 26% penetrance in heterozygotes.

Broader Issues. None of the investigators in this area sponsors a multiple gene theory, perhaps because it would be even less precise than theories requiring the notion of penetrance. The issue of multiple versus single gene inheritance is related to how schizophrenia is conceptualized as a clinical entity. Multiple gene heredity is presumed to underlie traits that are normally distributed in the population. Schizophrenia may be regarded as a combination of a number of essentially normal traits, in the same way that neurosis appears. Schizophrenia, so regarded, would be a collection of different syndromes, each determined by a combination of a number of genes. This approach sees schizophrenia and neuroses as essentially continuous, and in general rejects a disease concept of psychosis.

Major gene heredity, on the other hand, implies a disease concept of psychosis. Schizophrenia is seen as a fairly well-defined syndrome with certain classical features. The traits involved are *not* normally distributed in the population, and there is a discontinuity between neurosis and psychosis. This approach requires additional variables such as other genes, constitution, or environment, but the primary etiology is a specific, inherited, biological predisposition to schizophrenia. Kallmann (1953) has espoused this theory. He proposed that what is inherited is a generalized disposition to develop severe maladjustment, the specific symptom pattern (delusions, hallucinations, etc.) being attibutable to particular life experiences.

An alternate view (Rosanoff et al., 1934; Weinberg & Lobstein, 1943) assumes a different mechanism of heredity for each syndrome in schizophrenia; thus paranoids would have a different inheritance from catatonics. This second view assumes that there are several discrete disease processes lumped under the heading of schizophrenia, each disease having its own inheritance. Such an assumption requires the demonstration of reliability in diagnosing subtypes of schizophrenia, and, as noted earlier, this kind of diagnosis is somewhat unreliable. Therefore Kallmann's view seems to fit the facts better.

One variant of this second view is that there are two types of schizophrenia, one determined solely or largely by heredity and the other determined by environment. This hypothesis is obviously linked to the process-reactive dichotomy in schizophrenia. Thus process schizophrenics would have more serious symptoms, a poorer prognosis, and a strong inherited predisposition to schizophrenia; reactive schizophrenics would have mild symptoms, good prognosis, and no inherited predisposition to schizophrenia. A basic assumption is that process-reactive is a dichotomy, but, as we saw in Chapter 10, this is a moot point. It may be a dichotomy or a continuum. The hypothesis under consideration requires that a process-reactive *dichotomy* be demonstrated, and until this has been accomplished, the hypothesis is merely speculative.

Rosenthal (1959) attempted to pin down a similar hypothesis with previously obtained genetic data. He suggested that in identical twins there is concordance for catatonic schizophrenics but discordance for paranoid schizophrenics. Thus paranoid schizophrenia would be linked with milder thought disorder, less pychological deficit, and a weak genetic disposition, whereas nonparanoid schizophrenia would be linked with severer thought disorder, more psychological deficit, and a strong genetic disposition. However, two subsequent studies fail to confirm Rosenthal's hypothesis. Tienari (1963) and Kringlen (1964) both found complete discordance in the identical twins they studied. The schizophrenics were more or less evenly divided among hebephrenics, catatonics, and paranoids. This distribution is clearly in opposition to the hypothesis, which requires that discordance be restricted mainly to paranoids.

Affective psychoses and schizophrenia may be viewed either as distinct disease entities or as points on a continuum of psychosis, ranging from excessive affect to absence of affect. These opposing views are represented in the genetics of psychosis. One group of investigators (Kallmann, 1953; Slater, 1953) have reported data showing that the incidence of schizophrenia among relatives of affective psychotics is not greater than might be expected by chance. They conclude that the two psychoses have separate mechanisms of heredity. Another group has reported findings that lead to an opposite conclusion (Kant, 1942; Lewis, 1957): affective psychoses occur more frequently in the relatives of less disturbed schizophrenics than in the relatives of more disturbed schizophrenics, suggesting a relationship between mild forms of schizophrenia and affective psychoses. Furthermore, while affective psychotic parents do not necessarily have schizophrenic children, two schizophrenic parents often have affective psychotic children. This group of investigators espouses a single inheritance for both psychoses.

At present there is no way of deciding between these opposing theories. The results of the two groups clearly disagree, and the controversy is muddled by the lack of precise and consistent diagnostic procedures. In light of the ambiguity, genetic evidence should not be used to decide whether schizophrenia and affective psychoses are unitary or separate. Of greater relevance is evidence concerning prognosis. As we saw in Chapter 9, schizophrenia has a significantly poorer prognosis than affective psychoses, which is a reasonable basis for keeping the two distinct.

Although there are many controversies concerning the mode of inheritance of schizophrenia, the evidence clearly supports two conclusions: (1) there is an inherited component in schizophrenia, and (2) heredity alone cannot account for schizophrenia, which undoubtedly has an environmental component. These conclusions occupy a middle ground between those of extreme hereditarians and extreme environmentalists. Researchers in the genetics of schizophrenia admit that environmental variables may be of considerable importance in schizophrenia. They are not unduly concerned with the effects of environment because it is acknowledged that the inheritance of physiological or behavioral dispositions (ostensibly through neural structures) is different from the inheritance of anatomical traits. Eye color, for example, is not influenced by environment; but allergic physical reactions, which do have a hereditary component, are influenced by the environment.

Many clinicians, however, are upset by a demonstrated inherited component in schizophrenia. They believe that the presence of an inherited predisposition precludes an environmental explanation of schizophrenia. This view is obviously an exaggeration. Inheritance sets limits or preconditions within which the effects of environment operate, for example, intelligence. Nor does a genetic theory preclude environmental theories.

There is no genetic reason why the manifestations of schizophrenic psychosis should not be described in terms of narcissistic regression . . . Genetically it is also perfectly legitimate to interpret schizophrenic reactions as the expression of either faulty habit formations or of progressive maladaptation to disrupted family relations. The genetic theory explains only *why* these various phenomena occur in a particular member of a particular family at a particular time. (Kallmann, 1946, p. 320)

What kinds of heredity-environment interactions may we expect in schizophrenia? The clearest answer has been supplied by Meehl (1962), who distinguishes three concepts: *schizotaxia, schizotypy,* and *schizophrenia.* He suggests that what is inherited is a neural defect, probably in the integrative functioning of single nerve cells; he labels this defect *schizotaxia.* The individual's developmental history interacts with this neural defect to produce a personality organization called *schizotypy;* this consists of four tendencies which Meehl believes are present in all "schizophrenic personalities"—cognitive deficit, avoidance of others, inability to experience pleasure, and ambivalence. All schizotaxic individuals become schizotypes regardless of their developmental history.

Most schizotypes do not become schizophrenics. If there are favorable factors in the environment, or in themselves (tolerance for stress, physical rigor, etc.), or both, schizotypes do not develop the clinical symptoms of psychosis. They remain "peculiar" and somewhat idiosyncratic in their thought processes and personal relationships but do not become psychotic.

A minority of schizotypes have unfavorable constitutional or developmental history features, if not both, and they become *schizophrenic.* Thus Meehl combines genetic predisposition with neural defect, constitutional makeup, and unfavorable family environment in his theorizing about schizophrenia:

> All schizotaxics become, *on all actually existing social learning regimes,* schizotypic in personality organization; but most of these remain compensated. A minority, disadvantaged by other (largely polygenically determined) constitutional weaknesses, and put on a bad regime by schizophrenogenic mothers (most of whom themselves are schizotypes) are thereby potentiated into clinical schizophrenia. What makes schizotaxia etiologically specific is its role as a *necessary* condition. I postulate that a nonschizotaxic individual, whatever his other genetic makeup and learning history, would at most develop a character disorder or a psychoneurosis; but he would not become a schizotype and therefore could never manifest its decompensated form, schizophrenia (1962, p. 831)

Note the restriction Meehl places on schizophrenia at the end of the quotation: no one develops schizophrenia who does not have the hereditary predisposition. This is the essence of the genetic position: inheritance is a necessary but not a sufficient condition for the disease. This is the assumption contested by environmentalists, who claim that schizophrenia is a *learned* reaction. The nongenetic position is that although some schizophrenics may have an inherited predisposition, others do not. That is, schizophrenia can occur because of a vicious family environment in the absence of an inherited defect. The next chapter reviews the various theories stemming from this approach. Note that this view is not inconsistent with the evidence, for there is no proof that *all* schizophrenics have an inherited predisposition.

Here the matter rests. That there is an inherited component in schizophrenia appears highly probable, as does the notion that a poor environment can trigger schizophrenia in a predisposed individual. The controversial issue is whether schizophrenia can be learned in the absence of an inherited disposition. Adherents of the biological approach say no; adherents of the social-interpersonal approach say yes.

CONSTITUTION

It has been believed for more than a hundred years that physique is one of the determinants of psychosis. The most important formulation historically was Kretchmer's assertion (1925) that schizophrenics tend to be somewhat smaller and thinner than the average person. There has been much resistance to this hypothesis, and certainly the evidence for it is not unequivocal. Part of the problem is deciding which system of classification to use in analyzing the components of physique.

In this country the best known system is that of Sheldon (1940). He divides people into three body types. The *ectomorph* is thin, relatively long-boned, and without much fat or muscle. The *mesomorph* has an athletic build, with powerful torso and skeletal muscles. The *endomorph* is round, soft, and fat. A fourth category, *dysplasia,* includes those whose different body parts are not harmonious, namely, ectomorphic head and endomorphic body. These brief descriptions cannot do justice to the classification system, and Sheldon should be consulted for details.

The evidence concerning Kretchmer's hypothesis about the relationship between ectomorphy and schizophrenia is mixed. Rees (1957) noted that the proportion of endomorphs found among schizophrenics is considerably higher than would be predicted on the basis of the hypothesis. Bellak and Holt (1948), who compared schizophrenic and normal corpses, concluded that the schizophrenics tended to be mesomorphic ectomorphs. Brottgärd (1950), comparing various neurotics, found that those with schizoid tendencies were more ectomorphic than those without such tendencies.

Kline and Tenny (1950) examined hundreds of male schizophrenics in a military setting and discovered the following proportions among them:

ectomorph	26%
mesomorph	46%
endomorph	13%

The remainder could not be classified. They suggested that the reason for the predominance of mesomorphs was the selection process preceding induction into service. They also found that mesomorphs tended to be diagnosed paranoid schizophrenic and had a better prognosis; endomorphs had a poorer prognosis. A follow-up study two years later (Kline & Oppenhein, 1952) showed that the relationship between mesomorphy and a good prognosis did not stand up, although the relationship between endomorphy and a poor prognosis did.

One aspect of their findings was corroborated by Wittman (1948), who showed that the more mesomorphic schizophrenics in her sample were classified as reactives on the Elgin Prognostic Scale, and that they tended to be diagnosed as paranoid or catatonic. Process schizophrenics, who of course had a worse prognosis, tended to be diagnosed hebephrenic or undetermined, and they were more ectomorphic. In a study with women schizophrenics, Betz (1942) showed that there was a greater proportion of ectomorphs than in normal persons and that the patients were of smaller stature.

After reviewing the literature, Rees (1957) concluded that Kretchmer's hypothesis had been partially substantiated: there is a relationship between schizophrenia and ectomorphy, as well as dysplasia, but the number of schizophrenics who are endomorphic weakens the hypothesis. Constitution may well be a determinant, or at least a concomitant, of onset and prognosis. Ectomorphs tend to have an earlier age of psychotic breakdown, a greater degree of withdrawal, and perhaps a severer thinking disorder. Endomorphs have a later onset, more intact personality features, less withdrawal, and better preservation of affect. Mesomorphy appears to be unrelated to schizophrenia.

Concerning affective psychoses, the hypothesis is exactly opposite: endomorphs are more susceptible and ectomorphs, less so. It is known that as people age, they become more endomorphic. Since affective psychoses are known to occur with increasing frequency as individuals grow older, this is a possible confounding variable. Thus a relationship between affective psychoses and endomorphy may be attributed to either the age variable or the constitutional variable. Rees, on the basis of his own research, believed that the age variable makes the relationship appear stronger than it really is but that the relationship between constitution and manic-depressive psychosis is still there.

Thus the evidence suggests that there may be some validity to the constitutional hypothesis. Schizophrenics tend to be more ectomorphic, severer schizophrenics tend to be the most ectomorphic, and manic-depressives tend to be more endomorphic. It is still not clear how strong these relationships are, and the best guess at present seems to be that they are slight. It is probable that constitution is one of several inherited variables, including defects in chemicals involved in neural transmission and in autonomic functioning, which predispose the individual toward psychosis. Perhaps none of these variables is in itself a very strong determinant, but, taken together, they may lead to psychosis.

BIOCHEMICAL THEORIES OF PSYCHOSIS

There is evidence that psychosis is at least partially determined by heredity. But regardless of the specific *genetic* mechanism, there must be some biological defect which predisposes the individual to psychosis. It follows that the search for a biological defect should center on chemical substances in the body, specifically the chemical substances mediating transmission of neural impulses (*neurohumors*).

The notion that chemical substances are responsible for psychoses dates back more than a century. During the latter half of the nineteenth century the germ theory of disease explained the origin of a wide range of diseases, and it was inevitable that psychiatrists should come to believe that psychosis was caused by infection. This belief was strengthened by the discovery of the syphilitic basis of paresis, a disease with psychotic-like symptoms caused by a particular spirochete. However, the notion that infection causes psychosis has since been abandoned for lack of evidence.

Although the idea that *external* agents are responsible for psychosis has been discarded, the theory that *internal* substances cause psychosis (the endogenous toxic approach) has prevailed to the present time. Kraepelin, with appropriate reservations, suggested that schizophrenia was in part caused by toxic effects of the patient's disordered metabolism. Jung, in opposition to Freud, insisted that an unknown toxin underlay psychosis, the sequence being: emotional disorder—metabolic disorder—functional symptoms of psychosis.

Acceptance of the biochemical approach was an act of faith prior to the Second World War. Techniques were primitive and results contradictory, and those who maintained a belief in biochemical causation had difficulty in defending their position. After the Second World War there were breakthroughs in both techniques and knowledge about normal brain metabolism. By 1950 there were both the requisite techniques and knowledge needed for large-scale research on the biochemistry of psychosis. There followed an era of intense activity and investigation, and biochemical theories proliferated. A major impetus was provided by the discovery of *psychotomimetics* (drugs that mimic the symptoms of psychosis) and *tranquilizers* (drugs that quiet excited patients or energize depressed patients). Although such drugs had been used before in prescientific ways, now their chemical nature became known, and they could be investigated precisely and quantitatively. Further discoveries excited adherents of the biochemical approach: the pharmacological antagonism between some psychotomimetic drugs and some tranquilizers, and the chemical similarity between certain psychotomimetics and certain neurohumors (chemicals involved in the transmission of nerve impulses).

There are two major biochemical theories of psychosis, both dealing with neurohumors. One emphasizes adrenaline and its products, and the other focuses on serotonin. In addition, there are several compromise theories that attempt to combine the adrenaline and serotonin theories.

Adrenaline Metabolites

Hoffer, Osmond, and their collaborators (1954, 1958, 1959) elaborated the following theory based on the action of the metabolic products of adrenaline. When an individual is made anxious or is stressed, there is an excessive flow of adrenaline, ostensibly through stimulation of sympathetic ganglia. In normal persons the excess adrenaline is converted to harmless oxydized substances that minimize self-awareness of panic without interfering with cerebral metabolism. In schizophrenics an aberrant enzyme, probably due to faulty heredity, converts adrenaline to *adrenochrome*. It has been speculated that the enzyme may be *taraxein,* a substance reported by Heath et al. (1957) to be present only in schizophrenic blood. Adrenochrome crosses the blood-brain barrier, a chemical filter, and subsequently interferes with brain metabolism, but it is unstable and is converted to *adrenolutin.* Both adrenaline metabolites, adrenochrome and adrenolutin, ostensibly produce disturbed behavior, and they have been labeled psychotomimetics by Hoffer and Osmond.

These theorists claim that their postulates not only account for known facts but also suggest new facts that have ostensibly been verified. They distinguish between two kinds of psychotomimetics: (1) *lysergic acid diethylamide* (LSD) and *mescaline,* which produce hallucinations, and (2) adrenochrome and adrenolutin, which produce thought disorder and personality change with minimal hallucinations. The implication is that the adrenaline metabolites produce symptoms that resemble schizophrenia more closely than the symptoms produced by LSD and mescaline.

They established that schizophrenics convert most of the adrenochrome to adrenolutin which causes psychological disturbances; whereas normal persons convert adrenochrome, when it is administered to them, to nondisturbing substances. From these facts they speculated that schizophrenics have a chemical substance that inhibits the conversion of adrenochrome to neutral, nondisturbing products. It is possible that LSD works in precisely this fashion (inhibiting the destruction of adrenochrome), which means that more adrenochrome is converted to adrenolutin. Thus LSD is linked theoretically to adrenaline metabolites.

Two further facts are adduced to support the theory. First, schizophrenics have fewer allergies than normal persons. Since adrenochrome is an antagonist of *histamine,* which causes allergy, the relative absence of allergy in schizophrenia is indirect evidence for the theory. Second, it is known that nicotinic acid competes with *noradrenaline,* a neurohumor similar to adrenaline, and the presence of nicotinic acid should deplete the amount of adrenaline present. The smaller the amount of adrenaline, the smaller is the amount of adrenaline metabolites and therefore the fewer are the psychotic symptoms. Thus administering nicotinic acid should reduce psychotic symptoms. Hoffer and Osmond (1959) asserted that the injection of nicotinic acid definitely helped early schizophrenics, although it had no effect on chronic schizophrenics. Another deduction remains to be verified, namely, that barbiturates and tranquilizers decrease sensory input, thereby diminishing perceived stress, which in turn leads to a smaller adrenaline output and consequently fewer of the adrenaline metabolites that cause the psychotic symptoms.

The evidence for this theory is not as positive as its adherents believe. There is still some doubt about whether adrenochrome and adrenolutin produce psychotic-like symptoms. Nicotinic acid did help early schizophrenics, but the advantage was not maintained over time. Furthermore, it has been found that normal persons and schizophrenics have the same rates of utilization of both adrenaline and noradrenaline (Holland et al., 1958), and adrenochrome has been noted to be absent in schizophrenics as well as in normal persons (Axelrod et al., 1958). These findings weaken the theory and suggest it needs revision. The theory does explain a number of well-established facts and is therefore of value. However, at present it is not generally accepted because of the questionable status of adrenochrome and adrenolutin as substances peculiar to schizophrenics.

Serotonin

Serotonin theory was formulated by Woolley and Shaw (1954, 1957, 1962). It was originally suggested by the fact that lysergic acid diethylamide (LSD), which produces psychotic-like symptoms, is chemically related to serotonin. Serotonin is believed to be involved the the transmission of neural impulses in the brain, the evidence being its distribution in the brain and the distribution of the enzyme that destroys it (*monamine oxydase*). LSD resembles serotonin in chemical structure and interferes with its function as a neural transmitter; that is, serotonin is the metabolite and LSD, its antimetabolite.

The theory assumes that normal metabolism of serotonin in the brain is required for psychological normality; abnormal metabolism of serotonin results in schizophrenia. Although the disposition is inherited, it is assumed that it will become manifest only after several decades of life.

Schizophrenia is regarded as starting with a failure to form enough serotonin in the brain, and this is seen in the shyness and depression which are usually the forerunners of the disease. With sharply increased emotional strain, the control mechanism which governs the level of serotonin in the brain begins to fail. The production of serotonin may increase sharply (or its rate of destruction may decrease), and this probably coincides with the agitated phase. Subsequently, decreased production may again take place. (Woolley, 1962, pp. 183–184)

Thus both an excess and a deficiency of serotonin in the brain cause psychological abnormality. An excess causes agitation and hallucinations, such as are produced by psychotomimetic drugs like LSD. Woolley assumes that LSD and other drugs similar in chemical structure to serotonin act like serotonin in their effect on brain cells. The process is: a psychotomimetic drug (analogue of serotonin) produces an *excess* of serotonin-like effects, which in turn leads to excitement, hallucinations, and other aspects of the acute stage of schizophrenia. A *deficiency* of serotonin causes a depression of function such as is seen in catatonics. The substances related to serotonin but which act as antagonists (opposites) of serotonin produce this effect. For example, *reserpine,* which is a tranquilizer, is an antimetabolite of serotonin and has an opposite effect to serotonin on smooth muscle.

Thus the action of chemicals related to serotonin in exciting or depressing psychological functioning is evidence for serotonin theory. Another kind of evidence may be found in the effect of increasing the serotonin content of the brain, either by adding precursors or by reducing the amount of the enzyme that destroys serotonin (monamine oxydase). Woolley (1962) reports that increases in brain serotonin worsen the behavior of acute schizophrenics.

Serotonin theory has been severely criticized, and Woolley (1962) has attempted to meet various objections to his theory. It has been contended that psychotomimetic drugs such as LSD do not induce genuine psychotic symptoms in normal persons. Woolley agrees that taking a drug once does not produce symptoms identical to those seen in a chronic disease such as schizophrenia, but prolonged use of such drugs may produce similar patterns. The symptoms produced by drugs are perhaps best regarded as a *model* of the way symptoms might originate, not as features identical to those seen in psychoses that develop over a period of years.

Another question concerns why all of the chemicals similar to serotonin do not induce similar psychological changes. The answer, Woolley suggests, lies in differences in absorption of the substances in the body, in rate of elimination, and in whether the substance mimics or antagonizes serotonin.

Finally, there is the question of the amount of serotonin present in the brain. If the theory is correct, then schizophrenics should have more or less serotonin (depending on whether they are agitated or retarded), than normal persons in certain parts of the brain. There is no evidence to sustain such differential predictions, and Woolley admits that such evidence is crucial. Thus at present serotonin theory may be regarded as promising because it accounts for a set of psychological and pharmacological facts, but unproved because it lacks essential evidence.

Variations

Several other theories attempt to combine aspects of the adrenaline metabolites and serotonin theories, in each instance adding a variable not present in either of the two major theories. Marazzi (1955) suggested that the synapse, the point where impulses pass from one nerve to another, is the primary locus of action of both psychotomimetic and tranquilizing drugs. As evidence, he noted that adrenochrome and adrenolutin inhibit synaptic transmission, although with less potency than does serotonin. Disturbances at the synapse may be corrected by tranquilizing drugs, which counteract the inhibiting effects of psychotomimetic drugs, thereby restoring a proper balance.

Bulle and Konchegul (1957) examined the cerebrospinal fluid of psychotics. They found in schizophrenics a substance with properties like those of serotonin, and in manic-depressives a substance with properties like those of adrenaline; neither substance was present in normal persons. As the dosages of serotonin and adrenaline were increased, there were pronounced changes in the symptoms that appeared. They integrated these facts into the following theory. Schizophrenia is caused by the release of serotonin, or a similar substance, in the brain. A minute amount of serotonin depresses the highest cortical centers, resulting in thought disorder. A large amount of serotonin knocks out cortical inhibitory centers, releasing lower centers and thereby producing excitement and hallucinations. A still larger amount of serotonin depresses neural centers at all levels, producing a catatonic-like state of motor retardation. Affective psychoses are caused by the release of adrenaline, or a similar substance, in the brain. A small amount of adrenaline knocks out cortical inhibitory centers, releasing lower centers and causing manic excitement. A large amount of adrenaline depresses both cortical and lower centers, causing depression.

Brodie and Shore (1956) invoked the antagonism between the sympathetic and parasympathetic components of the autonomic nervous system. They assumed that the sympathetic system, which is involved in bodily arousal and increased activity in the face of threat, is controlled or modulated by noradrenaline; increased output of noradrenaline means increased activity of the sympathetic system. The parasympathetic system, which is involved in everyday restorative and vegetative bodily processes, was assumed to be controlled or modulated by serotonin; increased serotonin output means increased activity of the parasympathetic system. It was further assumed that an excess of noradrenaline leads to a sympathetic imbalance and therefore hyperactivity (psychotic-like behavior), whereas an excess of serotonin leads to a parasympathetic imbalance and therefore quiescence and lack of anxiety.

LSD acts by antagonizing serotonin, thereby blocking action of the parasympathetic system. This tips the balance in favor of sympathetic system, and the result is overactivity and psychotic-like symptoms. Chlorpromazine acts by antagonizing noradrenaline, thereby blocking sympathetic activity and tipping the balance in favor of the parasympathetic system. The result is relaxation and diminished motor activity.

It was assumed that LSD acts directly by blocking serotonin and chlorpromazine acts directly by blocking noradrenaline. LSD and chlorpromazine are apparently destroyed quickly by enzymes; their effects appear rapidly and disappear rapidly. The speed suggests that the action must be directly upon the neurohumors (serotonin and noradrenaline), else the effects would last longer. Reserpine, on the other hand, does have long-lasting effects, which endure after it has been destroyed in the brain. Presumably reserpine impairs the *storage* of serotonin and noradrenaline, and this has the effect of temporarily tipping the balance toward parasympathetic activity because serotonin is synthesized faster than noradrenaline.

Brodie and his colleagues agreed with Marazzi on the importance of the synapse as the locus of action. They suggested that imbalance in autonomic activity produces a shift in equilibrium at brain synapses. The synaptic disturbance might be caused by overproduction or underproduction of neural transmitting substances, impaired release from storage of these substances, or blocking after release.

The most recent theory is Rubin's attempt to consolidate the conflicting evidence concerning neurohumoral disturbance in psychosis (1962). He started with the usual assumptions about sympathetic and parasympathetic functioning. Sympathetic functioning is mediated by adrenaline and noradrenaline, hence the system is adrenergic. Parasympathetic functioning is mediated by *acetylcholine,* hence the system is cholinergic. When the organism is faced with stress or threat, the emergency calls forth action of the sympathetic system. Rubin added the assumption that optimal response to emergency requires a diminution of parasympathetic activity. He then applied these assumptions to chemical interactions in the brain, especially the *hypothalamus,* suggesting that serotonin is an adrenergic substance with respect to central (brain) representation of sympathetic functioning. With these assumptions as a base, he proceeded to the following theory.

When a normal individual is at rest, there is normal activity of both the sympathetic (adrenergic) and parasympathetic (cholinergic) systems. When a normal is stressed, there is an increase in adrenergic activity and a decrease in cholinergic activity as the organism prepares for emergency action. These are the normal patterns for rest and emergency. Psychotics may show disturbances in either aspect of the pattern, adrenergic or cholinergic, and the disturbance may be overactivity or underactivity. There are seven patterns of dysfunction in autonomic balance:

> excess cholinergic, excess adrenergic
> excess cholinergic, normal adrenergic
> excess cholinergic, deficient adrenergic
> normal cholinergic, excess adrenergic
> normal cholinergic, deficient adrenergic
> deficient cholinergic, normal adrenergic
> deficient cholinergic, deficient adrenergic

Thus there are several possible patterns of neurohumoral imbalance present in psychosis, and any group of psychotics probably contains individuals with each of the patterns.

Rubin then attempted to test his theory by investigating changes in the pupil of the eye in response to light and dark. It had already been established that pupillary constriction is a cholinergic response and that pupillary dilatation is an adrenergic response. It follows from the theory that there should be three levels of pupillary constriction—excessive, normal, and deficient—and three levels of dilatation. These are precisely what Rubin found (1961). He also found that all of his psychotic subjects showed impairment (excess or deficiency) in constriction, dilatation, or both.

Finally, Rubin speculated about the substances underlying these various imbalances:

The nature of the adrenergic impairment that characterizes some psychotics may be neurohumoral deficiency of some biogenic amine or some enzyme disorder such as monamine oxydase overactivity in the adrenergic centers of the brain. Other psychotics manifest adrenergic impairment by a neurohumoral excess of some sympathomimetic amine that may be the result of some enzyme disorder such as monamine oxydase underactivity in central adrenergic centers. Similarly, the cholinergic impairment of some psychotics may be characterized by excessive concentrations of brain acetylcholine or deficient acetylcholinesterase, while other psychotics may possess an inadequate level of acetylcholine or excessive acetyl-cholinesterase activity. (1962, p. 517)

Comments

These biochemical theories account for a variety of behavioral and pharmacological facts. Nevertheless, there are flaws in both the theories and the research on which they are based. Kline (1958) offered criticisms of both aspects. He noted that hospitalized psychiatric patients are a unique group, not only because of psychosis but also because of diet, lack of exercise, low grade infection, and general lack of social interaction. Diagnostic categories might lack reliability, and chemical indices are known to show periodic waxing and waning. Concerning control data, volunteers make poor control subjects because they have been shown to be different from non-volunteering normal persons. There is a need for base rates of normal chemical activity, without which it is difficult to know whether psychotics are deviant chemically.

Concerning interpretations of results, Kline mentioned that biochemical changes occurring in psychosis might be compensatory changes initiated after the onset of psychosis, rather than causes of the psychosis itself. His last point concerned the *post hoc* nature of much of the theorizing: accounting for data already collected, speculating about correlational data, or both.

Both Benjamin (1958) and Kety (1959) surveyed the literature in some detail and with a critical eye. Both cast doubt on the adrenaline metabolites theory but were more optimistic about the serotonin theory. Kety suggested that all differences in chemical activity between psychotics and normal persons disappear when the methodological issues cited above (diet, exercise, infection, etc.) are taken into account. These critiques have been hotly contested by proponents of the various biochemical theories.

Although the biochemical theories reviewed here are divergent, they all stem from a common base: the assumption that psychosis is caused by disturbances of the brain metabolism of substances involved in neural transmission. None of the theories has received unequivocal support over a period of years, but all appear to be testable. We must admire the precision and quantification of the methods of biochemical research and of the theories stemming from it. In evaluating these theories, we must bear in mind that the more testable a theory is, the more likely it is that contrary data will be discovered. Although none of them appears able to carry the full explanatory load yet, all of them make certain common assumptions that appear to be substantiated by facts. This is true especially of the assumption that psychotics have some kind of imbalance in the adrenergic-cholinergic systems.

In previous years one could easily deny the importance of biochemistry in psychosis, but today there is compelling evidence of biochemical changes in psychosis. Linking biochemical evidence with the leads derived from the genetic approach, we must give weight to the hypothesis that an important etiological factor in psychosis is an inherited defect in one or more enzyme systems that leads to faulty brain metabolism of neurohumors. The degree to which this inherited defect predisposes to psychosis remains a controversial issue.

PHYSIOLOGICAL THEORIES

The previous section dealt with "central" neural explanations of psychosis; the present section deals with more "peripheral" aspects, especially those related to malfunction of the autonomic nervous system.

The Adrenal Cortex and Stress

A group of researchers at Worcester, Massachusetts investigated schizophrenia in relation to stress and output of the adrenal cortex (Pincus & Hoagland, 1950). Their concept of stress was borrowed from Hans Selye (1956). He believes that the endocrine system is designed to handle any kind of stress, physiological or psychological, and the crucial organ in the endocrine system is the adrenal cortex. The adrenals are regarded as a kind of final common pathway for reactions to stress, and Selye collected impressive evidence showing that adrenal cortical functioning is crucial for adequate response to stress. He demonstrated that any stress leads immediately to the outpouring of products of the adrenal cortex. In the face of continued stress there is at first hypertrophy (excessive use) of this organ and then secondary atrophy (wasting away), as the organ can no longer cope on a continuous basis with demands for emergency functioning.

Pincus and Hoagland (1950) exposed normal persons and schizophrenics to a variety of physiological and psychological stresses and measured the output of the adrenal cortex. They found that under resting conditions there were no reliable differences between patients and normal subjects, although the patients did show much greater latitude in functioning (overactivity or underactivity). Under stress, two thirds of the schizophrenics were *under-reactive* in comparison to normal individuals. In reviewing this evidence, Hoskins concluded:

. . . it appears that the schizophrenic patient is handicapped in most cases by a failure of his adrenals to respond adaptively to the changing needs of the body. It is this characteristic rather than any marked failure of secretion that is impressive. (1946, p. 121)

The evidence is even stronger: Pincus and Hoagland reported that several measures of adrenal function showed a *fall* in output in response to stress, rather than merely no response or a normal increase.

The schizophrenic's adrenal insufficiency in the face of stress may be interpreted in two ways. First, there may be a basic defect in the ability of his endocrine system to tolerate emergencies, a defect that is perhaps inherited. Second, the defect in reactivity might be due to prolonged overactivity of the adrenal cortex, leading to the secondary atrophy that is part of Selye's *general adaptation syndrome*. This syndrome occurs when the organism is placed in a situation of prolonged stress and must respond physiologically with emergency mechanisms over an extended period of time. His endocrines, among other systems, cannot cope with the prolonged demands for emergency action, and eventually they become depleted. Subsequently, the organism is incapable of responding adequately to even a mild stress. This interpretation suggests a more psychogenic etiology: presumably the potential schizophrenic is placed in situations of continuous or oft-repeated threat, so that he is forced to make excessive emergency responses. This excessive use of emergency mechanisms results in permanent damage to the adrenal cortex, and the consequent inability to respond appropriately to stress leads to schizophrenia.

Pincus and Hoagland also suggested a relationship between the defect in adrenal cortex functioning and possible defects of neural transmission in schizophrenia:

. . . one of the most conspicuous indicies of failure in patients is the adrenal regulators of salt balance at the time of stress. The electrolyte, potassium, regulated by the adrenal cortex, is a substance of great importance in the excitability of nerve and in the generation and propagation of its action currents. . . . It is possible that faulty potassium metabolism in the face of the repeated stress of daily life may be an important cumulative factor in the development of a psychosis. (1950, pp. 649–650)

This speculation has not been followed up, either by its authors or by other investigators. It has apparently been dropped in favor of theories involving neural transmitters (for example, serotonin, noradrenaline).

The findings of the Worcester group were supported by other researchers, who also found evidence for diminished reactivity of the adrenal cortex in schizophrenics (Freeman, 1948). However, contrary evidence was also reported (Altschule, 1953): in response to stress, schizophrenics were found to have *higher* reactivity of the adrenal cortex than normal individuals, and in those patients who recovered, there was a diminution of reactivity.

There are two ways of reconciling these opposed findings. The most likely explanation is that the samples of patients varied along the dimension of acuteness-chronicity. Let us assume that the Worcester patients were chronic schizophrenics whose adrenal cortical mechanism for responding to stress had been worn out by excessive demands upon it. Assume further that Altschule's patients were acute schizophrenics and were therefore still responding to stress with excessive outpouring of the adrenal cortex. Ostensibly such continued over-reactivity by acute patients would eventually lead to a debilitation of their adrenal cortex, which would then become hyporeactive. This first explanation suggests that early *over-reactivity* is followed by later *under-reactivity* of the adrenal cortex, which fits the opposed findings on the assumption that the Worcester patients were chronic and the Altschule patients, acute.

A second explanation ignores the chronicity issue and suggests that schizophernics are *either* under-reactive *or* over-reactive:

Curiously enough, it is likely that in their own way all these authors are correct, since the most significant fact emerging from the investigation of schizophrenics is that the range of whatever somatic function one examines is considerably wider than that found in normal control groups. (Sands, 1957, p. 78)

This suggestion ignores the stress hypothesis of the Worcester group and emphasizes in its place the general tendency of schizophrenics to be deviant. However, this explanation is out of line with a large body of evidence on somatic arousal, which indicates that schizophrenics tend to be underreactive.

Somatic Arousal

The notion of somatic arousal is very old, but only in the last few decades has it been pinned down to specific physiological and neural events (Freeman, 1948; Lindsley, 1951; Hebb, 1955; Malmo, 1958; and Duffy, 1962). The behavioral continuum may be described as follows:

coma
deep sleep
light sleep

> drowsiness
> relaxed wakefulness
> alert attentiveness
> tension
> intense excitement

Behavioral efficiency is good in the wakefulness and attentiveness parts of the continuum, and poor in the other parts.

Somatic arousal is reflected in a number of body systems, the ones most frequently recorded being galvanic skin response, heart rate, blood pressure, and muscle action potentials. It has been shown that there are individual patterns of somatic arousal (Lacey & Lacey, 1958). Thus one person might show an elevated heart rate but only a small change in muscle action potentials, while another might show precisely the opposite pattern of somatic arousal. Nevertheless, in evaluating *group* trends, as in comparisons of schizophrenics with normal persons, any of the systems mentioned should suffice because all of them reflect group changes in arousal.

Heretofore there have been two opposing theories concerning somatic arousal in schizophrenia. One asserts that schizophrenics are underaroused and the other, that they are overaroused. These physiological theories parallel analogous psychological theories discussed in Chapter 12—undermotivation versus overmotivation in schizophrenia. The opposing motivational theories are incompatible, but it is possible to reconcile the opposing physiological theories. The key is a crucial distinction between activity and reactivity. *Activity* is defined as the person's habitual physiological level or basal amount of neuromuscular responding at rest; this is the characteristic level when there are no clearly defined stimuli impinging on the organism. *Reactivity* refers to the neuromuscular response of the individual to specific and clearly delineated stimuli. He is no longer at rest but is attending to and reacting to an environmental input.

This distinction may be used to combine the overaroused and underaroused theories. The assumption that schizophrenics are overaroused may hold only for resting levels. If this were true, the schizophrenic would best be characterized as *overactive:* his resting level of autonomic functioning would be abnormally high. Similarly, the assumption that schizophrenics are underaroused may hold only for situations involving a reaction to stimulus inputs. If this were true, the schizophrenic would best be described as *under-reactive:* his autonomic response to stimuli would be abnormally low.

Thus the opposing theories can be integrated into a single theory that assumes an abnormally high resting level (*hyperactivity*) and an abnormally low response to stimuli (*hyporeactivity*). This dual hypothesis can be checked against the physiological evidence, and for convenience of exposition the research has been grouped into three areas of physiological recording: galvanic skin response, cardiovascular response, and muscle action potentials.

Galvanic Skin Response. The galvanic skin response is the electrical conductance—or alternatively, the resistance—of the skin. We may oversimplify in the present context by saying that the more a person sweats, the lower is his skin resistance and the greater is his galvanic skin response. Sweating, although activated by the sympathetic nervous system, is under the control of cholinergic mechanisms, not adrenergic mechanisms. We saw earlier in the chapter that one theory of psychosis suggests the presence of an adrenergic-cholinergic imbalance (Rubin, 1962). If this theory were even partly true, there would be no clear pattern of galvanic skin response in schizophrenics.

The experimental evidence is in accord with this expectation, at least for activity level. Concerning *activity level,* three studies have shown that the resting galvanic skin response of schizophrenic is higher than that of normal persons (Hock, Kubis, & Rouke, 1944; Jurko, Jost, & Hill, 1952; and Howe, 1958). However, four studies reported no differences between schizophrenics and normal persons (Malmo & Shagass, 1949; DeVault, 1957; Pishkin & Hershiser, 1963; and Ray, 1963), and two researchers found lower galvanic skin responses in schizophrenics (Williams, 1953; Zahn, Rosenthal, & Lawlor, 1963).

These confusing and contradictory findings may be explained in two ways. It is possible that there are no differences in resting levels between schizophrenics and normal persons and the diverse findings merely represent sampling errors. On the other hand, the differences may be real and represent the state of affairs predicted from Rubin's theory: some schizophrenics are excessively cholinergic, some excessively adrenergic, and others balanced. These patterns would lead to higher than normal, lower than normal, and normal galvanic skin responses, respectively. At present this hypothesis is speculative, and it requires a demonstration that certain schizophrenics (paranoids, reactives, or acutes) are hypoactive, while others (nonparanoids, process, or chronics) are hyperactive.

Concerning *reactivity,* the evidence is consistent: when stimulated, normal persons have a greater increase in galvanic skin response than schizophrenics. In fact, it has been reported that schizophrenics respond to stimulation with a *reduced* galvanic skin response (Solomon, Darrow, & Blaurock, 1939; Hock et al., 1944; and Jurko et al., 1952). In two of these studies, improvement in the schizophrenics' clinical status led to increases in galvanic skin response reactivity. Paintal (1951) reported that psychotics had a reduced galvanic skin response to the threat of pain, but Ray (1963) failed to confirm this. Nevertheless, Ray found that the responses of normal persons increased more than those of schizophrenics when the instructions called for listening and responding to stimuli.

Thus the research on galvanic skin responses both confirms and fails to confirm the dual hypothesis. Schizophrenics are clearly less *reactive* than normal persons, but there is no unequivocal evidence that they are more *active*.

Cardiovascular Responses. Cardiovascular responding encompasses both heart rate and blood pressure. Concerning *resting level,* three studies have established that schizophrenics' heart rates are higher than those of normal persons (Jurko et al., 1952; Gunderson, 1953; & Williams, 1953). DeVault (1957) obtained similar results for chronic, reactive schizophrenics but not for process schizophrenics; but Reynolds (1962) found that normal individuals, reactives, and process schizophrenics lined up in increasing order of resting heart rate.

Resting blood pressure has also been found to be higher in schizophrenics than in normal persons. Malmo and Shagass (1952) reported higher diastolic blood pressure in chronic schizophrenics, as did Reynolds (1962) in process schizophrenics. Consistent with these findings are the reports of excessive constriction of peripheral blood vessels (Altschule & Sulzbach, 1949; Henschel, Brozek, and Keys, 1951).

Concerning *reactivity,* one large-scale study has shown that the cardiovascular response of schizophrenics is *less* than that of normal individuals (Astrup, 1962). There are also consistent differences within schizophrenics. In general, reactive schizophrenics tend to respond not very differently from normal persons, showing a marked increase in blood pressure when stimulated, whereas process schizophrenics show little or no increase in blood pressure (King, 1958; Reynolds, 1962). Reynolds also showed that the heart rate of process schizophrenics is hyporeactive compared to that of reactive schizophrenics and normal subjects.

Thus the research on cardiovascular responses supports the dual hypothesis. With rare exceptions, schizophrenics are *hyperactive* and *hyporeactive,* and the severer the psychosis (process, chronic), the greater are these two tendencies.

Muscle Action Potentials. Muscle action potentials are electrical impulses recorded from contracting muscles, which makes it difficult to investigate reactivity. Therefore most researchers have concentrated on resting levels. Malmo and his colleagues (1949, 1950, 1951) demonstrated that the resting muscle action potentials of schizophrenics were higher than those of normal persons, and that chronic patients had the highest levels. Reynolds (1962) showed that normal individuals, reactives, and process schizophrenics lined up in an increasing level of muscle action potentials. Other researchers have consistently found higher levels in schizophrenics (Jurko et al., 1952; Whatmore & Ellis, 1958; and Petursson, 1962).

Of particular interest is a study by Whatmore and Ellis (1964), who followed schizophrenics through periods of remission (no symptoms), relapse, and improvement. During remission there were intermittent elevations of resting muscle action potentials, despite the absence of clinical symptoms. During the weeks or months preceding relapse the level or the variability, if not both, of muscle action potentials rose and tended to become consistently high. Clinical symptoms appeared only after such high levels had been maintained and usually at the peak levels of muscle action potentials. Such high levels were maintained until a tranquilizing drug (chlorpromazine) was administered. Chlorpromazine resulted in a sharp drop in the level of muscle action potentials, and after a period of such reduction, the patients' clinical condition improved. Thereafter any worsening of the symptom picture was preceded by an increase in muscle action potentials. Note that these potentials are indicators of covert muscular activity which cannot be detected by the naked eye, and therefore such increases cannot be ascribed to increases in gross muscular movements such as might occur when patients become restless, excited, or uncontrolled. Whatmore and Ellis suggested that this overactive state of peripheral muscles might trigger an outbreak of schizophrenic symptoms. This is a plausible hypothesis in light of the time sequence—first overactivity, then symptoms. If this hypothesis were correct, it would push back the locus of explanation. We would have to determine what it is that initiates increases in covert muscular activity, and one answer would bring us back to the substances mediating neural transmission, for example, serotonin and adrenaline.

Muscular movements have also been recorded mechanically, without the aid of electrical sensors. Disturbances in finger movements have been reported by three groups of researchers (Malmo & Shagass, 1949; Edwards & Harris, 1953; and Gindis, 1960). Williams (1964) recorded the total energy imparted by gross movements of limbs and by skeletal muscle tension, and found the resting energy output of schizophrenics to be higher than that of normal persons and neurotics.

Thus the research on muscle action potentials and on muscular movements supports one part of the dual hypothesis—schizophrenics are *hyperactive*. Furthermore, we must seriously consider the possibility that excessive random movements lead to or at least precede the flare-up of schizophrenic symptoms. The second part of the hypothesis—that schizophrenics are hyporeactive—is more difficult to test because of technical problems of recording from muscles undergoing massive contractions.

The Theory of Excessive Sympathetic Tonus. The research on somatic arousal appears to support the dual hypothesis that schizophrenics are hyperactive and hyper-reactive. Although there are exceptions to this generalization, it appears to be the best statement summarizing a large body of research. The problem now is to integrate this conclusion into a larger theoretical framework.

Such a framework is supplied by the theory of excessive sympathetic tonus. For many years Wenger (1956, 1959) has maintained that imbalance of the autonomic nervous system in an important aspect of psychopathology. His own research demonstrated the familiar pattern of hyperactivity in the autonomic functioning of schizophrenics, and he was led to propose that schizophrenia is characterized by excessive activity of the sympathetic nervous system.

It may be speculated that excessive sympathetic tonus is a result of stimulation from higher neural centers, such as might occur as a consequence of faulty metabolism of the substances mediating neural transmission in the brain. The relevant biochemical theories were discussed earlier in the chapter, and there is no need to dwell upon them here.

What is of immediate relevance is an explanation of the under-reactivity that characterizes schizophrenia. If faulty metabolism of neurohumors underlies the autonomic overactivity of schizophrenics, then the same explanation cannot be invoked to account of hyporeactivity. Rather, the explanation seems to lie in the way the autonomic nervous system functions. In general, the higher the person's resting or basal level of autonomic *activity*, the less is his *reactivity*. This principle was first enunciated by Wilder (1950) as the Law of Initial Values, and it has since been confirmed by a number of investigators (Lacey, 1956; Malmo, 1958; and Benjamin, 1963). It has been further demonstrated that at extremely high resting levels of the autonomic nervous system, a stimulus tends to elicit either no autonomic response or a paradoxical decrease in autonomic level.

Thus the lack of autonomic reactivity is evidently not a *primary* characteristic of schizophrenia but a *secondary* one, resulting from an elevated resting level of autonomic functioning. The crucial assumption in the theory is that schizophrenics are hyperactive; their being hyporeactive follows from the known properties of the autonomic nervous system.

COMMENT

We have discussed four biological approaches to psychosis: heredity, constitution, biochemistry, and physiology. Concerning the inheritance of psychosis, a special problem is posed by diagnostic issues. There is some unreliability in diagnosing psychoses, which introduces error into data on heredity. The subjectivity of diagnosis is especially troublesome. An investigator who favors the hereditary approach might tend to see psychosis in the relatives of patients more than would an objective observer. An opposite bias by an environmentalist would also contaminate data. These sources of error can be corrected by "blind" diagnoses, in which the investigator does not know whether the individual is or is not a relative of a psychotic patient.

A more serious problem is the question of the homogeneity of psychoses.

Is there one affective psychosis or several? Mania and depression are grouped under one diagnostic heading, but perhaps each has its own heredity. Similarly, although involutional depression appears similar to psychotic depression, the two might have entirely separate mechanisms of heredity. There are varieties of schizophrenia, and it is not known whether the same inherited tendency underlies all of them. This is certainly one hypothesis: the generalized tendency toward schizophrenia is inherited, but the specific form it takes is determined by the environment. On the other hand, a separate inherited tendency might underlie each of the varieties of schizophrenia. This issue will not be resolved unless studies of heredity use finer diagnostic labels than *affective psychosis* or *schizophrenia*.

Concerning constitution, the evidence suggests that at best it is a weak variable. Many clinicians believe it exerts no influence at all. One reason for the lack of research is that few investigators wish to study a variable whose maximal influence is minor.

Concerning biochemistry and neurohumors, the research is promising, but it is still early—modern research dates back less than 20 years. There is a need for more knowledge of the normal functioning of neurohumors. In addition, there must be a stronger link between abnormal substances and psychotic symptoms. There is some evidence from research with psychotomimetics, but it is controversial. The symptoms produced by LSD and similar substances are similar but not identical to psychotic symptoms. How much similarity shall we demand? The answer depends upon the investigator's bias.

Research in this area is complicated by paradoxical pharmacological properties of some of the substances: a large dose may yield *opposite* effects of a small dose. The presence of the blood-brain barrier (a chemical filter) adds further complexity. In spite of these difficulties, there appears to be sufficient evidence to sustain the biochemical approach, at least as a working hypothesis that has explained some of the data.

Concerning physiology, the theory of excessive sympathetic tonus has much to recommend it, and it makes contact with interference theory (see Chapter 13). The schizophrenic's autonomic nervous system discharges at an abnormally high level while at rest, which renders him ineffective in responding physiologically to environmental stimuli. Of particular importance is the excessive muscle tonus, as revealed by muscle action potentials and other measures. It is known that there are optimal levels of muscle tonus, which enable the organism to respond quickly and efficiently to stimulus inputs. Insufficient "muscle background" leads to inefficient psychomotor responding, and excessive muscle tonus leads to even greater inefficiency. Thus the schizophrenic's deficit in a variety of psychomotor tasks may be ascribed to an abnormally high resting level of covert muscular contraction.

If the theory is correct, the schizophrenic's sense of muscular contraction (proprioception) must be disturbed. The ability to discriminate weights depends upon proprioception. Rosenbaum et al., (1966) found that schizophrenics were poorer at discriminating weights when the weights were light but not when they were heavy. Evidently, when the external stimuli (the weights) were sufficiently intense, they overrode the "internal noise;" but when the external stimuli were slight (light weights), the "internal noise" of excessive muscular contractions interfered with performance. The performance deficit was related to severity of psychopathology: the more disturbed schizophrenics showed more deficit than the less disturbed patients. These findings, derived from an experiment on psychological deficit, provide strong support for the theory of excessive sympathetic tonus.

The schizophrenic's high resting levels of heart rate, blood pressure, and muscle tension may be construed as excessive "biological noise," the analogy being to an automobile engine whose idler is set too high. Several authors have proposed that this excessive physiological activity directly accounts for some clinical symptoms. Angyal (1935, 1936) speculated that the high level of muscle contraction has been misinterpreted by schizophrenics, the misinterpretations taking the form of somatic delusions. Gould (1950) suggested that auditory hallucinations could be traced to a motor disturbance of the speech mechanism.

The notion of "biological noise" also fits Wishner's concept of efficiency (1955), which is defined as the ratio of focused to diffuse activity. Normal persons focus their activity on task requirements, and there is little random activity in the muscles or cardiovascular system. Schizophrenics direct less of their activity to the task, and a greater proportion of their total output is wasted in random, diffuse activity. The resultant deficit on a variety of tasks may thus be ascribed to an excessively high level of resting biological activity. This hyperactivity not only renders the schizophrenic less able to respond efficiently, but it also serves as a source of distraction. It seems likely that the schizophrenic is literally distracted by the excessive "idling" of his body machinery. We noted in the last chapter that the schizophrenic is hampered by intrusive and idiosyncratic associations. Now it appears that he is also distracted by interference from biological sources. One clinical symptom of schizophrenia is a tendency toward social withdrawal, and we may speculate that the schizophrenic is less susceptible to social stimuli because his attention is distracted by internal biological and associative stimuli.

REFERENCES

Altschule, M. D. *Body physiology in mental and emotional disorders.* New York: Grune & Stratton, 1953.

Altschule, M. D., & Sulzbach, W. M. Effect of carbon dioxide on acrocyanosis in schizophrenia. *Archives of Neurology and Psychiatry,* 1949, **61,** 44–45.

Angyal, A. The perceptual basis of somatic delusions in a case of schizophrenia. *Archives of Neurology and Psychiatry,* 1935, **34,** 270–279.

Angyal, A. The experience of the body-self in schizophrenia. *Archives of Neurology and Psychiatry,* 1936, **35,** 1029–1053.

Astrup, C. *Schizophrenia: Conditional reflex studies.* Springfield, Illinois: Thomas, 1962.

Axelrod, J., Perlin, S., & Szara, S. Is adrenochrome present in the blood? *American Journal of Psychiatry,* 1958, **115,** 162–163.

Bellak, L., & Holt, R. R. Somatotypes in relation to dementia praecox. *American Journal of Psychiatry,* 1948, **104,** 713–724.

Benjamin, J. D. Some considerations in biological research in schizophrenia. *Psychosomatic Medicine,* 1958, **20,** 427–445.

Benjamin, Lorna. Statistical treatment of the Law of Initial Values (LIV) in autonomic research: A review and a recommendation. *Psychosomatic Medicine,* 1963, **25,** 556–566.

Betz, B. Somatology of the schizophrenic patient. *Human biology,* 1942, **14,** 21–47, 152–234.

Böök, J. A. Schizophrenia as a gene mutation. *Acta Genetica,* 1953, 4, 133–139.

Brodie, B. B., & Shore, P. A. A concept for a role of serotonin and norepinephrine as chemical mediators in the brain. *Annals of the New York Academy of Science,* 1956–57, **66,** 631–642.

Brottgärd, S. O. Personality attitude and physical make-up. *Acta Psychiatrica Neurologica,* 1950, **25,** 339–354.

Bulle, P. H., & Konchegul, L. Action of serotonin and cerebrospinal fluid of schizophrenics on the dog-brain. *Journal of Clinical and Experimental Psychopathology,* 1957, **18,** 287–291.

Burch, P. R. F. Manic depressive psychosis: Some new etiological considerations. *British Journal of Psychiatry,* 1964, **110,** 808–817 (a).

Burch, P. R. F. Schizophrenia: Some new etiological considerations. *British Journal of Psychiatry,* 1964, **110,** 818–824 (b).

DeVault, S. Physiological responsiveness in reactive and process schizophrenia. *Dissertation Abstracts,* 1957, **17,** 1387.

Duffy, Elizabeth. *Activation and behavior.* New York: Wiley, 1962.

Edwards, A. S., & Harris, A. C. Laboratory measurements of deterioration and improvement among schizophrenics. *Journal of Genetic Psychology,* 1953, **49,** 153–156.

Freeman, G. L. *The energetics of human behavior.* Ithaca, New York: Cornell University Press, 1948.

Fuller, J. L., & Thompson, W. R. *Behavior genetics.* New York: Wiley, 1960.

Gindis, I. Z. The pathological changes in higher nervous activity in the various forms of schizophrenia. *Pavlov Journal of Higher Nervous Activity,* 1960, **10,** 434–439.

Gould, L. N. Verbal hallucinations as automatic speech. The reactivation of dormant speech habits. *American Journal of Psychiatry,* 1950, **107,** 110–119.

Gregory, I. Genetic factors in schizophrenia. *American Journal of Psychiatry,* 1960, **116,** 961–972.

Gunderson, E. K. Autonomic balance in schizophrenia. Unpublished doctoral dissertation, University of California, Los Angeles, 1953.

Heath, R. G., Martens, S., Leach, B. E., & Angel, C. Effect on behavior of humans with the administration of taraxein. *American Journal of Psychiatry,* 1957, **114,** 14–24.

Hebb, D. O. Drives and the CNS (conceptual nervous system). *Psychological Review,* 1955, **62,** 243–254.

Henschel, A., Brozek, J., & Keys, A. Indirect vasodilation in normal man and in schizophrenic patients. *Journal of Applied Physiology*, 1951, **4**, 340–344.

Hock, P., Kubis, J. F., & Rouke, F. L. Psychogalvanometric investigations in psychoses and other abnormal states. *Psychosomatic Medicine*, 1944, **6**, 237–243.

Hoffer, A. Epinephrine metabolites: Relationship of metabolites to schizophrenia. In Rinkel, M. & Denber, H. C. B. (Eds.) *Chemical concepts of psychosis*. New York: McDowell, Obolensky, 1958, pp. 127–137.

Hoffer, A., & Osmond, H. The adrenochrome model and schizophrenics. *Journal of Nervous and Mental Disease*, 1959, **128**, 18–35.

Hoffer, A., Osmond, H., & Smythies, J. Schizophrenia: A new approach. Part II Result of a year's research. *Journal of Mental Science*, 1954, **100**, 29–45.

Holland, R., Cohen, G., Goldenberg, M., Sha, J., & Leifer, I. Adrenaline and noradrenaline in urine and plasma of schizophrenics. *Federation Proceedings*, 1958, **17**, 378.

Hoskins, R. G. *The biology of schizophrenia*. New York: Norton, 1946.

Howe, E. S. GSR conditioning in anxiety states, normals and chronic functional schizophrenic subjects. *Journal of Abnormal and Social Psychology*, 1958, **56**, 183–189.

Jurko, M., Jost, H., & Hill, T. D. Pathology of the energy system: An experimental clinical study of physiological adaptiveness capacities in a non-patient, a psychoneurotic, and an early paranoid schizophrenic group. *Journal of Psychology*, 1952, **33**, 183–189.

Kallmann, F. J. The genetic theory of schizophrenia. An analysis of 691 schizophrenic twin index families. *American Journal of Psychiatry*, 1946, **103**, 309–322.

Kallmann, F. J. *Heredity in health and mental disorder*. New York: Norton, 1953.

Kant, O. Incidence of psychosis and other mental abnormalities in families of recovered and deteriorated schizophrenic patients. *Psychiatric Quarterly*, 1942, **16**, 176–186.

Kety, S. S. Biochemical theories of schizophrenia. Part II. *Science*, 1959, **129**, 1590–1596.

King, G. F. Differential autonomic responsiveness in the process-reactive classification of schizophrenia. *Journal of Abnormal and Social Psychology*, 1958, **56**, 160–164.

Kline, N. S. Non-chemical factors and chemical theories of mental disease. In Rinkel, M. & Denber, H. C. B. (Eds.) *Chemical concepts of psychosis*. New York: McDowell, Obolensky, 1958.

Kline, N. S., & Tenney, A. M. Constitutional factors in the prognosis of schizophrenia. *American Journal of Psychiatry*, 1950, **107**, 434–441.

Kline, N. S., & Oppenheim, A. N. Constitutional factors in the prognosis of schizophrenia: Further observations. *American Journal of Psychiatry*, 1952, **108**, 909–911.

Kretchmer, E. *Physique and character*. London: Kegan, Paul, Trench, Trubner, 1925.

Kringlen, E. Discordance with respect to schizophrenia in monozygotic male twins: Some genetic aspects. *Journal of Nervous and Mental Disease*, 1964, **138**, 26–31.

Lacey, J. I. The evaluation of autonomic responses: Toward a general solution. *Annals of the New York Academy of Science*, 1956, **67**, 123–164.

Lacey, J. I., & Lacey, Beatrice C. Verification and extension of the principle of autonomic response stereotypy. *American Journal of Psychology*, 1958, **71**, 50–73.

Lewis, A. J. The offspring of parents both mentally ill. *Acta Genetica*, 1957, **7**, 349–365.

Lidz, T., Wild, Cynthia, Schafer, Sarah, Rosenan, Bernice, & Fleck, S. Thought disorders in the parents of schizophrenic patients: A study utilizing the Object Sorting Test. *Journal of Psychiatric Research*, 1962, **1**, 193–200.

Lindsley, D. B. Emotion. In S. S. Stevens (Ed.), *Handbook of Experimental Psychology,* New York: Wiley, 1951, pp. 473–516.

McConaghy, N. The use of an object sorting test in elucidating the hereditary factor in schizophrenia. *Journal of Neurology, Neurosurgery and Psychiatry,* 1959, **22,** 243–246.

Malmo, R. B. Experimental studies of mental patients under stress. In M. L. Reymert (Ed.), *Feelings and emotions.* New York: McGraw-Hill, 1950, pp. 169–180.

Malmo, R. B. Measurement of drive: An unsolved problem in psychology. In M. R. Jones (Ed.). *Nebraska symposium on motivation.* Lincoln: University of Nebraska Press, 1958, pp. 44–105.

Malmo, R. B., & Shagass, C. Physiological studies of reaction to stress in anxiety states and early schizophrenia. *Psychosomatic Medicine,* 1949, **11,** 9–24.

Malmo, R. B., Shagass, C., & Smith, A. A. Responsiveness in chronic schizophrenia. *Journal of Personality,* 1951, **19,** 359–375.

Malmo, R. B., & Shagass, C. Studies of blood pressure in psychiatric patients under stress. *Psychosomatic Medicine,* 1952, **14,** 82–93.

Marrazzi, A. S., & Hart, E. R. The possible role of inhibition at adrenergic synapses in the mechanism of hallucinogenic and related drug actions. *Journal of Nervous and Mental Disease,* 1955, **122,** 453–457.

Meehl, P. E. Schizotaxia, schizotypy, schizophrenia. *American Psychologist,* 1962, **17,** 827–838.

Paintal, A. S. A comparison of the GSR in normals and psychotics. *Journal of Experimental Psychology,* 1951, **41,** 425–428.

Petursson, E. Electromyographic studies of muscular tension in psychiatric patients. *Comprehensive Psychiatry,* 1962, **3,** 29–36.

Pincus, G., & Hoagland, H. Adrenal cortical responses to stress in normal men and in those with personality disorders. I. Some stress responses in normal and psychotic subjects. *American Journal of Psychiatry,* 1950, **106,** 641–650.

Pishkin, V., & Hershiser, D. Respiration and GSR as functions of white sound in schizophrenia. *Journal of Consulting Psychology,* 1963, **27,** 330–337.

Planansky, K. Heredity in schizophrenia. *Journal of Nervous and Mental Disease,* 1955, **122,** 121–142.

Ray, T. S. Electrodermal indications of levels of psychological disturbance in chronic schizophrenia. *American Psychologist,* 1963, **18,** 393.

Rees, W. L. Physical characteristics of the schizophrenic patient. In D. Richter (Ed.) *Schizophrenia: Somatic aspects.* New York: MacMillan, 1957.

Reynolds, D. J. An investigation of the somatic response system in chronic schizophrenia. Unpublished doctoral dissertation, University of Pittsburgh, 1962.

Rosanoff, A. J., Handy, L. M., Plesset, I. R., & Brush, S. The etiology of so-called schizophrenic psychoses. *American Journal of Psychiatry,* 1934, **91,** 247–286.

Rosenbaum, G., Flenning, F., & Rosen, H. Effects of weight intensity on discrimination. *Journal of Abnormal Psychology,* 1965. In press.

Rosenthal, D. Some factors associated with concordance and discordance with respect to schizophrenia in monozygotic twins. *Journal of Nervous and Mental Disease,* 1959, **129,** 1–10.

Rosenthal, D. Problems of sampling and diagnosis in the major twin studies of schizophrenia. *Journal of Psychiatric Research,* 1962, **1,** 116–134.

Rubin, L. S. Patterns of pupillary dilatation and instruction in psychotic adults and autistic children. *Journal of Nervous and Mental Disease,* 1961, **133,** 130–142.

Rubin, L. S. Patterns of adrenergic-cholinergic imbalance in the functional psychoses. *Psychological Review,* 1962, **69,** 501–519.

Sands, D. E. Endocrine changes in schizophrenia. In D. Richter (Ed.) *Schizophrenia: Somatic aspects.* New York: MacMillan, 1957.

Selye, H. *The stress of life.* New York: McGraw-Hill, 1956.

Sheldon, W. H., Stevens, S. S., & Tucker, W. B. *The varieties of human physique.* New York: Harper & Row, 1940.

Shields, J., & Slater, E. Heredity and psychological abnormality. In H. J. Eysenck (Ed.) *Handbook of abnormal psychology.* New York: Basic Books, 1961.

Slater, E. The inheritance of manic-depressive insanity and its relation to mental defects. *Journal of Mental Science,* 1936, **82**, 626–633.

Slater, E. Psychiatry. In A. Sorsby (Ed.) *Clinical genetics.* London: Butterworth, 1953, 332–349.

Solomon, A. P., Darrow, C. W., & Blaurock, M. Blood pressure and palmar sweat (galvanic) responses of psychotic patients before and after insulin and metrazol therapy. *Psychosomatic Medicine,* 1939, **1**, 118–137.

Stern, C. *Principles of human genetics.* San Francisco: Freeman, 1960.

Tienari, P. Psychiatric illnesses in identical twins. *Acta Psychiatrica Scandinavica,* 1963, **39**, supplementum 171.

Weinberg, I., & Lobstein, J. Inheritance in schizophrenia. *Acta Psychiatrica Neurologica,* 1943, **18**, 93–140.

Wenger, M. A. *Evaluation of Project 6, Summary of Proceedings: Second Cooperative Psychological Research Conference.* Cincinnati: Veterans Administration Hospital, 1959.

Wenger, M. A., Jones, N. F., & Jones, M. H. *Physiological psychology.* New York: Holt, 1956.

Whatmore, G. B., & Ellis, R. M., Jr. Some motor aspects of schizophrenia: An EMG study. *American Journal of Psychiatry,* 1958, **114**, 882–889.

Whatmore, G. B., & Ellis, R. M., Jr. Some neurophysiologic aspects of schizophrenia: An electromyographic study. *American Journal of Psychiatry,* 1964, **120**, 1161–1169.

Wilder, J. The law of initial values. *Psychosomatic Medicine,* 1950, **12**, 392–401.

Williams, J. G. L. Use of a resonance technique to measure muscle activity in neurotic and schizophrenic patients. *Psychosomatic Medicine,* 1964, **26**, 20–28.

Williams, M. Psychophysiological responsiveness to psychological stress in early chronic schizophrenic reactions. *Psychosomatic Medicine,* 1953, **15**, 456–462.

Wishner, J. The concept of efficiency in psychological health and in psychopathology. *Psychological Review,* 1955, **62**, 69–80.

Wittman, Phyllis. Diagnostic and prognostic significance of the shut-in personality type as a prodromal factor in schizophrenia. *Journal of Clinical Psychology,* 1948, **4**, 211–214.

Woolley, D. W. *The biochemical bases of psychoses.* New York: Wiley, 1962.

Woolley, D. W., & Shaw, E. A biochemical and pharmacological suggestion about certain mental disorders. *Proceedings of the National Academy of Science,* 1954, **40**, 228–231.

Woolley, D. W., & Shaw, E. Evidence of the participation of serotonin in mental processes. *Annals of the New York Academy of Science,* 1957, **66**, 649.

Zahn, T. P., Rosenthal, D., & Lawlor, W. G. GSR orienting reactions to visual and auditory stimuli in chronic schizophrenic and normal subjects. *Psychophysiological Newsletter,* 1963, **9**, 48–50.

CHAPTER 15

Interpersonal and Social Approaches
to Psychosis

Man is a social animal. During infancy he requires parental assistance to survive biologically. Thereafter he requires relationships with his fellow man to survive psychologically. The first, and probably the most important, relationships occur in the family. Parents have the major share in socializing the child, in helping him to achieve a sense of reality and a sense of identity, and in meeting his needs for affection and attention. If the parents fail in these areas, it is reasonable to expect that the child will be psychologically damaged. If the impairment is sufficiently severe, the child will be disposed to become psychotic when he matures and must face the rigors of adult life. This, in very brief form is the *interpersonal approach*. It focuses on social relations and training within the family, and it identifies familial variables as determiners of psychosis.

The *social approach* deals with broader societal variables, for example, socioeconomic status. The individual is viewed as a member of society, more precisely of a particular stratum of society. His values, behaviors, and opportunities are in part determined by where he lives and his parents' place in the hierarchy of society. Those in disadvantaged positions are more likely to develop psychopathology because they face a much more difficult task in achieving their goals and in adapting to environmental requirements. Thus the emphasis is on extrafamilial variables in the social environment, especially on variables that can be assessed objectively and quantitatively. The social approach, as construed here, might also be called the *epidemiological* approach.

350

THE INTERPERSONAL APPROACH

Schizophrenia has been the focus of the interpersonal approach to psychosis, and the exposition will reflect this emphasis. The observations that require explanation are the schizophrenic's social withdrawal, poor contract with reality, and insecurity:

> The schizophrenic patient is inclined . . . to place a relatively low estimate on his personal power, to distrust himself, to experience the influence of others as emotionally coercive, and be somewhat moodily resentful of this imbalance. Now, it is a universal condition of human existence that we live *interdependently* in a social system characterized by *give and take* in personal leadership and cultural expectations; the schizophrenic, however, tends to avoid involvement with others and experiences a confused sense of frustration. In extreme moods he may react in desperate efforts to redress this imbalance by spasmodic self-assertion, actively or delusionally, but such efforts are likely to be poorly directed or ineptly sustained by reason of his basic self-distrust. More generally his attitude is manifested in passivity, lack of initiative, lack of hopeful expectation for the future, withdrawal, negativism, and resistance. Relationships with others tend to be reduced to watchful waiting. (Whitehorn, 1960, p. 76)

These characteristics occur ostensibly because of faulty personal relationships, which, in turn, are presumably due to defects in the family environment.

The Interpersonal Model

The interpersonal model of adjustment has two aspects. First, each person must develop a stable identity, which consists of feelings of trust of himself and of others, and a meaningful pattern of roles to play in society. Second, each person must be able to communicate with others, which requires an accurate perception of reality and the ability to send clear messages.

Identity. When parents are generous with their love and time spent with a child, the child can develop both a sense of being worthwhile and of trusting others. The feeling of self-worth can be acquired merely by imitating the parents' attitudes toward the child. If people as powerful and knowledgeable as his parents love him, then he must truly be lovable and intrinsically worthwhile. This positive evaluation of self serves as a foundation for continuing efforts to experience pleasure and to cope with rejection and failure in everyday life. Whatever the deficiencies in the child's abilities and whatever the tragedies and anxieties of daily living, the residual self-esteem laid down by parental affection should help in maintaining stability and equanimity. In brief, parental love and positive attitudes are major determiners of the child's ability to persevere in the face of defeat, to recover from a loss, and to face a world that is at times hostile, threatening, or rejecting.

Parental love and attention are also important in developing a sense of trust:

Mothers, I think, create a sense of trust in their children by that kind of administration which in its quality combines sensitive care of the baby's needs and a firm sense of personal trustworthiness within the trusted framework of their culture's life style. This forms the basis for a sense of identity. . . . (Erikson, 1950, p. 221)

Since man is a social being, he must find at least a few people whom he can rely on and regard without suspicion. The man who trusts no one lives in a threatening, dangerous world. Stability requires security from external threat, and ultimately this can be accomplished only by trusting those close to us.

Being able to trust others has its origin in parental love and attention. The absence of these weakens the child's sense of trust and self-esteeem. Parental rejection leads to the child's being pessimistic about his own abilities, which tends to make him passive and unable to initiate the activities needed for success in coping with life's challenges. Because of distrust of others, he will avoid close personal relationships and shy away from social interactions. Thus other things being equal, parental coldness and rejection predispose the child toward passivity and isolation, which may lead eventually to the social withdrawal and lack of affect characteristic of schizophrenia.

The process of adjustment, seen in interpersonal terms, consists of flexible role-taking. The adult must be prepared to play a variety of roles in everyday life and to be ready to switch from one to another as the occasion demands. In a single day he might move from a subordinate role in a conference with his boss, to a superordinate role in giving dictation to his secretary, to the familial roles of spouse and father in the home, and finally to the role of peer when neighbors visit.

From this perspective, the developmental sequence is a continuous process of acquiring new role behaviors and attitudes, and abandoning old ones. The young child is initially assigned the role of "baby of the family." Subsequently, he assumes a peer role with playmates and perhaps the role of parental helper. Eventually he will be expected to take roles involving varying degrees of status: leading, following, and equality.

An important determiner of adjustment is the individual's adequacy in role-taking, which is determined by three variables.

(1) *Talent:* Talent matters in role-playing only when the role is one

of leadership. The leader must be successful in competition, and this requires physical, social or intellectual ability. The roles of star athlete, lead debater, and successful officeholder all require at least some talent. However, if the individual is willing to accept a peer or subordinate role, then his physique, coordination, sociability, and intelligence need not be special. He needs little of these to be "one of the gang," whether it be in the home, school, or playground.

(2) *Models:* The models available for the child to copy are crucial to the development of sex roles and sex identification. Boys are at a disadvantage here because the male sex role appears to be more restrictive ("sissies" are regarded as being worse than "tomboys") and because child-rearing is mainly in the hands of women (mothers and women school teachers). Boys need an adult male model in order to assimilate the attitudes and behaviors of the male sex role in our society: toughness (being able to "take it"), sportsmanship, competitiveness. Girls need an adult model in order to develop the womanly attitudes of sexual attractiveness, compassion, and eventually, motherliness. Adequate models are necessary if the child is to acquire the roles appropriate to his age, sex, and status.

(3) *Parental Child-Rearing Practices:* Optimally, parents help the child to move from complete dependence in infancy to relative independence at maturity. The young child needs much attention and care; the older child and the adolescent require more freedom and independence. Some parents cannot grant the child increasing freedom from control as he matures. They continue to dominate and restrict the child, sometimes preventing the child from establishing good relations with peers. If the child does not fight such excessive parental domination, he may remain too dependent on his parents and fail to initiate independent social activities outside the home. Presumably, this tendency might lead to isolation from others and eventually, schizophrenia.

When all three determinants of role-playing—talent, models, and parental child-rearing practices—are favorable, the child should become a well-adjusted adult. He should be capable of playing a variety of socially approved roles, of moving easily from one role to another, and of initiating relationships outside the home.

When these three determinants of role-playing are unfavorable, the child may be disposed to become schizophrenic upon reaching adulthood. Only a small number of roles will be available to him, and he will be uncomfortable and inept in playing them. His sex identification will be diffuse and confused, and he will tend to be passive and lacking in initiative. He will be childlike in his reliance on others for assistance and in his relative inability to play responsible adult roles such as husband, father, or work leader. In brief, deficiencies in the learning of roles during childhood and adolescence tend to produce an emotionally apathetic adult who has too few roles available to him and who derives little satisfaction or security in playing them. Presumably, such a person will become schizophrenic with little environmental stress.

Communication. Communication includes both the sending of clear messages and the receiving of correct ones. The child must learn that there is a reality beyond himself, a reality he can depend on. Early in life the child's belief in his parent's omnipotence leads him to accept whatever they say as being literally true; this constitutes the beginning of a reality external to himself. If the parents interpret reality properly, distinguishing between legends and truths, the child should develop an adequate reality-testing mechanism.

Ideally, parental messages to the child are unequivocal; the child learns that "No" means just that. However, no set of parents can fully meet the ideal, and there are two sources of confusion in their communications. The first source, *vagueness,* is relatively harmless. The child is unsure of what he is being told because the parent's speech lacks precision; but eventually he comes to understand what is meant, and the messages can be received clearly regardless of how ambiguously they are sent.

The second source of confusion, *opposed messages,* is more serious. One part of the message may contradict the other part, or the vocal response may be contradicted by the facial and bodily response. In addition to simultaneously opposed messages, communications in sequence may oppose one another, for example, "Come kiss your mother," followed by "Your filthy hands dirtied my dress." Lastly, one parent's message may be contradicted by the other's message; the child can never be sure that the original communication will not be reversed by a later one from the other parent.

These various sources of confusion tend to produce a wary, uncertain child who seeks in vain a consistent set of incoming stimuli from the major figures in his life. He has difficulty in developing an enduring sense of reality because parental reality is ambiguous or contradictory. Eventually he tends to become suspicious that "things are not what they seem." Such a child, with only a tenuous grasp of reality, is disposed to become schizophrenic upon reaching adulthood.

The first investigators in this area tended to be psychoanalytic, and this led to a focusing on the oral period and the mother-infant relationship. Beyond infancy, the mother has the major responsibility of training the child, and to the extent that child-rearing practices lead to later schizophrenia, it appeared reasonable to blame the mother. This mother-blaming tendency was enhanced by clinicians who were too ready to accept the stories of maternal rejection and cruelty told by their schizophrenic patients. Mothers may be *schizophrenogenic* (tending to promote schizophrenia) in relation to their children, but we must demand better evidence than recitals of past history by schizophrenics.

Later investigators began to examine the father's role in the family of the schizophrenic patient. The most recent work has tended to involve the entire family, or at least both parents of the patient, and some researchers have insisted that schizophrenia can be understood only in the context of the interpersonal relationships among *all* members of the family. This brief history of research on the familial variables in schizophrenia brings us to the evidence itself. The exposition will follow the historical sequence: mothers, fathers, and then families.

Mothers

An obvious first step in attempting to discover the mother-child relationships involved in schizophrenia is to interview mothers of schizophrenics. This was done by a number of researchers (Gerard & Siegel, 1950; Reichard & Tillman, 1950; Tietze, 1949; Galvin, 1956; Limentani, 1956; and Lidz & Fleck, 1960). The picture that emerged was confusing and contradictory. Mothers were found to be both overprotective and rejecting, both overtly and subtly hostile, both neglectful of the child and intrusive into his activities, and both unduly and insufficiently restrictive.

There were two faults in these interview studies. First, most of them lacked a control group—mothers of normals. Second, the results were based on the interviewer's interpretations of the mother's verbalizations, which leaves room for interviewer bias. It is possible that these faults led to the contradictory results, and we must reserve judgment until the results of more rigorous studies can be examined.

Such studies have been carried out using questionnaires. The major impetus for this research was a report by Mark (1953), who compared the child-rearing beliefs of mothers of hospitalized schizophrenics with the beliefs of mothers of hospitalized normals. Mothers of schizophrenics were found to be more controlling and restrictive, but also more detached and more affectionate, devoted, and close to their children. Mark suggested that mothers of schizophrenics show pronounced ambivalence toward their children, being more loving and less involved than the mothers of normals.

These findings were partially corroborated by Freeman and Grayson (1955) who found that mothers of schizophrenics were more possessive and ignored their children more than did mothers of normals. Freeman followed up this study (Freeman, Simmons, & Berger, 1959) but failed to replicate it. Specifically, the items measuring possessiveness failed to check out; mothers of schizophrenics were not significantly more possessive than mothers of normals. Furthermore there was a negative correlation between possessiveness and education, and the authors suggested that the positive results in the first study may have stemmed from the lower socioeconomic status of the mothers.

Subsequently Shaefer and Bell (1958) developed the Parental Attitude Research Instrument (PARI) which has become the standard tool for research in this area. Zuckerman and his colleagues standardized the PARI and applied it to several populations (1958, 1960). Mothers of schizophrenics showed significantly less strictness than mothers of normals, but the most inportant result was the relationship between parental attitudes and educational level. The less educated the mother, the more authoritarian and controlling were her reported child-rearing practices. These findings were corroborated by Tolor and Rafferty 1963, who noted that with educational level controlled, mothers of schizophrenics were still more controlling and less strict than mothers of normals.

Clearly socioeconomic status and educational level of mothers importantly determine child-rearing attitudes. This conclusion is strengthened by other studies (Heilbrun, 1961; Garfield & Helper, 1962). Nevertheless, one difference does emerge in addition to education: mothers of schizophrenics report being more smothering, more restrictive, and in general fostering more dependency than mothers of normals.

Heilbrun (1960) investigated the beliefs of schizophrenic women concerning their mothers' child-rearing practices; the mothers also completed the PARI. On the basis of the mothers' reports there were no significant differences in child-rearing practices between mothers of schizophrenics and mothers of normals. The schizophrenics reported their mothers as being significantly more authoritarian and controlling than did the normal daughters. Garmezy, Clarke, and Stockner (1961) supplemented these data with material on schizophrenic males. Poor premorbid men reported more maternal dominance in their families than did good premorbids, who reported paternal dominance.

The only unequivocal finding to emerge from these investigations is that schizophrenics' mothers tend to be more controlling than mothers of normals. This fact may be interpreted in two ways. First, this over-restrictiveness may make it more difficult for the child to mature, to initiate new activities, to socialize, and in general to make his way in the world in a normal fashion. Consequently, the child has tendencies that may lead to schizophrenia.

The second interpretation assumes that the preschizophrenic child is *initially* deviant, and the mother's overcontrol is a *response* to the child's abnormal tendencies. The mother's response is presumably the kind of reaction we would expect to *any* deviance or illness in her child. For example, if the child had a chronic heart ailment, the mother would be forced to be restrictive and overcontrolling. This view is supported by Klebanoff's research (1959) with mothers of schizophrenics, brain-injured and retarded children, and normals. On the PARI the mothers of the non-normal children were all more possessive than the mothers of normals. Klebanoff suggested that mothers confronted with disturbed behavior in their children would develop similar attitudes, regardless of the nature of the disturbed behavior. Thus maternal attitudes toward preschizophrenic children may be an *effect* not a *cause*.

Fathers

Inspecting the role of fathers of schizophrenics has been part of the general trend toward *family interaction* as the major determiner of schizophrenia. After all, fathers play a role in child-rearing, and they must serve as a masculine model for their sons.

Fathers have been described in interview studies as insecure in their masculinity, weak and ineffectual, vacillating, and alternating between petty tyranny and helplessness (Lidz & Fleck, 1960). The major study that focused exclusively on the father (Lidz, Cornelison, Fleck, & Terry, 1957) derived five different paternal roles.

(1) The father is in conflict with his wife and is inconsistent with his children. If the daughter sides with the father, she usually becomes psychotic. She is prevented from identifying with her mother and taking a normal feminine role by the father's hostility toward the mother.

(2) The father is hostile toward the children and competes with them for the mother's attention. The children are confused and frightened by such competition, and they are insecure and wary.

(3) The father is a failure and is a nonentity in the home. The children may imitate him, thus acquiring nonadaptive patterns of behavior.

(4) The father has an exalted self-concept, and he remains aloof and isolated from the family. The wife often admires her husband but makes no effort to draw him into the mainstream of family life. The children are in effect deprived of their father.

(5) The father is passive and dominated by his wife. He provides a poor model for his sons and is resentful of the mother's pampering of the sons. Too weak to assert paternal authority, he retreats into malicious and sullen resentment.

The problem with research on the fathers of schizophrenics, as well as the interview studies mentioned earlier, is that control groups tend to be conspicuously absent. It is a rare study that compares the fathers of schizophrenics with the fathers of normals, the latter being difficult to obtain. Farahmand (1961) solved the problem by comparing fathers of schizophrenics with father's brothers, none of whom had schizophrenic children. Questionnaire results indicated that the schizophrenics' fathers were aggressive, punitive, and demanding, and less accepting, comradely, and permissive than their brothers. These findings raise the same issue that arose with the results for mothers: are the father's attitudes the cause or the effect of his child's deviance?

It is possible that neither parent, taken alone, is an important determiner of the children's later deviant behavior. Perhaps what is crucial is the *parental interaction,* not the isolated behaviors and attitudes of each parent.

Family Dynamics

Earlier the chapter introduced the communication approach to schizophrenia. This approach emphasizes the cognitive aspects of schizophrenia: a retreat into fantasy, inability to distinguish real from unreal or fantasied events, and hallucinations. These symptoms are presumably learned in a family that inadvertently forces the preschizophrenic child to accept and send confused and confusing messages.

The role-taking approach, also introduced earlier, focuses on the schizophrenic's social withdrawal. His isolation from others is ostensibly the result of inconsistent patterns of affection and rejection within the family. The isolation itself then leads to deviant thinking and other cognitive symptoms.

Thus the two approaches identify different fundamental causes of schizophrenia: the *direct* acquisition of irrationality because of communication problems with the family versus the *indirect* acquisition of irrationality through social isolation, which in turn is caused by faulty interactions within the family.

Communications. The flavor of this approach may be seen in a quotation from Lidz et al. (1957).

. . . the schizophrenic patient is more prone to withdraw through his symbolization of reality than other patients, because his foundation in reality is precarious, having been raised amidst irrationality and chronically exposed to intra-familial communications that distort and deny what should be the obvious interpretation of the environment, including the recognition and understanding of impulses and the affective behavior of members of the family. (p. 307)

Everyday normal interaction requires that individuals communicate with one another. Such communication requires fairly unequivocal messages sent by one person to another who can receive them clearly. It is precisely here that schizophrenics fail miserably. They manifest what Haley (1959) has called "an incongruence between elements of the message." This incongruence may show up in four different ways: source, message, receiver, and context. First, the schizophrenic may indicate that he really is not the *source* of the message, that he is only transmitting someone else's idea, that someone is influencing him or using his vocal cords as a transmitter of messages. Second, the schizophrenic may indicate that his words are not really a *message,* that is, he may talk gibberish or more often confuse the literal with the metaphorical meanings of messages. Third, the schizophrenic, when he receives a message, denies being the *receiver;* for example, by insisting that the person to whom he is talking is someone else. Thus he prevents any communication. This is seen most clearly in paranoid delusions such as "You are a member of the FBI, and you are after me." Fourth, the *context* in which the communication occurs is mislabeled by the patient, who insists that he is not in a hospital but in a palace or some other place.

How does an individual get this way? What sort of training is required in order to start out with what might be a normal child and turn out with a schizophrenic who is unable to send or to receive unequivocal messages. One answer may be found in the communication theory espoused by several different authors. To begin with, it is necessary to understand that most communications occur on at least two levels. What a person says and does are usually qualified by other things that he says, by his tone of voice, and bodily movements. All of these aspects of communication can qualify one another, sometimes enhancing, sometimes negating. A special problem occurs when they tend to negate one another. This problem is called the *double bind.*

Bateson et al. (1956) assume that in the family of schizophrenics the following characteristics are conducive to the double bind situation: (1) the child has a mother who is seductive or at least makes a loving approach to the child, and then withdraws as soon as the child responds to her; (2) the mother has feelings of both anxiety and hostility toward the child, neither of which is acceptable to her; and (3) there is no one in the family (for example, a strong, insightful father) who can intervene to support the child in the face of contradictory communications.

The mother usually expresses at least two opposing messages: hostile and withdrawing versus simulated loving or approaching. She uses the child's responses to affirm that her behavior is loving, thereby convincing herself that she is really a good mother. However, because the affection is simulated, the child cannot accurately interpret her communication if he is to maintain an adequate relationship with her. If the child correctly discriminates her conflicting signals, he must face the fact that she does not want him and is deceiving him by her loving behavior. This means he must deceive himself in order to support her in her deception. In order to survive with her, he must falsely discriminate his own internal messages and falsely discriminate the messages of others. The child is punished for discriminating both accurately and inaccurately: he is caught in a double bind. If he tries to respond to the simulated affection, the mother's anxiety will be aroused and she will punish him. However, if he does not make any overtures of affection, she feels threatened because it is a denial that she is loving. Such a denial arouses her anxiety, and she punishes the child for not making affectionate responses.

The double bind hypothesis has the following ingredients: two or more people, repeated experience, a primary negative injunction ("do not or I will punish"), a secondary injunction conflicting with the first at a more abstract level and, like the first, enforced by punishment or signals which threaten some kind of punishment (posture, gesture, or tone of voice), and a third negative injunction prohibiting the victim from escaping from the field. The complete set of ingredients is no longer necessary when the victim has learned to perceive his universe in double bind patterns. Almost any part of the sequence may then be sufficient to precipitate a panic. What the panic is about may be stated in conflict terms. The individual, receiving conflicting messages, has no clear course of action. Whatever he does, he will be punished.

The double bind is simply a communications way of construing the kind of conflict situation that might occur in the laboratory, that is, in experimental neurosis a discrimination is made impossible for an animal and then the animal's whole behavioral repertoire breaks down. The analogue is a good one, the only difference being in the details. For the animal the discrimination is usually between two different physical stimuli; for the child the stimuli to be discriminated are verbal and occur in an interpersonal situation.

The communication approach taken by Haley (1959) is somewhat broader, including other aspects of the interpersonal situation. He agrees with Bateson et al. in their double bind approach, but emphasizes the negation of the message of one member of the family by another. Thus different members of the family are consistently disqualifying what one another says. Typically if one says something, another indicates that it should not have been said or that it was said poorly. Since members of the family negate their own and one another's communications, any clear leadership in the family is impossible. For example, the mother may tend to initiate what happens, while indicating either that she is not doing this or that someone else should. The father will invite her to initiate something and then condemn her when she does. Often they suggest to the child that he take the lead and then disqualify any attempts of the child at leadership.

The family coalition against the outside world tends to break down rapidly. The family is unable to form any kind of alliance even within itself. The members behave as if any kind of alliance between two of them is a betrayal to the third person, and in general they seem to have difficulty functioning in any two-person relationship. What confines members so rigidly within their system is the prohibition against any alliance of one member with someone either inside or outside the membership, especially with someone outside the family. Thus members are prohibited from learning to relate to people outside the home and are confined within their own system of interaction.

Both the inability of the schizophrenic to relate to other people and his withdrawal behavior seem understandable in the context of a family situation in which: (a) whatever he did was disqualified by another member of the family, and (b) he was not allowed to relate to other people and thereby learn to behave differently. In brief, what is ostensibly unique about schizophrenic behavior is the incongruence of all levels of communication in social interactions.

Lidz et al. (1958), while accepting the double bind approach, have a different way of handling the development of schizophrenic thinking and speech:

> . . . our patients were not raised in families that adhered to culturally accepted ideas of causality and meanings, or respected the instrumental utility of their ideas or communications, because one or both parents were forced to abandon rationality to defend their own precarious ego structure. (1958, p. 315)

Lidz and his colleagues observed that the parents of schizophrenics maintain their own adjustment by limiting the environment and by rigidly preconceiving reality. It is necessary for them to retain a particular picture of themselves and their families in order to survive in society. The child must then imitate his parents and accept the parental evaluation of reality, or reject it and feel unwanted. Often the child must negate his own needs to support parental defenses. The real world must be denied and the child's reality distorted. The child is caught between the environment as it exists and parental interpretations of it. In other words, the child must accept mutually contradictory experiences, and this acceptance inevitably leads to distorted thinking.

Rigid defenses make the parents *impervious:* the parents listen but do not hear, and they are oblivious to all the unspoken aspects of communication. They exclude all aspects of verbal communications but those they need for their own defensive systems. They tend to use cliches and stereotypes to simplify the environment. For example they may label a child "the selfish one" or "the quiet one," toward whom they behave solely on the basis of these stereotypes.

The communication approach offers a plausible explanation of how the cognitive symptoms of schizophrenia are acquired. Incorrect and unrealistic reception of messages can be learned by *imitation,* which at least one parent being a deviant model for the child. In addition, contradictory messages from and between the parents place the child in the intolerable position of having to cope with at least two "realities." There is no reliable social consensus he can turn to, no foundation for testing the correctness of his perception of reality. Small wonder that the children of such families later become schizophrenics!

But do they? In the families observed by various communication theorists there was always at least one schizophrenic, but there were usually nonschizophrenic siblings, also. If the intrafamily pattern of communication is a determiner of schizophrenia, how did these siblings escape psychosis?

A related question pertains to normal families: are there communication problems in the families of normal children? Communication research has not answered this question because it has usually lacked control groups consisting of the families of normals. Nevertheless, it seems likely that no normal family is free of ambivalence and ambiguity in communication. The mother and father usually send out slightly different messages to their children, and either parent must at times qualify and negate his statements, either verbally or nonverbally. Surely, there are some normal families whose communications are as faulty as those described above. Why do the children not become schizophrenic?

One answer is that the normal child does not accept the faulty communications. He fights against being placed in a double bind and, if necessary, seeks his basic reality outside the family. The preschizophrenic child, however, accepts the double bind and is started on the road to psychosis. If this explanation is correct, then the family cannot be the crucial variable in schizophrenia. A poor family environment, acting on a potentially normal child, does not produce a schizophrenic. There must be some predisposition in the child which, when acted on by such variables as the double bind, leads to schizophrenia; otherwise *all* the children in a double bind family would become schizophrenic. The predisposition might be determined by either genetic factors or early familial factors.

Roles and Interpersonal Interactions. Lidz and his collaborators, in their study of the families of upper middle class schizophrenics (1957), formulated an interpersonal basis for the development of schizophrenia. They divided the families into those showing *schism,* and those showing *skew.*

The parents in a family showing *schism* resemble those seen in a divorce court. They show the following characteristics: recurrent threats of separation, antagonism of the spouses, derogation of one parent by the other parent, defiance of one parent by the other, one parent's seeking to coerce the other but being defied by the victim, one parent's ignoring the needs of the other, failure to share problems or satisfaction, competition for the children's loyalty and affections (sometimes to replace lost affections and sometimes to hurt the other spouse), and finally mutual distrust.

The child may react to this parental bickering and schism in one of four ways. First, he may fill the role of scapegoat, one whose difficulties preoccupy the parents and mask their basic dissatisfaction with each other. Second, he may insert himself into the split, seeking to widen the gap and gain one parent for himself. Third, he may devote attention to bridging the gap between the parents, dividing his loyalties, straddling the issues, and seeking to become a different person for each parent in order to fill the emotional needs of both. If he attempts to do this, he will have to give up his own independence completely. Fourth, he may be caught in a bind in which loyalty to one parent means rejection by the other. Because of opposing standards, he cannot satisfy one parent without arousing dissatisfaction and hostility in the other. The reasons why any particular child is caught in this marital schism of the parents are hard to state. All that is known is that once the preschizophrenic child does become involved in any of these four ways, this involvement relieves the other children in the family of much of the burden of dealing with their warring parents.

What happens to the child who is torn by this parental dissension? There are three possibilities. First, the child will probably not be able to model himself after one parent because to do so would antagonize the other parent. This, of course, will lead to faulty identification. Second, he will develop conflicting interpretations of reality because the interpretations suggested by one parent will be countered and negated by those of the other parent. Third, there will be excessive oedipal problems, because the child may be used by one parent to replace the other spouse or be used as a pawn in order to hurt the other parent. The parents fail to provide a satisfactory family environment because they cannot form a coalition as members of the parental generation and thereby maintain their appropriate sex-linked roles which are separate from those of the next generation. This failure to maintain boundaries between generations is one of the reasons for the development of bizarre oedipal problems. To maintain approval of the parent of the opposite sex, the child seeks to differentiate himself rather than identify with the parent of the same sex, and, lacking a positive sex-linked model which is necessary to gain maturity, he fails to develop the proper sex roles as a man or a woman. The parent of the opposite sex typically uses the child as a replacement for the unsatisfactory spouse, that is, in order to fill his own emotional needs, and this interferes with the child's development as an independent person.

In *skew* the serious pathology of one parent dominates the home, and the dependent spouse supports the weaknesses and pathology of the dominant parent. The dependent spouse gratifies the other's needs and forces the family to go along with a deviant interpretation of reality and the deviant model presented by the dominant parent. Potential sources of conflict are completely masked, and there is a denial of any difficulty. Thus the child gets a distorted view of reality and a model of parents that the child knows vaguely to be incorrect or at least incomplete. Lidz et al. found that the schizophrenic children of skewed families were predominately males. In these families the serious personality problems of the dominant parent were not countered by the spouse. The patient was the object of a particular intrusiveness by the dominant parent, who was usually the mother. This intrusiveness usually blurred the boundaries between parent and child and tied the patient to the dominant parent's deviant needs. The close tie with the mother is especially destructive for boys, who need to break clear of maternal domination and begin to assume a male identity based on imitation of the father. Their inability to do so because of the domination and the close tie to the mother leads to a confusion of sexual identity and excessive incestuous wishes.

This pattern of the skewed family is most nearly like what has been described, especially by earlier investigators, as the typical pattern of a schizophrenogenic mother and her preschizophrenic child. In this pattern the mother is demanding, excessively close to the child, and overly restrictive. In these early investigations the schizophrenics were almost exclusively men, which leads to a speculation concerning sex differences. Perhaps schizophrenic men and women differ sharply in their role difficulties. Cheek (1964) observed the familial interaction of schizophrenics and normal controls. Male schizophrenics manifested less dominance and activity (the equivalent of more withdrawal) than normal men. Female schizophrenics, on the other hand, were more dominant and active than normal women. Thus both male and female schizophrenics were deviant in their role-taking, the men being too passive and the women too active.

Fleck et al. (1963) reported similar role deviations in their schizophrenic sample and related them to disturbances in the family:

> We found that schizophrenic males often came from skewed families with passive, ineffectual fathers and disturbed, engulfing mothers, whereas schizophrenic girls typically grew up in schismatic families with narcissistic fathers who were often paranoid and, while seductive of the daughter, were disparaging of women, and with mothers who were unempathic and emotionally distant. (p. 6)

These authors suggest that family constellation alone is not sufficient to produce schizophrenia, which occurs only when a specific family pattern interacts with a child of specific gender. This notion may reconcile the discrepant findings concerning mothers and fathers of schizophrenics. If the hypothesis is correct, siblings of the same sex as the schizophrenic should be more disturbed than those of the opposite sex. Fleck et al. report that this is precisely what they found in their sample. Thus the skew versus schism dichotomy may have some validity.

Lu (1962) has formulated a *quadruple bind* theory to supplement the double bind theory of Bateson et al. (1956). Lu suggests that there are two sets of binds. One set consists of the parents' contradictory expectations of dependence and independence and the other, of the child's attempts to fulfill these expectations. She believes three conditions favor the development of schizophrenic symptoms in lower class American families: (1) contradictory parental expectations regarding dependence and independence, coupled with the child's persistent efforts to comply with both, that is, the *quadruple bind;* (2) certain expectations at birth or during infancy which incline both the parents and the preschizophrenic child to interact in these contradictory ways; and (3) certain sociocultural situations which heighten to the critical point the conflict between dependence and independence.

Concerning dependence, parents of preschizophrenic children expect a higher degree of obedience and submission from these children than from the nonschizophrenic siblings. The parents attempt to exercise authority over both the schizophrenic and nonschizophrenic child, but the schizophrenic child tends to be more passive and more dependent than his nonschizophrenic siblings. There is a generalized attitude on the part of the parent that the child must be perfect, that he must be upwardly mobile in a social sense, that he must achieve:

. . . parents always expected and even insisted that their preschizophrenic children be perfect, be the best, and be on top among their peers either educationally, occupationally, socially, or as a person. (1962, p. 222)

In addition to these generalized parental attitudes, there are attitudes toward concrete and specific tasks such as the handling of money, and household tasks. The preschizophrenic child tries desperately to live up to parental expectations that are naturally in conflict. He is expected to be obedient and dependent but also to achieve. Lu suggests that the generalized expectations play a prominent role for a long time before the development of symptoms, and then the specific concrete tasks occurring at a particular time, usually in adolescence, help precipitate the schizophrenic break.

The parents of these children tend to be more competitive with them in terms of status, power, and possessions than they are with the nonschizophrenic siblings. This competition adds another dimension to the parental bind. The child must be submissive, achieving, and also competitive with the parents.

What happens is that throughout childhood the preschizophrenic child can often live up to parental expectations for both obedience and achievement. However, the American culture deplores dependence, and as this child grows into adolescence there are pressures, usually from outside the family, for him to become more independent. Furthermore, competition becomes keener in adolescence; it is no longer as easy for the preschizophrenic child to achieve and to be at the top of his class. As he fails to meet these excessively high parental expectations, the child begins to sense his own failure, and this feeling of failure is enhanced by the praise his parents are beginning to give to the nonschizophrenic siblings.

The direct cause of the break is often a sudden demand for adult responsibility. There is often an increased financial or household burden, such as might happen if a parent were to leave, if the family moved, or if there were severe financial reverses in the family, and the child had to assume a major share of the load. Another direct cause is a loss of peers or other friends as a basis of emotional support. Friends move or enter the armed services, or the family of the preschizophrenic child moves. It is interesting to note in this context that the preschizophrenic child has usually been able to maintain at least some tenuous relationships, which served to offer some support beyond the family. Thus he was not a social isolate.

Why do the parents expect more of the preschizophrenic child? Lu speculates that as an infant the preschizophrenic child was often sick, often unusually large, or sometimes youngest. In other words, he had a rather special place in the family. Second, there was often tension between the parents or hardships in the home at the time of the birth of this particular child. Third, the preschizophrenic child was often slower in developing or more passive as a child and needed more adult help, and was therefore special among the other children.

These speculations have been supported by Pollin et al. (1965), who investigated identical male twins discordant for schizophrenia:

(1) The twin who became schizophrenic weighed less at birth. (2) He was perceived by his parents, particularly the mother, as vulnerable and his survival as imperiled. (3) In consequence, he was the focus of and recipient of more worry, involvement, and attention than the co-twin. (4) Early development was somewhat slower than the co-twin. (5) During successive stages of development, he tended to perform less successfully and to be perceived as the less competent, less capable, and less strong of the twins. (6) He tended to be the more docile and compliant of the two, was less independent, and had difficulty in achieving any degree of autonomy and separateness. (p. 66)

These findings greatly strengthen the interpersonal approach to psychosis because they supply a missing link. Earlier we noted that a vicious family environment could not fully explain the subsequent development of schizophrenia because rarely does more than one child in a schizophrenogenic family become psychotic. The child who does succumb must have some predisposition which renders him especially susceptible to a vicious family environment. Lu's hypothesis suggests that the predisposition consists of a special role in the family, that of the weak, sickly child who requires greater parental care. This explains why one child becomes the focus of poor parental practices and therefore moves in the direction of schizophrenia, whereas the siblings escape.

We have been concerned with schizophrenia in general rather than specific symptoms. Cameron (1943, 1947, 1959) has attempted to describe the development of delusions. He starts by assuming that the normal individual reacts to insecurity and threat by discussing the situation with someone he trusts. This person need not be a member of his family. By sharing his problems and anxieties, he can discover how realistic they are and perhaps obtain help in solving them. If he is to communicate with and understand others, he must be able to assume a variety of roles. Thus the basic assumption is that, ". . . skill in interpreting the attitudes and intents of another person depends chiefly upon skill in role-taking, since it is only by taking another person's role that we gain his perspective and see things approximately as he sees them" (Cameron, 1947, p. 437).

The potential delusional person is too isolated and deficient in role-taking to communicate or to gain perspective. In the face of threat or insecurity, he sees danger all around him and begins to imagine nonexistent changes. Those around him are organized into a fantasied or false community of persons who are endangering him; they constitute the *paranoid pseudocommunity*. The sole basis for his classifying unrelated persons in the same group is his incorrect assumption that their behavior and intentions all center on him. This pseudocommunity thus explains to him what would otherwise be unrelated events and actions, and this "explanation" is the delusion. Cameron's point is that the delusion can be traced back to deficient role-taking.

Comment

The interpersonal approach assumes that the schizophrenic is both deficient in role-taking and isolated from others. The isolation leads to a variety of cognitive symptoms, including delusions. Is there a single pattern of family interaction that leads to social withdrawal? The answer appears to be no. Schizophrenics seem to come from families of varying interpersonal patterns.

Weinberg (1960) suggests that the single common feature is the schizophrenic's feeling that he has been rejected and manipulated by his family. However, this interpretation, like the observations of familial patterns mentioned earlier, is made without reference to neurotics or normals. Many neurotics and normals feel rejected and manipulated, and surely many of their families manifest the same patterns seen in the families of schizophrenics. This is a repeated problem in research on the family background of schizophrenia: failure to include appropriate control groups. The absence of adequate controls makes it difficult to evaluate the evidence because the features seen in the families of schizophrenics might also occur in the families of normals or neurotics.

The symptom emphasized by the interpersonal approach is the schizophrenic's social isolation. Is this isolation the result of a vicious intrafamilial environment? The positions reviewed above assume that it is, the evidence being the presence of much bickering and conflict in the families of schizophrenics. However, it is possible that many schizophrenics are social isolates from the start and that family interaction does not cause this isolation but merely reflects it. Other schizophrenics, prior to the onset of the psychosis, may be no more isolated than normals.

These speculations are supported by two studies. Kohn and Clausen (1955) found that approximately one-third of a sample of adult schizophrenics had been social isolates during adolescence; the other two-thirds were not isolates, and none of the normals was an isolate. Thus social withdrawal in adolescence is not necessarily a predisposing factor in schizophrenia. Furthermore, the family patterns of the isolated schizophrenics were not different from those of the nonisolated schizophrenics. This suggests that faulty familial interactions do not necessarily result in social withdrawal.

Prout and White (1956) compared schizophrenics with nonpsychotic siblings. As children, the schizophrenics were found to be less social and more sensitive than their siblings, who were more independent, rebellious, and outgoing. There were painful events during the adolescence of many of the schizophrenics, but these were experiences common to most adolescents. The authors suggested that the mother attempted to overprotect and dominate the preschizophrenic child, and she succeeded. When she made similar attempts with the normal subject, he rebelled. Again the crucial difference appears to reside not in the parent-child interaction but in what the child was to begin with and in how he reacted to this interaction.

It seems clear that faulty family relationships are not sufficient to produce schizophrenia. There must be a predisposition, which itself may be the result of earlier family problems. Lu (1962) suggested that the preschizophrenic child might occupy a special place in the family because he is in some way unique. Once this special role is assigned, the child would be the only one to be caught in a quadruple bind and the only one eventually to become schizophrenic. This speculation answers the question of why only certain children in a family become schizophrenic. It is because they have accidently become the focus of parental conflicts and expectations and therefore the victims of the family's interpersonal problems.

An alternate assumption is that the predisposition is inherited. Specifically, the preschizophrenic child is presumably different from his siblings in sociability, attention, thinking, and independence. His special role in the family is not accidental; it is determined by the deviant behavior he displays in the home. He no doubt succumbs more easily to parental dominance because he is weak, passive, and incapable of dealing with threat. These characteristics ostensibly stem from an inherited temperament, which, together with a tendency toward cognitive difficulties, is the predisposition to schizophrenia. This view involves biological and interpersonal approaches. The predisposition is an inherited biological defect, but the precipitating variable is faulty family interaction. This is essentially Meehl's position (1962), as stated in the last chapter.

This issue bears on the process-reactive distinction. Let us assume that all schizophrenics have an inherited predisposition (the biological defect) which will lead to schizophrenia, even in a benign family environment. In the absence of family strife, the schizophrenic would be of the *reactive* type, which is defined in part by positive family features. Family strife would lead to a more severe and chronic type, the *process* schizophrenic. Thus the difference between process and reactive schizophrenics might reside in the adequacy of parental relationships.

Suppose the family consists of a passive father, a dominant mother, and preschizophrenic boy. The boy would not be able to identify with his weak father and would be trapped into an excessively close tie with his mother. He should become a severe (process) schizophrenic. When the father is dominant and the mother passive, the constellation is relatively benign. The preschizophrenic boy should be able to identify with his father, and he should become a mild schizophrenic, that is, reactive.

These are precisely the predictions made by Farina (1960). Parents of schizophrenics and normals were observed in a setting that revealed patterns of dominance and passivity. The parents of the normals were roughly equal in dominance, but the parents of the schizophrenics were unequal. The fathers of the reactive schizophrenics were dominant and the mothers, passive; but the mothers of the process schizophrenics were dominant and the fathers, passive. An incidental finding was the presence of more conflict between parents of the patients than between parents of the normals. These results were corroborated in a follow-up study (Farina & Dunham, 1963), which also found more conflict between parents of the process schizophrenics than between parents of the reactive schizophrenics. The presence of more conflict in parents of schizophrenics than in parents of neurotics and normals has also been observed by Fisher et al. (1959).

These studies support the hypothesis that family dynamics determine whether the schizophrenic will be process or reactive. Note that the hypothesis assumes that a predisposed child will eventually become at least a mild (reactive) schizophrenic even in the best family environment. This position relegates the family to a lesser role in schizophrenia, that is, a poor family environment is neither a necessary nor a sufficient condition for schizophrenia, but only a variable that increases its severity. Needless to say, most of the authors cited in this chapter would disagree with this position.

One aspect of the process-reactive issue that remains an enigma is the fear reaction of schizophrenics to each parent. As we saw in Chapter 10, process schizophrenics greatly fear their mothers and reactives fear their fathers. If mothers play the major role in dominating children who later become process schizophrenics, the patients have good reason to be upset by their mothers. Why, then, do reactive schizophrenics fear their fathers

but not their mothers? One possibility is that the father is the schizophrenogenic agent in reactive schizophrenia; his influence is less deleterious than
that of the mother, and the outcome is a more benign kind of schizophrenic
offspring—reactive. This speculation can be checked by studying the family
patterns of process and reactive patients. However, the hypothesis has only
an outside chance of being correct because it is difficult to believe that
all the differences between process and reactive schizophrenics are determined by which parent was schizophrenogenic.

A final point on family dynamics concerns heredity. The last chapter
provided abundant evidence that there is an inherited component in schizophrenia. This means that one parent of the preschizophrenic child is likely
to have schizophrenic tendencies. As we have seen, the parents of schizophrenics tend to be more disturbed, more deviant, and in greater conflict
than the parents of normals. Parental abnormality may make the child abnormal, and most of the theories considered here make this assumption.
However, an alternate assumption is also possible: parental abnormality
merely represents what would be expected if schizophrenia is inherited, and
this abnormality does not contribute *environmentally* to the child's later
schizophrenia. Since the parents who pass on their genes to the children
are the same ones who rear the children, it is difficult to test this hypothesis.
The only way to check it out would be to examine children of schizophrenics
who have been reared in foster homes with normal foster parents. So far
this has not been done. In any event, the hypothesis is too radical for most
psychologists, who believe there is enough evidence to indict the family as
one determiner of schizophrenia.

BROKEN HOMES AND MARITAL STATUS

As noted earlier, the social approach is roughly synonymous with the
epidemiological approach. Epidemiology is the study of the occurrence and
distribution of disease in different populations. The basic idea is to discover
where diseases flourish and under which circumstances they occur. Such
knowledge is of great importance in understanding disease, as has been demonstrated for a number of medical diseases. For example, the fact that ciga-
rette smokers have a higher incidence of lung cancer than nonsmokers impli-
cates certain chemicals (products of burning tobacco) as determiners of
cancer.

Epidemiology, as it has applied to psychopathology, has focused mainly
on such broad variables as residence, income, religion, education, and vocation. These are extrafamilial variables, in contrast to those discussed in the
last section, which were exclusively intrafamilial. However, epidemiology
has not neglected the family entirely, for there are familial variables
amenable to this approach. Broken homes and marital status, for example,

can be determined objectively, and their association with psychopathology can be ascertained. The discussion of these variables may serve as a bridge between the clinical study of families discussed in the last section and the sociological study of societal variables to be discussed shortly.

Broken Homes

At the beginning of the chapter we outlined an interpersonal model of adjustment, noting variables that might lead to psychosis, and in the last section we saw that the influence of both parents is assumed to be of great importance in the development of psychosis. It follows that an intact family is necessary for adjustment, and a broken home predisposes to later psychoses. *Broken home* refers to the loss of one or both parents by death, divorce, or hospitalization.

There is some evidence of an association between parental loss and later psychoses. Lidz and Lidz (1949) reported that 40% of their schizophrenic sample lost a parent before the age of 19, and Wahl (1956) reported a similar percentage before the age of 15. Approximately the same figure (40%) turned up in Brown's study (1961) of depressives, as contrasted with a figure of 12% for the general population. Blum and Rosenzweig (1944) found that female schizophrenics and affective psychotics had a greater percentage of parental loss than normals. Only one study (Oltman & Friedman, 1965) found similar parental deprivation in schizophrenics and normal persons.

These various investigations appear to support the hypothesis that a broken home is associated with the development of psychosis. However, these studies have *not* established that separation from a parent tends to lead to psychosis, but only that it leads to a deviation from normality. A broken home might also be associated with other kinds of psychopathology, and in fact this is precisely what has been found.

Maternal deaths before the child reaches eight years occur more in both schizophrenics and neurotics than in normals (Barry, 1949), and schizophrenics and alcoholics are separated from their mothers at an earlier age than normals (Hilgard & Newman, 1963). On the other hand, the figures on separation from the mother before the age of six years are reported as 35% for schizophrenic women and 5% for neurotic women (Berg & Cohen, 1959).

Gregory (1958), on the basis of his review of the literature, concluded that psychotics, neurotics, and delinquents all suffer parental loss to a greater extent than normals. There is some evidence that the crucial period of loss is during the first seven years of life. Thus with the single exception of the Berg and Cohen study, all the research points to the conclusion that a broken home is a nonspecific stress which facilitates the subsequent development of many kinds of psychopathology.

This conclusion makes sense. It is obvious that parents vary greatly in their child-rearing practices and involvement with their children. A child's being separated from a warm, attentive parent surely has different effects from a child's being separated from a cold, inattentive parent. It follows that separation itself should be a nonspecific variable. We can easily accept the idea that a broken home may be conducive to later deviant behavior. The child is bound to receive less attention and have less opportunity to identify with an important model in a broken home than in an intact home. There is no basis, however, for believing that separation facilitates the development of psychosis rather than other kinds of psychopathology. If anything, the evidence points to a higher percentage of broken homes in conduct disorders (delinquency, alcoholism) than in psychosis.

Several investigators (Berg & Cohen, 1959; Hilgard & Newman, 1963) have emphasized maternal deprivation as a possible cause of schizophrenia. This hypothesis has been effectively answered by Oltman and Friedman (1965): "And if maternal deprivation is indeed such an important etiological factor, what of the 85% to 90% of schizophrenics who have not experienced that condition?" (p. 54).

In brief, the hypothesis that a broken home predisposes to psychosis is too specific and needs to be amended to read: A broken home predisposes to many kinds of deviance. Further inferences are based on mistaken interpretations of data. An obtained difference between normals and psychotics does not guarantee that the variable in question holds only for psychotics. Such an inference requires a demonstration that psychotics differ not only from normals but also from neurotics and those with conduct disorders.

A variation on the theme of broken homes is the *anniversary hypothesis* (Hilgard & Newman, 1961):

If a person has lost a parent by death in childhood, and that person subsequently marries, has children, and later becomes hospitalized for the first time for mental illness, the first hospitalization is likely to occur beyond chance expectance when the oldest child of that person is within one year of the age the person was when the parent dies. (p. 14)

A search of hospital records revealed that the hypothesis holds for women but not for men. The anniversary year of the parent's death is evidently very painful for women, and it may serve as a trigger for latent psychotic tendencies.

Marital Status

It has been known for many years that single people have a higher incidence of psychosis than married people (Dayton, 1940; Malzberg, 1940, 1964; Odegaard, 1946; Adler, 1953; and Rose & Stub, 1956). There are two ways of explaining this statistic: (1) marriage protects people from psychosis because of the positive values of sharing and affection; at the very least, a spouse may be cared for rather than hospitalized. (2) There is a selective factor; those predisposed toward psychosis are less likely to marry.

These hypotheses can be checked out against the detailed data. The sex differences are especially interesting. The incidence of psychosis or severe impairment in single men is much greater than the incidence in married men, but the difference in incidence between single and married women is small (Rose & Stub, 1956; Odegaard, 1956; and Langner & Michael, 1963). Since the man must be more active in initiating courtship, it follows that male prepsychotics would be less likely to marry than female prepsychotics, who are allowed a more passive role.

The incidence of psychosis among the divorced is as high (or higher) as among single people (Odegaard, 1953). This suggests that marriage is not necessarily protective. Furthermore, this incidence is consistent with the selection hypothesis: the tendency toward psychosis helps to break up the marriage.

The last sex difference concerns age. For women the higher incidence of single psychotics over married psychotics is independent of age, but for men it increases until the age range of 40–50 years (Odegaard, 1946). Odegaard commented that the number of single men is reduced by marriage, which removes the more normal men and leaves a greater proportion of those tending toward psychosis. Again the data favor the selection hypothesis.

Finally, the incidence figures for affective psychoses are different. Single and married men have roughly the same incidence of affective psychoses, and married women have a slightly higher incidence than single women. People with tendencies toward affective psychoses do not manifest the kind of shy, withdrawn, asocial features seen in preschizophrenics, and therefore there is no selective factor in marriage. The conclusion is clear, then, that the predominance of single male schizophrenics over married schizophrenics is due to a selection factor: the characteristics comprising the schizoid personality tend to keep these men away from the social situations that eventuate in marriage. It follows that marriage is a good prognostic sign in male schizophrenics because presumably the schizoid tendencies were not of sufficient severity to prevent heterosexual contacts. That being married indicates a better prognosis than being single has been established (see Table 1 in Zubin et al., 1959).

SOCIETAL VARIABLES

The socialization process consists of exposing children to the values, roles, and attitudes deemed important in the larger society and in the specific subculture. Children must learn which goals are desirable and which means can achieve these goals. Some children are at a great disadvantage because of the locale or the social class into which they are born. This disadvantage, together with any inherited predispositions, may result in psychopathology.

Precisely which features of society are important determiners of psychopathology has been a matter of considerable speculation. One approach emphasizes social disorganization, the assumption being that chaos in the community leads to chaos in the individual; a "sick society" leads to sick individuals. Another approach emphasizes social class, the assumption being that the differential training and opportunities offered by various social class strata affect both the incidence of psychopathology and the kind of symptoms that occur. A third approach tends to negate or minimize the importance of these societal variables, the assumption being that they are *effects,* not *causes* of psychopathology.

Social Disorganization

The basic assumption is that social disorganization leads to personal disorganization. It is not important whether the setting is rural or urban, agricultural or industrial. The crucial variable is *change.* Changes in the patterns of society do not occur in a planned, orderly fashion, and therefore one of the consequences is unstable, chaotic communities. The individual can no longer rely on rigid and enduring community structures to lend stability to his efforts to adjust and to provide a consensual basis for reality. Lacking societal support, he is more likely to develop psychopathology.

Some communities are relatively stable, and others manifest marked deterioration. How can we distinguish them? Leighton (1959) used the following indicators of community disintegration:

> poverty—instability, as well as level, of income
> cultural confusion—"old country" versus new country traditions
> absence of religious values
> frequency of broken homes
> few and weak associations with the group
> few and weak leaders
> little recreation or leisure time
> high frequency of aggressive acts
> high frequency of crime and delinquency
> weak and fragmented communications.

In comparing communities, it was found that the more deteriorated regions had a considerably higher proportion of "severely impaired" individuals. Assuming that the disorganization led to the psychopathology and not the opposite, this finding supports the notion that social disorganization produces personal disorganization. Supporting evidence has also been reported by Jaco (1954), who found that more disorganized communities had higher rates of schizophrenia.

So far we have been discussing the theory in its broadest terms, that is, that poor social conditions constitute one determinant of psychopathology. However, one variant of the theory is more specific in that it attempts to show that social disorganization leads to psychosis by isolating individuals. Faris (1944) suggested that social isolation enters at a late stage in the hypothetical sequence that leads to psychosis, especially schizophrenia. First, the parents spoil the child, thereby making it difficult for him to develop close social contacts outside the family. The spoiled child is then subjected to ridicule and exclusion by playmates, usually during the period when he starts school. The child's attempts to make friends are continually blocked, and eventually he gives up the attempt. He turns to solitary pursuits and remains isolated. This isolation prevents him from acquiring appropriate social roles and communication skills, and his personality remains seclusive. It is but a short step from seclusiveness to symptom formation, as we saw in the first section of this chapter.

Faris does not blame disorganization for the spoiling of the child.

What does vary in the different areas is the reaction of other children to the overprotected child. In the more integrated communities, the relations between adults and children are such as to promote some community cooperation, with the result that sympathy of adults may lead to the lessening of the natural discrimination against the socially deficient child. In slum areas, however, the lack of this cooperation, the mixture of nationalities, the tradition of "toughness" among the delinquent boys, and such factors constitute such a barrier to the establishment of social relations that many find it impossible, and are thus turned down the path that leads to psychosis. (1944, pp. 753–759)

It follows from this social isolation hypothesis that the worst areas of a city will breed the greatest amount of psychopathology. Faris and Dunham (1939) tested this prediction in Chicago, dividing the city into concentric rings. It had been previously established that the center of a city is the worst residential area and that residential neighborhoods improve with distance from the center. Therefore the central area should have the highest rate of psychopathology, the rate diminishing from ring to ring as the suburbs are approached. This is precisely what was found for schizophrenia, alcoholism, and psychoses associated with brain damage. The rates were highest in the central business district, lower in the adjacent rooming house neighborhoods, and lowest in the residential areas on the edges of the city. The affective psychoses, however, were randomly distributed throughout the city.

Dunham (1957) reported several confirming studies by other researchers in large cities. However, Clausen and Kohn (1959) surveyed a small city, Hagerstown, Maryland, and found no relationship between residential areas and schizophrenia. They pointed out that in the various studies on this topic the relationship was strongest in large cities, weaker in moderate size cities, and nonexistent in small cities. Perhaps residence, as a determinant of schizophrenia, is important only in a large urban center.

If the relationship holds mainly for large cities, it would be consistent with the theory of social problems that underlies the social isolation hypothesis. This theory assumes that in urban, industrial society there is a breakdown in the close family relationships that are typical of rural and small town society. Family ties and enduring friendships with neighbors are weak or absent, and persons tend to relate to each other in more formal and distant settings, if at all. There is a decreased frequency of home ownership and a corresponding tendency to move from one neighborhood to another. Thus there is greater social distance and mobility, and greater isolation of individuals from one another. In cities the breakdown in community interaction can lead to the isolation that predisposes toward schizoid, unsociable personalities. This brings us to the starting point of Faris' (1944) social isolation hypothesis.

The theory of community disorganization is acceptable to many epidemiologists, but it has its critics. Kennedy (1964), for example, contested the assumption that the mobility and instability usually found at the center of a city necessarily lead to psychopathology. This criticism has also been made in the context of the "drift hypothesis," which states that disturbed people tend to drift toward the unstable and low-rent areas of the city because they have been impoverished and cast out of their own homes and neighborhoods. Thus the residential findings are attributed to a causal sequence not of residence leading to psychopathology but of psychopathology leading to residence.

Gerard and Houston (1953) showed that single and divorced schizophrenics tended to move away from their families into the central, disorganized areas of a city. Thus the central area may attract rather than breed schizophrenics. However, Lapouse, Monk, and Terris (1956) showed that recent immigration to the poorer areas of a city could not account for the concentration of psychotics in these areas, and Hollingshead and Redlich (1958) found no evidence of special geographic movement in their schizophrenic sample. These contradictory findings prevent us from accepting or rejecting the drift hypothesis. In any event it is doubtful that migration could explain in full the excess number of schizophrenics who reside in disadvantaged neighborhoods. At best the hypothesis tends to weaken the residential hypothesis.

Kennedy also suggested that social isolation does not necessarily lead to psychopathology. Dunham (1944) reported that catatonic schizophrenics were isolated in their disorganized communities, which tended to have a high rate of delinquency. However, Weinberg (1960) could find no evidence from the histories of schizophrenics that they had been isolated. Kohn and Clausen (1955), in a careful study, interviewed psychotic patients and matched controls, seeking information about childhood friendships and community contacts. Using only those patients who reported being social isolates during early adolescence, they found no evidence that this isolation was caused by residential mobility or lack of available playmates. Rather, the isolation appeared to be an aspect of the patient's shy and fearful personalities. This study seriously weakens the social isolation hypothesis and the underlying theory. It strengthens the alternate position, namely, that psychopathology *starts* with certain dispositions of the individual, which are then intensified by the social environment. These dispositions, as we saw earlier, stem from either biological factors or the earliest family environment.

Implicit in the theory of social problems that underlies the disorganization hypothesis is the assumption that during the past hundred years modern industrial society has increased pressures on individuals. The breakup of stable patterns of agrarian life and of enduring small town patterns is believed to have dissociated individuals from close relationships, and competitive pressures have made them tense, anxious, and depressed over failure. It is generally believed that these developments have greatly increased the incidence of psychopathology and that this is the price that must be paid in our "age of anxiety."

This notion has been tested, at least as it applies to psychosis, by Goldhamer and Marshall (1953). They compared the rates of functional psychoses (schizophrenia and affective psychoses) during the 19th century and during the present century, with the following results:

When appropriate comparisons are made which equate the class of patients received and the conditions affecting hospitalization of the mentally ill, age-specific first admission rates for ages under 50 are revealed to be just as high during the last half of the 19th century as they are today. (1953, p. 91)

There has been a big jump in the rate of admissions for the age groups above 50 years, which may be attributed to both an increase in such diseases as arteriosclerosis and to an increased tendency to hospitalize patients with senile psychoses.

In any event it is the age groups in the 20–50 year range that are of immediate concern because it is this population that would be affected by social disorganization. Psychoses occurring after the age of 50 are presumably not caused by adverse social conditions but by personal conditions (life circumstances such as aging and money problems). Assuming that the Goldhamer and Marshall results are not due to any artifact (and there is no reason to assume they are), we must conclude that the adverse conditions of modern industrial life have not led to a greater incidence of psychosis than did the "low pressure" society of the 19th century. Furthermore, these results are indirect evidence that the social disorganization theory is incorrect or at least inadequate. As Goldhamer and Marshall point out, their results strengthen two kinds of theory: genetic theory, which emphasizes biological variables at the expense of social variables, and interpersonal and dynamic theories, which emphasize family interactions, regardless of the larger social environment.

Social Class

Faris' theory specifies social disorganization as a key variable in schizophrenia, but the disorganization itself is linked to social class. The slum areas, which in large cities seem to breed both criminals and psychotics, are precisely the areas inhabited by members of the lowest social class. The approach here differs from Faris' in that it emphasizes either social mobility or differential training and opportunities for lower class members, rather than social isolation due to disorganization.

To begin with, we must document the assumption that social class is related to psychosis. Tietze, Lemkau, and Cooper (1941) found that the rate of schizophrenia is higher among lower class persons. Affective psychoses were slightly more common in members of the upper class. In general, affective psychoses appear to be randomly distributed among the various social classes. However, an excess of schizophrenics in lower class samples has been reported by several investigators (Stein, 1957; Hollingshead & Redlich, 1958; Morris, 1959; Goldberg & Morrison, 1963; Dunham, 1964). In addition the Midtown Study (Srole et al., 1962) showed that the worse the father's socioeconomic status, the more impaired were his offspring's mental health.

The results have not all been positive. Jaco (1960) found that psychosis was more frequent in *both* his high and low status samples. Kleiner and Parker (1963) summarized several research projects in Australia, England, and Norway, none of which found a relationship between social class and schizophrenia; the relationship is also absent among Negroes.

In light of these negative findings with nonwhite and foreign populations, we may conclude that the relationship between social class and schizophrenia holds only for urban, white Americans. Mishler and Scotch (1963) summarized nine studies:

The most consistent finding, which emerges from eight of the nine studies, is that the highest incidence is associated with the lowest social class groupings in each study. In six studies it is the unskilled or laborers category, in a seventh it is the unemployed, and in the eighth it is the lowest of the four social classes— defined by an index of occupation, education, and residence—that produces the highest rate. (p. 326)

Note that there is an excess of schizophrenics in the lowest social class but not an inverse relationship between social class and schizophrenia. Many investigators divide social class into five groups—Class I to Class V. As Dunham (1964) has pointed out, there is no relationship between schizophrenia and class status for the top four classes. Thus the single unequivocal fact to emerge from this research is that the rate of schizophrenia is excessively high in Class V, the lowest social class.

There are two hypotheses that attempt to explain this fact. One uses the notion of social mobility, and the other emphasizes differential training and opportunity.

Social Mobility. Social mobility refers to a shift in class status, either upward or downward. In the present context we shall use it only to mean downward shifts. Thus we have a social class analogue of the residential drift hypothesis discussed earlier, namely, that schizophrenics tend to drift into lower statuses because they are incapacitated by psychopathology.

In order to prove this hypothesis, it must be shown that schizophrenics were originally of a higher status from which they dropped prior to being identified as psychotic. Neither Hollingshead and Redlich (1958) nor Clausen and Kohn (1959) could find evidence of such downward mobility in schizophrenics. Hollingshead and Redlich reported that 91% of their schizophrenic sample were of the same social class as their fathers. On the other hand, Lystad (1957) found that schizophrenics were more downwardly mobile than a comparable nonpsychiatric sample, and Jaco (1960) noted more downward mobility in communities with high rates of psychopathology. Morris (1959) reported that the fathers of schizophrenics showed the usual distribution into various social class statuses, whereas the schizophrenic sons were concentrated in the lower class.

All of these investigations are cross-sectional, that is, they represent findings for one point in time. One way of pin-pointing the drift hypothesis would be a longitudinal study, with periodic measures on the same individuals over time. This is precisely what Goldberg and Morrison (1963) attempted, using case histories and retrospective reports. They found the usual excess of schizophrenics in the lowest social class, but their fathers were distributed into the various classes in the same way as the general population. There was a clear downward drift in social status from father to schizophrenic son and also in the status of the son over time. The schizophrenics generally functioned well in school and remained in the same status as their fathers. However, after leaving school, they began to function poorly. They failed to develop professional or technical skills, and consequently were unable to qualify for better jobs. The drop in social class between school and admission to a psychiatric hospital was inevitable because they were able to qualify only for jobs associated with the lowest social status.

These results were partially corroborated by Dunham (1964). He found no evidence that schizophrenics were either upwardly or downwardly mobile. However, he did find a discrepancy in social class between fathers and sons. The social class status of the fathers was evenly distributed, but their schizophrenic sons were mainly in Class V, the lowest social class. Dunham suggested that, ". . . the psychiatric condition of the patient appears to determine his social class rather than his social class determining or influencing his disorder." (p. 641)

Note that these findings hold only for men, whose occupational status is a crucial variable in determining overall social status. There is no evidence that women would manifest a similar downward drift, and it is possible that a sex difference underlies the conflicting results reported above. Men may drift downward in social status considerably more than women, and the balance of men and women in any given sample of schizophrenics may determine whether the results show mobility or not.

In any event, it seems safe to conclude that at least some schizophrenics are downwardly mobile, at least relative to their parents. Therefore the drift hypothesis has some validity. This means that there is some truth in the assertion that psychopathology can determine social class as well as the opposite. In light of what we know about the schizophrenic's psychological deficit and general inefficiency, it is not surprising to discover that he tends to filter down to the lowest social class. However, while acknowledging the validity of the drift hypothesis, we must hasten to add that it is only partially valid. It does not account for *all* of the excess incidence of schizophrenia in the lower class. Part of the explanation must be in the training and opportunities available in lower class culture.

Training and Opportunities. Although many researchers have focused on social class variables as antecedents of psychopathology, we shall rely mainly on the conceptualizations and results of the Midtown Study (Srole et al., 1962; Langner & Michael, 1963). The theory consists of speculations about class differences that might lead to differential psychopathology in middle and lower class persons, specifically speculations about the variables of *taming, identity, communication,* and *opportunities.*

The Midtown Study showed that middle and upper class groups were more likely to develop neurotic symptoms, whereas lower class people were more likely to develop psychoses or conduct disorders. These differences might be due in part to differences in the degree or kind of socialization (the *taming* of say, aggressive and sexual tendencies).

Our tentative hypothesis is that the anxiety found in the middle and upper levels may be due to the relatively severe suppression and accompanying repression and redirection of sexual and aggressive instincts; a sort of "over-socialization." (Langner & Michael, p. 422)

Under-socialization in the lower class is presumably responsible for the social
and antisocial acts characteristic of conduct disorders.

Middle class children are taught indirect and covert ways of aggressing,
and they are punished for direct, physical aggression. Sexuality is channeled
into petting and masturbation. Lower class children are often rewarded for
direct, physical aggression, and they are not taught covert and sly ways
of punishing others. Their sexual behavior is not diverted from coitus, and
activities like masturbation and petting are discouraged. The taming of
sexual and aggressive drives in middle class children is accomplished at
the cost of considerable anxiety. Direct expression of drives is not only punished but subjected to moral injunctions. Thus the middle class child may
be burdened with both anxiety and guilt for his "uncivilized" impulses.
This burden constitutes a disposition toward neurosis.

Psychosis may also be construed as a *loss of identity*. If psychosis is
more prevalent among the lower class population, might this be due to
faulty or insufficient training for identity? This question may be answered
by pointing out the positive features of middle class development and their
relative absence in lower class development. A strong sense of identity is
fostered by middle class parents in several ways. There are fewer children
in the family, which means that each child is treated more as an individual
than as a member of a large group. Middle class children can mark the
important events in their lives with celebrations (birthday parties, gradu-
ation parties, etc.), whereas lower class children tend not to have such clear
recognition of their life progress. Similarly, middle class families tend to
record events in their children's lives by means of photographs, souvenirs,
and scrapbooks, whereas lower class parents do not. Middle class children
usually have many possessions of their own (especially toys, games and
clothes), which help to foster a clear self-image ("myself and my private,
unshared goods"); in contrast, lower class children have few possessions,
and clothes are often "hand-me-downs." In brief, middle class development
fosters a strong sense of identity and lower class, a weak sense of identity.
Insofar as identity problems are an important aspect of schizophrenia, this
differential development accounts for the greater incidence of schizophrenia
among lower class persons.

Language is obviously basic to *communication*. Middle class children
learn to talk earlier than lower class children, and middle class children are
allowed more freedom to complain and to express resentments and jeal-
ousies. Lower class children are usually punished severely for complaining,
and there is less communication among members of lower class families.
This lack of communication may breed suspiciousness and a tendency to
withdraw from social contacts and into fantasy, and these, in turn, dispose
the individual toward conduct disorders and psychosis.

So far, the class differences have concerned childhood, but there are also important class differences in adult experiences. The lower class adult is, by definition, economically poorer than the middle class adult. Since in our society, money and goods constitute a major basis of evaluating an individual's worth, the lower class adult is branded as less worthy, not only by others but also by himself. He has neither the economic status nor the *opportunity* of the middle class adult to improve his status. His self-confidence is low, and his prospects for the future, dim. The lack of self-worth and the feelings of futility and hopelessness experienced by many lower class people are tendencies that may lead to social withdrawal and eventually to psychosis.

Other Variables. Several other class differences in psychopathology need to be mentioned. Social class appears to be related to prognosis. Hardt and Feinhandler (1959) showed that lower class patients had significantly longer periods of hospitalization than middle and upper class patients. They were able to rule out the variables of hospital admission policies, clinical features, and level of improvement at discharge. In the absence of these variables as explanatory factors, it seems likely that the poorer prognosis for lower class patients is due to either severer stresses before hospitalization (leading to severer and chronic psychopathology) or more stresses after hospitalization (leading to a greater likelihood of a subsequent breakdown), or both.

Despite the control for clinical features, Hardt and Feinhandler did observe that upper class patients were overrepresented in the depressed-suicidal group, and lower class patients were overrepresented in the quiet-idle and disturbed-destructive categories. Presumably, the depressed-suicidal category corresponds roughly to affective psychoses, and the other two correspond roughly to schizophrenia and conduct disorders. If these assumptions are correct, the class differences are substantially the same as those reported by Srole et al. (1962), namely, a greater incidence of schizophrenia and conduct disorders among lower class persons. Furthermore, it has been believed for many years that affective psychotics are generally middle or upper class in their background. Two studies have offered support for this belief. Parker et al. (1959) found the majority of their sample of affective psychotics to be of at least lower middle class background; only 16% were from the lowest social class. Zigler and Phillips (1960) divided symptoms into Self-Deprivation and Turning Against the Self, Self-Indulgence and Turning Against Others, and Avoidance of Others; these categories approximate the diagnoses of affective psychosis, conduct disorder, and schizophrenia, respectively. Through these diagnostic terms, it was found that affective psychosis was associated with the best histories of employment, occupation, and education (these three, together with residence, usually constitute the index of social class). Schizophrenia occupied a middle position, and conduct disorder was associated with the worst histories of employment, occupation, and education. Thus affective psychoses appear to occur more in mid- ✗ dle and upper class groups, and schizophrenia and conduct disorders, more in lower class groups.

One of the salient variables contributing to social class is occupation. Frumkin (1956) found that income is less important than the prestige associated with the occupation. On the basis of his comparisons of different occupational groups, he concluded that lower class groups tend to develop psychopathology of "sociogenic origin," whereas upper class groups tend to develop psychopathology of "psychogenic origin." Presumably what is meant is that lower class status tends to promote social isolation and schizoid tendencies such as are seen in schizophrenia, as well as asocial and antisocial tendencies such as are seen in conduct disorders; on the other hand, upper class groups tend to become involved with more personal difficulties such as anxiety, guilt, feelings of failure, and similar manifestations often seen in the affective psychoses. Middle class groups suffer from psychopathology of both sociogenic and psychogenic origin and therefore should manifest all the various psychopathologies.

The Midtown Study (Langner & Michael, 1963) demonstrated that ✓ the relationship between stress variables and class status affects the incidence of psychosis. The stress variables were factors believed to have a deleterious effect on adjustment: parents in poor physical or mental health, poor physical health in childhood, broken home, etc. A stress score was derived by summing the presence of these variables, and then the effect of stress on high and low status subjects was examined. When the stress was low (very few negative features in the present or past environment), the proportion of psychotics was slightly higher in the lower class than in the high class group, but in both groups the proportion of psychotics was very low. As the stress increased (more and more negative environmental features), the proportion of psychotics in the lower class group rose steadily, but in the high class group the proportion remained very low. These findings may be interpreted in terms of Frumkin's sociogenic-psychogenic dichotomy. If lower class individuals tend to develop psychopathology of sociogenic origin, then the more negative the social variables, the greater should be the tendency to become psychotic. If upper class individuals tend to develop psychopathology of psychogenic origin, then social variables should have little effect. A negative social environment would not increase the tendency to become psychotic because this tendency is affected only by psychological (presumably nonsocial) variables.

The variable of environmental stress is of interest in its own right, and we shall add a parenthetical note that is unrelated to class status. Langner (1961), in commenting about the results of the Midtown Study, noted that they were opposed to the concept of a single trauma as the cause of psychopathology.

If single traumatic events such as the death of a parent or severe childhood illness could be the sole trigger for mental disturbance, then we would find that certain factors were associated with very great mental health risk, no matter what other factors entered the picture. This "all or none" principle is illustrated nowhere in our data. Events in the life history seem to "pile up" but there is no one event which automatically spells mental disaster for the individual. (1961, p. 39)

He went on to add that there was no crucial point at which the addition of another stress would tip the balance, as in "the straw that breaks the camel's back." The relationship between stress and impairment is continuous, which casts doubt on the psychoanalytic notion of crucial repressed incidents or traumata.

COMMENT

It is clear that family relationships are one determinant of schizophrenia. Parents may predispose their children toward schizophrenia by forcing them to play a childlike, dependent role, thereby preventing the children from acquiring necessary modes of adjusting. Presumably, when the child is kept from interacting with playmates and must acquire virtually all his social behavior in a disturbed family, he will develop a schizoid personality. This kind of personality constitutes a predisposition to schizophrenia, the psychotic breakdown itself being triggered by the environmental pressures of adolescence.

Parents may also predispose their children toward schizophrenia by teaching them irrationality. The child may be forced to accept illogical verbalizations and distorted views of the world in order to retain parental affection and to avoid parental rebuff. There may also be parental training in faulty communication, the child failing to acquire habits of correct sending and receiving of messages.

Social class is also important. The lowest social class has a disproportionately high rate of schizophrenia (and probably psychosomatic and conduct disorders). Social class is unrelated to affective psychoses, and neurosis is probably less frequent in the lowest social class. There is considerable controversy over whether social class is a cause or an effect of schizophrenia. The lowest social class does place its members at a disadvantage in their attempts to adjust to a world that demands what they do not possess: money, goods, influence, education, etc. Furthermore, the family patterns of the lowest social class tend to have many of the elements that have been labeled *schizophrenogenic*. Nevertheless, it is difficult to establish that these variables cause schizophrenia, and so far this has not been done.

Concerning social class as an effect of schizophrenia, the argument is persuasive. A schizophrenic is at a disadvantage in competing with others in school, in social situations, and in work situations. Thus the *outcome* of psychotic tendencies is presumably a filtering down to the lowest social class. Lending weight to this explanation are the social statuses of schizophrenics and their fathers: the schizophrenics are predominantly of the lowest social class, whereas the fathers are distributed among the various social classes.

Social class and family have been considered without reference to cultural variables, which are beyond the scope of this book. Nevertheless, we should point out that cultural variables may be important in determining the *form* if not the presence of psychosis. Opler and Singer (1956) and Fantl and Schiro (1959) have found different patterns of psychopathology in Italian and Irish persons. Sanua (1963) compared Jewish and Protestant schizophrenics and parents. There was more psychopathology among Protestant fathers than mothers, but the reverse was true for Jewish parents. Thus differences among ethnic and religious groups should be considered in any interpersonal-social theory of psychosis. Cultural variables add complexity to theories which are already complex. Future studies will have to control for a number of variables: type of psychosis, family constellation, intactness of the home, social class, and such cultural variables as race, religion, and national origin.

This chapter has reviewed the major interpersonal and social approaches to psychosis, and the previous chapter reviewed the major biological approaches. We may now compare the biological and social models of psychoses.

The pure biological model views psychosis as a disease, the psychological symptoms being analogous to the medical symptoms of systemic disease. The tendency to become psychotic, which is inherited, is a necessary but not a sufficient cause of the psychosis. The necessary condition is some kind of nongenetic defect: chemical or mechanical damage to the fetus, birth injury, physique, or possibly systemic illness. The model is vague about the nature of the additional variable needed to combine with the inherited predisposition. However, such a variable must be a part of the biological model because hereditary alone cannot explain the rates of occurrence of psychosis. Certainly discordance in identical twins cannot be explained by heredity alone. Therefore it is assumed that those who do become schizophrenic suffer from an auxilliary, nongenetic anomaly as well as from an inherited tendency toward schizophrenia.

The pure biological model must account for social class and familial variables. The predominance of schizophrenics in the lowest social class is presumably caused by their downward mobility—the result of biological faults that render them unable to compete for status. A vicious family environment can also be explained in biological terms. Presumably it is caused by the deviant behavior of the same parent who passed on the tendency toward schizophrenia through the genes. Concerning the social maladjustment of psychotics, it is important to remember that they are inefficient in *all* areas of functioning. Thus they are as incompetent in impersonal situations (see Chapters 12 and 13) as in interpersonal situations.

The pure social model views psychosis as a failure of psychological adjustment. Low social class may so handicap the individual as to prevent successful adjustment. Similarly, his family may force him to play roles or develop modes of communication that lead to social isolation and cognitive symptoms.

How does this model account for the biological symptoms of schizophrenia? It assumes that they are analogous to psychosomatic symptoms. The individual who is isolated and fearful of social contact presumably develops physiological reactions to match these psychological states. His anxiety renders him hyperactive, and his lack of psychological response to the environment renders him physiologically hyporeactive.

These two pure models represent extreme positions, and most investigators lean toward some combination of biological and social variables. Although there are many possible combinations, there are two modal kinds. The first assumes that psychosis is more or less homogeneous. The predisposition to become psychotic is inherited as some biochemical fault, but it must be triggered by a vicious social environment. Psychosis is seen as being caused by a predisposing biological variable in combination with a precipitating social variable.

The second combined model assumes that there are two types of psychosis. The first is more or less a biological disease. It is determined mainly by heredity, and the environmental component is absent or weak; prognosis is poor. The second type of psychosis is more or less a social maladjustment. It is determined mainly by social and interpersonal variables, and the inherited component is absent or weak; prognosis is good. This model is based on the familiar process-reactive distinction, which is based on a reliable body of evidence (see Chapter 10).

REFERENCES

Adler, Leta M. The relationship of marital status to incidence of and recovery from mental illness. *Social Forces,* 1953, **32,** 185–194.

Barry, H., Jr. Significance of maternal bereavement before age eight in psychiatric patients. *Archives of Neurology and Psychiatry,* 1949, **62,** 630–637.

Bateson, G., Jackson, D. D., Haley, J., & Weakland, J. Toward a theory of schizophrenia. *Behavioral Science,* 1956, **1,** 251–264.

Berg, M., & Cohen, B. B. Early separation from the mother in schizophrenia. *Journal of Nervous and Mental Disease,* 1959, **128,** 365–369.

Blum, G. S., & Rosenzweig, S. The incidence of sibling and parental deaths in the anamnesis of female schizophrenics. *Journal of General Psychology,* 1944, **31,** 3–13.

Brown, F. Depression and childhood bereavement. *Journal of Mental Science,* 1961, **107,** 754–777.

Cameron, N. The paranoid pseudocommunity. *American Journal of Sociology,* 1943, **49,** 32–38.

Cameron, N. *The psychology of behavior disorders.* Boston: Houghton Mifflin, 1947.

Cameron, N. The paranoid pseudocommunity revisited. *American Journal of Sociology,* 1959, **65,** 52–58.

Cameron, N. *Personality development and psychopathology.* Boston: Houghton Mifflin, 1963.

Cheek, Frances E. A serendipitous finding: Sex roles and schizophrenia. *Journal of Abnormal and Social Psychology,* 1964, **69,** 392–400.

Clausen, J. A., & Kohn, M. L. Relation of schizophrenia to the social structure of a small city. In Pasamanick, B. (Ed.). *Epidemiology of mental disorders.* Washington, D. C.: American Association for the Advancement of Science, 1959, pp. 69–86.

Dayton, N. A. *New facts on mental disorders.* Springfield, Illinois: Thomas, 1940.

Dunham, H. W. The social personality of the catatonic schizophrenic. *American Journal of Sociology,* 1944, **49,** 508–518.

Dunham, H. W. Methodology of sociological investigations of mental disorders. *International Journal of Social Psychiatry,* 1957, **3,** 7–17.

Dunham, H. W. Social class and schizophrenia. *American Journal of Orthopsychiatry,* 1964, **34,** 634–642.

Erikson, E. *Childhood and society.* New York: Norton, 1950.

Fantl, Bertha, & Schiro, J. Cultural variables in the behavior patterns and symptom formation of 15 Irish and 15 Italian female schizophrenics. *International Journal of Social Psychiatry,* 1959, **4,** 245–253.

Farahmand, S. S. Personality characteristics and child-rearing attitudes of fathers of schizophrenic patients. Unpublished doctoral dissertation, Washington State University, 1961.

Farina, A. Patterns of role dominance and conflict in parents of schizophrenic patients. *Journal of Abnormal and Social Psychology,* 1960, **61,** 31–38.

Farina, A., & Dunham, R. M. Measurement of family relationships and their effects. *Archives of General Psychiatry,* 1963, **9,** 64–73.

Faris, R. E. L. Ecological factors in human behavior. In Hunt, J. McV. (Ed.) *Personality and the behavior disorders.* New York: Ronald, 1944.

Faris, R. E. L., & Dunham, H. W. *Mental disorders in urban areas.* Chicago: University of Chicago Press, 1939.

Fisher, S., Boyd, Ina, Walker, D., & Sheer, Dianne. Parents of schizophrenics, neurotics, and normals. *Archives of General Psychiatry,* 1959, **1,** 149–166.

Fleck, S., Lidz, T., & Cornelison, Alice. Comparison of parent-child relationships of male and female schizophrenic patients. *Archives of General Psychiatry,* 1963, **8,** 1–7.

Freeman, R. V., & Grayson, H. M. Maternal attitudes in schizophrenia. *Journal of Abnormal and Social Psychology,* 1955, **50,** 45–52.

Freeman, H. E., Simmons, O. G., & Berger, B. J. Possessiveness as a characteristic of mothers of schizophrenics. *Journal of Abnormal and Social Psychology,* 1959, **58,** 271–272.

Frumkin, R. M. Occupation and mental disorder. In Rose, A. M. (Ed.). *Mental health and mental disorder.* London: Routledge & Kegan Paul, 1956, pp. 136–160.

Galvin, J. Mothers of schizophrenics. *Journal of Nervous and Mental Disease,* 1956, **123,** 568–570.

Garfield, S., & Helper, M. M. Parental attitudes and socioeconomic status. *Journal of Clinical Psychology*, 1962, **18**, 171–175.

Garmezy, N., Clarke, A. R., & Stockner, Carol. Child rearing attitudes of mothers and fathers as reported by schizophrenic and normal patients. *Journal of Abnormal and Social Psychology*, 1961, **63**, 176–182.

Gerard, D. L., & Houston, L. G. Family setting and the ecology of schizophrenia. *Psychiatric Quarterly*, 1953, **27**, 90–101.

Gerard, D. L., & Siegel, J. The family background in schizophrenia. *Psychiatric Quarterly*, 1950, **24**, 45–73.

Goldberg, E. M., & Morrison, S. L. Schizophrenia and social class. *British Journal of Psychiatry*, 1963, **109**, 785–802.

Goldhamer, H., & Marshall, A. *Psychosis and civilization.* Glencoe, Illinois: The Free Press, 1953.

Gregory, I. Studies of parental deprivation in psychiatric patients. *American Journal of Psychiatry*, 1958, **115**, 432–442.

Haley, J. The family of the schizophrenic: A model system. *Journal of Nervous and Mental Disease*, 1959, **129**, 357–374.

Hardt, R. H., & Feinhandler, S. J. Social class and mental hospital prognosis. *American Sociological Review*, 1959, **24**, 815–821.

Heilbrun, A. B., Jr. Perception of maternal child-rearing attitudes in schizophrenics. *Journal of Consulting Psychology*, 1960, **24**, 169–173.

Heilbrun, A. B., Jr. Maternal authoritarianism, social class, and filial schizophrenia. *Journal of General Psychology*, 1961, **65**, 235–241.

Hilgard, Josephine, & Newman, Martha F. Parental loss by death in childhood as an etiological factor among schizophrenic and alcoholic patients compared with a non-patient community sample. *Journal of Nervous and Mental Disease*, 1963, **137**, 14–28.

Hollingshead, A. B., & Redlich, F. C. *Social class and mental illness.* New York: Wiley, 1958.

Jaco, E. G. The social isolation hypothesis in schizophrenia. *American Sociological Review*, 1954, **19**, 567–577.

Jaco, E. G. *The social epidemiology of mental disorders.* New York: Russell Sage Foundation, 1960.

Kennedy, M. C. Is there an ecology of mental illness? *International Journal of Social Psychiatry*, 1964, **10**, 119–133.

Klebanoff, L. B. Parental attitudes of mothers of schizophrenic, brain-injured, and retarded, and normal children. *American Journal of Orthopsychiatry*, 1959, **24**, 445–454.

Kleiner, R. J., & Parker, S. Goal-striving social status and mental disorder: A research review. *American Sociological Review*, 1963, **28**, 189–203.

Kohn, M. S., & Clausen, J. A. Social isolation and schizophrenia. *American Sociological Review*, 1955, **20**, 265–273.

Langner, T. S. Environmental stress and mental health. In Hoch, P. H. & Zubin, J. (Eds.). *Comparative epidemiology of the mental disorders.* New York: Grune & Stratton, 1961, pp. 32–44.

Langner, T. S., & Michael, S. T. *Life stress and mental health.* Glencoe, Illinois: The Free Press, 1963.

Lapouse, Rema, Monk, Mary A., & Terris, M. The drift hypothesis and socio-economic differentials in schizophrenia. *American Journal of Public Health*, 1956, **46**, 978–986.

Leighton, A. *My name is legion.* New York: Basic Books, 1959.

Lidz, Ruth, & Lidz, T. The family environment of schizophrenic patients. *American Journal of Psychiatry,* 1949, **106,** 332–345.

Lidz, T., Cornelison, Alice R., Terry, Dorothy, & Fleck, S. The intrafamilial environment of the schizophrenic patient. I. The father. *Psychiatry,* 1957, **20,** 329–342.

Lidz, T., Cornelison, Alice R., Fleck, S., & Terry, Dorothy. The intrafamilial environment of schizophrenic patients. II. Marital schism and marital skew. *American Journal of Psychiatry,* 1957, **114,** 241–248.

Lidz, T., Cornelison, Alice, R., Terry, Dorothy, & Fleck, S. The intrafamilial environment of the schizophrenic patient. VI. The transmission of irrationality. *Archives of Neurology and Psychiatry,* 1958, **79,** 305–316.

Lidz, T., & Fleck, S. Schizophrenia, human integration, and the role of the family. In Jackson, D. D. (Ed.). *The etiology of schizophrenia.* New York: Basic Books, 1960. pp. 323–345.

Limentani, D. Symbiotic identification in schizophrenia. *Psychiatry,* 1956, **19,** 231–236.

Lu, Yi-Chang. Contradictory parental expectations in schizophrenia. *Archives of General Psychiatry,* 1962, **6,** 219–234.

Lystad, Mary H. Social mobility among selected groups of schizophrenic patients. *American Sociological Review,* 1957, **22,** 282–292.

Malzberg, B. *Social and biological aspects of mental disease.* Utica, New York: State Hospital Press, 1940.

Malzberg, B. Marital status and the incidence of mental disease. *International Journal of Social Psychiatry,* 1964, **10,** 19–26.

Mark, J. C. The attitudes of mothers of male schizophrenics toward child behavior. *Journal of Abnormal and Social Psychology,* 1953, **48,** 185–189.

McPartland, T. S., & Hornstra, R. K. The depressive datum. *Comprehensive Psychiatry,* 1964, **5,** 253–261.

Meehl, P. E. Schizotaxia, schizotypy, schizophrenia. *American Psychologist,* 1962, **17,** 827–838.

Mishler, E. G., & Scotch, N. A. Sociocultural factors in the epidemiology of schizophrenia. *Psychiatry,* 1963, **26,** 315–351.

Morris, J. N. Health and social class. *Lancet,* 1959, **1,** 303–305.

Odegaard, O. Marriage and mental disease. A study of social psychopathology. *Journal of Mental Science,* 1946, **92,** 35–59.

Odegaard, O. New data on marriage and mental disease: The incidence of psychosis in the widowed and the divorced. *Journal of Mental Science,* 1953, **99,** 778–785.

Odegaard, O. The incidence of psychoses in various occupations. *International Journal of Social Psychiatry,* 1956, **2,** 85–104.

Oltman, Jane E., & Friedman, S. Report on parental deprivation in psychiatric disorders. *Archives of General Psychiatry,* 1965, **12,** 46–56.

Opler, M. K., & Singer, J. L. Ethnic differences in behavior and psychopathology: Italian and Irish. *International Journal of Social Psychiatry,* 1956, **2,** 11–23.

Parker, J. B., Spielberger, C. D., Wallace, D. K., & Becker, J. Factors in manic-depressive reactions. *Diseases of the Nervous System,* 1959, **20,** 1–7.

Pollin, W., Stabenau, J. R., & Tupin, J. Family studies with twins discordant for schizophrenia. *Psychiatry,* 1965, **28,** 60–78.

Prout, C. T., & White, Mary A. The schizophrenic's sibling. *Journal of Nervous and Mental Disease,* 1956, **123,** 162–170.

Reichard, Suzanne, & Tillman, C. Patterns of parent-child relationships in schizophrenia. *Psychiatry,* 1950, **13,** 247–257.

Rose, A. M., & Stub, H. R. Summary of studies on the incidence of mental disorders. In Rose, A. M. (Ed.). _Mental health and mental disorder._ London: Routledge & Kegan, Paul, 1956, pp. 87–116.

Sanua, V. D. The socio-cultural aspects of schizophrenia: A comparison of Protestant and Jewish schizophrenics. _International Journal of Social Psychiatry,_ 1963, **9,** 27–36.

Shaefer, E. S., & Bell, R. Q. Development of a parental attitude research instrument. _Child Development,_ 1958, **29,** 339–361.

Srole, L., Langner, T. S., Michael, S. T., Opler, M. K., & Rennie, T. A. C. _Mental Health in the metropolis: The Midtown Manhattan study._ New York: McGraw-Hill, 1962.

Stein, Lilli, "Social class" gradient in schizophrenia. _British Journal of Preventive and Social Medicine,_ 1957, **11,** 181–195.

Tietze, Trude. A study of mothers of schizophrenic patients. _Psychiatry,_ 1949, **12,** 55–65.

Tietze, C., Lemkau, P., & Cooper, M. Schizophrenia, manic-depressive psychoses and social-economic status. _American Journal of Sociology,_ 1941, **47,** 167–175.

Tolor, A., & Rafferty, W. The attitudes of mothers of hospitalized patients. _Journal of Nervous and Mental Disease,_ 1963, **136,** 76–81.

Wahl, C. W. Some antecedent factors in the family histories of 568 male schizophrenics of the U. S. Navy. _American Journal of Psychiatry,_ 1956, **113,** 201–210.

Weinberg, S. K. Social psychological aspects of schizophrenia. In Appleby, L., Scher, J. M., & Cumming, J. (Eds.). _Chronic schizophrenia._ Glencoe, Illinois: The Free Press, 1960, pp. 68–88.

Whitehorn, J. C. Studies of the doctor as a crucial factor for the prognosis of schizophrenic patients. _International Journal of Social Psychiatry,_ 1960, **6,** 71–77.

Zigler, E., & Phillips, L. Social effectiveness and symptomatic behaviors. _Journal of Abnormal and Social Psychology,_ 1960, **61,** 231–238.

Zubin, J., Burdock, E. I., Sutton, S., & Cheek, Frances. Epidemiological aspects of prognosis in mental illness. In Pasamanick, B. (Ed.). _Epidemiology of mental disorder._ Washington, D. C.: _American Association for the Advancement of Science,_ 1959.

Zuckerman, M., Ribback, Beatrice B., Monashkin, I., & Norton, J. A., Jr. Normative data and factor analysis in the Parental Attitude Research Instrument. _Journal of Consulting Psychology,_ 1958, **22,** 165–171.

Zuckerman, M., Barrett, Beatrice H., & Braziel, R. M. The parental attitudes of child guidance cases: I. Comparisons with normals, investigations of socio-economic and family constellation factors, and relations to parents' reactions to the clinics. _Child Development,_ 1960, **31,** 401–417.

CHAPTER 16

Psychosomatic Disorders

This chapter deals with an unusual set of complaints. The symptoms are medical, involving organ systems of the body, but they are intimately associated with psychological variables—hence the term *psychosomatic*. A rough definition that has served as well as any is the one suggested by Halliday:

A bodily disorder whose nature can be appreciated only when emotional disturbances, that is, psychological happenings, are investigated in addition to physical disturbances, that is, somatic happenings. (1948, p. 45)

This definition excludes all psychoses because psychotic symptoms do not involve dysfunction of such body systems as circulation, respiration, or digestion. Most neurotic complaints are excluded on the same basis. The somatic symptoms of hysteria are another matter; for example, paralysis of an arm is obviously a physical disturbance. The bodily symptoms of hysteria mimic those seen when the central nervous system is damaged. As we saw in Chapter 4, the symptoms of conversion hysteria usually involve voluntary response patterns such as perception and movement of the limbs and vocal cords. These response patterns, being voluntary, are under the control of the central nervous system. Their voluntary nature is one reason for difficulty in distinguishing some cases of hysteria from malingering. In any event, the somatic symptoms of hysteria occur in structures innervated by the central nervous system. In contrast, the symptoms of psychosomatic disorders occur in structures innervated by the autonomic nervous system: the stomach, the bronchioles of the lungs, the skin, and peripheral arteries. These organs are of course not under voluntary control. Thus we should add to Halliday's definition the phrase, "disorder of organs or organ systems innervated by the autonomic nervous system." This excludes hysteria.

The list of psychosomatic complaints can be small or large, depending upon the inclusiveness of the compiler. We shall focus on four of the most prevalent disorders, the ones on which most research has been done: bronchial asthma, peptic ulcer, essential hypertension, and neurodermatoses.

Asthma is a respiratory illness marked by wheezing, shortness of breath, coughing, gasping, and the sensation of choking. These symptoms are all due to decreases in the diameter of the bronchia, through which air passes to the lungs. These decreases, in turn, are caused by swelling of the bronchial mucosa or by contraction of the broncho-constrictor muscle. Asthmatic-like symptoms often accompany respiratory infections, and, indeed, obstruction of air passages is one of the commoner ailments known to man. Respiratory infections are of great importance in asthma. Rees (1964) found that 80% of his asthmatic sample had had respiratory infections prior to the development of asthma, in contrast to only a 30% rate of respiratory infection in nonasthmatic controls.

A peptic ulcer is a lesion or focal inflammation of the lining of the stomach or the upper part of the small intestine. Such ulcers are quite common, but in many instances they are "quiet," causing no pain or distress, and are therefore unnoticed and unreported. However, ulcers often cause severe pain and, when they perforate, serious internal bleeding results, which can cause death. Other symptoms are nausea and vomiting. It is believed that peptic ulcers are the result of excessive secretion of acid. The stomach produces acid to aid in digestion. The walls of the stomach and upper intestine can ordinarily resist the mildly corrosive effects of the acid. However, in some individuals the acid eats away the protective mucous lining, dissolving tissue in addition to food. This abnormal condition may occur because the particular site is no longer resistant to the acid or because the output of acid is excessive.

Hypertension consists of a chronically elevated blood pressure, which may be caused by kidney dysfunction (*renal* hypertension) or other physiological or anatomical abnormalities. *Essential* hypertension is high blood pressure for which there is no known cause. Three stages of development have been distinguished (Hambling, 1952). The first, *diastolic reaction,* occurs in *prehypertensives,* who react to psychological stress or the pain of the cold pressor test (immersion of hand or foot in ice water for one minute) with a diastolic blood pressure of more than 95 (mm. of mercury). The second stage, *benign hypertension,* is marked by a labile blood pressure, a *permanent* diastolic blood pressure above 95, and a slight thickening of small arteries (in response to the additional pressure). In the third stage, *malignant hypertension,* diastolic pressure is permanently above 130, and this abnormal pressure initiates damage to the kidneys, retinae of the eyes, and other sensitive organs.

Neurodermatoses are a group of syndromes all known to have psychological components. *Neurodermatitis* consists of chronic, nonallergenic reddening and thickening of the skin, exudation of liquid, and intense itching. Other symptoms included under the heading of neurodermatoses are nonallergenic hives, certain scalp conditions, and horniness of the skin.

PSYCHOSOMATIC DISORDERS AND SYSTEMIC DISEASES

The symptoms of psychosomatic disorders are similar and in some instances identical to those seen in systemic diseases. On what basis do we label essential hypertension a psychosomatic disorder and renal hypertension a systemic disease? The basis is clearly etiology. Renal hypertension has a known cause: kidney malfunction. Essential hypertension has no known medical cause, although it is ostensibly related to the psychological variables of anger and fear. In this instance it is relatively easy to distinguish between psychosomatic disorder and systemic disease, but in other instances the distinction is blurred.

The issue here is that of differentiating between two types of patients with somatic symptoms: psychosomatic and nonpsychosomatic patients. Some investigators make a sharp distinction, and others make no distinction at all. Stern (1964) has listed three usages of the term *psychosomatic*. The first reserves the term for symptom patterns that have clearly been linked to psychological causes, as have the four syndromes considered in this chapter. The second usage includes organic diseases believed to be affected but not caused by psychological variables, such as tuberculosis. The third usage is extremely diffuse, for it includes all diseases on the untestable assumption that psychological variables must be involved in all forms of illness and abnormality. We shall adhere to the first usage, which restricts *psychosomatic* to syndromes in which psychological variables are of etiological significance.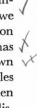

Of course, the fact that psychological variables *may* cause somatic symptoms does not mean that they are a necessary antecedent to the symptoms. The symptoms may be caused by psychological variables in some instances but not in others. Thus bronchial asthma, peptic ulcer, essential hypertension, and the neurodermatoses may be caused by psychological factors, but not necessarily. Psychological variables are best regarded as sufficient but not necessary causes of certain somatic symptoms.

This point is illustrated by the results of a study by Rees (1964) on child asthmatics and controls. Examination of the histories of these patients revealed three causal factors: allergic, infective, and psychological. The allergic factor (substances cause a chemical reaction whose end point is partial closing of the bronchia) was dominant in 17% of the cases and the sole factor in 5% of the cases. The infective factor was dominant in 42% of the cases, and 35% had their initial asthmatic attack during a respiratory infection. As noted earlier, 80% of the asthmatics had had previous respiratory infections, in contrast to only 30% of the controls. The psychological factor was dominant in 42% of the cases, and played a subsidiary role in another 30%. Thus psychological and infective factors are of great importance in the genesis of childhood asthma. In a small percentage of cases the allergic factor is the only important one, and these cases represent systemic disease, not psychosomatic disorder.

The line between the two is even more blurred in the three other syndromes discussed in this chapter. Some cases of peptic ulcer are caused solely by chemical and physiological factors, as are some cases of hypertension and skin disorder. That it is difficult to distinguish these cases from true psychosomatic patients testifies to the difficulties in this area and to our ignorance of the details of the process whereby psychological variables lead to somatic symptoms and even to changes in tissues.

In distinguishing between psychosomatic disorders and systemic diseases we have chosen a single criterion: the presence or absence of psychological variables as causes. There are other possible bases for this distinction, and Halliday (1948) has listed seven.

(1) Emotion as a precipitating factor. This consists of a single psychological variable, anxiety-laden events. Presumably, psychosomatic patients always have dramatic, traumatic (painful) events that serve to initiate their symptoms. This is debatable, and Halliday admits that at least a minority of psychomatic patients have not experienced such undue stresses.

(2) Personality type. Each psychosomatic disorder is ostensibly associated with a particular type of personality. As we shall see, there is little evidence to sustain this hypothesized link between traits or groups of traits and somatic symptoms.

(3) Sex ratio. The incidence of a given psychosomatic syndrome is presumably greater in one of the sexes. There are data to sustain this assumption. Ulcers are commoner in men, and neurodermatoses are commoner in women. However, sex differences also occur in a variety of diseases that have no psychological components, as well as in certain anomalies. For example color blindness occurs more frequently in men than in women. Therefore, in spite of evidence consistent with this assumption, it is not necessarily correct. Different sex ratios may be related to "personality" and "emotions" as they affect psychosomatic disorders, but on the other hand sex ratios may be completely unrelated to psychological variables.

(4) Relationship to other psychosomatic disorders. Psychosomatic disorders, it is assumed, do not usually occur together in the same individual.

They either alternate, occur in sequence, or do not occur jointly at all. This assumption is probably true, for most patients do not suffer from multiple major diseases. However, this is as true for organic diseases as for psychosomatic disorders.

(5) Family history. Most patients ostensibly come from families with a high incidence of similar psychosomatic disorders, or at least a high incidence of such predisposing states as "weak stomach" and "tendency toward high blood pressure." It is not known whether this is true, and beyond this, it remains to be established whether such familial patterns, if they exist, will be explained by heredity or early experience.

(6) Phasic manifestation. The disease waxes and wanes, and there is no regularity in these changes. This is true of most diseases, both psychosomatic and systemic, for there are very few diseases that manifest a clear cyclical pattern whose regularity is easily discerned.

(7) Prevalence is related to psychological and social changes in the community. Presumably the social and interpersonal environment constitutes an important determinant of psychosomatic disorders. This is reasonable and is probably true of all the disorders falling in the domain of psychopathology. In fact, it merely reiterates what is implicit in the term *psychosomatic*.

Examination of Halliday's criteria reveals that six of them are unproved, disproved, or hold for systemic diseases as well as psychosomatic disorders. Criteria of psychosomatic disorders must exclude nonpsychosomatic conditions if the criteria are to be useful. The only criterion that accomplishes this is the seventh one, and it is the one used earlier in defining psychosomatic disorders. These conclusions will be documented as the exposition proceeds. Halliday's assumptions constitute a sort of theory in that he attempts to relate a number of variables to psychosomatic disorders. His position includes variables from several theories we shall discuss presently.

Theories about psychosomatic disorder may be divided into biological and psychological. The biological approaches focus on the kinds of variables considered in Chapter 14: inherited physiological dispositions and constitutional defects. Obviously, psychological variables cannot be ignored in these theories, because the symptoms to be explained are psychosomatic. Nevertheless, the emphasis is on biological variables as the fundamental determinants of symptom patterns.

Psychological approaches focus on the personality attributes of patients, environmental events, faulty communication, regression, learning, and similar psychological determinants. Of course biological aspects cannot be ignored in these theories because the symptoms are somatic, but it is assumed that the fundamental determinants are psychological in nature.

Most of the theories can easily be classified as biological or psychological. Two theories are borderline in that they embody both kinds of variables. They have been labeled *psychological* because, on balance, the psychological aspects seem to be more important.

BIOLOGICAL THEORIES

There are four biological approaches to psychosomatic disorders. The first points to physique as the crucial factor; the second, to weak organs or organ-systems; the third, to inherited autonomic patterns; and the fourth, to stress and emergency reactions.

Physique

As might be expected, Sheldon (1940) attempted to relate body build to psychosomatic disorders. Specifically, he suggested that peptic ulcer patients are endomorphic mesomorphs, a combination of round, broad, fatty elements and athletic, muscular, strong elements. Draper and his colleagues (1944) agreed on the mesomorphic component but added ectomorphic (thin, linear) elements. Thus patients with ulcers are endomorphic mesomorphs for Sheldon and ectomorphic mesomorphs for Draper.

Brouwer (1957) tested these hypotheses with asthma and peptic ulcer patients, and with controls. His ulcer patients proved to be not mesomorphic but slightly ectomorphic; however, they were no more ectomorphic than the controls. In fact the differences among ulcer patients, asthmatics, and controls were small and random. Thus there is no evidence to sustain the notion that physique is a determinant of psychosomatic disorders.

Weak Organs

As White (1964) has noted, the simplest theory is that a psychosomatic disorder occurs because of a bodily weakness. The special vulnerability may be in an organ (the lungs in asthma) or an organ-system (the cardiovascular system in essential hypertension).

The defect may be inherited or it may come about because of adverse events in the medical history of the individual. The latter possibility is easier to check, especially in certain diseases. We saw earlier that 80% of Rees' (1964) sample of asthmatics suffered from previous respiratory infection. Such illness might well have weakened the respiratory apparatus, making the individual more susceptible to subsequent development of asthma. Unfortunately, studies like Rees' are rare, perhaps because in other psychosomatic conditions it is more difficult to trace a prior illness that is unequivocally related to the subsequent psychosomatic disorder. For example, which disease would render the cardiovascular system more vulnerable to essential hypertension?

Thus the notion of a special weakness owing to disease (or even accidents) is difficult to test. Similarly, the hypothesis of hereditary weakness is difficult to evaluate. It is not sufficient to observe that a particular disorder "runs in families." On the negative side, the influence of environment must be ruled out; on the positive side, there must be a demonstration of genetic regularity, such as increasing incidence with increasing blood kinship.

The theory of organ inferiority has an indeterminate status. It has a common sense appeal, but it is too vague to be tested. In any event, it would not be a sufficient explanation. If persons developed somatic complaints only because of special organ vulnerability, the disease would be medical, not psychosomatic. The organ weakness theory attempts to account for the *location* of the psychosomatic condition, not for its genesis.

Inherited Autonomic Patterns

A more precise variant of the weak organ theory is the theory that patterns of autonomic reactivity are inherited. This approach is based largely on the works of Lacey, Wenger, and Malmo, who have demonstrated pronounced individual differences in autonomic reactivity in both normals and psychiatric patients. Lacey and his colleagues (Lacey, Bateman, & Van Lehn, 1963; Lacey & Lacey, 1958) have shown that most of their college student subjects manifest patterns of autonomic activity that are stable from one situation to the next. One subject might show the greatest reaction to stress by a rise in blood pressure, with lesser changes in galvanic skin response and heart rate; this hierarchy of reactivity would show up regardless of the stressful stimuli used to induce the physiological changes. Another subject might show precisely the opposite autonomic pattern, again stable across situations.

These findings have been corroborated by Davis, Lundervold, and Miller (1957), although there was not as much stability. Malmo and Shagass (1949) showed that patients with cardiovascular symptoms reacted to stress with a greater cardiovascular response than a muscle tension increase, whereas patients with headaches had the opposite pattern. Further corroboration has come from research by Wenger et al. (1961), who noted that response specificity is due not only to individual differences but also to the method of measurement.

There is thus support for the notion of response specificity. However, the research cited does not necessarily indicate that these individual differences are inherited. It is possible that such differences are acquired in the course of development and are affected by a variety of psychological and social variables. One way of testing this hypothesis would be to study autonomic patterns in infants. If stable patterns exist in infants prior to the impact of the long process of socialization, the patterns are probably inherited.

Richmond and Lustman (1955) recorded the autonomic reactions of neonates (new born) three to four days old. They found large, stable individual differences in reflex circulatory and pupillary dilatation to loud sounds. Thus there appear to be clear cut, identifiable patterns of autonomic reactivity long before socialization could possibly have an impact. It seems reasonable to assume that these patterns are inherited.

This assumption receives strong support from research by Mirsky (1958). He demonstrated that the *pepsinogen*[1] level of ulcer patients is significantly higher than that of nonulcer patients. Then he showed that there were marked individual differences in the pepsinogen level of neonates, the measurements being taken through the umbilical cord. A high pepsinogen level in the child was related to high familial incidence of excessive pepsinogen.

Thus there seems to be an inherited tendency to oversecrete pepsinogen. The next step was to establish that oversecretors tend to develop ulcers. This is precisely what Mirsky did in two different populations. The first consisted of newly inducted soldiers, from which oversecretors and undersecretors were selected. By the end of four months of basic training, 14% of the oversecretors had developed ulcers, but none of the undersecretors had. The second population consisted of children and civilian adults, from which the top and bottom 2% of pepsinogen secretors were selected. They were followed over time, and again a large number of oversecretors developed ulcers, whereas none of the undersecretors did.

Mirsky's research demonstrates that physiological over-reactivity, which is probably inherited, is a major determinant of ulcer formation. However, not all ulcers are psychosomatic. Mirsky reported that the oversecretors tended to be dependent, "oral" personalities and that for some of them the ulcer was precipitated by painful life experiences. Thus we may conclude that (1) physiological over-reactivity predisposes the individual to develop ulcers, and (2) in many instances the ulcers are psychosomatic.

Since this section concerns autonomic patterns, we should note in passing that oversecretion of pepsinogen is probably due to excessive parasympathetic activity. Later in the chapter we shall consider the role of the parasympathetic nervous system more fully.

The importance of enduring autonomic patterns has been established only for ulcers; there has been no comparable set of results for asthma, essential hypertension, or neurodermatoses. Work such as Mirsky's would appear to be a next step in the study of these three psychosomatic disorders. Prospective studies, in which initially healthy individuals are followed for

---

[1] Pepsinogen is one of three stomach secretions, the other two being mucin and a weak solution of hydrochloric acid. An excess of pepsinogen may be one cause of ulcers.

years, appear to be of considerable value. The major deterrents are the prohibitive amounts of time and money involved, as well as the possibility that the original measures may become obsolete before the long-term research is completed.

Stress

The body reacts to a threatening stimulus by mobilizing its physiological resources. It meets stress with emergency reactions that are ordinarily of short duration. If the stress is prolonged, the emergency mechanisms become exhausted, and a variety of symptoms may appear.

This in capsule form is the stress theory of Selye (1956), who divides the organism's reaction to noxious stimuli into three stages. The first, *alarm reaction,* starts with a shock phase in which body temperature drops, the heart beats faster, and sometimes stomach or intestinal ulcers form. Then adrenaline is liberated, and the organism begins to meet the emergency through the arousal of organs innervated by the sympathetic nervous system. The second stage, *resistance,* is characterized by continuing emergency reactions to the persisting stress. The adrenal cortex becomes enlarged, and emergency mechanisms begin to approach exhaustion. The third stage, *exhaustion,* occurs only if the stress is of extreme duration. Now the adaptive mechanisms can no longer function; they must fail because they are designed for short-term emergency action, which cannot be sustained over time. What ensues is a variety of symptoms that Selye calls *diseases of adaptation.* One of these is likely to be essential hypertension, since blood pressure elevation is part of the alarm reaction or first stage.

Selye's theory has had little application to psychosomatic disorders, probably because it is nonspecific. It fails to specify why one individual would develop an *adaptation syndrome* and another, not; why one individual would become hypertensive and another, asthmatic. Wolff (1953) suggested that the answer might lie in inherited patterns of weakness, a position similar to inherited weak organs. He assumed that a *particular reaction to stress* was inherited.

. . . the individual and his clan meet life in a particular way different from members of other stocks. An individual may have been a potential "nose reactor" or "colon reactor" all his life without ever actually having called upon a particular protective pattern for sustained periods because he did not need to. A given protective pattern may remain inconspicuous during long periods of relative security, and then with stress, become evident as a disorder involving the gut, the heart and vascular system, the vasorespiratory apparatus, the skin or general metabolism. (1953, p. 35)

This theory is a variant of the theory of inherited autonomic patterns. The basic assumption—that there are inherited weaknesses in particular physiological systems—is plausible, but at present there is no unequivocally positive evidence for it. Thus its status is indeterminate, and an evaluation must await further research.

PSYCHOLOGICAL THEORIES

Psychological theories of psychosomatic disorders may be divided into two types. The first are general approaches to the area, suggesting that a particular viewpoint is valuable in dealing with these syndromes. The second are specific theories, involving one or more of the psychosomatic disorders under consideration.

General Approaches

Substitution. Groen (1957) divides reaction patterns of the organism into five types.

(1) *Neuromuscular*—instrumental behavior leading to reward, for example, food-seeking.
(2) *Mimical expressions*—facial and bodily expression of the emotions, for example, happiness, anger.
(3) *Vocal expressions*—vocal responses indicating emotions or signals for help.
(4) *Changes in visceral organs*—these are innervated by the autonomic nervous system.
(5) *Changes in hormone output*—these are innervated by the central nervous system.

The first three reaction patterns are voluntary and are part of the organism's adjustment to everyday problems. Mimical and vocal expressions can be used for substitute gratification when the neuromuscular pattern fails. The last two patterns are exclusively physiological and are not under voluntary control.

The normal individual can control, inhibit, and redirect the neuromuscular, mimical, and vocal reaction patterns, thereby finding adequate discharge for his impulses. The neurotic tends to overinhibit neuromuscular responding and must attempt discharge of impulses through mimical or vocal channels; this results in neurotic symptoms. The psychopath fails to inhibit, and his neuromuscular responses get him into trouble with society.

The potential psychosomatic individual cannot discharge his impulses in a normal fashion. In fact, according to Groen, he is inclined to react in a neurotic or psychopathic fashion but for some reason cannot do so.

. . . when psychopathic and psychoneurotic reaction patterns to frustration are thus inhibited from discharge, *somatic* reaction patterns are substituted in an increased intensity and duration, so that they are called diseased, and thus bring the individual to the family doctor or specialist. (1957, p. 91)

To recapitulate, Groen postulates five reaction patterns, at least one of which must occur in response to stimulation. When the first three (voluntary) patterns are inhibited, at least one of the last two (involuntary, somatic) patterns must occur. Thus an involuntary, somatic reaction is substituted for a voluntary, psychological reaction.

This formulation has testable consequences. It suggests that the psychosomatic patient has strong impulses which are denied expression in normal, psychopathic, or neurotic fashion. He must suffer from an overwhelming tendency to inhibit instrumental and expressive behavior. He should be timid, cautious, and emotionally unresponsive. He should manifest none of the symptoms associated with neurosis or conduct disorders. It is here that this approach comes to grief. The literature on psychosomatic disorders is filled with cases whose descriptions include a variety of neurotic complaints, ranging from hysterical to obsessive-compulsive symptoms. If such symptoms are present, there is no need for the substitution of somatic reaction patterns. Nevertheless, many psychosomatic patients do have neurotic symptoms. Thus Groen's substitution theory appears to be incorrect. His classification of reaction systems is of potential value in the analysis of the organism's response to everyday problems, but these reactions should not be considered as mutually exclusive.

Communication. Adjustment may be construed in terms of interpersonal communication, and, as we saw in the last chapter, deviance may be interpreted in terms of a breakdown in communication. Ruesch (Ruesch & Bateson, 1951) has applied communication theory to psychosomatic disorders. He assumes that psychosomatic patients, being immature, have failed to master an adequate system of communicating with others. This failure turns them away from the usual psychological channels of interaction and toward their own bodies as a source of messages. The genesis of this state of affairs is as follows.

The individual is unable to express himself by means of verbal symbols, perhaps because of poor observation of others and therefore a relative inability to imitate proper expression and correct poor expression. He becomes dependent on others in interpersonal situations, being the receiver but not the sender of messages. This dependent role tends to make him regard most messages from others as threatening or demanding, which alienates him further from verbal exchanges.

He gradually inverts his attention, focusing more on his own body than upon relations with others. Perception of bodily movements and noises comes to predominate over perceptions of the social environment. Value judgments come to be based on inner processes, not social consensus. Information tends to be received more from mechanical and chemical senses than from visual and auditory senses. Physiological boundaries become diffuse, and bodily signs assume greater importance than visual and verbal symbols. Finally, the body becomes the main instrument of communication, both sending and receiving messages. Communication occurs through physiological rather than psychological processes. The chronic overactivity of particular bodily systems, called psychosomatic disorder, is due to their being used for the purpose of communication.

Ruesch's theory offers an interesting parallel to Groen's substitution theory. Groen regards visceral overactivity as a substitute for blocked activity of the neuromuscular system; Ruesch regards visceral activity as a substitute for blocked communication through normal symbolic channels. Ruesch's theory is less specific, less testable, and more of a generalized approach to psychosomatic disorders.

Specific Theories

Regression. A theory of regression, as we saw in Chapters 5 and 11, assumes that there is a fixed developmental sequence. Maturity represents the endpoint of the sequence, and psychopathology represents a return to an earlier developmental stage. Now it is an established fact that the homeostatic mechanisms of infants are crude and allow for wide deviations in the internal environment. For example, temperature regulation is not as precise as it becomes later in development, and the temperature range of infants exceeds that of adults. Thus crude regulatory mechanisms represent an early developmental stage. Psychosomatic disorders may be regarded in terms of regression to earlier physiological eras, just as neuroses may be regarded in terms of regression to earlier psychological eras.

. . . psychosomatic symptoms are regressive psychophysiological states. Repressed fantasies of function return as psychophysiological components of mood and affect states. The more archaic the fantasy of function, the more autonomously the organ functions, and the less central integrative regulation participates. The brain, so to speak, disregards the organ which ceased to operate in the interests of a coordinated economy. The organ acts as though infantile homeostatic boundaries were present. The tissues, however, have lost their tolerance for infantile fluctuations. Hence, a decompensating situation develops and disability is the result. (Margolin, 1953, p. 33)

 Regression theories tend to equate severer symptoms with a greater depth of regression. Margolin, making this assumption, states that emotions associated with the oral period would lead to symptoms associated with dependency, that is, vague gastrointestinal symptoms. If inhibition of emotions occurs later in development, the somatic symptoms tend to be more focal and specific.

Margolin's regression theory is based on the developmental sequence: crude somatic regulation to precise, refined somatic regulation. Alternately, it may be assumed that infants are *vagotonic,* that is, their visceral activity is dominated by the parasympathetic nervous system. This theory was first formulated by Michaels (1944), but it has received its most extensive elaboration from Szasz (1952). He employs the concept of *specific, localized parasympathetic overactivity,* a state that presumably characterizes infancy. Szasz prefers the adjectives *specific* and *localized* in order to limit the concept to certain organs and thereby avoid the pitfalls of a complete parasympathetic-sympathetic dichotomy. He presents the following outline of regressive reaction to stress.

The organism overreacts parasympathetically, which is phylogenetically an older way of reacting. The somatic response is not adaptive to the organism's present requirements but represents a regression to infancy or to man's phylogenetic past. This regressive innervation is the final common pathway for various kinds of stress, and the outcome is a group of regressive somatic syndromes including ulcer, asthma, and neurodermatoses.

In terms of tissue changes, there are two effects of regressive innervation. The first is the liberation of *acetylcholine,* which mediates parasympathetic neural transmission. The acetylcholine, in turn, leads to increased activity and secretion in the hollow visceral organs. Oversecretion of acid in the stomach could cause ulcers; oversecretion of fluid in the bronchia could cause asthma. Acetylcholine also effects the release of histamine to cells, which could cause flooding and elevated temperature in the skin, thus leading to neurodermatoses. The second effect of regressive innervation is the production of lysozyme, an enzyme that dissolves mucous membranes. This could be another cause of ulcers.

Szasz contrasts regressive, parasympathetic innervation with phylogenetically younger, sympathetic innervation, which is diffuse and not focused on any specific organs. The normal response to stress is not cholinergic (regressive) but adrenergic (concomitant). Concomitant innervation prepares the organism for emergency action; it does not lead to disease unless the emergency is chronic or discharge is blocked. Under these circumstances, essential hypertension may develop. Thus two kinds of psychosomatic disorders are delineated: regressive (ulcer, asthma, and neurodermatoses) and concomitant or nonregressive (essential hypertension). As to which particular regressive psychosomatic disorder will develop, the answer is supplied by Michaels:

. . . the choice of organ or organ system . . . may be dependent upon its fusion with an emotional process at a labile period when the organ or organ system had not yet attained its full maturation. (1944, p. 61)

These regression theories are interesting but highly speculative. The crucial explanatory variables are difficult to investigate because they reside in a complex psychological-physiological interaction occurring early in childhood. Nevertheless, a basic assumption of the Michaels-Szasz theory can be checked, namely, the assumption that the infant is *vagotonic* (dominated by parasympathetic activity).

Richmond and Lustman (1955) studied the autonomic reactivity of three and four day-old infants, and found wide individual differences, including both sympathetic and parasympathetic dominance, as well as neither being dominant. They concluded:

> It would seem appropriate, therefore, to caution against basing psychosomatic theory on a "biological regression" or upon the concept that the infants' gastrointestinal tract is "vagotonic." (p. 270)

This research slices away the underpinning of regression theory, which appears to have speculated incorrectly about the somatic functioning of infants.

Specificity. Franz Alexander, being a psychoanalyst, was sympathetic to the regression approach. He accepted the sympathetic-parasympathetic dichotomy as a fundamental basis for distinguishing types of psychosomatic disorder, but he went on to postulate specific personality conflicts for each disorder.

Alexander (1950) distinguished two emotional reactions to stress. The first is emergency preparation for fight or flight, presumably mediated by the sympathetic nervous system. After such emergency action, physiological processes return to their resting state. In the absence of action, however, the organism remains for some time in a state of heightened physiological activity. If preparation for action is persistently followed by no action, the heightened physiological state may become chronic. Ostensibly, this is what occurs in essential hypertension.

The second emotional reaction to stress is withdrawal from outwardly directed activity to a dependent, vegetative existence. Such physiological activity is precisely the opposite of what is needed to meet the stress. It represents a regressive reaction in that it constitutes a revival of processes characteristic of infants; it is a vegetative existence. Note that this assumption has been disproved by the research of Richmond and Lustman (1955). The regressive reaction to stress may lead to ulcers or bronchial asthma. (Alexander does not include neurodermatoses.)

The distinction between emergency and withdrawal syndromes constitutes the first part of Alexander's theory. The second part deals with conflict situations believed to be specific to each psychosomatic disorder.

Regarding ulcer, it would appear that the crucial factor in the pathogenesis of ulcer is the frustration of the dependent, help-seeking, and love-demanding desires.

When these desires cannot find gratification in human relationships, a chronic emotional stimulus is created which has a specific effect upon the functions of the stomach. (Alexander, 1950, p. 103)

Alexander assumed that all ulcer patients have intense dependency needs, but that there are two kinds of reactions to this dependency. The first is the classical "ulcer personality": the desire to be cared for is opposed by more overt tendencies toward ambition, independence, aggression, and achievement. There is a reaction formation to childish needs for help, which takes the form of assuming excessive responsibility. The longing for parental love is repressed, and this repressed impulse causes the parasympathetic overactivity which leads to ulcers. Physiologically, the stomach is continuously preparing to receive food, which is symbolically equated with parental love.

The second reaction involves no overcompensation; the individual accepts his dependency needs and is clinging and demanding. However, this childish role is not acceptable to others, and his need for parental love is not met. He is frustrated because as an adult he cannot play the role of a child. This is common to both types of reaction to dependency needs: the first type is frustrated by a conflicting need to show independence, and the second type is frustrated by the refusal of others to furnish parental affection to an adult.

This theory of ulcer formation is based on observations of patients undergoing psychoanalysis. No doubt many ulcer patients manifest the dependency conflicts outlined, but if the theory is correct, dependency must be the core problem in virtually *all* ulcer patients. However, other investigators have reported other kinds of conflicts as determinants of ulcers. Specifically, anger and hostility have been pointed out in four studies as being responsible for excessive stomach motility and ulcer formation (Mittelmann, Wolff, & Scharf, 1942; Wolf & Wolff, 1943; Szasz, Levin, Kirsner, & Palmer, 1947; and Margolin, 1951). These studies all involved psychiatric or psychoanalytic interviews, and in three of them there was direct observation of the stomach by means of a gastric fistula.

Alexander insisted that the dependency conflicts of ulcer patients are deep and unconscious, and therefore only "depth interviews" and projective techniques should be used to test his hypothesis. In addition to the studies cited which used interviews, there are several negative studies using projective techniques. Streitfeld (1954) found that ulcer patients and controls did not differ in conflicts over oral-dependent needs. The ulcer patients did have intense oral-aggressive tendencies, but so did many of the control subjects. Mednick, Garner, and Stone (1959) compared ulcer patients, colitis patients, and orthopedic patients on a projective experimental task. There were no differences among the groups in dependence or conflicts about dependence. Marshall (1960) compared ulcer patients with controls, and the only reliable difference was the ulcer patients' tendency to describe themselves as more emotionally inhibited and more conforming.

Several investigators have shown that fear induces excessive stomach activity and ulcers. (We shall discuss the research in detail in a later section). Thus ulcers have been related not only to conflicts over dependency but also to anger, hostility, and fear. When rigorous experimental design is adhered to in research, specifically the presence of control subjects, ulcer patients are sometimes found to have no special conflicts or personality features. Therefore we may conclude that Alexander's hypothesis is incorrect.

Regarding asthma, the basic underlying conflict, according to Alexander, is an intense, unresolved, childlike relationship with the mother. The patient may defend against this infantile dependence, thereby developing traits of aggressiveness, hostility, or over-sensitivity. The unconscious wish is not so much a desire to be fed, as in ulcer patients, but a desire to be nurtured and protected. Asthma patients wish to be cuddled and kept warm by a maternal figure who will shield them from a cold, distant, and potentially threatening world. What they fear most is separation from the mother, and their histories always contain evidence of inconsistent maternal rejection.

Why should nurturance needs and separation fears lead to asthma? The answer lies in crying. The potential asthmatic has a strong impulse to cry for his mother, but he is prevented from doing so because of guilt or shame; or he lets himself go and then cannot stop crying. An asthmatic attack superficially resembles an attempt to hold back tears or to stop crying. The breathing patterns are similar: quick, shallow respiration, wheezing, and sniffling. In both instances the normal respiratory pattern is disturbed, and the similarity has been used by psychoanalysts to strengthen the case for asthma's being caused by a suppressed desire to cry, based on an unconscious need for a protective mother.

There is no doubt that some asthmatics have the particular dynamic conflict just described, and, indeed, some of the reports in the literature support Alexander's conceptualization. However, other kinds of conflicts are also present in asthmatics. Miller and Baruch (1950) found intense hostility in their asthmatic patients, and Barendregt (1957), in a Rorschach study, showed that asthmatics were more constricted and more hostile than controls. Knapp and Nemetz (1957) reported a variety of conflicts and disturbances in their asthmatic sample, with no single dynamic pattern being outstanding.

Although Alexander's hypothesis may have validity for some asthmatics, it does not hold for all, or even a large majority, of asthmatics. Again, the specificity hypothesis appears to be incorrect.

Regarding essential hypertension, we noted earlier that it is regarded as a disease of "concomitant innervation," not "regressive innervation." This means that it is a consequence of an overactive sympathetic nervous system, not an overactive parasympathetic nervous system. The problems do not concern everyday needs, such as food or affection; they concern emergency situations such as fight or flight.

Alexander postulated that rage is the central emotion underlying essential hypertension. The individual, for one reason or another, has hostile impulses that he is unable to discharge.

> The damming up of his hostile impulses will continue and will consequently increase in intensity. This will induce the development of stronger defensive measures in order to keep pent-up aggressions in check . . . Because of the marked degree of their inhibitions, these patients are less effective in their occupational activities and for that reason tend to fail in competition with others, so that envy is stimulated and their hostile feelings toward more successful, less inhibited competitors is further intensified. (Alexander, 1950, p. 150)

As we shall see shortly, there is considerable evidence for Alexander's principal assumption: that suppressed rage underlies essential hypertension. There has been no support, outside of Alexander's own writings, for the assumed feelings of inferiority and dependence.

Alexander's hypothesis, although essentially correct, fails to bridge the gap between temporary rises in blood pressure and chronic elevation of blood pressure. It is an oversimplification to state that chronic resentment leads to chronic high blood pressure. The theory must specify how this comes about, and the following formulation (Buss, 1961, Chapter 12) attempts to do just that.

The potential hypertensive individual has an excessively mobile blood pressure, as shown by his response to the cold pressor test. Like anyone else, he reacts to an anger stimulus with an elevation in blood pressure, but the blood pressure rise is considerably higher than average. Because the deviation from resting blood pressure is greater, more time is required to return to resting level than the average person. Because he is fearful of the consequences of anger, either punishment or his own guilt, the prehypertensive individual suppresses expressions of rage. Unlike the neurotic, he has no systematic defense against anger stimuli or his own tendency to aggress. He cannot retreat into rituals as does the compulsive person, nor can he avoid specific anger stimuli as does the phobic person. Instead, the prehypertensive individual works himself up to the final stages of physiological preparation for attack and in the absence of an attacking response or a temper tantrum, his tension state remains at a high level for some time. Thus his blood pressure remains high not only because it deviates so far from resting state but also because the tension state is not alleviated by an explosive behavioral reaction. This is the first stage—diastolic reaction.

Since the prehypertensive individual tends to suppress aggression, it follows that he is more sensitive than the average person to the presence of anger stimuli. The person who fears the consequences of venting rage tends to perceive anger stimuli in the neutral stimuli that impinge on him. The prehypertensive person should therefore become angry oftener than the average person, which means that his blood pressure should rise oftener. With the passage of time, the cycle proceeds toward more frequent elevation in blood pressure and longer periods during which it is high. This period continues for years, with the intervals between successive elevations of blood pressure becoming smaller and smaller. It becomes more and more difficult to distinguish resting blood pressure from temporary rises. The excessive and prolonged increases in blood pressure activate minor changes in the arterioles, which tend to thicken in response to the additional stress placed upon them. This thickening constricts the arteriolar bed, thus elevating resting blood pressure.

Eventually the intervals between successive blood pressure elevations become so small that blood pressure does not have time to return to resting level before another anger stimulus initiates the next rise in blood pressure. Blood pressure is still excessively mobile, but resting level in now higher. The peaks and the valleys are the same as before, but resting diastolic level is above 95—the stage of benign hypertension. Once this second stage has been reached, the cycle usually proceeds to the third stage, malignant hypertension, by means of bodily reactions to the abnormally high blood pressure: more thickening of the arterioles and the arteries, interference with kidney filtration, and so on.

This account of the etiology of essential hypertension makes three assumptions. First, the potential hypertensive individual has a labile blood pressure. This has been reported in Harris et al. (1953), and it evidently carries through to the second stage—hypertensives are hyperreactive on the cold pressor test[2] (Thacker, 1940). Second, potential hypertensives are more susceptible to anger, being resentful, jealous, and oversensitive to slights. They are driven into anger more quickly than the average person. Third, they cannot cope with rage, failing to express aggression against those they blame. They are too insecure and frightened of retaliation, too guilt stricken to launch an attack against those who anger them. Helpless to curb their recurrent rages or to alleviate tension by exploding into aggression, they remain tense and uncomfortable.

There are two kinds of evidence bearing on this formulation. The first comes from the laboratory, in which subjects are angered and their cardio-

[2] The cold pressor test consists of immersing one hand in ice water for one minute, which elevates blood pressure through constriction of peripheral blood vessels.

vascular reactions measured. The second comes from clinical studies of hypertensives.

Schachter (1957) divided laboratory subjects into three groups: hypertensives, 140/90 or over; potential hypertensives, initially 140/90 or over but dropping to below 135/85 after 30 minutes of rest; and normals, below 140/90 at all times (average blood pressure is 120/80). His anger situation involved an assistant's verbally abusing and jostling the subjects. Only systolic blood pressure yielded significant differences in anger; hypertensives increased the most, followed by potential hypertensives, and then normals. Diastolic pressure rose in all three groups, and the differences among groups were not significant. There was also a fear stimulus, and there were significant differences among groups in diastolic pressure; normals increased less than the other two groups. These findings offer only partial support for the dynamic formulation of hypertension mentioned earlier. The differential rise of systolic pressure in anger is supportive, but the failure of diastolic pressure to rise differentially and the significant diastolic changes in fear suggest that the formulation needs amending. Evidently fear is as much a cause of large jumps in blood pressure as is anger.

Neiberg (1957) compared hypertensive subjects and patients with middle ear infection in an anger arousing situation. Subjects were failed randomly while taking a test, with the experimenter making nasty, derogatory comments about their performance. Blood pressure increased approximately the same for both groups, the hypertensives' resting and final levels being higher than those of the controls. The discrepancy between these findings and Schachter's may be due to either the difference in measures or the difference in anger-arousing situations.

Two other studies used anger arousal in the laboratory with hypertensive patients, but in neither instance was blood pressure the dependent variable. Matarazzo (1954) badgered hypertensives and controls during a TAT administration but found no differences in TAT aggression. Harris et al. (1953) had potential hypertensive women and controls role play in a situation that induced anger, and their behavior was rated by judges. The potential hypertensives were judged as being more irritable, more resentful, and less controlled in their emotional responses. In both these studies the dependent variable was personality characteristics, and in the four studies mentioned so far, anger was aroused in the laboratory. In the following investigations, hypertensives were stressed in clinical situations, and the dependent variable was blood pressure change.

Schneider and Zangari (1951) interviewed a normotensive anxiety hysteric and a hypertensive patient, in both instances bringing up affect-laden material during the interviews. The anxiety hysteric manifested no systematic fluctuation in blood pressure. When the hypertensive patient became anxious and resentful, both diastolic and systolic blood pressure rose steeply, returning to the resting state only after strong reassurance.

Wolf and Wolff (1951) interviewed a large number of hypertensives and controls. After a period during which the subject was placid, there was an abrupt switch to a discussion of significant and disturbing interpersonal problems. The subjects were divided into two groups on the basis of their reported reactions to this stress. One group reported being menaced and trapped, feeling not only anxious but also resentful. Their blood pressure rose sharply: hypertensives' blood pressure increased from a mean of 165/103 to 189/117 and controls' from 119/76 to 131/81. The other group reported feeling defeated and overwhelmed, experiencing no resentment but only terror and despair. The blood pressure of both hypertensive and control subjects in this group fell below what it had been during the placid state. Note that both groups were anxious, but whereas the first group was also angry, the second group was not. Thus with anxiety held more or less constant, resentment elevated blood pressure and despair or depression lowered it. This is the strongest evidence available for the role of suppressed anger in the etiology of essential hypertension.

Moses et al. (1956) recorded the blood pressure of essential hypertensives undergoing psychoanalysis, attempting to relate blood pressure changes to the anxiety and anger that occurred during therapy. They found that rage and resentment predominated when blood pressure in the 160/100—200/130 range, but anxiety predominated in the 140/90—160/100 range. During the course of therapy excessive rage reactions diminished, with a concomitant drop in blood pressure. Blood pressure never descended below borderline hypertensive levels, but it was accompanied by persistent anxiety. The investigators concluded that anxiety raises blood pressure to hypertensive levels, but rage elevates it beyond these levels.

Oken (1960) demonstrated the role of suppressed anger in elevating blood pressure. The subjects, psychiatric patients with normal blood pressure, were angered and made anxious during psychiatric interviews. Blood pressure readings revealed that elevated blood pressure was consistently related to inhibition or suppression of anger.

These various laboratory studies raise two issues that are difficult for any dynamic formulation of hypertension to resolve. First, there is evidence that in anger the blood pressure increase of normals is often no less than that of hypertensives. There are reasons, however, for believing that hypertensives have a more labile blood pressure than normals. It has been demonstrated that the blood pressure reaction of hypertensives to the cold pressor test is considerably more intense than that of normals (Thacker, 1940). Those with a normal resting blood pressure but an overlabile reaction to the cold pressor test have been shown to be especially susceptible to hypertension in later years. Furthermore, Engel and Bickford (1961) demonstrated that hypertensives have an overreactive blood pressure response to stresses (noise, exercise, problems to be solved) in comparison to normals. They also showed that hypertensives have greater response stereotypy, as shown by maximal activation in a given physiological system, than do normals; this response specificity is, of course, in their blood pressure reactivity.

The absence of a differential rise in blood pressure between hypertensives and normals may be due to artifacts. Because of sampling errors, a particular group of normal subjects might be more susceptible to anger than a given group of hypertensives; in this event, the lability of the hypertensives' blood pressure would be canceled out by the greater psychological reactivity of the normals. Another kind of artifact is more systematic. Lacey (1959) has discovered a negative relationship between resting level and amount of increase in a number of physiological measures, including blood pressure. He found that the higher the resting level, the smaller is the increase during experimental arousal. This effect is evidently so pervasive that Lacey has proposed a regression equation as a statistical means of canceling it. Thus, if an investigator used essential hypertensives whose blood pressures were extremely high, he would have difficulty in demonstrating a differential increase over that of normals. This may account for the discrepancy in findings—some investigators reporting a differential increase and others not—when hypertensives and normals are angered in laboratory situations.

The second difficulty for a dynamic formulation of essential hypertension is the tendency of blood pressure to rise not only in anger but also in fear. There is evidence (Davis & Buchwald, 1957) that a variety of psychological stimuli initiate a blood pressure response, the cardiovascular system being mobile. Maximal blood pressure response to psychological stimuli occurs in the presence of anger and fear. Fear was not included in the dynamic formulation described earlier, yet it evidently does elevate blood pressure. Any formulation of the dynamics of essential hypertension must explain why fear does not lead to hypertension. The formulation presented earlier must therefore be amended, as follows.

Consider the sequence of events that begins with an anger stimulus. The individual immediately reacts with anger, his blood pressure soaring as part of the general preparation for attack. If the attack occurs, it will dissipate the physiological tension of anger, returning blood pressure to its resting level. This has been demonstrated in the laboratory by Hokanson and Burgess (1962, 1963). College students were angered, and then half were allowed to aggress and half were not. The blood pressure of those who aggressed tended to drop, but the blood pressure of the others remained elevated.

Another way of relieving tension is to go through all the motions of attack without attacking anyone—a temper tantrum. Whether the response is a coordinated attack or a violent flailing about, as in a temper tantrum, blood pressure should return to its resting level. What happens if neither of these responses occurs? Once the anger stimulus is removed, the tension state should start to dissipate, but in the absence of a temper or attack response, some time will elapse before resting level is reached. Note that only violent action (temper tantrum or attack) dissipate the tension state of anger.

Now consider the sequence that is initiated by a fear stimulus. In fear the individual's blood pressure also rises and it remains high so long as the fear stimulus continues to impinge on the individual; but, like anger stimuli, fear stimuli occur quickly and then are removed. When the fear stimulus disappears, tension level drops quickly to resting level. If the fear stimulus persists, two kinds of instrumental responses might reduce tension. The first is aggressive action, that is, eliminate the fear stimulus by destroying it or removing its source from the scene. The second is flight, that is, escape from the noxious stimulus by placing distance between it and the self. These alternatives represent the familiar fight-or-flight reactions.

Let us compare the two sequences. In anger, removal of the anger stimulus does not lead to an immediate diminution of blood pressure. Reduction of tension is achieved principally by making one type of instrumental response, attack. If the attack is not made, considerable time is required for blood pressure to return to normal. In fear, on the other hand, removal of the fear stimulus initiates an immediate drop in blood pressure. The instrumental response that diminishes fear consists of any action that eliminates the noxious stimulus. So long as the stimulus is removed by any means, blood pressure will start to return to resting level. In contrast, anger is not dissipated by the mere removal of the noxious stimulus. Fear can be reduced by a variety of instrumental escape responses, anger only by aggression or a temper tantrum. Note that when the anger stimulus is removed, it may be impossible for aggression to occur because the object of aggression (source of the anger stimulus) is no longer available. There are many reasons for an aggressive response not to occur: removal of the object of aggression, guilt concerning aggression, fear concerning retaliation, etc. On the other hand, there are few reasons for an escape response not to occur. Not only is it proper to protect oneself from noxious stimuli, but also escape does not require the interpersonal situation that aggression does.

Thus it is easier to make the instrumental responses that diminish fear than those that diminish anger. Although blood pressure is elevated by both fear and anger, it should remain elevated longer in anger than in fear. This hypothesis has not been tested, perhaps because investigators are more interested in arousal than in the time taken to return to a resting state. A comparison of the time taken to return to a resting state after fear and after anger stimuli should provide data bearing on the hypothesis. Once the arousing stimuli cease, it follows that blood pressure should return to its resting level faster in fear than in anger, so long as the individual is prevented from attacking.

The clinical studies may be divided into those using interviews and those using tests. The former were conducted in clinical settings, and they usually lacked objectivity, controls, and statistical tests. Two studies did employ controls. Saul (1939) reported on hypertensives and neurotic normotensives who were undergoing psychoanalysis. Both groups had essentially the same conflict, passivity versus aggressiveness. Saul suggested that the neurotics avoided high blood pressure by being more accepting of their passivity and also by employing defense mechanisms. Gressel et al. (1949) compared essential hypertensives with two control groups; one consisted of psychiatric outpatients and the other of medical outpatients. The hypertensives were found to differ from the medical patients on five out of six personality variables, but they differed from the psychiatric patients only on assertiveness and obsessive-compulsiveness. The hypertensives were subnormally assertive and unable to verbalize anger or hostility even to their physicians.

Unlike these two investigations, most clinical studies have not had control subjects, and there is no way of knowing whether the personality patterns reported are unique to essential hypertension. Therefore, the value of these studies lies in whether they are consistent with the hypothesized hypertensive dynamics, namely, that anger and resentment are intense but unexpressed.

Robbins (1948) and Schwartz (1940) reported on hypertensive patients undergoing psychoanalysis, noting the typical pattern of suppressed rage. Suppressed rage was also mentioned by Weiss (1942) in his review of 144 cases of essential hypertension. Engel (1953) followed a case of essential hypertension for 9 years and reported that attacks usually occurred in a setting of unexpressed anger accompanied by guilt. Suppression of aggression was also noted by Binger et al. (1945) and Tucker (1949). Wolf and Wolff (1946) reported an appearance of affability in hypertensives that overlay suspicion and strong desires to act out aggressively. Hambling (1951) found suppressed rage directed toward the parental figure whom the hypertensive saw as rejecting. Reiser et al. (1951) concluded that the predominant conflict in hypertensives concerned ambivalence toward parental figures, with hostility being only one source of conflict.

Taken together, these studies offer evidence consistent with the hypothesis that suppressed anger is basic to the development of essential hypertension. Most of the studies mentioned other personality characteristics, and the total number of characteristics ascribed to hypertensives is large. Examination of all the personality variables reported in these studies leads to no consistent finding, with the sole exception of unexpressed anger. Thus there is no "hypertensive personality," but hypertensives tend to suppress range, however else they differ among themselves.

Turning to studies with tests, one of the earliest was that of Ayman (1933). He had essential hypertensives and normals fill out a personality inventory and found that hypertensives reported themselves as being more sensitive, quick-tempered, and hyperactive than normals. Storment (1951) found no significant differences between hypertensive and medical patients on the Guilford-Martin personality inventories. The only positive trend was for hypertensives and rheumatic heart patients to describe themselves as overcritical and intolerant.

In a large-scale, well-controlled investigation, Hamilton (1942) studied three groups of normal subjects: those with high, normal, and low blood pressure (the highs and lows not being pathologically so). Only a few items in a trait rating scale significantly distinguished the highs from the normals, but the differences were sufficiently reliable to appear again on cross validation. The potential hypertensives (highs) showed low dominance, low assertiveness, and susceptibility to anger in comparison to normals. The lows were in the opposite direction, showing high dominance, high assertiveness, and unsusceptibility to anger. The tendency of the lows to have personality characteristics opposite to those of the highs is a striking result, and it corroborates the hypothesis that aggressiveness and control of anger are crucial in the etiology of essential hypertension.

Six studies used projective techniques to assess personality trends in hypertensive patients (Kemple, 1945; Modell & Potter, 1949; Schweers, 1950; Saul et al., 1954; Leary, 1957; and Thaler et al., 1957). The only consistent finding was difficulty in handling anger and aggression: either excessive or insufficient aggression.

In summary, the studies with tests tend to support the notion that hypertensives are caught in an intense approach-avoidance conflict concerning anger. They are covertly resentful and cannot prevent intense bouts of rage, but neither can they act out their aggressive tendencies. When the clinical studies are considered as a whole, the picture is the same, with few exceptions. When the laboratory studies are added, there is further confirming evidence concerning the role of suppressed anger in the etiology of essential hypertension. It may be concluded that a passive-aggressive conflict is the hypertensive's core problem, and it is doubtful that further clinical studies would add to knowledge in this area. Rather, more laboratory studies are needed to bridge the gap between diastolic reaction and benign hypertension.

Most of the evidence supports part of Alexander's theory and our more specific formulation. Nevertheless, the hypothesized pattern fits many neurotics as well as hypertensives. Most neurotics tend to suppress aggressive responses because of guilt and fear of retaliation. Although they are resentful of others, they tend to be nonaggressive. Neurotics may attack others in devious ways, but they are not directly aggressive. However, neurotics and essential hypertensives are only superficially similar in their handling of anger and aggression. The neurotic has defenses that help him to avoid anger-arousing situations. Once he becomes involved with anger stimuli, he has defenses that prevent him from developing uncontrolled rage. The phobic tends to avoid situations that are fraught with the danger of attack, either by himself or others; the compulsive becomes involved with his rituals, thereby avoiding both anger and aggression. The obsessive mulls over the pros and cons of action, displacing his anger and putting sufficient psychological distance between himself and the anger stimulus for him to remain relatively placid.

Unlike the neurotic, the essential hypertensive has no well-developed defenses against becoming enraged. Though he is aware of his burning anger, he tends neither to admit it nor to act it out against the targets of anger. Unable to deal with his aggressive tendencies by either action or neurotic defenses, the hypertensive must rely on suppression at the last possible moment. After he is worked up with rage and all the physiological preparations for attack have been made, he makes a last-ditch attempt to suppress his anger. The attempt is usually successful, and he remains bottled up in a state of impotent rage. The neurotic, in contrast, does not attain such peaks of prolonged rage because his attempts to cope with anger are made much earlier in the sequence.

Regarding neurodermatoses, Alexander tentatively suggested that hostility, masochism, and severe conflicts might be important, but he admitted that, "Attempts at generalizations are not yet successful." (1950, p. 166). Dunkel (1949) concluded that the major psychological component in neurodermatitis is guilty suppression of hostility. Lynch et al. (1953) also emphasized repressed hatred. However, Kepecs et al. (1951) focused on sexual conflicts in skin disorders, and McLaughlin et al. (1953) suggested a combination of sexual and aggressive conflicts. Thus, there is no generally accepted dynamic formulation for neurodermatoses, and we shall not attempt to evaluate the various hypotheses. Rather, we shall consider neurodermatoses in detail in a subsequent section.

There is sufficient evidence to evaluate Alexander's specificity theory. His hypotheses about peptic ulcer and bronchial asthma are not acceptable on two counts. First, they do not hold for most of the patients with these diagnoses. Ulcer and asthma patients have conflicts over aggression as well as dependency, and many are extremely anxious. Alexander overlooked these possibilities because he omitted a control group of neurotics from his observational studies. This was a recurrent theme in the early research on abnormal populations, but recent research has been more sophisticated.

If psychosomatic patients and neurotics have similar conflicts, the presence of a particular conflict is obviously not a sufficient condition for the development of psychosomatic symptoms. As best, a particular conflict might be a necessary but not a sufficient condition. However, studies demonstrating nondependency conflicts in ulcer and asthma patients lead to the conclusion that there are no specific conflicts underlying these two syndromes.

Part of Alexander's specificity hypothesis about essential hypertension appears to be correct. Chronic high blood pressure is likely to develop in individuals who have difficulty in venting anger through aggression. However, the other part of Alexander's hypothesis, the presence of inferiority feelings and competitiveness, has not been supported. Thus it is unexpressed rage that appears to be a necessary condition for essential hypertension. The other necessary condition, as in all psychosomatic disorders, seems to be a predisposition to have an overreactive cardiovascular system.

Thus Alexander's hypothesis about the disorder of *concomitant innervation,* (hypertension) has been corroborated, whereas his hypothesis about disorders of *regressive* innervation (ulcers and asthma) has not. The reason for this appears to lie in the close association between anger (and to a lesser extent, fear) and a rise in blood pressure. It has been well established that elevated blood pressure is part of an individual's anger reaction. With anger and blood pressure being correlated, it is not surprising that essential hypertension should be linked to suppressed anger.

The relationship between inhibited dependency needs and physiological reactivity is quite different; there is no close tie between the two. It was assumed by psychoanalysts that dependency would involve specific physiological reactions because of the symbolism involved. Needing love symbolically would mean needing food and therefore the stomach readies itself. Crying out for one's mother or half suppressing the cry would mean bronchial constriction and wheezing. These hypotheses, which occur naturally in a psychoanalytic context, have been proven to be incorrect. The psychoanalytic emphasis on the "symbolic functioning" of the gastrointestinal and respiratory systems is evidently mistaken. A more appropriate emphasis would be on the physiological concomitants of fear and rage, or on the physiological concomitants of "attitudes."

Attitudes. A variation of specificity theory is the "specific attitudes" theory of Graham and his colleagues (Grace & Graham, 1952; Graham, Graham, & Kabler, 1960). They define an attitude as what the individual feels is happening to him and what he wants to do about it. Their basic assumption is that every attitude toward a disturbing situation has an associated physiological pattern of change and therefore a specific psychosomatic disorder. Concerning the four psychosomatic syndromes we are dealing with, the hypothesized attitudes are:

> *bronchial asthma*—feeling unloved and left out, and wishing to shut the other person out.
> *ulcer*—feeling deprived and resentful, and wanting revenge.

essential hypertension—feeling threatened by ever-present danger, and needing to be on guard, watchful, and prepared.

skin disorders—being treated unfairly, taking a beating, being frustrated, and no desire to do anything about it.

If this theory is correct, it follows that inducing a particular attitude should elicit its associated physiological reaction. This reaction should eventually lead to the associated psychosomatic condition, for example, feeling threatened and being on guard should elicit an elevated blood pressure, which should eventually lead to essential hypertension. It also follows that patients with specific psychosomatic disorders should have the hypothesized attitudes. Graham and his colleagues have collected evidence on both these points.

Graham, Stern, and Winokur (1958) compared attitudes ostensibly associated with two skin diseases, Raynaud's disease (cold hands, poor circulation) and hives. The hypotheses were: (1) an attitude of wanting to take direct hostile action would elicit a drop in hand temperature such as might lead to Raynaud's disease, and (2) an attitude of seeing oneself mistreated and being injured, without wishing to take action would elicit a rise in hand temperature such as might lead to hives. Healthy men were hypnotized and told to assume one of the above attitudes; subsequently, the second attitude was assumed. The hostile attitudes resulted in a drop in hand temperature, and the passive attitude, a rise in hand temperature. Thus both hypotheses were confirmed.

A follow-up study (Stern, Winokur, & Graham, 1960) also included an attitude presumably associated with essential hypertension: the subject was told, under hypnosis, that the doctor was going to do something painful or harmful to him and that he could only wait and watch, but not prevent it. Again skin temperature dropped with the hostile attitude (Raynaud's disease), but this time it also dropped with the hives attitude (passive reception of mistreatment). Skin temperature rose with the hypertensive attitude. Thus only the effect of the Raynaud's disease attitude was replicated; the hives attitude yielded a rise in temperature in the first study and a drop in the second one. The rise in temperature associated with the hypertensive attitude in the second study, together with the rise in temperature associated with the hives attitude in the first study, suggests that physiological reactions are not specific to particular attitudes.

In the second study diastolic blood pressure was also recorded. It rose with both the Raynaud's disease and hypertensive attitudes and did not change with the hives attitude. Thus the results of the two studies both support and weaken the theory of specific attitudes. The support derives from the attitudes eliciting different physiological reactions, and the weakening derives from the same physiological reaction being elicited by different attitudes.

A third study (Graham, Kabler, & Graham, 1962) was unequivocally positive. Again the hives and hypertension attitudes were suggested under hypnosis, and again the subjects were healthy men. The hives attitude elicited a greater increase in skin temperature than the hypertension attitude, and the hypertension attitude elicited a greater rise in diastolic blood pressure than the hives attitude. These results constitute strong support for the theory of specific attitudes.

Further support comes from a clinical study (Graham, Lundy, Benjamin, Kabler, Lewis, Kunish, & Graham, 1962). Psychosomatic patients were interviewed and judges attempted to predict the diagnoses solely on the basis of typescripts of the interviews. The basis of prediction was a knowledge of the attitudes ostensibly associated with each syndrome. The judges did significantly better than chance, indicating that there is a definite association between the syndromes and the specific attitudes. However, there were many errors, which suggests that the association may not be strong.

In discussing their theory, Graham and his colleagues have mentioned its compatibility with Alexander's psychoanalytic specificity approach, Lacey's emphasis on individual differences, and the situational specificity emphasized by Ax and Schachter (physiological patterns for each emotion). They maintain that the specific attitudes theory is better than these other approaches because it not only can account for previous results but can predict the kind and direction of physiological change. Their argument is persuasive because of an impressive array of positive findings, both in the laboratory and in the clinic. Nevertheless, there are some negative features. The first consists of the conflicting findings mentioned. The second has to do with the diffuseness of physiological reactions. Graham and his colleagues have listed a large number of specific attitudes (we have dealt only with those relevant to the four disorders under consideration). It is doubtful that the dozen or so attitudes could each have an associated, specific physiological pattern. Some of their own evidence is consistent with this; the Raynaud's disease attitude and the hypertension attitude yielded similar physiological changes. There simply are not enough discrete physiological reactions to satisfy the number demanded by the theory. Therefore the theory will probably have to be amended in the direction of less specificity.

One other aspect of the theory deserves comment. We may well ask how it is that individuals develop the consistent patterns described by Lacey and Lacey (1958). The answer given is that

. . . individuals have patterns peculiar to themselves because they are more likely to adopt certain attitudes than others. (Graham, Kabler, & Graham, 1962)

This assumption denies the presence of inherited autonomic patterns and suggests that individual differences in physiological reactivity are due to psychological dispositions.

There is no direct evidence but there is some indirect evidence bearing on this hypothesis. As we saw in an earlier section, individual differences in physiological reactions have been established in young infants (Richmond & Lustman, 1955) and in children (Lacey & VanLehn, 1952). Surely children do not have the variety of attitudes posited by Graham, and certainly infants do not. Thus the developmental evidence favors inherited autonomic patterns and is opposed to this aspect of the theory of specific attitudes.

On balance, the theory appears to be promising. It is true that part of it will have to be amended and that there is some negative evidence. This is what must be expected of any theory stated precisely enough to be tested. The positive findings, especially the predictive research in the laboratory with normal subjects, are impressive. It seems likely that this experimental approach will eventually furnish the answers, rather than the correlational approach with clinical populations.

Body Image. Fisher and Cleveland, in their book (1958) and in other publications, have attempted to relate psychosomatic disorders to body image. They are interested mainly in the *boundary* aspect of body image:

. . . the individual may view his body as clearly and sharply bounded, with a high degree of differentiation from non-self objects. But contrastingly, he may regard his body as lacking demarcation from what is "out there." (Fisher, 1963, p. 62)

They use the Rorschach Ink Blot Test to select persons with a high barrier (definite boundary) image, as reflected in such responses as *turtle shell, man with armor,* and *mummy wrapped up. Penetrability* of the body is reflected in such responses as *torn coat, broken body,* and *person bleeding.* Thus the Rorschach can be used to select those with high and low barriers, and those with high and low penetrability of the body image. The more definite the boundary of the body image, the higher is the barrier score and the lower the penetration score.

The boundary aspect of the body image is presumably related to the site of symptoms. Strong boundaries are associated with symptoms close to the skin and weak boundaries with symptoms deep in the body:

[The] sequence involved in exterior versus interior site determination begins with the nature of the body image boundaries established by the individual early in his socialization. The greater the definiteness of his boundaries and of his consequent degree of psychological investment in the exterior body layers, the more likely are these layers to become the target for persistent tonuslike activation and to be selectively important for the channeling of excitation. A low degree of body definiteness may be presumed, on the contrary, to be associated with minimal responsiveness of the outer layers and a selectively higher degree of activation of the interior. (Fisher & Cleveland, 1960)

This theory has two testable propositions: (1) psychosomatic patients with internal symptoms (for example, ulcers) will have a lower barrier score than those with external symptoms (for example, skin disorders); and (2) normals with a high barrier score will show greater physiological reactivity peripherally than deep in the body, and the opposite will be true for those with a low barrier score. These two propositions have received some research confirmation.

Fisher and Cleveland (1955) gave Rorschachs to patients with internal symptoms (stomach disturbance and ulcerative colitis) and external symptoms (arthritis and neurodermatoses). The patients with external symptoms had higher barrier scores and lower penetration scores than those with internal symptoms. Two other groups were also tested: patients with back pain and with skin damage, the symptoms having been caused by injuries. These were used as control groups on the assumption that the symptoms, being due to mechanical injuries, were not related to body image. The assumption turned out to be correct. The arthritic patients had higher barrier scores than patients with back pain, and neurodermatitis patients had higher barrier scores than the skin damage patients. These differences in barrier score suggest that body image is an enduring part of the individual's personality, rather than a reflection of disturbance in a particular part of the body.

In a subsequent study Cleveland and Fisher (1960) found ulcer patients had lower barrier scores and higher penetration scores than arthritics. The ulcer patients also reacted to stress (a loud sound) with greater increases in heart rate and less of a galvanic skin response than the arthritics. The authors assumed that heart rate is a measure of interior reactivity and galvanic skin response is a measure of exterior reactivity. If these assumptions are correct—and they appear straightforward—the results constitute clear positive evidence for the validity of the body image concept.

Williams (1962) replicated the Rorschach results for the two psychosomatic groups: ulcer patients had lower barrier and higher penetration scores than arthritics. The ulcer patients also reacted to some stimuli with higher heart rates and lower muscle action potentials than did arthritics.

Eigenbrode and Shipman (1960) also attempted to replicate the barrier score findings. They compared skin disorder patients with a group of interior symptom patients (predominantly ulcer and ulcerative colitis) and found no differences in barrier scores. The clinical population from which they drew their sample is mainly of lower class status, whereas the hospital population sampled in previous research is mixed. This sampling difference might account for the failure to replicate, but in any event this is the only study that failed to obtain positive results.

Two laboratory studies have extended the body image concept to normals. Davis (1960) selected high and low barrier scorers from a sample of college men. Several physiological measures were obtained during rest and during stress (failure and critical comments from the experimenter). During rest the high barrier subjects had greater muscle action potentials and smaller heart stroke volumes than the low barrier subjects. The stress produced the following changes: high barrier subjects were greater in muscle action potentials and lower in heart rate, stroke volume, and total heart output than low barrier subjects. This experiment is important because it not only shows the relationship of body image to physiological reactivity but also does so in normal subjects, whose body image could not possibly be determined by ongoing somatic symptoms.

Fisher (1959) tried a similar procedure with adolescent girls. High barrier subjects had greater galvanic skin responses and lower heart rates during stress than did low barrier subjects. Cassell and Fisher (1963) injected histamine into the forearms of college men and women in order to study the intensity and size of the subsequent skin (flare) reaction. For women the higher the barrier score, the more intense was the flare reaction; the barrier score was unrelated to the flare reaction for men. There is no apparent reason for the sex difference, and the results are only partially supportive of body image theory.

Summarizing, of the seven studies cited, five are clearly positive, one is partially supportive, and one is negative. This is an excellent record for any theory in the area of psychosomatic disorders. Furthermore, there is a body of research unrelated to psychosomatic disorders that tends to corroborate and extend the body image concept (Fisher, 1963). There are problems that the theory must grapple with—the variability of the relationships with autonomic measures from one study to the next and the issue of whether syndromes such as asthma are interior or exterior—but at present body image theory is as good a theory as there is to account for the site of psychosomatic symptoms.

Fear. All psychological theories of psychosomatic disorders include fear as one of the determinants of somatic complaints. Fear (anxiety) usually plays the negative role of preventing the expression of impulses in behavior. Thus there are dependency versus fear conflicts and anger (or aggression) versus fear conflicts, presumably underlying ulcers and essential hypertension, respectively. In addition, the fear of separation, or alternatively, the fear of crying, presumably underlies asthma.

The theory we now consider is specific to ulcers. It states that chronic anxiety leads to an excessive outpouring of acid, which in turn leads to ulcers. Its major exponent is Mahl, who outlined the four postulates of his theory:

> (a) the gastric function essential for peptic ulcer etiology is positively associated with chronic anxiety; (b) if these two associated processes persist, peptic ulcer will develop; (c) it is not essential what the source of the anxiety is . . . ; (d) while the preceding factors might vary it is essential that the chronic anxiety be unrelieved by the development of adequate defense mechanisms or by changes in the stimulus conditions. (1950, p. 158)

Mahl himself produced evidence in three different species that anxiety leads to an outpouring of hydrochloric acid in the stomach. Using dogs as subjects (1949), he paired a buzzer with a strong electric shock. The time interval between buzzer and shock varied, and sometimes the buzzer occurred alone. The dogs manifested a variety of anxiety reactions: trembling, loss of sleep, phobic behavior, awkward postures, and urination and defecation with the onset of the stimulus. The acid concentration of their stomachs increased concomitantly with this anxiety.

Three monkeys were given the same buzzer-shock pairing, but they could learn to avoid the shock by making an instrumental response after the buzzer sounded (1952). One monkey learned the avoidance response and showed neither fear behavior nor excessive hydrochloric acid secretion. The other two monkeys failed to learn to avoid the shock, and they showed both fear behavior and excessive hydrochloric acid secretion.

The third experiment involved college students (1950), some of whom were to take an examination later in the day (experimental group) and some of whom were not (control group). The free hydrochloric acid in the stomachs of the experimental (anxious) students was greater than that of the control (nonanxious) students. Two of the experimental subjects were unconcerned about the examination and therefore not anxious; their acid concentration was lower than that of the remainder of the experimental group, all of whom were anxious.

In addition to Mahl's own research, there is corroboration from studies on avoidance conditioning with both animal and human subjects. Brady (1958), using pairs of monkeys, trained one member of the pair to make a response that would avoid the shock for both of them; the other member of the pair could do nothing about the shock. Only the "executive monkey" in each pair developed ulcers, presumably because of the chronic anxiety over avoiding the forthcoming shock. A similar avoidance experiment with single monkeys (Brady et al., 1958) also demonstrated that the conditioned avoidance situation could elicit ulcers. A third study (Brady, 1963) used the same procedure, but measured free acid concentration. While the monkeys were in the avoidance situation, the acid concentration dropped from its preavoidance level, but as soon as they were removed, the free acid concentration rose higher than its level during avoidance and even higher than in the preexperimental period. Thus it was only during the "time-off" from the actual threatening stimulus that the stomach functioned abnormally.

The last study used humans as subjects (Davis & Berry, 1963) in a situation similar to the "executive monkey" experiment. One college student in each pair was given avoidance training, while the other member of the pair could not avoid the oncoming noxious stimulus (white noise). The measure was muscle action potentials associated with movements of the stomach. The "executive students" had a larger gastric response than their partners, but only during the avoidance task itself. Unfortunately, there was no measure of free acid concentration, which makes this study difficult to compare with previous ones.

These various experiments offer considerable support for Mahl's contention that anxiety is the cause of ulcers. Mahl admits that this relationship is contrary to what might be expected as part of the organism's reaction to threat. The typical reaction is to mobilize emergency physiological resources. These involve the sympathetic nervous system, the stimulation of which results in a *decrease* in hydrochloric acid secretion. Mahl agrees that *acute anxiety* is accompanied by sympathetic dominance and a decrease in impulses through the vagus nerve, and therefore a decrease in stomach acid. However, he suggests that *chronic anxiety* is accompanied by parasympathetic dominance, increase in impulses through the vagus nerve, and increased stomach acid. This hypothesis is supported by the research cited, which showed that stomach acid increased only after *prolonged* anxiety or avoidance conditioning. For example in Mahl's study with dogs (1949) the rise in hydrochloric acid secretion occurred only on the fifth day of conditioning, accompanying chronic, not acute anxiety.

The notion that autonomic reactions change as emotional responses become chronic is not novel. Investigators are aware of the complex feedback mechanisms that regulate activity of the autonomic nervous system. Initial drops in activity may be compensated for by later rises that proceed well beyond the prestimulus or preexperimental level. Thus Mahl's position is consistent with the functioning of the autonomic nervous system, and it is supported by data involving several species.

Nevertheless, why do some anxious individuals develop ulcers and others not? Presumably, the answer lies in physiological dispositions, which are not ruled out by Mahl. Thus to be complete, Mahl's hypotheses must be combined with a notion such as inherited autonomic patterns, namely, ulcers occur in individuals whose stomachs tend to oversecrete and who are chronically anxious. This approach is in sharp contrast to specificity theories, which assume that particular conflicts or attitudes are essential to the development of ulcers. Mahl insists that it is chronic fear, regardless of the source. Our evaluation must favor Mahl, who has virtually all the experimental evidence on his side.

COMMENT

As we have seen, there are several ways of classifying the four psychosomatic disorders considered here: sympathetic-parasympathetic, interior-exterior (body image), and concomitant-regressive. Another way is to distinguish involuntary from voluntary reactions. Involuntary reactions lead to the symptoms of ulcers, essential hypertension, and neurodermatoses; voluntary, or at least partially voluntary, reactions lead to asthma.

Respiratory patterns can be manipulated by the individual, and in fact asthma-like wheezing can be simulated. This means that the response is easily conditioned; it can easily be linked to a variety of conditioned stimuli. As Turnbull (1962) has suggested, an *allergen,* which causes wheezing because of a physiological reaction, may serve as the unconditioned stimulus. This unconditioned stimulus may be preceded by a neutral stimulus, which, after appropriate pairing, comes to elicit the wheezing response. Once the wheezing response is conditioned, it can be maintained by reinforcement (being cared for, escaping from burdensome duties, etc.).

This kind of learning approach is not so applicable to the other three syndromes. Although it is possible that high blood pressure, excessive stomach acid, and skin disorders can be conditioned, they cannot be conditioned *easily.* The difficulty of such learning leads us to seek explanations elsewhere, specifically in approaches that emphasize excessive autonomic reactivity.

We must give more than lip service to physiological dispositions as the necessary condition for the development of psychosomatic disorders. This is not to deny the role of psychological variables as important determinants of such symptoms. Nevertheless, it may well be that the individual's pattern of physiological reactivity is the crucial determinant of whether he develops a psychosomatic disorder and if so, which one.

Whatever one's theoretical bias may be in these matters, the conclusion is inescapable that we need more laboratory research and less clinical research. The only clinical research that might be of value are studies that seek to classify patients *within* a particular disorder. For example, Purcell and his colleagues (Purcell, Bernstein, & Bukantz, 1961; Purcell, Turnbull, & Bernstein, 1962; Purcell & Metz, 1962) have distinguished between asthmatic children who require drugs to control the symptoms and those who do not, and Block et al. (1964) have dichotomized asthmatic children on the basis of a short inventory. Such research should cut down the heterogeneity that characterizes psychosomatic populations, and hopefully it will offer leads that might be pursued in the laboratory.

It is in the laboratory that the basic research must be conducted, for it is there that most of our reliable knowledge has accrued. Freeman et al. (1964) reviewed 195 studies of psychological aspects of allergy and concluded that most of them were of little worth; the few substantive findings emerged from laboratory research. This conclusion is supported by the material reviewed in this chapter. Clinical research is necessary at the start, but it must give way to laboratory research, with its emphasis on control and quantification. This is not to derogate clinical research but to place it in proper perspective as a predecessor to laboratory investigation.

References

Alexander, F. *Psychosomatic medicine. Its principles and applications.* New York: Norton, 1950.

Ayman, O. Personality type of patients with arteriolar essential hypertension. *American Journal of Medical Science,* 1933, **186**, 213–223.

Barendregt, J. T. A cross-validation study of the hypothesis of psychosomatic specificity, with special reference to bronchial asthma. *Journal of Psychosomatic Research,* 1957, **2**, 109–114.

Binger, C. A. L., Ackerman, N. W., Cohn, A. E., Schroeder, H. A., & Steele, J. M. Personality in arterial hypertension. *Psychosomatic Medicine Monographs,* 1945, No. 8.

Block, Jeanne, Jennings, P. H., Harvey, Eleanor, & Simpson, Elaine. Interaction between allergic potential and psychopathology in childhood asthma. *Psychosomatic Medicine,* 1964, **26**, 307–320.

Brady, J. V. Ulcers in "executive" monkeys. *Scientific American,* 1958, **199**, 95–100.

Brady, J. V. Further comments on the gastrointestinal system and avoidance behavior. *Psychological Reports,* 1963, **12**, 742.

Brady, J. V., Porter, R. W., Conrad, D., & Mason, J. W. Avoidance behavior and the development of gastroduodenal ulcers. *Journal of the Experimental Analysis of Behavior,* 1958, **1**, 69–72.

Brouwer, D. Somatotypes and psychosomatic diseases. *Journal of Psychosomatic Research,* 1957, **2**, 23–24.

Buss, A. H. *The psychology of aggression.* New York: Wiley, 1961.

Cassell, W., & Fisher, S. Body-image boundaries and histamine flare reaction. *Psychosomatic Medicine,* 1963, **25**, 344–350.

Cleveland, S. E., & Fisher, S. A comparison of psychological characteristics and physical reactivity in ulcer and rheumatoid arthritis groups: I. Psychological measures. *Psychosomatic Medicine,* 1960, **22**, 283–289.

Davis, A. D. Some physiological correlates of Rorschach body-image productions. *Journal of Abnormal and Social Psychology,* 1960, **60**, 432–436.

Davis, R. C., & Berry, F. Gastrointestinal reactions during a noise avoidance task. *Psychological Reports,* 1963, **12**, 135–137.

Davis, R. C., & Buchwald, A. M. An exploration of somatic response patterns: stimulus and sex differences. *Journal of Comparative and Physiological Psychology,* 1957, **50**, 44–52.

Davis, R. C., Lundervold, A., & Miller, J. D. The pattern of somatic response during a repetitive motor task and its modification by visual stimuli. *Journal of Comparative and Physiological Psychology,* 1957, **50**, 53–60.

Draper, G., Dupertuis, C. W., & Caughey, J. L. *Human constitution in clinical medicine.* New York: Hoeber, 1944.

Dunkel, Mary L. Casework help for neurodermatitis patients. *Journal of Social Casework,* 1949, **30**, 97–103.

Eigenbrode, C. R., & Shipman, W. G. The body image barrier concept. *Journal of Abnormal and Social Psychology,* 1960, **60**, 450–452.

Engel, B. T., & Bickford, A. F. Response specificity: Stimulus-response and individual-response specificity in essential hypertensives. *Archives of General Psychiatry,* 1961, **5**, 478–489.

Engel, G. L., Hamburger, W. W., Reiser, M., & Plunkett, J. Electroencephalographic and psychological studies of a case of migraine with severe pre-headache phenomena. *Psychosomatic Medicine,* 1953, **19**, 337–348.

Fisher, S. Prediction of body exterior versus body interior reactivity from a body image scheme. *Journal of Personality,* 1959, **27**, 56–62.

Fisher, S. A further appraisal of the body boundary concept. *Journal of Consulting Psychology,* 1963, **27**, 62–74.

Fisher, S., & Cleveland, S. E. The role of body image in psychosomatic symptom choice. *Psychological Monographs,* 1955, **69**, No. 17, (Whole No. 402).

Fisher, S., & Cleveland, S. E. *Body image and personality.* Princeton, New Jersey: Van Nostrand, 1958.

Fisher, S., & Cleveland, S. E. A comparison of psychological characteristics and physiological reactivity in ulcer and rheumatoid arthritis groups. II. Differences in physiological reactivity. *Psychosomatic Medicine,* 1960, **22**, 290–293.

Freeman, Edith H., Feingold, B. F., Schesinger, K., & Gorman, F. J. Psychological variables in allergic disorders: A review. *Psychosomatic Medicine,* 1964, **26**, 543–576.

Grace, W. J., & Graham, D. T. Relationship of specific attitudes and emotions to certain bodily diseases. *Psychosomatic Medicine,* 1952, **14**, 242–251.

Graham, D. T., Graham, Frances, K., & Kabler, J. D. Experimental production of predicted physiological differences by suggestion of attitude. Paper presented at American Psychosomatic Society meetings, 1960.

Graham, D. T., Kabler, J. D., & Graham, Frances K. Physiological responses to the suggestion of attitudes specific for hives and hypertension. *Psychosomatic Medicine,* 1962, **24**, 159–169.

Graham, D. T., Lundy, R. M., Benjamin, Lorna S., Kabler, J. D., Lewis, W. C., Kunish, Nancy O., & Graham, Frances K. Specific attitudes in initial interviews with patients having different "psychosomatic" diseases. *Psychosomatic Medicine,* 1962, **24**, 257–266.

Graham, D. T., Stern, J. A., & Winokur, G. Experimental investigation of the specificity of attitude hypothesis in psychosomatic disease. *Psychosomatic Medicine,* 1958, **20**, 446–457.

Gressel, G. C., Shobe, F. O., Laslow, G., Dubois, P. H., & Schroeder, H. A. Personality factors in arterial hypertension. *Journal of the American Medical Association,* 1949, **140**, 265–272.

Groen, J. Psychosomatic disturbances as a form of substituted behavior. *Journal of Psychosomatic Research,* 1957, **2**, 85–96.

Halliday, J. L. *Psychosocial medicine: A study of the sick society.* New York: Norton, 1948.

Hambling, J. Emotions and symptoms in essential hypertension. *British Journal of Medical Psychology,* 1951, **24**, 242–253.

Hambling, J. Psychosomatic aspects of arterial hypertension. *British Journal of Medical Psychology,* 1952, **25**, 39–47.

Hamilton, J. A. Psychophysiology of blood pressure. *Psychosomatic Medicine,* 1942, **4**, 125–133.

Harris, R. E., Sokolow, M., Carpenter, W. G., Freedman, M., & Hunt, S. P. Response to psychological stress in persons who are potentially hypertensive. *Circulation,* 1953, **7**, 874–879.

Hokanson, J. E., & Burgess, M. The effects of three types of aggression on vascular processes. *Journal of Abnormal and Social Psychology,* 1962, **64**, 446–449.

Hokanson, J. E., Burgess, M., & Cohen, M. F. Effect of displaced aggression on systolic blood pressure. *Journal of Abnormal and Social Psychology,* 1963, **67**, 214–218.

Kemple, C. Rorschach method and psychosomatic diagnosis. *Psychosomatic Medicine,* 1945, **7**, 85–89.

Kepecs, J. C., Rabin, A., & Robin, M. Atopic dermatitis. *Psychosomatic Medicine,* 1951, **13**, 1–9.

Knapp, P. H., & Nemetz, S. J. in collaboration with Gilbert, R. R., Lowell, F. C., & Michelson, A. L. Personality variations in bronchial asthma. *Psychosomatic Medicine,* 1957, **19**, 443–465.

Lacey, J. I. Psychophysiological approaches to the evaluation of psychotherapeutic process and outcome. In Rubinstein, E. A., & Parloff, M. B. (Eds.) *Research in psychotherapy.* Washington, D. C.: American Psychological Association, 1959.

Lacey, J. I., Bateman, Dorothy E., & VanLehn, Ruth. Autonomic response specificity. *Psychosomatic Medicine,* 1953, **15**, 8–21.

Lacey, J. I., & Lacey, Beatrice C. Verification and extension of the principle of autonomic response stereotypy. *American Journal of Psychology,* 1958, **71**, 50–73.

Lacey, J. I., & VanLehn, Ruth. Differential emphasis in somatic response to stress. *Psychosomatic Medicine,* 1952, **14**, 71–81.

Leary, T. *Interpersonal diagnosis of personality.* New York: Ronald Press, 1957.

Lynch, F. W., Hinckley, R. G., & Cowan, D. W. Psychosomatic studies in dermatology: B. Psychobiologic studies of patients with atopic eczema (disseminated neurodermatitis). *Archives of Dermatology and Syphilology,* 1953, **51**, 251–257.

Mahl, G. F. Chronic fear and gastric secretion of HCL in dogs. *Psychosomatic Medicine,* 1949, **11**, 30–44.

Mahl, G. F. Anxiety, HCL secretion, and peptic ulcer etiology. *Psychosomatic Medicine,* 1950, **12**, 158–169.

Mahl, G. F. Relationship between acute and chronic fear and the gastric acidity and blood sugar levels in *Macaca mulatta* monkeys. *Psychosomatic Medicine,* 1952, **14**, 182–210.

Malmo, R. B., & Shagass, C. Physiologic study of symptom mechanisms in psychiatric patients under stress. *Psychosomatic Medicine,* 1949, **11**, 25–29.

Margolin, S. G. The behavior of the stomach during psychoanalysis. *Psychoanalytic Quarterly,* 1951, **20**, 349–373.

Margolin, S. G. Genetic and dynamic psychophysiological processes. in Deutch, F. (Ed.) *The psychosomatic concept in psychoanalysis.* New York: International Universities Press, 1953, pp. 3–36.

Marshall, S. Personality correlates of peptic ulcer patients. *Journal of Consulting Psychology,* 1960, **24**, 218–223.

Matarazzo, J. O. An experimental study of aggression in the hypertensive patient. *Journal of Personality,* 1954, **22**, 423–447.

McLaughlin, J. T., Shoemaker, R. J., & Guy, W. B. Personality factors in adult atopic eczema. *Archives of Dermatology and Syphilology,* 1953, **68**, 506–516.

Mednick, S. A., Garner, A. M., & Stone, H. K. A test of some behavioral hypotheses drawn from Alexander's specificity theory. *American Journal of Orthopsychiatry,* 1959, **29**, 592–598.

Michaels, J. J. A psychiatric adventure in comparative pathophysiology of the infant and adult. *Journal of Nervous and Mental Disease,* 1944, **100**, 49–63.

Miller, H., & Baruch, Dorothy W. A study of hostility in allergic children. *American Journal of Orthopsychiatry,* 1950, **20**, 506–519.

Mirsky, I. A. Physiologic, psychologic and social determinants in the etiology of duodenal ulcer. *American Journal of Digestive Diseases,* 1958, **3**, 285–314.

Mittlelmann, B., Wolff, H. G., & Scharf, M. Emotions and gastroduodenal functions. *Psychosomatic Medicine,* 1942, **4**, 5–61.

Modell, A. H., & Potter, H. W. Human figure drawings of patients with arterial hypertension, peptic ulcer, and bronchial asthma. *Psychosomatic Medicine,* 1949, **11,** 282–292.

Moses, L., Daniels, G. E., & Nickerson, J. L. Psychogenic factors in essential hypertension: methodology and preliminary report. *Psychosomatic Medicine,* 1956, **28,** 471–485.

Neiberg, N. A. The effects of induced stress on the management of hostility in essential hypertension. Unpublished doctoral dissertation, Boston University, 1957.

Oken, D. An experimental study of suppressed anger and blood pressure. *Archives of General Psychiatry,* 1960, **2,** 441–456.

Purcell, K., Bernstein, L., & Bukantz, S. C. A preliminary comparison of rapidly remitting and persistently "steroid-dependent" asthmatic children. *Psychosomatic Medicine,* 1961, **23,** 305–310.

Purcell, K., & Metz, J. R. Distinctions between subgroups of asthmatic children: Some parent attitude variables related to age of onset of asthma. *Journal of Psychosomatic Research,* 1962, **6,** 251–258.

Purcell, K., Turnbull, J. W., & Bernstein, L. Distinctions between subgroups of asthmatic children: psychological test and behavior rating comparisons. *Journal of Psychosomatic Research,* 1962, **6,** 283–291.

Rees, L. The importance of psychological, allergic and infective factors in childhood asthma. *Journal of Psychosomatic Research,* 1964, **7,** 253–262.

Reiser, M. F., Rosenbaum, M., & Ferris, E. B., Jr. Psychologic mechanisms in malignant hypertension. *Psychosomatic Medicine,* 1951, **13,** 147–159.

Richmond, J. B., & Lustman, S. L. Autonomic function in the neonate: I. Implications for psychosomatic theory. *Psychosomatic Medicine,* 1955, **17,** 269–275.

Robbins, Lewis L. Psychological factors in essential hypertension. *Bulletin of the Menninger Clinic,* 1948, **12,** 195–202.

Ruesch, J., & Bateson, G. *Communication, the social matrix of psychiatry.* New York: Norton, 1951.

Saul, L. J. Hostility in cases of essential hypertension. *Psychosomatic Medicine,* 1939, **1,** 153–161.

Saul, L. J., Sheppard, Edith, Selby, Dorothy, Lhamon W., Sachs, D., & Master, Regina. The quantification of hostility in dreams with reference to essential hypertension. *Science,* 1954, **119,** 382–383.

Schachter, J. Pain, fear, and anger, in hypertensives and normotensives: a psychophysiological study. *Psychosomatic Medicine,* 1957, **29,** 17–29.

Schneider, R. A., & Zangari, Violet M. Variations in clotting time, relative viscosity, and other physiochemical properties of the blood accompanying physical and emotional stress in the normotensive and hypertensive subject. *Psychosomatic Medicine,* 1951, **13,** 288- 303.

Schwartz, L. A. An analyzed case of essential hypertension. *Psychosomatic Medicine,* 1940, **2,** 468–486.

Schweers, R. Some personality correlates of essential hypertension. Unpublished master's thesis, University of California, 1950.

Selye, H. *The stress of life.* New York: McGraw-Hill, 1956.

Sheldon, W. H., Stevens, S. S., & Tucker, W. B. *The varieties of human physique.* New York: Harper & Row, 1940.

Stern, J. A., Winokur, G., Graham, D. T., & Graham, Frances K. Alterations in physiological measures during experimentally induced attitudes. *Journal of Psychosomatic Research,* 1960, **5,** 73–82.

Stern, P. J. *The abnormal person and his world.* Princeton, New Jersey: Van Nostrand, 1964.

Storment, C. T. Personality and heart disease. *Psychosomatic Medicine,* 1951, **13,** 304–313.

Streitfeld, H. S. Specificity of peptic ulcer to intense oral conflicts. *Psychosomatic Medicine,* 1954, **16,** 315–326.

Szasz, T. S. Psychoanalysis and the autonomic nervous system. *Psychoanalytic Review,* 1952, **39,** 115–151.

Szasz, T. S., Levin, E., Kirsner, J. B., & Palmer, W. L. The role of hostility in the pathogenesis of peptic ulcer: Theoretical considerations with the report of a case. *Psychosomatic Medicine,* 1947, **9,** 331–336.

Thacker, E. A. A comparative study of normal and abnormal blood pressure among university students, including the cold pressor test. *American Heart Journal,* 1940, **20,** 89–97.

Thaler, Margaret, Weiner, H., & Reiser, M. F. Exploration of the doctor-patient relationship through projective techniques. *Psychosomatic Medicine,* 1957, **19,** 228–239.

Tucker, W. I. Psychiatric factors in essential hypertension. *Diseases of the Nervous System,* 1949, **10,** 273–278.

Turnbull, J. W. Asthma conceived as a learned response. *Journal of Psychosomatic Research,* 1962, **6,** 59–70.

Weiss, E. Psychosomatic aspects of hypertension. *Journal of the American Medical Association,* 1942, **120,** 1081–1086.

Wenger, M. A., Clemens, T. L., Coleman, D. R., Cullen, T. D., & Engel, B. T. Autonomic response specificity. *Psychosomatic Medicine,* 1961, **23,** 185–193.

White, R. W. *The abnormal personality.* New York: Ronald, 1964.

Williams, R. L. The relationship of body image to some physiological reactivity patterns in psychosomatic patients. Unpublished doctoral dissertation, Washington University, 1962.

Wolf, G. A., Jr., & Wolff, H. G. Studies on the nature of certain symptoms associated with cardio-vascular disorders. *Psychosomatic Medicine,* 1946, **8,** 293–319.

Wolf, S., & Wolff, H. G. Evidence on the genesis of peptic ulcer in man. In Tompkins, S. S. (Ed.) *Contemporary Psychopathology.* Cambridge: Harvard University Press, 1943.

Wolf, S., & Wolff, H. G. A summary of experimental evidence relating life stress to the pathogenesis of essential hypertension in man. In Bell, E. T. (Ed.), *Hypertension: A symposium.* Minneapolis: University of Minnesota Press, 1951.

Wolff, H. G. *Stress and disease.* Springfield, Illinois: Thomas, 1953.

CHAPTER 17

Conduct Disorders

As the title indicates, this chapter deals with behavior that society does not tolerate. We shall consider three classes of such behavior: psychopathy (irresponsible, amoral behavior), alcoholism, and sexual deviance. They all share the same criterion of abnormality, bizarreness. They all involve acts which society proscribes not necessarily as criminal acts but as acts reprehensible to others. Thus although conduct disorders touch upon criminality, we shall not discuss criminals and delinquents as such. The emphasis here is on bizarreness, not criminality.

PSYCHOPATHY

The terms *psychopath* and *psychopathic personality* have been severely criticized. It has been suggested that clinicians cannot agree on their definition, that their usage is vague, and that psychopathy is a wastebasket category for cases that are difficult to diagnose. However, Albert et al. (1959) analyzed 70 published papers on psychopathy and found substantial agreement on the definition of the term. Certainly there is no more disagreement and controversy over this diagnostic label than over others previously discussed.

Symptoms and Personality Features

There are two kinds of symptoms in psychopathy. The first consists of asocial and antisocial behavior, some of which might be found in any conduct disorder, such as excessive drinking and bizarre sexual behavior.

430

The second kind comprises a set of personality traits, all of which indicate immaturity or lack of socialization—for example, absence of guilt or shame. Previously we have been careful to separate personality traits from symptoms because psychopathology should be defined by deviance rather than personality features common to both normal and psychologically disturbed persons. However, psychopathy is exceptional in that the personality features themselves are abnormal. For example, some normal individuals lack warmth and feeling for their fellow beings, but the psychopath is alone in his tendency to treat others as objects rather than as fellow human beings. Thus a description of psychopathy must include both symptoms and personality features. We shall start with symptoms and then move on to personality traits, noting in advance that the former gradually merge with the latter.

The psychopath typically engages in one or more illegal acts. What distinguishes him from the ordinary criminal is his impulsiveness. The antisocial behavior is not planned; it is an impetuous response to an immediate situation, with no thought of the consequences to either the victim or the psychopath himself. The gain may be small and the risk of discovery large, but the momentary impulse is too strong to resist.

The psychopath's crimes are usually petty and deceitful. There may be thievery, but the most frequent acts are fraud, forgery, and failure to pay debts. When in a tight situation, the psychopath simply runs away. He may desert his wife and children without a qualm, or he may run away from debtors or from colleagues who are depending on him.

When escape is impossible, the psychopath resorts to lying as a means of escaping blame and punishment. His lying is not restricted to such situations; he may falsify to enhance his reputation or merely to boast to new friends. He is a pathological liar who cannot be trusted because of a complete disrespect for the truth. There is no feeling of sanctity about the truth or about promises. All promises are hollow in that they are designed only to obtain immediate gain in money or esteem. The psychopath can proceed through the entire ritual of swearing on his honor after years of chronic lying—all this with apparent candor and sincerity.

It is evident that the psychopath does not play by the rules. He makes a mockery not only of truth but also of all authority and institutions. He behaves as if rules did not apply to him and as if discipline were something to be applied only to others. Thus, he is without the checks and balances that give pause to most persons. Lacking the psychological means to control his impulses, he is at their mercy; lacking inhibitory mechanisms, he tends to act on the aggressive and sexual urges most persons have. His behavior is precisely opposite to that of a neurotic, who tends to inhibit most sexual and aggressive urges. In fact, the dimension of control of impulses may be pictured as follows:

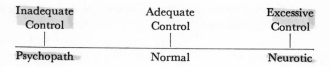

The neurotic denies himself gratification because he fears its consequences. The normal person sometimes denies gratification or delays it because of negative consequences, but he may seek immediate gratification of impulses. The psychopath demands immediate gratification of each passing impulse. Beyond the childlike inability to delay or to deny satisfaction, the psychopath often actively seeks thrills. This tendency leads him to over-indulge in alcohol and drugs, as well as to attempt dangerous exploits. His lack of inhibition is accompanied by a disdain of negative consequences. The psychopath simply does not anticipate injury or punishment; such consequences are apparently beyond his comprehension.

Furthermore, he does not seem to learn from bitter experience and repeatedly engages in acts that eventually lead to injury or punishment. If he disdains possible negative consequences for himself, he is even more callous about the consequences to others. There is no compunction about deserting a fiancé, a family, or a friend who has loaned money. These asocial acts usually involve no crime, and there is no legal punishment. The psychopath's victims are reluctant to discuss what has been done to them, and consequently, the psychopath is free to prey on others. Thus, it may require years before he is sufficiently well-known to be recognized and avoided. He must generally keep moving, either because he becomes known to a community or because he must escape from a situation established by his own lies, borrowing, or thievery.

Although the psychopath and the neurotic are at the opposite poles of several dimensions (such as control of impulses or guilt), they are alike in one respect: neither seems to learn from experience. The neurotic maintains his immature attempts to avoid anxiety in spite of their ineffectiveness. The psychopath maintains a pattern of lying, swindling, and deserting although he is usually caught and punished. In fact, he is often careless about being caught, making little or no effort to conceal his wrongdoing. There is a tendency to behave as though under the special protection of a guardian angel or as though guaranteed special immunity to punishment.

This poor judgment concerning *behavior* is accompanied by a paradoxically good judgment concerning *verbal* or abstract situations. The psychopath can distinguish right from wrong and knows about justice and morality. He simply cannot apply this knowledge and use his good judgment when it conflicts with an immediate impulse whose gratification cannot be delayed. This point is illustrated in a study of delinquent girls and student nurses (Simon et al., 1951). All the girls were asked to complete a series of items that opposed social values with personal needs, to wit, "Lucy had forgotten to give her mother an important message, but her friends were waiting for her so she . . . ." The delinquent girls tended to answer more in the direction of satisfying the personal need than fulfilling the social duty. A multiple choice version of the items indicated that the delinquent girls knew the socially acceptable answers, but when they had no guideline, as in the incomplete sentence version, their answers were in accord with their psychopathic behavior.

Let us summarize the symptoms of psychopathy:

(1) thrill-seeking behavior and disregard of conventions
(2) inability to control impulses or delay gratification
(3) rejection of authority and discipline
(4) poor judgment about behavior but good judgment about abstract situations
(5) failure to alter punished behavior
(6) pathological lying
(7) asocial and antisocial behavior

These features may be called symptoms, although they also include aspects of personality; for example, impulsivity is clearly a personality trait. Now we turn to characteristics of psychopathy which are more personality features than symptoms: personal relationships, guilt, insight, and the facade of maturity.

The psychopath has defective personal relationships, which is another way of saying that he has a fundamental incapacity for love or true friendship. The ability to love comprises several related features. One is tender feelings toward another person—feelings of warmth and protectiveness. Related to tenderness is a tendency toward altruism which may be reflected in behavior that ranges from unselfishness to self-sacrifice. Such behavior could not occur in the absence of empathy—a feeling of sharing the joy and suffering of the other person. The other side of the coin is gratefulness and appreciation of affection and help from others. Finally, there is delight in the company of others, not as mere objects of pleasure but as fellow human beings.

If capacity to love underlies adequate personal relations, an extension of self to others underlies the capacity to love. Self-interest must be extended to include others, or else there can be no tender feeling, no altruism, no empathy—in brief, no capacity to love and therefore no adequate social relationships. It is here that the psychopath fails. He is as self-centered, selfish, and unaware as a newborn infant of others as fellow humans. He regards others as being fundamentally no different from objects, that is, only as sources of pleasure or escape from pain. There is no basic distinction between humans and nonhumans. Other persons are manipulated for gain, without any concern for their pain, discomfort, or disappointment. There are a few situations that require the temporary suspension of the "human attitude." A surgeon, for example, must regard his patient merely as a biological machine so long as he is in the operating room. Once outside surgery, the physician resumes his attitude toward the patient as a human being. The psychopath behaves as though he were always in the operating room: he dehumanizes others by treating them as objects rather than as fellow men.

The basic problem is an inability to extend self-interest beyond the self. The psychopath's own needs and wants are paramount; those of others are too trivial to warrant attention. This extreme vanity prevents the psychopath from having any empathy. Unable to extend his self, he cannot place himself in the position of the other person. The combination of vanity and lack of empathy appears to underlie much of the psychopath's faulty judgment. His demand for immediate gratification is so imperious that others cannot comprehend it. He does not have the empathy that would allow him to anticipate how others might react to his unusual behavior. Therefore he finds it difficult to predict which acts will lead to punishment, and his behavior reflects his poor judgment.

It also follows from his inability to take the role of the other person that the psychopath has no self-insight. Insight involves a recognition of oneself as a social object, as well as awareness of one's impulses and motives. The psychopath, having no empathy, cannot see himself as others do. His own egocentricity prevents him from recognizing how childishly selfish his own demands really are.

Related to the selfishness is an absence of guilt or shame. We have described some of the asocial and antisocial acts typical of psychopathy: desertion, bad debts, thievery, and fraud. There is usually a trail of immorality, broken promises, and obvious breaches of a moral code to which the psychopath gives lip service. In the face of such a record, there is a denial of any wrongdoing and an air of injured innocence. Although there may be a hollow mouthing of acceptance of blame, there is neither true remorse nor subsequent change in behavior. The psychopath is truly amoral and accepts no personal responsibility for his action. He is adept at finding excuses and trite rationalizations, but these are only to convince others. He need never rationalize to himself because there is no responsibility, no blame, and thus no basis for guilt.

At this point we may ask how the psychopath is able to deceive anyone. In light of his immorality, deceitfulness, and occasional criminality, how does he obtain jobs, loans, and positions of trust? The answer lies in his facade of competence and maturity. He is usually of average or above average intelligence and has a superficial grasp of subjects which may deceive the unwary. There are no indications of either neurotic or psychotic symptoms, and in fact, there is often a zest for life which implies superior mental health. There is usually considerable charm and attention to the formalities of social relations. The mask is that of a well-mannered gentleman. We have already mentioned the psychopath's tendency to lie; he does so with disarming candor and sincerity which serve to bolster the impression of competence, maturity, and reliability.

Of course, he is inconsistent and unreliable. The psychopath can usually make a good start in any endeavor—a new job, a new project, or a new relationship. However, he has no staying power and cannot maintain the facade. He is fundamentally too restless and thrill seeking to abide day-to-day routines. Sooner or later he leaps impetuously into an escapade which reveals his true self. He squanders money, quits his job, deserts his family, runs out on bad debts, tells wildly improbably stories, or engages in criminal activity. He has no consistency, no long-term goals, no loyalty, no guilt—in brief, none of the qualities of trustworthiness and responsibility that mark an adult human being.

These personality features constitute a complex pattern which contains three manifest characteristics.

(1) *The psychopath is a hollow, isolated person.* He feels no abiding affection for others and can engage in only mimicry of genuine personal relations—the exterior form but not the substance. This absence of the capacity to love is accompanied by a lack of the ability to identify with others, either individually or in groups. Thus, his relationships are necessarily superficial; he has no loyalty to either individuals or groups; and he does not belong to any person or social group.

(2) *The psychopath has no fundamental identity of his own.* Being hollow and lacking substantive relationships, he can never develop an adequate self-concept. He has no sense of himself as a person with values and long-range goals and therefore cannot develop insight, guilt, or a sense of responsibility.

(3) *The psychopath cannot bind time.* He cannot wait; he cannot surrender a smaller present pleasure for a greater distant goal. He cannot abide routine for long and takes no comfort in a stable, recurrent regime of daily living. He has no sense of time, especially of the future; he senses only the here and now. This makes him prey to almost any momentary temptation or escape from tension, regardless of subsequent consequences. He simply cannot bridge the gap between present pleasure and future punishment. In this respect he is similar to the neurotic who buys a temporary respite from anxiety now at the cost of greater punishment later. The major difference is that the neurotic's motivation is to escape anxiety, whereas the psychopath's motivation is to achieve immediate gratification of an impulse.

Anxiety

There has been some debate about whether psychopaths are anxious. Albert et al. (1959) found that some clinicians listed anxiety as a symptom of psychopathy, but others did not. Cleckley (1964), who is recognized as an authority on psychopathy, has stated that anxiety is conspicious by its absence. Karpman (1941) agreed that *primary* psychopaths have no anxiety, but he distinguished another type, *secondary* psychopaths, who manifest anxiety and other neurotic features. This distinction has been supported by experimental evidence.

Lykken (1957) divided psychopaths into primary and secondary types, the later scoring higher on an anxiety inventory. Both groups were compared with normal subjects on galvanic skin-response (GSR) conditioning and an avoidance learning task that employed electric shock. In the face of electric shock, it was assumed that normal subjects would be most anxious (which is realistic), secondary psychopaths next, and primary psychopaths least anxious. Presumably, the higher the anxiety level is, the faster the GSR conditioning and avoidance learning. On both tasks the normal subjects were best, the secondary psychopaths next, and the primary psychopaths worst. The avoidance findings were partially replicated by Schoenherr (1964).

The assumption that anxiety is necessary for avoidance learning is generally accepted. The lower the level of anxiety, the worse the learning. Hetherington and Klinger (1964) compared normal subjects having some psychopathic tendencies with subjects having none (high versus low scores on the Psychopathic Deviate Scale of the Minnesota Multiphasic Personality Inventory). When the correct response was rewarded, the two groups learned at the same rate; but when the incorrect response was punished, the more psychopathic subjects learned at a slower rate. Hare (1965) selected subjects in the same way and presented the numbers 1 through 12 in succession. Subjects were told that painful electric shock would be given at number eight, and their GSRs were recorded (as a measure of anxiety). The GSRs of the more psychopathic subjects began latter in the number sequence, were slower, and were of lesser amplitude than the GSRs of the less psychopathic subjects.

It is clear from these laboratory studies that primary psychopaths have little anxiety. This lack of anxiety explains their inability to learn and their tendency to repeat the same mistake although it inevitably leads to punishment. Evidently, stimuli that warn of subsequent punishment do not elicit sufficient anxiety to inhibit the tabooed response.

Secondary psychopaths, who do manifest anxiety, should be regarded as a mixture of psychopathy and neurosis. What we described earlier was classical psychopathy, just as previously we described classical hysteria or classical depression. The "textbook psychopath" does not show anxiety, whereas the psychopath with neurotic features does. Thus it seems best to list absence of anxiety as an attribute of psychopathy. When anxiety accompanies psychopathic features, it should be regarded as an indication that the individual has some potential for correcting his mistakes. Thus it is a benign sign, just as depression is benign when it occurs in the context of psychotic symptoms.

Theories

We shall discuss three kinds of theories: interpersonal, learning, and biological. Interpersonal theories emphasize early parent-child relationships; learning theories emphasize specific aspects of training; and biological theories emphasize heredity, brain waves, or both.

Interpersonal Theories. Psychoanalytic theory has little to say about psychopathy. It comes as no surprise that a faulty superego presumably underlies psychopathy; the superego is either "bribed" into accepting id impulses, or isolated from the ego and instinctual strivings. No particular fixation or regression points are specified, and the major causal variables are identified as ". . . a frequent change of milieu, a loveless environment, or very inconsistent environmental influence . . ." (Fenichel, 1945, p. 374).

Although there is a paucity of psychoanalytic theorizing about psychopathy, psychoanalysts have presented neopsychoanalytic explanations of it. Greenacre (1945) offers the following account of the family background of the psychopath. Typically, the father is a successful man, a leader in the community who is distant and fear-inspiring to his son. The mother is frivolous, indulgent, and pleasure-loving. Both parents are self-centered, and their relations with each other and the child are poor. What passes for parental affection is really parental indulgence of the child. Pride substitutes for love, and excessive importance is given to appearances, especially as they reflect on parental reputation. The child is treated as an extension of the parent, and he learns to be an exhibitionist. He learns that appearance is more important than reality and that charm is better than competence or achievement. The father is so successful that the child must be a failure by comparison, but any failure is denied or concealed by the parents. This family background should produce a typical middle-class psychopath. Note that the theory emphasizes parent-child relationships to the exclusion of the standard psychoanalytic concepts.

Frankenstein (1959) focuses on the mother as the basic factor underlying psychopathy. He distinguishes 11 different types of psychopathy, but we shall discuss only the six that meet the generally accepted criteria mentioned earlier.

(1) *The morally indolent psychopath.* This type is caused not by a particular kind of mother but by a congenital absence of anxiety. He is

completely at the mercy of his impulses, without the inhibiting influence of fear or guilt. Presumably, he is born this way.

(2) *The brutally destructive psychopath.* He is hostile and aggressive; cruelty and destruction are sources of intense satisfaction. The brutality is caused by maternal rejection that starts at birth. The child reacts by rejecting everything that is nonself, taking as a model his aggressive mother. He feels rejected and responds with generalized hatred and vindictiveness.

(3) *The egocentric psychopath.* He represents the ultimate in selfishness: a person who regards the whole world as his own. In contrast to the brutal psychopath, he does not reject the nonself but attempts to incorporate it as part of his own identity. He lives only in the present, depending solely on sense impressions of the moment to establish his identity, his self. All this is a reaction to a sudden loss of his mother through death, illness, or separation during infancy, before he could establish his own separate identity.

(4), (5), and (6) *Psychopaths who assume others' identities.* Frankenstein distinguishes three types, but the differences among them appear to be slight. In all three types there is a fundamental lack of identity, which leads to borrowing the identity of others. The psychopath may merely imitate or he may perpetrate a full-scale swindle, using another's credentials to obtain money or position fraudently. The mother may be apathetic or indulgent; or she may have been replaced by "multiple mothers," which occurs with institutionalized children.

White (1964) also emphasizes mother-child relationships, suggesting, ". . . a very early injury to affectionate relations, a serious deficit of gratifying love and care perhaps even in the first year" (p. 372). This deficit presumably prevents the child from identifying first with his mother, then with other members of the family, and finally with friends. Deprived of membership in the two-person group of mother and child, he remains outside of all subsequent groups and has no abiding affection or involvement with any other person.

The last interpersonal theory is that of Gough (1948), who assumes the psychopath to be deficient in role-playing ability. He is unable to regard himself as a social object or to identify with another's point of view. Reed and Cuadra (1957) obtained objective support for this assumption. They showed that psychopathically oriented student nurses were less successful in predicting how others would describe them than nonpsychopathically oriented nurses. Gough suggests that because the psychopathic lacks role-playing ability, he cannot experience embarrassment, contrition, or loyalty. The absence of these "social emotions" results in a lack of inhibitions and an inability to live by the social rules necessary in any society. Unfortunately, Gough's theory does not suggest the causes of the psychopath's inability to play roles.

Learning Theories. The major learning theory of psychopathy is that of Eysenck (1957). He assumes that two temperament variables are basic: introversion-extraversion and neuroticism. An individual's position on these two dimensions, which is presumably inherited, forms the basis of subsequent personality development. The psychopath is assumed to be extremely extraverted. Extraverts condition slowly, build up reactive inhibition quickly, and dissipate it slowly. Assuming socialization to be dependent upon conditioning, the extravert should suffer from a lack of conditioning and should therefore be undersocialized.

The neurotic is assumed to be anxiety prone and hence to develop neurotic symptoms. Putting together neuroticism and extraversion, Eysenck arrives at the syndromes of hysteria and neurotic psychopathy. Neurotic or secondary psychopaths were previously described as being both asocial and anxious. Eysenck assumes that primary psychopaths, being nonanxious, differ from secondary psychopaths on the neuroticism dimension: primary psychopaths are low on neuroticism, and secondary psychopaths are medium to high.

We need not present further details of Eysenck's approach because it was discussed in Chapter 6. It does account for the salient aspects of psychopathy: lack of anxiety, undersocialization, and inability to learn new behavior. It is a learning approach, but it assumes inherited temperaments. The temperament variables are the basic causes of psychopathy, in contrast to the family interaction emphasized by interpersonal theories.

An alternate learning approach is nontheoretical. This one specifies the learning variables needed to produce a psychopath, without espousing a particular learning theory. The three central variables are imitation, reward, and punishment.

Parents serve as models for many aspects of a child's behavior. Two kinds of parental behavior foster the development of psychopathy. The first is being cold and distant with the child, allowing no warm, close relationship to develop. If the child imitates the parental model, he will become cold and distant in his personal relations. He will learn the formal attributes of social situations without ever becoming involved with the give-and-take that lends meaning to what are otherwise hollow amenities.

The second kind of parental behavior is inconsistency. Parents may be capricious in supplying affection, rewards, and punishments. They may be unstable in the enactment of their roles so that the child has difficulty in finding a consistent model to imitate. Such parental inconsistency causes the child's identity to remain diffuse, and he develops no consistent self-concept to help him cope with the chaotic events of childhood and adolescence.

The parents may reward behaviors that lead to psychopathy by reinforcing both superficial conformity and underhanded noncomformity.

The child learns to avoid punishment by lying. Rewards are less important here than punishments. The child may be punished for seeking close contact with the parents or with siblings or playmates; only formal, unemotional relationships are allowed. In meting out punishment the parent may be arbitrary and inconsistent, punishing on the basis of a momentary mood. Thus, the child does not learn right from wrong but only how to avoid blame and punishment.

One aspect of this regime is a lack of close supervision. The child who is not checked can learn to be devious, to conceal wrongdoing, to lie his way out of punishment, etc. Furthermore, when he is caught, he can make superficial expiatory responses; "I am sorry, and I won't do it again." If such verbal expiation is rewarded in the absence of any genuine feeling of wrongdoing, the child will learn how to escape punishment without feeling guilt or altering his behavior. In brief, psychopathy consists of a set of behaviors that can be shaped by the parents through imitation, rewards and punishments. Just as these variables can produce a guilty, inhibited neurotic (see Chapter 7), so can they produce a guiltless, uninhibited psychopath.

Biological Theories. It was once believed that psychopathy was an inherited constitutional defect. The evidence for this belief is scant (Shields & Slater, 1961), and virtually no one maintains it. One variant of a hereditary approach does have adherents. Eysenck (1957) assumes that extraversion, the temperament underlying psychopathy, is inherited. There is as yet little evidence that the extreme extraversion necessary for psychopathy is inherited, and at present Eysenck's is a minority view. This comment applies only to the heredity issue. His learning approach to psychopathy has much to recommend it and is consistent with clinical and experimental evidence.

Another biological theory suggests that psychopaths have minimal, diffuse brain damage. No one claims that psychopaths have focal lesions or anatomical damage that can be seen during brain surgery or autopsy. Nevertheless, there is strong evidence of brain abnormality in the deviant electroencephalograms (EEGs) reported in psychopaths (Silverman, 1943; Gottlieb et al., 1947; Hill, 1952; Erlich & Keogh, 1956; and Schwade & Geiger, 1956). It is known that one of the effects of brain damage is a loss of control. Children especially tend to become impulsive, asocial, and generally difficult to control as a consequence of illness or injury that affects the brain. It is only a short, logical step to attribute the psychopath's impulsiveness and asociality to diffuse brain damage.

This hypothesis has two flaws. First, although psychopaths as a group tend to have a higher frequency of deviant EEGs than normal persons, many psychopaths have entirely normal EEGs. The proportion of psychopaths with abnormal EEGs varies from one-half to four-fifths. If it is the lower proportion, then there are just as many psychopaths with normal

EEGs as with abnormal ones. Thus, mimimal brain damage can account for only a portion of psychopathy, perhaps only half.

Second, the EEG, which is recognized as an imprecise diagnostic device, is not a reliable indicator of minimal brain damage. This point is emphasized by the data for other abnormal samples. Hill (1952) found no EEG differences between psychopaths and a variety of psychotic patients, a finding corroborated by Shagass and Schwartz (1962). In both studies psychopaths and psychotics showed deviant EEG patterns.

Thus, the hypothesis of minimal brain damage as a cause of psychopathy is weakened by two sets of facts. However, the evidence indicates that the EEGs of many psychopaths are abnormal, and there is no obvious explanation. One speculation is that many seriously disturbed patients, whether psychopathic or psychotic, show deviance in a number of somatic systems. We saw in Chapter 14 that schizophrenics display a pattern of autonomic hyperactivity and hyporeactivity. Shagass and his colleagues have been investigating EEG disturbances in schizophrenics, and Shagass and Schwartz (1962) have reported that psychopaths' EEGs resemble those of schizophrenics more than those of neurotics. Since the presence of brain damage has not been established in schizophrenia, perhaps it is best to regard the abnormal EEGs of both schizophrenics and psychopaths as a *concomitant* of disturbed behavior rather than as a *cause*.

ALCOHOLISM

We shall discuss alcoholism as representative of all addictions. There are, of course, addictions to a variety of drugs, but the number of addicts involved is small compared to the number of alcoholics. Furthermore, although there are some differences between alcoholics and other addicts, both have similar problems, so that a discussion of alcoholism may serve as a discussion of all addiction.

Alcoholism may be defined as excessive drinking: any drinking that causes harm to the drinker. Harm in this instance refers not to "hangovers" but to repeated psychological inefficiency, bizarreness, or lasting physical symptoms. Another way of defining alcoholism is in terms of the use of alcohol as a drug rather than as a beverage.

Although millions of persons consume alcohol, only a small minority are alcoholics—the estimate is one million in this country. Thus, most drinkers are not alcoholics but *social drinkers*. They consume alcohol at the appropriate time, place, and occasion specified by the culture, and in appropriate amounts.

Why does anyone drink? The main reason is the pharmacological effects of alcohol, which is a "wonder drug" when taken in small amounts. It is a neural depressant, inhibiting first the higher brain centers and then the lower centers. When the higher brain centers are depressed, the lower centers are freed from inhibition. The individual feels more relaxed, less anxious, less guilty, and less inhibited. Alcohol in mild doses also stimulates the appetite and helps circulation by dilating peripheral blood vessels. There is also evidence that alcohol helps in resolving conflict (Conger, 1951). Lastly, the consumption of alcohol is linked with "good times" because of its use on festive occasions. In large amounts alcohol affects the lower brain centers, causing difficulty in sensory and motor activities. Eventually, it leads to unconsciousness, which may be welcomed by the drinker as preferable to remaining awake and aware of his problems.

Stages of Alcoholism

Alcohol, taken moderately, is beneficial to man; we label this *social drinking*. Alcohol, taken immoderately, is harmful; this we label *alcoholism*. How are the two distinguished? Jellinek (1952) has described the four stages in the progression from social drinking to alcoholism.

Prealcoholic Symptomatic Phase. There is periodic or continual drinking as a means of avoiding problems. At first alcohol is consumed to bolster confidence or diminish tension during infrequent crises. Subsequently, the crises occur oftener, and drinking becomes constant.

Prodromal Phase. Occasionally, heavy drinking leads to unconsciousness (blackouts). The individual begins to drink furtively, as alcohol becomes more a drug and less a beverage. As this stage proceeds, blackouts occur more frequently.

Crucial Phase. This phase is marked by a *loss of control:* once the individual takes the first drink, he continues to imbibe until he is too sick or too uncoordinated to take any more. He has not lost the *ability to abstain,* and he can still give up alcohol for weeks or even months. However, the first drink inevitably leads to complete intoxication.

At this point the alcoholic's adjustment begins to slide downhill. He starts drinking during the day, which impairs his work efficiency. His drunkenness becomes evident to his employer, family, and friends. His response to their recriminations or to his own guilt is to drink still more. He neglects his diet and begins to suffer from nutritional deficiencies. At some time during this phase he goes on a "bender" and is hospitalized for physical ailments caused by prolonged drinking. He develops *withdrawal symptoms* which can be alleviated only by alcohol, and he starts drinking in the morning.

Chronic Phase. Drinking is now continual; benders are frequent. Physiological changes occur, and now it requires less alcohol to induce unconsciousness. The alcoholic no longer cares about his job, his family, or his social status; he lives only to consume alcohol. He begins to experience psychological and physical symptoms caused by prolonged use of alcohol and by insufficient nutrition, and his only response is to continue drinking. Eventually, he comes to the attention of police and is hospitalized. After discharge if he continues to drink, he eventually develops serious physical symptoms and may die.

Types of Alcoholism

This sequence is typical of the pattern seen in alcoholics who may become members of Alcoholics Anonymous. It is only one pattern of alcoholism. Jellinek (1960) has described five different patterns, of which three are relevant here.

Alpha Alcoholism. This pattern is defined by four features:
(1) purely psychological dependence on alcohol as a means of easing tension
(2) the drinking pattern violates the rules of society as to when, where, and amount
(3) ability to abstain from drinking
(4) ability to control the amount consumed.

The harm caused by alpha pattern drinking consists of a drop in work efficiency, disturbed personal relations, or both. Although the drinker depends on alcohol as an escape mechanism, there is no progression to greater or more frequent drinking.

Gamma Alcoholism. The four features of this pattern are:
(1) an increased tolerance for alcohol, which means that it must be consumed in greater amounts to yield the desired effect.
(2) adaptive cell metabolism, in which the body becomes accustomed to the presence of alcohol and requires it for everyday functioning, which leads to withdrawal symptoms, which are extremely uncomfortable and lead to a craving for alcohol.
(3) ability to abstain from drinking.
(4) loss of control—the inability to stop after the first drink.

This pattern leads not only to psychological harm (inefficiency and poor personal relations) but also to physical harm (cirrhosis of the liver, intestinal complaints, and damage to nerves).

Delta Alcoholism. Again there are four features:
(1) an increased tolerance for alcohol
(2) adaptive cell metabolism
(3) withdrawal symptoms and craving
(4) inability to abstain

Note that the delta alcoholic cannot refrain from drinking but can regulate the amount he drinks. This contrasts with the pattern of the gamma alcoholic who can stop drinking for weeks or even months but who loses all control when he tries even a single drink. The delta pattern is typical of Latin countries and wine consumption; the gamma pattern is typical of Anglo-Saxon countries and whiskey consumption.

The alpha pattern involves only a *psychological* dependence on alcohol, but both gamma and delta patterns involve *physiological* dependence. Physiological dependence means that absence of alcohol produces withdrawal symptoms, the sign of true addiction. Godfrey et al. (1958) have outlined a *stereotyped withdrawal syndrome*, which consists of psychological and physiological symptoms:

(1) The patient is frightened, depressed, weak, restless, and unable to sleep. He feels "shaky inside," quivery, and gross tremors are usually present.

(2) There is an elevation of pulse rate and blood pressure, dilation of peripheral blood vessels, and a temporary elevation of body temperature. After a prolonged drinking bout there is always dehydration (dry mouth, sunken eyes, and wrinkled skin) and usually starvation. Alcohol relieves most of these symptoms, and once the alcoholic learns this, the craving cannot be extinguished. After a bender the alcoholic is a very sick person, and the only alternative to further drinking is hospitalization and immediate medical care.

This completes our account of the various stages and types of alcoholism. One aspect of alcoholism needs no explanation. This is physiological craving, which is based on some kind of change in cell metabolism. Isbell calls it:

. . . a "physical" or nonsymbolic craving which occurs in persons who have been drinking excessive amounts of alcohol for long periods of time, and is manifested by symptoms on withdrawal of alcohol. This type of craving is believed to be due to physiological alterations, the mechanism of which is not yet understood. The chief importance of physical craving is that it tends to make drinking bouts even more protracted and continuous. (1955, p. 42)

This kind of craving explains the inability of delta alcoholics to abstain from drinking.

Two other aspects of alcoholism still require explanation. First, what is the *origin* of excessive drinking? Why does an individual cross the line from social drinking to undisciplined drinking? A related question is why a former alcoholic starts drinking again. Second, what is the explanation for uncontrolled drinking. Why is a single drink enough to initiate the entire sequence of intoxication in a gamma alcoholic?

Theories of Alcoholism

There are four kinds of theories of alcoholism: dynamic (including psychoanalytic, neopsychoanalytic, and interpersonal theories), learning, biological, and cultural.

Dynamic Theories. Orthodox psychoanalytic theory assumes that alcoholics are narcissistic persons who are fixated at the oral phase of development (Fenichel, 1945). Male alcoholics (and men predominate) have homosexual tendencies which arise from the presence of a frustrating mother. The boy turns from his frustrating mother to his more easygoing father, and this development fosters unconscious homosexual impulses.

Classical psychoanalytic theory emphasizes orality and homosexuality in the genesis of alcoholism, but modern versions of psychoanalytic theory are broader. Levy (1958) lists seven functions of alcohol:

(1) *A discharge function.* Alcohol weakens the forces of repression, thereby releasing unconscious material. Anxiety, guilt, and shame are blunted, and previously repressed material can be expressed in cathartic fashion.

(2) *A narcotizing function.* Alcohol inhibits perception and eventually leads to unconsciousness. Thus it can protect the ego from anxiety-laden internal or external stimuli.

(3) *An orally gratifying function.* Levy parts company with orthodox psychoanalysts in that he denies the importance of oral ingestion in alcoholism. The real issue, he argues, is a recreation of infantile modes of experience; as with the infant, the alcoholic passively takes in the pleasures of the world. Alcohol diminishes the constraints of reality testing, and the individual can experience infantile feelings of being omnipotent, immortal, and lovable.

(4) *A masochistic function.* If the alcoholic has any guilt or needs self-punishment, the effects of drinking supply the need. There is the immediate discomfort of a hangover or such long range punishments as losing a job, ruining a career, or breaking up a marriage.

(5) *A hostile function.* Drinking may release repressed aggressive urges; the hostility may also be expressed indirectly. The long-range effects of alcohol (loss of job, break up of family, etc.) also serve to punish those closest to the alcoholic.

(6) *A homosexual function.* Again Levy deviates from orthodox psychoanalytic theory, which insists that homosexuality is basic to alcoholism. He suggests that such urges are merely easier to express under the influence of alcohol; there is no special relationship between alcohol and homosexuality.

(7) *An identification function.* Frequently the father of an alcoholic is also an alcoholic. This means that the son's drinking offers a means of identifying with his father. The identification may be more diffuse, an assertion of manhood. One concept of "being a man" includes being rough, tough, and a heavy drinker. The challenge, "I can drink you under the table" is an important part of masculinity for many men. Thus, drinking may help the alcoholic's shaky masculine identification.

Zwerling and Rosenbaum (1959) conducted a clinical study of alcoholics and arrived at the following formulation of an alcoholic's personality development:

Disruption of the mother-child relationship in the period of dependency sets in motion a series of developmental trends evolving into sequences of (1) distrustful withdrawal, with attendant experiences of isolation and estrangement in addition to persistence of atypical, magical thinking processes; (2) persistent passive-dependent longings, with resulting distortions in object relationships; (3) inevitable frustration of the insatiable omnipotence and dependency demands, with resultant impulsive grasping behavior and chronic rage; (4) conflict, ambivalent dependency relationships which must frequently be ruptured, repeatedly establishing the setting for depressive reactions; and (5) conflicted, ambivalent sexual role-playing with immature modes of sexual behavior. (p. 640)

The basic flaw in these dynamic theories is that they are not specific for alcoholics. Orality, homosexuality, disturbed parent-child relationships, and dependency problems are found in neurotics, psychotics, and patients with psychosomatic disorders. Any theory of alcoholism must state what is special about alcoholics. A dynamic approach must state one or more dynamic variables that occur in alcoholics but not in others. Button (1956) attempts to do this:

A. *Early factors, general:*
    1. A pregenital fixation, as a result of which oral objects (the breast and its equivalents; milk and its equivalents) are cathected as the greatest source of primal satisfaction.
    2. "Castration complex," contributing to which are primal fears—specifically of emasculation, and more generally of destruction.
    3. A weak, psychologically or physically absent, or unduly feared father; and a rigid, puritanical mother, dominant or rejecting (or both). Or conversely, a rigid, dominant father and a weak, submissive mother.
    4. *Some special factors:*
        a. A family constellation in which the patient tends to be the youngest, or the most protected, in the sense of prolonging his dependency and denying his gradual and smooth individualization.
        b. The specific aura given to alcohol, as well as to other symbols of "sin," of "forbidden fruit," rendering them unduly attractive.
B. *An incomplete masculine identification,* manifested by
    1. The wish to be a complete man ("masculine protest"), alternating with
    2. The wish to be receptive-dependent ("latent homosexuality");
    3. Feelings of impotence, social and sexual; and
    4. Feelings of hostility, manifested
        a. *externally,* as psychopathic behavior (violence, aggression, amoral and antisocial conduct), and

b. *internally,* as self-destruction (drinking, suicide, and somatization: conversion and hypochondriacal symptoms).

This series of symptoms then leads to

C. The syndrome of "psychopathic anxiety," manifested by guilt, tension, hostility, depression, and feelings of futility, inadequacy, and inferiority. Also contributing to this syndrome seem to be

1. *Punitive measures* by the external world, such as hospitalization, imprisonment, etc; and

2. *A moralistic approach* by the external world, exemplified in criticism by the family, Alcoholics Anonymous, judges and doctors, and by the lay as well as some professional literature.

"Psychopathic anxiety"—a poor term, used only for lack of a better one—is an intolerable condition. It is met by

D. *The erection of a defense system.* This comprises in approximately the order of frequency of appearance:

1. *Hysterical defense,* including
   a. denial,
   b. repression, and
   c. suppression of feelings of "psychopathic anxiety," and
   d. conversion of these feelings into physical ills;

2. *Psychopathic defenses,* which are, in manifestation,
   a. behavioral, as in an inability to profit from experience, or
   b. ideational, as in those persons to whom an outward expression of hostility and amorality is too threatening, or both types;

3. *Projective defenses,* in which the alcoholic's hostility is assumed by him to be emanating from the outside world, often with good reason;

4. *Schizoid defenses,* manifested by
   a. individualism—"egotism,"
   b. withdrawal-isolation-constriction of output; and
   c. distorted perceptions of "reality";

5. *Dependency* as a defense, which serves to obviate the patient's and his family's expectations that he will function as a responsible, adult, aggressive, and successful male, and excuse his failure to live up to them;

6. *Psychasthenic defenses,* manifested by obsessive thinking or compulsive behavior, frequently both. This has been listed at the end because it was less often noted in the present sample than the others, and also because it seems in some cases to be a defense against certain of the other defenses, notably the schizoid constellation of defenses.

One differentiating factor between alcoholics and nonalcoholics seems to be the fact that the above defenses are notably unsuccessful in reducing the alcoholic's painful self-perception as an inadequate hostile person. This hypothetical differentiation, however, is not based on evidence but on the impression gained from contact with alcoholics when compared with patients manifesting the other clinical syndromes named after their predominant defense systems; hysterics, psychopaths, paranoids, schizoid personalities, and so forth. These defenses in the alcoholic are, thus, relatively shortlived; there then occurs:

E. *The breakdown of the defense system,* contributing to which are:

1. An anxiety-producing *"insight"* or *"conversion experience"* whereby the patient suddenly develops the painful self-perception of impotence and inadequacy. This experience frequently occurs because the roots of alcoholism seem in many already perceptive alcoholics to be buried not too deep in the unconscious, at least when compared to the level of awareness of psychological causes in certain other psychopathological states, such as the psychoses.

2. *A perceived trauma,* real or fantasied, such as loss of job or wage-earning capacities, divorce or other marital upset, death or illness of some important environmental figure, disruption of some interpersonal relationship of importance to the patient, an accident or some physical disability, or the like.

3. *A temporal factor.* This means, basically, that some alcoholics (e.g., the "periodic" or the "week-end" alcoholic) seem to reach a point in the cycle of defense versus breakdown of defense where the two ends of this continuum meet—for no discernible reason. The cycle varies greatly in length with the individual.

4. Certain *physiological factors,* such as blood sugar level, androgen-estrogen balance, electrolyte balance, hypocorticalism, physical pain, fatigue, excitation patterns of the cerebral cortex, incipient disease processes, a disturbance of internal homeostasis, or the like, may play a part in the breakdown of the defense system. The evidence for this point, however, is markedly contradictory.

As a result of the breakdown of the defense system, the patient then begins

F. *Drinking to excess.* At this point, one step before "chronic alcoholism," by far the majority of patients interrupt the progression from bad to worse and erect again their chosen defense system or combination of defense systems. This re-erection seems to take the form of "repetition compulsion," in that most frequently the same defenses, now proven to the patient himself to be demonstrably unsuccessful, are again chosen. The cycle begins again, but this time, as with all succeeding times, the probability of its ending in the ultimate and probably irreversible condition of deteriorative alcoholism becomes increasingly greater. The choice of a defense system is not, of course, a voluntary one; certain factors leading to its re-erection do, however, seem to be at least partially dependent upon the patient's conscious wish to interrupt the cycle. These are such factors as institutionalization, voluntary or otherwise; resolution ("will power"); guilt, shame and remorse; punishment or coercion or both; and, temporarily, certain treatments, such as hormones, disulfiram, conditioned reflex, rest and sedation, vitamins, inspirational and intellectual methods, Alcoholics Anonymous techniques, group and individual psychotherapy, or any of the other countless techniques that have been tried with alcoholics.

If the drinking-to-excess pattern is not interrupted, however, and sometimes even if it is, there almost inevitably occurs, sooner or later, the condition of

G. *Confirmed and deteriorative alcoholism,* which at this point has probably become a "habit" and is relatively irreversible. By "habit" is meant that the original reasons for excessive drinking have become inaccessible or unimportant to the drinker, and that the once-painful act of drinking itself as well as the resultant hangover have become relatively gratifying in themselves. The whole organism, thus, has adapted itself, physically and psychologically, to a condition of chronic drunkenness. (pp. 672–675)

Button's schema is the most comprehensive dynamic account of alcoholism. It contains hypotheses specific enough to test, which makes it more valuable than previous theories. The theory was derived in part from clinical research, but it obviously needs empirical verification.

Learning Theories. There are two learning theories of alcoholism. The first is an application of the Dollard and Miller version of Hull's learning theory (see Chapter 6), and the second is a neutral, nonpartisan learning approach.

Conger (1956) applied the Dollard-Miller approach to alcoholism, but he dealt only with drive and reinforcement. In an earlier study (Conger, 1951) he found that alcohol helped rats to resolve a food-versus-punishment conflict. His interpretation was that fear of punishment was diminished by alcohol but hunger was not.

In the Dollard-Miller system a reduction in drive strength constitutes a reinforcement. The consumption of alcohol, which decreases fear drive, is therefore strongly reinforced. Concerning human drinking, why do the negative aspects of heavy drinking (hangover, loss of job, etc.) not weaken the drinking response? Conger invokes a temporal gradient of reinforcement as an answer. Responses reinforced immediately acquire greater strength than responses reinforced after long intervals. Drinking is immediately reinforced by a drop in anxiety, and the immediate reinforcement leads to a strong habit. Punishment occurs so much later than the response (hours for a hangover, months or years for a ruined career) that it has little effect on the response.

Conger's account may serve as an introduction to a learning theory of alcoholism, but it lacks details about the origin and pattern of drinking. Kingham (1958) offers a more complete theory, which makes three assumptions.

(1) The prealcoholic person has a strong desire to escape from reality and tends to have a cycloid personality. The first part of the assumption is in accord with clinical belief, which suggests that drinking represents an attempt to escape from conflict, anxiety, or unpleasant life situations. The second part has received some research support; alcoholics have been found to have elevated scores on the Manic or Depressive scales of the Minnesota Multiphasic Personality Inventory.

(2) *Blitz drinking,* defined as drinking so uncontrolled that it inevitably leads to complete intoxication or unconsciousness, is the dominant response in the drinking hierarchy. This response has presumably been learned over a period of years through trial and error, imitation, or rebellion.

(3) The Dollard-Miller system of drive-cue-response-reinforcement applies to drinking. The drive is some kind of psychological imbalance, such as frustration, fear, anger, loneliness, depression, or rejection. The cue is an alcoholic beverage. The response is blitz drinking. The reinforcement is a decrease in the tension state, a return of psychological balance.

Other learning concepts of importance are stimulus generalization, which helps the spread of the drinking in response to new and diverse drive states; the goal gradient, which accounts for the alcoholic's eliminating social drinking and moving directly to the goal (blitz drinking); and the temporal gradient of reinforcement, which accounts for the strength of the drinking response in the face of extremely adverse consequences that occur some time after the drinking response.

Storm and Smart (1965) attempt to account for alcoholism without using the concept of drive. They point out that the evidence from animal studies indicates little transfer of learning from the sober state to the alcoholic state or from the alcoholic state to the sober state. They label this lack of transfer *stimulus generalization decrement*. They assume that the larger the dose of alcohol, the greater is the decrement. They also assume that there is a learned discrimination between alcoholic and nonalcoholic states, citing Conger's study (1951) as evidence. Thus, what occurs in the drinking state is *dissociated* from what occurs in the sober state.

It follows from these assumptions that the longer the history of drinking and the larger the dose of alcohol, the greater is the dissociation between drunk and sober states. Thus behavior learned while drunk should generalize and hence occur at almost any level of intoxication, but *it should never generalize to the sober state*. Memory for occurrences of the drunken state should diminish and eventually disappear. Thus the inability to remember what happened while drunk (*blackout*) is explained by the learned dissociation of the two states. Similarly, what is learned during the sober state does not transfer to the drunken state. Consequently, injunctions against drinking, which are learned while the person is sober, have no effect once he starts to drink. This is one explanation for uncontrolled drinking, but there is another:

With increasing dissociation, and distinctiveness of behavior patterns under alcohol and when sober, moving by generalization down the gradient of alcohol dosage, the effect on behavior of any given amount of alcohol should become increasingly marked. The response of taking another drink, in particular, will have been frequently paired with the stimulus conditions produced by having taken a first one, thus establishing, by conditioning, the chaining of responses which is called loss of control. (Storm & Smart, 1965, p. 113)

Thus classical conditioning is used to account for loss of control. The pleasant effects of the last drink are paired with the act of taking the next drink. This pairing establishes the sequence:

pleasant effects of alcohol → taking another drink → pleasant effects, etc.

The chain of successive drinking responses is essentially the same as for eating peanuts. Virtually no one eats one peanut and then stops; usually the peanuts are eaten until the supply is exhausted. Similarly, the chain of drinking responses continues until the supply runs out or the person becomes unconscious.

The flaw in this approach is that it is too inclusive. It accounts for uncontrolled drinking but does not state why most persons who consume alcohol do not lose control. The flaw may be remedied by assuming individual differences in either the reinforcing or the aversive properties of alcohol. Some individuals have a strong need for the effects of alcohol (escape from problems, reduction of conflict, release of inhibition, relaxation, etc.), and therefore drinking is strongly reinforced. Others may benefit from the effects of alcohol without having the overwhelming need for it to escape from problems, release inhibitions, etc., and therefore drinking is only weakly reinforced. Other things being equal, strong reinforcement should lead to uncontrolled drinking and weak reinforcement should not.

The aversive properties relevant here are the relatively immediate effects of alcohol on the individual. Some persons suffer from nausea, vomiting, and dizziness after only a few drinks. If these physical symptoms occur after only a few drinks, they will be sufficiently aversive to counteract the beneficial effects of alcohol. The chain of drinking will be broken, and such individuals will never become uncontrolled drinkers. On the other hand, some individuals can consume large quantities of alcohol without showing signs of somatic distress. In the absence of any immediate aversive effects of alcohol, the chain of drinking is uninterrupted and may proceed to uncontrolled drinking.

Biological Theories. Biological theories of alcoholism have flourished. Jellinek (1960) has reviewed theories focusing on allergy, biochemistry, physiology, brain pathology, endocrinology, and nutrition. Most of them are highly speculative and supported by little or no evidence. We shall evaluate only the most prominent formulation, Williams' "genetotrophic" theory (1947, 1959), which is analogous to biochemical approaches to psychosis.

Williams assumed an inherited inability to produce certain enzymes. This biochemical defect leads to a nutritional problem because of an inability to digest certain nutrients. Consequently, the prealcoholic has a physiological need for the missing substances, which leads him to consume alcohol excessively. Thus, alcoholism is caused by an inherited enzyme defect that produces a physical craving for alcohol.

One fact adduced to support the theory is the wide individual differences in susceptibility to the effects of alcohol. However, the basic evidence has come from research on rats. Williams and other researchers have demonstrated that when rats are deprived of certain vitamins, they increase their consumption of alcohol, preferring it to water. The increase in consumption of alcohol occurs when the alternative to alcohol is water. Lester and Greenberg (1952) found that when the rats were offered a third choice (sugar water or saccharine water), they would *diminish* their intake of alcohol and increase their intake of sucrose (or saccharine). Thus Williams' basic experiment led to an incorrect conclusion. The correct conclusion is that rats deprived of vitamins will avoid water for *any* nutrient, and alcohol is not even preferred.

The genetic aspect of Williams' theory has also been refuted by evidence. Roe et al. (1945) studied children who were separated from their alcoholic parents and placed in foster homes. The rate of subsequent alcoholism in these children was no different from the rate in children of nonalcoholic parents.

Thus Williams' theory appears to be incorrect. Note that the theory attempts to explain the *origin* of alcoholism. The *origin* and the *maintenance* of alcoholism may well be distinct issues. Although a biological approach to the origin of drinking has not been found to be fruitful, a biological approach to maintenance makes considerable sense.

Consider the addictive aspects of chronic drinking. Jellinek (1960) reported that alcoholic patients require greater amounts of anesthetics than nonalcoholics to produce anesthesia. This is strong evidence for an increased tissue tolerance not only for alcohol but also for all substances that depress neural functioning. In addition to increased tissue tolerance, withdrawal symptoms are an important aspect of chronic alcoholism. Tissue tolerance and withdrawal symptoms constitute a reasonable basis for inferring a physiological craving for alcohol: addiction based on the biological consequences of prolonged, excessive intake of alcohol. Jellinek suggested that hereditary factors might account for the individual differences in the number of years required to reach the addictive state—3 to 15 years.

This biological approach to *addictive* alcoholism makes sense and accounts for known facts. It needs to be checked out in detail, and the necessary pharmacological and biochemical techniques are now available. Thus, although there appears to be no good biological theory of the *origin* of alcoholism, there may be a good biological theory of its *maintenance*, namely its addictive aspects.

Cultural Theories. The cultural aspect of alcoholism cannot be ignored. Alcoholism is a minor problem among Jews but a major one among the Irish; it is a more serious problem in France than in Italy. It is only a short step from these facts to the speculation that the prevailing cultural pattern facilitates or inhibits excessive drinking. In France wine is believed to be a positive good and perhaps even necessary for health, whereas in Italy the attitude toward wine is less rosy and more realistic. According to Jellinek (1960) it is a sign of bad manners to refuse a glass of wine in France but not in Italy.

The cultural approach emphasizes adoption of the prevailing pattern as a major factor in alcoholism. In certain countries children are introduced to alcohol early in their lives, and they can move toward excessive consumption merely by imitating older siblings, parents, and other models. In other countries the available models tend to be abstinent or at least moderate in their drinking.

Culture also appears to determine the *pattern* of alcoholism. As was noted earlier, gamma alcoholism, which involves a loss of control, is typical of Anglo-Saxon countries in which whiskey consumption predominates. Delta alcoholism, which involves inability to abstain, is typical of Latin countries in which wine consumption predominates. Thus the culture is a powerful variable in determining not only the amount but also the kind of drinking.

A study by McCord et al. (1959) bolsters the cultural approach. They followed up boys who were studied in childhood and then later in adulthood, and they sought early differences between those who subsequently became alcoholics and those who did not. There was no support for any of the biological appproaches—heredity, nutrition, or glandular functioning. There was no support for a dynamic approach; those who later became alcoholics were neither more "oral" nor more homosexual than those who did not. However, the cultural approach did receive support. Alcoholism was found to be related to social class (a higher rate among middle class than lower class) and ethnic background (a higher rate among Irish and native Americans). This support for the cultural approach is striking because of the absence of evidence favoring dynamic or biological approaches to the origin of alcoholism. One possible integration of these data and theories is:

(1) Alcoholism *originates* because of cultural variables acting in conjunction with learning variables (imitation and avoiding tension).

(2) Alcoholic *addiction* is caused by physiological changes in the individual as a consequence of many years of excessive drinking.

SEX DEVIANCE

At first glance it would appear to be a simple matter to define sex deviance; ask any adult, and he will give a straightforward answer. However, there would be considerable variability from one adult to the next, and it would surely turn out that, "Normality is what I practice, and deviance is what the other fellow practices." The legal definition, which varies from one state to another is excessively broad, including sexual activities that are considered normal by most persons. For example, sexual intercourse before marriage or outside of marriage is *fornication* in legal terms and subject to penalties, as is *common prostitution*. It is of interest to note that fornication is ordinarily prosecuted by the law only when money changes hands. Thus, in the interpretation of the law there is the leavening effect of a vague social definition of sex deviance. Psychologists tend to follow the social consensus on sexual deviance, including the various behaviors under two headings: deviant object and deviant response.

Deviant Object

In the course of normal development the maturing individual is required gradually to direct his sexual interest to members of the opposite sex. After puberty this rule is strictly enforced, with exceptions only for the indirect and playful activities of boys in locker rooms with boys and of girls at pajama parties. Genital activities with partners other than members of the opposite sex are regarded as deviant because the *normal* object is the opposite-sexed person. Deviance therefore includes homosexuality, animal contacts, and masturbation. Masturbation is deviant because of absence of the appropriate partner; because no one else is involved, it is considered only a minor sort of object deviance. Of course, sexual intercourse itself may be deviant even when the partners are of the opposite sex: between a man and a sufficiently young girl.

There are two kinds of homosexuality. The first consists solely of appropriate sexual activity with a partner of the same sex. *Appropriate* activity refers to sexual behavior consistent with the gender of the participant: the man takes the male role but does so with another man as partner, or a woman takes the female role but with another woman as partner. The second kind of homosexuality consists of an *inversion* of sexual activity: a man takes a passive feminine role with another man, or a woman takes an active, masculine role with another woman. This second kind is considered to be more abnormal than the first.

Deviant Response

In the behavior just mentioned, the sexual activity always involves genital stimulation; although the object is inappropriate, the response is appropriate. There are several kinds of sexual activity involving a deviant response regardless of the appropriateness of the partner.

(1) *Sadism* and *masochism* involve the giving or receiving of pain, respectively, in order to attain sexual pleasure. For those who indulge in these activities, sex is infused with a large element of aggression, and they may achieve orgasm through torturing someone or being tortured themselves.

(2) *Voyeurism* and *fetishism* both concern activities which may be one aspect of sexual arousal in normal individuals. When these activities displace

the normal outcome of sexual arousal (sexual intercourse), they are deviant. The *voyeur* derives intense pleasure from observing such sexually arousing sights as sexual activities of others or certain parts of the anatomy. Visual perception may be sufficient for him to achieve orgasm, and it may be the only means of achieving it. The *fetishist* becomes sexually aroused by touching or possessing garments or objects that are associated with sexual partners. Such arousal is no different from that expected in normal individuals when confronted with stimuli that symbolize sex. Fetishism is deviant in that contact with the symbols replaces sexual union itself.

(3) *Exhibitionism,* which is apparently limited to men, consists of exposing genitalia to women or children. There may be no sexual arousal in the individual who so exposes himself.

(4) *Transvestism,* which consists of dressing in the clothes of the opposite sex, also appears to be limited principally to men. There seem to be two kinds of transvestites. The first kind represents the extreme of fetishism in that touching of symbols and clothes associated with the opposite sex is not sufficient. The clothes must actually be worn to experience sexual arousal. In the second type there is an attempt to take over the superficial aspects of the feminine role. The man wishes to be a woman and takes the most direct and obvious way of achieving this—wearing a woman's clothes.

Abnormality

The three criteria of abnormality are discomfort, inefficiency, and bizarreness. The sexual deviant rarely suffers discomfort, and his unusual sexual outlet does not usually interfere with his job or the efficient playing of his various nonsexual roles. The essential criterion is therefore bizarreness. Society trains its members to be clean and to be disgusted at filth. Similarly, it trains them to regard heterosexual behavior between adults as normal and any other sexual outlet as disgusting and deviant.

We have distinguished two kinds of deviance, object and response deviance. Are they equally abnormal? In order to answer this question we must specify the characteristics of normal sexual behavior. We are born with a physiological sexual arousal system, but it is not oriented by nature toward partners of the opposite sex. In early childhood sexual arousal tends to be diffuse and at times difficult to distinguish from other arousal states. By adulthood the sensations of sexual arousal have become more or less localized in the genitalia. Thus, during maturation there is a progressive localization of sexual arousal, the final stage being what has been termed *genitality*. The appropriate adult sexual response is genital, regardless of the partner.

Society trains us to prefer members of the opposite sex as partners, and it punishes contacts with members of the same sex or with animals, as well as autoeroticism. Not all societies have these values, nor is our own society entirely homogeneous in this respect. When men or women are forced to endure long periods without members of the opposite sex, it is only natural that they should turn to homosexuality or masturbation for sexual outlet. Under extenuating circumstances, sexual behavior with a deviant object is not considered abnormal. It follows that the choice of a deviant partner (or no partner) is only moderately abnormal, such a choice being appropriate and normal under certain restricted conditions of living.

This is not true of deviant sexual *responses* such as fetishism or sadism. These behaviors are considered unacceptable under *any* circumstances. Whether or not the partner is appropriate, the behavior is clearly distinguishable from normal genital behavior. As such, it is more distant from normality than is behavior involving a deviant object and is therefore more abnormal.

Theories of Sexual Deviance

There are four approaches to sexual deviance: psychoanalytic theory, interpersonal theory, learning theory, and biological theory.

Psychoanalytic Theory. Psychoanalytic theory regards sexual deviance as a compromise between instinctual urges and forces of repression. The instinctual urges being blocked concern the Oedipal complex, and the motivation for repression is an unconscious fear of castration. When anxiety blocks normal heterosexual impulses, the individual regresses to infantile sexuality, specifically, sexual perversions. Subsequently, one aspect of infantile sexuality is overemphasized and used to aid repressing all other aspects of sexuality. The acting out of the perversion serves as a "demonstration" that there has been no castration.

Castration anxiety is the key to understanding perversions. The male homosexual fears women because, having no penises, they are a constant reminder of the threat of castration. Therefore it is possible to have sex only with a man who, having a penis, does not elicit castration anxiety. The male homosexual may also fear women because their genitalia unconsciously symbolize castrating instruments.

The male homosexual identifies with his mother. Whether he will be an active or passive homosexual depends on the nature of this identification. He may assume his mother's role in relation to himself and then treat young men and boys as he would be treated. This leads to active homosexuality. On the other hand, he may be fixated at the anal stage and therefore identify with the feminine aspects of his mother's role. This leads to passive homosexuality and a wish to be treated by men as his mother would want to be treated.

Castration anxiety is also basic to female homosexuality because it prevents any heterosexual behavior. The attraction to the mother may occur because of early fixation. Later, the attachment to a mother-substitute offers both security and sexual satisfaction, as the two women play "mother and child." Another possibility is the rejection of the mother for a masculine role. The woman, having to do without men because of castration fears, claims that she can do without men because she is a better man than they. This attitude accompanies the role-reversal type of female homosexuality.

Castration anxiety underlies not only homosexuality but all sexual perversions. Let us summarize the dynamics of four other entities:

(1) Fetishism—unconscious reassurance that there is still a penis, fetishes tending to be penis symbols.

(2) Exhibitionism—obtaining unconscious reassurance of having a penis by forcing others to react to the sight of it.

(3) Sadism—unconsciously castrating (punishing) others so that they cannot castrate the pervert himself.

(4) Masochism—acceptance of a lesser punishment in place of a possible greater one (castration), as well as pleasure "purchased" by pain.

The sexual pervert and the neurotic are similar in that both experience castration anxiety in relation to the Oedipus complex and both repress sexual interest in the parent of the opposite sex. The major difference is their defensive reactions to these intrapsychic events. The pervert regresses to infantile sexuality; the neurotic may regress but then uses a variety of defenses to prevent the expression of impulses. The pervert directly expresses some of his sexual impulses; the neurotic does not. The pervert has fewer defenses and consequently the underlying, unconscious castration anxiety is less covert than the neurotic's.

Interpersonal Theory. This approach distinguishes between sex outlet and sex role. Sex outlet refers to arousal and consummatory behavior, whether normal or abnormal. Sex role refers to the sets of personality traits that constitute masculinity and femininity. While sex role and sex outlet are distinguishable, society tends to merge them. Thus men are expected to be strong, active, and dominant (sex role) and motivated to pursue women for sexual pleasure (sex outlet). Women are expected to be soft, passive, and submissive (sex role) and motivated to tempt men toward sexual pleasure (sex outlet). The interpersonal approach focuses on sex role, making the assumption that deviations in role lead to deviations in outlet.

An understanding of deviations in sex roles requires knowledge about normal sex roles. A full discussion of normal masculine and feminine roles and their development is obviously beyond the scope of this book, and therefore we shall limit the discussion to a recent theoretical summary of findings by Johnson (1963). She distinguishes between two modes of relating to others, expressiveness and instrumentality.

Expressiveness refers to the tendency to respond so as to please others:

being tender, loving, rewarding, and understanding. This orientation toward the feelings and needs of others can be learned only in a relationship with an expressive person.

Instrumentality refers to the tendency to seek rewards and win in competition regardless of the feeling of others. This neglect of the needs of others is best learned in situations that reward the individual for succeeding rather than for becoming affectively involved with others.

Expressivity is the key to femininity; instrumentality is the key to masculinity. Johnson assumes that the father plays the crucial role in developing masculine and feminine sex roles in his children:

The mother is predominately expressive toward children of both sexes and uses, intentionally or not, "love oriented" techniques of control on both. It is in this first identification of both male and female children with the mother in a love-dependency relationship that the basic superego is laid down. Sex role differentiation then follows the initial mother identification and results from the identification of both sexes with the father in differentiated role relationships. The father adds the specifically feminine element to the female's initial expressiveness by rewarding her, by his appreciative attitude, not simply for being "good" but for being "attractive." With his son as with his daughter the father is solidary, but with his son he is also demanding, thus giving the extra push that instrumentalness requires. (1963, p. 324)

Thus the father is decisive in determining his children's sex roles. If he demands instrumentality (competitiveness, success, etc.) from his daughter, she will tend to have a masculine orientation. If he fails to demand instrumentality from his son, he will tend to have a feminine orientation.

In addition to specific training, interpersonal theory emphasizes identification and modeling. Boys must have an appropriate masculine model from whom they can copy male behaviors, and girls require a feminine model. If a boy's father is absent, distant, frightening, or rejecting, there will be a deficient masculine identification. Similarly, a girl's feminine identification depends upon the presence of a close, affectionate mother. Faulty parental training or lack of an appropriate model may lead to a weak or inappropriate sex role, which in turn may lead to a deviant sex outlet, especially homosexuality.

Learning Theory. There is no single, comprehensive learning theory of sex deviance, but behavior therapists believe that perversions can be cured by learning techniques (see Rachman's review, 1961). The histories of sex deviants abound with instances of sexual stimulation in the presence of stimuli which subsequently come to elicit sexual arousal. Thus in the development of perversions there seems to be a *pairing* of a sexually exciting stimulus with a neutral stimulus, followed by the response of sexual arousal. This appears to be the usual classical conditioning situation:

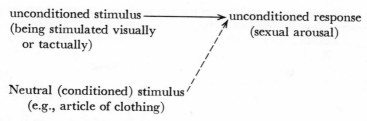

Initially the neutral stimulus does not elicit a sexual response, but after being paired with an unconditioned sexual stimulus, the neutral stimulus becomes a conditioned stimulus for a sexual response.

Such conditioning accounts for the wide variety of stimuli that excite sexual deviance. Classical conditioning also explains the arousal properties of sexual stimuli falling in the "normal" range. Most men are sexually aroused by seeing female breasts or genital organs or by reading about sexual experiences. There is nothing intrinsically arousing about such stimuli, and therefore their arousal properties must have been acquired through conditioning.

A more detailed learning approach has been outlined by McGuire et al. (1965). They assume that conditioning occurs only after some sexual experience, which is then used in fantasy during subsequent masturbation. If the sexual experience is a deviant one, it will tend to be the dominant fantasy during masturbation. Pairing of the fantasy of deviant sexuality with subsequent orgasm during masturbation enhances the stimulus value of the deviant fantasy.

Many deviant individuals believe that they are incapable of having normal sexual relations. This belief keeps them away from normal sexual outlets and intensifies satisfaction through deviant fantasies. Thus deviant behavior is strengthened by lack of reinforcement and opportunity. The following deductions stem from the theory:

(1) The theory makes no assumptions concerning previous sexual interest. In fact, two thirds of our patients recalled heterosexual interest before they had acquired their deviations, although the normal interest had usually disappeared by the time they were seen as patients. The deviations had also begun at various ages, with puberty the most common starting age.

(2) Any deviation can be acquired as hypothesized. We found no significant difference between deviations in the extent to which patients fitted the suggested pattern.

(3) A deviation acquired in this way should be able to be extinguished by deconditioning. This is supported by the success of aversion therapy carried out by ourselves and others.

(4) The theory explains why the deviant interest is not extinguished by the massive guilt that most of such patients experience. This is because the sexual pleasure from the masturbation of practice of the deviation comes at a more

effective moment, from a conditioning point of view, than the later guilt, no matter how intense or long-lasting this may be.

(5) A deviant who masturbates to fantasies as his main sexual outlet should be liable to develop other deviations. This was found among out-patients, many of whom had as many as three apparently unrelated deviations, though a link could often be found through the original fantasies.

(6) Since females masturbate to orgasm much less frequently than males (Kinsey, 1953) they should be less likely to develop sexual deviations. Apart from female homosexuality this is certainly true. We have not seen sufficient female homosexuals to account for the difference in that deviation. (McGuire et al., 1965, p. 187)

Biological Theory. The biological approach has focused mainly on homosexuality. There is abundant evidence from research on animals that sexual behavior depends largely on sex hormones (Ford & Beach, 1951). It is a short, logical step to assume that the cause of homosexuality in humans is some inherited defect in either sex organs or sex hormones.

Kallman (1953) presented evidence of an inherited component in homosexuality: greater concordance in identical twins than in fraternal twins. However, there has been some question about the representativeness of his sample and about the influence of nonhereditary variables. Furthermore, it is known that some individuals have moved from heterosexuality to homosexuality during adulthood, when hormonal changes are unlikely. There have also been changes in the opposite direction. If homosexuality is inherited, it is doubtful that such shifts in sexual outlet could occur.

Another hypothesis indicates variations in chromosomes as the cause of homosexuality. A normal male has an XY pattern and a normal female, an XX pattern of chromosomes. There are many abnormal variations in individuals with deviant anatomical sex characteristics: single X, a single Y, and XYY combination, etc. Analogizing from such abnormalities, some investigators have suggested that homosexuality is caused by abnormal chromosomes. For example, male homosexuals would have deviant chromosomal arrangements.

In recent years it has become possible to examine chromosomes directly. Pritchard (1962) checked the chromosomes of male homosexuals, most of whom had never had any heterosexual interest, and found the normal XY complement in every one of them. He also cited other genetic evidence (too complex to discuss here) against the hypothesis.

A final possibility for a biological explanation of homosexuality lies in deviant sex hormones. Normal males have a preponderance of androgens, and normal females have a preponderance of estrogens. Perhaps homosexuality is caused by excessive androgens in women and excessive estrogens in men.

Three kinds of evidence refute this hypothesis. First, there is no more hormonal imbalance in homosexuals than in heterosexual individuals. Second, hormone therapy, designed to correct the hypothetical imbalance, fails completely to alter homosexual behavior or interest (Money, 1961). Third, it is psychological role and not biological sex that determines the individual's sexual identification. Hampson (1963) studied men and women with biological sexual anomalies (anatomically bisexual or ambiguously sexual). These individuals had been reared as males or as females. When the biological sexual tendency clashed with the psychologically assigned sex role, the latter predominated. Thus none of the biological hypotheses has received support, and they have been discarded by most investigators.

COMMENT

Psychopathy, alcoholism, and sex deviance all involve immorality from society's point of view. They comprise behaviors that break written and unwritten rules: lying, cheating, stealing, irresponsibility, overindulgence, and immoral acts. All three involve breaches of conduct, which is the reason for their being discussed together. Nevertheless, they differ considerably in the way they deviate from society's norms.

The psychopath is unsocialized. He has learned the formal rituals of personal relationships but not the meaning of them. He fails to distinguish between human and nonhuman, treating both as objects. Children can be taught to do this, and such children become adults lacking one attribute of a socialized adult—humanity. The clearest example on a large scale is the Nazi Party of Germany, who regarded Jews in terms of "the Jewish question." The policy of genocide for Jews represents psychopathy on a large scale—treating human beings as objects to be exterminated.

Genocide is an extreme example of the psychopathic attitude. It exists to a lesser degree in all forms of prejudice; witness the Jim Crow belief that Negroes are inferior to and somehow less than human beings. Such prejudice is obviously learned, and we may infer that all psychopathy is learned. Children can be taught to treat others as objects, whether on a small scale as in ethnic or race prejudice (*some* humans are treated as objects) or on a large scale as in complete psychopathy (*all* humans are treated as objects).

In contrast to the psychopath, the alcoholic is socialized. Strictly speaking, he does not transgress or engage in tabooed activities. Drinking is quite acceptable; only overindulgence is not. Alcoholism was once considered immoral, but now it is regarded by most persons as an illness (and therefore more acceptable). Let us be clear about this issue. Addictive alcoholism may be considered a disease. It meets the requirements of a systemic disease such as diabetes: biological symptoms (withdrawal symptoms) in the absence of a chemical substance (alcohol) required for normal tissue metabolism. On the other hand, alcoholism without withdrawal symptoms should not be considered a disease, at least not in any medical sense, because it has no *biological* symptoms.

Alcoholism may be an escape from tension or anxiety. When an individual drinks to forget or otherwise escape from conflicts or fears, he resembles a neurotic. The neurotic uses various psychological means to avoid or escape from anxiety-laden situations; the alcoholic drinks. This kind of alcoholism is analogous to neurosis.

However, alcoholism may represent not an escape but a way of life. We saw earlier that heavy wine consumption is the normative pattern in France. Some individuals may be better indoctrinated and drift into alcoholism merely by adopting (too well) the prevailing pattern. Such alcoholism is unrelated to neurosis and can be explained solely on the basis of cultural variables.

The sex deviant may or may not be socialized. His sexual perversion may represent a failure to follow the usual developmental path to adult genital heterosexuality, in which event he is unsocialized. Perhaps he was seduced as a child and was thereby excessively rewarded for deviant sexuality; or perhaps he followed an incorrect adult model and ended up with a deviant sex role. Whatever the cause, this kind of sex deviance represents a lack of socialization.

On the other hand, the sex deviant may have turned away from normal heterosexual outlets because they were associated with punishment. The anxiety might have been generalized or specific to the Oedipal situation. The problem is not a lack of socialization but a fear of engaging in certain behaviors. This is analogous to neurotic behavior. The neurotic with phobias avoids anxiety by staying away from the objects of his fears. The variety of sex deviant we are discussing fears heterosexuality and therefore avoids it; he acnieves sexual pleasure by alternate means, which society labels abnormal.

It is clear that all three conduct disorders are defined by our particular culture. In certain other cultures the behaviors occur, but they are in no sense abnormal. The only exception is addictive alcoholism, which is a disease and therefore transcultural. It is possible that our cultural values will change in the direction of greater permissiveness and greater latitude concerning immorality. If this occurred, perhaps a textbook written 100 years hence would have no chapter on conduct disorders.

REFERENCES

Albert, R. S., Brigante, T. R., & Chase, M. The psychopathic personality: A content analysis of the concept. *Journal of General Psychology,* 1959, **60**, 17–28.

Button, A. D. The genesis and development of alcoholism. An empirically based schema. *Quarterly Journal of Studies on Alcoholism,* 1956, **17**, 671–675.

Cleckley, H. *The mask of sanity.* St. Louis: C. V. Mosby, 1964.

Conger, J. J. The effects of alcohol on conflict behavior in the albino rat. *Quarterly Journal of Studies on Alcohol,* 1951, **12,** 1–29.

Conger, J. J. Reinforcement theory and the dynamics of alcoholism. *Quarterly Journal of Studies on Alcohol,* 1956, **17,** 296–305.

Erlich, S. K., & Keogh, R. P. The psychopath in a mental institution. *Archives of Neurology and Psychiatry,* 1956, **76,** 286–295.

Eysenck, H. J. *The dynamics of anxiety and hysteria.* New York: Prager, 1957.

Fenichel, O. *The psychoanalytic theory of neurosis.* New York: Norton, 1945.

Ford, C. S., & Beach, F. A. *Patterns of sexual behavior.* New York: Hoeber, 1951.

Frankenstein, C. *Psychopathy—a comparative analysis of clinical pictures.* New York: Grune & Stratton, 1959.

Godfrey, L., Kissen, M. D., & Downs, T. M. Treatment of the acute alcohol-withdrawal syndrome. *Quarterly Journal of Studies on Alcohol,* 1958, **19,** 118–124.

Gottlieb, J. S., Ashby, M. C., & Knott, J. R. Studies in primary behavior disorders and psychopathic personality; inheritance of electrocortical activity. *American Journal of Psychiatry,* 1947, **103,** 823–827.

Gough, H. G. A sociological theory of psychopathy. *American Journal of Sociology,* 1948, **53,** 359–366.

Grenacre, Phyllis. Conscience in the psychopath. *American Journal of Orthopsychiatry,* 1945, **15,** 495–509.

Hampson, J. L. Determinants of psychosexual orientation (gender role) in humans. *Canadian Psychiatric Association Journal,* 1963, **8,** 24–34.

Hare, R. D. Psychopathy, fear arousal and anticipated pain. *Psychological Reports,* 1965, **16,** 499–502.

Hetherington, E. Mavis, & Klinger, E. Psychopathy and punishment. *Journal of Abnormal and Social Psychology,* 1964, **69,** 113–115.

Hill, D. EEG in episodic psychotic and psychopathic behavior. *EEG and Clinical Neurophysiology,* 1952, **4,** 419–442.

Isbell, H. Craving for alcohol. *Quarterly Journal of Studies on Alcohol,* 1955, **16,** 38–42.

Jellinek, E. M. Phases of alcohol addiction. *Quarterly Journal of Studies on Alcohol,* 1952, **13,** 673–678.

Jellinek, E. M. *The disease concept of alcoholism.* New Haven, Connecticut: Hillhouse Press, 1960.

Johnson, Mirriam M. Sex role learning in the nuclear family. *Child Development,* 1963, **34,** 319–334.

Kallman, F. J. *Heredity in health and mental disorders.* New York: Norton, 1953.

Karpman, B. On the need for separating psychopathy into two distinct clinical types: Symptomatic and idiopathic. *Journal of Criminology and Psychopathology,* 1941, **3,** 112–137.

Kingham, R. J. Alcoholism and the reinforcement theory of learning. *Quarterly Journal of Studies on Alcohol,* 1958, **19,** 320–330.

Lester, D., & Greenberg, L. Nutrition and the etiology of alcoholism. The effect of sucrose, saccharin and fat on self-selection of ethyl alcohol by rats. *Quarterly Journal of Studies on Alcohol,* 1952, **13,** 553–560.

Levy, R. I. The psychodynamic functions of alcohol. *Quarterly Journal of Studies on Alcohol,* 1958, **19,** 649–659.

Lykken, D. T. A study of anxiety in the sociopathic personality. *Journal of Abnormal and Social Psychology,* 1957, **55,** 6–10.

McCord, W., & McCord, Joan. *Origins of Crime.* New York: Columbia University Press, 1959.

McCord, W., McCord, Joan, & Gudeman, J. Some current theories of alcoholism. A longitudinal evaluation. *Quarterly Journal of Studies on Alcohol,* 1959, **20,** 727–749.

McGuire, R. J., Carlisle, J. M., & Young, B. G. Sexual deviations as conditioned behaviors: A hypothesis. *Behavior Research and Therapy,* 1965, **2,** 185–190.

Money, J. Components of eroticism in man. I. The hormones in relation to sexual morphology and sexual desire. *Journal of Nervous and Mental Disease,* 1961, **132,** 239–248.

Pritchard, M. Homosexuality and genetic sex. *Journal of Mental Science,* 1962, **108,** 616–623.

Rachman, S. Sexual disorders and behavior therapy. *American Journal of Psychiatry,* 1961, **118,** 235–240.

Reed, C. F., & Cuadra, C. A. The role-taking hypothesis in delinquency. *Journal of Consulting Psychology,* 1957, 21, 386–390.

Roe, Ann, Burks, B., & Mittelman, B. Adult adjustment of foster children of alcoholic and psychotic parentage and the influence of the foster home. *Memoirs of the Section on Alcohol,* Yale University, 1945.

Schoenherr, J. C. Avoidance of noxious stimulation in psychopathic personality. Unpublished doctoral dissertation, University of California, Los Angeles, 1964.

Schwade, E. D., & Geiger, S. G. Abnormal electroencephalographic findings in severe behavior disorders. *Diseases of the Nervous System,* 1956, **17,** 307–317.

Shagass, C., & Schwartz, M. Observations on somatosensory cortical reactivity in personality disorders. *Journal of Nervous and Mental Disease,* 1962, **135,** 44–51.

Shields, J., & Slater, E. Heredity and psychological abnormality. In H. J. Eysenck (Ed.) *Handbook of abnormal psychology.* New York: Basic Books, 1961, pp. 298–343.

Silverman, D. Clinical and electroencephalograph studies of criminal psychopaths. *Archives of Neurology and Psychiatry,* 1943, **50,** 18–33.

Simon, B., Holzberg, J. D., & Unger, Joan F. A study of judgment in the psychopathic personality. *Psychiatric Quarterly,* 1951, **25,** 132–150.

Storm, T., & Smart, R. G. Dissociation: A possible explanation of some features of alcoholism, and implication for its treatment. *Quarterly Journal of Studies on Alcoholism,* 1965, **26,** 111–115.

White, R. W. *The abnormal personality.* New York: Ronald, 1964.

Williams, R. J. The etiology of alcoholism: A working hypothesis involving the interplay of hereditary and environmental factors. *Quarterly Journal of Studies on Alcohol,* 1947, **7,** 567–587.

Williams, R. J. *Alcoholism. The nutritional approach.* Austin: University of Texas Press, 1959.

Zwerling, I., & Rosenbaum, M. Alcoholic addiction and personality. In S. Arieti (Ed.) *American handbook of psychiatry.* New York: Basic Books, 1959, pp. 623–644.

Name Index

Subject Index